The MICHELIN Guide

New York City
RESTAURANTS
2013

MICHELIN

Manufacture française des pneumatiques Michelin

Société en commandite par actions au capital de 504 000 004 EUR
Place des Carmes-Déchaux — 63000 Clermont-Ferrand (France)
R.C.S. Clermont-Fd B 855 200 507

© **Michelin, Propriétaires-éditeurs**
Dépot légal Octobre 2012
Made in Canada
Published in 2012

The MICHELIN Guide
One Parkway South
Greenville, SC 29615 USA
www.michelinguide.com
michelin.guides@us.michelin.com

Dear Reader

*W*e are thrilled to present the eighth edition of our MICHELIN Guide to New York City.

Our dynamic team has spent this year updating our selection to wholly reflect the rich diversity of New York City's restaurants and hotels. As part of our meticulous and highly confidential evaluation process, our inspectors have anonymously and methodically eaten through all five boroughs to compile the finest in each category for your enjoyment. While these inspectors are expertly trained food industry professionals, we remain consumer driven: our goal is to provide comprehensive choices to accommodate your comfort, tastes, and budget. Our inspectors dine, drink, and lodge as 'regular' customers in order to experience and evaluate the same level of service and cuisine you would as a guest.

We have expanded our criteria to reflect some of the more current and unique elements of New York City's dining scene. Don't miss the scrumptious "Small Plates" category, highlighting those establishments with a distinct style of service, setting, and menu; and the further expanded "Under $25" listing which also includes a diverse and impressive choice at a very good value.

Additionally, you may follow our Michelin Inspectors on Twitter @MichelinGuideNY as they chow their way around town. Our anonymous inspectors tweet daily about their unique and entertaining food experiences.

Our company's two founders, Édouard and André Michelin, published the first MICHELIN Guide in 1900, to provide motorists with practical information about where they could service and repair their cars, find quality accommodations, and a good meal. Later in 1926, the star-rating system for outstanding restaurants was introduced, and over the decades we have developed many new improvements to our guides. The local team here in New York enthusiastically carries on these traditions.

We sincerely hope that the MICHELIN Guide will remain your preferred reference to the city's restaurants and hotels.

Contents

© Peter L. Wrenn / MICHELIN

© John Peden / NYBG

Contents

5

The MICHELIN Guide

"*This volume was created at the turn of the century and will last at least as long*".

This foreword to the very first edition of the MICHELIN Guide, written in 1900, has become famous over the years and the Guide has lived up to the prediction. It is read across the world and the key to its popularity is the consistency in its commitment to its readers, which is based on the following promises.

→ Anonymous Inspections

Our inspectors make anonymous visits to hotels and restaurants to gauge the quality offered to the ordinary customer. They pay their own bill and make no indication of their presence. These visits are supplemented by comprehensive monitoring of information—our readers' comments are one valuable source, and are always taken into consideration.

→ Independence

Our choice of establishments is a completely independent one, made for the benefit of our readers alone. Decisions are discussed by the inspectors and the editor, with the most important decided at the global level. Inclusion in the guide is always free of charge.

→ The Selection

The Guide offers a selection of the best hotels and restaurants in each category of comfort and price. Inclusion in the guides is a commendable award in itself, and defines the establishment among the "best of the best."

How the MICHELIN Guide Works

→ Annual Updates

All practical information, the classifications, and awards, are revised and updated every year to ensure the most reliable information possible.

→ Consistency & Classifications

The criteria for the classifications are the same in all countries covered by the Michelin Guides. Our system is used worldwide and is easy to apply when choosing a restaurant or hotel.

→ The Classifications

We classify our establishments using XXXXX-X and 🏨🏨🏨-🏠 to indicate the level of comfort. The ✿✿✿-✿ specifically designates an award for cuisine, unique from the classification. For hotels and restaurants, a symbol in red suggests a particularly charming spot with unique décor or ambiance.

→ Our Aim

As part of Michelin's ongoing commitment to improving travel and mobility, we do everything possible to make vacations and eating out a pleasure.

The MICHELIN Guide

How to Use This Guide

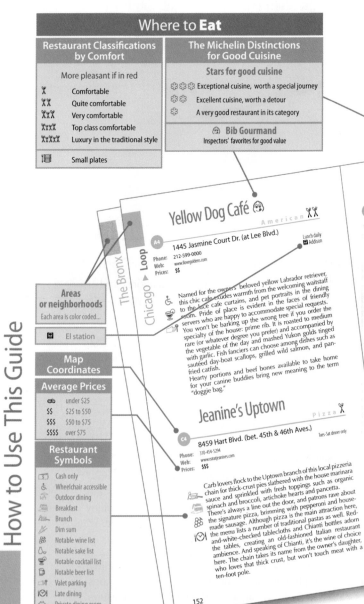

How to Use This Guide

Where to **Eat**

Restaurant Classifications by Comfort

More pleasant if in red

X	Comfortable
XX	Quite comfortable
XxX	Very comfortable
XxxX	Top class comfortable
XxxxX	Luxury in the traditional style
🗊	Small plates

The Michelin Distinctions for Good Cuisine

Stars for good cuisine

🏵 🏵 🏵	Exceptional cuisine, worth a special journey
🏵 🏵	Excellent cuisine, worth a detour
🏵	A very good restaurant in its category

🕃 Bib Gourmand
Inspectors' favorites for good value

Areas or neighborhoods
Each area is color coded...

🖸 El station

Map Coordinates

Average Prices

🕲	under $25
$$	$25 to $50
$$$	$50 to $75
$$$$	over $75

Restaurant Symbols

🔲	Cash only
⚿	Wheelchair accessible
⚘	Outdoor dining
🝢	Breakfast
🝝	Brunch
🝠	Dim sum
🝦	Notable wine list
⚲	Notable sake list
🍸	Notable cocktail list
🝧	Notable beer list
🝡	Valet parking
🝨	Late dining
⟳	Private dining room

Yellow Dog Café 🕃

American XX

A4

The Bronx

Chicago ▶ Loop

1445 Jasmine Court Dr. (at Lee Blvd.)

Lunch daily
🖸 Addison

Phone: 212-599-0000
Web: www.ilovegolden.com
Prices: $$

Named for the owners' beloved yellow Labrador retriever, this chic café exudes warmth from the welcoming waitstaff to the lace café curtains, and pet portraits in the dining room. Pride of place is evident in the faces of friendly servers who are happy to accommodate special requests. You won't be barking up the wrong tree if you order the specialty of the house: prime rib. It is roasted to medium rare (or whatever degree you prefer) and accompanied by the vegetable of the day and mashed Yukon golds tinged with garlic. Fish fanciers can choose among dishes such as sautéed day-boat scallops, grilled wild salmon, and pan-fried catfish.

Hearty portions and beef bones available to take home for your canine buddies bring new meaning to the term "doggie bag."

Jeanine's Uptown

Pizza X

C4

8459 Hart Blvd. (bet. 45th & 46th Aves.)

Tues-Sat dinner only

Phone: 310-454-5294
Web: www.eatatjeanines.com
Prices: $$$

Carb lovers flock to the Uptown branch of this local pizzeria chain for thick-crust pies slathered with the house marinara sauce and sprinkled with fresh toppings such as organic spinach and broccoli, artichoke hearts and pancetta. There's always a line out the door, and patrons rave about the signature pizza, brimming with pepperoni and house-made sausage. Although pizza is the main attraction here, the menu lists a number of traditional pastas as well. Red-and-white-checked tablecloths and Chianti bottles adorn the tables, creating an old-fashioned Italian restaurant ambience. And speaking of Chianti, it's the wine of choice here. The chain takes its name from the owner's daughter, who loves that thick crust, but won't touch meat with a ten-foot pole.

152

Where to **Stay**

Average Prices	Hotel Symbols	Hotel Classifications by Comfort
Prices do not include applicable taxes	**149 rooms** Number of rooms & suites	**More pleasant if in red**
$ under $200	♿ Wheelchair accessible	🏠 Comfortable
$$ $200 to $300	🏋 Exercise room	🏠🏠 Quite comfortable
$$$ $300 to $400	🧖 Spa	🏠🏠🏠 Very comfortable
$$$$ over $400	🏊 Swimming pool	🏠🏠🏠🏠 Top class comfortable
	🛏 Conference room	🏠🏠🏠🏠🏠 Luxury in the traditional style
Map Coordinates	🐾 Pet friendly	
	📶 Wireless	

...Palace ✿ ✿

Italian 🍴🍴🍴

...Pl. (at 30th Street)   Dinner daily

...ouspalace.com

David Burlington/Getty Images

...he cooked Italian never tasted so good than at this
...pretentious little place. The simple décor claims no big-
...he designers, and while the Murano glass light fixtures
...chic and the velveteen-covered chairs are comfortable,
...s isn't a restaurant where millions of dollars were spent
...the interior.

...stead, food is the focus here. The restaurant's name may
...ot be Italian, but it nonetheless serves some of the best
...asta in the city, made fresh in-house. Dishes follow the
...seasons, thus ravioli may be stuffed with fresh ricotta and
...herbs in summer, and pumpkin in fall. Most everything
...is liberally dusted with Parmigiano Reggiano, a favorite
...ingredient of the chef.

...For dessert, you'll have to deliberate between the likes
...of creamy tiramisu, ricotta cheesecake, and homemade
...gelato. One thing's for sure: you'll never miss your nonna's
...cooking when you eat at Sonya's.

153

Manhattan ▶ Chelsea

The Fan Inn

D1

135 Shanghai Street, Oakland

Phone: 650-345-1440 or 888-222-2424
Web: www.superfaninnoakland.com
Prices: $$

🏠🏠🏠

45 Rooms 5 Suites

🏋

🧖

John A. Rizzo/Getty Images

...oused in an Art Deco-era building, the venerable Fan Inn
...ently underwent a complete facelift. The hotel now fits
... with the new generation of sleekly understated hotels
...ing a Zen-inspired aesthetic, despite its 1930s origins.

...thing neutral palette runs throughout the property,
...uated with exotic woods, bamboo, and fine fabrics.
...e lobby, the sultry lounge makes a relaxing place for
...mixed cocktail or a glass of wine.

...ens and down pillows cater to your comfort, while
...n TVs, DVD players with iPod docking stations,
...less Internet access satisfy the need for modern
... For business travelers, nightstands convert to
...les and credenzas morph into flip-out desks.
...ater, fax or scanner? It's just a phone call away.
...st, the hotel will even provide office supplies.

...alf of the accommodations here are suites,
...xury factor ratchets up with marble baths,
...ng areas, and fully equipped kitchens.
...nn doesn't have a restaurant, the nearby
...rly everything you could want in terms of
...dumplings to haute cuisine.

315

San Francisco ▶ Civic Center

Where to Eat

Manhattan

Chelsea

Restaurants in this artsy neighborhood–the hub of New York's gallery scene–feature flavors from around the globe, encompassing everything from French bistros to sushi bars and contemporary Spanish fare. Old World Puerto Rican luncheonettes on and around 9th Avenue (where patrons are accommodated in English or Spanish, and the *café con leche* packs a heady wallop) provide a striking contrast to the mega-hip places that punctuate Chelsea today. For heavenly pizza, try the much-hyped **Co.**, home to iconoclast Jim Lahey's blistered and crispy pies. The Chef/owner and founder of **Sullivan Street Bakery**, fires his pizza in a wood-burning oven imported from Modena, and the lines of folks eager to taste them stretch out the door. If that's not hip enough, there's always the scene at **Buddakan**, that tried and trendy temple of modern Asian fare, brought to New York by Philadelphia restaurateur wunderkind Stephen Starr.

In the burgeoning area popularly referred to as the West Club District, patrons of nightspots like Mansion, Guest House, Home, and Marquee are grateful for all-night restaurants like the **Punjabi Food Junction**, offering a tasty self-serve Indian buffet. Also in the open-late category, quintessential New York spot **The Half King** dishes up good all-American grub. Named for an 18th century Seneca Indian chief, Half King also sponsors book readings on Monday nights, thanks to co-owner and writer Sebastian Junger, author of *War*, and co-director of the documentary, *Restrepo*.

Chelsea Market

No food-finding excursion to this area would be complete without a visit to the **Chelsea Market**. The 1898 Nabisco factory–where the Oreo cookie was first made in 1912–reopened in 1997 as an urban food market. Interspersed throughout its brick-lined arcades with stores selling flowers, meats, cheeses, artisan-made breads, and other gourmet essentials are cafés, bakeries, and eateries. Drop by to peruse their wares, stock your pantry, and have a bite to eat while you're at it.

Treat yourself to organic farm-fresh cuisine and biodynamic wines at **The Green Table** and **The Cleaver Co.** Seafood lovers can pick up a luscious lobster roll or some freshly steamed lobsters at **The Lobster Place**, New York's leading purveyor of these sea creatures. If you have kids in tow, a stop at **L'Arte del Gelato** is a must. Some new welcome additions to the market are **Dickson's Farmstand** for their serious meats and **Lucy's Whey** for fine cheeses. No matter your preference, a trip to the market will nourish you for hours of gallery-hopping on the district's western flank.

Chelsea

● Hotel
● Restaurant

UDSON

RIVER

PIER 63
PARK

HUDSON

CHELSEA
WATERSIDE
PARK

PIER 62

CHELSEA
PIERS

GARMENT
DISTRICT

MACY'S

MADISON
SQUARE
GARDEN

PENN
STATION

34 St-
Penn Sta

34 St-
Penn Sta

FASHION
INSTITUTE OF
TECHNOLOGY

MIDTOWN
SOUTH

Eventi

Hilton
Fashion District

GRAMERCY, FLATIRON
& UNION SQUARE

FLATIRON

UNION SQUARE

14 St-
Union Sq

Ovest
Pizzoteca

The
Americano

Hotel Americano

CHELSEA
PARK

Chop-Shop

The Red Cat

Trestle on Tenth

El Quinto Pino

Tia Pol

Txikito

Co.

La Promenade
des Anglais

Cookshop

Bombay Talkie

Blossom

Foragers
City Table

Del Posto

Tipsy
Parson

Naka Naka

Salinas

Rocking
Horse Cafe

Colicchio
& Sons

Morimoto

Cô Ba

Le Zie 2000

Socarrat

The Maritime

Sueños

CHELSEA
HISTORIC
DISTRICT

23 St

23 St

23 St

CHELSEA
MARKET

HIGH LINE
PARK

MEATPACKING

Gansevoort

Legend Bar &
Restaurant

Crema

La Nacional

da Umberto

Coppelia

HIGH
LINE
PARK

Horatio

Jane

GREENWICH, WEST VILLAGE
& MEATPACKING DISTRICT

UNION
SQUARE

Upstairs, the Chelsea Market pavilion houses the studios and test kitchens for the Food Network. Continue your stroll through Chelsea and follow the meaty scents to **Salumeria Biellese** for some great cured products. After these salty snacks, **La Bergamote Patisserie** is the perfect landing spot for satisfying a sweet tooth. And while in the neighborhood, consider dining with a view of Lady Liberty on one of the dinner cruises that departs from Chelsea Piers, an ever-evolving recreational waterfront area located along the West Side Highway between 17th and 23rd streets. Comprising four historic piers along the Hudson River, the complex now houses state-of-the-art sports facilities, including a spa, ice skating rink, and bowling alley. **Chelsea Brewing Company**, overlooking the Hudson River, is a glorious spot to close your day. Satiate your palate with one of their unique beers like the Checker Cab Blonde Ale.

The Americano

B1

518 W. 27th St. (bet. Tenth & Eleventh Aves.)

Subway: 23 St (Eighth Ave.)   Lunch & dinner daily
Phone: 212-216-0000
Web: www.hotel-americano.com
Prices: $$$

Within its all-mesh metal façade, The Hotel Americano's namesake restaurant is a striking home to contemporary dining in far west Chelsea, just steps from the High Line. Everything has the look of a custom-made, creative masterpiece. Envision high-design chandeliers over marble tables set with thick linens, delicate glasses, and an elevated back patio with bespoke picnic tables—an alfresco paradise. Meals might include fish tacos made with fragrant corn tortillas, smoky-spicy salsa *roja*, and perfectly grilled fish with fresh cilantro. Yet pastas may be where Americano shines brightest, as in translucent agnolotti filled with fava "pesto" floating in a Parmesan consommé that can only be described as flawless. The crisp, sweet madeleines are Proustian.

Blossom

B2

187 Ninth Ave. (bet. 21st & 22nd Sts.)

Subway: 23 St (Eighth Ave.)   Lunch Fri – Sun
Phone: 212-627-1144   Dinner nightly
Web: www.blossomnyc.com
Prices: $$

Blossom is sultry with just two rows of dim lights, an array of candles, and dark velvet curtains. Yet it remains a fantastic food oasis that is at once convivial yet hushed, and intimate without feeling tight. Whether a fanatic vegan or part-time vegetarian, trust that these dishes are always tasty and gratifying.

Framed mirrors lend an illusion of depth to these close-knit quarters. Shadowing the pleasant hum of diners is Blossom's dynamic cuisine. Nobly clad in black ensembles, servers might present the likes of parsnip *cappelletti*, parsnip and potato "hats" brushed with a shiitake-truffle oil; and pan-seared portobello "shank" rimmed by a tomato broth. Their vegan cheesecake will make you shun the classic version in a heartbeat.

Bombay Talkie

Indian ✗✗

B2

189 Ninth Ave. (bet. 21st & 22nd Sts.)

Subway: 23 St (Eighth Ave.)   Dinner nightly
Phone: 212-242-1900
Web: www.bombaytalkie.com
Prices: $$

Located in a landmarked Chelsea space designed by architect Thomas Juul-Hansen, this Indian spot knows the key to its popularity is in its consistency. Take a seat below the canvases from J.P. Krishna, and pick your meal off a menu boasting sections like "from the roadside" and "street bites."

Try a plate of *malai kofta*, dumplings stuffed with cheese and coconut, and bathed in a cashew-yogurt sauce; or *Bombay bhel*, served with wheat flour chips and rice puffs, tossed with a bright lime, mint, onion, and green mango salsa. The cocktail list piques diners' interest, as do the likes of Assam green tea and cardamom coffee.

This double-decker standby offers two stories of seating and a long communal table, but reservations are still recommended.

Chop-Shop

Asian ✗

B2

254 Tenth Ave. (bet. 24th & 25th Sts.)

Subway: 23 St (Eighth Ave.)   Lunch & Dinner Mon– Sat
Phone: 212-820-0333
Web: www.chop-shop.co
Prices: $$

Valued as one of the hippest nooks in town, Chelsea houses everything from art galleries to ethnic food delights. Like its locale, the setting is clean and laid-back, with reclaimed pine, vintage lights, concrete floors, large windows that flood the room with light, and a lovely backyard. Chop-Shop maintains a cool vibe through its delectably fresh and complex Asian menu.

The food meanders this vast continent, beginning with the likes of fresh summer rolls plump with shrimp to juicy pan-fried pork and bok choi dumplings licked with a spicy soy sauce. *Zha jian mia* tosses springy wheat noodles in a spicy ground pork sauce with refreshing cucumber; and a pan-fried sea bass fillet is tender, sweet, and topped with sour vinegar pepper strips.

Co.

B2

230 Ninth Ave. (at 24th St.)

Subway: 23 St (Eighth Ave.)
Phone: 212-243-1105
Web: www.co-pane.com
Prices: $$

Lunch Tue – Sun
Dinner nightly

Go ahead and heave a sigh of relief because Co. is not yet another wood-burning, Naples-aping pizzeria. In fact, it may be lauded as the bake shop that ushered in this Neapolitan-hailing, all-American food frenzy, where owner Jim Lahey (of the newly opened Sullivan Street Bakery, a few doors down) is wholly fixated on the art of bread-making.

The menu at this wood-paneled den–decked with mirrors, unconventional lights, and a cozy kitchen–may not be vast but the choices are plenty. A kindly staff presents such fine items as the "Popeye" pizza, served hot and crusty with fresh spinach, spicy crushed tomatoes, and a wealth of cheese. Adored by parents with children in tow is the pizza Bianca spread with olive oil, sea salt, and pickled vegetables.

Cô Ba 😊

B2

110 Ninth Ave. (bet. 19th & 20th Sts.)

Subway: 23 St (Eighth Ave.)
Phone: 212-414-2700
Web: www.cobarestaurant.com
Prices: $$

Lunch & dinner daily

Cô Ba may seem smaller than a bread-box, but this downright warm and friendly Vietnamese spot cleverly presents big, solid flavors and delectable cuisine. Inside, images of rural Vietnamese life, quirky conical rice paddy hats, and charming old photos of the motherland line the walls to decorate the room.

The menu is massive, covers all the familiar hits, and is sure to offer something for everyone, as in *rau nuong*, grilled eggplant with shiitakes and okra topped with basil, scallion oil, and a ginger-lime sauce; or Cô Ba beef done three ways (wok-seared with a sweet soy-sake marinade, wrapped inside grilled shiso leaves, or grilled sesame five-spice sirloin rolls). The steamed shrimp-coconut rice cakes with lime sauce are an absolute standout.

Colicchio & Sons

American XXX

A2

85 Tenth Ave. (bet. 15th & 16th Sts.)

Subway: 14 St - 8 Av
Phone: 212-400-6699
Web: www.colicchioandsons.com
Prices: $$$

Lunch & dinner daily

The design is dramatic, the large space can accommodate any mood or need, the taps are dispensing keg-wines from the Gotham Project, and the chef is Tom Colicchio. From the Tap Room's wood-burning pizza oven to the daylight-flooded dining room, everything seems inviting, clamor notwithstanding.

As one would hope and expect from this celebrity chef, the laborious and sophisticated menu is a marvel to peruse. Seasonal ingredients, like stinging nettles or truffles, are incorporated throughout. Expect dishes like roasted and braised Tamworth pork with green tomato chutney, dandelion greens, and *lardo* ravioli. Still, the tasting menu is where this kitchen shines, with the likes of Scottish wood pigeon with Brussel sprouts, black truffles, and chestnuts.

Cookshop

American XX

A2

156 Tenth Ave. (at 20th St.)

Subway: 23 St (Eighth Ave.)
Phone: 212-924-4440
Web: www.cookshopny.com
Prices: $$

Lunch & dinner daily

The beauty of Cookshop is that it still feels brand spanking new. With sunrays flooding its floors and soft lights by night, everybody looks pretty at this lively scene. Dressed-up with plants and flowers, Cookshop impresses its highbrow neighbors—the Desmond Tutu Center and High Line are in full view.

If you're here stag, settle at the bar to peruse a chalkboard stocked with menu items and their sources. Simple and seasonal is their essence and the outcome is worth it. Marrying soul with pride are such unique dishes as trap-caught Montauk squid with plump, flavorsome beans; fish tacos topped with a spicy jalapeño-cabbage slaw; and Italian plum buckle, a warm, lemony crumb cake filled with fresh plums and drizzled with buttermilk ice cream.

19

Coppelia

B3

207 W. 14th St. (bet. Seventh & Eighth Aves.)

Subway: 14 St (Seventh Ave.)
Phone: 212-858-5001
Web: www.coppelianyc.com
Prices: $$

Lunch & dinner daily

Visionary Chef Julian Medina (of Toloache fame) and his unstoppable team are still at it. Enter sensational Coppelia to find a breezy Caribbean vibe, moan-worthy dishes, and jaw-dropping desserts courtesy of the talented Pichet Ong. The space is reminiscent of a 50s luncheonette and rocks bright yellow walls, red-topped tables, checkered floors, and vintage-style banquettes. Grab a spot on the gorgeous marble bar and let the fiesta begin.

Favorites include superb guacamole with tortilla, yucca, and plantain chips; four variations of exquisite empanadas; cheese *croquetas*; decadent mac and cheese with *chicharrón*; and luscious pernil served over a yucca purée. The carrot cake with manchego cheese frosting and lime is simply out of this world.

Crema

C3

111 W. 17th St. (bet. Sixth & Seventh Aves.)

Subway: 18 St
Phone: 212-691-4477
Web: www.cremarestaurante.com
Prices: $$

Lunch & dinner daily

Hidden below street level on a Chelsea block dominated by consignment shops, Crema doesn't boast its charms to the world. Rather, this little restaurant relies on Chef Julieta Ballesteros' solid grasp of modern, upscale Mexican cooking to lure them in.

Inside, you'll find a narrow room with smooth, colorful walls, a cactus garden and a bar area sporting lovely glass vats of *agua loca*—a Mexican sangria not to be missed. All the better to wash down a perfectly balanced bowl of cream of corn bobbing with plump crab meat and micro cilantro; a tortilla pie layered with fresh ingredients and tender shredded chicken; or a decadent slice of pecan pie with spiced Mexican eggnog and vanilla ice cream. Come lunchtime, $15.95 scores you an entrée, soup, and side dish.

da Umberto

Italian ✖✖

C3

107 W. 17th St. (bet. Sixth & Seventh Aves.)

Subway: 18 St
Phone: 212-989-0303
Web: www.daumbertonyc.com
Prices: $$$

Lunch Mon – Fri
Dinner Mon – Sat

Now in its third decade, da Umberto still raises the bar for this city's understanding and love of Northern Italian cuisine, thanks to their exacting attention to detail and charming, sure-footed service. Expect regional favorites like *cacciucco*, the traditional fish soup; and a Napoleon, buttery and crisp, with Chantilly-whipped custard and sweet-tart raspberries. An interesting wine list, special antipasto bar, and recited specials are worthy highlights.

One would never expect all this from the exterior's rather old-fashioned lace curtains, but the inside is warm and sophisticated with bold flower arrangements and an inviting bar. A quiet restraint in both clientele and setting attests that here, you are among those who are in the know.

El Quinto Pino

Spanish 🍽

B2

401 W. 24th St. (bet. Ninth & Tenth Aves.)

Subway: 23 St (Eighth Ave.)
Phone: 212-206-6900
Web: www.elquintopinonyc.com
Prices: ⊜⊜

Dinner nightly

Chelsea has enough tapas joints to give the Barcelona metropolis a run for its money, but El Quinto Pino is a worthy member of this crowded landscape. This Lilliputian spot aims to return tapas to its original concept—these are quick snacks rather than sit-down meals. This is an ideal stop for a distinctively authentic *ración* or two and *una copa* or three.

Despite its lack of traditional table seating and constant reshuffling in the kitchen, this warm and narrow Spanish-tiled bar has been mobbed since its inception. And the credit goes to the small, creative blackboard menu listing tapas like uni panini, squeezed onto bread slathered with Korean mustard oil; or the Menu Turistico, featuring a revolving set of regional Spanish dishes.

Del Posto ✿

Italian 🍴🍴🍴🍴

85 Tenth Ave. (at 16th St.)

Subway: 14 St - 8 Av
Phone: 212-497-8090
Web: www.delposto.com
Prices: $$$$

Lunch Mon – Fri
Dinner nightly

Joe Vaughn

The wrought-iron doors are staffed, limos are lined up around the corner, and those Italian accents are real at Del Posto. In an unlikely feat of design and ambience, this western Manhattan mecca feels new and desirable, yet also like some theatrical episode from a bygone era: cue the tuxedo-clad gentleman, tickling the ivories. Sloping staircases, polished woods, and inlaid marble might seem intentionally heavy, but this vast and assertively masculine space has its charms in rich fabrics and traditional luxuries.

Tables are large, private, and posh with a few soft touches, like those floral-patterned plates that any *baronessa* would love. The menu strives to offer a tour of Italy, with pastas that can be interesting and downright amazing. Count on high-flying seasonal ingredients to make an appearance again and again: excellent black truffles land with sophistication and aplomb over beef carpaccio.

Every bite is right in lamb *alla Romana*, perfectly slow-roasted for 16 hours, served with Swiss chard, chickpeas, and garlicky yogurt. Desserts reveal silky, steamed chestnut nuggets, seasoned with Meyer lemon and tangerine zest over sweetened mascarpone.

Lunch menus are a genuine bargain.

Foragers City Table

Contemporary XX

300 W. 22nd St. (at Eighth Ave.)

Subway: 23 St (Eighth Ave.)
Phone: 212-243-8888
Web: www.foragerscitygrocer.com
Prices: $$

Lunch Sat – Sun
Dinner nightly

Foragers City Table brings a distinctly Californian philosophy to the heart of Chelsea. Glimpse through their long and lean glass panes, beyond the dining room, into a brimming market, and know that this place is for real. Flooded with avid foodies, it radiates utilitarian-chic via unencumbered windows and a boxy style.

Menu highlights include panko-fried spring onions with lemon-pepper spiked crème fraîche, and pork *crepinettes* composed of tender Boston lettuce wraps topped with juicy meatballs and batons of onion, cucumber, cilantro, and a revelatory Meyer lemon *nuac cham* sauce. The stunningly buttery and delicately smoked black cod atop a bed of freshly shelled peas and wedges of red zebra tomatoes reminds of all the flavors summer has to offer.

La Nacional

Spanish X

239 W. 14th St. (bet Seventh & Eighth Aves.)

Subway: 14 St (Seventh Ave.)
Phone: 212-243-9308
Web: www.lanacionaltapas.com
Prices: $$

Lunch & dinner daily

Housed on the ground floor of the Spanish Benevolent Society founded in 1868, La Nacional is not merely a cantina for homesick Spaniards, but city dwellers from all walks of life hooked on Iberian classics.

The bar is a fine spot for sangria-sipping while catching up on the latest football match, but the front dining room brings a more subdued experience.

The tapas are tasty, but La Nacional shines in its paella preparations—*paella de la casa* studded with seafood, strips of piquillo peppers, and sweet green peas; *arroz negro* enriched with squid ink and seasoned with *sofrito*; or *fideua* composed of broken thin noodles. Each features excellent ingredients and impressive cooking that produces mouthwatering *socarrat* (golden-crusted rice at the bottom).

La Promenade des Anglais

Mediterranean 🍴🍴

B2

461 W. 23rd St. (bet. Ninth & Tenth Aves.)

Subway: 23 St (Eighth Ave.)
Phone: 212-255-7400
Web: www.lapromenadenyc.com
Prices: $$$

Lunch Sat – Sun
Dinner nightly

The talented Chef Alain Allegretti's latest venture can be savored at La Promenade des Anglais. After an entire overhaul, the restaurant now wears a playful, carefree aura. Comfort and elegance are immediately evident in velvet booths, brass lamps, antique mirrors, and blue banquettes. The bar is long, fully stocked, and thus, enticing.

Named for the famed promenade in Nice, this getaway is at once casual and stunning. The kitchen boasts promise and surprise as coiffed servers deliver the likes of *vitello tonnato*, creatively spun with fried sweetbreads and crimson tuna; risotto with Sicilian olive oil and squid ragù all bathed in a creamy almond pesto; and a lovely, golden rum-laden *baba*, packed with fruit compote and laced with whipped cream.

Legend Bar & Restaurant

Chinese 🍴

B3

88 Seventh Ave. (bet. 15th & 16th Sts.)

Subway: 14 St
Phone: 212-929-1778
Web: www.legendrestaurant88.com
Prices: ☜☺

Lunch & dinner daily

The chefs manning these stoves are phenomenally well-versed in Sichuan food (one might suspect their skill inspired the name). Legend's superlative Sichuan menu may be laden with missable Vietnamese dishes, but that hasn't kept the masses away from this crowded Chelsea haunt. Happy hour is magnificent here, while the rest of the Asian-accented space caters to the Sichuan-seeking diners.

Vivid colors and a clean décor welcome you inside, while the lower level displays round tables outfitted with lazy Susans; and the orange upholstery pairs perfectly with such zesty offerings as spicy conch topped with slivered scallions; braised, diced rabbit with pickled peppers swimming in a red chili oil; and and rice balls of sesame paste floating in sweet milk.

Le Zie 2000

Italian ✗✗

B3

172 Seventh Ave. (bet. 20th & 21st Sts.)

Subway: 23 St (Seventh Ave.)
Phone: 212-206-8686
Web: www.lezie.com
Prices: $$

Lunch & dinner daily

Inside this pastel dining room, Le Zie 2000 continues to embody wholesome Italian cuisine. Outside, a small patio remains a fine place to while away the sunny days.

Begin meals in the Venetian tradition by sharing the antipasti sampling–*cicchetti*–which includes several of the region's savory classics and is served with its signature starch, grilled polenta. Among several fine *paste* and heartier *secondi piatti* is the ever-popular Le Zie mac 'n cheese with truffles.

With an entrance on 20th Street, Le Zie features a cute, dimly lit, very comfy back lounge with light tasting and cocktail menus, served by a friendly bartender. All wines from Le Zie's extensive list of some 200 labels representing all of Italy's viticultural regions are available here.

Morimoto

Fusion ✗✗✗

A2

88 Tenth Ave. (at 16th St.)

Subway: 14 St - 8 Av
Phone: 212-989-8883
Web: www.morimotonyc.com
Prices: $$$

Lunch Mon – Fri
Dinner nightly

Arriving at Morimoto is a singular experience. The music, the beautiful patrons, and inviting platters—it's all very chic indeed. Know that this culinary citadel will unearth its veritable feast for the senses as you glide through its cascading curtains and into the dusky, Japanese-rooted restaurant.

The juxtaposed dining levels are a telling commentary on minimalism—from a square, white room and backlit wall, to glass installations, and clear, acrylic chopsticks. Halogen spotlights lend warmth and delicacy to an ambitious lineup of toro tartare capped with caviar; wafer-thin tuna pizza flecked with olives; pork and garlic chive *gyoza* gussied up with crème fraîche; and happily unctuous ravioli stuffed with smoked salmon and trickled with yuzu gelée.

Naka Naka

A2

458 W. 17th St. (bet. Ninth & Tenth Aves.)

Subway: 14 St - 8 Av
Phone: 212-929-8544
Web: www.nakanakany.com
Prices: $$$

Dinner Tue – Sun

Naka Naka is a quaint, hidden Japanese gem that delivers Tokyo to Chelsea, albeit for a few hours. This infallible cocoon may see a less-than-largely native clientele, yet servers dressed in classic kimonos and faithful accents like Japanese lanterns, chopstick holders, origami "peace" cranes, and paper art deliver a faithful experience .

Dominated by an elevated platform adorned with brocade pillows, find seats at the bar or low-slung tables; jazz standards reveal the American infusion. Extricating this treasure from the rabble are such inventive dishes as *oshinko* tossing cool daikon, cucumbers, and pickled vegetables; a Naka Naka roll crested with crunchy crimson tobiko; and *ika uni ae*, cold, crunchy squid licked with sea urchin sauce and shaved ohba.

Ovest Pizzoteca

B1

513 W. 27th St. (bet. 10th & 11th Aves.)

Subway: 23 St (Eighth Ave.)
Phone: 212-967-4392
Web: www.ovestnyc.com
Prices: $$

Lunch & dinner daily

Fine fare is rare in these parts, so Ovest Pizzoteca's (of the lauded Luzzo's) is now firmly ensconced into Chelsea's Club Row. Open garage doors cede a glimpse of this chic, modern warehouse with a cement bar, industrial lighting, and a wooden ceiling. From the back of the large, spare dining room, a wood- and gas-burning oven crackles until first light. Ravenous revelers and diners of all stripes follow the alluring aromas of pies and panini, like the Peppino with *prosciutto cotto*, artichokes, and goat cheese. Expect tasty treats like *polpettine*—four plump, juicy meatballs bathed in an excellent, fresh-tasting tomato sauce with a sprinkling of parsley. The well-rounded menu goes on to offer *sfizzi*, antipasti, bruschette, salads, and pasta.

The Red Cat

American ✕✕

B2

227 Tenth Ave. (bet. 23rd & 24th Sts.)

Subway: 23 St (Eighth Ave.)
Phone: 212-242-1122
Web: www.redcatrestaurants.com
Prices: $$

Lunch Tue – Sat
Dinner nightly

This clever, cozy, and perpetually humming Jimmy Bradley joint is packed wall-to-wall seven nights a week. And no wonder: with its warm, sultry décor, a downright sexy cocktail list, and scrumptious, always inventive American fare, The Red Cat might be called a restaurant triple threat. A jovial red banquette extends along one wall, opposite a bar that dominates the room, lavishly outfitted with flower arrangements and Moorish light fixtures. Take a moment to study the artwork adorning walls and sculpture above the kitchen entrance.

Just remember to book ahead—highly publicized specialties like their deep-fried bacon tempura have only added to the wait. And save room for dessert; chocolate mousse with blackberry-lager sauce is yet another work of art.

Rocking Horse Cafe

Mexican ✕

B2

182 Eighth Ave. (bet. 19th & 20th Sts.)

Subway: 14 St - 8 Av
Phone: 212-463-9511
Web: www.rockinghorsecafe.com
Prices: $$

Lunch & dinner daily

This easygoing Chelsea standby serves up solid Mexican fare in a vivid, sophisticated dining space fitted out with shimmering blue mosaic tiles, tangerine-colored walls, beet red accents, and creamy jumbo lanterns. At the bar, big mesh containers hold mounds of the house-made tortillas and a cheerful crowd lines the stools, downing seriously good (and strong) margaritas while they wait to be seated.

In the dining room, couples and friends line the tables, tucking into creative spins on Mexican favorites like a marvelous *ensalada de calamares*, spiked with fresh cracked black pepper, cool cilantro, and a lick of *crema*; a fresh batch of Niman Ranch pork *carnitas*; or a traditional, but irresistible *tres leches con platanos* strewn with candied pecans.

Salinas

Spanish 🍴🍴

B2

136 Ninth Ave. (bet. 18th & 19th Sts.)

Subway: 18 St
Phone: 212-776-1990
Web: www.salinasnyc.com
Prices: $$$

Lunch Sat – Sun
Dinner Tue – Sat

You'll be salivating over the Spanish food (and the scantily clad hostesses) in no time at Salinas. Set behind wrought-iron gates on a busy stretch of Ninth Ave., this restaurant invites diners to an Iberian world of delicious treats and seductive spaces. Sure, it's tapas, but Chef Bollo's elegant take is a tad different than the tried and true classics found throughout the city.

There's a host of seasonal starters (summer months showcase clams with *pocha* beans and artichokes beside a spicy and oh-so-yummy ceviche). From Spanish flatbread peppered with thyme, dry aged Mahón cheese, to *porcella*, slow-roasted suckling pig matched with grilled apricots and bathed in a wine reduction, there is nothing like sampling a cavalcade of culinary delights.

Socarrat

Spanish 🍴

B2

259 W. 19th St. (bet. Seventh & Eighth Aves.)

Subway: 18 St
Phone: 212-462-1000
Web: www.socarratpaellabar.com
Prices: $$$

Lunch & dinner daily

Tapas bars have been taking over the city, yet Socarrat– named for the delicious crust that forms at the bottom of a pan–is a worthy addition by virtue of its irresistible paella. Like its siblings, this is a friendly and familiar spot, where long communal tables are packed with your newest old friends and tapas-loving locals. Glossy walls reflect the room's gentle light, while mirrors and portraits lend depth and color.

Octopus rounds crowned with spices is a perfect opener for paella Socarrat, a crisp layer of caramelized rice mingled in a fragrant stock with spicy chorizo and briny clams. Happy Hour Mondays keeps everyone beaming by pairing the likes of *croquetas de setas* (mushrooms) or crispy pork belly with sangria for around $10.

Sueños

Mexican

311 W. 17th St. (bet. Eighth & Ninth Aves.)

Subway: 14 St - 8 Av
Phone: 212-243-1333
Web: www.suenosnyc.com
Prices: $$

Dinner Tue – Sun

With its entrance tucked down an alley and requiring a walk along a virtual gangplank, Sueños is as downright good as it is audacious to succeed in its somewhat tired state, amid more fashionable neighbors. Nonetheless, this is a bright and charming Mexican spot that rises above the more familiar ethnic eateries that dot the boroughs.

In a city dominated by male chefs, Sue Torres brings success and life to her dishes through the little touches, like the fresh tortillas being churned out by hand in the dining room; or the guacamole, made to order with ripe chunks of avocado and bright tomato, paired with a basket of salty, house-made chips. An interesting chile-tasting menu and chile-rubbed goat with sweet plantain purée are not to be missed.

Tia Pol

Spanish

205 Tenth Ave. (bet. 22nd & 23rd Sts.)

Subway: 23 St (Eighth Ave.)
Phone: 212-675-8805
Web: www.tiapol.com
Prices:

Lunch Tue – Sun
Dinner nightly

 You can't shake a stick in Chelsea without hitting a tapas joint these days, but Tia Pol sets the standard. Although the bare bones space, a narrow dining room tucked behind a steel-patch door on Tenth Avenue, isn't much to marvel at—one whirl with Tia Pol's affordable Spanish wine list and delicious Basque small plates and you'll be rubbing elbows at the perpetually packed bar in no time.

Kick the night off with a cheese and charcuterie platter loaded with silky hams and garlicky chorizo; then dig into dishes like a chewy, toasted baguette laced with pickled onions and tender veal tongue, cooked *a la plancha*; smoky, paprika-dusted slices of chorizo finished in a sherry reduction; and tender lamb skewers rubbed with fragrant Moorish spices.

Tipsy Parson

American 🍴🍴

B2

156 Ninth Ave. (bet. 19th & 20th Sts.)

Lunch & dinner daily

Subway: 18 St
Phone: 212-620-4545
Web: www.tipsyparson.com
Prices: $$

For food that is as soulful as it is playful, the Tipsy Parson, a jewel in Chelsea compliments of Tasha Gibson and Julie Wallach, is a homey, multi-room place dressed in flowery fabrics, bric-à-brac, and French doors. The dark, masculine bar is shelved with premium spirits and actual books.

The Southern menu may begin with the trio of spreads like pimento cheese, deviled tasso, and black-eyed pea salad with house-made herb crackers. The buttermilk-chive biscuits with honey-butter are not to be missed, though entrées are equally pleasing, as in broiled shrimp with stone-ground grits, fried green tomatoes, and tomato vinaigrette. Though not on the menu, brunch-time diners can request the Luther burger (apparently named for the late Vandross himself).

Trestle on Tenth

Contemporary 🍴🍴

B2

242 Tenth Ave. (at 24th St.)

Lunch & dinner daily

Subway: 23 St (Eighth Ave.)
Phone: 212-645-5659
Web: www.trestleontenth.com
Prices: $$

This inviting little gem is tiny in comparison to the behemoth restaurants thriving in and around Chelsea these days, but it packs a mighty big punch. Duck inside and you'll find an intimate, minimally dressed interior featuring a wall of exposed brick; contemporary art; blonde wood ceilings; and a pretty outside garden that opens up seasonally.

Grab a seat and tuck into exceptional fare like a silky cauliflower soup, bobbing with fragrant herbs and tender, garlicky escargots; the homemade *metzgete* plate (served for a short window in January) utilizing every part of the pig, which might include exceptional blood sausage, liver sausage, and pork belly; or crispy roast chicken with summer vegetables in a fragrant, beautifully clear consommé.

Txikito

B2

Spanish ✗

240 Ninth Ave. (bet. 24th & 25th Sts.)

Subway: 23 St (Eighth Ave.)
Phone: 212-242-4730
Web: www.txikitonyc.com
Prices: $$

Lunch Tue – Sun
Dinner nightly

Manhattan ▶ Chelsea

First thing's first: they aren't tapas, they're *pinxtos*, and they're outstanding. Give thanks to the gifted Basque chef/owners, Alexandra Raij and Eder Montero, for their superb creations, which represent the duo's deep connection to the region.

Hunker down in the cool, wood-paneled space and order up a frenzy of these tummy-satisfying delights, many of which are made with locally sourced ingredients. The anchovies in any incarnation are a must, but also try the *txipiron encebollado*—long, tender ribbons of squid with sweet onion and pine nuts; *lomo adobado*, house-cured pork loin grilled with sweet-smoky piquillo peppers; or the *pil pil*, fish cheeks finished with a tart-sweet sauce. Drop in for *hamaiketako*–Basque brunch–for poached eggs with chorizo.

Good food without spending a fortune? Look for the Bib Gourmand 😊.

Chinatown & Little Italy

As different as *chow mein* and chicken cacciatore, these two districts are nonetheless neighbors, though in recent years, their borders have become blurred with Chinatown voraciously gulping up most of Little Italy.

The end of California's Gold Rush brought the arrival of New York's first Chinese in the 1870s. The immigrant influx arrived energetically, setting up garment factories, markets, and restaurants in the quarter, which has inexorably spread into Little Italy and the Lower East Side. It is documented that New York cradles the maximum number of Chinese immigrants in the country and specifically, Queens, followed by Manhattan, holds one of the largest Chinese communities outside Asia. Immigrants from Hong Kong and mainland China (most recently Fujian province), populate Manhattan's Chinatown, each bringing their own distinct regional cuisines.

Chinatown Chow

Chowing in Chinatown can be both delectable and delightfully affordable. Elbow your way through the crowded streets and find a flurry of food markets, bubble tea cafés, bakeries, and eateries both large and small. Feast on freshly pulled noodles; duck into an ice cream parlor for a scoop of avocado or black sesame; or breeze past a market window and gander the crocodile meat and frogs on display (with claws!). Haggle over the freshest fish and produce at the storefronts and then sneak under the Manhattan Bridge for a *banh mi*. Klezmer meets Cantonese at the Egg Rolls and Egg Creams Festival, an annual summer street celebration honoring the neighboring Chinese and Jewish communities of Chinatown and the Lower East Side. Partygoers pack the streets for Chinese New Year (the first full moon after January 19th), with dragons dancing down the avenues accompanied by costumed revelers and fireworks.

LITTLE ITALY

The Little Italy of Scorsese's gritty, authentic *Mean Streets* is slowly vanishing into what may now be more aptly called Micro Italy. The onetime stronghold of a large Italian-American population (once spanning from Canal Street north to Houston, and from Lafayette to the Bowery) has dwindled to a mere corridor—Mulberry Street between Canal and Broome streets. Chinatown is quickly devouring Mulberry Street, the main drag and the tenacious heart of the area. But the spirit of the origins still pulses in century-old family-run markets, delis, gelato shops, and mom-and-pop trattorias. Established in 1892, **Alleva Dairy** (known for their homemade ricotta) is the oldest Italian cheese

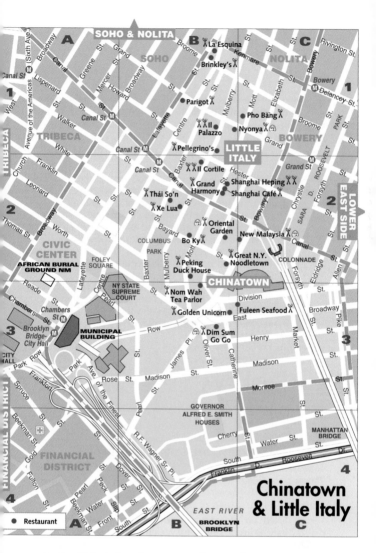

Chinatown & Little Italy

store in the U.S. A few doors down at **DiPalo's Fine Foods** find imported *sopressata*, *salumi*, and stunning wine selections. Renowned for its Italian pastries and strong espresso, devotees frequent the beloved **Ferrara's Bakery and Café** on Grand Street. On weekends from May to mid-October, Mulberry Street is a pedestrian zone, creating one big alfresco party—the Feast of San Gennaro in September is particularly raucous. While these days you can get better Italian food elsewhere in the city, tourists still gather to treasure and bathe in the nostalgia of Mulberry Street.

Bo Ky

B2

80 Bayard St. (bet. Mott & Mulberry Sts.)

Subway: Canal St (Lafayette St.)   Lunch & dinner daily
Phone: 212-406-2292
Web: www.bokynyc.com
Prices: 🍜

Bo Ky is a total dive... but in a good way. It's the kind of place that everyone wants to know about, where Chinese-born families and savvy locals go for great, cheap food.

The service can seem gruff and the space itself may appear dingy, but no one seems to mind as they gather around large communal tables (set with plastic and disposable dishes), leaning over massive soup bowls brimming with meat, vegetables, and noodles. The menu includes fish ball soup infused with sesame oil, ginger, and scallions, bobbing with flat noodles. Fatty and silky-tender hunks of country-style duck, braised in a briny liquid stocked with star anise, clove, and peppercorns, are so enjoyably tender that they have truly earned their own window display.

Brinkley's

B1

406 Broome St. (bet. Centre & Lafayette Sts.)

Subway: Prince St   Lunch & dinner daily
Phone: 212-680-5600
Web: www.brinkleysnyc.com
Prices: $$

Fixed on the culture-clash nib of Chinatown and Little Italy, Brinkley's is an easygoing gastropub tailored for cool, alternative kids as well as upmarket hipsters. But, most everyone here is struck by their rummage sale-chic décor where metallic stools line a lengthy zinc-topped bar and white subway tiles punctuated by blackboards don the walls. The requisite black-and-white checked floor and burgundy leather booths prime you for such ingenious grub as gourmet sausages wrapped in puff pastry, or grilled pita wedges spread with deliciously creamy roasted garlic hummus.

In the back, a communal table allows laptop lizards to linger over lunch, which usually entails a salad or sandwich like smoked Nova Scotia salmon capped with crème fraîche and dill.

34

Dim Sum Go Go

Chinese

5 East Broadway (at Chatham Sq.)

Subway: Canal St (Lafayette St.)   Lunch & dinner daily
Phone: 212-732-0797
Web: N/A
Prices:

Wake us up before you go-go to this Chinatown classic where the food is damn good. The dim sum is Hong Kong level, and the Cantonese is worth a sampling. With over 24 varieties of mouthwatering dim sum served well into the evening (dim sum is traditionally a lunch thing) and a killer Cantonese menu, this bright, funky restaurant is a guaranteed good time; even if you do have to spend a little more than you would out in Sunset Park.

Head upstairs for a lively dinner scene or duck into the sleek downstairs room for a quick bite. Silky cellophane noodles arrive laced with crab and Chinese chives; while crab meat soup bobbing with tender bits of smoked ham, is served with fried Shanghai bread. Oh and you simply must not miss the otherworldly roast pork buns.

Fuleen Seafood

  Chinese

11 Division St. (bet. Catherine & Market Sts.)

Subway: Canal St (Lafayette St.)   Lunch & dinner daily
Phone: 212-941-6888
Web: N/A
Prices:

From their variety of hard- and soft-shell crab dishes to the ever-popular snails in black bean sauce or geoduck clams "two different ways," this Cantonese kitchen does impressive things with gourmet ingredients. The large round tables of this Chinatown mainstay are filled with gregarious groups from the local, discerning Chinese community—a testament to its success. Yet all are welcome here, as the polite staff graciously guides you through the menu, making helpful recommendations.

Garlicky, green vegetables are an essential accompaniment to meals here, perhaps complementing a whole fish, presented tableside before being expertly steamed and dressed with ginger and scallions. Landlubbers will unearth plenty of options on the sizeable menu.

Manhattan ▶ Chinatown & Little Italy

Golden Unicorn

Chinese   🍴

B3

18 East Broadway (at Catherine St.)

Subway: Canal St (Lafayette St.)   Lunch & dinner daily
Phone: 212-941-0911
Web: www.goldenunicornrestaurant.com
Prices: $$

This age-old dim sum parlor, spread over many floors in an office building, is one of the few Cantonese spots that actually has the space and volume to necessitate its parade of steaming carts brimming with treats. While Golden Unicorn's system is very efficient and part of the spectacle, arrive early to nab a seat by the kitchen for better variety and hotter items. A helpful brigade of suited men and women roam the space to offer the likes of exquisitely soft roast pork buns, or congee with preserved egg and shredded pork. Buzzing with locals and visitors, it is also a favorite among families who appreciate the kid-friendly scene as much as the delectable, steamed pea shoot and shrimp dumplings, pork *siu mai*, and rice rolls stuffed with shrimp.

Grand Harmony

Chinese   🍴

B2

98 Mott St. (bet. Canal & Hester Sts.)

Subway: Canal St (Lafayette St.)   Lunch & dinner daily
Phone: 212-226-6603
Web: N/A
Prices: 🍴🍴

Is this, hands down, *the* best dim sum in Gotham? Probably not. Still, Grand Harmony pleases and teases its Chinese troops with an attractive banquet hall bedecked in red and gold, overflowing with chintzy decorations, gilded accents, and vibrant columns. Come midday, the huge space jams with crowds pouring in for that daytime indulgence—dim sum.

Dinner unveils a mélange of Cantonese food, but dim sum (at pretty prices) is the going game. Keep an eagle eye on those expert ladies rolling around carts of delicious *gai lan* (steamed Chinese broccoli, perfectly crisp, with oyster sauce); piping hot barbecue pork buns; fried tofu skin wrapped around pork, shrimp, and cabbage; or vermicelli tossed with pickled vegetables, dried squid, seafood, and scallions.

Great N.Y. Noodletown

Chinese ✗

B2

28 Bowery (at Bayard St.)

Subway: Canal St (Lafayette St.)

Phone: 212-349-0923

Web: N/A

Prices: 🍜

Lunch & dinner daily

You don't come for the ambience. With its closely jammed seats, roast ducks hanging in the window, and menus tucked under glass-topped tables, Great N.Y. Noodletown is down-market Chinatown at its drabbest. What you come for is the food–which, served daily from 9:00 A.M.-4.00 A.M.–is not only delicious but remarkably cheap. Who could argue with a big bowl of perfectly roasted duck and tender noodles in steaming broth for $4?

Best bets include any of the roasted meats served over fluffy rice; and, of course, duck, in all its crispy, fatty succulence. Don't miss the specials written on the table tents, where you'll find irresistible house delights like salt-baked soft shell crabs (a must do when it's in season) and Chinese flowering chive stir-fries.

Il Cortile

Italian ✗✗

B2

125 Mulberry St. (bet. Canal & Hester Sts.)

Subway: Canal St (Lafayette St)

Phone: 212-226-6060

Web: www.ilcortile.com

Prices: $$

Lunch & dinner daily

Beyond this quaint and charming façade lies one of Little Italy's famed mainstays, ever-popular with dreamy eyed dates seeking the stuff of Billy Joel lyrics. The expansive space does indeed suggest a nostalgic romance, with its series of Mediterranean-themed rooms, though the most celebrated is the pleasant garden atrium (*il cortile* is Italian for "courtyard"), with a glass-paneled ceiling and abundant greenery.

A skilled line of chefs present a wide array of familiar starters and entrées, from eggplant *rollatini* to chicken Francese; as well as a range of pastas, such as *spaghettini puttanesca* or *risotto con funghi*. More than 30 years of sharing family recipes and bringing men to one bent knee continues to earn Il Cortile a longtime following.

Il Palazzo

B1

151 Mulberry St. (bet. Grand & Hester Sts.)

Subway: Canal St (Lafayette St.)　　　　　　　　Lunch & dinner daily
Phone: 212-343-7000
Web: N/A
Prices: $$

This "palace" on Little Italy's celebrated Mulberry Street rises to every expectation of a good, traditional Italian-American meal. A tuxedo-clad host ushers guests into a long room with stucco walls and linen-draped tables. Beyond, the sunken dining room recalls a winter garden of lush greenery and natural light. Sidewalk seating is beloved among tourists watching tourists.

Old-world dishes reign here, beginning with a basket of focaccia and bowl of *stracciatella alla Romana*. The classics continue with the likes of *vitello alla pizzaiola* (veal scallopini sautéed with tomato, onions, mushrooms, roasted peppers, and fresh basil); or *gamberoni alla scampi* (jumbo shrimp sautéed in a garlic-white wine sauce). Lunchtime frittata specials offer good value.

La Esquina

B1

106 Kenmare St. (bet. Cleveland Pl. & Lafayette St.)

Subway: Spring St (Lafayette St.)　　　　　　　Lunch & dinner daily
Phone: 646-613-7100
Web: www.esquinanyc.com
Prices: $$

When La Esquina opened in 2005 it was a breath of bright air, offering enjoyably fresh cuisine that stood tall among the paltry selection of Manhattan Mexican. Thankfully, the city's south-of-the-border dining scene has evolved since then. However, La Esquina remains a worthy option. More playground than restaurant, the multi-faceted setting takes up an iconic downtown corner and draws a hip crowd to the grab and go taqueria, 30-seat café, and lively subterranean dining room and bar amplified by a nightly DJ soundtrack.

The spirit here is not just alive but kicking with classic renditions of tortilla soup; *mole negro enchiladas* filled with excellently seasoned chicken; as well the likes of *carne asada* starring black Angus sirloin with *mojo de ajo*.

New Malaysia

🍴

C2

46-48 Bowery (bet. Bayard & Canal Sts.)

Subway: Canal St (Lafayette St.)
Phone: 212-964-0284
Web: N/A
Prices: 💶

Lunch & dinner daily

Mad for Malaysian? Head to this lively dive, sequestered in a Chinatown arcade. Proffering some of the best Malaysian treats in town, including all the classics, New Malaysia sees a deluge of regulars who pour in for a massive offering of exceptional dishes. Round tables cram a room furnished with little more than a service counter. Still, the aromas wafting from flaky *roti canai* and Melaka crispy coconut shrimp keep you focused on the food.

Capturing the essence of Chinatown are fast (brusque?) servers who deliver abundant yet authentic bowls of spicy-sour *asam laksa* fragrant with lemongrass; *kang-kung belacan*, greens infused with dried shrimp and chili; and *nasi lemak*, the national treasure starring coconut rice, chicken curry, and dried anchovies.

Nom Wah Tea Parlor

🍴

B3

13 Doyers St. (bet. Bowery & Pell St.)

Subway: Canal St (Lafayette St.)
Phone: 212-962-6047
Web: www.nomwah.com
Prices: 💶

Lunch & dinner daily

Possibly the most senior dim sum den along the still, back streets of Chinatown, Nom Wah Tea Parlor endured a face-lift when old man Wally handed over charge to young Wilson Tang. Resembling an old diner-meets-coffee shop, the room features a counter, parade of pleather booths, and tables topped with red-and-white vinyl that spikes a nostalgic sense.

"The original egg roll" is a massive hit (literally) and includes delicious tofu skin wrapped around crunchy vegetables, doused in a tempura batter, and fried to crisp perfection. Cheery servers deliver other dim sum like a rice roll in fried dough splashed with sweet soy; or fried eggplant stuffed with shrimp paste. While the house special pan-fried dumplings are salty, they are some of *the* best in town.

Nyonya 😊

B1

199 Grand St. (bet. Mott & Mulberry Sts.)

Subway: Canal St (Lafayette St.)   Lunch & dinner daily
Phone: 212-334-3669
Web: www.ilovenyonya.com
Prices: 😊😊

S

A Southeast Asian marvel in Manhattan, Nyonya is replete with regulars and City Hall suits. True to the Chinatown aesthetic, the space is large and bright with gruff servers. But keep faith, as they hold the keys to some magnificent Malaysian food.

Teasing your taste buds is a fluffy oyster omelette anointed with sweet chili sauce. A specialty from the massive menu and perfect for the prudent is beef *satay* with peanut sauce; while the house special crabs massaged with ground chili and dried shrimp is best for the bodacious.

A lineup of classic beverages gorgeously complements such faithful fare as *Assam laksa* rich with herbs, lemongrass, noodles, and sardine flakes; and *nasi lemak*, a mélange of coconut rice, chicken, anchovies, veg, and eggs.

Oriental Garden 😊

B2

14 Elizabeth St. (bet. Bayard & Canal Sts.)

Subway: Canal St (Lafayette St.)   Lunch & dinner daily
Phone: 212-619-0085
Web: www.orientalgardenny.com
Prices: $$

A single room makes up this garden of Chinese delights. Robed in warm shades of beige and red, and packed with tables that expand just as readily as your waistline, Oriental Garden is a precious jewel much sought-after both for daytime dim sum and top-quality Cantonese.

Jammed by noon, dim sum is ordered from carts or the printed menu. The carts carry crowd-pleasers but tune them out and opt for steamy chive dumplings, crisp-baked roast pork triangles, and juicy roast duck. After the dumplings digest, Cantonese takes over. The fish tanks lining the entryway are a good indication of where to start. First-rate preparations of these global swimmers include the seasonal Australian crystal crabs, oysters with ginger and scallions, or lobster "country style."

Parigot

French ✗

B1

155 Grand St. (at Lafayette St.)

Subway: Canal St (Lafayette St.)   Lunch & dinner daily
Phone: 212-274-8859
Web: www.parigotnyc.com
Prices: **$$**

In the neck of Nolita, Parigot is that hugely favored French bistro teeming with traditional fare. Francophiles come here to be comforted by classics such as mussels Parigot; escargot with garlic-parsley butter; Basque omelette; and *coq au vin*. Smaller groups from around the way might share an *assiette de charcuterie* or *assiette de fromages* served with warm slices of toasted bread, all the while picturing themselves cruising along the glorious Seine.

With French music wafting through a wood-furnished dining room whose cheerful walls are hung with photos of quaint cafés, a meal at Parigot feels like a mini escape to the Côte d'Azur, beautifully capped with a traditional and fresh salad Niçoise, a side of fantastic fries, and a glass of crisp rosé.

Peking Duck House

Chinese ✗

B2

28 Mott St. (bet. Chatham Sq. & Pell St.)

Subway: Canal St (Lafayette St)   Lunch & dinner daily
Phone: 212-227-1810
Web: www.pekingduckhousenyc.com
Prices: **$$**

Only rookies open the menu at Peter Luger steakhouse—and the same ought to apply to any restaurant named after a menu item. So, while you may stumble onto a few gems like the sautéed string beans with minced pork, the bird is the word at this group-friendly Chinatown joint.

Despite its rather odd name, the Peking Duck House is a touch classier than her Chinatown sisters, with a contemporary polish that won't frighten your Midwestern cousin. Service may slow down at the more elegant midtown location, but both wheel out the golden brown duck with proper flare, and carve it into crisp-skinned mouthwatering slices. Your job is easy: fold into fresh pancakes, sprinkle with scallion, cucumbers, and a dash of hoisin sauce...then devour.

Pellegrino's

Italian ✗✗

B1

138 Mulberry St. (bet. Grand & Hester Sts.)

Subway: Canal St (Lafayette St)

Lunch & dinner daily

Phone: 212-226-3177
Web: N/A
Prices: $$

Pellegrino's offers a well-done meal that puts her gaudier neighbors to shame. Both regulars and tourists frequent this local mainstay, and on a sunny day the quaint sidewalk tables look upon the pulsating heart of Little Italy. Inside, deep red walls dotted with three-dimensional art takes you back in time. The staff is courteous and children are welcome; in fact, half portions are offered for smaller appetites.

The food stays true to its Italian-American roots with heaping portions—grilled portobello topped with caramelized fontina and a drizzle of balsamic vinegar; or fettuccine Giovanni in a cream sauce accented by prosciutto and asparagus. The cannoli is a classic finish, even if it is presented with a rote zigzag of custard and strawberry sauces.

Pho Băng

Vietnamese ✗

C1

157 Mott St. (bet. Broome & Grand Sts.)

Subway: Bowery

Lunch & dinner daily

Phone: 212-966-3797
Web: N/A
Prices: ⌘⌘

Hangover? Craving? In need of a quick, tasty meal? Pho Băng is where it's at for restorative bowls of bubbling *pho*, served up in a flash and on the cheap. Park it in the simple space and start with a plate of delicious fried Vietnamese spring rolls (*cha gio*) served with lettuce and mint leaves for wrapping; or try the tasty rice "crêpe," (*bahn cuon nhan thit cha lua*), stuffed with black mushrooms, pork, sprouts, and ham—a real treat and rare find here in New York, so don't skip it.

Finally, follow the lead of your fellow diners and slurp up one of seventeen varieties of hearty *pho*. Try the *pho tai gau*— fresh eye of round, brisket, and rice noodles in a flavorful beef broth, served with sprouts, basil, and lemon, all for less than eight bucks.

Shanghai Café

Chinese 🍴

B2

100 Mott St. (bet. Canal & Hester Sts.)

Subway: Canal St (Lafayette St.)
Phone: 212-966-3988
Web: N/A
Prices: 🥢🥢

Lunch & dinner daily

Clean, simple, and updated, this café is where one should head when in the mood for well-priced, Shanghai-style food. Appreciably more attractive than its neighbors, Shanghai Café prides itself on a pretty interior featuring a few booths and tables armed with bamboo steamers cradling those classic handmade buns—perhaps filled with tender pork, crab, and ginger with a steaming rich and fatty broth.

Groups gather here with an intent to eat and their tables quickly disappear under the avalanche of dishes like sea cucumber drowned in a brown sauce infused with shrimp roe. A savory soup bobbing with bean curd, dried scallops and thick noodles; chewy rice rounds in a clear and delicious pork broth and spicy beef tendons are favorites of those in the know.

Shanghai Heping

Chinese 🍴🍴

B2

104 Mott St. (bet. Canal & Hester Sts.)

Subway: Canal St (Lafayette St.)
Phone: 212-925-1118
Web: N/A
Prices: $$

Lunch & dinner daily

Head downtown to Chinatown to fully appreciate the swank Shanghai Heping—a stylish and contemporary restaurant decked in lime green accents, faux-granite tabletops, and tiled floors. Friendly staff and a proficient chef ensure tasty renditions of Shanghainese dishes.

Quality ingredients and great skill shine through menu items like chilled and crunchy-salty bamboo shoots braised in a soy-based brown sauce abundant with Chinese spices; and knots of chewy tofu skin stewed with pork belly cubes in a rich, velvety sauce, wonderfully flavored with cloves, star anise, and ginger. Large slices of green opo squash (long gourd) sautéed in garlic sauce are so tender, delicate, and simply tasty that you might just see them atop every table in the house.

43

Thái So'n

B2

89 Baxter St. (bet. Bayard & Canal Sts.)

Subway: Canal St (Lafayette St.)   Lunch & dinner daily
Phone: 212-732-2822
Web: N/A
Prices: 🆎

Thái So'n is by far the best of the bunch in this Vietnamese quarter of Chinatown. It's neither massive nor fancy, but it's bright, clean, and perpetually in business. One peek at the specials on the walls (maybe golden-fried squid strewn with sea salt) will have you begging for a seat in the crammed room.

Speedy servers scoot between groups of City Hall suits and Asian locals as they order the likes of *cha gio*, pork spring rolls with *nuoc cham*; or *goi cuon*, fantastic summer rolls filled with poached shrimp and vermicelli. Naturally, *pho* choices are abundant, but the real star of the show is *pho tai*—where raw beef shavings are cooked to tender perfection when combined with a scalding hot, savory broth replete with herbs, sprouts, and chewy noodles.

Xe Lua

B2

86 Mulberry St. (bet. Bayard & Canal Sts.)

Subway: Canal St (Lafayette St)   Lunch & dinner daily
Phone: 212-577-8887
Web: www.xeluanewyork.com
Prices: 🆎

A cheery orange sign splashed in yellow, blue, and green blazons this lovely spot's name in both English and Vietnamese, while tropical themes outfit the interior in royal blue, bamboo, and a floor-to-ceiling mural of boats, sea, and sky.

The expansive menu features a flavorful assortment of appetizers, stir-fries, clay pots, noodles, and rice dishes, with headings like "Porky," "Froggy Style," and "Chicken Little" to express their quirky humor. Dive into one of fourteen varieties of *pho*—these steaming bowls of rice noodle soup are all under seven dollars. Heartier appetites are satisfied with the *pho xe lua*, a massive bowl of noodles, brisket, tendon, tripe, and meatballs swimming in a rich beef broth. The staff is pleasant, quick, and efficient.

East Village

This storied bohemia is no longer rampant with riots, rockers, and radical zeitgeist, but remains crowned as Manhattan's uncompromising capital of counter-culture. East Villagers may seem tamer now that CBGB is closed, but they are no less creative, casual, and undeniably cool.

The neighborhood's bars and eateries exhibit the same edge, and denizens craving a nightly nosh have plenty to choose from. **Momofuku Milk Bar** turns out a spectrum of delectable baked goods and soft serve ice cream in seasonal flavors like cereal milk and caramel apple until midnight. Sauces like curry-ketchup and smoked-eggplant mayo heighten crispy Belgian fries from **Pomme Frites**. For burgers, **Paul's** may have the best in town. **Crif Dogs**–open until 4:00 A.M. on weekends– deep-fries their dogs for the perfect post pub-crawl snack. Many eateries, cafés, second-hand shops, and vendors line these blocks with specialties from pork (**Porchetta**) to macaroni & cheese (**S'mac**) in a distinctly East Village way. Speaking of cheese, **The Bourgeois Pig** draws celebrities on the "down-low" with its pots of fondue; equally stellar is **Luke's Lobster**, a seafood shack offering the freshest of product directly from Maine. Perhaps most spirited, and in keeping with the kitschy downtown feel, is Japantown—a decidedly down-market and groovier "Harajuku" version of its Midtown East sibling. Along St. Marks Place, look for the red paper lanterns of hip yakitori spots like **Taisho**, or smell the takoyaki frying and sizzling okonomiyaki at **Otafuku**; and explore divey izakayas like **Village Yokocho**. Among the area's sultry sake dens, few can rival subterranean **Decibel**— serving an outrageous selection of sake and shochu in its hideaway setting. Devout bargain-hunters will relish **Xi'an Famous Foods**— their menu is made up of regional Chinese cuisine from the Shaanxi province, an area made famous after the discovery of the Terracotta Army.

Flavor Smackdown

While Japantown may tuck its lounges down a nondescript stairway, everything along the "Curry Row" stretch of East Sixth Street smacks of festivities, with spices as bold as the neon lights that dot the awnings. While these inexpensive spots may cater to NYU students, they also offer a great spread of South Asian food.

For a bit of old-world flavor, an afternoon at **Veniero's Pasticceria & Caffé** is in order. Established in 1894, this friendly staple draws long lines (especially around

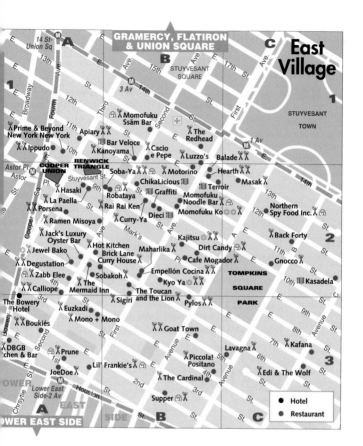

East Village

(Map labels:)

14 St-Union Sq

STUYVESANT SQUARE

3 Av 14th

STUYVESANT TOWN

Prime & Beyond New York New York
Ippudo
Apiary
Bar Veloce
Kanoyama
Cacio e Pepe
Momofuku Ssäm Bar
The Redhead
Luzzo's
Balade
COOPER UNION
RENWICK TRIANGLE
Stuyvesant
Soba-Ya
Motorino
Hearth
Masak
Hasaki
ChikaLicious
Graffiti
Terroir
La Paella
Robataya
Momofuku Noodle Bar
Porsena
Rai Rai Ken
Dieci
Momofuku Ko
Northern Spy Food Inc.
Ramen Misoya
Curry-Ya
Jack's Luxury Oyster Bar
Kajitsu
Dirt Candy
Back Forty
Jewel Bako
Hot Kitchen
Brick Lane Curry House
Maharlika
Cafe Mogador
Gnocco
Degustation
Zabb Elee
Sobakoh
Empellón Cocina
TOMPKINS
Calliope
The Mermaid Inn
Kyo Ya
Kasadela
The Bowery Hotel
Sigiri
The Toucan and the Lion
Pylos
SQUARE
PARK
Euzkadi
Boukiés
Mono + Mono
Goat Town
Kafana
DBGB chen & Bar
Prune
Lil' Frankie's
Lavagna
JoeDoe
Piccola! Positano
Edi & The Wolf
The Cardinal
Supper
LOWER EAST SIDE
Lower East Side-2 Av

● Hotel
● Restaurant

---

holiday time) for its traditional Italian baked goods. **Sigmund Pretzel Shop** is famed for its handmade pretzels dressed with dips like beet-horseradish mayo. The beloved, family-run **Veselka** has been serving Ukrainian treats for over 50 years, representing the area's former Eastern European population. For specialty items, **East Village Cheese** is a premier vendor—find an ample selection here, minus the mark-up of gourmet emporiums. It goes without saying that liquor flows freely

in the East Village. There are an abundance of dive bars, but those with a more urbane palate will be happy that this neighborhood is at the nexus of cutting-edge mixology. Speaking of which, **Angel's Share** (hidden in a Japanese restaurant on Stuyvesant Street); **PDT**, or Please Don't Tell (accessed through Crif Dogs); **Death & Co.** on East Sixth Street; and **Mayahuel** (with its south-of-the-border spin) all offer an epicurean approach to cocktail service garnering them accolades.

47

Apiary

60 Third Ave. (bet. 10th & 11th Sts.)

Subway: 14 St - Union Sq
Phone: 212-254-0888
Web: www.apiarynyc.com
Prices: $$

Dinner nightly

Bringing a unique elegance and maturity to its East Village locale, Apiary's intimate space is buzz-worthy. Envisioned by Ligne Roset, the sleek and contemporary room features burgundy- and brown-upholstered chairs beneath chandelier-shaped plastic sconces that in turn cast sultry shadows on the walls.

The modern menu follows suit, with the likes of golden brown sweetbreads with deep-crimson romesco sauce—its alluring flavors a wonderful departure from tradition. From the emerald green olive oil and excellent breads to thick-cut, caramelized pork chops with black beans and chunky guacamole, to desserts like a buttery blackberry financier, Executive Chef Scott Bryan keeps the menu concise and tasty. Prix-fixe and tasting menus are also offered.

Back Forty

190 Ave. B (at 12th St.)

Subway: 1 Av
Phone: 212-388-1990
Web: www.backfortynyc.com
Prices: $$

Lunch Sat – Sun
Dinner nightly

Chef/owner Peter Hoffman sates city slickers seeking the country life with this popular tavern's array of fresh-from-the-farm themed preparations. The casual setting evokes heartland charm with its tables topped by brown paper mats that display the menu, walls adorned with found objects and agricultural tools, as well as an inviting backyard dining area. Though Back Forty is billed as a grass-fed burger joint, the menu offers much more than spicy homemade ketchup. Starters feature garden-fresh ingredients; while seasonality and sustainability drives the rest of the menu with the likes of Catskill trout and East Coast hake with local clams and salsa verde.

A new SoHo location resides at the corner previously occupied by Savoy (also from the same chef).

Balade

Lebanese

208 First Ave. (bet. 12th & 13th Sts.)

Subway: 1 Av   Lunch & dinner daily
Phone: 212-529-6868
Web: www.baladerestaurants.com
Prices: ⊂⊙

Honing in on the cuisine of Lebanon, Balade is a welcoming and tasty Middle Eastern experience fronted by a cheerful red awning. The spotless room is accented with tile, brick, and wood; and each table bears a bottle of private label herb-infused olive oil.

The menu begins with a glossary of traditional Lebanese ingredients and the explanation that *Balade* means "fresh, local." The mezze; grilled meat-stuffed sandwiches; and Lebanese-style pizzas called *manakeesh* topped with the likes of lean ground beef, chopped onion, and spices are all fresh-tasting indeed. House specialties are also of note, like the *mujaddara crush*—a platter of lentils and rice topped by crispy fried onions and a salad of cool chopped cucumber and tomato.

Bar Veloce

Italian

175 Second Ave. (bet. 11th & 12th Sts.)

Subway: Astor Pl   Lunch & dinner daily
Phone: 212-260-3200
Web: www.barveloce.com
Prices: ⊂⊙

Bar Veloce closed last year but has re-emerged to offer a larger setting and just-as-enjoyable light Italian plates. The wine bar features communal tables and a U-shaped counter, while grey walls and concrete lend an industrial flair. Bottles of wine on display stimulate your thirst.

Behind the bar, cooks in cream blazers dress greens, slice an inexhaustible amount of ciabatta, and continuously work the panini press—Bar Veloce's carte is delicious in its simplicity. Begin the day with breakfast pastries, then delight in a salad of fresh baby arugula slicked with zesty vinaigrette and shards of Grana Padano; or a toasty sandwich of pistachio-flecked mortadella, crushed green olives, and aged provolone, all washed down by a glass of crisp *vermentino*.

Boukiés

A3

Greek ✗✗

29 E. 2nd St. (at Second Ave.)

Subway: Lower East Side - 2 Av
Phone: 212-777-2502
Web: www.boukiesrestaurant.com
Prices: $$

Lunch Sat – Sun
Dinner nightly

Owner Christos Valtzoglou has rejiggered this corner of East Village real estate into a contemporary, inviting, and Aegean-inspired space for sampling inventive meze. White marble, bright-blue rattan furniture, and linen banquettes comfortably convey the geographical focus of Boukiés, where Greek food authority Diane Kochilas has consulted on the menu.

Among the carte du jour's many highlights are claypot-baked chickpeas and eggplant in minty, cinnamon-seasoned tomato sauce; a savory plate of neatly crisped and buttery cigar-shaped mushroom pies; or head-on prawns with a roasted red pepper-and-almond sauce. Semolina cake with caramelized pineapple and sweet vanilla-flecked yogurt is best enjoyed with a dark Greek coffee.

Brick Lane Curry House

A2

Indian ✗

306-308 E. 6th St. (bet. First & Second Aves.)

Subway: Astor Pl
Phone: 212-979-2900
Web: www.bricklanecurryhouse.com
Prices: $$

Lunch & dinner daily

Located on Curry Row and named after London's own, Brick Lane is a 6th Street standout featuring numerous influences lifted from across the pond. Beers are available by the half or full pint, an Underground map adorns the wall, and meltingly soft cheddar cheese stuffs the tasty *paratha*.

Despite the Anglo-culinary whimsy, Brick Lane's heart belongs to curry with a selection of fifteen varieties that include Goan, spiked with green chilies and a tangy bite. Prepared with your protein of choice, the selection even includes the *phaal*, said to be so spicy it is accompanied by a disclaimer warning guests of "physical or emotional damage" that may result. However, this may also be a reminder of the thoughtful, friendly, and efficient service staff here.

Cacio e Pepe

B1

Italian ✗

182 Second Ave. (bet. 11th & 12th Sts.)

Subway: 3 Av
Phone: 212-505-5931
Web: www.cacioepepe.com
Prices: $$

Dinner nightly

With its subdued temperament and pleasant service, this casual and charming Italian can be trusted to satisfy, from the warm greeting everyone receives upon entering to the cannoli—a lovely finale to any meal here. The rustic menu of traditional Roman dishes features a house specialty from which the establishment takes its name: homemade *tonnarelli* tossed with pasta water, olive oil, cracked black pepper, and a showering of pecorino cheese. Yet there is much more to be discovered, such as cuttlefish over soft polenta or *bucatini all'Amatriciana*.

The wine list is short but carefully selected to highlight less-familiar producers in the most notable Italian regions. In warm weather, the pretty backyard garden makes an idyllic dining area.

Cafe Mogador

B2

Moroccan ✗

101 St. Mark's Pl. (bet. First Ave. & Ave. A)

Subway: 1 Av
Phone: 212-677-2226
Web: www.cafemogador.com
Prices:

Lunch & dinner daily

Since 1983, this family-run neighborhood favorite has graciously served reasonably priced breakfast, lunch, and dinner daily while exuding an inviting coffeehouse vibe. Inside, Moorish lanterns, spice jars, black-and-white photos, and exotic bric-a-brac impart an air of North Africa that spills onto the pleasant sidewalk seating.

Moroccan and Middle Eastern specialties include platters of merguez, hummus, and falafel dressed with harissa and pita. Grilled skewers of marinated meats are definitely tempting, but the lamb couscous with chickpeas, vegetables, and raisins; or the chicken tagine with lemon and olives should also be given serious consideration.

Brooklynites can now boast their very own outpost of Cafe Mogador in Williamsburg.

Calliope

French XX

A2

84 E. 4th St. (at Second Ave.)

Subway: Lower East Side - 2 Av
Phone: 212-260-8484
Web: www.calliopenyc.com
Prices: $$

Lunch Sat — Sun
Dinner nightly

Husband-and-wife team Eric Korsh and Ginevra Iverson have moved into Belcourt's old corner and bring with them an unabashed bistro experience that's easy to love. Oysters, beef tongue with sauce *gribiche*, or Provençal tomato tart are all fine starting points, before moving on to pleasing entrées that may include spoon tender lamb neck braised in a spirited broth of tomato, red wine vinegar, and chili flakes. The *baba au rhum* is a thing of beauty—presented warm, crowned by perfectly whipped cream, and soaked (right before your eyes) with Venezuelan rum.

A communal table supplements seating in the charming dining room that is decorated with vintage mirrors and French doors that make for a relaxed and breezy experience when the weather cooperates.

The Cardinal

Southern X

B3

234 E. 4th St. (bet. Aves. A & B)

Subway: Lower East Side - 2 Av
Phone: 212-995-8600
Web: www.thecardinalnyc.com
Prices: $$

Lunch Sat — Sun
Dinner nightly

Southern cuisine continues to make further Manhattan inroads with the arrival of this new Alphabet City spot named after the North Carolina state bird. The restaurant's motif is clear, with the state's flag proudly brandishing one wall and a menu of down-home treats built around a brief list of entrées paired with a slew of choices for sides.

The barbecue plate is a meaty delight—spilling over with dry-rubbed pork ribs smoked in-house for six hours, toothsome brisket infused for three times as long, and a link of house-made pork sausage. A trio of sauces is provided to dress-up an already satisfying plate and give equal representation to Tennessee, Texas, and North Carolina. Regional sodas, like Cheerwine, are sure to make some feel nostalgic.

ChikaLicious

Contemporary

B2

203 E. 10th St. (bet. First & Second Aves.)

Subway: Astor Pl
Phone: 212-475-0929
Web: www.chikalicious.com
Prices: ⊜⊗

Dinner Thu – Sun

Named for Pastry Chef/owner Chika Tillman, this sweet spot presents an all-encompassing dessert experience that somehow manages to impress without overkill. The chic white space offers counter seating overlooking a lab-clean kitchen where the team prepares elegant jewels that start as butter, sugar, and chocolate. À la carte is offered, but the best way to appreciate this dessert bar is to select the prix-fixe menu. Feasts here may begin with an amuse-bouche of Darjeeling tea gelée with milk sorbet, followed by a mascarpone semifreddo topped with espresso granita, then finish with the pillowy cubes of coconut-marshmallow petits fours.

Dessert Club across the street tempts with cookies, cupcakes, and shaved ice for a grab-and-go fix.

Curry-Ya

Japanese

B2

214 E. 10th St. (bet. First & Second Aves.)

Subway: Astor Pl
Phone: 866-602-8779
Web: www.nycurry-ya.com
Prices: ⊜⊗

Lunch & dinner daily

From the co-owner of Soba-Ya, comes this tasty newcomer, specializing in Japan's unique version of curry—*yoshoku*. This culinary icon belongs in the repertoire of Western-style dishes that have become a part of the Japanese palate. Characterized by a mild sweetness and restrained heat, Curry-Ya's rich sauce is garnished with pickled vegetables, short grain rice, and is available with a selection of accompaniments like *panko*-crusted Berkshire pork cutlet, organic chicken, and grilled hamburger. The small menu also offers inspiring starters like a salad of *yuba* and snow peas with green olive dressing.

The bright space, warmed by pale pink walls and blond wood stools, offers seating for 14 at a marble counter set in front of the white-tiled kitchen.

DBGB Kitchen & Bar

French ✗✗

A3

299 Bowery (bet. First & Houston Sts.)

Subway: Lower East Side - 2 Av
Phone: 212-933-5300
Web: www.danielnyc.com
Prices: $$

Lunch & dinner daily

Superstar Chef Daniel Boulud's popular take on casual downtown eats features an earthy shaded dining room that evokes the Bowery's past as a hub for restaurant supplies: shelves are stocked with dry goods and crockery, the wraparound exposed kitchen displays gleaming surfaces, and the restroom walls recall pages of vintage cookware catalogs. The kitchen's playful spirit is evident in the eclectic menu of impressive dishes, including mouthwatering burgers, a globally-inspired selection of sausages, and grown-up ice cream sundaes. More gilded fare has featured the likes of velvety potato soup seasonally embellished with green garlic, sweet peas, and ramps; and a richly satisfying bowlful of house-made saffron tagliolini with veal Bolognese.

Degustation

Spanish ✗✗

A2

239 E. 5th St. (bet. Second & Third Aves.)

Subway: Astor Pl
Phone: 212-979-1012
Web: N/A
Prices: $$

Dinner nightly

Arriving courtesy of the proprietors of Jewel Bako, this elegant tapas bar wholly clad in squares of slate and counter seats radiates East Village-chic—all the better to take in the show that pivots around the *plancha*, which is in constant use to toast bread, sear proteins, and caramelize *torija*.

Long a local darling and adored date-night spot, Degustation has welcomed a new talent to lead the brigade and she in turn proves that change is delicious. Well-executed small plates include Nantucket Bay scallops cooked in duck fat; or squid stuffed with braised oxtail propped on steel-cut oats cooked risotto-style and enriched with squid ink. Crisp-skinned quail perched atop *arroz brut* (dirty rice flavored with liver and jus) is a match made in heaven.

Dieci

Fusion

B2

228 E. 10th St. (bet. First & Second Aves.)

Subway: Astor Pl
Phone: 212-387-9545
Web: www.dieciny.com
Prices:

Dinner nightly

Dieci fuses Italian and Japanese cuisines for a successful marriage of taste and creativity. The tiny step-down setting is easy to miss but conquers its spatial challenge with comfortable seating centered on a dark-wood dining counter that juts out from the kitchen; a handful of small tables bolster the accommodations.

The menu is under the direction of Chef Takanori Akiyama and presents a unique array of small plates that include meaty bites such as yuzu-pepper organic chicken *kara-age*; unexpected sushi, as in shrimp and uni wrapped in prosciutto; and pastas such as an intermingling of slender, springy ramen and spicy lamb Bolognese. Desserts are also impressive, as in silky Earl Grey crème brûlée with house-made Tahitian vanilla bean gelato.

Dirt Candy

Vegetarian ✗

B2

430 E. 9th St. (bet. First Ave. & Ave. A)

Subway: 1 Av
Phone: 212-228-7732
Web: www.dirtcandynyc.com
Prices: $$

Dinner Tue – Sat

Accommodating fewer than twenty in a boutique-sized space, Chef/owner Amanda Cohen keeps a watchful eye on each and every diner as she skillfully crafts vegetarian fare from the tiny rear kitchen. Certified by the Green Restaurant Association, the bright room has glass-paneled walls and closely packed tables furnished with Arne Jacobsen chairs.

Both devotees and skeptics alike are impressed by this menu of unique items featuring such preparations as portobello mousse with truffle oil-slicked toast and pickled pear compote; or golden-crisped blocks of semi-firm tofu draped with Kaffir lime beurre blanc. Yield to temptation with desserts like light and spongy zucchini-ginger cake served à la mode with deliciously smooth cream cheese ice cream.

Edi & The Wolf

Austrian Austrian

C3

102 Ave. C (bet. 6th & 7th Sts.)

Subway:	1 Av	Lunch Sat – Sun
Phone:	212-598-1040	Dinner nightly
Web:	www.ediandthewolf.com	
Prices:	$$	

Chefs Eduard Frauneder and Wolfgang Ban, the dynamic duo behind Seäsonal, have brought their wares downtown with the arrival of this *heuriger*—a casual neighborhood wine tavern common in Austria. The dark and earthy den is chock-full of reclaimed materials including a 40-foot rope salvaged from a church, now coiled above the tiny bar.

The crux of the offerings is comprised of small and shared plates such as cured and dried *landjäger* sausage accompanied by house-made mustard and pickles. Entrées fall under the heading of "schnitzel & co." and offer a highly recommended wiener schnitzel, which starts with a pounded filet of heritage pork encased in an incredibly delicate and crunchy coating, finished by Austrian-style potato salad and lingonberry jam.

Empellón Cocina

Mexican

B2

105 First Ave. (bet. 6th & 7th Sts.)

Subway:	Lower East Side - 2 Av	Lunch Sat –Sun
Phone:	212-780-0999	Dinner nightly
Web:	www.empellon.com	
Prices:	$$	

Chef Alex Stupak's follow-up to his rousingly successful Taqueria serves a "taco-free" and utterly creative Mexican experience. A circular bar dispenses one of the largest selections of tequila and mescal in the city, while the dining room's décor conveys a cool vibe with its white walls and dark wood furnishings accented by splashes of blue.

The menu is mostly a fork-and-knife affair, though there are tasty exceptions like *chicharrónes* with tomatillo-caper salsa. Meals are built around groupings of small plates such as ruby red shrimp dressed with fruity-spicy dried chili and a crisp ribbon of masa filled with luscious uni mousse; or rabbit roulade with shiitake-poblano stuffing and creamy salsa verde studded with crumbles of green chorizo.

Euzkadi

A3

Basque

108 E. 4th St. (bet. First & Second Aves.)

Subway: Lower East Side - 2 Av
Phone: 212-982-9788
Web: www.euzkadirestaurant.com
Prices: $$

Dinner nightly

Haven't heard of Euzkadi? Maybe you've been living in a cave. While some restaurants dish out great food but disappoint in the décor department, this one-of-a-kind place delivers both. With textured, exposed walls painted with prehistoric-style cave drawings, thick, velvet curtains shutting out all sunlight, and soft, low lighting, diners can be cave dwellers—even if just for the evening. This cocoon-like restaurant is a great find, despite its cramped quarters.

Of course, no caveman ever ate this well. The menu covers all the bases of traditional Basque cooking, including tapas and the house specialty, *paella mariscos*. Loaded with fish and shellfish, and redolent of saffron, the paella comes sized for two in a traditional cast-iron pan.

Manhattan ▶ East Village

Gnocco

C2

Italian

337 E. 10th St. (bet. Aves. A & B)

Subway: 1 Av
Phone: 212-677-1913
Web: www.gnocco.com
Prices: $$

Lunch Sat — Sun
Dinner nightly

This quaint Alphabet City Italian is a top local hangout, perfectly suiting the casual, neighborhood vibe. The dining room's rustic charm is accented by rough hewn plank flooring, exposed brick, and large windows that overlook the colorful scenes of Tompkins Square Park. In summer, the shaded back terrace with vine-covered walls and pretty murals is a great place to enjoy the namesake specialty, *gnocco*: crispy, deep-fried pillows of dough served with thin slices of *prosciutto di Parma* and salami.

Enjoyable homemade pastas, a lengthy listing of thin-crusted pizzas, and heartier main dishes comprise the tasty offerings here, served by an attentive and gracious staff. The fluffy and creamy lemon and mint semifreddo is always a pleasant finish.

Goat Town

B3

511 E. 5th St. (bet. Aves. A & B)

Subway: Lower East Side - 2 Av
Phone: 212-687-3641
Web: www.goattownnyc.com
Prices: $$

Lunch Sat – Sun
Dinner nightly

This Alphabet City bistro boasts a rustic-chic amalgam of hand-built, salvaged furnishings awash in a perfectly calibrated glow. Fashioned by a Brooklyn-based design firm, the backdrop is enhanced by a lively crowd and an infectious playlist.

The 50-seat dining room serves a well-made and seasonally influenced selection that might include specials dressed with freshly snipped herbs grown out back. Expect starters such as seared mackerel with olive oil breadcrumbs, and entrées like braised goat shoulder cleverly paired with bread salad punched up by anchovies, dried cranberries, and walnuts. Dessert showcases the evening's sundae special–think dark-roast coffee ice cream draped with caramel, cake bits, and salted pretzel–and is not to be missed.

Graffiti

B2

224 E. 10th St. (bet First & Second Aves.)

Subway: 1 Av
Phone: 212-464-7743
Web: www.graffitinyc.com
Prices: $$

Dinner Tue – Sun

Credibly doted on since it's inception in 2007, this cub of Chef/owner Jehangir Mehta is still going strong and baby boy is quite the dreamboat. Dressed with tightly-packed square communal tables and beaded ceiling lights, petite Graffiti may be dimly lit, but an exposed brick wall glossed with a metallic finish and hugging framed mirrors is all brightness.

Feeding a pack of 20 on newspaper-wrapped tables are Indian-inspired sweet and savory small plates of watermelon and feta salad cooled by a vibrant mint sorbet; eggplant buns spiked with toasty cumin; green mango *paneer*; and zucchini hummus pizza. If you forget to order the addictive green chili shrimp, you can hit "Mehtaphor" in the Duane Street Hotel for a taste of this spiced delight.

Hasaki

210 E. 9th St. (bet. Second & Third Aves.)

Subway: Astor Pl
Phone: 212-473-3327
Web: www.hasakinyc.com
Prices: $$$

Lunch Wed – Sun
Dinner nightly

 Opened in 1984 and still going strong, this unassuming, no-reservations spot on a tree-lined stretch of the East Village is quietly housed just below street level. The dining room has a clean and spare look, with seating available at a number of wood tables or at the sizeable counter manned by a personable chef.

Hasaki's longevity is attributed to the high quality of its products, which infuses the dining experience with a sense of seriousness and purpose. Skillfully prepared and reasonably priced, delicate sushi and sashimi share the spotlight with shabu-shabu, green tea noodles, and crisp tempura. The menu is supplemented by fascinating daily specials that tend to sell out quickly. Before 6:30 P.M., the generous "Twilight" menu is cherished.

Hearth

403 E. 12th St. (at First Ave.)

Subway: 1 Av
Phone: 646-602-1300
Web: www.restauranthearth.com
Prices: $$$

Dinner nightly

 Simple wooden tables; walls lined with wine glasses and copper pots; a cozy little bar overlooking the kitchen—Hearth's welcoming, candlelit interior sets the stage for the comforting Mediterranean meal to come.

The menu effortlessly skates between old-world classics and seasonal dishes punched up with inspired touches of creativity. The result is a beautiful and harmonious spring onion soup, bobbing with rich knobs of sea urchin and tender brioche croutons; fresh Columbia River sturgeon wrapped in crispy prosciutto and paired with ruby red beets, horseradish, and trout roe; or homemade lasagna, fat with fresh ricotta, saffron, and lemon rind. Paired with a gorgeous red plucked off the temptingly descriptive wine list? Mediterranean bliss.

Hot Kitchen

Chinese ✕

 A2

104 Second Ave. (bet. 6th & 7th Sts.)

Subway: Astor Pl
Phone: 212-228-3090
Web: www.hotkitchenny.com
Prices: $$

Lunch & dinner daily

This newly opened spot brings a dash of Sichuan cooking to a neighborhood already rife with international options. Whitewashed brick walls accented by chili red beams and ebony furnishings detail the tidy space.

Steer clear of the Chinese-American portion of the menu, and partake in Hot Kitchen's offering of classic Sichuan dishes bolstered by a portion of nicely done house specialties. Expect the likes of wok-fried quail liberally seasoned with cumin and salt; steamed whole fish slathered in a deluge of minced pickled red peppers; and shredded crispy duck studded with green onions and fried fresh ginger. Hot Kitchen uses the seasons to influence its roster of specials that have featured an autumnal bowl of braised spareribs with yam.

Ippudo

Japanese ✕✕

A1

65 Fourth Ave. (bet. 9th & 10th Sts.)

Subway: 14 St - Union Sq
Phone: 212-388-0088
Web: www.ippudo.com/ny
Prices: ⊜⊜

Lunch & dinner daily

 A wall covered in soup bowls is your clue of what to order at this first stateside outpost of the popular Japanese chain, opened by the renowned "King of Ramen" Shigemi Kawahara. Ramen-hungry diners are given a boisterous welcome from the youthful, energetic staff upon entering; expect the same at the farewell. With most seating arranged at communal oak-topped tables and prominently displayed open kitchen, Ippudo feels laid-back and fun yet sleek. The classic *shiromaru* ramen is a deeply satisfying bowl of rich pork broth and excellent, slender, fresh-made noodles garnished with sliced pork and cabbage.

If left with a bowlful of extra broth, simply tell your server "kae-dama" and for a small charge you'll receive an additional bowl of noodles.

Jack's Luxury Oyster Bar

Seafood

A2

101 Second Ave. (bet. 5th & 6th Sts.)

Subway: Lower East Side - 2 Av   Dinner nightly
Phone: 212-253-7848
Web: N/A
Prices: $$

An enticing collection of seafood creations await at Jack Lamb's intimate dining den where a romantic glow is cast over the cabin-chic setting punctuated by plaid walls, painted wainscoting, and glass votive holders all in red.

An offering of oysters precedes the oft-changing selection that has revealed a velvety smooth bowlful of potato chowder: steamed cockles, silken leeks, and petite salt and vinegar chips buoyed in potato cream. A seared slice of octopus-packed terrine with pickled cauliflower and braised baby turnips is a tasty prelude to deconstructed apple pie composed of crumbled white cheddar cheese pastry, caramelized apple pearls, and smooth vanilla ice cream. A chef's tasting menu further showcases the kitchen's chops.

JoeDoe

A3

Contemporary

45 E. 1st St. (bet. First & Second Aves.)

Subway: Lower East Side - 2 Av   Lunch Sat – Sun
Phone: 212-780-0262   Dinner Tue – Sun
Web: www.chefjoedoe.com
Prices: $$

The snug setting of this downtown gem from Chef/owner Joe Dobias has an appealingly rustic and rugged aura. Wood and brick construct a stage that is sprinkled throughout with whimsical and nostalgic bric-a-brac. Seating is bolstered by the comfortable bar-cum-dining counter. Speaking of which, don't miss out on a spread of killer cocktails.

The highly enjoyable menu emerges from a tiny but organized kitchen and displays a vibrant personality in dishes that have featured a gorgeous chilled carrot soup, thick and creamy with ground almonds, and flecked with cacao nibs for a bitter crunch; or slow-roasted rabbit sauced with tomatillo salsa and matched with a round of fried dough.

For a takeout treat, check out the chef's new sandwich shop, JoeDough.

Jewel Bako ✿

Japanese 🍴

A2

239 E. 5th St. (bet. Second & Third Aves.)

Subway: Astor Pl

Phone: 212-979-1012

Web: N/A

Prices: **$$$**

Dinner Mon - Sat

Swee Phuah

Unceremoniously wedged amidst two nondescript façades, find a lighted glass window displaying a single flower and door discreetly marked "Jewel Bako." Maybe it's the fish shipped daily from Japan, or the very committed owners, Jack and Grace Lamb. Whatever it is, this eminent *sushi-ya* only gets better with each meal. Everything from the décor to the glassware evidences the Lambs' immaculate style.

With one chopstick planted firmly into tradition and the other dipping playfully into whimsy, this is a "jewel" among sushi savants. The counter in the back is their favored nest where they indulge in the day's freshest sushi or pristine omakase—a cube of daikon braised in dashi and dabbed with miso elicits many beams.

Jewel Bako's greatest feat is its spectacular consistency. The quality of fish is superb, seasonal variety is appropriate, and depth of flavor seems unending. Expect the likes of unctuously rich blue fin topped with fresh ginger or chopped mackerel crested with scallion. Polite servers show an eye for detail and just the right interest to ensure an enjoyable meal. Let them guide you to the perfect sake, so spirited, that the sashimi before you threatens to come back to life.

Kafana

Eastern European

 Manhattan ▶ East Village

C3

116 Ave. C (bet. 7th & 8th Sts.)

Subway: 1 Av
Phone: 212-353-8000
Web: www.kafananyc.com
Prices: $$

Lunch Sat – Sun
Dinner nightly

Translating to "café" in Serbian, Kafana has a heartwarming ambience that beckons one to stay for a while. Exposed brick walls decorated with mirrors, vintage photographs, rough-hewn wood tables topped with votives and flowers, and boldly patterned banquettes outfit the intimate space, attended by a genuinely friendly staff. In one corner sits the small bar, with a charmingly low-tech antique cash register.

Kafana offers worldly diners an exotic cuisine not often found in Manhattan. The list of hearty Serbian specialties includes a phyllo pie filled with cow's milk feta and spinach, grilled meats, or slow-cooked stews prepared with large, tender white beans perfumed with garlic and paprika, topped with slices of smoky peasant sausage.

Kanoyama

Japanese

B1

175 Second Ave. (at 11th St.)

Subway: 3 Av
Phone: 212-777-5266
Web: www.kanoyama.com
Prices: $$

Dinner nightly

Offering an impressive lineup of excellent quality and deftly prepared fish, this popular sushi den now claims greater capacity following a recent expansion. In a space that is simply done but spotless and well-maintained, the focus here is on a parade of pristine cuts that are bolstered by a passage of daily items such as rich baby shad from Japan and tender, mild American white bonito. Also find a generous listing of oysters; starters such as *wakasagi* tempura (fried baby smelts) sprinkled with green tea-salt; and a handful of cooked entrées. The value-conscious omakase is highly recommended.

Besides being tempting, the website is very informative: it presents diverse fish facts, photos, and recommendations for seasonality and preparation.

Kajitsu ✿

414 E. 9th St. (bet. First Ave. & Ave. A)

Subway: 1 Av

Dinner Tue – Sun

Phone: 212-228-4873

Web: www.kajitsunyc.com

Prices: $$$

Kajitsu

The true Shojin cuisine of Buddhist monasteries can be an otherworldly event of serenity, timelessness, and pleasure. Here at Kajitsu, there are neither spotlights nor music—this is a place for contemplation of the intricate and often subtly flavored four- and seven-course kaiseki vegetarian menus. The current décor is extraordinarily simple and yet personal, with natural materials and the unmistakable whiff of fresh wood in the air (Note there are plans to relocate in 2013).

Somehow, the limits of eating a cuisine that "does not take life" are forgotten as the courses become more complex. The essence of summer is reflected in a stunning, creamy chilled corn soup served unseasoned to highlight the exceptional natural sweetness of the corn, with snap pea tempura and fresh chives. Satisfying and hearty, two fried rounds of golden brown yuba filled with morels and wheat gluten are sprinkled with *sansho* pepper and served in a pool of inky *hijiki* sauce.

Nearing the end of meals, a rice course may combine a perfect balance of crunchy, salty, sweet, and sour vegetables and pickles. Fragrant apricots cleverly tucked with sweet white miso and topped with a clear jelly are a memorable finale.

Kasadela

Japanese

C2

647 E. 11th St. (bet. Aves. B & C)

Subway: 1 Av
Phone: 212-777-1582
Web: www.kasadela.com
Prices: 💰💰

Dinner nightly

This simply furnished, low-key *izakaya* offers an array of traditional Japanese snacks best washed down with an iced cold beer or sake; just remember that here, your glass of sake can be embellished with gold leaf for a small fee, said to promote better health.

Located in Alphabet City, the space is often quieter early in the evening and stays open late enough to satisfy the cravings of the neighborhood's nocturnal scenesters. Patrons arrive here seeking honest, good-valued satisfaction, in the likes of creamy and smooth Japanese-style potato salad; addictively sweet and salty glazed chicken wings; or *tori kawa*: charred skewers of rich chicken skin. Finish with a delicious crème caramel that would do any talented pastry chef proud.

La Paella

Spanish

A2

214 E. 9th St. (bet. Second & Third Aves.)

Subway: Astor Pl
Phone: 212-598-4321
Web: www.lapaellanyc.com
Prices: $$

Lunch Wed – Sun
Dinner nightly

On a street known for Asian dining spots, La Paella recalls the charm of an old-world Iberian inn with rustic furnishings, wooden ceiling beams draped with bundles of dried flowers, and wrought-iron accents. A fresco of a picador on the parchment-colored wall completes the scene. Ideal for groups (though often crowded with them), the menu encourages sharing with its sizable tapas offering as well as the house specialty: paella, sized for two or more. Several variations of this namesake dish include the Basque, with chorizo, chicken, and clams over saffron-scented rice.

The cozy, dimly lit space makes it a delicious date spot for couples enjoying a bottle of Spanish wine, immune to the spirited sounds of sangria-fueled merrymaking.

Kyo Ya ✿

B2

94 E. 7th St. (bet First Ave. & Ave. A)

Dinner nightly

Subway: Astor Pl
Phone: 212-982-4140
Web: N/A
Prices: $$$

Kyo Ya

Its discreet location on a quiet block is an apt locale for this very special Japanese gem, where skill, artistry, and quality are exuded from every facet. The interior is meticulous yet warm with inlaid wood floors and a vaulted brick ceiling, while the Japanese team emanates hospitality.

It is no secret that Kyo Ya offers an extraordinary, order-in-advance kaiseki menu; however, it holds the à la carte offerings to the same standard and esteem. Here, seasonal ingredients from America and Japan appear decadent, bright, and in a range of colors and textures that tease the palate from first glance.

If sashimi suits you, expect almost luminescent *tai*; tender, fatty hamachi; or creamy-orange Arctic char that is literally akin to butter—melting, fresh, and outrageously rich. Seared, marinated mackerel pressed sushi is topped with the whole fish from nose to fin, highlighting the differing textures and flavors of fatty belly and tail, with alternating garnishes of pickled ginger, wasabi, and chive blossoms in each mouthful. Yet in this art, there is also balance, as in a plate of powerful Tokyo Bay *anago* smoked in-house, delicately contrasted with asparagus, radishes, and a yuzu-miso dressing.

Lavagna

Italian

 C3

545 E. 5th St. (bet. Aves. A & B)

Subway: Lower East Side - 2 Av
Phone: 212-979-1005
Web: www.lavagnanyc.com
Prices: $$

Lunch Sat – Sun
Dinner nightly

Instantly evidencing Lavagna's popularity is its steady stream of regulars who seem smitten with this delightfully discreet trattoria. Open since 1999, the staff is ever gracious, greeting guests by name, but the same courtesy is offered to first-timers as well. A wood-burning oven flickers in the elfin kitchen thereby elevating Lavagna's sense of snug comfort.

Speaking of snug, the Italian menu offers a terse listing of *pizzette*, perhaps capped with roasted mushrooms, fontina, and white truffle oil. Antipasti unveils cool, shaved octopus massaged with fresh lemon and extra virgin olive oil; while entrées vie for center stage as in an al dente twirl of *fedelini fini* with slow-cooked tomatoes and toasted garlic slices; or oven-roasted fish, flambéed tableside.

Lil' Frankie's

Italian

 A3

19 First Ave. (bet. 1st & 2nd Sts.)

Subway: Lower East Side - 2 Av
Phone: 212-420-4900
Web: www.lilfrankies.com
Prices:

Lunch Fri – Sun
Dinner nightly

Dinnertime always seems like a party at this offshoot of the ever-popular Frank, featuring a greenery-adorned dining room and a bar area lovingly nicknamed after owner Frank Prisinzano's father, "Big Cheech." The classic East Village space is furnished with a combination of wood and marble-topped tables, colorful benches, and brick walls with black-and-white portraits, fashioning a shabby-chic backdrop.

Cooked to crispy perfection in a wood-burning oven, Naples-style pizza, with toppings like homemade sausage and wild fennel, star on the menu. Equally impressive is the lineup of antipasto and pastas, handmade with the freshest ingredients. Come with a crowd or expect to wait, reservations are accepted only for parties of six or more.

Luzzo's

Pizza ✗

B1

211-13 First Ave. (bet. 12th & 13th Sts.)

Subway: 1 Av
Phone: 212-473-7447
Web: www.luzzospizza.com
Prices: 🍴🍴

Lunch Tue – Sun
Dinner nightly

Luzzo's is easily spotted by its long line of hungry faces patiently waiting to score a table, especially on a Friday night when the rustic setting of rough-hewn plank flooring and exposed brick adorned with copper cookware can suddenly feel like an NYU dining hall.

Despite the masses, this consistently top-rated pizzeria is a fun night out. Its Naples-born owner and noted *pizzaiolo* does things his own way to produce a stellar pie while defying some of the strict mandates set by the Neapolitan-pizza politburo, most notably baking his pizzas in a mix of wood *and* coal. The results are delectable, as in the pizza *diavolo*—crusty, puffy, and tender with a hint of smoke and topped with tomato, creamy mozzarella, and salty-spicy slices of hearty salami.

Maharlika

Filipino ✗

B2

111 First Ave. (bet. 6th & 7th Sts.)

Subway: Astor Pl
Phone: 646-392-7880
Web: www.maharlikanyc.com
Prices: $$

Lunch & dinner daily

A wall-mounted blackboard announcing the Tagalog word of the day (*karne*=meat) efficiently sums up Maharlika, known and loved for its array of hearty Filipino preparations. The cordial staff may outshine their décor-deficient setting, yet fans of this soulful cuisine keep returning time and again for such classic specialties as chicken *adobo*, and *Pampangan-style sizzling sisig*—a hot skillet heaped by a trio of finely chopped pig parts (ear, snout and belly) arranged around a fried egg that is stirred together tableside.

A bowl of garlic fried rice accompanies the hearty repast as does a bottle of zingy sugarcane vinegar infused with garlic, ginger, and chilies. If, after all that you're not ready to bust, the incredible flan is worth the indulgence.

Masak

Singaporean ✗

C2

432 E. 13th St. (bet. First Ave. & Ave. A)

Subway: 1 Av	Lunch Sat – Sun
Phone: 212-260-6740	Dinner Tue – Sun
Web: www.masaknyc.com	
Prices: $$	

More than a uniquely delicious homage to the cuisine of this Singaporean chef, Masak's accomplished kitchen prepares its own modern interpretation of Southeast Asian food and all its Indian, Chinese, Malay, post-Colonial glory. Batik print wallpaper, bent cane chairs, and painted wood shutters accent the petite setting which features design cues inspired by the iconic British Colonial décor typified in Singapore's early 20th century "black and white" homes.

The chili crab dip is a must—a lusty bowlful of sweet chili and crab stew accompanied by fried knobs of steamed bread for dipping. Other treats include Grandma's chicken curry; oxtail noodles, and refreshing coconut sorbet afloat in mango purée thickened with sago pearls and Thai basil.

The Mermaid Inn

Seafood ✗

A2

96 Second Ave. (bet. 5th & 6th Sts.)

Subway: Astor Pl	Dinner nightly
Phone: 212-674-5870	
Web: www.themermaidnyc.com	
Prices: $$	

When schedules or seasons don't allow for a trip to the Cape, The Mermaid Inn offers a polished yet comfortably rustic take on those familiar sea-sprayed fish shacks. Dark wood furnishings, walls decorated with nautical maps, and a quaint backyard dining area give the setting an undeniable charm. The concise menu begins with a first-rate raw bar and continues with deftly prepared offerings like P.E.I. mussels steamed in an aromatic broth, or the lobster sandwich served on a grilled bun. Their addictive crunchy, golden, Old Bay fries are an essential side dish. A complimentary demitasse of creamy pudding ends things sweetly.

Two additional Manhattan locations (in Greenwich Village and the Upper West Side) continue to spread the wealth.

Momofuku Ko ⁂ ⁂

B2

163 First Ave. (bet. 10th & 11th Sts.)

Subway: 1 Av
Phone: 212-777-7773
Web: www.momofuku.com
Prices: $$$$

Lunch Fri – Sun
Dinner nightly

Noah Kalina

Chef David Chang's celebrated destination could reside in an unmarked basement and dedicated foodies would still ferret it out. As it is, the sliver of a restaurant is shielded behind a metalwork façade with that iconic peach serving as a clear enough indicator of the wonderland within.

Diners who have successfully navigated the egalitarian online reservation system are offered a spot along the 12-seat dining counter. Framed by varnished plywood and brushed slate, the room is understated by design, placing the spotlight on the crazy-talented kitchen team as they prepare a knockout ten-course spectacle.

Keep your expectations high because these chefs rarely falter, which is impressive considering how daring these oft-changing creations are. Stimulating bites like oysters with apple vinegar commence the procession that can be followed up by a puff of steamed egg afloat in mouthwatering bacon dashi; homemade orecchiette with decadent black truffle and aged-cheddar sauce; and luscious squab breast and beer-braised leg with sunchoke cream. Memorable desserts reveal a rice pudding-filled cone crowned by white miso ice cream, with a root beer chaser made from locally foraged herbs and maple syrup.

Momofuku Noodle Bar 😄

Asian ✗

B2

171 First Ave. (bet. 10th & 11th Sts.)

Subway: 1 Av
Phone: 212-777-7773
Web: www.momofuku.com
Prices:

Lunch & dinner daily

This spot launched Chef David Chang's ascent into celebrity chef-dom. The ever-popular destination restaurant is still a "lucky peach" (the name's Japanese translation) to its hoards of fans hungering for ramen and steamed buns. Momofuku's gutsy menu is fashioned with Asian street food in mind: goat ramen with piquillo pepper, red shiso, and soy egg; or brisket buns with horseradish, pickled red onion, and cucumber. The trendsetting chef elevated humble fried chicken to legendary status, with his order-in-advance feast featuring two treatments of the bird with sauces and greenmarket sides. Whether sitting at the counter or communal tables, join the devotees slurping noodles elbow-to-elbow and watching the chefs' sleight of hand in the open kitchen.

Momofuku Ssäm Bar 😄

Contemporary ✗

B1

207 Second Ave. (at 13th St.)

Subway: 3 Av
Phone: 212-777-7773
Web: www.momofuku.com
Prices: $$

Lunch & dinner daily

Restless Chef David Chang always manages to wow the taste buds of even the most jaded foodies. At this freewheeling culinary playground, he offers an exuberant contemporary menu so far-reaching that it somehow all makes sense. Yet this space has grown up, offering more room and a mouthwatering list of libations relished by the trendsters in the adjacent lounge, Booker and Dax.

Small plates include raw bar preparations like Santa Barbara uni with tomato, mustard oil, and *chawan mushi*. Entrées like braised goat with *azuki* beans, feta, and Agrinio olives show what all the buzz is about. An order-in-advance rotisserie duck is a weekday lunch highlight.

Loud and crowded, the minimalist space is perpetually mobbed by its sophisticated clientele.

Mono + Mono

A3

116 E. 4th St. (bet. First & Second Aves.)

Subway: Lower East Side - 2 Av

Phone: 212-466-6660

Web: www.monomononyc.com

Prices: ⊜⊜

Dinner nightly

This surprising, fun, and low-key Korean fried chicken spot is tucked within a quaint walk-up along a tree-lined street. Step inside and be surprised, as its proportions feel deep, dark, and downright cavernous, fashioning a thoroughly industrial vibe. Music accentuates the experience here: running the entire length of one wall is a boundless library of jazz vinyl, and overhead find a revolving rack of record jackets.

Settle in with a *shoju*-based cocktail like the Billie Holiday—sweetened with rose water, raspberries, and champagne—then prepare to feast on twice-fried chicken that is crackling crisp and brushed with either soy garlic or spicy sauce. Snacks like kimchi-fried brown rice, savory pancakes, and *japchae* round out the eats.

Motorino

B2

349 E. 12th St. (bet. First & Second Aves.)

Subway: 1 Av

Phone: 212-777-2644

Web: www.motorinopizza.com

Prices: ⊜⊜

Lunch & dinner daily

This East Village annex of Mathieu Palombino's Neapolitan-style pizzeria may not be as fetching as the shuttered Williamsburg original, but the pies turned out here are certainly a tasty treat. Simply beautified with a pressed-tin ceiling and bold green-and-white striped walls, the room's blackboard specials convey a more complex and product-focused sensibility that is applied here—fresh ramps have been a seasonally-tuned topping.

Cold and hot antipasti (octopus salad tossed with potatoes, celery, and chili oil; or roasted peppers with capers and parsley) bolster the mouthwatering pizza selection topped with the likes of *fior di latte*, caramelized Brussels sprouts, and diced pancetta.

The weekday lunch special is an especially good value.

Northern Spy Food Co.

American 🍴

C2

511 E. 12th St. (bet. Aves. A & B)

Subway: 1 Av
Phone: 212-228-5100
Web: www.northernspyfoodco.com
Prices:

Lunch & dinner daily

Espousing a country kitchen aesthetic, this inviting café is framed by reclaimed hickory flooring, a wood-slat banquette painted robin's egg blue, and tables fashioned from salvaged bowling alley lanes.

The value-driven menu of seasonal, locally sourced fare is always enjoyable. Lunchtime offerings unveil impressive sandwiches such as the crispy chicken thigh and poached egg or wild mushroom and cheddar, washed down by an old-timey coffee seltzer. Dinner serves up house-made head cheese; heritage pork meatballs with marinara; and Long Island market fish with anchovy butter. A list of local beers accompanies the wine list; and Sunday nights bring a three course prix-fixe menu that has featured eggplant caponata, a rabbit pot pie, and chocolate-beet cake.

Piccola! Positano

Italian 🍴

B3

235 E. 4th St. (bet. Aves. A & B)

Subway: 1 Av
Phone: 212-933-4669
Web: www.piccolapositano.com
Prices: $$

Lunch Sat – Sun
Dinner nightly

If seeking refuge from the noisy East Village streets, find yourself lured into warm Piccola Positano. The wide and windowed space is filled with sleek wrought-iron details, unique décor, and rustic, roughhewn walls covered in festive murals. Low lights lend a dusky mien to the oven-dominated room, which keeps with the 'hoods spirit and buzzes at night as clusters dig in with gusto.

Alongside the oven is a comfy bar strewn with diners devouring a proper rendition of *lenticchie e scarola*, an earthy lentil and curly escarole soup drizzled with olive oil. Churned out of the mighty pizza oven is the blistered *Caruso* topped with crisped potatoes and fluffy eggs; while *capellini* mingled with zucchini and tender shrimp offers pure, delicious comfort.

Porsena

Italian ✗✗

21 E. 7th St. (bet. Second & Third Aves.)

Subway: Astor Pl   Dinner nightly
Phone: 212-228-4923
Web: www.porsena.com
Prices: $$

New Yorkers love Sara Jenkins. Her cooking is adroit, uncomplicated, and just so good—a combination that has diners flocking to her winning trattoria, Porsena. Bigger than closet-sized Porchetta, this spot, furnished with a mix-and-match assortment of chairs and touches of red and grey as well as a comfortable bar counter, is a hugely accommodating space.

Inspired by the chef's childhood time in Rome, the menu starts off with the likes of wilted escarole salad, bitter and smoky, dressed with garlic vinaigrette. The heart of the menu is its focus on *pasta asciutta* (dried pasta) that may be deliciously prepared as *pennette col cavolfiore*—a lusty balance of mini penne, roasted cauliflower, capers, and black olives showered by toasted breadcrumbs.

Prime & Beyond New York

Steakhouse ✗

90 E. 10th St. (bet. Third & Fourth Aves.)

Subway: Astor Pl   Lunch Wed – Sun
Phone: 212-505-0033   Dinner nightly
Web: www.primeandbeyond.com
Prices: $$$

This location of the Fort Lee, NJ original brings great steak to the East Village. Appropriate for the locale, the setting eschews the standard men's club swagger of most steakhouses for a look that's spare and cool. Despite the chillax vibe, expect to see suits; the meat is that good. In fact, it's procured from the same purveyor that supplies Peter Luger and Keens.

Aged in-house for six weeks, the USDA prime Porterhouse is presented hot off the grill but well rested, richly flavored, tender, and juicy. Myriad cuts satisfy all preferences, while sides like kimchi, spicy scallion salad, and fermented cabbage stew are especially appealing and honor the owners' heritage. The lunch menu is pared down but offers Korean-style soups and stews.

Prune

Contemporary ✗

A3

54 E. 1st St. (bet. First & Second Aves.)

Subway: Lower East Side - 2 Av
Phone: 212-677-6221
Web: www.prunerestaurant.com
Prices: $$

Lunch & dinner daily

Packed with simple furnishings and attended to by a friendly staff, the popularity of this endearing breadbox of a restaurant never seems to fade. On a warm day when the front doors open, few Manhattan restaurants can match its ambience. From her kitchen in back, Chef/owner (and best-selling author) Gabrielle Hamilton has impressed serious diners since 1999.

The deceptively modest menu changes often but the chef's signature style shines through in items that are fuss-free yet display an undeniable level of skill and talent. A meal here may feature a crisp-skinned fillet of Tasmanian sea trout set atop a bundle of frisée and crowned by a dollop of perfect homemade mayonnaise; or a creamy, sweet/tart lime custard graced with crumbly oatmeal shortbread.

Pylos

Greek ✗✗

B3

128 E. 7th St. (bet. First Ave. & Ave. A)

Subway: Astor Pl
Phone: 212-473-0220
Web: www.pylosrestaurant.com
Prices: $$

Lunch Wed – Sun
Dinner nightly

Taking its name from the Greek translation of "made from clay," this contemporary taverna features a ceiling canopy of suspended terra-cotta pots and whitewashed walls with lapis-blue insets. The restrained décor produces a chic Mediterranean vibe that perfectly suits its lusty, home-style, deliciously refined cuisine—courtesy of noted Greek food authority Diane Kochilas.

Moussaka, a classic Greek comfort favorite, is beautifully presented here as a dome filled with layers of browned meat and silky eggplant, encrusted in slender potato slices, finished with layer of golden-browned béchamel. Sides may include *spanakorizo*, wilted spinach rice flecked with feta crumbles; while custard-filled phyllo drenched in mountain honey ends things sweetly.

Rai Rai Ken

B2

Japanese ✗

218 E. 10th St. (bet. First & Second Aves.)

Subway: Astor Pl
Phone: 212-477-7030
Web: N/A
Prices: 🍜

Lunch & dinner daily

Rai Rai Ken isn't quite what it used to be—it's bigger and much more comfortable. Just a few doors east of the former location, the new room boasts a fresh and tidy look with blond wood seating plus the signature red vinyl stools. An array of pots remain bubbling and steaming behind the counter.

Rest assured the menu's star attraction–those thin, toothsome ramen noodles–are just as delicious, served with four near-addictive, fantastically complex broth variations: *shio, shoyu,* miso, and curry. Each bowlful is chock-full of garnishes, like slices of roasted pork, boiled egg, nori, fishcake, and a nest of springy noodles. Grab a business card before leaving as loyal diners are rewarded with a complimentary bowl after ten visits.

Ramen Misoya

A2

Japanese ✗

129 Second Ave. (bet. St. Marks Pl & 7th St.)

Subway: Astor Pl
Phone: 212-677-4825
Web: www.misoyanyc.com
Prices: 🍜

Lunch & dinner daily

With 30 locations worldwide, Ramen Misoya now brings its trademark ambrosial bowlfuls to New York City. The earthy dining area dons a bamboo-lined ceiling as well as a TV monitor that is internally looped to broadcast the kitchen's every move.

The ramen offering here differentiates itself by centering on a trio of miso-enriched broths: *shiro* is a white miso fermented with rice koji (starter); richer tasting *kome-miso;* and *mame-miso,* a strictly soybean product. The mouth-coating soup is delicious alchemy. Each slurp is a multifaceted distillation of pork and chicken bones with savory-salty-sweet notes, stocked with excellent noodles, vegetables, and the likes of panko-crusted shrimp tempura, fried ginger chicken, or slices of house-made *cha-su.*

The Redhead

 American

 B1

349 E. 13th St. (bet. First & Second Aves.)

Subway: 1 Av
Phone: 212-533-6212
Web: www.theredheadnyc.com
Prices: $$

Dinner nightly

At long last, a comeuppance for redheads tired of those endless jokes. This redhead makes its namesake beam with pride. Tucked into a diminutive space, it has cornered the market on charm with a rustic exposed brick-and-bistro table-décor. The vibe is laid-back and lures a crowd that packs this little spot and makes it loud, loud, loud. Wait times, even on weeknights, can seem interminable, but the gleaming all-American bar is the perfect antidote.

The address says East Village, but the bold menu says deep South. Selections like hush puppies filled with sour cream and caviar, or buttery oyster pot pies bathed in Pernod show off a North-meets-South flair; while entrées like low country shrimp and grits or roasted duck gumbo keep things civil.

Robataya

 B2

Japanese

231 E. 9th St. (bet. Second & Third Aves.)

Subway: Astor Pl
Phone: 212-979-9674
Web: www.robataya-ny.com
Prices: $$

Lunch Wed – Sun
Dinner nightly

This latest and fun venture from restaurateur Bon Yagi features a front room with a 26-seat counter lined with salivating diners and platters of ultra fresh vegetables, fish, and meats to be grilled and served by a paddle wielding team of chefs perched behind the counter.

The *robatayaki* menu offers up flavorfully grilled dishes, from silky eggplant to sheets of dried sardines, seasoned with imported salt, brushed with soy or teriyaki, or dressed with miso. The menu shows a plethora of options but is usually supported by cold, warm, and seasonal appetizers; fried dishes like *yuba gyoza*; and iron pots of steamed rice (*kamameshi*) topped with snow crab, perhaps.

Table seating is available in the rear dining room for those who prefer a more serene experience.

Sigiri

Sri Lankan 🍴

B2

91 First Ave. (bet. 5th & 6th Sts.)

Subway: 1 Av   Lunch & dinner daily
Phone: 212-614-9333
Web: www.sigirinyc.com
Prices: 💰💰

For a delicious taste of something different, round the corner of 6th Street to First Avenue, and climb to Sigiri's small second floor dining room. This humble Sri Lankan establishment stands above its neighbors for wonderfully prepared, intriguingly fragrant cuisine that needs neither a colorful light display nor boisterous greeter. Instead, the warm and sedate room features sienna walls and simple tables with bright cloths.

Specialties are numerous and may include *string hopper kotthu*, a stir-fry of impossibly thin and fluffy rice noodles tossed with eggs, chicken, and vegetables, accompanied by a cup of coconut gravy; or spoon-tender chunks of eggplant *moju*, spiced with dried red chili. In lieu of alcohol, fruit cordials or apple-iced tea is offered.

Sobakoh

Japanese 🍴

A2

309 E. 5th St. (bet. First & Second Aves.)

Subway: Lower East Side - 2 Av   Lunch Fri – Sun
Phone: 212-254-2244   Dinner nightly
Web: N/A
Prices: 💰💰

Before entering Sobakoh, stop for a minute to appreciate Chef/owner Hiromitsu Takahashi, sequestered to his temperature- and humidity-controlled glass booth, forming layers of organically grown buckwheat flour dough into first-rate noodles. This ritual is performed several times daily by the smiling chef and is the foundation of the seasonally arranged offerings at this Japan-meets-East Village soba spot. Service can be sluggish, so start with a classic Japanese snack, like the refreshing daikon salad dressed with yuzu, wasabi, and bonito flakes, while waiting for your bowlful of *uni ikura soba*—chilled buckwheat noodles heaped with creamy sea urchin and plump salmon roe.

The inexpensive prix-fixe menu offered nightly is even cheaper before 7:00 P.M.

Soba-Ya 😊

Japanese ✗✗

B2

229 E. 9th St. (bet. Second & Third Aves.)

Subway: Astor Pl

Phone: 212-533-6966

Web: www.sobaya-nyc.com

Prices: 😊😊

Lunch & dinner daily

In a neighborhood replete with tempting Japanese dining options, Soba-Ya has been sating noodle cravings with awesome buckwheat soba and hearty udon–all homemade daily–for more than a decade. Enterprising co-owner Bon Yagi, also of Curry-Ya, favors authenticity over flash in his establishments, and this popular soba spot fashioning a traditional Japanese aesthetic is no exception.

Sit among the largely Japanese lunchtime clientele to savor and slurp cold, refreshing soba attractively served in a red-black bento box neatly stocked with the likes of dashi-poached vegetables, fresh and deliciously glazed salmon, or crisp shrimp tempura. Complete this meal with a pot of hot broth added to your remaining soy-based dipping sauce for a warming finish.

Supper 😊

Italian ✗

B3

156 E. 2nd St. (bet. Aves. A & B)

Subway: 1 Av

Phone: 212-477-7600

Web: www.supperrestaurant.com

Prices: $$

Lunch Sat – Sun
Dinner nightly

If you lived by Supper, you'd be supping there all the time. Replete with character, warmth, and regulars, this neighborhood spot has it all: its modest menu is deliciously appealing; preparations are simple yet, perfect; flavors run large; and its prices are affordable. With three East Village hits in hand, the Frank crew means business.

A substantial menu keeps company with nightly specials and a killer wine list; diners pack the low-lit, sultry front room for a slice of action from the open kitchen. Find more intimacy in the back, or pick the private room for a dinner party starring veal *polpettini* bobbing in *sugo*; roasted chicken massaged with rosemary and garlic; and *spaghetti al limone*, sauced with white wine, cream, lemon zest, and Parmesan.

Terroir

Italian

B2

413 E. 12th St. (bet. First Ave. & Ave. A)

Subway: Astor Pl   Dinner nightly
Phone: 646-602-1300
Web: www.wineisterroir.com
Prices: $$

Step inside Terroir, from Hearth partners Chef Marco Canora and sommelier Paul Grieco, and you will be seduced by the spirit of this place; the passion is palpable. What else would you expect from a sommelier who describes this wine bar as his sandbox? Park yourself on one of the 24 seats and enjoy flipping though the whimsical menu—a vinyl binder adorned with stickers and markings galore that looks like the work of a trouble-making grade-schooler.

The clever lineup of fermented beverages includes Kosher wines, cider, and mead; and is accompanied by enjoyably prepared morsels like crunchy red wine risotto balls strewn with braised oxtail; or a slice of strawberry tart that was featured as part of a seasonal Riesling-inspired prix-fixe.

The Toucan and The Lion

Fusion

B2

342 E. 6th St. (bet. First & Second Aves.)

Subway: Lower East Side - 2 Av   Dinner Wed – Mon
Phone: 212-375-8989
Web: www.thetoucanandthelion.com
Prices: $$

A fanciful flourish of creativity and a mighty mash-up of flavors are some of the treasures in store at this clever and current boîte. The space is small, done in a bleached palette and furnished with a quirky smattering of accents including patio furniture and ceiling light pendants that double as terrariums, but the overall aesthetic is akin to a crowded urban terrace.

While tables are barely large enough to accommodate one plate, you'll want to order many: excellent quality head-on prawns draped in luscious tamarind and sweet chili sauce, is best accompanied by toasted *bao* for sopping; and goat "pot pie" features a small skillet filled with tender goat meat and root vegetables in delicious coconut-rich Massaman curry, served with warm *roti*.

Zabb Elee

 A2

Thai ✗

75 Second Ave. (bet. 4th and 5th Sts.)

Subway: Astor Pl	Lunch & dinner daily
Phone: 212-505-9533	
Web: www.zabbelee.com	
Prices: 💰💰	

Proclaim you've found a great new Thai spot, and people listen; announce it's in Manhattan, and crowds race you to the door. This spicy sparkler eschews the high design look common to others in its category, opting instead for a reticent look of pale tones jazzed up by patterned tile and light green shutters.

The food speaks, or should we say shouts, for itself, honing in on Northern Thailand for a vibrant profusion of Isaan specialties. Chef Ratchanee Sumpatboon delivers knockouts such as *som tum poo plara* (green papaya salad with preserved crab and fried pork rind); *pukk boong moo korb* (sautéed morning glory with crispy pork); and *pad ped moo krob* (fried pork mingling with Thai eggplant in a ginger curry sauce fragrant with green peppercorns).

Look for our symbol 🍸, spotlighting restaurants with a notable cocktail list.

Financial District

Widely considered the financial center of the world, the southern tip of Manhattan is flooded by hard-driving Wall Street types. When it's time to eat, they love a hefty steak, especially when expense accounts are paying the bill. And though expense accounts may be shrinking these days, bigger is still better at stalwarts like **Delmonico's** which opened in 1837 as America's first fine-dining restaurant. The institution that introduced diners to now-classic dishes such as eggs Benedict, lobster Newburg, and baked Alaska, continues to pack 'em in for the signature Angus boneless rib eye, aka the Delmonico steak.

Reinventing the Public Market

New is replacing old as the publicly owned Tin Building and New Market Building–home to the former Fulton Fish Market–house tenants in the form of **The New Amsterdam Market**, a seasonal marketplace where butchers, grocers, fishmongers, artisan cheese producers, and other vendors hope to create a regional food system. With a stated mission "to reinvent the public market as a civic institution in the City of New York," this non-profit organization dedicates itself to promoting sustainable agriculture and regionally sourced food, while offering space for independent purveyors to sell on behalf of farmers and producers. Check their website (www.newamsterdampublic. org) for event dates. One of the district's largest tourist draws, South Street Seaport is surrounded by eateries from family-friendly Irish pubs to the historic **Fraunces Tavern**. Innkeeper Samuel Fraunces purchased this three-story, 18th century brick mansion at the corner of Pearl and Broad streets in 1762.

The Financial District has traditionally catered to power-lunchers by day and business travelers by night. However, that's all changing rapidly as the area becomes increasingly residential. What you will discover is a smorgasbord of bars, restaurants, and food services catering to the local residents. These blossoming culinary gems incite buttoned-up Wall Street suits to loosen their collars and chill out over a glass of wine at **Pasanella and Son**—considered and revered by many as "the best wine shop" in town. Front Street has also attracted a surprising spate of Italian eateries counting **Il Brigante**, with its dough-spinning *pizzaiolo* who belongs to the United States Pizza Team, among their number. Another paesan, **Barbarini Alimentari** raises the bar with gourmet groceries and an upscale menu of Italian fare. The ultimate in express lunch, NY's food-carts are hugely popular in the FiDi. For a quick nosh at a bargain price, follow your nose to **Alan's Falafel Cart** on Cedar Street.

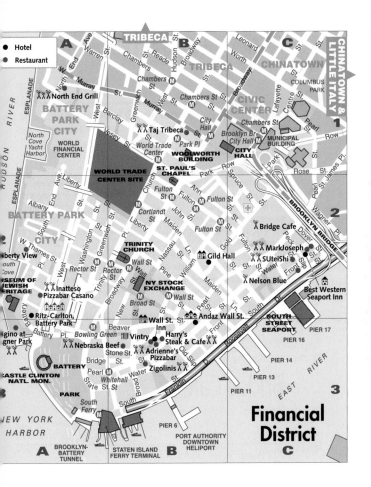

A — TRIBECA — **B** — **C** CHINATOWN & LITTLE ITALY

Leonard St

Worth St

TRIBECA

CHINATOWN

COLUMBUS PARK

Warren St

North End Ave

W End Ave

Murray St

✕✕✕ North End Grill

Chambers St

Reade St

Hudson St

Broadway

Worth St

Centre St

Lafayette St

Pearl St

Row

1

BATTERY PARK CITY

North Cove Yacht Harbor

WORLD FINANCIAL CENTER

Greenwich St

West St

Barclay St

Murray St

Chambers St M

West St

Vesey St

✕✕ Taj Tribeca

World Trade Center

Park Pl

City Hall

Brooklyn Br-City Hall M

Chambers St

MUNICIPAL BUILDING

CIVIC CENTER

Broadway

WOOLWORTH BUILDING

ST. PAUL'S CHAPEL

CITY HALL

Park Row

Centre St

Pearl St

James Pl

WORLD TRADE CENTER SITE

Rose St

Fulton St M

Ann St

Spruce St

Park Row

BATTERY PARK CITY

Albany St

South End Ave

Liberty St

Cortlandt M

John St

Liberty St

Maiden Ln

Fulton St M

Fulton St

BROOKLYN BRIDGE

Wagner Pl

Pearl St

St James Pl

2

iberty View

W Thames St

outh Cove

Washington St

Greenwich St

Rector St

TRINITY CHURCH

Trinity Pl

Wall St

Pine St

Nassau St

William St

Gold St

Fulton St

✕ Bridge Cafe

Dover St

Peck Slip

✕✕ MarkJoseph

✕ SUteiShi

Water St

Front St

Ship

BROOKLYN BRIDGE

MUSEUM OF JEWISH HERITAGE

✕✕ Inatteso
● Pizzabar Casano

Rector St

Broadway

NY STOCK EXCHANGE

Broad St

Wall St

Pearl St

Maiden Ln

Gild Hall 🏨

✕ Nelson Blue

Front St

South St

Best Western Seaport Inn

● Ritz-Carlton, Battery Park

New St

Beaver St

🏨✕ Wall St. Inn

Andaz Wall St.

SOUTH STREET SEAPORT

PIER 17

gino at gner Park

Battery Pl

Bowling Green M

🍴 Vintry

Broad St

Stone St

Harry's Steak & Cafe ✕

Old Slip

Roosevelt Dr

PIER 16

✕✕ Nebraska Beef

Bridge St

Pearl St

✕✕ Adrienne's Pizzabar

Zigolinis ✕✕

Water St

PIER 14

BATTERY

Whitehall St

State St

Broad St

Front St

Franklin Dr

PIER 13

EAST RIVER

CASTLE CLINTON NATL. MON.

PARK

South Ferry M

PIER 11

3

NEW YORK HARBOR

South St

PIER 6

Financial District

BROOKLYN-BATTERY TUNNEL

STATEN ISLAND FERRY TERMINAL

PORT AUTHORITY DOWNTOWN HELIPORT

A — **B** — **C**

Then for something sweet, head to **Financier Patisserie** on charming, cobblestoned Stone Street, one of the narrow, sinuous streets laid out in the 17th century by New York's Dutch settlers. While here, take your pooch for a drink at **Growler Bites & Brews** and after, wash it down with an espresso at **Zibetto's**. Despite the economic downturn, restaurants downtown are as busy as ever, with former Wall Street wonders drowning their worries in martinis and Manhattans; and reviewing their portfolios over burgers and beer. Events like the Stone Street Oyster Festival, sponsored by the same folks who operate Financier Patisserie and Ulysses pub, play to the area's strengths. What better way to lift your spirits and celebrate the local Blue Point harvest in September than by slurping oysters and swilling libations outdoors on Stone Street?

Adrienne's Pizzabar

Manhattan ▶ Financial District

Pizza ✕✕

B3

54 Stone St. (bet. Coenties Alley & S. William St.)

Subway: Bowling Green   Lunch & dinner daily
Phone: 212-248-3838
Web: www.adriennespizzabar.com
Prices: 💰

Come midday at Stone Street and Coenties Alley, Adrienne's is abuzz with Financial District business types hungering for delectable pizzas. With their thin-crusts, slightly chunky sauce, and fresh toppings, these pies are a classic—even the square shape is true to the venerable Sicilian-American version.

With increasing residences in this nook, Adrienne's is just as packed at night, when diners linger to appreciate the mosaic-steel bar, stiff-backed leather banquettes, polished marble, or lovely outdoor tables. Choosing between their four hearty ravioli selections can be a challenge, when deciding between lobster, cheese, spinach-cheese, or sausage-broccoli rabe. Desserts are divine, which is no surprise as the owners are also behind Financier Patisserie.

Bridge Cafe

American ✕

C2

279 Water St. (at Dover St.)

Subway: Brooklyn Bridge - City Hall   Lunch Sun — Fri
Phone: 212-227-3344   Dinner nightly
Web: www.bridgecafenyc.com
Prices: $$

Set along the touristy cobblestoned street that is today's Water Street, the Bridge Cafe–which claims to be New York's oldest drinking establishment–was standing here when the area was better known for brothels and saloons than J. Crew and Banana Republic.

And so if the food is simply good, but not heroic, at this Manhattan mainstay, one can let a few details slide—especially for brown liquor enthusiasts looking to cruise the restaurant's extensive list of Bourbons, malts, and Scotches. The menu lists some refreshingly light fare like a soft shell crab BLT; grilled wild Pacific salmon; and avocado and watercress salad. But a spot-on buffalo burger, topped with chili, bacon, and pepper jack on a chipotle aïoli-slathered bun really hits the spot.

84

Gigino at Wagner Park

Italian ✗✗

A3

20 Battery Pl. (in Wagner Park)

Subway: Bowling Green
Phone: 212-528-2228
Web: www.gigino-wagnerpark.com
Prices: $$

Lunch & dinner daily

Move over out-of-towners, locals are wising up to this hidden gem, where harbor views, a dedicated staff, and a scrumptious Italian menu make for a fantastic experience. The serenely lit room is outfitted in muted whites, with high ceilings and large windows that peek out at the shimmering water (in warmer seasons, snag a seat on the gorgeous terrace for the best views).

Dine on tasty arugula salad with pear slices, shaved Parmesan, and candied walnuts; *cosciotto di pollo*—tender chicken braised in white wine and vegetable ragù; pan-sauteed artichoke hearts with garlic, flat-leaf parsley, and olive oil; or gnocchi tossed in a veal and beef meatball-laden tomato ragù. Save room for a fresh lemon tart, with whipped cream and slices of strawberry.

Harry's Steak & Cafe

American ✗✗

B3

1 Hanover Sq. (bet. Pearl & Stone Sts.)

Subway: Wall St (William St.)
Phone: 212-785-9200
Web: www.harrysnyc.com
Prices: $$

Lunch & dinner Mon – Sat

Mornings may begin with a bell, but Wall Street's powerbrokers ring in its end at Harry's Steak & Cafe. A beloved watering hole for decades, this Wall Street institution was reincarnated into two distinct spaces: a café and a steakhouse. Handsome and clubby with a gleaming black walnut bar and copper ceilings, the café defines relaxed elegance, while the more serious steakhouse feels secreted away with a sophisticated intimacy.

Beef is what's on tap at Harry's, so expect old-fashioned boys' club dining and precise service. The more casual café menu features a few deep-pocketed riffs on American favorites like the Kobe hot dog (only on Wall Street), while the steakhouse focuses on classic preparations of its excellent quality, rich, and juicy beef.

Inatteso Pizzabar Casano

Italian 🍴🍴

A2

28 West St. (at 2nd Pl.)

Subway: South Ferry
Phone: 212-267-8000
Web: www.inattesopizzabar.com
Prices: **$$$**

Lunch & dinner daily

Aside from its convoluted name, everything at Inatteso is delightfully unassuming. The endearing room co-stars a slender though spirited bar at the entrance. Enchanting vistas of the venerable Statue of Liberty and Ellis Island, appropriate lighting, and lattice-like wood paneling augment the overall allure.

The staff within this contemporary, well-designed haunt may not be perfect, but their kindly manner when presenting the likes of a classic and delicious pizza Margherita will win you over. An arugula salad tossed with baked figs stuffed with Gorgonzola *dolce* and wrapped in prosciutto; swordfish *contadina* glistening with an herbaceous olive oil and laid atop broccoli rabe; or sweet vanilla-infused ricotta cheesecake are some of their other big wins.

Liberty View

Chinese 🍴

A2

21 South End Ave. (below W. Thames St.)

Subway: Rector St (Greenwich St.)
Phone: 212-786-1888
Web: N/A
Prices: **$$**

Lunch & dinner daily

As befits what is becoming one of the city's most vital and investment-loving neighborhoods, local eateries are cleaning up their act, including this authentic Sichuan option—now more dining scene than just a takeout spot. Long-standing Liberty View, positioned on one of *the* best promenades in the city, offers solid Chinese in a clean and comfortable space.

Scores of surrounding FiDi suits frequent these freshly dressed tables set by windows replete with panoramic views. Don't let their marvelous vista of the Statue of Liberty detract you from the likes of cold beef tripe in a spicy pepper oil; Macau rice cooked with barbecue pork, scallions, and eggs; or Shanghai noodles glistening with mushrooms and shiny soy-glazed mustard greens.

MarkJoseph

Steakhouse

C2

261 Water St. (bet. Peck Slip & Dover St.)

Subway: Brooklyn Bridge - City Hall
Phone: 212-277-0020
Web: www.markjosephsteakhouse.com
Prices: $$$

Lunch Mon – Fri
Dinner nightly

Rising from the shadows of the Brooklyn Bridge in the South Street Seaport Historic District, MarkJoseph's caters to both Wall Street wunderkinds and tourists with deep pockets. The cozy dining room is a notch above the standard steakhouse design, with art-glass vases and pastoral photographs of the wine country adding sleek notes.

At lunch, regulars devour hearty half-pound burgers (though a turkey variety is also offered). At dinnertime, a prime dry-aged Porterhouse, sized for two to four, takes center stage. Classic accompaniments may include crisp salads, seafood cocktails, and sides like creamed spinach. The wine list offers a nice choice of hefty varietals, as well as some interesting old-world selections to accompany that bone-in ribsteak.

Nebraska Beef

Steakhouse

B3

15 Stone St. (bet. Broad & Whitehall Sts.)

Subway: Bowling Green
Phone: 212-952-0620
Web: www.nebraskasteakhousenyc.com
Prices: $$$

Lunch Mon – Fri
Dinner nightly

It's easy to miss the door that marks the entrance to this beloved Financial District watering hole-cum-steakhouse (look for the red and gold sign out front), but not the raucous happy hour crowd that floods the narrow bar leading to the restaurant. Smile and squeeze through, to discover a much calmer scene inside: a dark, wood-paneled dining room with a clubby, in the know vibe.

This is one Wall Street oasis where the past and present comfortably co-exist—the martinis flow freely, the garlic bread melts in your mouth, and the hand-picked, 28-day, dry-aged ribeye still arrives sizzling, perfectly charred, and juicy as sin. If you're short on time or looking for lunch options, you can also grab a steak sandwich, salad, or burger on the fly.

Nelson Blue

C2

233-235 Front St. (at Peck Slip)

Subway: Fulton St   Lunch & dinner daily
Phone: 212-346-9090
Web: www.nelsonblue.com
Prices: $$

Tucked into a bustling old corner of Front Street near the South Street Seaport dominated by old pubs and workhorse happy hour restaurants, Nelson Blue offers a quirky, delicious detour from the usual haunts. The solid fare and never-ending beer taps are the main draw here, but the fun-loving ambience–notice hand-crafted artifacts like a Maori war canoe, a handsome oval bar, and a long communal wood table–only adds to the fun.

The New Zealand-based menu offers a range of straightforward fare like a Thai chicken soup humming with coconut, curry, lotus root, lemongrass, and sizzling rice; tender grilled lamb lollipops laced with a delicious rosemary-mustard sauce; and Nelson Blue's classic curried lamb pot pie paired with creamy mashed potatoes.

North End Grill

A1

104 North End Ave. (at Murray St.)

Subway: Chambers St (West Broadway)   Lunch & dinner daily
Phone: 212-747-1600
Web: www.northendgrillnyc.com
Prices: $$$

North End Grill presents straightforward, aromatic American fare. From the moment you enter and until you leave (preferably after grilled pineapple slathered with cashew butter) find yourself cloaked in global scents. With Chef Floyd Cardoz (of Tabla fame) in charge, this serious, stunning newbie is already thriving in its rather odd locale.

Glitzy lights mark the door to this state-of-the-art abode. But, before the bar seizes you, take a moment to admire their busy yet collected kitchen. Cuddle into a midnight blue banquette and inspect the menu, rife with an eggscellent section of...you guessed it...eggs. Other picks unveil fresh octopus curls atop a lentil salad; tender cubes of seared Mangalista bacon; and soft shell crab with spicy papaya tangles.

SUteiShi

C2

Japanese ✗✗

24 Peck Slip (at Front St.)

Subway: Fulton St
Phone: 212-766-2344
Web: www.suteishi.com
Prices: $$

Lunch Mon – Sat
Dinner nightly

In a neighborhood starved for good eats, this colorful and spacious haven makes the grade. Make no mistake: it's not mind-blowing sushi you will find here. But, guests who stick to the inventive rolls or lunchtime bento boxes will be rewarded with a very good meal in a welcoming atmosphere. Make your way into SUteiShi's sleek, red lacquer-accented dining room to discover a sushi bar with a wood-weaved backdrop, a few bonsai plants, and the requisite Maneki-neko (beckoning cat). Don't miss the *ikura* roll wrapped with King salmon and topped with bright salmon roe; the super-fresh uni; or an intriguing black sesame brulée that reads more like a pudding, and arrives accompanied by two sesame wafers, bright slices of strawberries, and ripe blueberries.

Taj Tribeca

B1

Indian ✗✗

18 Murray St. (bet. Broadway & Church St.)

Subway: Park Place
Phone: 212-608-5555
Web: www.tajtribeca.com
Prices: $$

Lunch & dinner daily

The scene may not impress, but this Indian spot is heads above other neighboring eateries that line these bare streets of this fast-changing neighborhood.

A small, lovely bar greets diners as they enter Taj Tribeca, and an exposed brick wall, adorned with heavy wood-framed mirrors, adds a sense of space. Sitar and sarod tunes, sconces, and splashes of fuchsia, green, and red add some allure and softness to this long, deep room with wonderfully high ceilings.

Creative dishes might include *lasooni gobhi*, cauliflower florets stir-fried with a touch of garlic and finished in a fragrant tomato base; crispy vegetable *pakoras*; and *Kashmiri roganjosh*, tender cubes of lamb simmered in a sensational stew of fennel seeds, chili powder, and ginger.

89

Vintry

Contemporary

B3

57 Stone St. (bet Coenties Alley & Hanover Sq.)

Subway: Bowling Green
Phone: 212-480-9800
Web: www.vintrynyc.com
Prices: $$

Lunch & dinner daily

Vintry is a gem in a sea of standard bars on the very charming, pedestrian-only, cobbled Stone Street, with a sparkle that is light years away from the typical frat party-style taverns that dominate this stretch. From its rare African redwood and rainforest marble bar to its bone-like maple vines, the interior combines rare elements to fashion a swanky yet unique setting.

First and foremost, this is a temple to brown booze (no clear spirits served here) and boasts tremendous whiskey and wine lists. Bigwigs and budget-conscious alike can find something to fit their tastes (note the wire-covered wall cabinet housing the big guns). The concise menu has everything from lamb meatballs, truffle mushroom *cavatelli*, and swordfish *au poivre* to complement.

Zigolinis

American

B3

66 Pearl St. (at Coenties Slip)

Subway: Wall St (William St.)
Phone: 212-425-3127
Web: www.zigolinis.com
Prices: $$

Lunch & dinner Mon – Fri

With its lovely chandeliers, silk fabric, and picture windows overlooking historic Pearl Street, this sexy and spacious downtown restaurant is a breath of fresh air among the staid options that typify the Financial District dining scene. The nightly cocktail specials and vibrant happy hour prove its worth. The Italian-leaning American menu is broad and appealing, with a tasty offering of sandwiches and burgers at lunch. Dinnertime "pub fare" is always popular for groups, with options like their celebrated lollipop wings, cheeseburger sliders, and crispy-fried mozzarella.

These owners know they've found a good thing: note their quick-serve "deli" outpost located next door, as well as a casual Zigolinis serving Neapolitan-style pizza in Hell's Kitchen.

Gramercy, Flatiron & Union Square

Gramercy Park, anchoring its namesake neighborhood, is steeped in history, old-world beauty, and tranquility. But, its extreme exclusivity is the stuff of legends among life-long New Yorkers, few of whom have set foot on its pretty yet private paths. This may be where tourists have an advantage, because outside of the residents whose home address faces the square, Gramercy Park Hotel guests are among the few permitted entrance. The staff accompanies guests to the daunting cast-iron gate, allows them in, and reminds them of the number to call when they wish to be let out again, perhaps to explore this lovely enclave filled with charming cafés and beautiful brownstones. Still this is New York, so walk a few blocks in any direction to discover the neighborhood's diverse offerings like Maury Rubin's **City Bakery**—a popular spot revered for its excellent pastries, hot chocolate, and signature pretzel croissant.

Curry Hill

North of the park is Gramercy's very own "Curry Hill" with an authentic range of satisfying, budget-friendly restaurants. Food enthusiasts should visit **Kalustyan's**—a spice-scented emporium specializing in a mind-boggling wealth of exotic products ranging from orange blossom water, to thirty varieties of dried whole chilies. A few blocks to the west, find the very open, tranquil, and welcoming Madison Square Park, which boasts its own unique history and vibe. This was the home of the city's first community Christmas tree in 1912, the original location of Madison Square Garden arena, and site of New York's very first baseball club, the Knickerbockers of 1845. It is therefore only fitting that greeting park visitors is the original and scrumptious **Shake Shack**, serving its signature upscale fast food to a legion of followers from an ivy-covered kiosk. Burgers and Chicago-style dogs are always popular, but the house-made creamy custard has its cultish followers checking the online "custard calendar" weekly for their favorite flavors. Barbecue fans should time their visits here with the Big Apple Barbecue Block Party held in June. This weekend-long event features celebrity pit masters displaying and serving their talents to throngs of hungry aficionados. One of this neighborhood's most famous and frequented features is **Eataly NY**, founded by Oscar Farinetti and brought stateside by business partners Mario Batali and Joe Bastianich. This massive mecca offers a glamorous marketplace and dining hall replete with Italian products and aromatic food stalls showcasing fresh pasta, organic breads, domestically raised meats, fresh fish from the Fulton Fish Market, Neapolitan-style pizza, and a coffee bar.

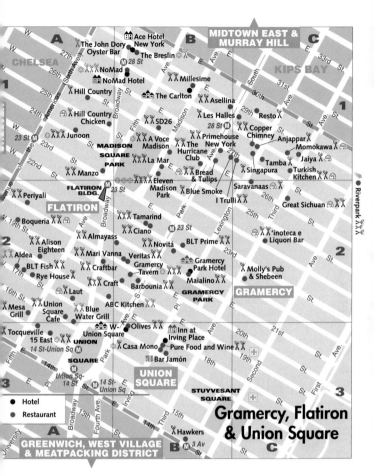

Gramercy, Flatiron & Union Square

Nearby Union Square may be known as an historic downtown park with playgrounds and tiered plazas that occasionally hosts political protests and rallies, but today the square is best known for its year-round **Greenmarket**. Housed in the newly renovated Union Square Park is a beautiful array of seasonal produce, baked goods, fresh meat, seafood, dairy, plants, and flowers that are still available every Monday, Wednesday, Friday, and Saturday. Early in the day, it is not uncommon to spot chefs dressed in their whites selecting the day's supplies. Beyond the market's borders, find a nice bottle of wine to complement that farm-to-table meal from the comprehensive **Union Square Wines and Spirits** or the regionally-specific **Italian Wine Merchants**. Further testament to Union Square's reputation as the center of Manhattan food shopping is the presence of **Whole Foods** and the city's very first **Trader Joe's**, all within blocks of one another.

ABC Kitchen

Contemporary 𝄜𝄜

 A2

35 E. 18th St. (bet. Broadway & Park Ave. South)

Subway: 14 St - Union Sq Lunch & dinner daily
Phone: 212-475-5829
Web: www.abckitchennyc.net
Prices: $$

The super-busy Super-Chef Jean-Georges Vongerichten weaves a bit of green into his rich tapestry of dining venues with this invigorating eatery at ABC Carpet & Home. Rooted in a farm-to-table ethos, the jet set sups here on an assortment of seasonal and consciously procured small plates like raw summer squash salad with Parmesan dressing and herbs; wood-fired whole wheat pizza with Jersey tomatoes, buffalo mozzarella, and basil; or seared salmon with crushed market peaches and chili-lime tomatoes.

The chic setting showcases a whitewashed interior warmed by reclaimed ceiling beams, soy candles, and that trademark ABC touch: mix and match chandeliers. The room's furnishings and handmade service pieces are available for purchase online.

Alison Eighteen

Contemporary 𝄜𝄜

A2

15 W. 18th St. (bet. Fifth & Sixth Aves.)

Subway: 14 St - 6 Av Lunch & dinner daily
Phone: 212-366-1818
Web: www.alisoneighteen.com
Prices: $$

Steadfast restaurateur Alison Price Becker has returned with this venture designed by the team responsible for the look of her first operation, Alison on Dominick Street, which served as a launching pad for a notable lineup of culinary talent still working their collective magic today. The feel is fresh yet warm with aubergine-tinted booths, espresso-shaded tables, and walls lined with bespoke toile wallpaper.

The kitchen presents a roster of seasonally inspired au courant hits. Anson Mills polenta is topped with foraged mushrooms; spit roasted chicken is rubbed with spices and garnished with wilted spinach and a rainbow of carrots; and desserts include a chocolate caramel tartlet. Alison Eighteen's front kiosk serves weekday morning coffee and pastries.

Aldea ✿

Mediterranean 🍴🍴

31 W. 17th St. (bet. Fifth & Sixth Aves.)

Subway:	14 St - 6 Av	Lunch Mon – Fri
Phone:	212-675-7223	Dinner Mon – Sat
Web:	www.aldearestaurant.com	
Prices:	**$$**	

Jerry Errico

Everything is primo yet pleasant at Aldea—making this Iberian favorite an idyllic complement to its tony Gramercy locality filled with choice shops and restaurants.

The contemporary interior reflects Chef George Mendes' cooking through light woods, cool tones, and a semi-open kitchen adding to the room's warmth and sense of anticipation. Expect to see publishing types casually negotiating at neighboring tables; even business lunches feel nicer, not too serious and never loud. The vibe here is that delicious.

The kitchen's talent in presenting refined cooking with local, seasonal, and Mediterranean sensibilities is great; its ability to highlight single ingredients with complex flavors that never overpower is extraordinary. This approach is clear in exquisitely textured Spanish octopus, poached and seared *a la plancha*, served alongside cubes of roasted celery root, sliced Fuji apple, and squid ink-lemon purée. Nothing detracts from the excellent ingredients when New Bedford diver scallops arrive with roasted trumpet mushrooms, pickled radish, and citrus. Impeccable technique is clear in the ultra-thin pastry crust and salted caramel ice cream that surround the very elegant pecan tart.

Almayass

Lebanese XX

B2

24 E. 21st St. (bet. Broadway & Park Ave. South)

Subway: 23 St (Park Ave. South)   Lunch & dinner Mon – Sat
Phone: 212-473-3100
Web: www.almayassnyc.com
Prices: $$

Hot or cold, fresh and flavorful, the extensive choice of mezze at Almayass showcases the riches of Lebanese cuisine accented by Armenian influences, thereby reflecting the heritage of this family-run operation with global outposts. A selection from the spreads and dips is a must, as in the *moutabbal*—eggplant seasoned with lemon, sesame paste, and garlic, redolent of smoke, and topped with jewel-like pomegranate seeds. Other items to seriously consider include *subereg* (a baked dish of four cheeses); oven-baked *mantee* traditional; or charbroiled beef kebab laced with sour cherries.

Polished wood accents, vivid artwork, servers attired in candy-hued shirts, and tables sized for feasting produce a distinctly upscale vibe within this delicious dining room.

Anjappar

Indian X

C1

116 Lexington Ave. (at 28th St.)

Subway: 28 St (Park Ave. South)   Lunch & dinner daily
Phone: 212-265-3663
Web: www.anjapparusa.com
Prices: $$

This new Curry Hill settlement is the third stateside location (there are two others in NJ) from a chain of restaurants based in Chennai. Not much to look at from the outside, Anjappar's interior is festive with bold red accents and carved woodwork that pep up the tidy dining room.

South Indian (Chettinad) cuisine typified by non-vegetarian preparations rich in freshly ground and blended spices set Anjappar's distinct specialties in a league of its own. While you may find a bevy of biryanis and flaky breads, creations like egg masala (sliced boiled eggs sautéed in a pungent onion-and-tomato gravy); and chicken *sukka varuval*, stir-fried chicken vibrantly seasoned with curry leaf, ginger, chili, and black pepper have the diners returning time and again.

Manhattan ▶ Gramercy, Flatiron & Union Square

Asellina

Italian ✕✕

B1

420 Park Ave. South (at 29th St.)

Subway: 28 St (Park Ave. South)
Phone: 212-317-2908
Web: www.togrp.com/asellina
Prices: $$

Lunch & dinner daily

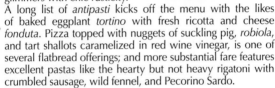

From hospitality company The One Group, and housed in the glassy new Gansevoort Park Avenue hotel, Asellina offers a gratifying and updated vision of Italian dining. Bedecked with terra brick walls, concrete flooring, exposed filament bulbs, and sienna-toned leather furnishings, the lofty room glimmers with chic rusticity.

A long list of *antipasti* kicks off the menu with the likes of baked eggplant *tortino* with fresh ricotta and cheese *fonduta*. Pizza topped with nuggets of suckling pig, *robiola*, and tart shallots caramelized in red wine vinegar, is one of several flatbread offerings; and more substantial fare features excellent pastas like the hearty but not heavy rigatoni with crumbled sausage, wild fennel, and Pecorino Sardo.

Barbounia

Mediterranean ✕✕

B2

250 Park Ave. South (at 20th St.)

Subway: 23 St (Park Ave. South)
Phone: 212-995-0242
Web: www.barbounia.com
Prices: $$

Lunch & dinner daily

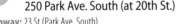

Favored by the nearby business crowd and residents alike, this big and bustling space boasts exotic touches throughout. Fat columns and arched openings abate the room's scale, while pillow-lined banquettes, a knobby-wood communal table, and open kitchen equipped with a wood-burning oven allude to the menu's bazaar of Mediterranean flavors, highlighting Greece and Morocco as well as Southern France and Italy.

The sunny flavors of the region shine in the selection of creamy spreads accompanied by a slab of freshly baked flatbread. Branch out to explore a tempting array of meze, oven-roasted whole fish, or house specialties like lamb terra-cotta—a stew perfumed with sweet spices, covered with a crusty bread lid, and baked in an earthenware dish.

A Voce Madison ✿

Italian ✕✕

B1

41 Madison Ave. (entrance on 26th St.)

Subway: 28 St (Park Ave. South)
Phone: 212-545-8555
Web: www.avocerestaurant.com
Prices: $$$

Lunch Mon – Fri
Dinner Mon – Sat

Evan Sung

Adjacent to the oasis that is Madison Square Park, A Voce seamlessly meshes classic modernity with its warm, rustic Italian menu. Though the polished tables can feel tightly spaced in the earthy room, larger ones are perfectly suited to the business lunches and publishing deals often sealed here. The bar is a marvelous, carved hunk of wood that is outstanding for solo dining. Service is well-orchestrated rather than indulgent.

Helmed by Chef Missy Robbins, this kitchen's bold confidence and intelligence shine through every dish. Eggy and springy house-made linguine twirl about razor clams, crisp-fried artichokes, Calabrese chili powder, fresh mint, lemon zest, and toasted breadcrumbs with sublime results. *Bollito misto* is fantastically contemporary and praiseworthy here, with braised brisket, duck, and tongue all deeply flavored and slow-cooked to perfection, served with an ingenious squash *mostarda*. When the time is just right, indulge in *tarocco*–wintertime blood oranges harvested on Etna–with black olives, yogurt mousse, tarragon, and blood orange sorbet.

Different seasonal and regional menus serving reasonably priced specialties during the week can be a diamond in the rough.

Bar Jamón

 Spanish

 B3

125 E. 17th St. (at Irving Pl.)

Subway: 14 St - Union Sq
Phone: 212-253-2773
Web: www.barjamonnyc.com
Prices: $$

Lunch Sat – Sun
Dinner nightly

A nibble at tiny Bar Jamón, with its brilliant by-the-glass list of Spanish wines (shared with big sister Casa Mono next door), may convince you that Chef Andy Nusser is the unsung hero of the Batali empire. Though the restaurant is the size of a closet, everything is done deliciously and with panache.

This mouthwatering menu so creatively breaks the tired tapas mold that arrival more than 15 minutes past opening almost guarantees a wait (stick to weekend off-hours). Luscious slices of *jamón serrano* or the famed Iberico from Spain's *pata negra* (black hoofed) pigs and a long list of cheeses and accompaniments star on a menu of small plates washed down by more than 600 choices of Spanish wine. A *cuarto* from the impressive list is de rigueur.

BLT Fish

 Seafood

 A2

21 W. 17th St. (bet. Fifth & Sixth Aves.)

Subway: 14 St - 6 Av
Phone: 212-691-8888
Web: www.bltfish.com
Prices: $$$

Lunch Mon – Fri
Dinner Mon – Sat

Now under the domain of ESquared Hospitality, this civilized canteen offers a two-tiered approach to fish-focused dining. The boisterous ground floor Fish Shack embraces an easy-breezy look and flavor with its raw bar, lobster rolls, and bowlful of salt-water taffy. Upstairs, the elegant dinner-only setting boasts a retractable glass roof, open kitchen, and mocha-hued furnishings.

Appetizers come both raw, like kampachi sashimi, and cooked, as in Santa Barbara uni risotto. Entrées may feature tomato-based cioppino stocked with Alaskan king crab and Maine lobster, or whole fish for two, priced by the pound. Nightly blackboard specials serve up greenmarket-influenced cooking, as in a decadent broccoli and white cheddar gratin.

99

BLT Prime

B2

111 E. 22nd St. (bet. Lexington Ave. & Park Ave. South)

Subway: 23 St (Park Ave. South)　　　　　　　　　　Dinner nightly
Phone: 212-995-8500
Web: www.bltprime.com
Prices: $$$

Like its aquatic cousin, this handsome rendition of a steakhouse is also under new direction yet hasn't missed a beat in sating carnivores with meals of sizzling broiled steaks served in cast iron and glazed by melting herbed butter. Starters such as a heap of baby spinach salad tossed with meaty bacon bits, blue cheese, hard-boiled egg, and warm bacon-vinaigrette; as well as the choice of a slew of sauces and sides offer much in the way of embellishment. In a fitting wave of decadence, dinners are bookended by oversized Gruyère cheese popovers and plates of petite cookies.

A chic yet cozy mien pervades with a warm lighting scheme illuminating the room stocked with earth-toned furnishings, gleaming zebrawood tables, and lively open kitchen.

Blue Smoke

B1

116 E. 27th St. (bet. Lexington Ave. & Park Ave. South)

Subway: 28 St (Park Ave. South)　　　　　　　　　Lunch & dinner daily
Phone: 212-447-7733
Web: www.bluesmoke.com
Prices: $$

Blue Smoke, where hickory and applewood infuse the "low and slow" smoked meats in a real barbecue pit, proves that jazz and barbecue are nothing if not a winning combination. The proof lies in the ravishing pulled pork platter—think of a mountain of tender, shredded meat studded with bits of crisped skin heaped precariously atop a slice of house-baked white bread and accompanied by a caddy of sauces. Starters like deviled eggs and shrimp corn dogs, as well as stellar desserts by pastry chef Jennifer Giblin bookend this fabulous feast.

Families and groups may choose the upstairs dining, but the same food can be enjoyed downstairs at Jazz Standard, complete with live music. Owner Danny Meyer stamps the restaurant with his signature of gracious service.

Blue Water Grill

Contemporary 🍴🍴

A2

31 Union Sq. West (at 16th St.)

Subway: 14 St - Union Sq
Phone: 212-675-9500
Web: www.bluewatergrillnyc.com
Prices: $$

Lunch & dinner daily

Facing the Union Square Greenmarket, perennially popular Blue Water Grill is housed in a former, century-old bank, whose grand rooms now bustle with eager guests and a well-trained service team. Still, it retains a stately air with its soaring molded ceiling, gleaming marble, and windows overlooking the terraced dining area, ideal for warmer weather.

The crowd-pleasing menu focuses on seafood, but offers something for everyone. Highlights include a raw bar and sushi or maki selections, as well as fish entrées, simply grilled or accented with international flavors, as in big eye tuna with miso-black garlic vinaigrette. Find live jazz nightly in the downstairs lounge; or private group dining in the Vault Room, a former repository for gold bullion.

Boqueria

Spanish 🍴🍴

A2

53 W. 19th St. (bet. Fifth & Sixth Aves.)

Subway: 18 St (Seventh Ave.)
Phone: 212-255-4160
Web: www.boquerianyc.com
Prices: $$

Lunch & dinner daily

Channeling the little bars that surround the legendary *Mercat de la Boqueria* in Barcelona, this upscale tapas spot is among the city's better destinations for an Iberian bite. Despite the crush of occupants each evening, the attractive setting provides a comfortable perch either in the rear room furnished with high tables or at the front counter flaunting plates of *tortilla Española*.

The kitchen is in the capable hands of a Barcelona native who boasts an impresive resume. Treats here have featured crunchy *croquetas* filled with a creamy combination of octopus and tomato; house-made pork sausage paired with crisped yet creamy garbanzo beans and syrupy red wine reduction; and *torrija*, a stunning Spanish rendition of French toast.

Bread & Tulips ☺

Italian ✗✗

365 Park Ave. South (at 26th St.)

Subway: 28 St (Park Ave. South)
Phone: 212-532-9100
Web: www.breadandtulipsnyc.com
Prices: $$

Lunch Mon – Fri
Dinner Mon – Sat

Tucked away on the lower level of the Hotel Giraffe, the inspired Italian cooking at Bread & Tulips sets it apart from the host of workaday dining options lining this stretch of Park Avenue South. The windowless room creates an air of seclusion and contemporary good looks through exposed brick, darkly polished woods, and filament light fixtures.

The kitchen shows its chops with a short list of pizzas that emerge charred, moist, and chewy from the brick oven, topped with the likes of hen of the woods mushrooms, pickled ramps, wild watercress, and creamy Taleggio cheese. Nightly specials include house-made pastas and entrées such as Muscovy duck breast seared to a beautiful crisp, with grappa-soaked Concord grapes atop a dollop of dense polenta.

Ciano

Italian ✗✗

45 E. 22nd St. (bet. Broadway & Park Ave. South)

Subway: 23 St (Park Ave. South)
Phone: 212-982-8422
Web: www.cianonyc.com
Prices: $$$

Lunch Mon – Fri
Dinner Mon – Sat

Terra-cotta tile, warm sunset hues, a crackling fireplace topped with fresh herbs scenting the room—is this a Tuscan farmhouse? Not quite, but close: It's Ciano.

Chef Shea Gallante heads up this charming dining room that proffers a rousing display of market-inspired Italian creations. House-made pastas can be scene-stealing with the likes of *cortecce*—each toothsome oval precisely coated with a mouthwatering combination of thinly sliced baby octopus, finely diced fennel and pancetta, and garlic breadcrumbs. The short list of entrées may offer Berkshire pork tenderloin with polenta and a sweet potato fritter; and desserts always please, as in the supple vanilla panna cotta paired with white chocolate sorbet that shines against blueberry compote.

The Breslin ✿

Gastropub ✗

B1

16 W. 29th St. (at Broadway)

Subway: 28 St (Broadway)
Phone: 212-679-1939
Web: www.thebreslin.com
Prices: $$

Lunch & dinner daily

Melissa Hom

Staying at the perpetually hip Ace Hotel can be quite a thrill in itself, but to be merely steps away from the foodie-mobbed and beloved Breslin is a supreme luxury. This (at times painfully) trendy gastropub has NYers waxing poetic about the big, bold flavors and beautifully crafted dishes. As a result, all who sojourn here know they're in for a wait—The Breslin never stands still.

Gorgeous from every angle, this urban burrow manages to look timeless and friendly at the same time. The presence of heavy, handsome, and worn-in wood juxtaposes well with the sleek, open kitchen. Tables are jammed, so if you're not in the mood for eavesdropping, retire to a booth sequestered away from the bedlam.

Also drawing you in are sultry lights and pleasing plates that are worth every bit of hype like the infamous Caesar salad paired with a char-grilled lamb burger topped with feta and cumin mayo. Pleasant and practiced servers move to the whim of businessmen, visitors, and hipsters as they devour razor clams cooked *a la plancha* with fiery serranos and garlic aïoli; or warm and perfectly crisp sugar doughnuts served with a trio of lemon curd, raspberry jam, and dark chocolate sauces for dipping.

Casa Mono ✿

Spanish 🍴

52 Irving Pl. (at 17th St.)

Subway: 14 St - Union Sq
Phone: 212-253-2773
Web: www.casamononyc.com
Prices: $$

Lunch & dinner daily

Peter Siskos

While there are quite a few restaurants lucky enough to be settled on this stretch of Irving Place, it is virtually impossible to miss this bold (read: vibrant awning) beauty whose tantalizing whiffs are known to lure in passersby. Casa Mono is tiny but coveted as a precious gem. It boasts only a smattering of sturdy dark wood tables, though seating is nearly doubled by the two counters: one faces the open, aromatic, orderly kitchen; another is a wine bar awash with Euro sophisticates sipping Albariño.

Casa Mono may be petite, but its wall of windows, orange accents, and distressed mosaic floor are mighty seductive. One step inside and feel as if you're back in *España* gnawing on crisped, golden brown duck confit, slow-poached in olive oil for six hours before being poised atop a knob of "hashbrowns." The exquisitely tender duck meat that falls from the bone lands deftly into a smooth and creamy sesame-studded winter squash *mole* spread across the plate.

Stylish servers are precise in delivering the likes of rich cod cheeks *pil pil* in an outstanding garlic-lemon-accented sauce; or a cast-iron skillet of bread and orange-infused custard in *pudín de naranja*, which is an absolute winner.

Copper Chimney

Indian ✗✗

126 E. 28th St. (bet. Lexington Ave. & Park Ave. South)

Subway: 28 St (Park Ave. South)
Phone: 212-213-5742
Web: www.copperchimneynyc.com
Prices: ⊗⊗

Lunch & dinner daily

This attractive and sleek dining room with a hip décor and fun vibe impresses with Northern and Southern Indian fare that stands well above the array of local options. The appetizer selection may include lovely *malai kofta*, perfectly browned and simmered in a delicious, creamy saffron sauce. Main courses incorporate a wide range of traditional ingredients, while emphasizing refined preparation and elegant presentation. Non-meat eaters will be happy with the ample selection of flavorful vegetarian items. Delicately puffed *kulcha*, served hot and dusted with cilantro and mint, is a great foil to any rich, leftover sauces (and the best way to sop them up).

The contemporary setting is further enhanced by a second floor lounge area.

Craft

American ✗✗✗

43 E. 19th St. (bet. Broadway & Park Ave. South)

Subway: 14 St - Union Sq
Phone: 212-780-0880
Web: www.craftrestaurant.com
Prices: $$$$

Dinner nightly

This hot spot from celebrity Chef/owner Tom Colicchio is honest-to-goodness city chic. It's dim and moody—reading the menu in the dark can make you feel older than that harried exec in the corner. It's American as only a city chef can do, with more twists and turns than a drive on the autobahn. Colicchio's a good guy though—note the shout-outs to farmers and producers of these quality ingredients.

Confused by the seemingly simple choices? Broken down, it's really just sophisticated snacks with a "pick and choose" mentality. It was Miss Scarlet in the Library with a candlestick holder, er, it's halibut, braised in beurre blanc, in a copper dish. Keep grazing...you'll go from pork trotter and crisp-a-licious shishito peppers to s'mores stat.

Craftbar

A2

Contemporary 🍴

900 Broadway (bet. 19th & 20th Sts.)

Subway: 14 St - Union Sq
Phone: 212-461-4300
Web: www.craftrestaurant.com
Prices: $$

Lunch & dinner daily

Flaunting Craft's trademark style, Craftbar offers fine cooking garnished by the space's industrial good looks and pretty occupants—all a perfect match for its Gramercy environs.
With an extensive menu of something for just about everyone, it's no wonder that Craftbar always draws a crowd. Raw, cured, and fried snacks, local cheeses, and small plates offer a tasty prelude to the range of product-focused fare that has featured stuffed rabbit saddle dressed with golden raisin chutney; and pan-seared branzino draped over a peak of ratatouille. Brown sugar cake with a caramelized pineapple ring and crème fraîche ice cream makes saving room for dessert a requisite indulgence.
Revel in the boundless wine list, with many selections by the glass.

Great Sichuan 😊

C2

Chinese 🍴

363 Third Ave. (bet. 26th & 27th Sts.)

Subway: 28 St (Park Ave. South)
Phone: 212-686-8866
Web: www.greatsichuan.com
Prices: $$

Lunch & dinner daily

This under-the-radar Sichuan restaurant, tucked into a bustling stretch of Third Ave., is a find you'll want to tell your friends about stat. A simple dining room, fitted out in wood details, white linens, and stone tile floors, belies the bold and flavorful fare ahead. Dishes are fresh and authentic—not to mention spicy enough to put some hair on your chest.
Skip the American-style offerings and set your sights on one of the chef's Sichuan specialties; or the authentic Mao section, which features mouthwatering goodies like cured pork with green garlic shoots, or braised pumpkin with ginger and scallions. Another highlight is the whole steamed fish, smothered in pickled chili peppers, sweet red bell peppers, caramelized white onion and green scallion.

Eleven Madison Park ✿ ✿ ✿

Contemporary XXXX

B1

11 Madison Ave. (at 24th St.)

Subway: 23 St (Park Ave. South)
Phone: 212-889-0905
Web: www.elevenmadisonpark.com
Prices: $$$$

Lunch Mon – Fri
Dinner Mon – Sat

Francesco Tonelli

Truly deserving of its stately and iconic façade, Eleven Madison Park is a worthy pinnacle of New York dining. Inside, the striking high ceilings of a grand ballroom rise above art deco lanterns, hand-stenciled borders, restored terrazzo floors, and a crowd who appreciates that no detail has been overlooked. Miles Davis plays softly in the background—a distant song suggesting that he would be trying to get in here, too. Amid such opulence, the menu's lack of description seems to be the only thing holding back.

Yet under Chef/owner Daniel Humm, the cuisine is regal, beautiful, and breathtakingly delicious. A canapé might arrive as a "smoky and sweet" brioche topped with fried quail egg, bacon, smoked-apple and celery-infused tea with an itsy-bitsy bundle of raffia-tied thyme—fit for the king of Lilliput. "Cobia" might reveal a pan-roasted baton of fish with king trumpet mushrooms, dry-roasted garlic, all earthy yet vibrant with cress sprigs. The transition to dessert brings elegant tableside service; a mini egg cream prepared with flair—an example of the ability here to interpret cuisine with a sophisticated style and whimsical touches.

Service is not merely observant, but anticipatory.

15 East ❀

A3

Japanese ✗✗

15 E. 15th St. (bet. Fifth Ave. & Union Sq. West)

Subway: 14 St - Union Sq
Phone: 212-647-0015
Web: www.15eastrestaurant.com
Prices: $$$

Lunch Mon — Fri
Dinner Mon — Sat

Michel Ann O'Malley

Classic talent, youthful dedication, and the chefs' calm intensity of purpose culminate at 15 East in meals that reflect a sense of Japanese tradition rarely found in the US. At the same time, modern touches enliven the dining experience.

The sushi counter offers prime seating, with prized views of the kitchen team at work in their white-tiled space, grating that wasabi root immediately before presenting your sashimi. The dining area is less mesmerizing, but is cozier with linen-shaded windows and mottled-grey fabrics.

Meals may open with a seasonal trio of house-made yuba topped with uni, slow-poached octopus, and a perfectly summery gazpacho purée. The array of sashimi reveals yellowtail, fluke, and sea scallop all expertly cut and delicious, alongside a shrimp so fresh that it still is filled with life before delicately surrendering. Be sure to indulge in some of the city's best tempura (the impossibly light batter barely appearing to cover each morsel of fish or ginger shoot) fried to crisp, seasoned with green-tea salt and lemon. Homemade desserts like almond-tofu with blood orange sorbet and sake syrup, are a lovely reflection of this kitchen's broad range and depth of skill.

Gramercy Tavern ✿

Contemporary 🍴🍴🍴

B2

42 E. 20th St. (bet. Broadway & Park Ave. South)

Subway: 23 St (Park Ave. South)
Phone: 212-477-0777
Web: www.gramercytavern.com
Prices: $$$

Lunch Mon – Fri
Dinner nightly

Ellen Silverman

Gramercy Tavern sits in a stately building set steps away from the esteemed Gramercy Park. Pass through its lively foyer, decorated with seasonal produce and foliage, and the world melts away.

The Tavern area has the relaxing warmth of an early American saloon, with exposed wood beamed ceilings, colorful murals, and a long bar that stretches the back wall. Thick drapes, copper sconces, and early American portraits lend intimacy and a sense of history to the three formal dining rooms. Here, know that you are rubbing elbows with an assemblage of bigwigs, celebrities, and affluent locals, as polished servers arrive at your table with an almost bookish knowledge of Chef Michael Anthony's delightfully simple menu.

Each dish is superbly unfussy, as in starters like plump buckwheat ravioli filled with an enticing blend of ground smoked duck and Romano bean purée, tossed with halved sungold tomatoes, more beans, and a buttery jus. Entrées include Arctic char cooked with extraordinary skill, served in a warm buttermilk broth with fresh English peas and caramelized Tasso ham. For dessert, a warm chocolate bread pudding is presented steaming from the oven, alongside creamy cacao nib-studded ice cream.

Hawkers

B3

A s i a n 🍴

225 E. 14th St. (bet. Second & Third Aves.)

Subway: 14 St - Union Sq   Lunch & dinner daily
Phone: 212-982-1688
Web: www.hawkersnewyork.com
Prices: 〰️

Hawkers takes its cue from the open-air food stalls strutting local specialties that are customary throughout Southeast Asia. The slender room, embellished by a collection of silhouettes and street-theme graffiti art set against a bright red background, showcases a two-sided dining counter and a laid-back crew.

The menu is gently priced and serves up a variety of fresh and tasty snacks such as Thai sausage, chicken *satay* burger, and five-spice pork roll encased in a delicately crisp bean curd skin. Several fried rice and noodle preparations form the heart of Hawkers' offerings: the Maggi, named after a popular brand of instant noodles, features ramen served up as a fluffy stir-fry stocked with sliced tomato, egg, bean sprouts, and green onion.

Hill Country

A1

B a r b e c u e 🍴

30 W. 26th St. (bet. Broadway & Sixth Ave.)

Subway: 28 St (Broadway)   Lunch & dinner daily
Phone: 212-255-4544
Web: www.hillcountryny.com
Prices: $$

This Texas-size roadhouse has won over the hearts and stomachs of smoked brisket deprived New Yorkers. Always a rollicking good time, Hill Country's food stations, dispensing some of NY's best barbecue and country fare, set it above the booming competition.

The crew behind the stoves here have clearly honed their skills— successfully fueling Hill Country's massive smokers with cords of oak to recreate a truly Texan Hill Country experience. Grab Flintstone-size ribs by the pound, sausages by the link, stamp your meal ticket, and head to the trimmings counter for home-style sides. Then, settle in for some live country music, making this a festive spot for groups and families.

Those seeking a more subdued setting can order takeout or delivery.

Hill Country Chicken

American

A1

1123 Broadway (at 25th St.)

Subway: 23 St (Broadway)
Phone: 212-257-6446
Web: www.hillcountrychicken.com
Prices:

Lunch & dinner daily

The city's fried chicken rivalry has gotten more delicious with the arrival of Hill Country Chicken. Like its barbecue-themed sibling, Texas serves as the inspiration for this self-described chicken joint, which can accommodate 100 in a country kitchen-style space in sunny yellow and sky blue. Service involves lining up to order, but the crew is swift and friendly. The first order of business is deciding on a variety of naturally raised chicken (classic or Mama El's rocking a skinless, cracker-crumb crust), but there's no wrong choice. Each piece is crunchy, juicy, and incredibly flavorful.

Pimento cheese-topped mashed potatoes; biscuits baked on premises; and a slew of awesome pies proves that this joint is much more than a one hit wonder.

The Hurricane Club

Asian

B1

360 Park Ave. South (at 26th St.)

Subway: 28 St (Park Ave. South)
Phone: 212-951-7111
Web: www.thehurricaneclub.com
Prices: $$

Lunch Mon – Fri
Dinner nightly

A tiki bar as envisioned by the design impresarios at AvroKO and Chef Craig Koketsu (of Park Avenue), The Hurricane Club offers the sips and eats of faraway lands in a pretty setting worthy of a movie backdrop. The multi-room space, vast by NYC standards, is embellished with glossy black and dark croc-embossed banquettes brightened by mirror panels, potted greenery, and large windows dressed with cascading ivory shades; the center bar is crowned by strands of crystal beads.

The assortment of libations provide a quenching prelude to an upscale Polynesian-ish menu of pu pu platters stocked with *croque monsieur* spring rolls; and family-style preparations of sticky and succulent ribs, noodles, and rice. Order-in-advance luau dinners are also offered.

'inoteca e Liquori Bar ☻

Italian ✗✗

C2

323 Third Ave. (at 24th St.)

Subway: 23 St (Park Ave. South)
Phone: 212-683-3035
Web: www.inotecanyc.com
Prices: $$

Lunch Sat – Sun
Dinner nightly

The most sophisticated of its clan, 'inoteca e Liquori Bar brings its beloved small plates to Gramercy. Awash in candlelight, the chic dining space is an earthy rainbow of marble paneling; the separate, bustling bar is a bright corner with large windows and marble tables. With a cocktail menu of more than thirty-five masterful classic and vintage libations, heightened with fresh juices, infusions, and chilled with crystal clear blocks of ice, this is where 'inoteca is at its best.

To complement the skillfully crafted wines, the excellent Italian wine bar cuisine features *antipasti*, panini, and decadent pastas, like baked rigatoni with cauliflower and herbed breadcrumbs. Sidewalk dining is a lovely spot for the inexpensive, prix-fixe brunch.

I Trulli

Italian ✗✗

C1

122 E. 27th St. (bet. Lexington Ave. & Park Ave. South)

Subway: 28 St (Park Ave. South)
Phone: 212-481-7372
Web: www.itrulli.com
Prices: $$$

Lunch Mon – Fri
Dinner nightly

Equal parts dining room and *enoteca*, the charming I Trulli has been going strong for almost 20 years. From the roaring fireplace to the breezy outdoor garden, this place oozes warmth and the ambience is chic country comfort. Every detail including the domed white walls and oven is designed to recall the distinctive architecture of the region's *trullo*, or stacked-stone homes.

I Trulli celebrates the wine and food of Southern Italy's Puglia region. The wine bar has a terrific selection of all-Italian wines and a tempting taste of small dishes, while the dining room focuses on heartier selections, handmade pastas, and regional specialties like *fave e cicoria*.

Desserts show off the chef's proud roots as a pastry artist and provide a strong and sweet finish.

Jaiya

Thai

C1

396 Third Ave. (bet. 28th & 29th Sts.)

Subway: 28 St (Park Ave. South)
Phone: 212-889-1330
Web: www.jaiya.com
Prices:

Lunch Mon – Fri
Dinner nightly

This forever-mobbed Thai hot spot is adored for its spicy and sumptuous cooking. While the furnishings may feature deep-hued woods, dark tables, padded beige walls, and a sleek contemporary bar, rest assured that the vast, budget-friendly menu remains as delicious as ever.

Start with a hot and crisp spring roll filled with glass noodles and bean sprouts while considering the proteins for customizing Jaiya's heaping stir-fried dishes fragrant with basil, garlic, and Kaffir lime. Curry listings encourage the same liberty, highlighting a host of creamy coconut curries, spiced with chilies and sweet with fresh basil, filled with the likes of succulent shrimp and fresh tilapia.

Upper East Siders now have a Jaiya to call their own on Second Avenue.

The John Dory Oyster Bar

Seafood

B1

1196 Broadway (at 29th St.)

Subway: 28 St (Broadway)
Phone: 212-792-9000
Web: www.thejohndory.com
Prices: $$

Lunch & dinner daily

Located in a corner of the Ace Hotel, Chef April Bloomfield's oyster bar is loads of fun. The high-ceilinged boîte boasts original details like a mosaic tile floor as well as chic touches—ebony-stained subway tiles, comfy crayon blue-and-green seating, and a bar flanked by two globe aquariums. The menu adheres to its eponymous concept and offers an array of seafood-centric small plates that everyone piles high on copper-topped tables. Dishes include crispy, salty rock shrimp mounded atop a brioche roll lined with butter lettuce, bacon, and herbed mayonnaise; and the luscious oyster pan roast that quickly became a signature.

For groups, the chef's table can be reserved for a full-on feast of briny bounty, fittingly anchored by a whole-roasted John Dory .

Junoon ✿

A1

27 West 24th St. (bet. Fifth & Sixth Aves.)

Subway: 23 St (Sixth Ave.)
Phone: 212-490-2100
Web: www.junoonnyc.com
Prices: $$$

Lunch Mon – Fri
Dinner nightly

Composition - B Productions

Following in the footsteps of its fabulous Flatiron environs, Junoon is simply stunning. From the moment you step inside this striking sanctum until you depart, find yourself engulfed in grandeur. Serenity also prevails in shimmering pools arranged as a corridor dividing the two dining rooms: one is sleek and spare; the other more opulent.

Junoon's design and culinary creations are a magnificent marriage of modern elegance and classic Indian artistry. Dusky lighting, banquettes with wood frames, and muted colors convey an almost grave tone. Majesty is restored with ornate mirrors, an extravagant wine cabinet, and embellished tables laden with some of the best breads in town.

As for the food, the kitchen exerts every effort to ensure flawless and flavor-ridden fare. The staff is perhaps a tad less rapt, but when you're reveling in deep-fried mushroom and coconut *pakoras* or goat *handi* steeped in a rich, garlicky pomegranate sauce...where was I again? Lamb becomes a standout of sweet delight in *pathar ka gosht*, seasoned with their signature, holy blend of *garam masala*, with tandoori pineapple and roasted onion chutney; while a *gianduja parfait* delivers an explosion of flavor and texture.

La Mar

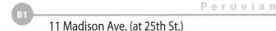

Peruvian XXX

B1

11 Madison Ave. (at 25th St.)

Subway: 23 St (Park Ave South)
Phone: 212-612-3388
Web: www.lamarcebicheria.com
Prices: $$$

Lunch & dinner Mon – Sat

Undaunted by the notorious challenge that New York City poses to imported chefs, regardless of pedigree, Peru's own celebrity chef and culinary ambassador, Gastón Acurio, brings his sunny specialties to the former home of Tabla. The grand space features a lounge pouring intoxicating pisco-based cocktails capped by a citron and turquoise-shaded dining room.

The kitchen, helmed by Chef Acurio's most trusted lieutenant, presents pleasingly updated classics like bracing ceviches, as in the *nikei*, made with diced yellowfin tuna awash in tamarind-sparked *leche de tigre*. Entrées might feature the *tacu tacu a la pobre*, grilled hanger steak, crisped cake of rice and lima beans tinted with *aji amarillo*, quail egg, and fried plantain.

Laut 😊

A2

Asian X

15 E. 17th St. (bet. Broadway & Fifth Ave.)

Subway: 14 St - Union Sq
Phone: 212-206-8989
Web: www.lautnyc.com
Prices: $$

Lunch Mon – Fri
Dinner nightly

Laut's simple façade doesn't prepare you for the hospitable spirit that resides within. But, one look at the line of diners voracious for their marvelous treats, and you know why this spot is assured a place on top.

Inside, find a tastefully decorated room where the walls are painted red, the brick is exposed, and the artwork evokes faraway lands. Loud music and a peppy bar keep the vibe upbeat as pleasant servers whizz around with such tasty, family-style Malaysian fare as *roti canai*, deliciously flaky crêpes served with a spicy coconut chicken curry. Glazed ceramic dishes reveal other exceptional standards like beef *rendang* enriched with coconut milk and herbs; or *sambal petai*, prawns coated in a warmly spiced sauce with savory shrimp paste.

115

Les Halles

C1   French 🍴

411 Park Ave. South (bet. 28th & 29th Sts.)

Subway: 28 St (Park Ave. South)   Lunch & dinner daily
Phone: 212-679-4111
Web: www.leshalles.net
Prices: $$

Gramercy's long-lived, long-loved French brasserie never lets up—it's open all day and boisterous crowds are the rule, not the exception. Do as the regulars do and dig into luscious beef tartare prepared tableside; a steaming pot of mussels; gut-busting *cassoulet "Toulousain"*; and, of course, a heap of golden and crispy pomme frites. Stick to the classics and you're in for an enjoyable experience.

Known as home base to celebrity Chef-at-large Anthony Bourdain, well known for his bestselling *Kitchen Confidential* and numerous television gigs, the room is dressed in dark tones. Expect carved wood accents, leather banquettes, and checkerboard terrazzo flooring that combine to produce an atmospheric room that looks dusky even on the sunniest afternoon.

Maialino

B2   Italian 🍴🍴

2 Lexington Ave. (at 21st St.)

Subway: 23 St (Park Ave South)   Lunch & dinner daily
Phone: 212-777-2410
Web: www.maialinonyc.com
Prices: $$

Danny Meyer's reworking of the Gramercy Park Hotel's dining venue has rendered a chicly casual Italian spot with a rustic theme conceived by the Rockwell Group. Accessed by a separate street entrance, the expanse up front is bright and lively with plenty of counter seating at the bar; while the back area, with its glossy dark wood accents, is furnished with tables dressed in blue-and-white checked tablecloths.

An alumnus of Babbo and Gramercy Tavern rules the kitchen; and the Roman trattoria menu offers a selection of salami and *antipasti*. This is followed by pastas symbolic of the region such as an excellent *tonnarelli cacio e pepe*, and a short list of hearty *secondi* that includes crispy fried suckling pig's foot with braised lentils.

Manzo

  Italian XX

200 Fifth Ave. (at 23rd St.)

Subway: 23 St (Broadway)
Phone: 212-229-2180
Web: www.eataly.com
Prices: $$$

Lunch Mon – Fri
Dinner nightly

 Eataly New York (brought to you by Mario Batali and friends) is a perpetually bustling emporium brimming with Italian products. The rollicking scene rarely lets up and navigating through the hordes of visitors entranced by the sights and scents of the abundance on offer may prove to be overwhelming for some.

For sit down dining, steer yourself straight toward Manzo, tucked away from the fray. "Beef" in Italian, Manzo offers a meaty take on Italian. Pastas are numerous and impressively prepared; and the weekday lunch prix-fixe is highly recommended—baby artichokes with plump cranberry beans; charred New York strip with Barbaresco vinaigrette; and silken vanilla panna cotta. Pair your meal with a pour from the comprehensive wine selection.

Mari Vanna

 Russian XX

41 E. 20th St. (bet. Broadway & Park Ave. South)

Subway: 23 St (Park Ave South)
Phone: 212-777-1955
Web: www.marivanna.ru/ny
Prices: $$

Lunch & dinner daily

 The bar is stocked with urns of house-infused vodka (apricot, seaberry, and cucumber-dill to name just a few) and the main dining room is often fully occupied by large groups. Despite the revelry, the ambience at Mari Vanna persuades its occupants to sit back and enjoy themselves in the shabby-chic room, done in a bleached palette complemented by embroidered seat backs and glowing chandeliers.

Traditional Russian specialties abound with the likes of Olivier salad, *salo* (house-smoked fatback), borscht, and plump *pelmeni* with herbed butter and sour cream. The kitchen's serious effort shines through, as in entrées like *golubtzi*, featuring two neat bundles of braised cabbage stuffed with ground beef and rice and draped with a lush coat of tomato cream.

Mesa Grill

A2

Southwestern 🍴🍴

102 Fifth Ave. (bet. 15th & 16th Sts.)

Subway: 14 St - Union Sq

Lunch & dinner daily

Phone: 212-807-7400

Web: www.mesagrill.com

Prices: $$$

Responsible for launching Chef Bobby Flay to cookbook and Food Network stardom, Mesa Grill still buzzes nightly even after two decades of service—a particularly impressive achievement in this fickle city. The lofty room, colored with Southwest accents, sees its share of tourists hoping to catch a glimpse of the famous celebrity chef and native Manhattanite; but even if the chef is absent, a glass-walled kitchen entertains with views of his team putting a creative spin on Southwest cuisine.

Flay's trademark style results in a solid menu of vibrant preparations that can include a roasted garlic shrimp tamale; grilled mahi mahi with refreshing pineapple and onion salsa alongside creamy roasted poblano rice; or a moist, toasted-coconut layer cake.

Millesime

B1

Seafood 🍴🍴

92 Madison Ave. (at 29th St.)

Subway: 28 St (Park Ave. South)

Lunch Mon – Fri

Phone: 212-889-7100

Dinner Mon – Sat

Web: www.millesimenyc.com

Prices: $$$

This elegant brasserie takes its name from the French word for "vintage" and is housed on the second floor of the Carlton Hotel. Lipstick red banquettes, tables topped with Eiffel Tower-shaped salt and pepper shakers, and a mouthwatering raw bar are spaciously laid out over a 100-year old mosaic tile floor and crowned by a Tiffany-style glass dome skylight dating back to 1904.

Diners compose their own meals by choosing from a selection of excellent quality fish fillets that are grilled on the *plancha* and dressed with a choice of sauces. An inexpensive lunch and dinner prix fixe may bring finely chopped salmon tartare with shaved fennel and sweet mustard; linguine piperade with rock shrimp; and a chocolate espresso bar with raspberry ice cream.

Molly's Pub & Shebeen

C2

Gastropub ✗

287 Third Ave. (bet. 22nd & 23rd Sts.)

Subway: 23 St (Park Ave. South) Lunch & dinner daily
Phone: 212-889-3361
Web: www.mollysshebeen.com
Prices: ⊜⊜

A stop at Molly's Pub & Shebeen isn't just for celebrating St. Patrick's Day-style revelry the remaining 364 days of the year. The utterly charming setting, friendly service, and heartwarming fare make it much more than the standard Irish watering hole. The setting, first established in 1895, has had various incarnations but has been sating a loyal following since 1964. Wood smoke perfumes the air, rustic furnishings are arranged on a sawdust-covered floor, and a seat at the original mahogany bar couldn't be more welcoming. The ambience of this pub (or *shebeen*, which is an illicit drinking establishment) has few peers.

Stick with the list of house specialties (lamb stew, corned beef and cabbage, and Shepherd's pie) for an authentic experience.

Momokawa ☺

C1

Japanese ✗

157 E. 28th St. (bet. Lexington & Third Aves.)

Subway: 28 St (Park Ave. South) Dinner nightly
Phone: 212-684-7830
Web: www.momokawanyc.com
Prices: $$

Fans of Japanese cuisine will cheer at the authenticity of the expansive menu served at this impressive charmer. The location may come as a surprise, tucked away on a busy Curry Hill block, but the sparsely decorated small room is reminiscent of the type of place Tokyo salarymen might frequent for drinks and a delicious bite before the long commute home.

You can opt for one of their set menus (either the $60 prix-fixe or $55 seasonal course menu) or go for the à la carte affair kicking things off with seasonal appetizers such as miso eggplant, or soy-marinated rice cake; from there sashimi follows; and then cooked items like simmered beef with daikon, fried sardines with shishito peppers, and beef sukiyaki make for a lovely finish.

NoMad

B1

1170 Broadway (at 28th St.)

Subway: 28 St (Broadway)	Lunch & dinner daily
Phone: 212-796-1500	
Web: www.thenomadhotel.com	
Prices: $$$	

The NoMad

At NoMad, Eleven Madison Park's meritorious duo Chef Daniel Humm and restaurateur Will Guidara bring their magic to the F & B operations of the hot and of-the-moment boutique hotel of the same name.

The setting dates back to 1903 and the series of dining rooms bear a decadent Gilded Age luxe as interpreted by noted designer Jacques Garcia. Each offers a unique experience; the Atrium is bright and relaxed but it's the romantic Fireplace room with its hearth lifted from a French château, and regal Parlour with its dark oak, wine red velvet, and pressed herb-lined walls that are the preferred seats.

The kitchen astonishes with its lot of elegant à la carte creations. It's all deliciously tempting; so at the risk of becoming mired by indecision, just order. Refreshing, fragrant, and complex strawberry gazpacho was nothing short of genius; a gorgeous square of suckling pig dressed with pickled mustard seeds and plump cherries was crowned by a sheet of crispy, translucent skin; and dessert brought a how'd-they-do-that lemon tart encased in a satiny sheen of toasted almond shortbread.

The hotel's cupola is the scene of a weather-dependent five-course tasting menu served under the stars.

Novitá

B2   Italian ✗✗

102 E. 22nd St. (bet. Lexington Ave. & Park Ave. South)

Subway: 23 St (Park Ave South)
Phone: 212-677-2222
Web: www.novitanyc.com
Prices: $$

Lunch Mon – Fri
Dinner nightly

For a solid Italian meal in Gramercy, this sweet little trattoria is worth wandering into. Tucked just below street level, along quiet 22nd Street, Novitá is delightfully unpretentious given its tony zip code, with a pretty, straightforward décor featuring sunny yellow walls, wide windows, and beautiful fresh flowers strewn about the room.

Ditto on the food. The daily specials can be pricey (be sure to ask in advance) but are lovely additions to a regular menu that might reveal crimson red tuna, fried in paper-thin pastry and served with a silky mayo and balsamic reduction; perfectly roasted Australian rack of lamb with sautéed baby spinach and garlic; or a soft square of *millefoglie* sporting rich vanilla cream and fresh sprigs of mint.

Olives

B3   Contemporary ✗✗

201 Park Ave. South (at 17th St.)

Subway: 14 St - Union Sq
Phone: 212-353-8345
Web: www.olivesnewyork.com
Prices: $$$

Lunch & dinner daily

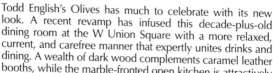

Todd English's Olives has much to celebrate with its new look. A recent revamp has infused this decade-plus-old dining room at the W Union Square with a more relaxed, current, and carefree manner that expertly unites drinks and dining. A wealth of dark wood complements caramel leather booths, while the marble-fronted open kitchen is attractively set with a wood-burning oven. A communal dining nook sits across the kitchen and looks upon gleaming plate glass windows.

The enterprising chef's brand of interpretive Mediterranean cuisine remains the menu's trademark in items such as diver scallop crudo dressed with segments of crimson grapefruit, slivered red chili, and shaved fennel; and tagliatelle draped with a savory, slow-cooked rabbit-and-porcini ragù.

Periyali

A2

Greek

35 W. 20th St. (bet. Fifth & Sixth Aves.)

Subway: 23 St (Sixth Ave.)
Phone: 212-463-7890
Web: www.periyali.com
Prices: $$$

Lunch Mon – Fri
Dinner nightly

Bright, airy, and standing strong for over twenty years, Periyali has maintained not only its popularity but a high standard of cuisine and service—quite a feat in NYC. The tranquil, fresh space evokes the Mediterranean with whitewashed walls, colorful banquettes, and billowing white fabric draped across the ceiling. Natural light floods the breezy atmosphere.

Starters include the likes of *fava kremidaki*, an outstanding blend of puréed fava beans with red onion, lemon, and aromatic olive oil. The fantastic rabbit stew (*kouneli stifado*) is served spoon-tender in thick and rich tomato gravy, with perfect little white pearl onions.

Dessert cookies may be honey-drenched and sprinkled with walnuts, little nut-filled cigars, or almond-rich baklava.

Primehouse New York

B1

Steakhouse XX

381 Park Ave. South (at 27th St.)

Subway: 28 St (Park Ave. South)
Phone: 212-824-2600
Web: www.primehousenyc.com
Prices: $$$

Lunch & dinner daily

Ditch stodgy for chic at this nonetheless grand steakhouse that sets itself apart from the recognizable herd of traditionalists. The multi-room space sports a black-and-white bar area, bright and elegant dining room, and the impressively stocked, smoked glass-walled wine cellar. However, style does not trump substance.

The focus remains on cuts of Prime Black Angus beef from Creekstone Farms, KY, aged in-house in a Himalayan salt-tiled room. Non-steak options include wild Arctic char with English pea risotto, or Caesar salad prepared tableside by attentive servers. A tower of icy seafood from the raw bar and an order-in-advance soufflé, salted caramel perhaps, are fine bookends to a meal here.

The sexy bar/lounge is a top stop for after-work cocktails.

Pure Food and Wine

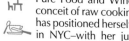

Vegan XX

54 Irving Pl. (bet. 17th & 18th Sts.)

Subway: 14 St - Union Sq
Phone: 212-477-1010
Web: www.purefoodandwine.com
Prices: $$

Lunch & dinner daily

Pure Food and Wine applies upscale sophistication to the conceit of raw cooking. Run by owner Sarma Melngailis, who has positioned herself as a high priestess of the raw movement in NYC–with her juice bar/takeout shop, cookbooks, and continuous Twitter posts–a meal here is sure to put the glow back in your cheeks.

To preserve vitamins, enzymes, minerals, and flavors in the food, nothing is heated above 118°F. Despite these constraints, the "cooking" is undoubtedly tempting. These delights include the spicy sesame salad, a slaw of cold-hardy vegetables sprinkled with ground cashew crunch and sparked by wasabi aïoli; or the classic zucchini- and tomato-lasagna, layered with basil-pistachio pesto and dairy-free macadamia nut and pumpkin seed ricotta.

Resto

Contemporary X

111 E. 29th St. (bet. Lexington Ave. & Park Ave. South)

Subway: 28 St (Park Ave. South)
Phone: 212-685-5585
Web: www.restonyc.com
Prices: $$

Lunch & dinner daily

At Resto, the friendly young staff is attired in whimsical T-shirts flaunting the motto, "Bringing fat back." This heart-on-the-sleeve mentality is utterly appropriate for a menu that proves its nose-to-tail ethos with dishes that have included a wildly flavorful pig's head Cuban sandwich, veal belly gyro, and crispy pig's ear salad. Though the cooking is best described as contemporary, there is a distinct Belgian vibe here, as in *moules frites* paired with an array of flavor-spiked mayonnaise, Liege waffles flecked with crunchy sugar, and a stellar beer selection to wash it all down.

The comfortable dining room's gleaming appointments–white marble bar counter, pressed-tin ceiling, and metal chairs–beckon to a steady stream of neighborhood residents.

Riverpark

Contemporary   XXX

C1

450 E. 29th St. (bet. First Ave. & the East River)

Subway: 28 St (Park Ave. South)
Phone: 212-729-9790
Web: www.riverparknyc.com
Prices: $$

Lunch & dinner daily

Perched over the FDR with a view of the sky-lit East River, this vast haven continues to fall under the radar. As the Alexandria Center for Life Sciences' anchor dining spot, Riverpark is also Tom Colicchio's latest contemporary vision. Accoutered with a sweeping staircase, high ceilings, comfortable tables, and friendly servers, the space is a mirage of beauty and fantasy. Riverpark's very own 15,000 square foot urban farm delivers the goods from just across the plaza to Chef Sisha Ortúzar. Begin a unique culinary tour with burnt cavatelli tossed with cauliflower and pecorino; or oyster tacos dressed with a spicy remoulade. If fluffy beignets coupled with espresso custard don't put you in a festive mood, the beer garden outside will do the trick.

Rye House

American   X

A2

11 W. 17 St. (bet. Fifth & Sixth Aves.)

Subway: 14 St (Sixth Ave.)
Phone: 212-255-7260
Web: www.ryehousenyc.com
Prices: $$

Lunch & dinner daily

As its name would suggest, Rye House offers a tavern-inspired look and easygoing vibe fueled by an impressive selection of amber liquor. The front bar provides a comfortable perch from which to sip a mint julep or single-malt Scotch, but those who wish to dine sacrifice the bar's ambience for the back area's greater comfort and enjoy the kitchen's concise and enjoyably prepared selection of playful pub grub.

The small plate offerings include the likes of crunchy and well-seasoned fried dill pickle slices, Sloppy Joe sliders, and drunken mussels bathed in Belgian-style ale. The list of entrées may be short but items such as roasted chicken dressed with spoonbread, braised greens, and buttermilk-enriched jus prove this is food to be savored.

Saravanaas

Indian ✗

81 Lexington Ave. (at 26th St.)

Subway: 28 St (Park Ave. South)   Lunch & dinner daily
Phone: 212-679-0204
Web: www.saravanabhavan.com
Prices: ⊖⊖

 With its corner location and attractive two-room setting, Saravanaas stands out from the Curry Hill crowd. The brightly lit room is set with lacquered tables and high-backed ivory upholstered chairs that seem a far cry from the taxi driver cafeterias dotting this strip of Lexington.

The reason this beloved Gramercy location is forever bustling with locals and tourists alike is for vegetarian food that is as good as it is serious, with a wide array of specialties, curries, breads, and weekend-only biryani on offer. However, table-long *dosas*, paired with a plethora of chuntneys (think coconut and chili) and fiery *sambar* are *the* main attraction. Don't miss the *aloo paratha*: this butter-drenched, puffy flatbread filled with spiced potatoes is excellent.

SD26

Italian ✗✗

19 E. 26th St. (bet. Fifth & Madison Aves.)

Subway: 28 St (Park Ave. South)   Lunch Mon – Fri
Phone: 212-265-5959   Dinner nightly
Web: www.sd26ny.com
Prices: $$

This regional Italian restaurant formerly known as San Domenico now inhabits a 14,000 square foot dining hall replete with a crowd-pleasing array of features—a wine bar, generously sized lounge area, multiple dining rooms, open kitchen, and jumbo *salumeria* station.

The offerings are as wide-ranging as the space, with good value found at both the lunch prix-fixe and small plates served at the wine bar. Given the size and scope of SD26, the service can sometimes flounder but here are three reasons that prove the kitchen gets it right: silky strands of whole wheat fettucine dressed with luscious wild boar ragout; braised beef cheeks, melt-in-your-mouth tender, paired with a dollop of white polenta; and a lovely *baba* with sweet, juicy orange sauce.

Manhattan ▶ Gramercy, Flatiron & Union Square

Singapura

C1

106 Lexington Ave. (bet. 27th & 28th Sts.)

Subway: 28 St (Park Ave. South)   Lunch & dinner daily
Phone: 212-684-6842
Web: www.singapuranyc.com
Prices: 🍜

Diners craving a dose of spice eagerly fill up this Curry Hill establishment for a taste of something different. Singapura's colorful and decorative accents along with its warm, hospitable spirit give the slender setting a cheerful countenance.

More *sambal* than masala, the emphasis here is on Southeast Asian flavors, particularly Singapore, Malaysia, and Thailand, with some Hakka Chinese specialties thrown in for good measure. The likes of *chili paneer*, cubes of semi-firm cow's milk cheese sautéed with a piquant blend of fried onion, scallions, green chilies, garlic, and lemongrass make for an apt starting point; while heartier plates unveil *sarawak sambal udang*, shrimp cooked in a tempting mélange of chillies, *belacan*, ginger, and lush coconut cream.

Tamarind

B2

41-43 E. 22nd St. (bet. Broadway & Park Ave. South)

Subway: 23 St (Park Ave. South)   Lunch & dinner daily
Phone: 212-674-7400
Web: www.tamarinde22.com
Prices: $$

   ♿

   🕐

A pioneer among the city's growing spate of upscale Indian restaurants, Tamarind has been putting an elegant spin on the flavors of Goa, Punjab, Madras, and Calcutta since 2001. Polished service and a glassed-in kitchen displaying the tandoor and its tempting creations combine to accentuate the grand setting.

Though perhaps not as impressive as her glitzier TriBeCa sibling, the extensive menu here is well-rendered and always delightful. Picture meaty fillets of *malai* halibut, seasoned with mace and cardamom, tandoor-roasted, and enveloped in a coconut milk-rich sauce imbued with ginger and turmeric.

For a casual bite, try next door Tea Room for light fare like sandwiches, pastries, and Indian specialties, each with a recommended tea pairing.

Tamba

Indian ✗

103 Lexington Ave. (bet. 27th & 28th Sts.)

Subway: 28 St (Park Ave. South)　　　　　　　Lunch & dinner daily
Phone: 212-481-9100
Web: www.tambagrillandbar.com
Prices: $$

Slow down in Curry Hill—Tamba is that cozy, sprightly spot one might easily pass, and miss the chance for excellent, wallet-friendly Indian cuisine, as well as great service that soars above other nearby *desi* diners.

Hindi for copper, Tamba showcases Indian delicacies as glorious and gleaming as the copper vessels that carry them. Leaving aside the insanely popular, inexpensive lunch buffet, true gourmands know to branch out and explore the extensive menu of Northern and Southern Indian specialties. From the tandoor oven comes succulent plates like *haryali tikka*—boneless pieces of chicken marinated with mint and coriander. The raita is made with the kitchen's own house yogurt; and Tamba's lemon rice is so popular it deserves its own Facebook page.

Tocqueville

Contemporary ✗✗

1 E. 15th St. (bet. Fifth Ave. & Union Sq. West)

Subway: 14 St - Union Sq　　　　　　　Lunch & dinner Mon – Sat
Phone: 212-647-1515
Web: www.tocquevillerestaurant.com
Prices: $$

Lovingly run by proprietors Chef Marco Moreira and his wife Jo-Ann Makovitzky since 2000, Tocqueville offers a creative and decidedly upscale approach to seasonal cuisine. The stately dining room, bedecked with starched, linen-draped tables, dove grey furnishings, and butterscotch walls, sits just a block away from the Union Square Greenmarket.

This advantageous locale persuades the skilled kitchen to reveal a bounty of delightful fare that might begin with warm brioche and butter (both house-made). Meals go on to include smooth and zesty tomato soup, elegantly poured tableside over a morsel of fried ricotta; or roasted baby pumpkin risotto with pan-seared wild mushrooms and toasted pumpkin seeds.

Lunch offers particularly good value.

Turkish Kitchen

Turkish XX

C1

386 Third Ave. (bet. 27th & 28th Sts.)

Subway: 28 St (Park Ave. South)
Phone: 212-679-6633
Web: www.turkishkitchen.com
Prices:

Lunch Sun – Fri
Dinner nightly

There are so many good Turkish restaurants floating around Manhattan's East Side these days, it's getting harder to choose among the competition. Here's a tip: you'll almost never go wrong placing your chips on this quirky, jewel-toned mainstay which boasts a lively dinner scene; an attentive service staff ready to walk newcomers through the extensive offerings; and a lunch menu stacked with great value (including a four-course prix-fixe).

The restaurant's grilled meats; stuffed cabbage; and *manti*, spiced ground beef dumplings in a rich dill chicken broth capped by a dollop of yogurt, are all standouts. Or try the *iskender* kebab—seasoned lamb, sliced paper-thin off a rotisserie and served over crispy pita bathed in garlic-yogurt and rich tomato sauce.

Union Square Cafe

American XX

A2

21 E. 16th St. (bet. Fifth Ave. & Union Sq. West)

Subway: 14 St – Union Sq
Phone: 212-243-4020
Web: www.unionsquarecafe.com
Prices: $$$

Lunch & dinner daily

This revered dining institution lies in the heart of widely trafficked Union Square. An elder member of the renowned Danny Meyer culinary family, the Café is well-loved, never outdated, and does not disappoint. From the warm service to the distinct spaces that feel bright, sunny, and even romantic across the downstairs and mezzanine levels, everything here seems smoother with the years.

The merry bar is as locally cherished as the room's vivid murals and city icons demolishing a yellowfin burger glossed with ginger-mustard. Dining here becomes even more enjoyable over plates of chili-soy-glazed pork belly with tender cuttlefish; a perfectly cooked NY strip with bone marrow mashed potatoes; or sweet, crusty pear dumplings in huckleberry compote.

Veritas

B2

43 E. 20th St. (bet. Broadway & Park Ave. South)

Subway: 23 St (Park Ave. South)
Phone: 212-353-3700
Web: www.veritas-nyc.com
Prices: $$$

Dinner Mon – Sat

This sophisticated member of New York's dining scene is a destination beyond such distinctive neighbors as cutting-edge art studios and high-end interior design shops. Still drawing a full dining room, Veritas is favored by an urbane, upscale clientele for its elegant space anchored by a lively bar, whitewashed brick walls accented with cork patchwork, and ebony-stained tables.

Warm colors and lovely jazz tunes add a sense of intrigue that is only elevated by its first-rate cuisine. Visual impact is clear in glistening slices of bass and coral-hued salmon artfully arranged with pickled cauliflower florets, or a perfectly seared scallop poised atop sweet parsnip purée. For an excellent and cleverly updated end, try a bittersweet peanut butter candy bar.

Look for our symbol 🍺,
spotlighting restaurants
with a notable beer list.

Manhattan ▶ Gramercy, Flatiron & Union Square

129

Greenwich, West Village & Meatpacking District

Artistic, poetic, and edgy: These ideals are the Village's identity. Thank the Beat Generation for this, because sixty years later, many still seek out this neighborhood for its beloved street cafés brimming with struggling artists, philosophical meanderings, and revolutionary convictions. Perhaps due to the prominence of NYU, local residents still embrace the liberal, intellectual, and bohemian spirit that, in many ways, is the heart of this city.

Nevertheless, the belly of this area is equally worthy of attention and praise; even the humble **Peanut Butter and Co. Sandwich Shop** flaunts its creative side with peanut-buttery concoctions like the Elvis, which is grilled with bananas and honey (bacon is optional). Or, pick up a jar to-go, flavored with the likes of maple syrup, white chocolate, and chili powder. Steps away, **Mamoun's** has been feeding NYU students some of the best falafel in town for generations; topping one with their killer hot sauce is a must. In Washington Square Park, savvy students and foodies stand shoulder-to-shoulder in line for **N.Y. Dosas**, wrapped in delicate rice- and lentil-flour crêpes, served with character and flair. Peer into the assortment of old-time Italian bakeries and shops along Bleecker Street, where **Faicco's Pork Store** has been offering its specialties for

over 100 years—take home a sampling of their fresh and perfectly seasoned sausages or a tray of *arancini* (fried rice balls), though etiquette dictates that one must be eaten warm, before leaving the store. Yet the neighborhood's most noteworthy storefront may be **Murray's Cheese Shop**. This is Manhattan's definitive cheesemonger, run by a deeply informed service staff, happy to initiate hungry neophytes into the art and understanding of their countless varieties (enthusiasts note that classes are also available, exploring the meaning of terroir or cheese-pairing fundamentals).

If seeking a more lowbrow spot, try **Dirty Bird To Go** for its sinfully fried or rotisserie chicken. Rest assured that these birds are locally sourced from an Amish farm, and are free-range, vegetarian-fed, and antibiotic free—all necessary qualifications for any self-respecting takeout joint in downtown bohemia. Of course, no Village jaunt is complete without pizza—with some of the finest to be found coal-fired and crisp, only by the pie, at the original **John's**. For a quick slice, stop by **Joe's**, another local institution, for their traditional and blistery thin-crust selections. A visit to **Cones** is equally enticing, where uniquely textured Argentine ice cream is available in both expected and unforeseen flavor combinations.

WEST VILLAGE

For a nearly royal treat, stop by **Tea and Sympathy**, offering tea-time snacks or full Sunday dinners comprised of roast beef and Yorkshire pudding. The storefront also sells prized English wares, ranging from teas to pots to jars of clotted cream. No matter where you grab your picnic, one of the best places to enjoy it is Hudson River Park, watching the urban vista of roller skaters and marathoners. Pier 45 is a particularly lovely spot, at the end of Christopher Street, across the Westside Highway. A stone's throw from here is **Il Cantuccio**, a boutique Tuscan bakery that boasts a regional variant of biscotti from Prato. The influential James Beard Foundation sits in the historic 12th Street townhouse that was once home to the illustrious food writer.

While strolling back through chic boutiques and camera-ready brownstones, peek down quaint Perry Street for yet another *very* NY moment: A glimpse at where Carrie Bradshaw (of *Sex and the City*) "lived." For a quick but excellent bite, be sure to stop in at **Taïm** for killer falafels and refreshing smoothies. Then, let the overpowering aromas of butter and sugar lead you to the original **Magnolia Bakery**. Filled with pretty little pastel-flowered cupcakes and prettier couples donning Jimmy Choo shoes, this is the Village's official date night finale.

Another sweet spot is **Li-Lac**, dispensing chocolate-covered treats and nostalgic confections since 1923. One of the West Village's most celebrated landmarks may be the **Corner Bistro**, whose pub fare has been at the heart of the "Best Burger in Town" debate for decades. Another "bar's bar" incarnate that strives to embody everything a cheap beer and retro juke hope to effuse is the **Rusty Knot**. Kick back and grab some Po' boys or pickled eggs to go with that pint. For a more refined late-night scene, expert mixologists can be found creatively pouring "long drinks and fancy cocktails" at **Employees Only**. Likewise, bartenders approach celebrity status at **Little Branch**, where an encyclopedic understanding of the craft brings dizzying and delectable results.

MEATPACKING DISTRICT

Further north is an area known as the Meatpacking District. Just two decades ago, its cobblestoned streets were so desolate that only the savviest young Manhattanites knew that its empty warehouses held the city's edgiest clubs. Young hipsters take note: The Meatpacking District has already arrived, repopulated, and regrouped with seas of sleekly designed lounges serving pricey cocktails to the fashionable minions, as if in defiance of these cautious times. Luxury hotels have risen, and storied bistros so infamously festive that they once defined the neighborhood have fallen. Completing this picture is the High Line, an abandoned 1934 elevated railway that is now transformed into a 19 block-long park.

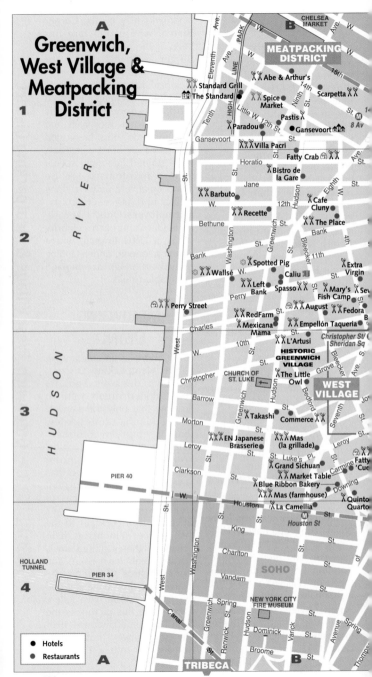

Greenwich, West Village & Meatpacking District

A

B

CHELSEA MARKET

MEATPACKING DISTRICT

1

Abe & Arthur's

Standard Grill
The Standard

Spice Market

Scarpetta

Paradou

Pastis

Gansevoort

Ganesvoort

Villa Pacri

Fatty Crab

Horatio St.

Bistro de la Gare

Jane St.

Barbuto

Cafe Cluny

W. 12th St.

Recette

The Place

Bethune St.

2

R I V E R

Bank St.

Spotted Pig

Wallsé

Caliu

Extra Virgin

Left Bank

Spasso

Mary's Fish Camp

Sev

Perry St.

August

Fedora

Perry Street

RedFarm

Empellón Taqueria

Charles St.

Mexicana Mama

L'Artusi

Christopher St/ Sheridan Sq

10th St.

HISTORIC GREENWICH VILLAGE

CHURCH OF ST. LUKE

The Little Owl

WEST VILLAGE

Christopher St.

3

H U D S O N

Barrow St.

Takashi

Commerce St.

Morton St.

Leroy St.

EN Japanese Brasserie

Mas (la grillade)

St. Luke's Pl.

Grand Sichuan

Leroy St.

Clarkson St.

Market Table

Fatty 'Cue

Blue Ribbon Bakery

PIER 40

Mas (farmhouse)

Quinto Quarto

La Camellia

Houston St

HOLLAND TUNNEL

King St.

4

PIER 34

Charlton St.

Vandam St.

SOHO

Spring St.

NEW YORK CITY FIRE MUSEUM

Dominick St.

Broome St.

● Hotels
● Restaurants

A

B

TRIBECA

132

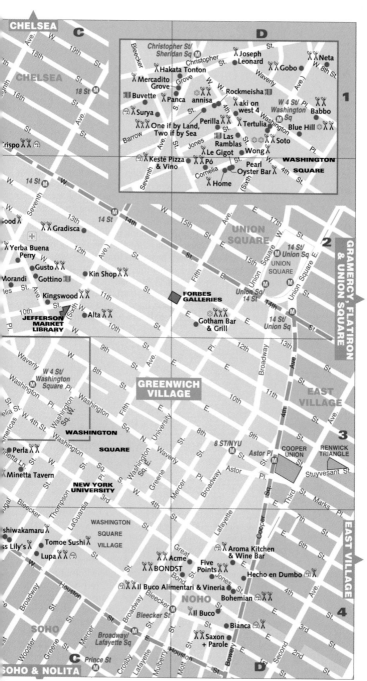

CHELSEA

CHELSEA C

Ave.

W. 19th St.
18th St.
18 St Ⓜ
16th St.

D

Christopher St/
Sheridan Sq
Christopher
Grove
Ⓧ Hakata Tonton
Ⓧ Mercadito
Grove
Ⓧ Buvette   Ⓧ Panca
Ⓧ Surya
ⓍⓍⓍ One if by Land,
Two if by Sea
Barrow
Ⓧ Kesté Pizza
& Vino
Seventh

Ⓧ Joseph
Leonard   ⓍⓍ Gobo   Ⓧ Neta
Waverly
W. 8th St.

Rockmeisha Ⓧ
ⓍⓍ annisa
Ⓧ aki on
west 4
Ⓧ Perilla   Ⓧ Tertulia
Jones
St.
Ⓧ Las
Ramblas
Ⓧ Le Gigot
Ⓧ Pó
Cornelia
St.

W 4 St/
Washington
Sq
Ⓧ Babbo
Blue Hill ⓍⓍ
Ⓧ Soto
Ⓧ Wong
Pearl
Oyster Bar Ⓧ
Ⓧ Home
(Sixth
St.

**WASHINGTON
SQUARE**

1

D

Crispo ⓍⓍ

14 St Ⓜ W.
Seventh
13th St.
ⓍⓍ Gradisca
14 St Ⓜ **14th**

Ⓧ Yerba Buena
Perry
Ⓧ Gusto ⓍⓍ
Morandi   Gottino
Kingswood ⓍⓍ
**JEFFERSON
MARKET
LIBRARY**
(Sixth
Ⓧ Alta ⓍⓍ
10th St.
W.
9th St.

12th
St.
Ⓧ Kin Shop ⓍⓍ
Fifth
11th
St.

**UNION
SQUARE**
17th St.
14 St/
Union Sq Ⓜ
UNION SQUARE
Union Square E.
Union Sq/
14 St Ⓜ
14 St/
Union Sq Ⓜ
E. 13th St.

2

**GRAMERCY, FLATIRON
& UNION SQUARE**

**FORBES
GALLERIES**
ⓍⓍⓍ
Gotham Bar
& Grill

Waverly
W 4 St/
Washington
Square Pl.
Washington
Sq.
celia St.
mericas
W. 4th St. Washington
WASHINGTON

**GREENWICH
VILLAGE**

Fifth
University
8th
Waverly
N.
12th
St.
11th
St.

**EAST
VILLAGE**

3

Ⓧ Perla ⓍⓍ
inetta Ln.
Ⓧ Minetta Tavern
**NEW YORK
UNIVERSITY**
Thompson
LaGuardia

SQUARE
Greene
St.
W.
Mercer
St.
8 ST/NYU Ⓜ
Astor Pl.
Astor
Broadway
Pl.
**COOPER
UNION**
Stuyvesant St.
E.
Third
St.
**RENWICK
TRIANGLE**
St. Marks Pl.

D

shiwakamaru Ⓧ
ss Lily's Ⓧ
Ⓧ Tomoe Sushi
Lupa ⓍⓍⓍ
ugal
Bleecker
Broadway
**WASHINGTON
SQUARE
VILLAGE**
3rd
St.

ⓍⓍ Acme
ⓍⓍ BONDST
Ⓧ Aroma Kitchen
& Wine Bar
Five
Points Ⓧ
ⓍⓍ Il Buco Alimentari & Vineria
Hecho en Dumbo Ⓧ
Bond
St.
NOHO
Bohemian ⓍⓍ
Bleecker St Ⓜ
Bleecker St.
Ⓧ Il Buco
E.
7th
St.
6th
St.
5th
St.
4th
St.
Ave.

**EAST
VILLAGE**

4

SOHO
Wooster
Greene
Mercer
Broadway/
Lafayette Sq
Ⓧ Bianca Ⓧ
ⓍⓍ Saxon
+ Parole
Lafayette
Prince St Ⓜ
Crosby
Mulberry
Houston
Mott
St.
Bowery
2nd
3rd

C   **Prince St**   D

SOHO & NOLITA

133

Abe & Arthur's

American 🍴🍴

B1

409 W. 14th St. (bet. Ninth & Tenth Aves.)

Dinner Mon – Sat

Subway: 14 St - 8 Av
Phone: 646-289-3930
Web: www.abeandarthurs.com
Prices: $$$

This sexy yet tasteful dining den installed in a former nightclub, offers an experience that feels a little Vegas—in a good and fun way. The look is glitzy and highbrow: picture a dark-wooded and glossy-tiled lounge leading into a soaring dining space adorned with butterscotch leather furnishings and walls boasting a series of backlit graffiti-esque scrims.

The menu's steakhouse slant frames a selection of dry-aged certified Black Angus beef procured from Creekstone Farms. Raw bar treasures and an ample list of non-steak entrées round out the menu with dishes like ricotta cavatelli with mushrooms, kale, and pine nut cream. Sides include roasted Brussels sprouts with Nueske's bacon and a tart kiss of lemon, proving everything does taste better with bacon.

Acme

Contemporary 🍴🍴

D4

9 Great Jones St. (bet. Broadway & Lafayette St.)

Lunch Sat – Sun
Dinner nightly

Subway: Broadway - Lafayette St
Phone: 212-203-2121
Web: www.acmenyc.com
Prices: $$

Retooled by the impresarios behind Indochine and BONDST, the new Acme looks wonderfully weathered and chic. Exposed brick and wood furnishings anchor this space fronted by a packed bar leading to the dining room fitted with rough-hewn plank flooring and studded leather banquettes.

The kitchen offers a unique and refreshingly tempting menu, run by Danish chef, Mads Refslund, buzzed for having co-founded Noma with René Redzepi. Items from the "Soil" include roasted black heirloom carrots draped with *lardo* and squeezed with blood orange. The "Sea" brings gorgeous pan-roasted black sea bass set upon pickled green tomato wheels, touched by cardamom, while sides like hand-cut fries with a pale green oyster-and-chive mayo are bound to leave you beaming.

aki on west 4

Japanese ✗

D1

181 W. 4th St. (bet. Barrow & Jones Sts.)

Subway: W 4 St - Wash Sq
Phone: 212-989-5440
Web: N/A
Prices: $$

Dinner nightly

Set in a red-brick row house, Aki's tiny dining room feels like an intimate parlor. Add to this a warm, polite staff and a menu that displays a distinct personality, and it is easy to see why this spot continues to attract a loyal following.

Chef/owner Siggy Nakanishi once served as private chef to the Japanese Ambassador to Jamaica and his menu reflects a sweet and sunny personality. Daily specials are presented as a tabletop photo display; the chef's menu offers a selection of creative preparations that may include the eel napoleon appetizer composed of panko-crusted tofu, delicate eel tempura, and pumpkin purée. Other dishes include finely prepared sushi and rolls, as in the Jamaica roll, stuffed with jerk chicken and hearts of palm, of course.

Alta

Contemporary ✗✗

C2

64 W. 10th St (bet. Fifth & Sixth Aves.)

Subway: Christopher St - Sheridan Sq
Phone: 212-505-7777
Web: www.altarestaurant.com
Prices: $$

Dinner nightly

Rusticity reinvented is the order of the day at this jam-packed tapas den where you'll need to squeeze your way past the sangria- and rosé-dispensing bar to reach the felicitous back dining room festooned by exposed brick, antique Moorish flooring, and wood-burning fireplace.

Alta's nimble kitchen churns out a parade of tastes with a thoroughly creative and contemporary spirit. There's grilled house-made merguez dressed with Lilliputian falafel, gelled red wine, and *lebne*; cavatelli sauced with celery root cream, a dab of wild boar ragù, and Parmesan crumbs; grape leaves wrapped around jasmine rice and chicken confit with a squiggle of grape molasses; and a cube of bronzed apple confit plated with crushed praline and vanilla bean ice cream.

Manhattan ▲ Greenwich, West Village & Meatpacking District

annisa ✿

Contemporary ✕✕

D1

13 Barrow St. (bet. Seventh Ave. South & W. 4th St.)

Subway: Christopher St - Sheridan Sq

Phone: 212-741-6699

Web: www.annisarestaurant.com

Prices: $$$

Dinner nightly

Julie Denthies

Beloved Annisa ("women" in Arabic) has come to be hallowed as one of the most resilient and relished Village options for sophisticated dining.

From its charming setting within a historic district, Annisa seems inviting, both outside and in, with large windows, upholstered walls, and a cozy yet exquisite elevated dining room. A polite, professional service team does not miss a beat in orchestrating meals here. The elegant wooden bar up front reigns supreme with a rare selection that applauds "women in wine"—most of these are crafted by female vintners or vineyard owners.

Chef Anita Lo's contemporary menu focuses on flavors and combinations that are thought-provoking and very tasty. Dinners reveal such understated and complex starters as barbecued squid fragrant with Thai basil and finished with peanuts, providing a perfect balance of sweet, savory, and earthy tastes. Miso-marinated sable floats in a delicious bonito broth with silken tofu, while a sautéed fillet of pollock is paired with braised bacon and spicy kimchi. Desserts are grounded by homey satisfaction and may even add a note of whimsy as in the poppy seed-studded bread and butter pudding brightened by a luscious lemon curd.

Aroma Kitchen & Wine Bar

Italian ✗

D4

36 E. 4th St. (bet. Bowery & Lafayette St.)

Subway: Bleecker St
Phone: 212-375-0100
Web: www.aromanyc.com
Prices: $$

Dinner nightly

Aroma Kitchen & Wine Bar is a welcoming spot that radiates an amiable vibe from its edge of the Village, thanks to co-owners Alexandra Degiorgio and Vito Polosa. Simple, warm, and rustic, the intimate room's focal point is its dark wood dining counter. On a warm, sunny day, the space opens to provide additional sidewalk seating and thereby alleviates the throng of enthusiastic regulars.

This wine bar menu begins with a host of hearty appetizers like juicy meatballs with a fragrant Neapolitan ragù and *scamorza*, along with expertly prepared pastas like Di Palo ricotta cavatelli tossed in a braised oxtail sugo, studded with zucchini and earthy cremini mushrooms. The unique and fairly priced wine list contains many varietals rarely found outside Italy.

August

Mediterranean ✗✗

B2

359 Bleecker St. (bet. Charles & 10th Sts.)

Subway: Christopher St - Sheridan Sq
Phone: 212-929-8727
Web: www.augustny.com
Prices: $$

Lunch & dinner daily

One may wonder how August has retained its long-standing popularity as a favored neighborhood destination? Well, it's not that hard to deduce. Wood and stone underscore the lived-in room that is both warm and chic with a wood-burning oven, and yet cooled by an inviting backyard garden. The staff is relaxed and sociable, never missing a step; and the kitchen remains under steady tutelage despite the inevitability of change.

August's farm-driven comfort fare is a little bit Americana and a little bit Euro revealing preparations that may bring crispy-fried squid salad drizzled with yuzu ranch; organic chicken roasted in the wood oven and sided with crinkly fried green beans; and a deliciously gooey warm chocolate cake for a classic and sweet *finis*.

137

Babbo

Italian Italian ✗✗

D1

110 Waverly Pl. (bet. MacDougal St. & Sixth Ave.)

Subway: W 4 St - Wash Sq
Phone: 212-777-0303
Web: www.babbonyc.com
Prices: $$$

Lunch Tue – Sat
Dinner nightly

Trends may come and go, but judging from the crowds that haven't subsided since its 1998 opening, Babbo's still got it. This Mario Batali mainstay doesn't cut any corners or lines— reservations are a must for table seating, though you can pop in and sit at the bustling bar. From the on-the-move staff to the rock-and-roll tunes, the place stays busier than Eataly on Christmas Eve.

Staff shuttle plates of pasta and other Italian specialties to eager customers who come as much for the convivial ambience as they do for the wild mushroom *sformato*, or specials like grilled veal chop with morels and black truffle vinaigrette. Can't decide between the *maccheroni all chitarra* and the beef cheek ravioli? Sit back and settle in for the eight course pasta menu.

Barbuto

Italian ✗✗

B2

775 Washington St. (at 12th St.)

Subway: 14 St - 8 Av
Phone: 212-924-9700
Web: www.barbutonyc.com
Prices: $$

Lunch & dinner daily

Those who wax poetic on the virtues of the perfect roast chicken need look no farther. Located on a quiet stretch of the West Village just steps from MePa, Chef Jonathan Waxman's Barbuto plays up its locale and industrial bones with concrete flooring, painted-over brick walls, and garage doors that open up to create an atmospheric indoor/outdoor vibe.

Still, that chicken is what best expresses Barbuto's refined simplicity—the roasted bird has a coarse pepper-freckled auburn skin and tender ivory flesh moist with flavorful juices, further enhanced by a splash of bright and briny salsa verde. This dish is admirably supported by the likes of grilled octopus salad with fennel and pink grapefruit or a cookie-like chocolate hazelnut *crostata*.

Bianca

 Italian

5 Bleecker St. (bet. Bowery & Elizabeth St.)

Subway: Bleecker St   Dinner nightly
Phone: 212-260-4666
Web: www.biancanyc.com
Prices: $$

 Curtained windows lead the way to this unassuming spot, perfect for a date or catching up with friends. With plank flooring, candlelit tables set with blue-striped kitchen towels used as napkins, shelf-lined walls displaying delicate floral-trimmed china, and an open kitchen tucked in the cozy back, Bianca's casual personality extends through to every detail, including the cuisine.

The Northern Italian-themed menu strives to remind guests that simplicity is always satisfying, especially with starters like *gnocco fritto*. Other specialties may include a traditional Emilia-Romagna style lasagna or fennel-studded sausage simmered with cannellini beans.

Generous portions and a moderately priced Italian-focused wine list contribute to Bianca's large following.

Bistro de la Gare

Mediterranean

626 Hudson St. (bet. Horatio & Jane Sts.)

Subway: 14 St - 8 Av   Lunch & dinner Tue – Sun
Phone: 212-242-4420
Web: www.bistrodelagarenyc.com
Prices: $$

 Equally talented and no less charming are Chef/owners Maryann Terillo and Elisa Sarno who have created a wonderfully low-key neighborhood bistro that exudes the aura of an old favorite even though it is new to the scene. The quaint room is simply done with tan walls hung with sepia photography, and is furnished with wooden chairs and white paper-topped tables. Like the décor, the menu follows suit lending a simplistic approach to a listing that boasts Mediterranean influences.

Starters include the likes of blistered-skin grilled sardines with a warm cannellini bean salad; entrées may offer a roasted baby chicken cloaked with walnut crumbs; and desserts feature a slice of olive oil cake decked in a compote of plumped raisins and dried figs.

Manhattan ▶ Greenwich, West Village & Meatpacking District

Blue Hill ✿

American 🍴🍴

D1

75 Washington Pl. (bet. Sixth Ave. & Washington Sq. Park)

Subway: W 4 St - Wash Sq   Dinner nightly
Phone: 212-539-1776
Web: www.bluehillnyc.com
Prices: $$$

Thomas Schauer

As a longtime proponent of local, seasonal ingredients, culinary crusader Chef Dan Barber and his devoted team prepare a bill of fare that relies almost solely on the small farm network located within a few hundred miles of the city. Of course, the daytrip-worthy farm at Stone Barns (home to Blue Hill's Westchester outpost) purveys the bulk of his eggs and salad greens, Berkshire pork, etc. However, exemplary product alone does not make this restaurant the destination that it is. Rather, the kitchen's talent and imagination have earned its accolades and attention.

There's no easing into dinner here which starts off with a smashing presentation of fresh-from-the-farm treats—the tiniest of just-plucked carrot, radish, or romaine; a mini-asparagus burger; and warm bread served with whipped *lardo* and beet-flavored salt. The sophisticated cooking continues with the likes of smoked spelt spaghetti tousled with organic shiitake mushrooms and pickled ramps; or crisped and velvety Hudson Valley duck breast, fanned over a mélange of chickpeas and fiddlehead ferns.

Chef Dan Barber's presence is felt not only in each dish, but also regularly observed in the understated and elegant dining room.

Blue Ribbon Bakery

Contemporary

B3

35 Downing St. (at Bedford St.)

Subway: Houston St
Phone: 212-337-0404
Web: www.blueribbonrestaurants.com
Prices: $$

Lunch & dinner daily

The origin of this very New York bistro begins with the discovery of an abandoned brick oven that brothers Eric and Bruce Bromberg found in the basement of a bodega. This sparked the idea for a bakery, and in 1998 Blue Ribbon Bakery joined the duo's family of popular and impressive dining venues. The sunny corner spot charms with mustard yellow walls and creaky wood-plank flooring; downstairs the heady aroma of freshly baked bread wafts throughout exposed brick alcoves.

Excellent sandwiches star on the roster of lunchtime fare, like shrimp salad with roasted tomato mayonnaise tucked into slices of lightly toasted challah. Dinner brings eclectic possibilities like leeks vinaigrette, grilled sardines, fried chicken, and ice cream parlor desserts.

Bobo

Contemporary

B2

181 W. 10th St. (at Seventh Ave.)

Subway: Christopher St - Sheridan Sq
Phone: 212-488-2626
Web: www.bobonyc.com
Prices: $$

Lunch Sat – Sun
Dinner nightly

This resilient Village gem has weathered numerous chef changes with aplomb, and currently hosts a toque that has reworked the carte to showcase a more classically minded hand. *Frisée aux lardons* and *steak au poivre vert* vie for your attention along with appetizing plates of asparagus salad gussied up with crispy shallots, accents of pickled red onion, shiitake mushroom, and crème fraîche. A recent dinner special revealed flavorful chicken tagine sparked by green olives, fresh mint, and slivered almonds; and desserts display a fun side, as in a decadent candy bar-inspired confection.

Despite the revolving door of talent, Bobo remains as pretty as ever with a second floor dining room awash in handsome dark wood, pale blue walls, and whitewashed brick.

141

Bohemian 🐵

D4

Japanese ✕✕

57 Great Jones St. (bet. Bowery & Lafayette St.)

Dinner nightly

Subway: Bleecker St
Phone: 212-388-1070
Web: www.playearth.jp
Prices: $$

♿ This intriguing dining den is secreted away down an unmarked hallway and fronted by a thick glass door. Despite the stealth locale, the staff couldn't be more welcoming or courteous as they attend to diners amid polished concrete floors, white walls, and mid-century furnishings in emerald green, turquoise, and cognac—in a space that once served as a studio for artist Jean-Michel Basquiat.

Bohemian's bill of fare features snacks and small plates such as a decadent mushroom croquette topped with uni. However, the true highlight is the exceptional *washugyu* from Japanese Premium Beef offered in several guises—as a sashimi of short rib; steak of the day; or as luscious mini burgers dressed with lettuce, slow-roasted tomato, and pecorino on tender brioche.

BONDST

D4

Japanese ✕✕

6 Bond St. (bet. Broadway & Lafayette St.)

Dinner nightly

Subway: Bleecker St
Phone: 212-777-2500
Web: www.bondstrestaurant.com
Prices: $$$

The white banner branded with a bold dot marking this edgy and upscale venue is just as swanky as the quintessentially cool, cobblestone corridor it sits on. This multi-floored brownstone features a ground floor lounge and upstairs dining room, whose minimalist setting suits the chill vibe and very pretty crowd.

Special sushi like, Alaskan king crab on crispy rice may sound interesting, but its best to stick to the straightforward array of good quality nigiri and sashimi arranged by fish type. Cooked fare attest to the kitchen's aptitude, as in a dazzling composition of tender and meaty grilled octopus, purple potato, and pink grapefruit; and entrées like pan-seared, sweet and silky Hokkaido scallops with twirls of *ika* soba and frothy uni sauce.

Buvette

French

 C1

42 Grove St. (bet. Bedford & Bleecker Sts.)

Subway: Christopher St - Sheridan Sq
Phone: 212-255-3590
Web: www.ilovebuvette.com
Prices: ⌾⌾

Lunch & dinner daily

Rolling stone Chef Jody Williams moves from Italy to France at her newest venture set in the former home of the Pink Teacup. Despite the diminutive space, Buvette oozes charm and all are well taken care of—the affable staff weaves lithely through the full house, greeting guests with a warm smile and displaying a chalkboard of daily specials to diners at the counter and low tables.

French tapas are the theme, including cheeses, charcuterie, tartines, and Escoffier-esque vegetable dishes such as artichokes à la Grecque. Heartier options may include coq au vin in a mini cast iron pot, stocked with all the classic elements. End on a sweet note with the chocolate mousse, dense enough to cut with a knife, and capped by a cloud of whipped cream.

Cafe Cluny

American ✗

 B2

284 W. 12th St. (at W. 4th St.)

Subway: 14 St - 8 Av
Phone: 212-255-6900
Web: www.cafecluny.com
Prices: $$

Lunch & dinner daily

  With its winsome glow and welcoming vibe, this quintessential neighborhood restaurant (from the owner of TriBeCa's Odeon) is one of the Village's most chic meeting spots, no matter the time of day. The popular corner-set bar and multi-room interior are lined with caricatures of celebrity regulars and a wall installation of shadowy bird cutouts that come alive in evening candlelight.

Open daily from 8:00 A.M. until midnight, the kitchen might begin with the breakfast club sandwich stuffed with fried egg, bacon, avocado, tomato, and spicy mayo. Seasons inspire bruschetta with roasted tomato and kale pesto, or the pancetta-wrapped pork tenderloin with roasted local Seckel pears and Swiss chard. Service is affable, able, and attracts a devoted following.

Caliu

B2

557 Hudson St. (bet. Perry & W. 11th Sts.)

Subway: Christopher St - Sheridan Sq

Phone: 212-206-6444

Web: www.calilutapas.com

Prices:

Lunch & dinner daily

The mission at this low-key tapas spot, helmed by a Peruvian chef and alum of Boqueria and Casa Mono, is to present a distinctive menu that is focussed and authentic in its offering of Spanish small plates. Served *frias* and *calientes*, the creative carte piques interest with the likes of *sobrassada*—a dense and chewy chorizo with an uncommonly rich spreadable center; and baguette toasts cradling dollops of roasted red pepper and almond romesco topped with fresh mint. Warm preparations include the likes of quick-sautéed calamari dressed with a jet black vinaigrette enriched with squid ink.

The room is spare but comfortable; tumblers of wine and a skilled kitchen ensure that diners leave this bona fide tapas den happy and sporting a warm, satisfied glow.

Commerce

B3

50 Commerce St. (near Barrow St.)

Subway: Christopher St - Sheridan Sq

Phone: 212-524-2301

Web: www.commercerestaurant.com

Prices: $$

Lunch Sat – Sun
Dinner nightly

Commerce sits on a picture perfect West Village block, and although it's only been open since 2007 the lovingly restored space dates back to being a depression-era speakeasy. Belly up to the bar with its backdrop of polished wood veneer; or grab a seat in the convivial dining room that shows off earthy-toned terrazzo flooring and walls accented with glazed ivory tile.

Chef Harold Moore's menu melds seasonal and global inspiration and brings forth items such as a BLT soup, a cool, creamy green purée livened by buttermilk and stocked with slivered heirloom tomatoes, crushed bacon, and brioche croutons. Entrées have featured a Korean-style pork chop; and desserts are fun—envision a tall wedge of birthday cake, adorned with a candle for deserving diners.

Crispo 😋

C1

Italian   ✕✕

240 W. 14th St. (bet. Seventh & Eighth Aves.)

Subway: 14 St (Seventh Ave.)   Dinner nightly
Phone: 212-229-1818
Web: www.crisporestaurant.com
Prices: $$

Its convenient 14th Street address may help draw crowds, but Chef/owner Frank Crispo's impressive Northern Italian fare is what keeps fans returning again and again. The large room fills up easily and is effortlessly comfortable with attentive service in a rustic ambience punctuated by filament light bulbs, mahogany panels, and vintage tile work.

The menu begins with a lengthy listing of small plates starring prosciutto, carved in the dining room on the chef's antique Berkel slicers, as well as daily specials like grilled artichokes glossed with a lemony butter sauce. Pastas are expertly prepared and may include a silky twirl of fettucine topped with sweet and plump head-on prawn scampi. For dessert, panna cotta is a voluptuous experience.

Empellón Taqueria

B2

Mexican   ✕✕

230 W. 4th St. (at 10th St.)

Subway: Christopher St - Sheridan Sq   Lunch & dinner daily
Phone: 212-367-0999
Web: www.empellon.com
Prices: $$

Alex Stupak, wd~50's former pastry chef extraordinaire, switches gears from sweet to savory at this venture and brings along a temptingly creative and heartfelt rendition of Mexican cuisine with creamy textures, sweet spices, and tangy roasted chiles aplenty. The tasteful setting features dark-stained furnishings in a whitewashed room with pizzazz from a colorful mural and a bar that gets plenty of action.

The kitchen prepares a roster of heavily stuffed tacos, such as a tasty mélange of shredded chicken with chili- and cilantro-spiked green chorizo. Other treats include a *queso fundido* of braised beef short ribs baked with a blanket of sheep's milk ricotta; or warm and crunchy chips with a duo of smoked cashew and roasted *arbol* chili salsas.

EN Japanese Brasserie

Japanese XXX

B3

435 Hudson St. (at Leroy St.)

Subway: Houston St
Phone: 212-647-9196
Web: www.enjb.com
Prices: $$$

Lunch & dinner daily

Industrial chic-meets-Tokyo mod in this hot spot *izakaya* with soaring heights, warm tones, brick walls, and regal fittings. EN's open kitchen pays homage to authentic Japanese palates, but also reveals ingenuity in its own inventions.

This West Village favorite draws a swank set with its sophisticated fare. Diners sip from the thorough sake selection and await specialties like house-made tofu, served warm or chilled and drizzled with *wari-joyu* (soy sauce and fish broth). A feast for the senses, the menu is extensive with sushi, noodles, stone-grilled meats, Kyoto-style tapas, and kaiseki options. The new brunch offerings might include *chawan mushi* with Kurobuta pork sausage and mushrooms, salt-grilled salmon, or skillet-baked *azuki* bean pancakes.

Extra Virgin

Mediterranean X

B2

259 W. 4th St. (at Perry St.)

Subway: Christopher St - Sheridan Sq
Phone: 212-691-9359
Web: www.extravirginrestaurant.com
Prices: $$

Lunch Tue – Sun
Dinner nightly

Co-owned by two Queens natives, this invitingly laid-back spot sits on an idyllic tree-lined corner. There are touches of rusticity throughout the space, with rough-hewn wood tables, exposed brick walls, and framed mirrors; the vibe here is as chill and enjoyable during days as evenings.

Extra Virgin's Mediterranean menu offers crowd-pleasing fare like a starter salad of warm pistachio- and breadcrumb-crusted goat cheese with roasted beets, generously showered with crisp, julienned Granny Smith apple. The kitchen's seriousness is evident in touches like the addition of bright and flavorful sweet peas, roasted yellow peppers, and black olives to the rigatoni with sausage; or the apple tart paired with sour cream ice cream and warmed dark caramel sauce.

Fatty Crab

Malaysian

B2

643 Hudson St. (bet. Gansevoort & Horatio Sts.)

Subway: 14 St - 8 Av   Lunch & dinner daily
Phone: 212-352-3592
Web: www.fattycrew.com
Prices: $$

Zak Pelaccio's signature dish could be made with mung beans and it would still knock the socks off the uninitiated. As it is, the namesake dish at Fatty Crab, a creative Malaysian joint tucked into a cozy storefront in the Meatpacking District, is made with mouthwatering chunks of Dungeness crab, bobbing in a rich, messy chili sauce that is part sweet, part savory—and wholly freaking amazing. Don't forget to grab the bread on your table to sop up every drop of this delicious specialty. For a neater bite, opt for the steamed pork buns with soy vinegar.

The front patio and small dining room filled with a few-too-many tables fill up fast, so arrive early for dinner. Or, swing by for a late afternoon lunch and you'll have the place mostly to yourself.

Fatty 'Cue

Barbecue

B3

50 Carmine St. (bet. Bedford & Bleecker Sts.)

Subway: Houston St   Lunch & dinner daily
Phone: 212-929-5050
Web: www.fattycrew.com
Prices: $$

This Manhattan outpost of the 'Cue brand hatched by Chef Zak Pelaccio and his "Fatty Crew" offers a more comfortable and upscale setting than the Williamsburg original (closed for some time to undergo renovations). The lusty take on Southeast Asian cuisine is built around locally sourced, humanely raised product that's smoked and spiced to the point where flavorful is an understatement.

Start off with a Fatty Manhattan combining rye, sweet vermouth, and smoked cherry cola or go the whole hog and flash out with Thai-style bottle service before supping on the likes of pork ribs brined in fish sauce and glazed with palm sugar; thinly sliced brisket trimmed by aged Gouda and warm Parker House rolls; or veal sweetbreads dressed with black pepper aïoli.

Fedora

B2

239 W. 4th St. (bet. Charles & 10th Sts.)

Subway: Christopher St - Sheridan Sq   Dinner nightly
Phone: 646-449-9336
Web: www.fedoranyc.com
Prices: $$

Originally opened in 1952, Fedora was recently taken over by Gabriel Stulman. The restaurateur has an affinity for all things vintage, and this freshened-up space has been kept lovingly intact, down to the blazing neon signage out front. The retro setting–polished brass, black-and-white photos, and jelly jars used as votive holders–pours creative libations at a mahogany bar and seats diners along a black leather banquette.

Rich and meaty plates abound as in Wagyu tongue with celeriac remoulade; crispy pig's head with sauce *gribiche*; and a "surf and turf" of fried sweetbreads and seared octopus with port wine-enriched butter sauce. If possible, save room for a creative dessert like the silky cheesecake panna cotta drizzled with passion fruit nectar.

Five Points

D4

31 Great Jones St. (bet. Bowery & Lafayette St.)

Subway: Bleecker St   Lunch & dinner daily
Phone: 212-253-5700
Web: www.fivepointsrestaurant.com
Prices: $$

The pulse of Chef Marc Meyer's first success continues to beat as strongly as when it opened in 1999. This neighborhood favorite blends relaxed ambience, polished service, and seasonal food with a near-Californian sensibility that is utterly irresistible to its nightly stream of food-savvy sophisticates.

Beyond the energetic bar is a quieter back dining room anchored by a tree trunk bedecked with greenery and surrounded by tables wrapped in brown paper. The menu winks at Chef Meyer's take on urbane rusticity as it boasts local, seasonal ingredients. Expect the likes of country-style pâté with house pickles, whole grain mustard, and toast; Montauk Point swordfish with slow-cooked broccoli and fig-almond *anchïoade*; or a Finger Lakes grass-fed beef burger.

Gobo

D1

401 Sixth Ave. (bet. 8th St. & Waverly Pl.)

Subway: W 4 St - Wash Sq
Phone: 212-255-3902
Web: www.goborestaurant.com
Prices: 💳

Lunch & dinner daily

With its nourishing global vegetarian cuisine and peaceful Zen-inspired décor, Gobo offers a tasty and tranquil timeout from Manhattan's bustle. Muted tones and warm wood accents dominate the airy dining room that is attended by a suitably laid-back staff.

Gobo's inexpensive menu of "food for the five senses" begins with healthy beverages like freshly squeezed juices and soy milk-based smoothies as well as organic wines. Ambitious starters easily tempt without pushing the vegetarian envelope in the likes of *roti canai* and homemade hummus. Larger plates offer an appetizing Asian influence in satisfying and flavorful vegetable protein dishes such as the healthful stir-fry of ginger-marinated seitan with lightly sautéed kale and steamed rice.

Good

C2

89 Greenwich Ave. (bet. Bank & 12th Sts.)

Subway: 14 St - 8 Av
Phone: 212-691-8080
Web: www.goodrestaurantnyc.com
Prices: $$

Lunch Tue – Sun
Dinner nightly

Yes, it's true: this charming neighborhood favorite lives up to its preordained reputation, and has done so since opening in 2000. The pale, earthy, and appealing dining room has a soothing, intimate, and laid-back air, as if to whisper, "Stop by anytime." This echoes through the cozy bar and stretch of sidewalk seating.

The menu proffers a greatest-hits list of comfort food favorites that are given a globally-inspired turn. Fish tacos are stuffed with the selection of the day; macaroni and cheese is studded with green chilies beneath a tortilla crumb-crust; and grilled lamb sirloin arrives with chickpea polenta and creamed Swiss chard.

Good offers a hearty lunch menu and nicely priced combo specials; weekend brunch is washed down by clever cocktails.

Gotham Bar and Grill ✿

Contemporary 𝕏𝕏𝕏

12 E. 12th St. (bet. Fifth Ave. & University Pl.)

Subway: 14 St - Union Sq
Phone: 212-620-4020
Web: www.gothambarandgrill.com
Prices: $$$

Lunch Mon – Fri
Dinner nightly

David Cavallo

Chef Alfred Portale has been at this helm since 1985—that kind of longevity is practically unheard of, and has enabled Gotham to survive the fickle restaurant scene by consistently remaining one of its beloved spots. The food here is serious, solid, and completely pleasurable with appealing flavors and classic preparations.

The unassuming exterior belies the fact that inside this lovely open space–dotted with chandeliers and floral displays worthy of contemplation–tables are humming with money and power. But, by the grace of servers who never stop smiling and a kitchen that doesn't disappoint, the business crowds are clearly focused on dining.

Artistic ensembles may begin with a wonderfully executed roasted wild mushroom risotto glistening with aged Gruyère and Niman Ranch bacon. Entrées divulge whole Maine lobster fragrant from the culminating layers of Kaffir lime, ginger, and seasonal vegetables. Rather than simply trying to sate a sweet tooth, desserts like a tropically themed mango soufflé highlight a range of tastes and textures with the addition of coconut sake sorbet and young coconut panna cotta.

Summertime brings a fab bargain in the two-course greenmarket prix-fixe for $25.

Gottino

Italian

 52 Greenwich Ave. (bet. Charles & Perry Sts.)

Subway: Christopher St - Sheridan Sq   Lunch & dinner daily
Phone: 212-633-2590
Web: www.ilmiogottino.com
Prices:

Despite the departure of its founding chef, this charming *enoteca* continues to serve as a lovely respite in which to savor a variety of highly enjoyable small plates. Knobby wood, a marble dining counter, and blackboard with wine list highlights set against exposed brick craft the rustically endearing setting.

An assortment of snacks is prepared on view by the skilled and attentive staff, and nibbling sophisticates will find much to choose from. Small bites include crostini, freshly toasted in a press and slathered with mint-flecked artichoke confit; and tiny roasted apples stuffed with savory pork sausage. Heartier plates feature *pizzoccheri*—a baked and bubbling intermingling of buckwheat pasta, melted green cabbage, speck, and fontina.

Gradisca

Italian

126 W. 13th St. (bet. Sixth & Seventh Aves.)

Subway: 14 St (Seventh Ave.)   Dinner nightly
Phone: 212-691-4886
Web: www.gradiscanyc.com
Prices: $$$

Grazie for Gradisca, an Italian trove filled with food like *mamma* used to make. Amid a sea of mediocrity, Gradisca still flickers due to its generosity, first-rate product, and knowledge. All who enter this below-street level dining enclave are struck by their masterful (if pricey) pasta parade. If that doesn't warm you, look around for the cheery Emiliani staff. Parted into three nooks, each dining room flows seamlessly into the other.

Awe-inspiring images of movie stars set against rich red walls lend a romantic vibe and invite you to dine on a rich corn-and-polenta *timbale* with pork sausage; ribbons of *tagliatelle* tossed with wild boar ragù; or brined rabbit with caper berries. Flaunting fine technique is a quivering vanilla-flecked panna cotta.

Grand Sichuan

B3

15 Seventh Ave. South (bet. Carmine & Leroy Sts.)

Subway: Houston St   Lunch & dinner daily
Phone: 212-645-0222
Web: www.thegrandsichuan.com
Prices: ⊛

The popularity of Sichuan cuisine shows no signs of abating, as evidenced by the continued profusion of regionally specific (and similarly named) eateries. This Greenwich Village outpost is part of a burgeoning mini-chain proffering spicy treats throughout the metropolitan area.

The menu is divided into three sections: "American Chinese", "Latest" and "Classic Sichuan." This last heading is especially tempting and should be your focus here. The full roster of specialties includes *dan dan* noodles stocked with spicy minced pork; braised fish with chili sauce; and shredded chicken breast mingling fresh Napa with sour-preserved cabbage.

The inexpensive lunch special is a big draw, and the availability of small and large portions is a thoughtful touch.

Gusto

Italian

C2

60 Greenwich Ave. (at Perry St.)

Subway: 14 St (Seventh Ave.)   Lunch & dinner daily
Phone: 212-924-8000
Web: www.gustonyc.com
Prices: $$

This slick trattoria has recently been freshened up both in the front of house and behind the line. The space now sports a more rustic scene fostered by a liberal use of polished dark wood complementing whitewashed brick walls, pink orchids, and a glittery chandelier at the center of it all.

Fried food–calamari, the signature artichokes, *prosciutto cotto*, and mozzarella beignets–anchors the selection of cooked starters. Following these are a bounty of mostly house-made pasta that may reveal baked orecchiette under a Parmesan crust; and several secondi evenly split between fish and meat, such as Alaskan halibut with green lentils and wild mushrooms.

On a warm afternoon, sitting outside on Gusto's sidewalk is a great spot to take in the Village scene.

Manhattan ▶ Greenwich, West Village & Meatpacking District

Hakata Tonton

Japanese

D1

61 Grove St. (bet. Bleecker St. & Seventh Ave.)

Subway: Christopher St - Sheridan Sq   Dinner nightly
Phone: 212-242-3699
Web: www.tontonnyc.com
Prices: $$

A new cuisine has taken root in New York. Enter this tiny red and yellow dining room to be educated in this other facet of the Japanese culinary repertoire: *tonsoku* (pigs' feet, ears, and the like).

Varied *tonsoku* dishes may include a luxurious slow-roasted pork or *oreilles du cochon* (French in name only) which are an explosion of crunchy, cool, creamy, sweet, sticky, and vinegary flavors. Truer to its Italian roots, *tonsoku* carbonara is made with smoky bacon and is a good choice for wary newbies. A "rare cheesecake" of piped cheese and sour cream is a very smart and completely delicious take on the traditional dessert.

The plain-Jane décor sits in stark contrast to the rich and porky fare that diners will come rushing back for.

Hecho en Dumbo

Mexican

D4

354 Bowery (bet. 4th & Great Jones Sts.)

Subway: Bleecker St   Lunch Sat – Sun
Phone: 212-937-4245   Dinner nightly
Web: www.hechoendumbo.com
Prices: $$

Obviously not housed in DUMBO anymore, this Mexico City-style spot sports an edgy downtown vibe with rustic reclaimed wood and quirky mismatched chairs. A back dining counter offers diners a view of the kitchen led by Mexico City native Daniel Mena.

Antojitos (small bites) and contemporary fare shape the made-from-scratch menu built around house-made tortillas, *bolillo* bread, and *queso Oaxaca*. Tasty treats may include *pescadillas*: fried turnovers of crispy tortilla filled with shredded tilapia, diced onion, and chiles. The *molletes* is (for lack of a better reference) the ultimate Mexican version of grilled cheese, served toasted and open-faced, topped with black bean purée, *queso* Chihuahua, and crumbles of homemade pork belly chorizo.

Home

D2

20 Cornelia St. (bet. Bleecker & W. 4th Sts.)

Subway: W 4 St - Wash Sq   Lunch & dinner daily
Phone: 212-243-9579
Web: www.homerestaurantnyc.com
Prices: $$

This intimate Cornelia St. dining room has persevered through
the years and continues to offer great tastes of Americana in
a setting that is welcoming and warm—all apt characteristics
for an eatery called Home. Everyone seated in their black
spindleback chairs or back garden seats, is happy to see this
unassuming, unpretentious whitewashed little space thriving.
The kitchen honors sourcing and seasonality in its range of
comforting specialties that have included a freshly prepared
vegan purée of tomato and sweet basil representing the soup
of the day; and a hearty oyster Po'boy featuring hefty, briny,
cornmeal-crusted Willapa Bay oysters and spice-tinged
rémoulade sauce, on a fresh ciabatta roll alongside a tangle
of Old Bay-sprinkled shoestring fries.

Il Buco

D4

47 Bond St. (bet. Bowery & Lafayette St.)

Subway: Bleecker St   Lunch Mon – Sat
Phone: 212-533-1932   Dinner nightly
Web: www.ilbuco.com
Prices: $$

Il Buco offers guests the idyllic Tuscan farmhouse fantasy
without leaving Manhattan. This artist's studio-cum-restaurant
shines with sunny charm and quirky warmth through chicly
rustic tables, wood floors, copper plates, and antiques.
However, with delightful service, an extraordinary sommelier,
and superlative market-driven Italian cuisine, Il Buco does
not rely on looks alone. The chef is a stickler for quality, and
the product-focused menu celebrates the seasons, as in an
amazingly simple salad of crisp and earthy Tuscan black kale
with anchovy vinaigrette. Plentiful appetizers are followed by
homemade pastas and daily-changing entrées, such as pan-
fried prawns with Sicilian sea salt, a hint of rosemary, and
delicious kick of hot pepper.

Il Buco Alimentari & Vineria

Italian 🍴🍴

D4

53 Great Jones St. (bet. Bowery & Lafayette St.)

Subway: Bleecker St   Lunch & dinner daily
Phone: 212-837-2622
Web: www.ilbucovineria.com
Prices: $$

Il Buco's sure-footed new spinoff is an enticing option all its own. Showcasing a tempting store of artisanal products up front and an open kitchen in back, the bewitching room is rustic with terra-cotta tile and pressed copper imported from Italy, wooden communal tables, and the perfume of wood smoke used to fuel the oven and rotisserie.

Italian-inflected, seasonally-driven cuisine is clearly the driving force among the parade of ambrosial small plates. Dishes may include hearty puntarelle dressed with anchovy vinaigrette; perfectly cooked spaghetti slicked with a light, pink-tinged cream sauce emboldened with *bottarga di muggine*; or thinly sliced *porchetta alla Romana*, seasoned with fennel seeds and topped with amber-like shards of crisped skin.

Joseph Leonard

Contemporary 🍴

D1

170 Waverly Pl. (at Grove St.)

Subway: Christopher St - Sheridan Sq   Lunch & dinner daily
Phone: 646-429-8383
Web: www.josephleonard.com
Prices: $$

Joseph Leonard serves an enjoyable carte of well-prepared contemporary fare devoted to the season and bearing a faint French accent in country pâté with pickled onions and baguette; pan-seared Long Island fluke with creamy lemon rice and soy reduction; and a tall wedge of classic carrot cake. Breakfast is served as well and includes the likes of *saucisson à l'ail* with eggs and hashbrowns.

This chicly curated corner setting, owned by Gabriel Stulman, sports rough-hewn wood-plank flooring, raw walls, and book-filled shelves. The space is installed with a winsome assemblage of vintage pieces, including a zinc bar and fridge that looks like it was lifted from the set of *I Love Lucy*, that lend a unique air to this always-welcoming establishment.

Kesté Pizza & Vino

D2

Pizza 🍴

271 Bleecker St. (bet. Cornelia & Jones Sts.)

Subway: W 4 St - Wash Sq

Phone: 212-243-1500

Web: www.kestepizzeria.com

Prices: 🅰️🅰️

Lunch & dinner daily

If Neapolitans had a motto, it would be "*fà 'na cosa 'e journo,*" literally meaning to do something in a hurry. Pizza is the tangible derivative of that motto; and at Kesté, it is alive and well-translated in each of their 22 pies, one calzone, and daily specials. This Village delight may be a slim corridor, yet diners are allowed to linger and chat with the Italian-accented staff.

If NY is serious about its pizza, then Kesté leads the movement within its warm walls. Insatiable appetites lop up the likes of a Kesté pizza, salty and tangy with a pulpy smear of tomatoes, basil, and prosciutto; *salsiccia*, crumbled sausage atop sweet *salsa di pomodoro* and mozzarella; and Nutella, a perfect pizza dough packed with that beloved blend of chocolate and hazelnuts.

Kingswood

C2

Contemporary 🍴🍴

121 W. 10th St. (bet. Greenwich & Sixth Aves.)

Subway: 14 St (Seventh Ave.)

Phone: 212-645-0044

Web: www.kingswoodnyc.com

Prices: $$

Lunch Fri – Sun

Dinner nightly

Kingswood's mirthful spirit is evident from the moment you step inside. The inviting bar is habitually packed by a good-humored crowd, while beyond, the dining room is abuzz with its own sleek rusticity and warmth. Bathed in a flattering glow, diners sit at long communal tables and caramel leather banquettes set against a softly lit glass-walled installation and votive candles.

The contemporary menu displays boldly flavored accents while paying homage to its owner's native Australia, as in the house burger with cheddar and sweet chili sauce; Goan fish curry; and beer-battered fish and chips. Here, surf and turf may mean crisp-skinned salt cod and fork-tender pork cheeks dressed in a dark reduction of meaty jus with creamy, smoked mashed potatoes.

Kin Shop

Thai ✗✗

469 Sixth Ave. (bet. 11th & 12th Sts.)

Subway: 14 St (Seventh Ave.)
Phone: 212-675-4295
Web: www.kinshopnyc.com
Prices: $$

Lunch & dinner daily

Chef/owner Harold Dieterle has flirted with Thai food in the past at his lovely Perilla, but now fully affirms his serious commitment to this cuisine in Kin Shop. His buzzing venture gets its name from the Thai word "to eat," and one does it very well in their pretty dining room boasting whitewashed brick, batik canvases, and a beachy color scheme.

The approach is contemporary and offers a mouthwatering sojourn. Curries include banana leaf-steamed rabbit bathed in sour yellow curry with eggplant chutney; while noodles feature pan-fried rice vermicelli tangled with roasted chilies and crab. Even the condiments deserve undivided attention— the addictive chili jam is made even more delicious when paired with freshly griddled, buttery *roti*.

La Camelia

Mexican ✗

64 Downing St. (bet. Bedford & Varick Sts.)

Subway: Houston St
Phone: 212-675-7060
Web: www.lacamelianyc.com
Prices: ⊗⊗

Lunch & dinner daily

This cheery new spot edges out the plethora of workaday Mexican options with a number of advantages: a spacious and cordially attended setting, a comfortable bar stocked with a dizzying array of tequilas, and guacamole made-to-order in the dining room from a station stocked with a heap of ripe avocados among the display of fresh produce.

The selection of pleasing fare includes an array of tacos such as lamb *barbacoa*, braised in beer and chilies, stuffed into a handmade soft corn tortilla; chicken enchiladas draped with decadent and complex *mole poblano*, sided by rice and beans; and *camarones de Camelia* combining jumbo shrimp cooked in creamy goat cheese sauce with *rajas poblano*. Weekend specials bring the likes of pork tamales with *mole verde*.

Manhattan ▶ Greenwich, West Village & Meatpacking District

L'Artusi

Italian

B3

228 W. 10th St. (bet. Bleecker & Hudson Sts.)

Subway: Christopher St - Sheridan Sq
Phone: 212-255-5757
Web: www.lartusi.com
Prices: $$

Lunch Sun
Dinner nightly

L'Artusi's façade may be demure, but this attractive dining room offers a fun, buzz-worthy vibe to elevate its upscale rendition of Italian-rooted food, anchored by small plates. The large space, with gray and ivory stripes aplenty, offers three dining counters, table service, and a quieter mezzanine. An open kitchen adds to the lively air.

The impressive Italian wine list, complete with maps, is laid out with a gravitas that demands attention. The well-versed staff is pleased to suggest the best pairings to complement pastas such as buckwheat *pizzoccheri* with Brussels sprouts, fontina, and sage. Salads of chicory dressed in Parmesan, lemon, and anchovies, or crudo plates of beef carpaccio with horseradish *crema* are wonderful ways to start a meal here.

Las Ramblas

Spanish

D1

170 W. 4th St. (bet. Cornelia & Jones Sts.)

Subway: Christopher St - Sheridan Sq
Phone: 646-415-7924
Web: www.lasramblasnyc.com
Prices:

Dinner nightly

Sandwiched among a throng of attention-seeking storefronts, mighty little Las Ramblas is easy to spot, just look for the crowd of happy, munching faces; the scene spills out onto the sidewalk when the weather allows. Named for Barcelona's historic commercial thoroughfare, Las Ramblas is a tapas treat.

A copper-plated bar and collection of tiny tables provide a perch for snacking on an array of earnestly prepared items. Check out the wall-mounted blackboard for *especiales*. Bring friends (it's that kind of place) to fully explore the menu which serves up delights such as succulent head-on prawns roasted in a terra-cotta dish and sauced with cava vinegar, ginger, and basil; or béchamel creamed spinach topped by a molten cap of Mahón cheese.

Left Bank

B2

Contemporary 🍴🍴

117 Perry St. (at Greenwich St.)

Subway: Christopher St - Sheridan Sq
Phone: 212-727-1170
Web: www.leftbankmanhattan.com
Prices: $$

Dinner nightly

Although the name may conjure up images of rustic French fare, the cuisine of this admirable new bistro is deftly capricious. Cozily tucked away on a quiet corner, the minimalist space is framed by whitewashed brick walls dressed with a smattering of intriguing artwork and emboldened by a red-painted ceiling.

Find many pleasures within the global scope of Left Bank's carte. Offerings have included a decadent slab of pig's head terrine sided by a supple spoonful of bloomed mustard seeds; impressively prepared pastas like *paccheri* with slow-cooked pork and beef ragù; and mains like fillet of crackling-skinned wild striped bass propped by wild mushrooms and preserved lemon. For dessert, there's really only one option—the incredible maple syrup pie.

Le Gigot

D2

French 🍴

18 Cornelia St. (bet. Bleecker & W. 4th Sts.)

Subway: W 4 St - Wash Sq
Phone: 212-627-3737
Web: www.legigotrestaurant.com
Prices: $$

Lunch & dinner Tue – Sun

Looking perfectly at home on its quaint tree-lined street, Le Gigot is quietly and confidently alluring. The petite bistro boasts personable yet polished service, inlaid wood flooring, olive-colored velvet banquettes, and butter-yellow walls hung with blackboards displaying the day's specials, such as lobster salad or bœuf Bourguignon. This intimate setting is a perfect match for the classic French cooking.

The salad of endive, apple, and Roquefort, studded with toasted walnuts and dressed with sweet vinaigrette hinting of mustard seed, is simplicity at its most delicious. The duck confit, with its velvety rich meat cloaked with fabulously crisped skin and a bubbling, golden block of potato and celery root gratin, is one of the best in the city.

The Little Owl

Contemporary ✗

90 Bedford St. (at Grove St.)

Subway: Christopher St - Sheridan Sq   Lunch & dinner daily
Phone: 212-741-4695
Web: www.thelittleowlnyc.com
Prices: $$

Perched on a winsome corner of the West Village, Chef Joey Campanaro's Little Owl continues to hold a dear place in the hearts of diners near and far who appreciate that simple food and great food can be one and the same. The broccoli soup (a pure, silky purée enriched with a trace of cream and crowned by a crouton of bubbling, aged cheddar) is among the best examples of this.

The small corner room is quaint and despite this establishment's popularity, the service team is completely attitude-free. The wee kitchen is on display, and the focused crew turns out a rousing roster of preparations that bear an affinity for Mediterranean cuisine such as seared cod with *bagna cauda* vinaigrette, and gravy meatball sliders, a hands-down house specialty.

Lupa 😊

Italian ✗✗

170 Thompson St. (bet. Bleecker & Houston Sts.)

Subway: W 4 St - Wash Sq   Lunch & dinner daily
Phone: 212-982-5089
Web: www.luparestaurant.com
Prices: $$

This ever-popular Roman trattoria has been skillfully sating wolfish appetites for years and continues to fall under the hegemony of culinary heavyweights schooled in the immense bounty offered by the Italian table. Lupa's setting is rustic and charming with that timeless combination of sienna-toned walls, terra-cotta tile flooring, and wood furnishings. The service team is notable for their knowledge and courteousness.

Stop at the bar for a carafe of *vino* from the all-Italian wine list and nibble on house-cured specialties. Then move on to a focused selection of fare such as capon and pork terrine with celery *conserva*; and impressive *primi* like *tonnarelli* dressed with chunks of heritage pork ragù. A short list of *secondi* anchors the offerings.

Manhattan ▶ Greenwich, West Village & Meatpacking District

Market Table

American 🍴🍴

B3

54 Carmine St. (at Bedford St.)

Subway: W 4 St - Wash Sq
Phone: 212-255-2100
Web: www.markettablenyc.com
Prices: $$

Lunch & dinner daily

Sophisticated cooking is on display at this quaint and urbane café brought to you by Joey Campanaro and Chef Mike Price. Open all day, the bright, two-room space features brick walls lined with shelves of pantry staples, warm wood furnishings, large plate-glass windows, and a boisterous energy that rarely quiets down.

The kitchen, open for hungry eyes to enjoy, excels at turning out a seasonally respectful assortment of presentations that are just as skilled as they are simple. Case in point: the beet salad is composed as a rainbow of roasted roots paired with crunchy-creamy goat cheese fritters; and the strip steak is enhanced by an irresistible and decadent fontina-potato purée. Even a humble slice of apple pie will not only please but also impress.

Mary's Fish Camp

Seafood 🍴

B2

64 Charles St. (at W. 4th St.)

Subway: Christopher St - Sheridan Sq
Phone: 646-486-2185
Web: www.marysfishcamp.com
Prices: $$

Lunch & dinner Mon – Sat

Mary Redding opened this tiny Florida-style fish shack in a West Village brownstone in 2001 and has been enjoying wild success ever since. Her ever-debated lobster rolls are among the city's finest examples, overflowing with succulent chunks of meat, slathered in mayonnaise and piled on a buttery hot dog bun—messy but definitely worth it! Yet this small spot features an extensive menu that goes well beyond, with particular focus on Key West cuisine such as conch fritters, and the bounty of New England waters. Accompaniments like Old Bay fries and regional desserts reflect American flair with homespun simplicity.

Bear in mind that only seafood is served here, reservations are not accepted, and the counter couldn't be better for solo dining.

Mas (farmhouse)

B3

Contemporary

39 Downing St. (bet. Bedford & Varick Sts.)

Subway: Houston St   Dinner nightly
Phone: 212-255-1790
Web: www.masfarmhouse.com
Prices: $$$

Taking its name from the term used to refer to a country house or farm in Southern France, Mas fully embraces this theme in its menu and décor. Cloistered amid a picturesque West Village locale, the elegant and ever-popular dining room is shaded in an earthy palette and boasts a wooden communal table and rustic stone accents.

CIA-trained Chef Galen Zamarra, who honed his skills working in David Bouley's kitchen, pays homage to finely sourced ingredients by producing delicious, seasonal fare. Dinner may reveal a tartlet of trumpet royal mushroom and leek marmalade atop a buckwheat-pecan *sablée*; tidy bundles of seared rainbow trout stuffed with shiitake mushrooms and Swiss chard; or oven-warm quince frangipane cake with white chocolate ice cream.

Mas (la grillade)

B3

Contemporary

28 Seventh Ave. South (bet. Leroy & Morton Sts.)

Subway: Houston St   Lunch & dinner daily
Phone: 212-255-1795
Web: www.maslagrillade.com
Prices: $$

Fans of Chef Galen Zamarra are already well-versed in his sophisticated, seasonal, small farm-procured treats. At this fresh venture, he turns up the heat to showcase an array of contemporary creations blazoned with the kiss of fire, fueled by locally sourced hardwoods.

The attractive two-story dining room offers handcrafted millwork, tables elegantly appointed with faux bois china pieces and locally produced pottery, and a bar pouring thematically apt cocktails, as in a Rob Roy made from smoky Islay single malt. From the entirely wood-fired basement kitchen emerge the likes of spit-roasted Rocambole garlic with toast; grilled romaine with lamb bacon and buttermilk blue cheese dressing; and bone-in monkfish tail with smoked celery root purée.

Mercadito Grove

Mexican

D1

100 Seventh Ave. South (at Grove St.)

Subway: Christopher St - Sheridan Sq

Phone: 212-647-0830

Web: www.mercaditorestaurants.com

Prices: $$

Lunch Sat – Sun
Dinner nightly

Largest in the Mercadito chainlet, Grove has a devoted following that fills its pastel-painted chairs and corner sidewalk seating nightly. Starters range from a small list of fresh ceviches to flautas filled with chicken and black beans. Recommendations include any of the *platos fuertes* that make up the menu's concise selection like the *adobo*-marinated *pollo a las brasas*, available as a half or whole bird.

Tacos are likewise popular and are prepared with homemade tortillas, perhaps stuffed with beer-battered mahi mahi as in the *estilo Baja*. Hungry night owls should note that Mercadito offers an all-you-can eat taco special late in the evening.

Each dish attests to why Mercadito now includes outposts in Miami and Chicago.

Mexicana Mama

Mexican

B2

525 Hudson St. (bet. Charles & 10th Sts.)

Subway: Christopher St - Sheridan Sq

Phone: 212-924-4119

Web: N/A

Prices: 😊😊

Lunch & dinner Tue – Sun

Cute and charming, Mexicana Mama showcases the homespun flavors of the Mexican kitchen. The space, painted deep blue, barely seats 20 and is so small that a trip to the bathroom necessitates a walk through the open kitchen for an up close and personal view of the crew at work, where everything looks tidy and tempting.

A blackboard announces the day's mouthwatering specials like apricot- and chipotle-glazed chicken or coconut-marinated fish. The printed menu offers the likes of grilled corn slathered with chipotle mayonnaise and a showering of *cojito* cheese; or *queso flameado*—molten cheese topped with spicy Mexican chorizo and thin strips of roasted poblano pepper, attractively presented with fresh tortillas for a delicious and fun make-your-own feast.

Minetta Tavern ✿

C3

Gastropub 🍴

113 MacDougal St. (at Minetta Ln.)

Subway:	W 4 St - Wash Sq	Lunch Wed – Sun
Phone:	212-475-3850	Dinner nightly
Web:	www.minettatavernny.com	
Prices:	**$$$**	

Ngoc Ngo

First opened in 1937 but now under the charge of Keith McNally, Minetta Tavern's distinctly old New York vibe is a feather in the cap of the scene-setting restaurateur's oeuvre. This chic canteen bulges with a full house nightly, attracting a diverse social strata running from sharply suited powerbrokers to gaggles of tourists celebrating a night on the town.

To step into Minetta Tavern is to travel back in time. Grab a seat at the bustling oak bar (if only this original fixture could talk) and order a classic cocktail before being graciously steered through the closely set dining room—its salvaged beauty bears grace and warmth, donned in a wraparound mural of Washington Square Park.

The kitchen's steady stewardship is responsible for an array of impressive preparations that, like the setting, are deliciously timeless. A chilled block of oxtail terrine filled with buttery-sweet foie gras, scattered with celery root slivers and bloomed mustard seeds is a fine starting point before moving on to entrées like a flawless fillet of trout meunière crowned with jumbo lump crabmeat; or the signature Black Label burger. Finish with a slab of coconut layer cake with crème fraîche pastry cream.

Miss Lily's

132 W. Houston St. (at Sullivan St.)

Subway: Houston St
Phone: 646-588-5375
Web: www.misslilysnyc.com
Prices:

Lunch & dinner daily

At Miss Lily's, jerk chicken is brought to you by a scenester lineup that includes La Esquina's Serge Becker. Up front, the look conjures a retro takeout joint, with orange Formica booths, linoleum flooring, and a backlit menu board above the open kitchen. The back dining room is larger and has reggae record jackets lining the walls. Loud music, a gorgeous staff, and a blithe crowd create a festive vibe.

Glossy packaging aside, the Jamaican specialties served here are well-done. Curry goat brings bone-in pieces of pasture-raised meat in a tasty sauce bright with turmuric, sweet spices, and the slow burn of Scotch bonnet pepper. As for that chicken, it's charred and smoky, accompanied by mango-ginger chutney and a bottle of the tangy, spicy marinade.

Morandi

211 Waverly Pl. (bet. Charles St. & Seventh Ave. South)

Subway: 14 St (Seventh Ave.)
Phone: 212-627-7575
Web: www.morandiny.com
Prices: $$$

Lunch & dinner daily

Morandi has all the requisite charm one would expect from a Keith McNally trattoria that recalls Tuscany with all its glorious clichés, antique-tiled floors, brick archways, and walls lined with straw-wrapped Chianti bottles. Dotted with a mishmash of tables, well-dressed patrons shielded by designer shades are bathed in a warm glow even at high noon, thanks to parchment-shaded ceiling fixtures.

They come to pay homage to a rustic menu that may begin with seasonal *antipasti* before moving on to a classic panzanella marrying beefsteak and heirloom tomatoes, fresh basil, and slivers of red onions; *spaghetti neri,* squid ink pasta rolling with tender calamari, octopus, shrimp, and mussels; and light, spongy *budino limone* licked with buttermilk ice cream.

Neta

D1

61 W. 8th St. (bet. Fifth & Sixth Aves.)

Subway: W 4 St - Wash Sq   Dinner nightly
Phone: 212-505-2610
Web: www.netanyc.com
Prices: $$$

Chefs Nick Kim and Jimmy Lau have packed up their knives and headed downtown to venture out on their own, leaving behind the fabled dominion of legendary Chef Masa Takayama. Clean, modern, and spare, the setting is anchored by a maple dining counter overlooking a pastel rainbow of mouthwatering fish and gleaming steel appliances.

As one would hope (and expect) the emphasis here is on pristine, ocean-fresh morsels that can be ordered à la carte. Or, try the impressive omakase, which has revealed Florida mackerel *tataki* with ginger and tempura crumbs; Maine sea scallop warmed in its shell with garlic-butter and Santa Barbara uni; a savory nugget of flash-fried California blowfish *kara-age*; and nigiri of grilled tuna sinew brushed with soy sauce.

One if by Land, Two if by Sea

D1

17 Barrow St. (bet. Seventh Ave. South & W. 4th St.)

Subway: Christopher St - Sheridan Sq   Lunch Sat – Sun
Phone: 212-255-8649   Dinner nightly
Web: www.oneifbyland.com
Prices: $$$

Step into this oh-so-agreeable 18th century carriage house and it's easy to forget you're in Manhattan. Long known as one of the city's most romantic dining rooms, this establishment enjoys the reputation of being *the* place to pop the question, or at least the spot for a romantic rendezvous. The brick-lined space exudes old-world sophistication—tables are topped with a rose and taper candle, the room looks out onto an ivy-cloaked courtyard, and there's live piano music.

The food is delectable, whether you're in the mood for love or not, and proffers a contemporary slant in its collection of courses that can include Maine scallop sashimi with stone fruit; fettuccine with Sicilian pistachio pesto; and poached day boat cod with green garlic-citrus *nage*.

Panca

 D1

92 Seventh Ave. South (bet. Bleecker & Grove Sts.)

Subway: Christopher St - Sheridan Sq   Lunch & dinner daily
Phone: 212-488-3900
Web: www.pancany.com
Prices: $$

The exciting flavors of *Novo Andean* cuisine headline this contemporary spot, where Peruvian ingredients are prepared with Asian and American techniques. Outside, a sidewalk dining area sits along the hubbub of Seventh Avenue; the interior is simple and cool with citron walls and a stacked-stone bar displaying the bottles of *pisco* to be mixed into cocktails.

Discreetly tucked into the dining room's corner is the ceviche station, where ocean-fresh seafood inspires vibrant preparations of *tiraditos* like the five *elementos* made with the fish of the day, red onions, key lime juice, chiles, and pink Hawaiian sea salt. *Lomo saltado* highlights the cuisine's fusion in an entrée of beef tenderloin stir-fried with vegetables, *aji amarillo*, and soy sauce.

Paradou

B1

8 Little W. 12th St. (bet. Greenwich & Washington Sts.)

Subway: 14 St - 8 Av   Lunch Sat – Sun
Phone: 212-463-8345   Dinner Tue – Sun
Web: www.paradounyc.com
Prices: $$

Paradou offers a bit of Provence and a welcome respite from the spate of gargantuan, too-cool-for-school dining halls populating the Meatpacking District. Here, a casual yet energetic crowd revels in the carefree, distinctly French spirit while relaxing over crisp glasses of champagne and supping on plates of foie gras or bowls of *moules du jour.*

Most guests choose to head to the patio which doubles Paradou's seating capacity, but the intimate dining room is lovely as well. Regardless of your seat, the menu offers classic cooking, as in lamb ribs drizzled with truffle honey; sides such as cassoulet beans showered with herbed breadcrumbs presented in a cast iron skillet; and finales such as warming apple crêpes spiked with Calvados.

Manhattan ▶ Greenwich, West Village & Meatpacking District

Pastis

French ✕

B1

9 Ninth Ave. (at Little W. 12th St.)

Subway: 14 St - 8 Av
Phone: 212-929-4844
Web: www.pastisny.com
Prices: $$

Lunch & dinner daily

This lovingly recreated bistro is the first success story of the Meatpacking District, then a nascent neighborhood. Even now, it remains a trendy and popular place that is just as much fun during the day as evening, squeezing in a fashionable (and often famous) flock from breakfast through dinner. Inside, the timeless bistro décor (decorative mirrors, long zinc bar, walls lined with vintage Pastis ads) has that hip, informal charm so difficult to replicate; outside, the sidewalk seating was designed with Bellini-sipping and sunshine in mind.

The menu is good and satisfying, focusing on neighborhood favorites like steak *frites*. The cocktail list, as expected, leans heavily on the anise-flavored aperitif from which the restaurant takes its name.

Pearl Oyster Bar

Seafood ✕

D2

18 Cornelia St. (bet. Bleecker & W. 4th Sts.)

Subway: W 4 St - Wash Sq
Phone: 212-691-8211
Web: www.pearloysterbar.com
Prices: $$

Lunch Mon – Fri
Dinner Mon – Sat

In 1997, Chef/owner Rebecca Charles opened Pearl Oyster Bar in memory of her grandmother and the childhood summers they spent in Maine. Today, she serves a slice of New England to the heart of Manhattan; though many imitations and variations can be found, Pearl is a NY classic. This beloved eatery has a small dining room, a counter handling a brisk business for shellfish aficionados, an accompanying cookbook, and long lines out the door.

The classic New England menu offers small and large plates of pristine seafood as well as their hallowed lobster roll. Try this with one of their carefully selected wines or beers on tap. Pearl is a true, tried American restaurant, so don't even try to end meals with an espresso (the chef refuses to serve it).

Perilla

D1

9 Jones St. (bet. Bleecker & W. 4th Sts.)

Subway: W 4 St - Wash Sq

Phone: 212-929-6868

Web: www.perillanyc.com

Prices: $$

Lunch Sat – Sun
Dinner nightly

This casually elegant Village fave showcases its unaffected ambience alongside the talent and dedication of partners Chef Harold Dieterle and General Manager Alicia Nosenzo. He is a CIA graduate and the premier winner of the reality television hit *Top Chef*; she hails from San Francisco and has honed her front-of-house skills at impressive restaurants on both coasts.

The kitchen turns globally sparked inspiration into a suite of clever creations that have included crispy lamb sweetbreads with cumin-infused glazed carrots and ginger-spiked sweet and sour sauce; and a roasted bone-in pork chop paired brilliantly with luscious *tonnato* sauce. For dessert, a boozy brunch-inspired block of sour cream coffee cake with rum raisin ice cream is sheer pleasure.

Perla

C3

24 Minetta Ln. (at Sixth Ave.)

Subway: W 4 St - Wash Sq

Phone: 212-933-1824

Web: www.perlanyc.com

Prices: $$$

Lunch Fri – Sun
Dinner nightly

Staffed by cool, chatty servers, this restored Italian tavern is quietly set along a narrow Village street, yet it is vastly popular for its big, blowout spread. Quenching your thirst from the get-go is a well-stocked marble bar where enticing cocktails are routinely poured into sparkling stemware. Farther along, find an airy dining room whose white walls, wood floors, and brass-studded banquettes will have you besotted.

The energy is high, but everyone slows to appreciate the likes of gorgeous *garganelli*, neatly mounded and tossed with an excellent tomato sauce brimming with tripe and *guanciale*. Meat lovers will swoon over heartier secondi, such as silky, *saba*-glazed duck or thick slices of charred beef tongue laid atop creamy white beans.

Manhattan ▶ Greenwich, West Village & Meatpacking District

Perry Street 🐶

B2

176 Perry St. (at West St.)

Subway: Christopher St - Sheridan Sq

Phone: 212-352-1900

Web: www.jean-georges.com

Prices: $$

Lunch & dinner daily

This *way* West Village dining room, housed at the base of a modernist glass condo tower by Richard Meier, is the antithesis of Jean-Georges Vongerichten's cantankerous Spice Market. Cool, spare, and subdued, the ethereal setting is splashed with diffused sunshine during the day and grounded by plush, chocolate brown carpeting.

As one would expect, the service and tabletop are excellent; and the kitchen, headed by son Cedric Vongerichten, is impressive. The gently priced prix-fixe offers good value in its series of plates that may bring silken slices of king oyster mushroom carpaccio with creamy-ripe avocado, *fleur de sel*, and fresh thyme; or slow-cooked salmon sparked with jalapeño paste, caraway-flecked braised cabbage, and buttery fingerlings.

The Place

B2

310 W. 4th St. (bet. Bank & 12th Sts.)

Subway: 14 St - 8 Av

Phone: 212-924-2711

Web: www.theplaceny.com

Prices: $$

Lunch Sat – Sun
Dinner nightly

Set deep within the West Village, The Place is the kind of cozy, grotto-style den that makes you feel all grown-up. Rendezvous-like, guests climb below street level to find a bar aglow with flickering votive candles. Wander back a bit, and you'll find rustic beams and white tablecloth seating; two outdoor terraces beckon when the sun shines.

The guileless name of the "place" and timeless look of the century-old setting is nicely juxtaposed by a wholly contemporary menu that roams the globe: duck confit-filled parcels served with grain mustard and braised red cabbage is a lovely autumnal treat, while entrées please year-round with dishes like a cheddar-capped shepherd's pie; Long Island duck breast with tamarind sauce; and Cuban-style pork chops.

Pó

Italian ✗✗

D2

31 Cornelia St. (bet. Bleecker & W. 4th Sts.)

Subway: W 4 St - Wash Sq
Phone: 212-645-2189
Web: www.porestaurant.com
Prices: $$

Lunch Wed – Sun
Dinner nightly

This longtime neighborhood favorite, opened in 1993, continues to attract a devoted following for its understated yet sophisticated ambience and creative Italian fare.

During the day, the slender dining room is light and breezy, especially in warmer weather when the front door is propped open and ceiling fans swirl overhead. At night, this quaint spot tucked away on tree-lined Cornelia St. feels timeless and perfectly romantic.

Egg dishes and panini are available at lunch. The dinner menu features a contemporary slant that may include starters like house-cured tuna dressed with white beans, artichokes, and chili-mint vinaigrette; freshly made gnocchi draped with lamb ragù; and entrées that include grilled skirt steak with Gorgonzola butter.

Quinto Quarto

Italian ✗

B3

14 Bedford St. (bet. Downing & Houston Sts.)

Subway: Houston St
Phone: 212-675-9080
Web: www.quintoquarto.com
Prices: ⊖⊖

Lunch & dinner Tue – Sun

Informal, intimate, and inviting, this pleasing *"osteria Romana"* embraces every loving detail of its textbook rustic style. The 50-seat room boasts exposed brick walls, plank flooring, a beamed ceiling, and wood tables topped with bottles of fragrant olive oil.

Quinto Quarto's kitchen paves the way to the Eternal City with a range of regional plates that bear a homespun essence. Pastas here are always satisfying, with a bounty that includes *bombolotti* with onion, *guanciale*, pecorino, and red chili flakes. Straightforward entrées charm with their simplicity, as in *salsiccia vino bianco*, plump knobs of mild pork sausage cooked in white wine and served with roasted potatoes.

The lunch prix-fixe is a pared down affair, but includes a glass of wine.

171

Recette

Contemporary ✗✗

B2

328 W. 12th St. (at Greenwich St.)

Subway: 14 St - 8 Av
Phone: 212-414-3000
Web: www.recettenyc.com
Prices: $$$

Lunch Sun
Dinner nightly

Straddling a tree-lined corner in the heart of the West Village, Recette has a few things going for it straight off the bat: it's cute, intimate, and decidedly low-lit. Date-night anyone?

But with Jesse Schenker, a much buzzed about young chef on board, not to mention a pastry chef rumored to hail from Per Se, there's a lot more to Recette than looks and location. Its menu is a veritable recipe for success with a range of globally inspired small plates perfectly suited to share with friends or on your own. Partake in the likes of bigeye tuna sashimi (crack the lid of clementine ice to discover the ruby red flesh underneath); an ode to spring in the form of creamy ramp soup with pickled ramps; or spaghetti tangled with uni-enriched stewed tomatoes.

RedFarm

Asian ✗✗

B2

529 Hudson St. (bet. Charles & 10th Sts.)

Subway: Christopher St - Sheridan Sq
Phone: 212-792-9700
Web: www.redfarmnyc.com
Prices: $$

Lunch Sat – Sun
Dinner nightly

This eclectic Village-meets-MePa gem is tons of fun and reeks of creativity. Everything from its quirkily smart design, stylish staff, to the hipster crowd speaks to a trendy spirit. The vibe is loud and lively and communal seating means rubbing elbows with bright young things.

While for some this may recall those dreaded high school cafeteria scenes, it's a big part of the allure at this foodie hot spot. RedFarm gives Chinese food a slick and sexy makeover. The farmer's market runs head-on into the wok here, as the bustling kitchen sends out a succession of dishes such as lush, spicy jalapeño poppers packed with minced shrimp; duck-and-Fuji apple wraps, *shu mai* shooters, and spicy crispy beef tossed in an addictive glaze of vinegar and Grand Marnier.

Rockmeisha

Japanese

D1

11 Barrow St. (bet. Seventh Ave. South & W. 4th St.)

Subway: Christopher St - Sheridan Sq
Phone: 212-675-7775
Web: N/A
Prices: 🍜

Dinner nightly

Regional specialties hailing from the chef's homeland of Kyushu, the large island in Southern Japan, are the way to go at this laid-back, fun, and tasty *izakaya*.

Like its name, the menu takes on a musical theme in listing its dishes as "goldies" such as the likes of *takosu*, thick slices of dense octopus bobbing in a refreshing yuzu-zested soy vinegar sauce; while their "greatest hits" may feature the *tonsoku*, a crispy pork foot that is unctuous to the point of being voluptuous, accompanied by raw cabbage and a dab of citrusy-spicy *yuzu kosho* to cut the richness.

The intimate space is decorated with a touch of kitsch (think poison warning signs), curious little cartoon drawings lining the walls, and rock music pulsing in the background, of course.

Saxon + Parole

Contemporary ✗✗

D4

316 Bowery (at Bleecker St.)

Subway: Bleecker St
Phone: 212-254-0350
Web: www.saxonandparole.com
Prices: $$$

Lunch Sat – Sun
Dinner nightly

This new iteration of the short-lived Double Crown retains its key players in Executive Chef Brad Farmerie and the AvroKO Hospitality Group. Named after two 19th century racehorses, the handsome setting sports a limited use of color, and employs rich wood tones and warm lighting to achieve a suitably clubby atmosphere.

The crowd-pleasing menu, founded on grilled meats and seafood, boasts beginnings like a pot of velvety portobello mushroom mousse capped by a sheen of whiskey and black truffle jelly; and entrées such as whole-roasted branzino stuffed with Parmesan and smoked paprika-seasoned panko, sided by Brussels sprouts in chili caramel. Desserts play a deliciously whimsical note, as in steamed Christmas pudding with hard-sauce ice cream.

Scarpetta

Italian

B1

355 W. 14th St. (bet. Eighth & Ninth Aves.)

Subway: 14 St - 8 Av   Dinner nightly
Phone: 212-691-0555
Web: www.scottconant.com
Prices: $$$

Scarpetta moves to the beat of Chef Scott Conant, who is no stranger to gifted kitchens. Flanked by a MePa neighborhood that seems to have money tucked between the cobblestones to fund its constant development, Scarpetta remains an adored Italian treat. The restaurant is divided into two spaces: a stunning mahogany bar up front offers plenty of seats for the well-heeled patrons; in the main dining room, a retractable skylight crowns the plush tables dressed with a burnt orange motif-fabric.

If nestled at the bar, shoot the breeze with servers about braised duck with tender cavatelli; *capretto* bathed in a shimmering sauce of pancetta, mushrooms, and root vegetables; or a lush almond chocolate torte frilled with white balsamic marshmallows.

Sevilla

Spanish

B2

62 Charles St. (at W. 4th St.)

Subway: Christopher St - Sheridan Sq   Lunch & dinner daily
Phone: 212-929-3189
Web: www.sevillarestaurantandbar.com
Prices: $$

With a long and colorful history since first opening its doors in 1941, charmingly nostalgic Sevilla remains a rarity among Manhattan's dining scene. The roaming menu harks back to traditional Spanish fare, heaping and hearty; the kind enjoyed long before our commonplace exposure to the cuisine became focused on small plates.

The majority of Sevilla's reasonably priced dishes are built around simply prepared seafood and chicken dressed with a number of primary sauces featuring almond, garlic, wine, and the prominent green sauce—parsley-packed and punched with garlic. Starters include the *ajo* soup, a clear chicken broth infused with the nutty essence of roasted garlic and enriched with egg; while the smooth, classic flan is a fitting finale.

Soto ✿ ✿

Japanese ✗✗

D1

357 Sixth Ave. (bet. Washington Pl. & W. 4th St.)

Subway: W 4 St - Wash Sq
Phone: 212-414-3088
Web: N/A
Prices: $$$

Dinner Mon – Sat

Tokio Kuniyoshi

The experience of dining at Chef Sotohiro Kosugi's eponymous home is stunning, dramatic, and often surprising...as is its rather unexpected location behind the white façade of an unmarked storefront amid the tattoo parlors of lower Sixth Avenue. The diminutive interior is modern, immaculate (if antiseptic), and rightfully keeps the focus on the food. The staff is welcoming and notably deferential to the chef—their respect for his artistry is palpable.

The menu showcases the kitchen's understanding of traditions and sometimes creative, playful spirit through prime ingredients like caviar, lobster, and uni. Follow the chefs omakase direction here which might include the likes of black soybean yuba topped with supremely fresh Santa Barbara uni set afloat in shiitake broth; or thinly sliced fluke resting atop chives, shiso, ginger shoots, and *mizore* ponzu for a dish that exemplifies pure flavors and exceptional technique. Toro can be a sublime experience, silky and embellished with avocado coulis, luscious caviar, and a sesame ponzu.

No matter the night's offerings, there are no missteps in the parade of superbly handled, expertly formed, and perfectly chosen fish in each bite of nigiri.

Spasso

B2

Italian ✗✗

551 Hudson St. (bet. Perry & 11th Sts.)

Subway: Christopher St - Sheridan Sq   Lunch & dinner daily
Phone: 212-858-3838
Web: www.spassonyc.com
Prices: $$

This newcomer adds to the wealth of Italian small plates available in the West Village. Housed in the former home of Alfama, the convivial room boasts a gracious mien with a touch of rusticity; seating options include a comfortable bar and dining counter near the kitchen where one can watch prosciutto shaved, salads prepped, and gooey chocolate caramel *crostata* sliced and plated.

The kitchen, headed by an alum of Lupa and Convivio, serves up an array of contemporary Italian. Bites include eggplant *"arancini"* and whipped house-made ricotta flavored with the sweet taste of roasted tomato. There are plenty of heartier options as well, such as silky ravioli pockets filled with spring peas and chopped prawns; and *secondi* like trout saltimbocca.

Spice Market

B1

Asian ✗✗

403 W. 13th St. (at Ninth Ave.)

Subway: 14 St - 8 Av   Lunch & dinner daily
Phone: 212-675-2322
Web: www.spicemarketnewyork.com
Prices: $$

This former warehouse turned sexy Asian street food lair has spawned offshoots in London and Qatar, further facilitating Chef Jean-Georges Vongerichten's global reach. But here in NYC, the 2004 original is a 12,000 square-foot fantasy glammed up by carved wooden arches, jewel-toned fabrics, a teak pagoda, and sarong-wrapped staff. The scene still thumps nightly, crammed with fun-loving grazers supping on faraway specialties all crafted with the chef's trademark élan. The carte divulges a savory romp: shatteringly crispy shrimp spring rolls; salt and pepper skate, polished copper bowls of pork *vindaloo*; and fried rice crowned by a sunny-side egg ringed with gingery breadcrumbs.

Come to eat. Come to drink. Spice Market rarely disappoints.

Spotted Pig ❀

B2

314 W. 11th St. (at Greenwich St.)

Subway: Christopher St - Sheridan Sq
Phone: 212-620-0393
Web: www.thespottedpig.com
Prices: $$

Lunch & dinner daily

Spotted Pig

New York born and bred, this beloved facsimile of an English gastropub is as much an iconic neighborhood fixture as the Village Vanguard or Magnolia Bakery.

Hang your coat, grab a stool, and savor tasty preparations worth crooning about. Lunchtime is a quieter, more limited affair, but at dinner the place is habitually packed to the gills, so plan on a wait. That in mind, take a look around; the scene is worth savoring. An assemblage of porcine tchotchkes embellishes the speakeasy's frame that's dressed down with well-trodden plank flooring, crumbling brick, and exposed polished copper pipes.

Composed of house favorites and seasonally skewed specials, Chef-extraordinaire April Bloomfield seduces palates with her roster of glorious grub that zips throughout the wee space. A tart composed of dense ricotta curds warmed by just baked *pâte feuilletée*–a crisp shell of buttery air–draped by shaved prosciutto and young arugula makes a soigné start. Meals may move onto juicy grilled skirt steak accompanied by a dollop of biting horseradish cream, roasted beets of various hues, and their wilted, well-seasoned greens. End on a sweet note with warm ginger cake sided by whipped cream perfection.

Standard Grill

 B1

848 Washington St. (bet. Little W. 12th & 13th Sts.)

Subway: 14 St - 8 Av   Lunch & dinner daily
Phone: 212-645-4100
Web: www.thestandardgrill.com
Prices: $$

Classy comfort food is the name of the game at this jaunty grill that draws the "in" crowd. Despite the scene, the cooking is worth every penny. The raw bar or cheese fondue for a crowd make a fine start before moving on to the likes of grilled cobia fillet with a caramelized coating of *chermoula* marinade. Is that lobster Thermidor on the menu? Yes. And high- and lowbrow desserts include baked Alaska and cookies with local milk.

Perched beneath the Highline, the Standard Grill serves up a choice of seating: a bright and airy front lounge, breezy sidewalk, and knockout dining room–clubby and sophisticated–replete with wood-paneled walls, subway tile-clad vaulted ceiling, comfy red leather booths, and tables sporting menswear-inspired linens.

Surya 😊

C1

302 Bleecker St. (bet. Grove St. & Seventh Ave. South)

Subway: Christopher St - Sheridan Sq   Lunch & dinner daily
Phone: 212-807-7770
Web: www.suryany.com
Prices: $$

This sleek Indian restaurant serves a slice of the East with a definitive New York look (read: no bright colors and no sequin-studded artwork at Surya). Polished dark wood floors, a cushioned banquette, ivory walls, and a back garden fashion a clean aesthetic and very pleasant ambience. Toto, we're definitely not in Delhi anymore.

It might look New York, but the taste is pure India. Take one bite of the lamb Chettinad or the halibut *moli* and you'll be transported in no time. Choose from a variety of regional specialties and tandoor preparations. You'll find everything from the familiar (*vindaloo*) to the rare (*surra putto*, cubes of shark with green pepper and curry leaf).

It's more limited than at night, but the lunch menu delivers a good value.

Takashi

Japanese

B3

456 Hudson St. (bet. Barrow & Morton Sts.)

Subway: Christopher St - Sheridan Sq | Dinner nightly
Phone: 212-414-2929
Web: www.takashinyc.com
Prices: $$

 Chef Takashi Inoue's meaty array honors the *yakiniku* (Japanese for Korean-style barbecue) focus of his hot spot and allows diners to tap into their inner pyromaniac by way of tabletop grilling atop striated wood benches.

Start off cool, with say *yooke* (a mound of exquisitely fresh chuck eye steak tartare seasoned with a light, refreshing house sauce and topped with a quail egg) before moving on to sustainably raised cuts of beef which are either seasoned with salt, garlic, and sesame oil, or marinated in Takashi's special sauce. Some nightly specials require the chef's expert preparation, as in domestic Kobe chuck flat steak grilled rare and simply presented with lemon wedges, wasabi, and soy sauce—this well-marbled beauty needs nothing else.

Tertulia

Spanish

D1

359 Sixth Ave. (at Washington Pl.)

Subway: W 4 St - Wash Sq | Lunch & dinner daily
Phone: 646-559-9909
Web: www.tertulianyc.com
Prices: $$

 Chef Seamus Mullen has returned to the city's dining scene with this boisterous new eatery that has had fans heading here in droves since day one. Inspired by a *sidreria*, or cider house common to Northern Spain, Tertulia is a convivial gathering spot complete with a bar equipped with wood barrels dispensing Spanish wines, and sangria nicely finished off with a scoop of diced fresh fruit.

Cured meats and cheeses bolster the chef's ingredient-driven take on tapas that offers up *arroz a la plancha*, creamy Calasparra rice caramelized on a hot griddle; *rabo de toro*, spoon tender oxtail glazed with sherry jus and served with crushed smoked potatoes, brined olives, and shaved celery; or warm apple cake sided by rum raisin ice cream and cider caramel.

Tomoe Sushi

Japanese

C4

172 Thompson St. (bet. Bleecker & Houston Sts.)

Subway: Spring St (Sixth Ave.)
Phone: 212-777-9346
Web: N/A
Prices: 🍴

Lunch Tue – Sat
Dinner nightly

Tomoe focuses on value and quality rather than soigné appearances. Its tile floor has been dulled by a steady stream of sushi aficionados, the simple furnishings aren't conducive to leisurely meals, and the décor is limited to hand-drawn signs displaying specials. Still, regulars enthuse over these supple morsels prepared by the efficient team behind the counter and presented by swift, casual servers.

Characterized by pieces that err on the side of heft, this sushi has a foundation of rich, thickly cut slices of fish, minimal embellishment, and fine technique. The kitchen also prepares a long list of cooked dishes that display a creative hand, as in steamed buns filled with teriyaki-brushed silken tofu, pickled garlic, and a dollop of mayonnaise.

Ushiwakamaru

Japanese

C4

136 W. Houston St. (bet. MacDougal & Sullivan Sts.)

Subway: B'way - Lafayette St
Phone: 212-228-4181
Web: N/A
Prices: $$$$

Dinner Mon – Sat

Arrive early enough and you may find Ushiwakamaru's tables pre-assigned to reserved guests by way of post-its: most nights, this casual basement sushi-ya is packed with regulars craving Chef Hideo Kuribara's skillfully crafted morsels.

Sitting at the counter should influence you to indulge in the omakase, along with most of your neighbors. It is more interactive here than found at more traditional *sushi-ya*, allowing diners to tailor the experience based on their budget. Your *itamae* will send forth the likes of a sweet-tasting slice of giant clam; or wild baby yellowtail perched atop warm, loosely packed rice; and sashimi that may feature sliver-skinned horse mackerel; or slivers of toothsome octopus tentacle sided by pepper-flecked sea salt.

Villa Pacri

B1

Italian 🍴🍴🍴

55 Gansevoort St. (bet. Greenwich & Washington Sts.)

Subway: 14 St - 8 Av
Phone: 212-924-5559
Web: www.villapacri.com
Prices: $$$

Dinner Tue – Sat

Villa Pacri is proof that you can have it all. This multi-level restaurant-cum-lounge has a little bit of everything spread over five floors, from a basement/underground lounge to a rooftop deck, with a first-floor café and Villa Pacri–the grown-up's choice–in between. This inviting room looks like the offspring of an Italian villa and a California shabby-chic cottage.

It's a scene, and many are there for the people-watching, but the well-executed Italian cooking is delicious and the staff is well-trained. Irresistible pasta dishes like *p accheri alla Napoletana* draped in a lobster-enriched sauce will have you licking your plate clean, while desserts are worth the splurge—just beware that bills can be bigger than the next table's TriBeCa loft.

Wong

D1

Asian 🍴

7 Cornelia St. (bet. Bleecker & W. 4th Sts.)

Subway: W 4 St - Wash Sq
Phone: 212-989-3399
Web: www.wongnewyork.com
Prices: $$

Dinner Mon – Sat

Malaysian-born Simpson Wong's eponymous new spot is tucked away on one of the coziest blocks in Greenwich Village. Beyond its windowed façade, the cool space is framed by whitewashed brick walls. Diners sit at either communal tables or two counters, one of which overlooks the inner workings of the kitchen.

The menu utilizes local farm products for a concise presentation of contemporary-minded Asian cuisine. Expect the likes of lightly cooked Swiss chard with mildly spiced *sambal*, faintly sweet with gratings of toasted coconut; and novel creations like thick, chewy rice noodles tangled within a hearty, satisfying sauce of finely chopped pork, sea cucumber, and shiitakes. Desserts include roast-duck ice cream with star anise-poached plums—for real.

Wallsé ✿

Austrian ✗✗

B2

344 W. 11th St. (at Washington St.)

Subway: Christopher St - Sheridan Sq
Phone: 212-352-2300
Web: www.kg-ny.com
Prices: $$$

Lunch Sat – Sun
Dinner nightly

KGNY Restaurant Group

This Austrian sparkler is a real New Yorker. Situated on an idyllic corner that embodies what everyone dreams downtown neighborhoods should resemble, Wallsé resides among tree-shaded, cobblestoned streets and historic townhouses, all bathed in rose-colored light as the sun sets over the Hudson just blocks away. Inside, the two dining rooms juxtapose the easy-breezy locale with a décor that's strongly flavored. Dark carpeting and black velvet upholstery contrast gallery white walls, which are hung with bold, contemporary paintings.

The cuisine of Chef Kurt Gutenbrunner has been more sure-footed of late, as it has embraced an intriguingly modern approach to Austrian cooking. Expect creative twists applied to starters like vivid green sweet pea purée cradling an impossibly thin ravioli stuffed with lobster; or entrées such as an impressively refined rendition of oxtail goulash, presented as a block encasing a fluffy bread dumpling, and ringed by red and yellow sweet peppers.

Desserts certainly should not be skipped, especially with such incomparable preparations as *topfen palatschinken*, crêpes packed with a sweet cheese mousse and teased with vanilla bean-citrus syrup and kumquats.

Yerba Buena Perry

1 Perry St. (at Greenwich Ave.)

Subway: 14 St (Seventh Ave.)
Phone: 212-620-0808
Web: www.ybnyc.com
Prices: $$

Lunch Sat – Sun
Dinner nightly

Executive Chef Julian Medina mambos his way through the kitchens of not one, but six different restaurants, including Toloache and Coppelia; however, this tiny but oh-so-mighty restaurant takes the cake.

Mixing Cuban, Peruvian, Chilean, and Mexican influences and traditions, upscale Medina delivers a signature flavor. Even familiar dishes have unexpected flair as in the ribeye ceviche dressed with spicy red pepper sauce, completed with corn kernels and sea urchin lobes. In the hands of this kitchen, even simple shrimp assume a lobster-like meatiness, complemented with their own Rio de Janeiro-style tomato salsa.

The tightly packed room is comfortable but can feel cramped, so hope to make new friends to share the meaty *parrillada* and a trio of fab fries.

Look for the symbol 🍳 for a brilliant breakfast to start your day off right.

Manhattan ▶ Greenwich, West Village & Meatpacking District

183

Harlem, Morningside & Washington Heights

Flanked by Riverside and Morningside parks and home to stately Columbia University, Morningside Heights is a lovely quarter of the city, and known for some of the best breakfast spots in town. Sandwich shops and eateries line these avenues, where quick, inexpensive meals are a collegiate necessity. Resident academics and Ivy leaguers are found darting to and from class or lounging at the **Hungarian Pastry Shop** with a sweet treat and cup of tea. Considered a landmark, this old-world bakery has been open for more than three decades and is a focal point for students, locals, and visitors alike. Across the street, Saint John the Divine, a gorgeous Gothic revival and formidable presence on Amsterdam Avenue offers beauty, history, and wonderful community outreach programs. Special occasions call for an evening sojourn at L**ee Lee's Bakery**. Rather than be misled by its sterile locale, prepare yourself for a plateful of the most decadent rugelach ever. In the summer, enjoy a drink in the breeze on the alluring outdoor terrace. To the north is Harlem—a true feast for the stomach and soul. Fifth Avenue divides the neighborhood into two very unique areas: West Harlem, an epicenter of African-American culture; and East Harlem, a diverse Latin quarter affectionately known as "El Barrio."

WEST HARLEM

West Harlem still retains a kind of sassy edge as it gives way to slow and welcomed gentrification—one of its most visible borders is at **Fairway**, a Tri-State area staple that lures shoppers off the West Side Highway for their mind-boggling offerings and

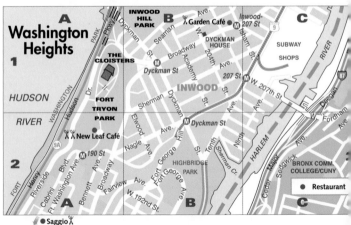

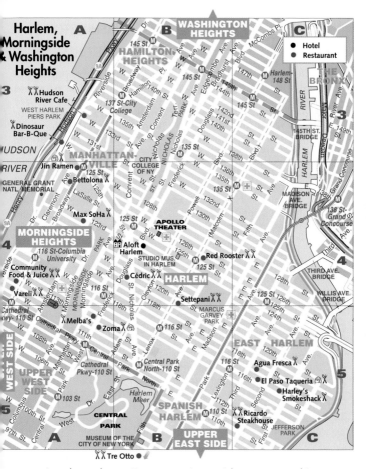

Harlem,
Morningside
& Washington
Heights

A B WASHINGTON
HEIGHTS

C

● Hotel
● Restaurant

145 St

HAMILTON
HEIGHTS

Harlem-
148 St

THE
BRONX

3

✗✗ Hudson
River Cafe

WEST HARLEM
PIERS PARK

137 St-City
College

145 St

145TH ST.
BRIDGE

3

✗ Dinosaur
Bar-B-Que

HUDSON

RIVER

MANHATTAN-
VILLE

Jin Ramen

135 St

125 St

138 St-
Grand
Concourse

GENERAL GRANT
NATL. MEMORIAL

Bettolona ✗

CITY
COLLEGE
OF NY

135 St

MADISON
AVE.
BRIDGE

Max SoHa ✗

125 St

MORNINGSIDE
HEIGHTS

APOLLO
THEATER

THIRD AVE.
BRIDGE

4

116 St-Columbia
University

Aloft
Harlem

Red Rooster ✗✗

125 St

4

Community
Food & Juice ✗✗

STUDIO MUS.
IN HARLEM

HARLEM

WILLIS AVE.
BRIDGE

Vareli ✗✗

116 St

Cédric ✗✗

Settepani ✗✗

125 St

Melba's ✗

Zoma ✗

116 St

MARCUS
GARVEY
PARK

WEST SIDE

UPPER
WEST
SIDE

Cathedral
Pkwy-110 St

Central Park
North-110 St

EAST HARLEM

Agua Fresca ✗

116 St

103 St

Harlem
Meer

El Paso Taqueria ✗

Harley's
Smokeshack ✗

CENTRAL
PARK

SPANISH
HARLEM

110 St

Ricardo ✗✗
Steakhouse

JEFFERSON
PARK

A

MUSEUM OF THE
CITY OF NEW YORK

B

UPPER
EAST SIDE

C

✗✗ Tre Otto ●

sensational produce. For a
taste of the area's history, sift
through the impressive literary
collection at The Schomburg
Center for Research in Black
Culture on Lenox Avenue, or
spend a sunny afternoon among
the quaint row houses in the
historic districts of Sugar Hill and
Hamilton Heights. When the
sun goes down, slip into famed
Patisserie des Ambassades
whose contemporary yet chic
interior and knack for flavors
is evident through breakfast,
lunch, and dinner. **Kuti's** also

entices with aromas wafting
from its familiar lamb shawarma
and plates of sizzling shrimp.
Harlem Week is an annual
festival that features art, music,
and food each August. While
here, cool off with a cone of
red velvet cake ice cream if
the natural ice cream stand is
around. Food factors heavily
into Harlem culture–both east
and west of Fifth Avenue–
and the choices are as diverse
as the neighborhood itself.
From Mexican to Caribbean
to West African, the culinary

delights abound. To further indulge your fried food fantasy, entrée famed **Charles** for Chef Charles Gabriel's acclaimed buffet and sinfully delicious fried chicken. For dangerously spiced Senegalese food, head to **Afrika Kine**; or shop around **Darou Salam Market** for West African groceries. **Carrot Top Pastries** seduces locals with sweet potato pies, while **Harlem Shambles**, a true-blue butcher shop, specializes and offers quality cuts of meat and poultry designed to enhance any dining experience.

EAST HARLEM

In East Harlem, Cuban cuisine- and culture-vultures should visit **Amor Cubano** for their tasty home-style creations including *lechon*, savored amidst a vibrant atmosphere of live Cuban music. For Caribbean delights stop into **Sisters**; or peruse the taco trucks and taquerias along the Little Mexico strip of East 116th Street in the heart of one of New York's many Mexican communities. A remnant of the former Italian population of East Harlem, **Rao's** is a New York institution. Run out of a small basement and frequented by the likes of Donald Trump and Nicole Kidman, Rao's is one of the most difficult tables to get in all of Manhattan. The original patrons have exclusive rights to a seat here and hand off their reservations like rent-controlled apartments. Better try to get in good with the owner if you can. **Patsy's** is still holding strong in Harlem, burning its coal oven and sometimes its pizza.

WASHINGTON HEIGHTS

The diverse Washington Heights offers a plethora of food choices from tasty trucks (**Patacon Pisao** for Venezuelan?) to charming restaurants, perfect for the late-night crowd. The Tony award-winning musical *In The Heights* pays loving tribute to the ebullient Washington Heights neighborhood where Dominican and Puerto Rican communities have taken root. Latin beats blast through the air; and bright, refreshing Puerto Rican piragua carts can be found selling shaved ice soaked in a rainbow of tropical flavors. Locals line up around the block at **Elsa La Reina del Chicharrón** for their deliciously deep-fried *chicharrón* featuring crispy pork chunks. Then, try *jugos naturales*–juices made from cane sugar and fresh fruits like pineapple and orange–for a healthy treat. Great fish markets and butcher shops dot the streets, and less than ten bucks will get you a delicious plate of *pernil* with rice and beans at any number of eateries. Duck into **La Rosa Fine Foods**, a wonderful Latin gourmet market, for fresh fish, meat, and produce; or **Nelly's Bakery** for a creamy cup of *café con leche* and a *guayaba con queso* (guava and cheese pastry). **Piper's Kilt**, a standing relic in Inwood, represents the former Irish and German population of the area. Settle into a booth at the lively "**Kilt**" with some Irish nachos and a perfect pint.

Agua Fresca

C5

Mexican ✗

207 E. 117th St. (bet. Second & Third Aves.)

Subway: 116 St (Lexington Ave.)   Lunch & dinner daily
Phone: 212-996-2500
Web: www.aguafrescarestaurant.com
Prices: 🍲

Agua Fresca is an out-of-this-world entrance into the sunny, authentic, and delicious flavors of Mexico. Thank Chef Adrian Leon, who also hails from this great land, for his menu's showcase of Nuevo Latin leanings along with solid, traditional fare.

Beyond the rather unimpressive, commercial locale, the dining space is cheery—everything seems kissed by bright colors and tastes from strawberry sangria to baked cinnamon churros with *dulce de leche*. Start with the fab guacamole trio: classic; smoky chipotle; and pineapple-shrimp. Other must-haves include *chilaquiles rojos al arbol* (crispy tortilla chips smothered in smoky arbol sauce, *queso fresco*, and juicy chicken in tomatillo sauce); or tender pork chop in *pasilla chile* sauce over sweet plantain mash.

Bettolona

A4

Italian ✗

3143 Broadway (bet. LaSalle St. & Tiemann Pl.)

Subway: 125 St (Broadway)   Lunch & dinner daily
Phone: 212-749-1125
Web: www.bettolona.com
Prices: $$

Bettolona has slowly but steadily built quite a fanfare, courtesy of an Italian team that bestows its authenticity. This hole-in-the-wall is ever-charming, with its mellifluous lighting, red banquettes, and rustic demeanor. The visible pizza oven also lends a hand in luring the locals for a home-style Regina Margherita spread with creamy *fior di latte* and silky San Marzano tomatoes.

Bare wood tables are tightly set, so this isn't ideal for an intimate date. Yet familiar and tasty classic pastas like spinach fettuccine mingled with sweet sausage, peas, and tomatoes in cream sauce; and *penne Siciliane* slathered with fresh ricotta and cubed eggplant in tomato sauce (just like *nonna* used to make) are hugely favored among the Columbia University crowd.

Manhattan ▶ Harlem, Morningside & Washington Heights

Cédric

B4

185 St. Nicholas Ave. (at 119th St.)

Subway: 116 St (Frederick Douglass Blvd.)　　　　　　Lunch & dinner daily
Phone: 212-866-7766
Web: www.cedricbistro.com
Prices: $$

With sensual interior accents like etched mirrors, gold and red splashes, and flashy chandeliers, Cédric oozes almost as much cool as its uptown home—it's impossible not to have a good time here. Stunning florals sit proudly at the bar as if it were a sign that austerity is not their style. While this Harlem sophisticate is hardly dull, the round-the-clock crowd can make the zinc bar and dining room feel snug.

Through the large pane windows, watch happy diners dive into a bowl of excellent mussels plumped with white wine and shallots. Seared salmon fillets quenched with balsamic and paired with ratatouille; or a staggeringly creamy crème brûlée studded with vanilla flecks are other reasons why this darling is so revered and well-attended.

Community Food & Juice

A4

2893 Broadway (bet. 112th & 113th Sts.)

Subway: Cathedral Pkwy/110 St (Broadway)　　　　　　Lunch & dinner daily
Phone: 212-665-2800
Web: www.communityrestaurant.com
Prices: $$

Community Food & Juice is among a handful of exciting places to arrive in this pocket of Morningside Heights. Not just because the highly sustainable, locally sourced food is spectacular, or because the owners arrive via the lauded Clinton Street Baking Company—but because the homey vibe makes you want to come back every night of the week.

Unfortunately, so does the rest of the neighborhood—and most nights, you'll find a healthy wait for a table (they don't take reservations). Your reward for all that patience? A piping hot, homespun matzo ball chicken soup dancing with tender carrots, celery, and fragrant herbs; a pan-seared Vietnamese chicken sandwich done *bahn mi*-style; or rich butterscotch pudding sporting a smooth dollop of whipped cream.

Dinosaur Bar-B-Que

Barbecue ✗

A3

700 W. 125th St. (at Twelfth Ave.)

Subway: 125 St (Broadway)
Phone: 212-694-1777
Web: www.dinosaurbarbque.com
Prices: $$

Lunch & dinner daily

Dinosaur Bar-B-Que is a Harlem institution, steps below the imposing Riverside Drive. Inside, it can get rowdy at times, and yet, their barbecue is as good as its rocking reputation and the welcoming staff is perfectly equipped to manage the scores of rib lovers waiting for tables. The décor feels timeless—complete with a line of Harleys parked outside.

Dinosaur's undiminished popularity is thanks to the menu of rich, lip-smacking specialties piled high with a range of Southern flavors, from sweet and smoky to tangy and sultry. Whether going for a full rack of dry-rubbed ribs glazed with their propriety sauce; Creole-spiced deviled eggs flecked with sour cornichons; or a Big Ass pork shoulder, all is quenched with a bevy of frosty beers.

El Paso Taqueria

Mexican ✗

C5

237 E. 116th St. (bet. Second & Third Aves.)

Subway: 116 St (Lexington Ave.)
Phone: 212-860-4875
Web: N/A
Prices: ✺✺

Lunch & dinner daily

Hidden in plain sight is this standout, serving some of Manhattan's best Mexican eats. Beyond the intricately designed wrought-iron gates lies the meticulous and adorably appointed interior, with its warming brick walls, ceramic accents, and inviting back patio.

Begin with the likes of steamed tamales packed with jalapeños and cheese, or the excellent and refreshing beef tripe soup in a tomato-chile *guajillo* broth topped with cilantro and onions. Other highlights might include the *cemita al pastor* of chipotle-marinated pork on a sesame seed bun with Oaxaca cheese, avocado, onions, and pineapple; or classic and delectable *chile rellenos*, cheese-stuffed, egg-battered poblano peppers in a smoky tomato sauce, sprinkled with ample crumbles of *cotija*.

Garden Café

Contemporary ✗

B1

4961 Broadway (bet. 207 & Isham Sts.)

Subway: Inwood - 207 St
Phone: 212-544-9480
Web: www.gardencafenyc.com
Prices: $$

Lunch & dinner daily

A chocolate brown awning dips over this sweet Inwood favorite, where a charming vibe and broad, contemporary menu that leans heavily on Latin American staples keep locals cheery. Inside, bare bistro tables and leather banquettes sit against golden-hued walls, while sultry jazz soothes the air.
Sit in the quaint outdoor garden and savor the special sangria and dark-grain breadbasket with tasty olive tapenade, but beware that dishes here are deliciously oversized. Peruse the daily specials or simply start with the likes of flavorful corn tortilla soup, before delving into the perfectly charred stuffed poblano—bursting with tender shrimp simmered in peppers and chorizo, served with Spanish rice, black beans, *pico de gallo*, and fresh corn tortillas.

Harley's Smokeshack

Barbecue ✗

C5

355 E. 116th St. (bet. 1st & 2nd Aves.)

Subway: 116 St (Lexington Ave.)
Phone: 212-828-6723
Web: www.harleyssmokeshack.org
Prices: $$

Lunch & dinner daily

This Harlem barrio is known for heart-thumping Latin eats, so the arrival of Harley's Southern barbecue was as refreshing as a glass of cold sweet tea. The exposed brick interior is dressed in cowboy trappings like boots, bull skulls, and leather saddles. It's a sight to behold—and to smell those tantalizingly smoky aromas.
The loud bar is best for those with a game and gulp in mind, while groups head to the back to devour the smoky Southern menu. Food here is a mouthwatering and gut-busting homage to this region, as in a barbecue-Frito pie piled with pulled pork, soft cheddar, and jalapeños. Expect shiny, dry-rubbed St. Louis-cut spareribs to carry a delicious dose of charred flavor, or hunks of brisket-stuffed meatloaf glazed with apple-barbeque sauce.

Hudson River Cafe

A3

Latin American 🍴🍴

697 W. 133rd St. (at Twelfth Ave.)

Subway: 125 St (Broadway)
Phone: 212-491-9111
Web: www.hudsonrivercafe.com
Prices: $$

Lunch Sat – Sun
Dinner nightly

There is nothing more NY than savoring tasty treats while basking in sunny Hudson River views. While the live music and occasional Amtrak rumble may elevate the decibels, lounging on the bi-level patio with a sweet cocktail or beer in hand restores the pleasure. Also lending a soothing aspect is their sleek interior dressed with wooden floors and mosaic tiles. Modern accents prevail with black, white, and red splashes.

Well-crafted fixtures cast a soft glow on flavorful Latin dishes, like *taquitos* stuffed with crispy coconut shrimp, or *costillas de buey*, braised short ribs in a pomegranate-Rioja reduction. Creations like *ceviche mixto* in a Bloody Mary *mojo* and a rich chocolate cake oozing at the center show the kitchen's love for purely fun fare.

Jin Ramen

A4

Japanese 🍴

3183 Broadway (bet. 125th St. & Tiemann Pl.)

Subway: 125 St (Broadway)
Phone: 646-559-2862
Web: www.jinramen.com
Prices: 💰💰

Lunch & dinner daily

This is the new kid on the newly revitalized block. Still, Jin Ramen's location at the foot of the 125th subway exit and the owners' ties to Columbia University are not the reasons why they see a constant stream of hungry diners. Nor is their success thanks to the divinely simple space with a few tables and dining counter set beneath warm, wood-textured walls. They just happen to be serving the best ramen anywhere above 59th Street.

Towering windows look upon Broadway, but bubbling stovetops may just be the view of choice here. Steaming bowls of *shio ramen* with bamboo shoots and a soy-flecked egg are churned out routinely by chefs who are all smiles when assembling *tonkotsu*, rich and salty with pork, or the exemplary *nankotsu kara-age* (fried chicken).

Max SoHa

A4

1274 Amsterdam Ave. (at 123rd St.)

Subway: 125 St (Broadway)   Lunch & dinner daily
Phone: 212-531-2221
Web: www.maxsoha.com
Prices: $$

It's wall-to-wall at this beloved trattoria, where cheerful patrons can be found slurping down heaping bowls of pasta in a lively atmosphere. A stone's throw from Columbia University, Max SoHa draws in a diverse crowd. The small, fetching space exudes a rustic air with its walls of exposed brick, weathered wood, mismatched dishware, and daily specials spelled out on chalkboards.

The Italian-only wine selection is terrific and well-priced, so sip a little *vino* to get things warmed up. Traditional Italian flavors get whipped into an array of antipasti, *risotti* (maybe salmon and zucchini?), and entrées such as grilled skirt steak with mushrooms and roasted potatoes. The house-made tiramisu gets a Cointreau kick, for a tasty twist on the original.

Melba's

A5

300 W. 114th St. (at Frederick Douglass Blvd.)

Subway: 116 St (Frederick Douglass Blvd.)   Lunch Sat – Sun
Phone: 212-864-7777   Dinner nightly
Web: www.melbasrestaurant.com
Prices: $$

This popular Morningside Heights joint stays elbow-to-elbow most nights despite small digs, loud music, and a slow-as-molasses staff. In fact, that's all part of the charm for the regulars that crowd into Melba's to listen to music, drink, and, of course, eat.

Solidly ensconced in what is recognized as Harlem's Gold Coast, Melba's custom chandeliers, plush banquettes, and exposed brick are cozy-chic incarnate. From the Southern bill of fare, go for down-home comfort, like Southern-fried chicken or eggnog waffles, while those looking to stay on the soulful lighter side stick to Melba's grilled vegetable Napoleon. No matter what, the heartbreakingly moist coconut layer cake infused with butter cream and dusted with coconut flakes is a must.

New Leaf Café

A2

American XX

1 Margaret Corbin Dr. (in Fort Tryon Park)

Subway: 190 St Lunch & dinner Tue – Sun
Phone: 212-568-5323
Web: www.newleafrestaurant.com
Prices: $$

Plumb in the heart of bucolic Fort Tryon Park stands the gorgeous stone edifice that houses New Leaf Café. Built in the 1930s and revitalized in 2001 by the New York Restoration Project, the cottage-like structure flaunts a vintage charm with its arched-brick doorways and windows, shaded by a bevy of lush trees. The interior is as enchanting with dark woods, stone walls, and seasonal artwork outfitting the amber-lit rooms; picturesque views of the verdant surroundings add to the allure.

Fresh, carefully sourced ingredients make for a wonderful menu of seasonal dishes. Savor the fantastically flavorful free-range chicken: moist on the inside, crisp on the outside—perfect. To end, the brioche bread pudding with homemade rum raisin ice cream is a must.

Red Rooster

B2

American XX

310 Lenox Ave. (bet. 125 & 126th Sts.)

Subway: 125 St (Lenox Ave.) Lunch & dinner daily
Phone: 212-792-9001
Web: www.redroosterharlem.com
Prices: $$$

Three cheers to Marcus Samuelsson, chef and Harlem resident, for his oh-so fun and enticing establishment that attracts a coterie of hip and savvy diners north of 96th St., adding to the already lively throng of proud Harlemites who've embraced this spot from the get-go.

Named after an old neighborhood speakeasy, the room boasts a bustling bar, an open kitchen, and a plethora of original works from neighborhood artists as well as a menu that follows its own rules. The melting pot of tweaked comfort favorites offers a bevy of options, such as the house Caesar smeared with smoked, *bottarga*-enriched dressing; a skillet piled high with jerked pork belly, baked beans, and fried egg; or the incredible fried yard bird with white gravy and hot sauce.

Manhattan ▶ Harlem, Morningside & Washington Heights

Ricardo Steakhouse

Steakhouse

C5

2145 Second Ave. (bet. 110th & 111th Sts.)

Subway: 110 St (Lexington Ave.) Dinner nightly
Phone: 212-289-5895
Web: www.ricardosteakhouse.com
Prices: $$

With an endless parade of regulars angling to score a seat at this bustling East Harlem steakhouse, a neighborhood cheer went up when Ricardo's announced it may-finally-be expanding next door with more seating. In recent years, this charming respite–with its cute backyard garden and cozy, exposed brick interior–has become a local hangout for the quickly gentrifying neighborhood scene.

Kick things off with flaky empanadas or a tender calamari salad, grilled *a la plancha*; and then get down to business with one of the house's spectacular cuts of beef. A T-bone special arrives perfectly charred, impressively thick and well-marbled, laced in a green peppercorn sauce and paired with mashed potatoes, French string beans, and a buttery handful of sautéed shrimp.

Saggio

Italian

A2

829 W. 181st St. (bet. Cabrini Blvd. & Pinehurst Ave.)

Subway: 181 St (Fort Washington Ave.) Lunch Sat – Sun
Phone: 212-795-3080 Dinner nightly
Web: N/A
Prices: $$

Washington Heights welcomed this Italian stallion with arms wide open—not surprising, given the area's Dominican culinary domination. Its arresting brown-and-white awning beckons from afar, while slim yet tall windows offer glimpses of this burgeoning strip.

Saggio sits on a sloping stretch, but that's where the bend ends. This is straightforward, solid Italian fare further evidenced by rich Mediterranean-style walls, dark parquet floors, and charming wrought-iron chandeliers. The space may be snug, but *lasagna verde* layered with creamy béchamel and salty pecorino; and deliciously moist *polpettone* braised in a rich tomato sauce emits *molto* heart.

While an apple tart streaked with cinnamon may be fairly standard, the genial staff is anything but.

Settepani

Italian XX

 B4

196 Lenox Ave. (at 120th St.)

Subway: 125 St (Lenox Ave.) Lunch & dinner daily
Phone: 917-492-4806
Web: N/A
Prices: $$

Settepani is a breath of fresh Italian air. Set in the Mount Morris Park Historic District and starring a sleek marble bar, ultra-modern banquettes, and fine linen tablecloths, it is lauded as a beacon of Harlem's "second Renaissance." Originally a café, this elegant restaurant now flaunts a stylish interior with slate and concrete flooring, towering windows draped with silk, and sultry lighting.

The backlit bar, premium sprits, and Romanesque-style busts are only part of the fun. Modern and ancient tunes blend happily in impressive classics like *pasta con sarde* perfectly infused with fennel fronds; *coniglio "a Purtusia"*, braised rabbit in an herbed wine broth; or *insalata alla melagrana*, bread salad mingling tomatoes, scallions, and pomegranate seeds.

Tre Otto

Italian XX

 B5

1408 Madison Ave. (bet. 97th & 98th Sts.)

Subway: 96 St (Lexington Ave.) Lunch & dinner daily
Phone: 212-860-8880
Web: www.treotto.com
Prices: $$

On this busy stretch of Madison find the quaint Tre Otto, displaying its own downtown charm in the heart of burgeoning Carnegie Hill. This kitchen shines with its collection of recipes gathered over time, with true Italian flare. That said, the focaccia is still the highlight and must be enjoyed no matter the mood. Their ample menu is sure to satisfy any taste.

Tables are tight at this narrow yet well-run spot. A display case adorned with panini and black slate bar is tantalizing to say the least. Boasting first-rate products are dishes like *polpette al sugo con crostini*, mini meatballs with grilled crostini; *penne con salsiccia e funghi*, penne tossed with sausage and mushrooms; and *torta di cioccolato*, a classic dark chocolate, flourless cake.

Vareli

A4

2869 Broadway (bet. 111th & 112th Sts.)

Subway: Cathedral Pkwy/110 St (Broadway)   Lunch & dinner daily
Phone: 212-678-8585
Web: www.varelinyc.com
Prices: $$

The dark wooden front sign indicates that Vareli is not your average Columbia University joint. Step inside this multi-level restaurant and wine bar and Morningside Heights seems a world away. In fact, you may feel that you are inside a wine vat, with curved wooden ceilings and a polished copper bar. Authentic Mediterranean wine barrels set for diners and a Japanese rock waterfall add to the intimate mood.

Let the well-chosen wine list complement a worthwhile starting selection of cheese and charcuterie; then proceed to an appetizer of flash-fried cauliflower served over tahini, chilies, and sage, drizzled with lemon juice. Finish with the expertly cooked duo of Hudson duck, served with an excellent peach-mint reduction and seasonal vegetables.

Zoma

A5

2084 Frederick Douglass Blvd. (at 113th St.)

Subway: 116 St (Frederick Douglass Blvd.)   Lunch Sat – Sun
Phone: 212-662-0620   Dinner nightly
Web: www.zomanyc.com
Prices: ⊆⊇

Ethiopian date night? If you're headed uptown to Harlem, look no further. Nestled among the new landscape of beer gardens and coffeehouses that flank this quickly-morphing area of Morningside Heights, sophisticated Zoma feels smart, cool, and modern—with a spare white interior lined in beautiful exotic relics and intricately woven fabrics.

The menu hits a similarly understated but classy note, with ample yet reasonably priced portions of authentic dishes like *timatim fitfit*, a refreshing starter of *injera* and tomato salad tossed with sweet onions, cilantro, and jalapeño peppers, dressed in a lemony olive oil; or *awaze tibs*, a slowly simmered lamb dish laced with onions, spicy green peppers, and the fragrant hint of cardamom and coriander.

Lower East Side

Clockwise from the north, this neighborhood is bounded by Houston Street, the East River, Pike Street, and the Bowery. While it has proudly retained the personality of its first wave of hard-working settlers, the area has embraced a steady change to its landscape brought on by artsy entrepreneurs lured to these formerly overlooked parts. A mostly low-lying neighborhood, with the exception of a few high-rise apartments and towering reminders of a recent real estate boom, the Lower East Side feels village-like in its stature with a palpable creative spirit.

Eastern European Eats

Before checking out the scene as it looks today, visit the Lower East Side Tenement Museum for a glimpse of the past. This restored structure dates back to 1863 and depicts what life was like for the swells of immigrant families, primarily Eastern European Jews that settled here in the early part of the last century fleeing famine and war, making this neighborhood the most densely populated area in the country. For a taste of yore, head to **Russ & Daughters** set on Houston Street. Opened in 1914, this beloved institution is a nosher's dream, and is famed for its holiday specialties, selection of smoked and cured fish, hearty bagels, and all things delicious, otherwise known as "appetizing."

ORCHARD STREET

Orchard Street, long the retail heart of this nabe was once dominated by the garment trade with stores selling fabrics and notions. Tailors remain in the area, offering inexpensive while-you-wait service, but boutiques selling handmade jewelry, designer skateboards, and handcrafted denim have also moved in. Shoppers looking to cool their heels should drop by **Il Laboratorio del Gelato** for an indulgent scoop—their gleaming location tempts residents and Houston Street passersby with a seasonally-changing roster of *gelati*.

For purchases with a more daily purpose, the **Essex Street Market** houses numerous purveyors of fresh produce, meat, and fish under one roof. The market is truly a gourmet's delight—it features two cheesemongers, a coffee roaster, a chocolatier, and **Shopsin's General Store**, a crazy joint notorious for its encyclopedic menu and cranky owner. By the 1950s, the melting pot that defined the Lower East Side became even more diverse with a new tide of immigrants, this time from Puerto Rico and other parts of Latin America. This population continues to be the dominant force today. For a sampling of home-style Latino fare (like *mofongo* and *pernil*), try **El Castillo de Jagua** on the corner of Essex and Rivington streets.

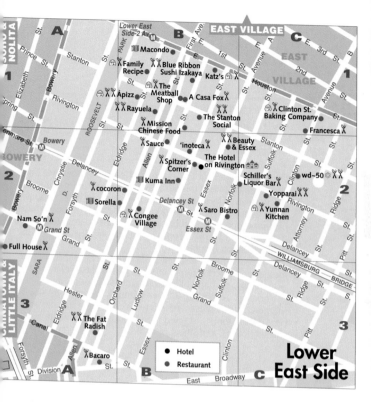

Lower
East Side

RIVINGTON STREET

Rivington Street embodies this area's hybrid of old and new. Located here is **Streit's Matzo Factory**, in operation since 1925, and **Economy Candy**, an emporium for old-fashioned sweets since 1937. During the day, the mood is pretty chill, perfect for idling in any one of the nearby coffee shops.

For a nutritious pick-me-up, **Teany** specializes in vegan vittles served in a café setting. Read: A plethora of teas and a super special brunch on weekends. Come evening, the street fills with meandering groups strolling to and from a number of popular dining spots. South of Delancey Street, Grand Street is home to well-maintained residential complexes and shops that cater to a cadre of longtime residents.

Carb-addicts should be afraid, very afraid, as this street is home to **Kossar's Bialys**, several kosher bakeries, and **Doughnut Plant**, where the owner offers an updated take on his grandfather's doughnut recipe in flavors like Valrhona chocolate. For that quintessential deli accent at home, head to **Pickle Guys** on the corner of Essex Street, stocked with barrel upon barrel of...you guessed it... pickles.

199

A Casa Fox

B1

173 Orchard St. (bet. Houston & Stanton Sts.)

Subway: Lower East Side - 2 Av
Phone: 212-253-1900
Web: www.acasafox.com
Prices: $$

Lunch Wed – Sat
Dinner Tue – Sun

Chef/owner Melissa Fox dishes out savory home-style Latin American cuisine in this attractive respite featuring a gracious service team. The setting is rustic as evidenced by its variously sized wooden tables topped with bottles of homemade *picante* sauce, exposed brick, and plaster-coated walls, and open kitchen. Family keepsakes offer a heartwarming glow by the working fireplace.

The menu reflects inspiration from the chef's Nicaraguan mother and offers a range of small plates like tender-crusted empanadas, perhaps filled with smoked Gouda and diced portobellos. A portion of the menu is devoted to slowly simmered stews presented in a terra-cotta bowl like the *arroz con pollo*—tomato-stained rice studded with white meat chicken, olives, and sweet peas.

Ápizz 🍴

B1

217 Eldridge St. (bet. Rivington & Stanton Sts.)

Subway: Lower East Side - 2 Av
Phone: 212-253-9199
Web: www.apizz.com
Prices: $$

Dinner Tue – Sun

It's hard not to fall in love with Ápizz. The room (dressed with honey-toned wood furnishings, amber glass votive holders, and slender mirror panels) has a bewitching rosy glow fueled by the star of the restaurant's open kitchen, a wood-fired brick oven. The motto here is "one room, one oven," and this area prettied by polished copper pots, dried flowers, and platters of produce is the command post for the preparations that follow on the menu.

The flame-kissed specialties bear a sophisticated rusticity as in a vibrant pile-up of warm octopus, diced potato, and cherry tomatoes; the L.E.S. pizza topped with chorizo; and *fazzoletti e granchio*—fresh handkerchief pasta with spicy tomato sauce and sweet nuggets of excellent quality lump crabmeat.

Bacaro

Italian

136 Division St. (bet. Ludlow & Orchard Sts.)

Subway: East Broadway
Phone: 212-941-5060
Web: www.bacaronyc.com
Prices: $$

Dinner Tue – Sun

From the owners of Peasant comes Bacaro, which takes its name and inspiration from the pub-like wine bars of Venice, and has a warm, inviting glow that sets it apart from its edgier surroundings. The sexy subterranean dining room (a former gambling parlor) evokes an ancient cellar with brick archways, weathered plaster, salvaged ceiling beams, and candlelit alcoves, which are perfect for groups. The marble-topped bar, illuminated by a blown glass chandelier, is a lovely spot to enjoy a *crostini di giorno*, or explore the all-Italian wine list.

The menu highlights Venetian traditions in offerings like tender octopus and cubed potato dressed with olive oil and parsley, or hearty dishes of creamy lasagna Treviso with smoked mozzarella and radicchio.

Beauty & Essex

Contemporary

146 Essex St. (bet. Rivington & Stanton Sts.)

Subway: Delancey St
Phone: 212-614-0146
Web: www.beautyandessex.com
Prices: $$

Lunch Sat – Sun
Dinner nightly

Chef/partner Chris Santos (also of The Stanton Social) shows off his prowess at creating utterly intriguing small plates at this chic multi-room bôite. The tempting roster offers ginger-glazed General Tso's monkfish garnished with broccoli and rice croquettes; sashimi of tuna, *tonnato*-style; and braised short rib tamales. The extensive menu is also hearty as in dishes like *garganelli* with spicy veal ragù baked in an earthenware crock.

A vestibule fashioned as a pawn shop fronts the dazzling setting which is outfitted in an earthy palette contrasted with metallic touches; upstairs there's a bar arranged against a backdrop of crystal decanters, and a small dining room featuring a collection of vintage lockets hung on the walls.

Blue Ribbon Sushi Izakaya

Japanese ✗✗

B1

187 Orchard St. (bet. E. Houston & Stanton Sts.)

Lunch & dinner daily

Subway: Lower East Side - 2 Av
Phone: 212-466-0404
Web: www.blueribbonrestaurants.com
Prices: $$

The newest member of the Blue Ribbon family calls the sleek Thompson LES hotel home. Boasting an understandably lounge-y mien the crepuscular setting thumps with beats and chatter. The counter offers more intimacy than the dining room, and the chefs here are not bashful about striking up a conversation. Coral upholstered furnishings accentuate the brightly colored fillets stocking the station along with speckled quail eggs and shelves of wood platters.

The hearty menu offers nigiri such as *Kindai akamai*, along with plenty of cooked tastes, like braised strips of tender tripe in tamari butter; sesame-glazed pork meatball *kushi-yaki*; or a fluffy bowlful of liver, bacon, and onion fried rice topped by a finely grated showering of hard-boiled egg.

Clinton St. Baking Company 😊

American ✗

C1

4 Clinton St. (bet. Houston & Stanton St.)

Lunch daily
Dinner Mon – Sat

Subway: Lower East Side - 2 Av
Phone: 646-602-6263
Web: www.clintonstreetbaking.com
Prices: 🍴🍴

Stop by this L.E.S. institution on just about any afternoon and chances are pretty good that you'll be greeted by a crowd waiting patiently for a table and their turn to partake in a menu of brunch-y delights, offered until 4:00 P.M. daily (6:00 P.M. on Sundays). Revered for his skill with carbohydrates, Chef Neil Kleinberg crafts buttermilk biscuits, brioche French toast, *huevos rancheros*, and an assortment of pancakes (think wild Maine blueberry or chocolate chunk) that are, in a word, awesome.

Simple wood furnishings and two small dining counters outfit the room, and the service is as gracious as one would hope. Dinnertime brings a quieter scene and comfort food favorites like fish tacos; spicy shrimp and grits; or buttermilk fried chicken.

cocoron

J a p a n e s e ✕

B2

61 Delancey St. (bet. Allen & Eldridge Sts.)

Subway: Delancey St
Phone: 212-925-5220
Web: www.cocoron-soba.com
Prices: 💰💰

Lunch & dinner Tue – Sun

Heartwarming soba is the specialty at this stall-sized spot. The room offers a handful of tables and is dominated by a hefty counter facing the busy little kitchen. Service is all smiles, and those needing assistance in making their selections are in good hands.

Four varieties of soba are offered. Besides being delicious, each one claims to have special restorative powers like the warm stamina soba—a pot of meaty rich broth boasting a sweet and salty essence and stocked with exceptional pork (ground and sliced), *tsukune*, burdock root, and shiitake, accompanied by buckwheat noodles for ample slurping. Side dishes are very fresh and include snacks such as kimchi, miso coleslaw, potato salad, and *okara*—the pulp leftover from soy milk production.

Congee Village 🙂

C h i n e s e ✕

B2

100 Allen St. (at Delancey St.)

Subway: Delancey St
Phone: 212-941-1818
Web: www.congeevillagerestaurants.com
Prices: 💰💰

Lunch & dinner daily

The menu at Congee Village is vast and its Cantonese focus is clear. The soothing namesake, rice porridge, is well-represented with 30 varieties offering a full spectrum of embellishments, from healthy vegetarian to pig's blood, to name a few. In addition to prized delicacies, find dim sum treats like delicately flaky Hong Kong-style scallion pancakes. Other ample offerings include chicken steamed in lotus leaf with mushrooms and diced Chinese sausage, slicked with soy sauce, ginger, and scallions; bitter melon stir-fried with black bean sauce; or specialties like pork ribs seasoned with shrimp paste and fried until crispy.

From the fringe of Chinatown, the multi-level setting trimmed with bamboo, brick, and stone is well-maintained and inviting.

Family Recipe 😊

J a p a n e s e ✗

B2

231 Eldridge St. (bet. Houston & Stanton Sts.)

Subway: Lower East Side - 2 Av
Phone: 212-529-3133
Web: www.familyrecipeny.com
Prices: $$

Lunch Sun
Dinner Tue – Sun

Large windows reveal Family Recipe's simple but chic setting that is framed by blond wood accents, glossy gray tables, and mod black plastic chairs. Lime green seating adds a pop of color at the L-shaped dining counter surrounding the open kitchen where Chef Akiko Thurnauer turns out her heartfelt home-style cooking.

Built upon a range of small plates, the menu offers several specials like mushroom and dried oyster dumplings with a delicate, translucent wrapping; or tempura rolls of thin green tea noodles wrapped around uni and accompanied by sheets of nori tempura. The rock shrimp and squid ink *okonomiyaki* is fantastic, and even Brussels sprouts excite— here they're pan-roasted with capers, pine nuts, and shallots and plated with miso.

The Fat Radish

C o n t e m p o r a r y ✗✗

A3

17 Orchard St. (bet. Canal & Hester Sts.)

Subway: East Broadway
Phone: 212-300-4053
Web: www.thefatradishnyc.com
Prices: $$

Lunch & dinner daily

When this former sausage factory was transformed into a handsome boîte brimming with a chic coterie, The Fat Radish became a classic Lower East Side success story. Bedecked with a poured concrete bar, exposed brick walls, and touches of salvaged wood, the space is embellished with fresh flowers, warm candlelight, and colorful art softening the room's industrial carriage.

The free-spirited kitchen tickles the palate with a gift of radishes dressed with olive tapenade. The eclectic carte presents an intriguing array that may include handmade tagliatelle tossed with chunky puréed broccoli rabe, sundried tomato, and anchovy breadcrumbs; or tart and fragrant monkfish *vindaloo* over a toothsome mound of wild rice accompanied by *raita* and long bean chutney.

Francesca

Spanish

C1

17 Clinton St. (bet. E. Houston & Stanton Sts.)

Subway: Lower East Side - 2 Av
Phone: 212-253-2303
Web: www.francescanyc.com
Prices: $$

Dinner Tue – Sat

The Franks (Castronovo and Falcinelli) turn to Spain, particularly the Basque country, at their re-tooled Clinton Street *spuntino*. *Pintxos* headline a compact slew of snacks like tuna-stuffed piquillo peppers; while small plates may yield a bowlful of warm bean ragout, each legume exquisitely soft yet solely intact, bobbing in roasted red pepper- and garlic-laced broth and strewn with herb oil. A smear of lush ricotta cuddling a dollop of *dulce de leche* dotted with bits of salted Marcona almonds hits all the right notes for a sweet sendoff. Francesca offers a convivial bar and separate, quieter, dining area; and throughout the location polished wood furnishings, sangria red walls, and a list of sherry-based cocktails produce an invitingly rustic charm.

Full House

Chinese

A2

97 Bowery (bet. Grand & Hester Sts.)

Subway: Grand St
Phone: 212-925-8083
Web: www.fullhousecafenyc.com
Prices: 🍴

Lunch & dinner daily

Can't pick between Shanghainese or Cantonese? Head down to Chinatown's Full House, a bright and modern restaurant that prepares both of these regional cuisines with an equally authentic hand. Dishes here may range from juicy pork and crab dumplings served with black vinegar and grated ginger, to vegetarian mock duck (tofu skin) roll infused with soy-based braising broth, and sautéed fresh eel with shaved yellow leeks in a soy and oyster sauce. Highlights include the sweet sautéed pumpkin, celery, and lotus root coated in garlic sauce.
Illuminated by neon accent lights, the main dining room features comfy booths and spacious tables ideal for families. Up a flight of glass-enclosed stairs is a second, semi-private room that also caters to larger groups.

'inoteca

Italian ✗

B2

98 Rivington St. (at Ludlow St.)

Subway: Delancey St
Phone: 212-614-0473
Web: www.inotecanyc.com
Prices: ⊜⊚

Lunch & dinner daily

This foodie favorite is a beloved dining destination thanks to the winning lineup of owners Jason Denton and Chef Eric Kleinman. Highly coveted wraparound sidewalk seating and knobby wood furnishings perfect the classic wine bar ambience that invites guests to stop by anytime.

Small plates make for an enjoyable repast and feature a range of cheeses, panini, *tramezzini*, and antipasti such as grilled calamari with soppressata and a spicy tomato vinaigrette. An array of heartier items like juicy slices of luscious *porchetta* plated with roasted sweet baby carrots atop a refreshing bundle of parsley flecked with grated horseradish offer highly satisfying sustenance.

Whether it's for a snack or spread, 'inoteca always serves up a reason to drop by.

Katz's ⊕

Deli ✗

B1

205 E. Houston St. (at Ludlow St.)

Subway: Lower East Side - 2 Av
Phone: 212-254-2246
Web: www.katzdeli.com
Prices: ⊜⊚

Lunch & dinner daily

One of the last-standing, old-time Eastern European spots on the Lower East Side, Katz's is a true NY institution. It's crowded, crazy, and packed with a panoply of characters weirder than a jury duty pool. Tourists, hipsters, blue hairs, and everybody in between flock here, so come on off-hours. Because it's really *that* good.

Walk inside, get a ticket, and don't lose it (those guys at the front aren't hosts—upset their system and you'll get a verbal beating). Then get your food at the counter and bring it to a first-come first-get table; or opt for a slightly less dizzying experience at a waitress-served table.

Nothing's changed in the looks or the taste. Matzoh ball soup, pastrami sandwich, potato latkes—everything is what you'd expect, only better.

Kuma Inn

Asian

B2

113 Ludlow St. (bet. Delancey & Rivington Sts.)

Subway: Delancey St   Dinner nightly
Phone: 212-353-8866
Web: www.kumainn.com
Prices:

 A veteran of Daniel and Jean Georges, New York City-born Chef/owner King Phojanakong presents ambrosial pan-Asian tapas that reflect the multicultural influences of his Thai-Filipino background.

Come as you are—Kuma Inn doesn't put on airs. The discreetly marked setting is located on the second floor of a nondescript walk-up. The menu is best suited for grazing so bring reinforcements to ensure a sampling of the chef's signature items—perhaps cubes of firm tofu sautéed with earthy wood ears and fragrant Thai basil sliced by spicy soy and mirin; slices of Chinese sausage bathed in a Thai chili-lime sauce; or drunken shrimp imbibed in chili-sparked sake. Genteel service and a playlist of the chef's favorite tracks add to the mood of this spartan room.

Macondo

Latin American

B1

157 E. Houston St. (bet. Allen & Eldridge Sts.)

Subway: Lower East Side - 2 Av   Lunch Sat – Sun
Phone: 212-473-9900   Dinner Mon– Sat
Web: www.macondonyc.com
Prices: **$$**

 The vibe at this fun spot from the owners of Rayuela matches that of its high-traffic location. Weather permitting, the front bar opens onto the street and is abuzz with thirty-somethings sipping fruit-forward cocktails (think fresh strawberries and pisco spiked with jalapeño, lemongrass, and Kaffir lime leaf). Inside, the long, narrow space features shelves of Latin provisions, an open kitchen, rows of communal tables, and low, lounge-like booths.

Perfect for a group, crowds come here to linger (until 2:00 A.M. on weekends) over the pan-Latin small plates covering all the bases: ceviches, tacos, arepas, and *cocas* (flatbreads). A large plate of *mofongo de pulpo* shows off mashed green plantain with octopus, olive-caper-tomato sauce, garlic and bacon.

The Meatball Shop 😋

B1

84 Stanton St. (bet. Allen & Orchard Sts.)

Subway: Lower East Side - 2 Av   Lunch & dinner daily
Phone: 212-982-8895
Web: www.themeatballshop.com
Prices: 😑😑

It is hard to imagine a restaurant truer to its name than this. The focal point of everything here is the mighty meatball, perhaps served as the classic beef with prosciutto and fresh ricotta; spicy pork studded with pickled cherry peppers; chicken flavored with white wine and fennel seeds; a vegetarian option; or daily special. These five incarnations have a choice of five sauces, such as classic tomato, spicy meat, mushroom gravy, Parmesan cream, and pesto. Dessert means ice cream—in floats or sandwiches.

The compact room is a perfect fit for its cool, comfortable locale and is equipped with a communal table, dining counter, brick red walls, vintage photos, and an open kitchen. The success has spilled over to Greenwich Village and Williamsburg outposts.

Mission Chinese Food

B1

154 Orchard St. (bet. Rivington & Stanton Sts.)

Subway: Lower East Side - 2 Av   Lunch Fri – Tue
Phone: 212-529-8800   Dinner Thu – Tue
Web: www.missionchinesefood.com
Prices: $$

Danny Bowien created a sensation with his Mission Chinese Food in San Francisco and now brings his wares cross country to Manhattan. What looks like a banal takeout shop is in actuality the hotly anticipated spot, whose tiny threshold is hung with a backlit display menu and crammed with boxes of...what else...takeout containers.

After patiently waiting in line, you are led past the kitchen (Chef Bowien may be in the house) to a small room crowded with ravenous foodies downing *shochu* cocktails, and small tables piled high with such uniquely aggressive cooking that may yield delicious Shanghainese rice cakes tossed with thrice-cooked bacon and chili oil-soaked tofu skin; or a sizzling platter of lamb breast billowing cumin-scented smoke.

Nam Sơn

A2

Vietnamese ✗

245 Grand St. (bet. Bowery and Chrystie St.)

Subway: Grand St
Phone: 212-966-6507
Web: N/A
Prices: 🍘

Lunch & dinner daily

Nam Sơn will have you wishing you lived closer to Chinatown—enormous praise given the chaos flanking these "mean streets." But if you did, you'd be eating here all the time. This fresh, flavorful Vietnamese spot off the Doyers-Baxter trail may have like neighbors, yet they shine by dint of a pleasant interior and speedy staff.

The value here is incredible. With prices that can't be beat, Nam Sơn fills its ample, brightly-lit room with typical faves like *goi cuon*, a summer roll bursting with poached shrimp and pork and a rice noodles wrapped in paper. *Cha gio*, well-seasoned pork and vegetable spring rolls with *nuoc cham* for dipping; and *pho tai*, deliciously spiced beef broth floating with noodles are nothing short of a savory triumph.

Rayuela

B1

Latin American ✗✗

165 Allen St. (bet. Rivington & Stanton Sts.)

Subway: Lower East Side - 2 Av
Phone: 212-253-8840
Web: www.rayuelanyc.com
Prices: $$

Lunch Sat – Sun
Dinner nightly

This sleek Lower East Side gem helped kick off the neighborhood's wave of Pan-Latin fusion spots—and locals quickly embraced its hip vibe and deeply flavorful food. Years later, the loyalty remains: despite more and more competition, Rayuela continues to pack them in.

What's the secret? For starters, dark wood, sexy lighting, and great music make this a comfortable setting for an important date or night out with friends. Moreover, the food continues to be solid: Try the red snapper, marinated in a ginger-soy-citrus sauce with a flurry of bright julienned peppers, cucumbers, and red chili peppers; the gorgeous seafood paella humming with lemongrass, coconut milk, and ginger; or mouthwatering corn arepas with *cabra* cheese and sweet agave nectar.

Saro Bistro

102 Norfolk St. (bet. Delancey & Rivington Sts.)

Subway: Delancey St
Phone: 212-505-7276
Web: www.sarobistro.com
Prices: $$

Lunch Sat – Sun
Dinner Tue – Sun

 Inspired by the cooking of his Bosnian grandmother, Israeli-born Chef/owner Eran Elhalal serves cuisine that tours the Balkans from his quaint bistro. The petite 22-seat room is comfortable and pleasantly arranged with papered walls, wood furnishings, and dried flower arrangements. Tables are set with vintage flatware, mismatched floral-rimmed china, and a glass filled with slender green chilies to spice up your meal.

The menu offers a rich trip through this unique and eclectic region with specialties that include a daily offering of savory pie accompanied by kefir; grilled *cevapcici* kebabs served with zucchini fritters and a quenelle of fresh cheese; homemade linguini with clams; and slow-roasted lamb shoulder with braised cabbage.

Sauce

78-84 Rivington St. (at Allen St.)

Subway: Lower East Side - 2 Av
Phone: 212-420-7700
Web: www.saucerestaurant.com
Prices:

Lunch & dinner daily

 Frank Prisinzano (of Supper and Lil' Frankie's) adds another venue to his clique of simply named restaurants with this new arrival. Already looking well lived-in (even a bit disheveled at times) the décor tilts toward homey with mismatched wallpaper and lacy café curtains dressing the corner setting.

The ingredient-driven menu proudly reads like a red-sauce joint with a range of zesty Italian-American fare. "Sloppy sandwiches" are a tasty lunchtime option, while heartier appetites will be sated by grandmother's tomato gravy ladled over a heap of fresh *cencione* pasta sided by an order of ragù by the piece—grass-fed beef meatballs, Italian sausage, or braciole. House-butchered meats are showcased in the likes of a gutsy *bollito misto*.

Schiller's Liquor Bar

European

C2

131 Rivington St. (at Norfolk St.)

Subway: Delancey St
Phone: 212-260-4555
Web: www.schillersny.com
Prices: $$

Lunch & dinner daily

Schiller's, like Keith McNally's wildly successful Balthazar and Pastis, touts a magical mix; like the most popular girl in school, this spot knows how to pop in a crowd. However, its components are breezy retro-bistro good looks, comfort food favorites, and a prime location straddling a choice corner of the Lower East Side. The straightforward menu makes things easy with choices like chicken pot pie, fish and chips, or steak with perfect frites.

As to how best to describe the atmosphere that draws locals, day trippers, and low-key celebrities alike, we direct you to the cheeky house wine list, categorized into *cheap, decent,* or *good.* A terrific cocktail selection rounds out the drink list. Pastries from Balthazar Bakery are a brunch-time hit.

Sorella

Italian

B2

95 Allen St. (bet. Broome & Delancey Sts.)

Subway: Delancey St
Phone: 212-274-9595
Web: www.sorellanyc.com
Prices: $$

Dinner Tue – Sun

For leisurely yet serious small plates, step inside Sorella's recently expanded, whitewashed brick dining area and glass-enclosed atrium. The Northern Italian menu brings a range of cheeses, meats, and *qualcosina*, which translates as "a little something." These finely tuned dishes may include the likes of Hearst Ranch beef carne *cruda* (note the owner here is Emma Hearst, great-great-granddaughter of William Randolph). Expect pastas like *tajarin* with lamb ragù, black pepper ricotta, pistachios, and mint. Special two-course prix-fixe meals are offered Tuesday through Saturday.

Explore the expansive selection of wines by the glass, with twenty choices priced under $15.

Next door, Stellina is a sweet spot for a pick-me-up.

Spitzer's Corner

Gastropub ✗

101 Rivington St. (at Ludlow St.)

Subway: Delancey St
Phone: 212-228-0027
Web: www.spitzerscorner.com
Prices: 😑

Lunch & dinner daily

This modern New York gastropub strives to highlight its honest, local sensibilities; but most importantly, this spot perfectly complements the casual cool of a weekend night on the Lower East. With old pickle-barrel slats for walls and a zinc bar, the multi-room space is effortlessly stylish and comfortable, much to the pleasure of the trendy crowds who pile in, despite the no-reservations policy. Happily, they chill at the bar or settle into a long, sleek bench while nursing a selection from the 40 smartly chosen beers on tap, or the small but studied by-the-glass wine list.

The menu offers a host of salads and sandwiches, but those looking for a proper meal can go with plates of hand-cut French fries, truffled mac' and cheese, and Kobe sliders.

The Stanton Social

Fusion ✗✗

99 Stanton St. (bet. Ludlow & Orchard Sts.)

Subway: Lower East Side - 2 Av
Phone: 212-995-0099
Web: www.thestantonsocial.com
Prices: $$

Lunch Sat – Sun
Dinner nightly

A beloved haunt in the LES, The Stanton Social has a richly tailored design that pays homage to the haberdashers and seamstress shops that once dotted this trendy nabe. Vintage hand mirrors, woven leather straps, and wine shelves laid out in a herringbone pattern outfit the low-lit, dark-wood furnished cave.

Opened in 2005, this grand boîte is still going strong; a testament to the enjoyable cuisine on offer. The generous order of globally-inspired preparations, executed under the watch of Chef/partner Chris Santos, brings on cooking with gusto and includes sliders, a house signature; hand-pulled chicken arepas kicked with tomatillo sauce and pickled jalapeños; and rounds of crispy eggplant Parmesan finished with mozzarella, micro basil, and basil oil.

wd~50 ✿

Contemporary 🍴🍴

C2

50 Clinton St. (bet. Rivington & Stanton Sts.)

Subway: Delancey St   Dinner nightly
Phone: 212-477-2900
Web: www.wd-50.com
Prices: $$$$

Travis Huggett

The history of Clinton Street's evolution into an impressive restaurant row dates back to 1999 and stars Chef Wylie Dufresne whose renegade cooking turned heads at the gone but not forgotten 71 Clinton Fresh Food. wd~50 opened in 2003 as the pioneer of molecular gastronomy in New York and has been thrilling diners ever since. Recently, the chef has turned the page to a new chapter by revamping the experience, switching to a tasting menu in lieu of an à la carte listing. Nostalgic diners can find solace in the prix-fixe of classics, "From the Vault."

The room hosts sophisticated guests in an environment warmed by wood furnishings with a pop of cobalt and sienna. Take a peek in the kitchen; chances are the chef is in house.

wd~50's 12-course sequence displays, as much as ever, the chef's unique trademark of skill and wit: a twirl of lobster roe "noodles" and coriander-infused brown butter is perched atop the most flavorful celery ever; fragrant *pho* enriched with foie gras is propped up by pickled bean sprouts and puffed beef tendon; and chalk white slow-cooked turbot is set against black licorice *pil-pil*. Desserts dazzle with a mad scientist slant, as in an amazing hunk of yuzu milk ice.

Yopparai

151 Rivington St. (bet. Clinton & Suffolk Sts.)

Subway: Delancey St   Dinner Mon – Sat
Phone: 212-777-7253
Web: www.yopparainyc.com
Prices: **$$**

Classic Japanese minimalism and reverent service set this sake pub apart from other fun but more boisterous *izakaya*. Press the buzzer to enter and step inside to find a comfortable room in a soothing palette of pale grey and blue. A seat at the counter is the best option, but tables are also available.

The array of small plates is striking, as in "Yopparai-style" sashimi made with toro chopped so finely that the taste is almost cloud-like, mixed with green onion, pickled daikon, and served on ice with sheets of warmed nori for wrapping. *Yaki onigiri* are crisp, golden brown with brushed soy, and deliciously hot from the grill.

And to drink, go with sake. The chefs' backdrop is stacked with *masu* and an arrangement of opened bottles awaiting your selection.

Yunnan Kitchen

79 Clinton St. (bet. Delancey & Rivington Sts.)

Subway: Delancey St   Dinner Wed – Mon
Phone: 212-253-2527
Web: www.yunnankitchen.com
Prices: **$$**

This classy new Chinese offering hones in on the province of Yunnan, located in Southwestern China and bordering Vietnam, Laos, and Myanmar. The kitsch-free dining room features windows framing the Clinton Street scene. Inside, find a focused menu that might feature such fresh and flavorful creations as wide ribbons of firm tofu tossed with an abundance of fresh cilantro, mint, and smoky chili oil; delicious and delicate potato croquettes dusted with a mouthwatering blend of salt and spices; and spicy pork *shao kao*—pounded nuggets grilled on a skewer.

The day's market bounty is displayed on the carte and has included a bowl brimming with fluffy, minimally-seasoned fried rice stocked with chopped garlic and plump, bright green sweet peas.

Midtown East & Murray Hill

Started by the Vanderbilt's in the 19th century, then saved from the wrecking ball with the help of Jacqueline Kennedy Onassis in the 20th century, Grand Central Terminal has somehow become a 21st century foodie haven.

Grand Central Terminal

A perfect day at the world's largest train station begins with a coffee amid the work-bound masses from **Joe's** (**Oren's** also showcases some first-rate beans). Lunch options range from the multi-ethnic food court offerings (**Café Spice** for Indian, **Mendy's** for kosher, **Zocalo** for Mexican), to the prized concourse restaurants situated beneath the celestial ceiling murals. Nonetheless, one of Manhattan's most beloved icons, the **Oyster Bar**, has been tucked into the cavernous lower level since 1913. While they may be the most beloved spot for all things bivalve, it is really their famed oyster stew that has crowds returning time and again. But first, be sure to visit the "whispering gallery" located near its entrance, where low, ceramic arches allow whispers to sound like shouts.

Come happy hour, Grand Central continues to inspire with **Campbell Apartment**—for those who meet the dress code. This 1920s office of railroad mogul John W. Campbell was restored and re-opened as one of the area's swankier stops for a famously dry martini.

Those seeking a quiet night of home cooking can simply walk across the concourse to visit the market, for a stunning array of gourmet items. Fishmongers, produce stands, butchers, bakeries, florists, and possibly the best spices in the city are all found here.

Grand Central Terminal is also a perfect microcosm of its eastern midtown home, because stretching through this neighborhood is the same diversity of shopping and dining. Even Eli Zabar has its very own outpost here, namely **Eli's Bread** that boasts a host of homemade bread, breakfast pastries, and creamy coffee cakes. Residents of Beekman and Sutton are also proud of their very own top fishmonger (**Pisacane Seafood**), cheese shop (**Ideal Cheese**), butcher (**Simchick Meats**), bagel and lox shop (**Tal Bagels**), and to complete any dinner party, florist (**Zeze**). One of the area's better-kept secrets is **Spices and Tease**, a boutique store specializing in myriad varieties of exotic teas, spices, and spice blends. If you missed Mexican street cart **El Rey del Sabor**'s notoriously heart-warming huaraches, be sure to hunt them down and get your fill for the following day. **Schnitzel & Things** follows suit with a truck-full of classic yet creative schnitzels crisped to golden brown perfection. Also, find some of the sweetest treats in town, from cupcakes at **Magnolia** and **Crumbs**, to chocolates at **Teuscher**'s. While **Dag Hammarskjöld Plaza**

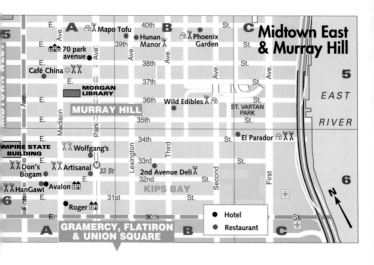

Within the map:

E. Ave. **A** Mapo Tofu 40th St.
Hunan Manor 39th **B** Phoenix Garden St.
E. 70 park avenue 38th
Café China 37th
MORGAN LIBRARY
Madison Park E. 36th Wild Edibles
MURRAY HILL ST. VARTAN PARK
E. 35th
Lexington Third E. 34th St. El Parador
EMPIRE STATE BUILDING Wolfgang's
Don's Bogam Artisanal 33rd 33 St 2nd Avenue Deli
Second First E. 32nd St.
HanGawi Avalon KIPS BAY
Roger E. 31st St.
E. 30th St.
Fifth

A GRAMERCY, FLATIRON & UNION SQUARE **B**

• Hotel
• Restaurant

EAST

RIVER

N

Greenmarket may by dwarfed by Union Square, it has just the right amount of everything to satisfy its neighbors.

Japantown

Within these overtly commuter, residential, and internationally-focused midtown nooks, is a very sophisticated Japantown, with casual *izakayas* and secreted-away hostess clubs lining the area east of Lexington. For a light lunch or snack, sample the ultimate *onigiri* (rice balls) at **Oms/b**. True Japanophiles should stop by **Cafe Zaiya** for their mouthwatering array of udon dishes (maybe the *kitsune*?); or the reputed **Japanese Culinary Center** filled with gorgeous Japanese tabletop items like glassware, gleaming knives, shiny ceramics, as well as kitchenware, unique ingredients, and other imported delicacies. Finally, another udon hot spot is **Onya** that showcases a massive selection from *kamaage* and curry udon, to fragrant vegetable soup udon.

MURRAY HILL

Younger and quieter than its northern neighbor, Murray Hill has its own distinct restaurant vibe. Here, faster and casual finds thrive by dint of hungry twenty-somethings craving pizza or cheesesteak. Afterwards, they move on to their favored Third Avenue watering holes to hoot and holler with buddies over Bud Lights while catching the snowboarding finals. This is the Murray Hill of recent college grads spilling out onto sidewalks of **Bar 515** or **Third and Long**. But, this is only one Murray Hill. The other rises with the sun over pristine brownstones and apartment towers, awakening young families who gather amid blooming flowers at St. Vartan Park or chat with neighbors over chopped liver and smoked fish at **Sarge's Deli**. These are the (slightly) senior locals of Murray Hill—they love it here and will remain faithful residents until well-after the frat party has ended.

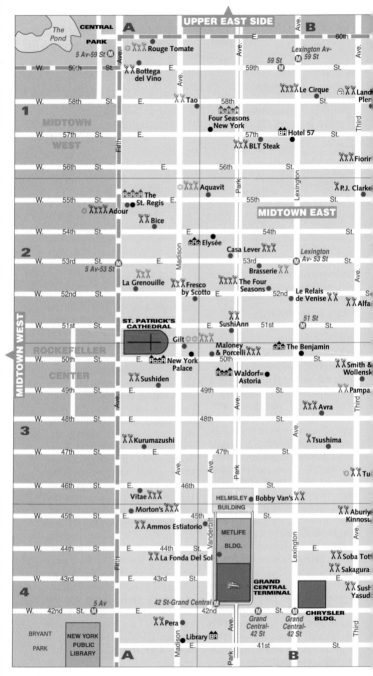

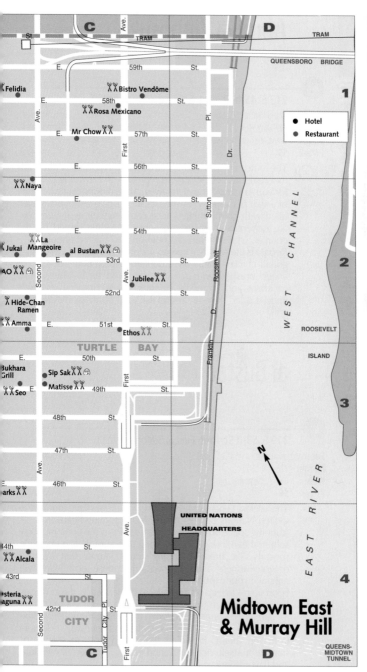

C · Ave. · D

St. · TRAM · TRAM

QUEENSBORO BRIDGE

Felidia

E. · 59th · St.

✕✕ Bistro Vendôme

E. · 58th · St.

✕✕ Rosa Mexicano

Mr Chow ✕✕

E. · 57th · St.

First · Dr.

E. · 56th · St.

Ave.

● Hotel
● Restaurant

✕✕ Naya

E. · 55th · St.

Sutton

E. · 54th · St.

Jukai · ✕✕ La
Mangeoire · al Bustan ✕✕

E. · 53rd · St.

Roosevelt

Second

Ave.

AO ✕✕ · Jubilee ✕✕

52nd · St.

Hide-Chan
Ramen

D

✕✕ Amma

E. · 51st · St.

Ethos ✕✕

WEST CHANNEL

TURTLE · BAY

50th · St.

Franklin

ROOSEVELT

Bukhara
Grill

Sip Sak ✕✕

First

ISLAND

✕✕ Seo · E. · Matisse ✕✕ · 49th · St.

48th · St.

47th · St.

N

E. · 46th · St.

arks ✕✕

Ave.

UNITED NATIONS
HEADQUARTERS

EAST RIVER

4th · St.

✕✕ Alcala

43rd · St.

steria
aguna ✕✕

Second

TUDOR

42nd · Tudor City Pl. · St.

CITY

First

**Midtown East
& Murray Hill**

QUEENS-
MIDTOWN
TUNNEL

C · D

Aburiya Kinnosuke

Japanese ✗✗

B4

213 E. 45th St. (bet. Second & Third Aves.)

Subway: Grand Central - 42 St
Phone: 212-867-5454
Web: www.aburiyakinnosuke.com
Prices: $$

Lunch Mon – Fri
Dinner nightly

The route may be dark and narrow, but this particular one leads to a real and honest *izakaya* replete with crowning cocktails for you to sample the night away. Aburiya Kinnosuke has a bit of a split personality: by day, it's an upscale bento box haven filled with chirpy midtowners; come nighttime, it turns into an authentic, intimate lair. Serious foodies should hit the counter, while the rest can peel-off into a private nook.

Robata is the real deal here so go for the *tsukune*—deliciously grilled chicken meatloaves dunked in cold poached egg, or *anago* brushed with spicy wasabi and fresh lemon. Also excellent and incredibly popular are top-quality products (maybe dried skate fin or cod fish roe?) cooked on a *shichirin* grill.

al Bustan 😀

Lebanese ✗✗

C2

319 E. 53rd St. (bet. First & Second Aves.)

Subway: Lexington Av - 53 St
Phone: 212-759-5933
Web: www.albustanny.com
Prices: $$

Lunch & dinner daily

This tireless Lebanese favorite and longtime staple among the United Nations power crowds, is still turning heads from its stunning space. Whether sipping drinks in the contemporary subterranean lounge, or indulging in one of their home-style specials (like the outstanding *kouzy*), know that a sense of graciousness and old-school Lebanese hospitality will enhance your experience.

Food seems to leap off the plate, as evidenced by the gorgeous Lebanese mezze of fattoush, *hommos bi lahmeh*, *foul medamas*, or *samboussek jibneh* (tasty little dumplings). Prix-fixe options at $45 or $50 a head offer a nice way to sample from the menu, including the mixed grill, *mashawi*, for sharing. In itself, rice can sound boring, but here the texture and flavor is fantastic.

Adour

French 𝗫𝗫𝗫𝗫

A2

2 E. 55th St. (at Fifth Ave.)

Subway: 5 Av – 53 St	Dinner Tue – Sat
Phone: 212-710-2277	
Web: www.adour-stregis.com	
Prices: $$$$	

Bruce Buck

Entering through the St. Regis Hotel only enhances the grandeur of dining at Adour. Within the ballroom setting, elaborate moldings, floor-to-ceiling etched glass screens, and wine display cabinets convey a sense of old-world luxury. There is an inescapable feeling of wealth and opulence in the central room, where moneyed regulars and residents are seated (solo diners are relegated to a satellite alcove). No matter where you sit, the smartly uniformed servers are at times overly scripted, but always precise and formal.

This carefully prepared cuisine reflects a classical and refined cooking with modern interpretations. Skill and talent are paramount in a dish of pan-fried sweetbreads atop bright green sweet peas, diced carrots, and veal jus; or a lush cocotte of soft-cooked farm egg with a splash of cream, melting layers of Gruyère, caramelized ham, and toast points that are perfect for sopping up the velvety yolk.

Desserts may dazzle with deep bowls that arrive topped with a thin chocolate cookie lid and gold leaf at the center—tableside, the server ladles a robust coffee granite through this to reveal dark chocolate sorbet, crème Chantilly, and marshmallow hidden beneath.

Alcala

C4

246 E. 44th St. (bet. Second & Third Aves.)

Subway: Grand Central - 42 St
Phone: 212-370-1866
Web: www.alcalarestaurant.com
Prices: $$$

Lunch Mon – Fri
Dinner nightly

Alcala de Henares is a central Spanish city as diverse as the UN itself. Ironically, this chirpy restaurant of the same name also caters to a global clientele. What Alcala lost in size (now in smaller quarters), they have gained with an ever-courteous service staff. That said, reservations are a must in this cozy spot dressed with buttery yellow walls, hand-painted ceramics, and a tiny bar dripping with Spanish wines. Serving the rustic cuisine of Northern Spain, the menu has included *salmonrejo*, a tangy, chilled gazpacho topped with chopped Serrano ham; *vieras a la plancha*, seared diver scallops drizzled with a piquillo pepper sauce; or simple and none-too-sweet almond and hazelnut *semifreddo de almendras*, with crisp batons of puff pastry.

Alfama

B2

214 E. 52nd St. (bet. Second & Third Aves.)

Subway: Lexington Av - 53 St
Phone: 212-759-5552
Web: www.alfamanyc.com
Prices: $$

Lunch & dinner daily

Neighborhood locals and Portuguese patrons love Alfama's relaxed yet elegant setting. There's no mistaking that inimitable Portuguese flair—blue-and-white ceramic tiles, communal tables crafted from pristine marble, and pottery add rustic touches, while the illuminated glass tile map of the world on the wall is an attractive focal point.
Choose from *petiscos*–the Portuguese version of tapas–like brandy flambéed sausage, shrimp turnovers, and juicy rabbit meatballs. Comforting seafood stews, and cod and shrimp gratin are heartier choices. *Galito gerlhado*, grilled chicken with *piri piri* and fried yucca, is one of many faves, but seafood is the star. Three courses for under $30 at lunch, makes Alfama popular with midtowners.

Amma

Indian

C2

246 E. 51st St. (bet. Second & Third Aves.)

Subway: 51 St
Phone: 212-644-8330
Web: www.ammanyc.com
Prices: $$

Lunch & dinner daily

Make your way up a few stairs to enter Amma's home, an elegant parlor arranged with close-knit, white-robed tables set atop carpeted floors. This is indeed Indian food—brought to you in a colonial-style townhouse in frenzied midtown. Amma's "living room" feels bright with big windows, saffron-tinted walls, chaste artwork, and a chandelier twinkling upon an affluent set.

Brimming at lunch with delicacies like *prawn masala* steeped with coconut, Amma becomes romantic at night. In keeping with its mien, warm yet vigilant servers present you with Indian hospitality at its finest—in the form of *tandoori* sea bass with plantain dumplings; *bagharey baingan* (eggplant stuffed with a spicy peanut sauce); and *bhindi ka raita*, all soaked up by a basket of breads.

Ammos Estiatorio

Greek

B4

52 Vanderbilt Ave. (at 45th St.)

Subway: Grand Central - 42 St
Phone: 212-922-9999
Web: www.ammosnewyork.com
Prices: $$$

Lunch & dinner Mon – Sat

Duck into sunny and sophisticated Ammos, right across from Grand Central Terminal, and leave gray skies behind. Favoring a certain modern Mediterranean-meets-Manhattan elegance, this upscale Greek brightens the midtown lunch crowds with white market umbrellas hanging from the ceiling, warm yet efficient service, and a well-run kitchen serving time-honored favorites with contemporary flair.

The fresh and modern boosts are clear in *spanikopita*, prepared with tangy feta and spinach between two crisp, golden layers of phyllo, jazzed up with light tomato sauce and mint olive oil. Salads, the Ammos fries, and a three-course prix-fixe are most popular at lunch, while quieter dinners feature a large selection of entrées and fresh fish by-the-pound.

Aquavit

Manhattan ▶ Midtown East & Murray Hill

B2

65 E. 55th St. (bet. Madison & Park Aves.)

Subway: 5 Av - 53 St
Phone: 212-307-7311
Web: www.aquavit.org
Prices: $$$$

Lunch Mon – Fri
Dinner Mon – Sat

Evan Sung

With so much ado made of Nordic cuisine in recent years, Aquavit might have rested on its laurels as New York's steadfast home to contemporary Scandinavian cooking. To the contrary, everything here seems to have been enlivened and reconfigured, from the modern and elegantly functional dining rooms, to the precise presentations from Chef Marcus Jernmark on dishes that recall elements of nature through slabs of slate and deep grey ceramics. What was becoming perhaps a bit tired now feels incredibly cool and of the moment. Service remains warm and well-trained.

Expect to be fascinated from the first delicious bite, which might be a small jam jar opened at the table to reveal a plume of enticing smoke infusing juniper-crusted tuna with a dollop of caviar. A fantastic composition of flavors and textures combine in the sweet-cured herring with American *löjrom*, steamed potatoes, *västerbotten* cheese, dill, rye crisps, pickled shallots, and citrusy foam. *Lardo*-baked halibut is so impossibly tender that it verges on the consistency of silky-salty custard, with deep, earthy beets.

Desserts are equally inspired, as in the salmonberry trio with macadamia "snow" and sour cream panna cotta.

Artisanal

French ✗✗

2 Park Ave. (entrance on 32nd St.)

Subway: 33 St
Phone: 212-725-8585
Web: www.artisanalbistro.com
Prices: $$

Lunch & dinner daily

Terrance Brennan's much-loved restaurant serves a whole roster of bistro delights (think chicken paillard, tuna niçoise, and steamed mussels) but the real fans of Artisanal treat the place like their own private cheese club. Brennan has a passion for the stuff, and the restaurant has oodles of varieties as well as an on-site cheese cave—that you can enjoy it in a lively, upscale brasserie only makes it even more fun.

Choose a glass of wine from the extensive list, and get to work on a perfectly prepared basket of *gougères*, followed by one of the house fondues; or an irresistible *croque monsieur*, sporting tender prosciutto, soft Gruyère, and a delicious lick of browned béchamel, paired with a crunchy stack of house-made chips.

Avra

Greek ✗✗✗

141 E. 48th St. (bet. Lexington & Third Aves.)

Subway: 51 St
Phone: 212-759-8550
Web: www.avrany.com
Prices: $$$

Lunch & dinner daily

Let's face it. Midtown, awash in gray and black, can sometimes have you singing the blues. But wait! Next time you're feeling a little low, get your dose of sunshine inside Avra. This appealing and bright *estiatorio*, with plenty of outdoor seating, brings the warmth of the Greek islands to the concrete jungle.

This dressed-up taverna is always jammed with midtowners, business types, and tourists who come for the comfortable sophistication and the pleasing menu. Whether here for brunch, lunch, or dinner, the mostly Greek menu is large and offers everything from *saganaki* and souvlaki to fresh grilled fish (on display at the back).

High prices and the less-than-sunny staff could be seen as drawbacks, but the delicious food and pleasant setting shine through.

Bice

Italian XX

7 E. 54th St. (bet. Fifth & Madison Aves.)

Subway: 5 Av - 53 St
Phone: 212-688-1999
Web: www.bicenewyork.com
Prices: $$$

Lunch & dinner daily

In a neighborhood teeming with subdued, upscale façades, Bice cuts a cheerful figure with its bright canopies and streams of people tucking to and fro. Perhaps it can't help but give off some of that upbeat Milan bustle—the restaurant, which now boasts over 30 locations world-wide, began in Italy's most fashionable city.

Judging from the longevity of this location, the formula (solid upscale Northern Italian cuisine) works. Open for lunch and dinner, Bice stays thumping day and night with fashionable diners tucking into tender tagliolini with lobster, shiitake mushrooms, blistered tomatoes, chunky tomato sauce, and a float of basil chiffonade. Desserts range from simple to decadent crispy *cantuccini* laced with roasted almonds, or tiramisu *della* Bice.

Bistro Vendôme

French XX

405 E. 58th St. (bet. First Ave. & Sutton Pl.)

Subway: 59 St
Phone: 212-935-9100
Web: www.bistrovendomenyc.com
Prices: $$

Lunch & dinner daily

Bistro Vendôme brings a breath of fresh air to stuffy Sutton Place with this sunny and quaint multi-level townhouse. Bright and airy (they have also have a picturesque outdoor terrace on the top), this classic restaurant nails the European bistro in its look and feel. While neighborhood denizens (of a certain age) with their dashing beaus may crowd the place, it remains surprisingly family friendly day or night.

The kitchen delivers the classics exactly as they were conceived. From the escargot bathed in a rich and fragrant parsley and garlic-butter sauce, to mussels Provençale with crispy frites, and floating islands of meringue in crème anglaise with toasted almonds and spun sugar—each dish is solid, traditional, and just as it should be.

BLT Steak

Steakhouse XXX

B1

106 E. 57th St. (bet. Lexington & Park Aves.)

Subway: 59 St
Phone: 212-752-7470
Web: www.e2hospitality.com
Prices: $$$$

Lunch Mon – Fri
Dinner nightly

Pass the lengthy bar and Mondrian-style panels to reach the heart of this power lunch spot, beloved more by jackets than jeans. The handsome floors and polished striated tables at BLT Steak offer an idyllic stage for that steady din of corporate chatter. Augmenting the machismo are black-and-white pics of immortal NY scenes including the "Charging Bull" invoking images of power and money...and meat.

Hanger steak moistened with maitre'd butter is a darling among expense accounts, while the "B" in BLT may as well stand for their double-cut smoked bacon. Tuna tartare becomes highbrow when paired with *gaufrettes*; and the mashed potatoes are deeply gratifying, so don't hold back. Same for the peanut butter chocolate mousse licked with banana ice cream.

Bobby Van's

Steakhouse XX

B3

230 Park Ave. (at 46th St.)

Subway: Grand Central - 42 St
Phone: 212-867-5490
Web: www.bobbyvans.com
Prices: $$$$

Lunch Mon – Fri
Dinner Mon – Sat

This scene is so powerful that it intoxicates. A regular flock of bankers and brokers (entering through the passageway beneath the Helmsley Building at 46th and Park) seeks this clubby and boisterous haunt for its crowd, pricey wines, and those towering shellfish platters, served with flourish and perhaps a gruff edge.

After starters like the popular steakhouse Iceberg wedge salad with fried onions and bacon, arrives the meaty main attraction. These steaks are cooked exactly as ordered and carved tableside, with sides like fried zucchini served family-style.

After work, the bar is adorned with addictive homemade potato chips and offers a lighter menu as it comes alive with well-shaken martinis.

Note that Bobby Van's has four other locations in Manhattan.

Bottega del Vino

 A1

7 E. 59th St. (bet. Fifth & Madison Aves.)

Subway: 5 Av - 59 St   Lunch & dinner daily
Phone: 212-223-2724
Web: www.bottegadelvinonyc.com
Prices: $$$$

Amidst a sea of overpriced, mediocre, and stuffy Italian-feigning restaurants, Bottega del Vino is a welcome relief tendering some genuine Italian fare. Naturally, such authenticity comes at a price, and a costly one at that. The primo location, off Fifth Avenue, makes this a magnet for shoppers, tourists, and boutique investment bankers.

With the panini-cappuccino menu up front, Bottega del Vino's back quarters are close-knit with nooks and banquettes. Dark wood and engravings lend warmth to this European-loving oasis whose classic Italian menu unveils *insalata di mare* with shaved celery in a light lemon dressing; *risotto del giorno* gleaming with asparagus and mascarpone; and a flawless version of the oft-clichéd tiramisu.

Brasserie

B2

100 E. 53rd St. (bet. Lexington & Park Aves.)

Subway: Lexington Av - 53 St   Lunch & dinner daily
Phone: 212-751-4840
Web: www.rapatina.com/brasserie
Prices: $$$

Whether it's Brasserie's location in the Seagram building or the simple fact that this has been a midtown fixture since 1959, everyone here seems to expect Don Draper to walk in at any moment. And what an entrance he would make, since guests must descend into the dry room en route to their table. Mod in that "meet George Jetson" kind of way, Brasserie is a see-and-be-seen spot for suits.

Strike a deal or schmooze with clients over this country club-style cuisine. With offerings like onion soup gratinée chock-full of caramelized onions beneath bubbling Gruyère; white asparagus crêpes topped with chervil-lemon-butter sauce and lobster; and striped bass over a bed of new potatoes, this food may seem familiar but therein lies the appeal.

Bukhara Grill

C3

Indian ✗✗

217 E. 49th St. (bet. Second & Third Aves.)

Subway: 51 St
Phone: 212-888-2839
Web: www.bukharany.com
Prices: $$

Lunch & dinner daily

Blazing Bukhara Grill's dusky space exudes sophistication, drama, and a dash of kitsch. The upper level leans contemporary; while the rustic and timbered dining room is dressed in tables carved from tree-trunks, Indian artwork, and stoneware. Sink into a booth and gaze at imposing cooks manning fiery tandoors.

Waiters in traditional garb present hungry diners with foods from India's Northwest Frontier region. Bite into juicy chicken *malai kebab* marinated in ginger, garlic, and spices; *aloo bukhara korma* starring saucy lamb chunks dancing with apricots and potatoes; and the forever beloved *kurkuri bindi*—crispy okra tossed with onions, spices, and coriander. Piles of puffy bread, straight out of the oven, reveal a committed chef and kitchen.

Casa Lever

B2

Italian ✗✗✗

390 Park Ave. (entrance on 53rd St.)

Subway: Lexington Av - 53 St
Phone: 212-888-2700
Web: www.casalever.com
Prices: $$$

Lunch & dinner Mon – Sat

In the basement of the landmark Lever House, sleek Casa Lever showcases a unique, retro-modern dining room shaped like a hexagon. Here, amid large brightly-colored Andy Warhol portraits of prominent figures, Blackberry-clad bankers clink glasses in slick, elevated booths—the elegant Italian dishes seem to have taken a step in a very delicious direction.

Kick things off with a plate of nicely seared calamari, served with fresh spring peas, sautéed baby carrots, and rendered pieces of *guanciale*; and then move on to perfectly al dente pockets of homemade ravioli filled with braised duck and laced with brown butter and mushrooms. Finish with a fresh square of moist tiramisu that arrives plated with lovely *langue du chat* and *palmier* cookies. *Perfetto.*

Café China ✿

Chinese XX

A5

13 E. 37th St. (bet. Fifth & Madison Aves.)

Subway: 34 St - Herald Sq	Lunch & dinner daily
Phone: 212-213-2810	
Web: www.cafechinanyc.com	
Prices: $$	

Yiming Wang

Shanghai glam of yesteryear comes alive in this gracious space, daintily edged by wood-framed doors, bamboo planters, and Chinese calligraphy. Upon entering Café China, find thoughtful inflections from soft sea foam walls and antique portraits to a lofty ceiling adorned with an elegant brass chandelier. Touches of glossy black and Chinoiserie convey an art deco take on Shanghai in the 30s.

The menu eschews ubiquitous Americanized favorites in favor of a refined take on Chinese cuisine. Young and engaging servers deliver such carefully prepared dishes as diced rabbit tossed in a supremely flavorful and lip-numbing red chili oil with scallions and roasted peanuts; sole fillets in a wonderfully subtle soy bath, paired with snow pea shoots and sliced green chilies; and texturally exquisite julienne jellyfish coated in a fresh, tangy scallion pesto. The cumin lamb is spicy, tender, and intensely good.

Odes may follow from the flavor explosion in spicy Chengdu wontons—silky parcels of ground pork and finely chopped scallions. These dumplings slicked with chili oil might be fire engine red, but don't be dissuaded—flavors here are not so much a wallop of heat as a range of deep, lingering tastes.

Don's Bogam

Korean   ✗✗

17 E. 32nd St. (bet. Fifth & Madison Aves.)

Subway: 33 St   Lunch & dinner daily
Phone: 212-683-2200
Web: www.donsbogam.com
Prices: $$

K-town gets a kick in the pants from this exciting, group-friendly mod spot. The contemporary room features a few different seating options, but big parties will want to head for the sleek, modern floor-level tables fitted out with tabletop grills and specially designed cavities for dangling your feet.

The menu is typically massive—with a bevy of lunch and dinner specials (served both à la carte and as sampler barbecue combos) and a *banchan* parade accompanying everything. Find great quality and freshness arriving in plates like *mandu*, traditional Korean pork and vegetable dumplings; grilled and marinated barbecue shrimp; or barbecue *bulgogi*, a heavenly pile of tissue-thin beef flash-cooked with cabbage, sprouts, and noodles.

El Parador

Mexican   ✗✗

325 E. 34th St. (bet. First & Second Aves.)

Subway: 33 St   Lunch & dinner Mon – Sat
Phone: 212-679-6812
Web: www.elparadorcafe.com
Prices: $$

For over 50 years, El Parador has been pleasing generations of New Yorkers with killer margaritas, tasty Mexican food, accommodating staff, and its "you want it, you got it" ethos (don't hesitate to order something not found on the menu).

Do not be deterred by its Midtown Tunnel location or façade that suggests it is a spot where real drinkers drink. Its warm interior offers some of the best tasting Mexican-influenced food around, as in the taco tray—spilling with savories from beef *picadillo* to chorizo, it is as fun and satisfying to prepare as to eat. Equally tasty are the nachos: crisp tortillas spread evenly with toppings and cleanly sliced for easy eating. Wash it down with a sip (or several) of their excellent tequila and perfect margaritas.

Ethos

Greek ✗✗

C2

905 First Ave. (at 51st St.)

Subway: 51 St
Phone: 212-888-4060
Web: www.ethosrestaurants.com
Prices: $$

Dinner nightly

Ethos has been reborn! A renovation brought sparkle to this standby (just across from Beekman and its ritzy residents) and transformed the lifeless room to a vibrant picture of Mykonos with whitewashed walls, cozy cushions, and light wood trim. Gleaming china, glassware, and an upbeat soundtrack finish off the polish, and transport you to the Greek islands...for a night.

While the meze makes for a delicious meal on its own, the menu remains appealing (minus a few favorite kitchen items) with abundant salads and grilled whole fish. *Pikilia* (assortment of spreads) is as tasty as before, and those Ethos chips of zucchini and eggplant with *tzatziki* are a must. The new servers can be pushy, but hopefully a face-lift is planned for them as well!

Felidia

Italian ✗✗

C1

243 E. 58th St. (bet. Second & Third Aves.)

Subway: Lexington Av - 59 St
Phone: 212-758-1479
Web: www.felidia-nyc.com
Prices: $$$

Lunch Mon – Fri
Dinner nightly

Felidia's burnt-orange awning, red brick patio, and tiny olive trees instantly make it the most attractive spot on the block. Inside, the space is bright and warm with a long wood bar, cherry red leather chairs, and colorful Venetian glass sconces. Expect to glimpse owner and matriarch Lidia Bastianich, herself, adding to the friendly ambience.

The consistent menu is filled with top ingredients handled with straightforward care, as in fresh *burrata* topped with a fried egg—its warm, runny yolks drips down to meet perfectly blanched asparagus and crisp bacon; or *cacio e pere* featuring tender ravioli filled with pear purée and finished with showers of pepper. Classic desserts get a fantastic twist, as in tiramisu flavored with limoncello rather than coffee.

Fiorini

B1

Italian ✗✗✗

209 E. 56th St. (bet. Second & Third Aves.)

Subway: Lexington Av - 53 St
Phone: 212-308-0830
Web: www.fiorinirestaurantnyc.com
Prices: $$$

Lunch Mon – Fri
Dinner Mon – Sat

Lello Arpaia and his son, Dino, are masters at the hospitality trade, and they run their Italian eatery, Fiorini, (which translates to little flower) so tightly that you can't help but leave with a special fondness for the place. Make your way past the elegant front bar, and you'll find an intimate, honey-toned dining room aglow in warm pastels and buzzing with a quietly professional service staff.

Modern, straightforward Italian best describes the menu, where you'll find any number of comfort classics along with a lineup of fresh, silky pastas like a perfectly luscious al dente spaghettini *alla carbonara*, tossed with organic eggs, Pecorino Romano, fresh cracked pepper, and sweet crumbles of bacon. Polished off with the house espresso? Perfect!

The Four Seasons

B2

American ✗✗✗✗

99 E. 52nd St. (bet. Lexington & Park Aves.)

Subway: 51 St
Phone: 212-754-9494
Web: www.fourseasonsrestaurant.com
Prices: $$$$

Lunch Mon – Fri
Dinner Mon – Sat

In a day when restaurants try to draw in crowds by populist appeal, The Four Seasons is unabashed in its embrace of power and privilege. Opened in 1959, this time capsule of mid-century swagger is a design delight. Those who go already know that the walnut-paneled Grill Room is *the* place to be for lunch, while the iconic tree-anchored Pool Room is a great scene for evening dining.

Diners who don't circle the same orbit as the cast of powerhouse regulars may bristle at the astronomic prices of the menu. But it's still worth a visit, for seasonal preparations such as plump sweet corn ravioli with rock shrimp and chanterelles; delicately crisped fried soft shell crabs; refreshingly tart raspberry summer pudding; or just a leisurely cocktail at the bar.

Fresco by Scotto

A2

34 E. 52nd St. (bet. Madison & Park Aves.)

Subway: 5 Av - 53 St
Phone: 212-935-3434
Web: www.frescobyscotto.com
Prices: $$$

Lunch Mon – Fri
Dinner Mon – Sat

Despite a location near Rockefeller Center that draws on expense accounts and nearby NBC executives (perhaps the same ones who just produced the Scotto family recipe demonstrations on The Today Show), Fresco by Scotto oozes a comfortable yet cosmopolitan aura. Unobtrusive service and sound Italian-American cuisine enhance the dining room's simple elegance.

Lunch and dinner menus list rustic and robust dishes, including "Fresco Originals" like penne gratin, a hearty pasta with julienned *prosciutto di Parma*, peas, fontina, provolone, and Parmigiano finished with cream and cracked pepper. Equally enticing are their grilled sweet sausages, seasoned with cheese and parsley, in a roasted pepper and onion ragù. Try Fresco on the go for a quick lunch fix.

HanGawi

A6

12 E. 32nd St. (bet. Fifth & Madison Aves.)

Subway: 33 St
Phone: 212-213-0077
Web: www.hangawirestaurant.com
Prices: $$

Lunch Mon – Sat
Dinner nightly

Don't worry about wearing your best shoes to HanGawi; you'll have to take them off at the door before settling in at one of the restaurant's low tables. In the serene space, decorated with Korean artifacts and soothed by meditative music, it's easy to forget you're in Manhattan.

The menu is all vegetarian, in keeping with the philosophy of healthy cooking to balance the *um* and *yang*. You can quite literally eat like a king here starting with vermicelli delight (sweet potato noodles), perfectly crisp kimchi and mushroom pancakes, devastatingly delicious tofu clay pot in ginger sauce, and the regal kimchi stone bowl rice made fragrant with fresh veggies. Of course, you'll have to rejoin the crowds outside. Still, it's nice to get away... now and Zen.

Gilt ❀ ❀

A3

455 Madison Ave. (bet. 50th & 51st Sts.)

Subway: 51 St
Phone: 212-891-8100
Web: www.giltnewyork.com
Prices: $$$$

Dinner Tue – Sat

The New York Palace

What was the private residence of a railroad baron that became the storied and celebrated Le Cirque is now home to Gilt—a restaurant that lives up to every detail of its history and design. The Italian Renaissance revival exterior and iconic circular drive are impossible to miss and provide a perfect introduction to the 19th century carved walnut paneling, plaster friezes, leaded glass, and glittering Gilded Age accents housed within. Futuristic touches like a dramatic fuchsia shell rising above the bar, surprise and enliven the space.

The contemporary cuisine keeps pace with top-shelf ingredients, a skillful touch, and meticulous refinement. Meals may begin by upending expectations with "bacon and eggs"—creamy eggs sit at the bottom of an artistic composition layering a crisp potato-Parmesan disc with glistening white sturgeon roe, smoked bacon wisps, and *cippolini* compote. Cobia with "flavors of Thailand" is worthy of an ode, haunting and seductive with green curry, slippery coconut gel, nests of crisp taro ribbons, charred romaine, and fish that is as pure and white as a pearl.

Desserts like the coffee ice cream bar sound simple, but are alluring, complex, and absolutely worth it.

235

Hide-Chan Ramen

C2

Japanese

248 E. 52nd St. (bet. Second & Third Aves.)

Subway: Lexington Av - 53 St
Phone: 212-813-1800
Web: N/A
Prices: 😊

Lunch Mon – Fri
Dinner nightly

Food is everyone's focus at this buzzing ramen shop. Climb a flight of stairs to arrive at this cozy canteen, and perch at the counter or a private table (surrounded by textured cement walls and paper signs advertising sake and specials), as you wait for steamed buns wrapped around an excellent slice of pork, drizzled with kewpie mayo.

While their menu offers a few Japanese delicacies (maybe the best *gyoza* in town), regulars come here for one item alone: the deliciously slurpy ramen. You can customize yours (fatty broth please!), but to skip the classic *Hakata tonkotsu*, with its delectable piggy flavor, would be such a shame. Likewise, the *Hakata kuro ramen* is really something special—splashed with a nutty black garlic purée, it approaches divinity.

Hunan Manor

Chinese

B5

339 Lexington Ave. (bet. 39th & 40th Aves.)

Subway: Grand Central - 42 St
Phone: 212-682-2883
Web: www.hunanauthentic.com
Prices: 😊

Lunch & dinner daily

Hunan cuisine is now making an appearance in the midtown mix. Located only steps from bustling Grand Central Terminal, Hunan Manor (baby sibling of Flushing's Hunan House) is forever busy at lunch, so be sure to get here early to snag a spot. Even when this tight-knit space is packed with an obvious blend of local suits and zealous foodies, the staff remains adept and affable.

Like its surrounds, presentations and prices are delightfully modest. The Manor's menu is massive, so bring friends to share plates of Hunan-style spicy pickled cabbage; probably *the* best scallion pancakes in town; outstanding and silky *mai fun* in a spicy-sour broth of string beans and ground pork; or white pepper-smoked duck, fantastically fragrant with dried turnips and chilies.

Jubilee

C2

French

948 First Ave. (bet. 52nd & 53rd Sts.)

Subway: Lexington Av - 53 St
Phone: 212-888-3569
Web: www.jubileeny.net
Prices: $$

Lunch Sun – Fri
Dinner nightly

After decades, Jubilee has finally moved into a fresh, new home whose charm and warm style seem light years away from its former outdated space. The character-rich décor straddles the line between nautical and residential with sisal carpets, blue and beige splashes, leather settees, and a wall of painted anchors with blackboards listing nightly specials worthy of consideration.

The menu remains the same—crowd-pleasing Belgian classics like eleven varieties of *moules* paired with perfect house frites, or an asparagus "napoleon" starring asparagus layered with crispy speck and florets of Parmesan foam. The chef adeptly demonstrates classic skills in his fish soup, rich in texture and flavor, paired with *croutes*, *rouille*, and grated Gruyère.

Jukai

C2

Japanese

237 E. 53rd St. (bet. Second & Third Aves.)

Subway: Lexington Av - 53 St
Phone: 212-588-9788
Web: www.jukainyc.com
Prices: $$$

Lunch Tue – Fri
Dinner Mon – Sat

This little restaurant is a happy secret among Japanese expats seeking the taste of home. Situated down a flight of stairs and in the basement of a midtown structure, Jukai is tiny but mighty sweet. Furnished with just a handful of tables, the best seats in the house are at the L-shaped counter, right before Chef Hiro and his skilled cadre.

This is among the rare local spots to pay such extraordinary homage to Japanese traditions—so call ahead to order the tasting menu. Expect meals to begin with a succulent, truly giant oyster (to be quartered before eaten) with ponzu, followed by superbly fresh sashimi, and perhaps a bowlful of turtle soup. The white sesame blancmange is a delicate and delicious finish, especially with a perfect cup of green tea.

Kurumazushi

A3

Japanese ✗✗

7 E. 47th St., 2nd fl. (bet. Fifth & Madison Aves.)

Subway: 47-50 Sts - Rockefeller Ctr
Phone: 212-317-2802
Web: www.kurumazushi.com
Prices: $$$$

Lunch & dinner Mon – Sat

The second-floor location up a steep set of stairs may seem pure Tokyo, but the business clientele and foreign tourists have no problem finding their way to this stalwart of traditional, Edo-style sushi. The room is simple (if outdated) but a warm welcome to your seat at the sushi bar before the extraordinary Chef Toshihiro Uezu is all that's needed. A *washitsu* room is available for private parties.

While à la carte may suffice, Kurumazushi is regaled for its omakase (though there are dramatic variations in pricing, so be sure to communicate a budget). Each taste of this precious sushi–from kampachi and sea scallop to sweet shrimp, giant clam, and uni–holds its place within the upper eschelons of NY sushi dining. The toro is a worthy specialty.

La Fonda Del Sol

B4

Spanish ✗✗

200 Park Ave. (entrance on Vanderbilt Ave.)

Subway: Grand Central - 42 St
Phone: 212-867-6767
Web: www.patinagroup.com
Prices: $$

Lunch Mon – Fri
Dinner Mon – Sat

It's a two space/two menu affair here at La Fonda Del Sol. One is the "dining room," with its upscale vibe and continental menu; the other is the "tapas lounge," with attentive service, an upbeat and cheery ambience, and Spanish-influenced bites. Situated in the mix of office buildings surrounding Grand Central Terminal, both remain popular among the midtown business crowd, area residents, and touristy types.

Stop in the tapas lounge and tuck into the ceviche of the day– the fresh fish changes daily–which could be thinly sliced fluke topped with grapefruit, sea salt, and olive oil. Or, choose a more upscale experience in the main dining room replete with such luscious entrées as buttery poached lobster over frisée and drizzled with apple cider dressing.

La Grenouille

French

 A2

3 E. 52nd St. (bet. Fifth & Madison Aves.)

Subway: 5 Av - 53 St
Phone: 212-752-1495
Web: www.la-grenouille.com
Prices: $$$$

Lunch Tue – Fri
Dinner Tue – Sat

Like the Judi Dench of French dining, La Grenouille is a respected holdout from another era in Manhattan's fine dining scene—one where white-coated servers fussed over you in a setting fit for royalty. But as over-the-top as the dining room might appear nowadays (think high coffered ceilings, plush red banquettes, and opulent flower arrangements), there is something comforting for the well-heeled regulars who have been calling this Masson family mainstay its second home (one where you're required to wear jackets) since 1962.

Quickly disappearing old-world dishes like *quenelles* and *rognons* share menu space with dishes like duck confit, served over warm green lentils; and tender chicken paillard, paired with crispy sage and tender squash gnocchi.

La Mangeoire

French

 C2

1008 Second Ave. (bet. 53rd & 54th Aves.)

Subway: Lexington Av - 53 St
Phone: 212-759-7086
Web: www.lamangeoire.com
Prices: $$$

Lunch Sun – Fri
Dinner nightly

 Cozy and warm, La Mangeoire is the French bistro that everyone dreams of having in the neighborhood. This delightful farmhouse in harried midtown is now updated and slightly more modern with sunlight drenching its floors and French artifacts dotting its walls.

As if to prove their authenticity, they also have a fully French staff who are adept, friendly, and even flirty in their relaying of the classic menu. Rillettes of smoked salmon are delicious and rustically served in a little jar with toasted baguette. Still, the roast chicken should be the stuff of culinary legends: gorgeously dark and crisp-skinned, juicy, served with an accompanying pitcher of jus to pour as desired. A rich yet lightly textured milk chocolate mousse is decadence incarnate.

Land of Plenty ☺

Chinese ✕✕

B1

204 E 58th St. (bet. Second & Third Aves.)

Subway: 59 St
Phone: 212-308-8788
Web: www.landofplenty58.com
Prices: $$

Lunch & dinner daily

Housed in restaurateur Donatella Arpaia's old mainstay, Mia Dona, Land of Plenty lucked out with an exceedingly elegant and fully decorated space. With the attractive interior left nearly untouched, it now has an inviting bar and intimate tables, and can boast not only surprisingly delicious Sichuan cuisine, but a remarkably fast and well-humored staff.

If your wisecracking waiter lists Sichuan *douhua* as a special, be sure to get it—the soft tofu is topped with chili oil, fried soybeans, and crushed Sichuan peppercorns. Showcasing excellent products and solid techniques are crunchy jelly fish strips tossed in chili oil and citrus vinaigrette; tender poached chicken in peanutty chili oil; and a bubbling vat of savory beer-braised duck meat.

Le Cirque

Contemporary ✕✕✕✕

B1

151 E. 58th St. (bet. Lexington & Third Aves.)

Subway: 59 St
Phone: 212-644-0202
Web: www.lecirque.com
Prices: $$$$

Lunch Mon – Fri
Dinner Mon – Sat

At this NYC citadel, also lauded as Sirio Maccioni's cathedral of contemporary cuisine, menu classics are showcased with both a description and date of birth ("Flounder le Cirque, est. 1974") that serve as further testament to Le Cirque's culinary eminence. This ultra-chic stalwart never ceases to stun, beginning with its limousine-lined central courtyard entrance.

The décor is a classy and tasteful throw-back of sorts that manages to invent a "circus-chic" aesthetic through rich fabrics, handsome paneling, and many, many monkeys. Speckled with glitterati, the dining room seduces with a warm artichoke soup finished with tarragon; excellent *lasagnette* of lamb braised with aromatics and fresh herbs; and gingerbread profiteroles atop fluffy whipped cream.

Le Relais de Venise

Steakhouse ✗✗

B2

590 Lexington Ave. (at 52nd St.)

Subway: 51 St
Phone: 212-758-3989
Web: www.relaisdevenise.com
Prices: $$

Lunch & dinner daily

There is no menu at Le Relais de Venise L'Entrecôte, a Parisian restaurant with a prime location set along thumping Lexington Avenue. There is only one $24.95 option, but it is a delightful option indeed—green salad with tangy mustard vinaigrette and walnuts, followed by juicy steak served in two parts (because you wouldn't want the rest of it to get cold, would you?) laced in the house's mouthwatering secret sauce, with all the crunchy frites you can eat.

With a Parisian décor and waitresses darting around in saucy French maid get-ups, this is a lively joint—all the more reason to pluck a glass of *vin* off the extremely affordable list, sit back and relax. By the time the dessert menu rolls around, you'll have forgotten how stressful decisions can be.

Maloney & Porcelli

American ✗✗✗

B3

37 E. 50th St. (bet. Madison & Park Aves.)

Subway: 51 St
Phone: 212-750-2233
Web: www.maloneyandporcelli.com
Prices: $$$

Lunch Mon – Fri
Dinner nightly

Much more than a steakhouse, this upbeat and versatile spot is sure to exceed expectations. Note that the first sign of the "excess" is evidenced in entrée-sized starters, like their signature chopped salad and clams Casino, as well as a Flintstone-sized, Roquefort-crusted filet mignon. Pleasant surprises are equally evident in crowd-pleasing and carb-worthy offerings like bacon gnocchi (weight can be gained by just reading this menu). Lunchtime includes the "angry shrimp" cobb salad and M&P lobster roll.

Enormous wine glasses and peppermills likewise imply that more is more—a philosophy that, unfortunately, extends to the check. Nonetheless, it is jammed with an expense-account crowd, and the bar remains very popular post-work.

Mapo Tofu

B5

338 Lexington Ave. (bet. 39th & 40th Sts.)

Subway: Grand Central - 42 St   Lunch & dinner daily
Phone: 212-867-8118
Web: N/A
Prices: 🥢

Just when you think you're sated, this Sichuan Shangri-la bestows you with another boon. At Mapo Tofu it's not just about tofu, but their sumptuous feast. Their forte also includes the expert marriage of spices, wafting into a simple though neat room adorned with tables and slapdash servers. Their genius locale and superior spread hoists it into a league of its own.

Start this Sichuan safari with sliced conch steeping in roasted chili vinaigrette; string beans with bamboo shoots and pork are an incredible item; and braised fish, tofu, and cellophane noodles carry a fiercely flavorful chili broth. Camphor tea-smoked duck; *dan dan* noodles with pork; and wok-tossed prawns with spiced salt and Sichuan peppercorns are stunning, flavor-ridden plates.

Matisse

C3

924 Second Ave. (at 49th St.)

Subway: 51 St   Lunch & dinner daily
Phone: 212-546-9300
Web: www.matissenyc.com
Prices: $$

Matisse might be smack dab in midtown, but this tightly packed, sun-filled bistro looks and feels more downtown. Informal without being casual, this single room restaurant with a front row seat to the action of Second Avenue has that typical New York lack of elbow room, but forever lively and whizzing spirit.

Young and old area denizens are lured by the simple and classic French cooking with a reasonable price tag. The menu presents an appealing range of comfort foods, such as a caramelized onion tarte and *croque monsieur*. Sunday brunch delivers the goods with omelets and French toast alongside other usual suspects.

Some of the dishes are presented on delightfully rustic wooden boards and exude charm thereby displaying Matisse's stylish flair.

Morton's

Steakhouse ✗✗✗

A4

551 Fifth Ave. (entrance on 45th St.)

Subway: 5 Av
Phone: 212-972-3315
Web: www.mortons.com
Prices: $$$

Lunch Mon – Fri
Dinner nightly

Part of a Chicago-born chain with outposts across the country, Morton's understands exactly how to empower the weekday corporate crowds and charm weekend tourists with its fun, formulaic experience.

It all starts with a cart: as the servers recite and explain the menu, a cart is rolled to your table, bearing plastic-wrapped samples of the exact cuts of Prime aged beef, which will be prepared exactly to your liking. Alongside these meats are virtually every raw ingredient used to round out the menu, from massive potatoes to live lobsters. Gimmicks aside, the food here is high quality and delicious.

As one of the older siblings, this midtown Morton's embraces a clubby décor of mahogany paneling and jewel tones that sets the steakhouse standard.

Mr Chow

Chinese ✗✗

C1

324 E. 57th St. (bet. First & Second Aves.)

Subway: 59 St
Phone: 212-751-9030
Web: www.mrchow.com
Prices: $$$$

Dinner nightly

Oh Mr Chow, how you hook the hordes with your flavorful fusion and fancy prices! Perhaps it's the retro scene decked in black-and-white, lacquered Asian-accented chairs, and glinting mirrors. Or, maybe it's the noodle guy's theatrical display of hand-pulling? Whatever the hype, Mr Chow still has it and Sutton suits along with their wealthy wives party here like it's 1999.

Attentive service and flowing drinks keep everything moving as fans nibble away on the well-priced Beijing duck prix-fixe with four starters plus entrées. Tender orange chicken satay and water dumplings with seafood are tasty, but Dungeness crab sautéed with egg whites, and *ma mignon*, cubes of tender fried beef tossed in a sweet-spicy sauce laced with scallions truly get the crowd going.

Naya

Lebanese XX

C2

1057 Second Ave. (bet. 55th & 56th Sts.)

Subway: Lexington Av - 53 St
Phone: 212-319-7777
Web: www.nayarestaurants.com
Prices: $$

Lunch & dinner daily

Amid this bland stretch of cheap booze and loud beats lies Naya, a tiny and mod neighborhood spot with tasty Lebanese fare. Inside, the streamlined décor feels smart and attractive, with white pleather booths contrasting against shiny dark tables. This sleek aesthetic runs to the back where a large table is best for suit-donning groups.

Most love Naya for its vast choice of Lebanese mezze and daily specials featuring home-style food with modern flair. It is clear that this is no amateur show, as obliging waiters present you with the likes of a "quick Naya" lunch special unveiling generous portions of *fattoush*, *labné*, and *baba ghannouj*. A chicken shawarma sandwich reaches epic scopes when paired with their deliciously tangy homemade pickles.

OBAO 😊

Asian XX

C2

222 E. 53rd St. (bet. Second & Third Aves.)

Subway: Lexington Av - 53 St
Phone: 212-308-5588
Web: www.obaony.com
Prices: 💷

Lunch & dinner daily

Who knows what possessed Michael Huynh to drop this fantastic and delightful Vietnamese restaurant in the harried streets of Midtown East, but anyone tired of slogging downtown is in for one heck of a treat.

The restaurant has a contemporary urban feel, with a smattering of booths and a communal table toward the center of the back room; and while the Vietnamese dishes are the strongest (especially the *pho*), the menu also dabbles in cuisine from Laos and Singapore, adding creative touches that truly work. Don't miss the fragrant curried catfish satay; the Laos beef salad tossed with pineapple, shallots, and mint; or the beef *luclak* with tomatoes and crisp watercress, washed down with Vietnamese coffee or coconut juice straight from the shell.

Osteria Laguna

Italian ✗✗

209 E. 42nd St. (bet. Second & Third Aves.)

Subway: Grand Central - 42 St
Phone: 212-557-0001
Web: www.osteria-laguna.com
Prices: $$

Lunch Mon – Fri
Dinner nightly

A little bit corporate (it is midtown, after all) and a little bit casual (daytrippers from nearby Grand Central), Osteria Laguna has nailed its audience and delivers a perfect blend to suit both worlds. Inside, it's delightfully rustic, complete with the requisite Italian ceramic plates and wooden chairs with rush seating.

Crowd-pleasers like pastas, pizzas from the wood-burning oven, *antipasti*, salads, and grilled meats and fish dishes comprise the menu at this better-than-average Italian. The friendly service can be spotty, but the perfectly crisped wood-fired pizzas are always spot on. The portions are abundant, perhaps even too much given the tiny tables, but the prices aren't, so you can treat your out-of-town friend and keep the change.

Pampano

Mexican ✗✗

209 E. 49th St. (bet. Second & Third Aves.)

Subway: 51 St
Phone: 212-751-4545
Web: www.modernmexican.com/pampano
Prices: $$$

Lunch Mon – Fri
Dinner nightly

Pampano is a proven pick among corporate types craving upscale, seafood-centric Mexican food. An army of hostesses may greet you at the entry but leave you feeling cool. No matter, they might as well have escorted you to Acapulco, otherwise known as a table upstairs—think whitewashed ceilings, giant wicker chairs, and overhead fans. While the bar is very popular at happy hour, the mediocre downstairs "botaneria" seating and menu should be skipped in favor of the superior upstairs setting.

Expect the likes of red snapper-packed *quesadillas de pescado* oozing with Oaxaca cheese and spicy salsas. *Huarache de hongos* topped with mushrooms and goat cheese; or a dark chocoflan with candied peanuts are tasty studies in presentation and texture.

Pera

Turkish ✕✕

 A4

303 Madison Ave. (bet. 41st & 42nd Sts.)

Subway: Grand Central - 42 St
Phone: 212-878-6301
Web: www.peranyc.com
Prices: $$

Lunch & dinner daily

This perennially-packed Mediterranean brasserie attracts a loud lunchtime crowd of office workers, while at nighttime the scene is populated by intimate pairs. The establishment, named after an upscale neighborhood in Istanbul, warms the heart with its chocolate-brown color scheme and grand display kitchen boasting an open flame grill station.

The expert cooks churn out a throng of mouthwatering fare, like fig *pidette*—a dense flatbread spread with strips of Turkish-style dried beef, *rucola*, dried figs, and cumin-infused yogurt drizzles; the cubed watermelon and feta salad massaged with fragrant basil oil is a warm weather must; and roasted whole fish is offered to be de-boned and comes delightfully dressed with blistered tomatoes and candied lemon.

Phoenix Garden 🐵

Chinese ✕

B5

242 E. 40th St. (bet. Second & Third Aves.)

Subway: Grand Central - 42 St
Phone: 212-983-6666
Web: www.thephoenixgarden.com
Prices: 🐚

Lunch & dinner daily

You can take the restaurant out of Chinatown, but you can't take the Cantonese out of this midtown favorite—which serves up authentic dishes at a great value. By day, the office suits set pours in for quick lunches; by dinner, Phoenix Garden lights up with a fun, diverse crowd looking to check out the mouthwatering daily specials.

While the house's tasty Peking duck is not always on the menu, you can certainly try to request it—a deliciously crispy affair that gets rolled into neat little pancakes with hoisin, scallion, and cucumber. Meanwhile, don't miss the steamed chive dumplings, plump with tender shrimp; the succulent pepper and salty shrimp; or the sautéed snow pea shoots in a lovely crabmeat sauce, with tender mushrooms and snow peas.

P.J. Clarke's

Gastropub

915 Third Ave. (at 55th St.)

Subway: Lexington Av - 53 St
Phone: 212-317-1616
Web: www.pjclarkes.com
Prices: $$

Lunch & dinner daily

The original is always the best: that's why it's been duplicated. It might sound trite, but this midtown institution started serving drinks and meals to men in suits before your father's father was born. It feels old and traditional because it is, yet somehow this spot manages to keep improving. No fluff, no fuss, no reservations at P.J. Clarke's, where the staff is likely to throw a "hon" or two into the conversation.

The crowd-pleasing menu offers old-time classics like chilli and tasty burgers (note the fries are extra), but seafood and steakhouse classics are popular. Salads and appetizers are not only numerous, but those thick-cut potato chips with salty Maytag blue cheese dip and massive chopped salads seem to get better with each visit.

Rosa Mexicano

Mexican

1063 First Ave. (at 58th St.)

Subway: 59 St
Phone: 212-753-7407
Web: www.rosamexicano.com
Prices: $$

Dinner nightly

Rosa may have spread her wings, but one thing remains gospel: her original location is the "wind beneath" and the only one where the food is not just good, it's great. Despite the expansion, Rosa upholds her excellence by virtue of a titanic roster of delicious dishes, those stellar margaritas, and hospitable ambience. Warm and worn in a distinctly Mexican style, find the front room flocked with booths, tables, and a bar packed three deep.

The tortilla lady and her *comal* live in an adjacent room, while the back space whispers intimacy. Lights are low here but the flavors are as bright as *guacamole en molcajete*. Captivating plates of *queso fundido* with *chorizo y rajas*; *plantanos* topped with *crema*; and *budin de pollo*, complement their unhurried service.

Rouge Tomate ✿

Contemporary XXX

A1

10 E. 60th St. (bet. Fifth & Madison Aves.)

Subway: 5 Av
Lunch & dinner Mon – Sat
Phone: 646-237-8977
Web: www.rougetomatenyc.com
Prices: $$$

Serge Anton

Expressions like "eye-popping" and "jaw-dropping" are best reserved for the experience of entering Rouge Tomate's stunning space for the first time. Architectural feats reveal themselves in red elevated dining cubes that appear suspended over the main room, and a curving walnut bar facing a glass-enclosed display of tantalizing fruit, bound for cocktail crowds. The look is light, airy, and clean; the cuisine follows suit.

While the menu does focus on healthful eating, the food is innovative, meticulously composed, and scientifically balanced (you won't miss that butter and cream). The effort behind each dish is as formidable as the pleasure.

Starters are not merely a lovely piece of art, but an intricate layering of flavors, as in meaty and luscious Guinea hen and black truffle terrine served with a purple quenelle of shallot-prune marmalade. A talented hand and balanced tastes shine through the perfectly cooked sunchoke ravioli, with black trumpet mushrooms and crispy knobs of veal sweetbreads—their decadent richness kept at bay by pickled carrot ribbons. Desserts will dazzle: think sumptuous passion fruit pudding topped with pineapple and mango cubes, coconut, and julienned shiso.

Sakagura

Japanese ✕✕

B4

211 E. 43rd St. (bet. Second & Third Aves.)

Subway: Grand Central - 42 St
Phone: 212-953-7253
Web: www.sakagura.com
Prices: $$$

Lunch Mon – Fri
Dinner nightly

With its killer sake list and delicious small plates, this unassuming Japanese den has gotten deservedly popular in the last few years. For those who can find it (hint: it's in the basement of that office building), plan for a swinging night out in Tokyo by way of midtown. Grab a seat at the counter to amp up the fun and watch the libations flow.

Though the menu is built to complement the sake, the food more than merits its own applause. A soft boiled egg bobs alongside fresh uni and salmon roe in a lovely dashi (*onsen tamago*); while grilled eel is layered with Japanese cucumber and seaweed in a light rice wine vinegar vinaigrette (*uzaku*); and chicken is marinated in sake and ginger-infused soy sauce, then fried to sweet perfection (*tori karaage*).

2nd Avenue Deli

Deli ✕

B6

162 E. 33rd St. (bet. Lexington & Third Aves.)

Subway: 33 St
Phone: 212-689-9000
Web: www.2ndavedeli.com
Prices:

Lunch & dinner daily

While the décor may be more deli-meets-deco and there's a tad less attitude, this food is every bit as good as it was on Second Avenue. Ignore the kvetching and know that this is a true Jewish deli filled with personality, and one of the best around by far.

The menu remains as it should: Kosher, meat-loving, and non-dairy, with phenomenal pastrami, pillowy rye, tangy mustard, perfect potato pancakes, and fluffy matzoh balls in comforting broth. Have the best of both worlds with the soup and half-sandwich combination.

Carve a nook during midday rush, when in pour the crowds. The deli also does takeout (popular with the midtown lunch bunch), and delivery (grandma's pancakes at your door). Giant platters go equally well to a bris or brunch.

Seo

C3

249 E. 49th St. (bet. Second & Third Aves.)

Subway: 51 St
Phone: 212-355-7722
Web: N/A
Prices: $$

Lunch Mon – Sat
Dinner nightly

For home-style Japanese food in a delightful setting, head to Seo. This hospitable hideaway wears no airs; its kitchen is wholly dedicated to the cooking and conservation of their little lair. While Westerners may misconstrue it for a sushi bar (glimpse the long wraparound counter), Seo is anything but. Make your way beyond a steamy kitchen to a small dining room neatly attired with a few tables and a glass wall overlooking a traditional and very tranquil Japanese garden. Amid this serenity, eat your way through crunchy, salty edamame followed by tender *inaniwa udon* or superb salmon sashimi atop rice with wasabi and shiso. Like its Zen backyard, a lick of the red bean-green tea ice cream will deliver you far from the maddening midtown streets.

Sip Sak

C3

928 Second Ave. (bet. 49th & 50th Sts.)

Subway: 51 St
Phone: 212-583-1900
Web: www.sip-sak.com
Prices: $$

Lunch & dinner daily

It's as if Chef/owner Orhan Yegen treats Sip Sak like his personal design project—primped, preened, and never left alone. Yet this is working. Everything feels warmer now, with Turkish artifacts on mellow-toned walls and an imposing floral arrangement. The lights are low, but cast a pretty glow upon marble-topped tables, bistro chairs, and small front bar. With the master on set, the staff is nimble (if sometimes robotic) in delivering a recital of their tasty eats. Appetizer platters are ideal for groups, and throw in a shepherd salad featuring spicy cubanelles. If the stuffed cabbage stars, try it, otherwise feta-packed *borek* and soft *manti* filled with spiced beef in yogurt are equally delightful.
Find more of the same at their casual sib, Bi Lokma.

Smith & Wollensky

Steakhouse ✕✕

B3

797 Third Ave. (at 49th St.)

Subway: 51 St
Phone: 212-753-1530
Web: www.smithandwollensky.com
Prices: $$$$

Lunch Mon – Fri
Dinner nightly

Long before Manhattan's steakhouse craze reached epic proportions, there was Smith & Wollensky. The NY flagship opened in 1977, and over 30 years later, it is still jumping—it's historic green and white façade is a welcome beacon to neighborhood power players during the week; while families and tourists keep businesss booming over the weekends. Now you too can have your "Devil Wears Prada" moment as they deliver to your desk, no assistant required!

The owners may have plucked the names Smith and Wollensky out of a phone directory, but they were considerably more careful choosing their USDA Prime beef, which they dry-age and hand-butcher on premises. The result, paired with mouthwatering mashed potatoes or hashbrowns, is steakhouse nirvana.

Soba Totto

Japanese ✕✕

B4

211 E. 43rd St. (bet. Second & Third Aves.)

Subway: Grand Central - 42 St
Phone: 212-557-8200
Web: www.sobatotto.com
Prices: $$

Lunch Mon – Fri
Dinner nightly

This traditional Japanese restaurant arrives courtesy of the family behind Aburiya Kinnosuke and other Totto outposts. The simple, modern, and stylish space has a dining counter for a view of the action, and well-spaced tables filled with expats enjoying faithful renditions of incredibly fresh Japanese specialties.

At lunch, soba noodles are the focus, served as a value-driven set or as an accompaniment—always in generous portions of excellent quality. Come evening, consider planning ahead and reserving a special course menu, available in a range of prices. Otherwise, just sit back and let the nice selection of sake, shochu, and Japanese beer ease your way through the yakitori, salads, soba, and specials offered in limited quantity each night.

Sparks

Steakhouse ✗✗

 C3

210 E. 46th St. (bet. Second & Third Aves.)

Subway: Grand Central - 42 St
Phone: 212-687-4855
Web: www.sparksnyc.com
Prices: $$$$

Lunch Mon – Fri
Dinner Mon – Sat

Sparks isn't contrived or outdated. This venerable steakhouse lives up to its reputation and very little has changed—even their service team remains as efficient as it is obliging. This place is a loud and loveably gruff slice of NY history that once the backdrop of an historical mob hit. Today, suits and regulars seem to grab the spotlight. The main dining room meanders into cozy corners but still reeks of the Old World with dark wood and rich carpets.

This is straight steakhouse fare with some salads (a Caesar topped with salty anchovies) and seafood (flavorful baked clams combined with shrimp scampi in lemon, butter, and garlic) to start. Get a perfectly cooked sirloin drowned in its own juices, paired with an side of excellent creamed spinach.

SushiAnn

Japanese ✗✗

B2

38 E. 51st St. (bet. Madison & Park Aves.)

Subway: 51 St
Phone: 212-755-1780
Web: www.sushiann.com
Prices: $$

Lunch Mon – Fri
Dinner Mon – Sat

Lucky are those who wander into this large midtown den helmed by one of the best sushi teams in town—even luckier are those regulars at the counter, who know that despite the Americanized menu options, there is a depth of authenticity rare in these parts. Such standby sushi classics as SushiAnn know just how to balance tradition, pleasure, and expectation. For an adventure, sit at the counter (where there is a $30 minimum) and don't hesitate to express interest in the more authentic dishes. This is just the right place to go for the omakase: fresh mackerel served with ponzu and minced ginger; fatty bluefin fanned over shiso leaf and kelp; smoky slices of grilled giant clam; or rich torched sardine—all carefully explained by the knowledgeable staff.

Sushiden

Japanese

A3

19 E. 49th St. (bet. Fifth & Madison Aves.)

Subway: 5 Av - 53 St
Phone: 212-758-2700
Web: www.sushiden.com
Prices: $$$

Lunch Mon – Fri
Dinner Sun – Fri

Forget everything you think you know before stepping into this traditional *sushi-ya* in the heart of midtown—there won't be a California roll in sight. Be sure to reserve ahead, as tables are buzzing with businessmen at lunch, though treating yourself to omakase at the sushi bar is the best way to watch and appreciate the chefs' magic.

Soothing wood accents keep perfect company with their soft-spoken, kimono-clad staff and quiet, expert chefs. Menus may reveal such outrageously fresh fish as four silky slices of bonito sashimi (*hagatsuo*); a fresh, live scallop sliced into three rounds with a touch of freshly ground wasabi; mild and delicate branzino nigiri; and *benisake*, deep orange sockeye salmon, sweet in flavor and pleasantly rich in texture.

Sushi Yasuda

Japanese

B4

204 E. 43rd St. (bet. Second & Third Aves.)

Subway: Grand Central - 42 St
Phone: 212-972-1001
Web: www.sushiyasuda.com
Prices: $$$$

Lunch Mon – Fri
Dinner Mon – Sat

Attention rule breakers: this glorious sushi spot ain't for you. Late for your reservation? It will be forfeited. Lingering too long after eating? You will be informed that time is up. Sushi-loving diehards can handle the tough love though, and come back time and time again for the spectacularly fresh fish. Left in the capable hands of Mitsuru Tamura after Naomichi Yasuda's departure, this beloved spot still maintains its loyal following.

Grab a spot on the sleek bamboo sushi counter and give over to the chef's superb recommendations, which will be circled on the menu. Tasty slices of kanpachi (amberjack) and *aji* (mackerel) are brushed with soy and served over rice; while the exquisite *hotate* (scallop) is sprinkled with a touch of sea salt.

253

Tao

A1

Asian 🍴🍴

42 E. 58th St. (bet. Madison & Park Aves.)

Subway: 59 St
Phone: 212-888-2288
Web: www.taorestaurant.com
Prices: $$$

Lunch Mon – Fri
Dinner nightly

♿ This former cinema is now (literally) a lively, massive, and über-popular temple of all foods pan-Asian, dramatically outfitted with a Chinese scroll draped across the ceiling and 16-foot statue of Buddha towering over a reflecting pool. The theater's former balconies remain packed, accommodating 300 diners on three levels. The fusion cuisine has a crowd-pleasing combination of Hong Kong, Chinese, Thai, and Japanese dishes, including sushi and sashimi. Perfect for sharing, the well-prepared menu offers everything from small plates of shrimp tempura with garlic-chili sauce and squab lettuce wraps, to wasabi-crusted filet mignon.

The loyal after-work business crowd turns younger and trendier on weekends, ordering hip libations like the lychee martini.

Tsushima

B3

Japanese 🍴

141 E. 47th St. (bet. Lexington & Third Aves.)

Subway: Grand Central - 42 St
Phone: 212-207-1938
Web: N/A
Prices: $$

Lunch Mon – Fri
Dinner nightly

Once frequented by a handful of in the know diners, Tsushima is a sleeper no more. This midtown Japanese lair is jam-packed with business diners and neighborhood dwellers seeking fantastic value (especially at lunch) and terrific quality. It's not big, but it is bright and upbeat with a long, narrow space that is stylish in a spare Tokyo-meets-Manhattan way. Service is speedy, which is perfect for those who need to get back to a meeting after slurping some soup and nibbling some sushi—options are authentic but will nod if needed to spicy tuna-craving Americans. Lunch specials are generous, plentiful, and inexpensive. The omakase for dinner is well worth the extra expense, when the sushi chefs are less rushed and the quality is turned up big time.

Tulsi ❀

211 E. 46th St. (bet. 2nd & 3rd Aves.)

Subway: Grand Central - 42 St
Phone: 212-888-0820
Web: www.tulsinyc.com
Prices: $$

Lunch Mon – Sat
Dinner nightly

Melissa Hom

Nimbly set on a quiet midtown street just blocks from the United Nations, this elegant Indian eatery is sanctified by suits and global business cliques. Basking in sultry spotlights, Tulsi's tables dominate the heart of the room, whereas elusive, sheer muslin-veiled banquettes dwell on the fringes. While the food is a definite hook–imagine a tangy *kala chole* (black chickpea) and tomato salad spiced with *chaat masala*, lemon, and mint–Tulsi's décor is just as exciting with a pageant of exotic copper accents, intricate relics, and lush greenery.

True to the midtown aesthetic, sparkling flatware poses atop clean and crisp linen-covered tables. And though the staff may falter, their warmth and smiling service begs forgiveness. A complex and flavorful plate of masala-stuffed eggplants bathed in a piquant tomato-and-tamarind sauce paired with vegetable pilaf evidences pure ambrosia.

Indian diners come in droves during the day, when the feel is at its finest, solely for the likes of their exquisitely unembellished *tadka dal* and spicy Bombay chicken curry. Chasing this down with a coconut- and lemongrass-*faluda* laced with basil seeds offers a burst of flavors, spice, and all things nice.

Vitae

A3

Contemporary

4 E. 46th St. (bet. Fifth & Madison Aves.)

Subway: Grand Central - 42 St   Lunch & dinner Mon – Sat
Phone: 212-682-3562
Web: www.vitaenyc.com
Prices: $$$

This swanky newcomer has quickly become part of the neighborhood, attracting a lively post-work crowd for excellent cocktails served downstairs and impressive, quieter, dining upstairs. The room diverges from its cavernous midtown location with an intimate setting embellished with terrazzo flooring and teal upholstered furnishings; a pleasant and knowledgeable staff further elevates the exclusive vibe here.

Chef/owner Edwin Bellanco illustrates his skilled hand in Vitae's carte that has offered a massive bronzed sea scallop dressed with caramelized cauliflower florets, toasted cashews, and sweet-spicy green coconut curry; as well as a pasta course starring a nest of toothsome *chitarra*, tossed with fresh chickpeas and moist chicken-ricotta meatballs.

Wild Edibles

B5

Seafood

535 Third Ave. (bet. 35th & 36th Sts.)

Subway: 33 St   Lunch & dinner daily
Phone: 212-213-8552
Web: www.wildedibles.com
Prices: $$

Wild Edibles is plain neat. This utterly charming fish shop, smack dab in harrowing midtown, is flooded with warmth. With stations in Grand Central, this fabulous retailer remains unequalled—notice a smattering of dark-wood tables, subway tiles, and a bar joined to the seafood counter unveiling the freshest (and finest) treats.

Relish the quiet at lunch, and do as the regulars do in seeking out straight-from-the-source specials. Take off with an outstanding warm seafood salad mingling fennel, arugula, and creamy white beans; and then fly high with the Canadian club oyster flight with three pours of wine or beer. The New England (or New Orleans) mussels are sumptuously sopped up by Old Bay fries. Rushed? Take your 'catch' and sauce to-go.seafood

Wolfgang's

4 Park Ave. (at 33rd St.)

Subway: 33 St
Phone: 212-889-3369
Web: www.wolfgangssteakhouse.com
Prices: $$$$

Lunch & dinner daily

What started for the fomer waiter of the esteemed Peter Luger has evolved into now five locations going strong—a decision that has yielded mouthwatering results. Located in the former Vanderbilt Hotel dining room, this 1912 landmark space is dressed with elegant tables and showcases a gorgeous terra-cotta ceiling courtesy of famed architect, Rafael Guastavino.

The setting is handsome, but the steak's arrival refocuses all attention on the strapping Porterhouse (for two, three, or four) served sizzling and paired with fried onion rings; sautéed mushrooms; and German potatoes...extra crispy please! If you really want something to knaw on before the meat makes its way, order a perfect martini and slice by slice of Canadian bacon—you're not here for a diet.

Look for our symbol 🍇,
spotlighting restaurants
with a notable wine list.

Manhattan ▶ Midtown East & Murray Hill

Midtown West

Manhattan ▶ Midtown West

This New York is a city of incomparable diversity, evident in every tree-lined neighborhood, ethnic enclave, and luxury high-rise. The truth remains, however, that there is only one street in all five boroughs to be boldly hailed Restaurant Row. Considering that its famed location–where celebrity chefs prepare all-you-can-eat pasta alongside promising sushi bars–is in a neighborhood named Hell's Kitchen is further testament to its dedication to great food.

Restaurant Row

Still, this is an area that insists on reinvention. Hence, Restaurant Row (perhaps due to its uneven reputation) is becoming known as Little Brazil near Sixth Avenue, where samba and street food are celebrated late summer each year on Brazilian Day. A few steps farther west and the city's eclectic identity comes to life again, where a walk down Ninth Avenue offers a world of goods. A wonderful start (or finale) can be found at **Amy's Bread**, whose crusty baguettes supply countless restaurant kitchens, while colorful cakes or cookies tempt passersby. Meanwhile across the avenue, **Poseidon Bakery** is rumored to be the very last place in America to still make its own phyllo dough by hand—a taste of the *spanakopita* will prove it. Regardless of its name, **Sullivan Street Bakery**'s one and only retail outlet is actually on 47th, between 10th and 11th avenues (a location so perilously far west in the Manhattan mindset that its success proves its worth in gold). Absolutely anything artisanal and delicious can be found nearby at the **Amish Market**, filled with fine produce, meats, and an array of specialty items. A sweet side-trip is the **Little Pie Company**, whose treasured wares are rolled, filled, and baked in its glass-paneled display kitchen. While this stretch of Hell's Kitchen is rich with markets and restaurants, those highlights familiar to any theater-going tourist or Lincoln Tunnel-bound commuter who has been stuck in its traffic, include "the hamburger you must try before you die" at **The Counter**. Tucked into the basement at Macy's is **De Gustibus**, a cooking school and stage for a range of culinary legends. While **La Boîte**'s exotic spice blends are ever-luring, **Sergimmo Salumeria**'s first-rate *salumi* and *formaggi* will warm the soul. Travel south of Port Authority Bus Terminal and unearth a string of pleasures starting with **Ninth Avenue International Foods**. These olives, spices, and spreads are a serious business, but it is the renowned *taramosalata* (as if prepared by the gods atop Mount Olympus themselves) that finds its way into restaurants throughout the city. Stop by **Giovanni**

Esposito and Sons meat market for a sampling of their Italian sausages. For sandwiches, **Manganaro**'s is the true inventor of the original six-foot Italian-American "hero." These are among the family-owned landmark businesses that have quietly been shaping New York's food scene for a better part of the century. Truffle fiends will find a spectacular selection at stylish **Urbani Truffles**, happily located on West End Avenue and 60th Street.

Street Eats

While this is an area often choked by traffic and hungry office workers, NYers demand outstanding food, no matter the venue. Under the guidance of the Vendy Awards and the blog midtownlunch.com, discover a moveable line of fast, satisfying street food vendors. Highlights include sausage and schnitzel from **Hallo German Food Stand** and the **Treats Truck** (check the web or follow on Twitter for upcoming locales). Those seeking a more stable location to grab a juicy burger, fries, or milkshake will not be disappointed at Le Parker Meridien's **burger joint**. Foodies in need of a rarer treat know to head south to K-town—the type of neighborhood that sneaks up and floors you. Its instant, unmistakable Asian vibe owes largely to the prominence of karaoke bars, authentic grocers, and countless spots for fresh tofu or handmade dumplings. Throughout Midtown West, it is clear that equal attention is paid to cuisine as to arranging storybook holiday mannequins

behind the velvet ropes of Saks Fifth Avenue. As if to illustrate the point, the Japanese bakery, **Minamoto Kitchoan**, channels elegance and subtlety in its beautiful rice cakes, bejeweled with plum wine gelée. The exquisite packaging makes these the penultimate hostess gift. On the other end of the spectrum, **AQ Kafé** puts every effort into serving three outstanding meals a day to its midtown devotees (four, if counting the fab pastries). French-influenced **Petrossian Boutique** offers caviar and croissants to their patrons; and **Marketa** is great for Greek food fans, after which an espresso shot at **FIKA** (where the Swedes display their passion and skill for the Italian elixir) tastes divine. Wind up the affair with a stirring cocktail at the chic **Empire Room** housed in the Empire State Building.

TIME WARNER CENTER

No visit here is complete without a tribute to the gargantuan feat that is the Time Warner Center, presiding over regal Columbus Circle. Here, world-renowned chefs indulge both themselves and their patrons with earth-shattering success. The good news is that the economic downturn has eased demands for reservations (the bad news is the price tag). Still, a range of pleasures can be found here, from **Bouchon Bakery**'s classic French macarons, to the eye-popping style and sass of **Stone Rose Lounge**.

Midtown West

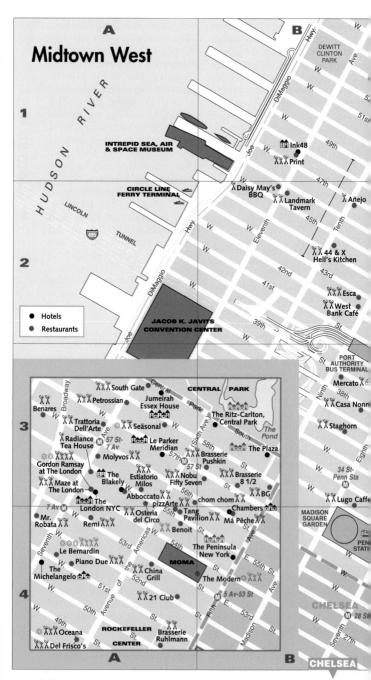

HUDSON RIVER

INTREPID SEA, AIR & SPACE MUSEUM

CIRCLE LINE FERRY TERMINAL

LINCOLN TUNNEL

I-495

DEWITT CLINTON PARK

Joe DiMaggio Hwy.

W. Hwy.

Eleventh

Tenth

Ninth

W. 51st

49th

47th

45th

43rd

41st

42nd

39th

38th

Ink48

Print

Daisy May's BBQ

Landmark Tavern

Añejo

44 & X Hell's Kitchen

Esca

West Bank Café

JACOB K. JAVITS CONVENTION CENTER

PORT AUTHORITY BUS TERMINAL

Mercato X

Casa Nonn

Staghorn

Lugo Caffe

- ● Hotels
- ● Restaurants

Inset map

Broadway

Central Park S.

CENTRAL PARK

South Gate

Petrossian

Jumeirah Essex House

The Ritz-Carlton, Central Park

The Pond

Benares

Trattoria Dell'Arte

Seäsonal

Radiance Tea House

57 St-7 Av

Le Parker Meridian

Sixth Ave.

Gordon Ramsay at The London

Molyvos

The Blakely

Estiatorio Milos

Brasserie Pushkin

The Plaza

57th St.

Brasserie 8 1/2

Maze at The London

Abboccato

pizzArte

Nobu Fifty Seven

chom chom

BG

The London NYC

7 Av

Osteria del Circo

Tang Pavilion

Má Pêche

Chambers

Mr. Robata

Remi

Benoit

The Peninsula New York

Seventh

Le Bernardin

Piano Due

China Grill

MOMA

The Modern

E. 55th St.

MADISON SQUARE GARDEN

PEN STATI

34 St-Penn Sta

Eighth

Ninth

38th

W. 28 S

CHELSEA

The Michelangelo

21 Club

Fifth Ave.

Madison

5 Av-53 St

53rd

Oceana

Del Frisco's

ROCKEFELLER CENTER

Brasserie Ruhlmann

49th

50th

51st

52nd

53rd

Avenue of the Americas

CHELSEA

260

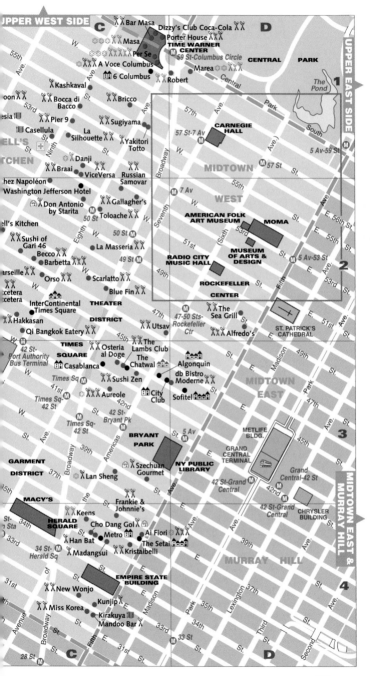

Abboccato

Italian

 A3

136 W. 55th St. (bet. Sixth & Seventh Aves.)

Subway: 57 St
Phone: 212-265-4000
Web: www.abboccato.com
Prices: $$$

Lunch Mon – Sat
Dinner nightly

Housed within Blakely Hotel, Abboccato is smart, attractive, and expertly run under the watchful eye of seasoned restaurateurs—the Livanos family (also behind nearby Oceana). An elegant yet rustic dining room, bar area ripe for people-watching, attentive service, and pretty *terrazza* that almost swings onto the sidewalk boast their characteristic style and provide a sophisticated antidote to this bustling midtown location.

The Italian menu meanders through the Peninsula, and each offering is a regional specialty like spaghetti carbonara, made here with house-cured duck prosciutto. An additional menu is dedicated exclusively to *cicchetti*. The dessert offerings are not extensive but remember the classics, such as tiramisu or cannoli.

Alfredo's

 Italian

D2

4 W. 49th St. (bet. Fifth & Sixth Aves.)

Subway: 47-50 Sts - Rockefeller Ctr
Phone: 212-397-0100
Web: www.alfredos.com
Prices: $$$

Lunch & dinner daily

No matter how busy it gets, Alfredo's has certain assets in spades: their consistent success is thanks to the love and attention of a polished, professional kitchen and warm servers passionate about the cuisine.

Make your way past the hungry tourists that mob its scene and be rewarded with pizza and pasta delicious enough to make your *ragazza* blush. Their classic fettuccine Alfredo is worth braving the wilds of 30 Rock. Still, the wise gourmand goes further to explore the likes of a Baccanale tasting menu, based on the flavors of imperial Rome (think crisp seafood sausage or house-made lasagna with white veal Bolognese and a Marsala wine reduction).

To avoid these midtown crowds and prices, try the gloriously gargantuan TriBeCa sibling, Trattoria Cinque.

Ai Fiori

Italian 〰️ XXX

C4

400 Fifth Ave. (bet. 36th & 37th Sts.)

Subway: 34 St - Herald Sq
Phone: 212-613-8660
Web: www.aifiorinyc.com
Prices: $$$$

Lunch & dinner daily

Ted Axelrod

Chef Michael White's stunner may be sequestered in the dark-shaded, glossily finished Setai Fifth Avenue located just blocks away from the famed Empire State building, but its soul belongs "among the flowers" (hence the name).

Perched above the hotel's lobby, Ai Fiori is accessed by ascending a gently winding limestone staircase. The room is spaciously arranged with plenty of surrounding windows lending lightness to the stylish setting gilded with plush napery, gorgeous floral arrangements, and an elegant bar that's perfect for a solo repast.

Through a modern Italian menu, Chef White expresses his ability to cull an expert team capable of great things. Dishes find inspiration from the Italian and French Rivieras, balancing rustic favorites with elegant presentations. Pasta is a standout, as in a bowlful of *pansotti*–pot-bellied pockets– glistening in silky veal jus and plumped by a filling of braised snails. Entrées have revealed roasted rack of lamb *en crepinette* sided by a stack of black pepper-flecked *panisse*. Meals come to a strong close with sweet finales such as *sformato di cioccolato*, chocolate mousse studded with preserved cherries and encased in devil's food cake.

Añejo

B2

668 Tenth Ave. (at 47th St.)

Subway: 50 St (Eighth Ave.)
Phone: 212-920-4770
Web: www.anejonyc.com
Prices: $$

Lunch Sat – Sun
Dinner Tue – Sun

Fact: things are sprouting fast in NY's Mexican food realm and heart-stopping, buzz-worthy Añejo is at the head of the pack. The keyed-in kitchen keeps this delicious trajectory alive and well. Adding sensory fuel is the hand-painted Day of the Dead mural in the rear. Sturdy communal tables are chockablock so after one (or three) of their excellent cocktails, your neighbor may be a new best friend.

The rustic room is softened by chandeliers and puts you in the right mood for such notable food as fluffy corn dumplings floating in a meaty porridge of chorizo and Oaxaca cheese. The guacamole trio starring tomatillos and roasted pineapple is a salty addiction; while mushroom-*huitlacoche* tacos raised a notch by smoky mayo elicit countless "oohs" and "aahs."

Ardesia

C1

510 W. 52nd St. (bet. Tenth & Eleventh Aves.)

Subway: 50 St (Eighth Ave.)
Phone: 212-247-9191
Web: www.ardesia-ny.com
Prices: $$

Lunch Sat – Sun
Dinner nightly

Thanks to the talented ladies of Ardesia, this far western stretch of Hell's Kitchen bears a trace of industrial grit, yet is suddenly stylish and chic. Parked amid glistening high rises and the Daily Show studio with Prada's offices but one block away, this sleek spot is the result of owner Mandy Oser and Chef Amorette Casaus' (trained under Gray Kunz) collective hard work, and a favorite for locals seeking scrumptious small plates.

Sit and savor a glass at the white marble bar and admire the floor-to-ceiling blackboards displaying their terrific wine selection. Lounge on a sexy brown velvet banquette while nibbling homemade NY-style pretzels with Maldon salt, spicy Dijon, and cheddar-Gruyère sauce. Or, learn how to make them at the chef's special class.

Aureole

Contemporary 🍴🍴🍴

C3

135 W. 42nd St. (bet. Broadway & Sixth Ave.)

Subway: 42 St - Bryant Pk
Phone: 212-319-1660
Web: www.charliepalmer.com
Prices: $$$$

Lunch Mon – Fri
Dinner nightly

Eric Laignel

The signage may be spare, but the Bank of America tower's ground floor windows are sure to reveal Aureole's bustling scene within. Find casual bar dining in front, and a more intimate and muted back room with upholstered banquettes and shimmering pillows.

The large mezzanine is dedicated to displaying a bright wall of wine. Few restaurants attain the consistency of Aureole: dining here is a pleasure from start to finish. The contemporary menu may highlight the global influences of ruby red shrimp with coconut, lemongrass, and Asian pear. Presentations are attractive and enticing—silky pockets of pasta squares are delicate enough to see the spoon-tender short-rib filling inside. Nutty ribbons of pecorino, roasted chestnuts, and pomegranate droplets bring tart and earthy complexity to this excellent dish. Fish is beautifully cooked, as in golden-crisped skin branzino set atop an emerald green herb purée, dressed with shaved fennel, red onion, and a scattering of dandelion leaves.

Starry-eyed dessert lovers will find their bliss in the *gianduja*: hazelnut cake piped with bittersweet chocolate ganache, served with a chocolate mousse-filled caramelized tuile and chocolate-hazelnut ice cream.

A Voce Columbus ✿

Italian 𝗫𝗫𝗫

C1

10 Columbus Circle (in the Time Warner Center)

Subway: 59 St - Columbus Circle   Lunch & dinner daily
Phone: 212-823-2523
Web: www.avocerestaurant.com
Prices: $$$

Bruce Buck

There is a palpable warmth upon entering this third-floor Time Warner respite. The space is comfortably chic and always busy, but no matter, the hosts and servers never waver as guests continue to pile in. Dark mosaic tiles, natural light, and metals create a visual balance that is at once very contemporary and very Italian. Ask for a window table, but know that every seat will share a stunning view of this prime position over Columbus Circle. As grand as the vista may be, remember to also glance at neighboring tables, dominated by Europeans, area residents, and media powerhouses (their deep discussions are well-articulated and worthy of a little eavesdropping).

On the menu, Chef Missy Robbins' talent and passion shine through a mix of fashionably rustic dishes with swirls of true Italian modernity. Pastas might include springy house-made linguine nestled around a rich shellfish sugo with spicy heat and garlicky breadcrumbs. Expect entrées such as pearly white hake poached in olive oil, with earthy white beans, tomato *conserva*, and black pepper vinaigrette.

Prix-fixe menus are only available at lunch, though a luscious panna cotta crested with grapefruit segments is offered all day.

Barbetta

C2

Italian XXX

321 W. 46th St. (bet. Eighth & Ninth Aves.)

Subway: 50 St (Eighth Ave.)   Lunch & dinner Tues – Sat
Phone: 212-246-9171
Web: www.barbettarestaurant.com
Prices: $$$

Standing proud since its 1906 opening, Barbetta proves that the "new" in New York need not be taken literally. From its gilded furnishings to its candelabra and crystal chandeliers, this dining room celebrates an old-world aesthetic. At the ornate tables, find true-blue New Yorkers who, as regulars, have been treated like family here for more than century (though outsiders may detect a hint of indifference from the service staff).

Consistency is the theme here, and some of the menu items, such as *minestrone giardiniera*, have been served since the very beginning. Good, traditional Italian food with a few throwbacks–capped off by a selection from the dessert trolley–prove that this just might be your grandfather's favorite Italian restaurant.

Bar Masa

C1

Japanese XX

10 Columbus Circle (in the Time Warner Center)

Subway: 59 St - Columbus Circle   Lunch & dinner Mon – Sat
Phone: 212-823-9800
Web: www.masanyc.com
Prices: $$$

Bar Masa is practically an elder of the Time Warner Center—the mall that many NYers derided but is now a gourmet harbor attracting moneyed foreign tourists and locals alike. Booming with banter, Bar Masa fills with shoppers craving a modern and more American take on Japanese cuisine. Dining here is a decidedly different experience from its eponymous neighbor.

Limestone floors and wood accents warm the space with a convivial aura; a row of tables sit behind billowing fabrics and relaxing perches are set at the bar. The chefs offer no showmanship here: from behind curtains, a masterpiece of oysters bathed in a citrus-mirin sauce, dancing shrimp sprinkled with chili salt, and squat glasses of cocoa- and black sesame-ice cream magically appear.

Manhattan ▶ Midtown West

267

Becco

Italian

C2

355 W. 46th St. (bet. Eighth & Ninth Aves.)

Subway: 50 St (Eighth Ave.)   Lunch & dinner daily
Phone: 212-397-7597
Web: www.becco-nyc.com
Prices: $$

Designed for the throngs of tourists, Becco may verge on brusque but is all about business. Given the bold and big-named eateries lining Restaurant Row, the competition rages on and Becco reigns supreme with one secret behind its success: Lidia Bastianich. Amid dishes piled high and a bread basket that could choke an *anatra*, patrons are visibly content throughout her multi-nook arena.

Ms. Bastianich deserves accolades for this well-oiled machine. Expect the likes of mozzarella in *carrozza*, deep-fried bread slices sandwiching mozzarella and served over pesto; grilled swordfish covered with sautéed onions and poised atop roasted sweet potatoes; and *strudel di mele*, an apple purée studded with raisins in bread-like pastry and cinnamon ice cream.

Benares

Indian

A3

240 W. 56th St. (bet. Broadway & Eighth Ave.)

Subway: 59 St - Columbus Circle   Lunch & dinner daily
Phone: 212-397-0707
Web: www.benaresnyc.com
Prices: $$

Christened after the holy city set on the banks of the Ganges, seafood-focused Benares brings a sacred slice of India to the heart of Hell's Kitchen. With scarce competition and by virtue of its sultry mien, the polished eatery soars to great peaks—picture turmeric-toned chairs and walls dressed in vibrant Benarasi saris. Large green plants feel lush and gold-veined tiles lend a bit of glitz. Accoutrements include the small service bar, lively kitchen, and tasty repertoire of vegetarian dishes, like creamy Kashmiri soup with roasted turnips.

Meat and (especially) fish seekers can rest easy, as these play prominent roles in the *safed gosht*, a Rajasthani specialty featuring marinated lamb in cardamom-almond sauce; and *sevai kurma* brimming with seafood.

Benoit

A4

French XX

60 W. 55th St. (bet. Fifth & Sixth Aves.)

Subway: 57 St
Phone: 646-943-7373
Web: www.benoitny.com
Prices: $$

Lunch & dinner daily

What started as the Manhattan outpost of a century-old Parisian classic has grown, matured, and indeed come into its own as an elegant French bistro with genuine New York style. One step inside reveals layer upon lovely layer of red accents, polished brass, frosted glass, and modern chairs that combine to make this a very special place.

Be sure to begin with a range of hors d'oeuvres that showcase the kitchen's potential, from lentil salad topped with quail eggs to the excellent rillettes and *baccalau*. While some dishes are touched with innovations, others highlight good quality and tradition, as in the hand-cut steak tartare. Desserts are not to be missed—the rum *baba*, topped tableside with rum and dollops of whipped cream, is simply outstanding.

BG

B3

American XX

754 Fifth Ave. (at 58th St.)

Subway: 5 Av - 59 St
Phone: 212-872-8977
Web: www.bergdorfgoodman.com
Prices: $$$

Lunch & dinner daily

The inviting and inventive *carte du jour* is never lost on its discerning clientele at posh and stunning BG. Afternoon tea is all the rage within this Parisian-style brasserie that oozes panache with its ornate seats and hand-crafted wallpaper. If tea's not your taste, stop at the bar for an excellent *croque monsieur* dressed with béchamel and organic greens, then gaze into those Central Park vistas.

BG's setting is exquisite and certainly not a secret, especially among its bevy of Bergdorf blondes. Neither are their heavy-hitting chefs who employ the finest ingredients in the main event, like a Gotham salad tossing chicken, Gruyère, and beets; or lobster Napoleon featuring fresh pasta frolicking with meaty lobster, mushrooms, and truffle butter.

Blue Fin

Seafood ✗✗

C2

1567 Broadway (at 47th St.)

Subway: 49 St
Phone: 212-918-1400
Web: www.bluefinnyc.com
Prices: $$$

Lunch & dinner daily

It's inside the W Hotel so you know it's going to look good and Blue Fin doesn't disappoint with its two-tiered dining room, sweeping staircase, and baby grand piano. The scene is buzzy on the first floor and at the sushi bar, so if you're looking for quieter digs, head upstairs.

Blue Fin is a seafood spot—would you have guessed? Maybe it's the light blue walls with the motion of the ocean hanging installation. There's sushi and a raw bar, as well as an assortment of everything from grilled octopus salad to Atlantic striped bass. Desserts, like the key lime mojito tart, are where it's at. Honestly, who can resist the adorable "going to the theater" treat with selections like gooey and warm chocolate chip cookies or caramel popcorn to-go?

Bocca di Bacco

Italian ✗✗

C1

828 Ninth Ave. (bet. 54th & 55th Sts.)

Subway: 50 St (Eighth Ave.)
Phone: 212-265-8828
Web: www.boccadibacconyc.com
Prices: $$

Lunch Sat – Sun
Dinner nightly

If hunting for a true-blue trattoria, Bocca di Bacco is the ideal entrant. Their quarters may be cramped and a bit dark but are flanked with admirable traits: a great wine list to match an agreeable menu. The décor is a hark back to those Italian *cantine* with oak barrels and wooden accents. The bar up front affords lovely wining and dining and is an alluring roost for what ever hue your mood exudes.

Even if the staff vanishes, rest assured they will return with a rustic repast. Dishes verge on the small side so feel free to over order. Shellfish-stuffed ravioli in a brandy sauce; herb-roasted lamb shank matched with mashed potatoes; and an irresistible walnut and chocolate *tartufo* decked with whipped cream are only some of their big hits.

Braai

South African ✗✗

C1

329 W. 51st St. (bet. Eighth & Ninth Aves.)

Subway: 50 St (Eighth Ave.)
Phone: 212-315-3315
Web: www.braainyc.com
Prices: $$

Lunch Fri – Sun
Dinner Tue – Sun

From its ground floor townhouse home, Braai is adored for its tantalizing South African cuisine. Two tables sit up front in a snug patio, which dovetails into a long and slender dark wood space. Drawing inspiration from its region, wide planks make up the flooring while the arched ceiling is thatched with straw. Yet the African décor in the dining room, set with marble-topped communal tables, is anything but kitschy.

The menu is resplendent with new and balanced flavors that are at once evident in *frikkadel*, a classic dish of baked meatballs in broth; or calamari drenched in a lovely wine-lemon emulsion. Speaking of mainstays, *bunny chow*, a street treat of lamb curry ladled into a bread bowl, is a favorite here as well as at nearby sibling Xai Xai.

Brasserie 8 1/2

Contemporary ✗✗✗

B3

9 W. 57th St. (bet. Fifth & Sixth Aves.)

Subway: 57 St
Phone: 212-829-0812
Web: www.brasserie8andahalf.com
Prices: $$$

Lunch Sun – Fri
Dinner nightly

Nestled into the unique Skidmore building, the sweeping, tangerine-colored staircase that delivers you into Brasserie 8 1/2 is a bit more theatrical than the menu's predictable performance, but this Patina Group restaurant impresses nonetheless. Settle into the main dining room–with its eye-popping hues and original artwork of Henri Matisse and Fernand Léger–to find solid, contemporary, and prettily plated offerings. From the seasonal game menu, expect the likes of stuffed pheasant with apples, foie gras, cabbage, and an apple cider reduction.

Though its thoughtful design and well-spaced tables will impress company, it also caters well to solo guests, whether at the handsome, elevated mezzanine or one of the two sleek bars anchoring the room.

Brasserie Pushkin

 B3

41 W. 57th St. (bet. Fifth & Sixth Aves.)

Subway: 57 St
Lunch & dinner daily
Phone: 212-465-2400
Web: www.brasseriepushkin.com
Prices: $$$

Brasserie Pushkin is a grand labor of love. Lucratively set steps from venerable Carnegie Hall, this opulent arena successfully delivers gratifying Russian classics. If silky *pelmeni* in broth, served with sour cream comes to mind, you are starting to get the drift.

Large window panes reveal an enchanting patisserie counter filled with sweet macarons. Other delights in store like parquet floors, gilded sconces, and a Murano chandelier further uplift a cheery bar scene rife with soft murmurs, perhaps about a flawless consommé pocked with flaky salmon; or braised veal blintzes licked with a ginger-vodka sauce. The service may verge on fussy, but nothing takes away from the delicious art behind the Cafe Pushkin cake crested with raspberry geleé.

Brasserie Ruhlmann

🍴🍴

A4

45 Rockefeller Plaza (bet. Fifth & Sixth Aves.)

Subway: 47-50 Sts - Rockefeller Ctr
Lunch daily
Phone: 212-974-2020
Dinner Mon – Sat
Web: www.brasserieruhlmann.com
Prices: $$$

Named for the French designer, Emile-Jacques Ruhlmann, this midtown brasserie sweeps you from the cacophony of touristy Rockefeller Center and into a heady vision of old-school Paris, surrounded by magnificent art deco touches, dark chocolate colors, faux ebony walls, and perhaps a few personalities from nearby NBC Studios.

A commendable team heads the kitchen, spinning a tandem of brasserie classics into delicious artistry. The daily specials (*plats du jour*) should be seriously considered during weekdays—starting with Monday's beef short rib Bourguignon and ending with Friday's lemon-rosemary seabass. A decadent cookie plate almost prepares you for the outside world again, with hazelnut-lemon stars, rich chocolate triangles, and creamy lemon squares.

Bricco

Italian   ✕✕

C1

304 W. 56th St. (bet. Eighth & Ninth Aves.)

Subway: 57 St - 7 Av
Phone: 212-245-7160
Web: www.bricconyc.com
Prices: $$

Lunch Mon – Fri
Dinner nightly

It's a bit of a challenge to spot this cozy nook in the swirling hubbub of nearby Columbus Circle, but its well worth the effort. Romantic little spots like Bricco are a rarity in this neck of the woods, and owner, Nino Catuogno, knows it—those autographed lipstick kisses lining the ceiling and popular, female-friendly bar prove it.

Couples can head back to the intimate main room for a comforting menu of delicious pizzas (maybe prosciutto, arugula, and creamy mozzarella?) visibly made to order in the brick oven; fat ribbons of whole wheat pasta in meaty ragù; or tender filet mignon dancing in brandy and cream, and sprinkled with crunchy peppercorns. Save room for a fragrant dessert of deep purple pears, poached in wine and liqueur.

Casa Nonna

Italian   ✕✕

B3

310 W. 38th St. (bet. Eighth & Ninth Aves.)

Subway: Times Sq - 42 St
Phone: 212-736-3000
Web: www.casanonna.com
Prices: $$

Lunch Mon – Fri
Dinner nightly

This sprawling arena may be steps from the blaring Port Authority Bus Terminal, yet it maintains its welcoming demeanor through a meandering series of rooms and nooks donned with decorative plates, plush banquettes, and framed artifacts. There is a dish for every taste at Casa Nonna, whose attractive menu is replete with satisfying and well-prepared Italian-American classics.

Heralding the faithful are "spiedini" of grilled fontina wrapped with speck and licked with syrup-sweet *saba* made of grape must reduction; spaghetti entwined with roasted cauliflower, garlic, and chili flakes; swordfish topped with roasted red peppers and olives, and a tangy *tartaletta* adorned with marshmallow cream.

Lavish cocktails and an infinite wine list make for fine pairings.

Casellula

American

C1

401 W. 52nd St. (bet. Ninth & Tenth Aves.)

Subway: 50 St (Eighth Ave.)
Phone: 212-247-8137
Web: www.casellula.com
Prices: $$

Dinner nightly

Casellula oozes with warmth in both look and feel. Dark wood tables, exposed brick, and flickering votives are a sight for sore eyes, while the delightful staff is so attentive and friendly, that you may never want to leave.

Small plates are big here, while medium plates feature yummy sandwiches (crunchy *muffulettas* stuffed with fontina and savory cured meats) and tasty shrimp tacos splashed with salsa verde. Pity the lactose intolerant, as dessert (pumpkin ice cream "sandwich" pecked with brown butter caramel?) along with cheese (and lots of it) are part and parcel of the special experience at this petit place. Feeling blue? They've got that and much more with over 50 different varieties, perfectly complemented by an excellent and vast wine list.

Chez Napoléon

French X

C2

365 W. 50th St. (bet. Eighth & Ninth Aves.)

Subway: 50 St (Eighth Ave.)
Phone: 212-265-6980
Web: www.cheznapoleon.com
Prices: $$

Lunch Mon – Fri
Dinner Mon – Sat

When a restaurant affectionately refers to its matriarch as "Chef Grand-mere," you can expect a virtual time warp into that ageless gastronomy of tried and true dishes like Dover sole and soufflés. Chez Napoléon may not be nouvelle, yet the Bruno family continues to work their magic in this old-school cream sauce favorite.

From the bartender's bellowing French accent to the décor featuring green walls dotted with sepia photos and historic maps, the petite bistro feels well-worn and beloved. Staying true to its tune, the food is equally authentic: think *escargots de Bourgogne*, meaty snails in garlicky parsley-butter; *rognons Dijonnaise*, hearty and deliciously seasoned veal kidneys; and *pêche Melba* with vanilla ice cream and raspberry coulis.

China Grill

 A4

Asian

60 W. 53rd St. (bet. Fifth & Sixth Aves.)

Subway: 7 Av
Phone: 212-333-7788
Web: www.chinagrillmgt.com
Prices: $$$

Lunch Mon – Sat
Dinner nightly

Opened more than 20 years ago, this first China Grill continues to be a perennial favorite and serves as the flagship of Jeffrey Chodorow's international restaurant organization. The sprawling interior, designed by Jeffrey Beers, is housed on the ground floor of the CBS building and features a multi-level dining room of soaring 30-foot ceilings accented with white canopy light fixtures. The long bar area is a popular spot to unwind after a long day at the office.

Large tables provide the perfect spot to dine with a group; the food is good, fun, and is best enjoyed when shared. Served family style, the Asian-influenced menu may include perfectly fried rice topped with creamy, diced avocado, or delicate pancakes generously filled with tender lobster.

Cho Dang Gol

C4

Korean

55 W. 35th St. (bet. Fifth & Sixth Aves.)

Subway: 34 St - Herald Sq
Phone: 212-695-8222
Web: www.chodanggolny.com
Prices: ⊜⊜

Lunch & dinner daily

K-town may boast its barbecue joints, but Cho Dang Gol has its own calling in tofu, that creamy little bean curd that sets hearts a-jumping. The restaurant is named for a South Korean village famous for this specialty; one imagines those locals would approve of this fresh, silky house-made version. Here, tofu finds its way into more than two dozen dishes, including hot and crispy pancakes, filled with ground pork and vegetables; or a cast iron pot, loaded with sweet and spicy octopus. A spicy prime rib casserole is perfect for sharing.

At first glance, Cho Dang Gol is warm and sentimental with cute Korean artifacts and rustic wooden tables, but don't expect like-minded service. When the house gets packed, servers respond with brusque efficiency.

chom chom

A3

40 W. 56th St. (bet. Fifth & Sixth Aves.)

Subway: 57 St   Lunch & dinner daily
Phone: 212-213-2299
Web: www.chomchomnyc.com
Prices: $$

Somehow, chom chom landed well north of its K-town compatriots to happily bring its soul-shaking Korean cuisine to a neighborhood away from the clamor. The vibe at this Korean corridor is mod and folksy (vertically cut trees drape the walls), but the food is flavorfully faithful. Sip a soju at the bar before diving into a menu that favors fun over tradition.

Chom chom wears many hats, but everything is crested with serious ingredients. Begin with a few "kapas" (Korean tapas) like spicy pork buns; succulent sweet potato *japchae* with paper-thin beef and vegetables; and *bo ssäm* with braised and seared pork belly, spicy batons of root vegetables, and fresh Boston lettuce. Simpler dishes highlight amazing quality, as in broiled wild salmon.

Daisy May's BBQ

B2

623 Eleventh Ave. (at 46th St.)

Subway: 50 St (Eighth Ave.)   Lunch & dinner daily
Phone: 212-977-1500
Web: www.daisymaysbbq.com
Prices: ⊖⊘

Trek to the ends of the earth (known to some as Eleventh Avenue), and the barbecue gods will reward you. Welcome to Daisy May's BBQ USA—where Chef/owner (and cookbook author) Adam Perry Lang's smoky, succulent 'cue served up in a big old dining hall (think school lunchroom-meets-barn) counts everyone from Oprah to bike messengers to midtown suits as fans.

Three chalkboards list the pig specials: a whole pig for up to 12 people (should you be blessed with so many friends); half a pig; and a few daily specials. The house pulled pork, a mound of tender, glistening sweet and smoky pork, is a fan favorite for good reason. A limited selection of beer and wine is available to wash it all down, but our money's on the irresistibly sweet and minty iced tea.

Danji

C1

346 W. 52nd St. (bet. Eighth & Ninth Aves.)

Subway: 50 St (Eighth Ave.)
Phone: 212-586-2880
Web: www.danjinyc.com
Prices: $$

Lunch Mon – Fri
Dinner Mon – Sat

James Park

Heralding the entrance to this energetic and fun foodie destination is a perpetual queue of hungry devotees. While the menu is their main draw, the room itself has über charm. Amid a cozy stage of concrete floors and whitewashed walls, Danji is both elegant and edgy with wire-caged lights and a beautiful display of earthenware. Still, everyone is here for the distinctly modern Korean fare, courtesy of Chef/owner Hooni Kim.

Two communal blond wood counters readied with sleek white-framed stools provide most of the seating, and a smaller cluster of tables reside in the back. Small white plates and disposable chopsticks might be your only tabletop frill, but after tackling a hunk of Danji-braised short ribs, where the slow-cooked meat is so deliciously tender that it slips from the bone onto delicately cooked vegetables, what more can one need?

Clean, yet vibrant flavor is lucidly conveyed in yellowtail sashimi (procured from Tokyo's Tsukiji market) dressed with slivers of jalpeño and *cho jang*, a sweet and spicy red chilli paste. But really, it's the kimchi trio (daikon, Napa cabbage, and buttery cucumber) with its compelling flavors and fresh crunch that brings you back time and again.

277

db Bistro Moderne

D3 Contemporary ✕✕

55 W. 44th St. (bet. Fifth & Sixth Aves.)

Subway: 5 Av
Phone: 212-391-2400
Web: www.danielnyc.com
Prices: $$$

Lunch & dinner daily

This stylish Daniel Boulud bistro is an ideal upscale spot for drinking and dining pre- or post-theater—after 9:00 P.M., try the champagne and dessert pairings. Its moneyed European clientele and service that is beyond reproach befits the sophisticated space, divided into a lively, red-accented front room and quieter, more refined back.

Boulud's French-inflected menu showcases consistency and formidable skills in dishes like country duck pâté that somehow becomes richer and more decadent with each bite. The chocolate clafouti is garnished with outstanding vanilla ice cream and chocolate sorbet. Yet most famously, the humble burger is reinvented when ground sirloin is filled with braised short ribs, foie gras, and black truffles on a Parmesan bun.

Del Frisco's

A4 Steakhouse ✕✕✕

1221 Sixth Ave. (at 49th St.)

Subway: 47-50 Sts - Rockefeller Ctr
Phone: 212-575-5129
Web: www.delfriscos.com
Prices: $$$

Lunch Mon – Fri
Dinner nightly

Prime, aged, corn-fed beef is the main attraction at this sprawling, outrageously successful outpost of the Dallas-based steakhouse chain. Portions range from the petite filet to a 24-ounce Porterhouse to make any Texan proud. The menu may begin with a suitably rich feast of crab gnocchi or caviar, but then does an about face with offerings of angel hair pasta or creamed corn. Lunch is an affordable way to sample their classics.

Complementing its McGraw-Hill Building home, Del Frisco's flaunts a masculine look with its large L-shaped bar, dramatic wrought-iron balcony, wood accents, and floor-to-ceiling windows. The mezzanine dining area, accessible by a sweeping staircase, enjoys a quieter ambience.

Also try Del Frisco's Grille in Rockefeller Plaza.

Dizzy's Club Coca-Cola

C1

Southern

10 Columbus Circle (in the Time Warner Center)

Subway: 59 St - Columbus Circle   Dinner nightly
Phone: 212-258-9595
Web: www.jalc.org
Prices: $$

It's probably one of the better ways to spend a night on the town: reserve a modestly priced ticket, request a perch at the bar or stage-facing table, and you will start to understand what all the fuss is about at this modern and swanky "club." From the alluring lights and cars dotting Columbus Circle, to a dizzying show of Southern staples and jazz artists, the audience is entranced at this formidable home to America's equally formidable art form.

And can there be anything better than crispy Louisiana hot wings, roasted duck with a salty side of andouille étouffée, and a buttery pecan pie to go with such serious tunes? Everybody is here for the top performances, taking in the dreamy views of Central Park along with a Genever splashed with white cranberry.

Don Antonio by Starita

C2

Pizza

309 W. 50th St. (bet. 8th & 9th Aves.)

Subway: 50 St (Eighth Ave.)   Lunch & dinner daily
Phone: 646-719-1043
Web: www.donantoniopizza.com
Prices: $$

Get on your knees and thank the pizza gods for this divine addition to the Neopolitan pie scene. The place has serious street cred—the original in Naples has been open since 1901, and its current owner, Antonio Starita, is a renowned instructor. The dark, narrow space rocks a polished but raw style, with deep reds, exposed brick, and spider-like light fixtures. It's also packed, so expect a wait.

The delectable offerings include the *girella*, a homemade mozzarella-filled crust topped with pecorino, *prosciutto cotto*, grape tomatoes, and arugula; and *montanara Starita*, fried pizza dough crowned with smoked buffalo mozzarella and tomato sauce. Though pies are the main draw, appetizers like potato croquets are always tasty. Gluten free crust is on offer.

Esca

B2

Seafood ✗✗

402 W. 43rd St. (bet. Ninth & Tenth Aves.)

Subway: 42 St - Port Authority Bus Terminal
Phone: 212-564-7272
Web: www.esca-nyc.com
Prices: $$$

Lunch Mon – Sat
Dinner nightly

The spicy Gaeta olives and white bean bruschetta at Esca could sustain a foodie for days, but lucky for us, they also proffer a swarm of seafood that vows to nourish for years. This butter-colored and wood-planked outpost via Dave Pasternack is divinity for fish lovers. Wine cabinets at every turn and excitable servers dressed in neckties are sure to lure the trendsters.

Most dishes are delightfully literal letting the *pesci* shine. It's best to bring helpers to sample their schools of crudo (amberjack glazed with olive aïoli and sea salt) and antipasti like seared monkfish liver with logs of soft-cooked rhubarb. But, it's not all about sharing as crisp, golden brown flounder fillets accentuated simply with sautéed mushrooms and leeks are all yours.

Estiatorio Milos

A3

Greek ✗✗✗

125 W. 55th St. (bet. Sixth & Seventh Aves.)

Subway: 57 St
Phone: 212-245-7400
Web: www.milos.ca
Prices: $$$

Lunch Mon – Fri
Dinner nightly

Estiatorio Milos is a Greek restaurant with such deliciously singular focus on the sea that it may best be described as sunbleached. Beyond a giant urn stationed at the entrance, there are no shawarmas or moussakas in sight; however, the gleaming dining room is dramatic, amid 30-foot ceilings and a swarm of hovering suits that part like the Red Sea at the hostesses' command. Then, of course, there are the iced beds of fish: pink, gold, clear-eyed, and flecked with silver, they are a tableau of the Agean's bounty.

The dining room casts a spare glow on such tasty portions as grilled St. Pierre, wonderfully fleshy and crisp with a squeeze of lemon and hint of smoke; or the Lavraki and Petropsara soup, a classic treasure hailing from Santorini.

etcetera etcetera

Italian

C2

352 W. 44th St. (bet. Eighth & Ninth Aves.)

Subway: 42 St - Port Authority Bus Terminal
Phone: 212-399-4141
Web: www.etcetcnyc.com
Prices: $$

Lunch Wed & Sun
Dinner nightly

Hip and modern, etcetera etcetera is a breath of fresh air in the often staid Theater District. The modern and contemporary design punctuated by pops of bright orange has a Milan-meets-Miami sensibility, but the crowd is never too cool for school.

The kitchen turns out seriously solid and well-prepared meals. Pasta and risotto dishes, such as the homemade basil spaghetti with jumbo lump crab and sweet roasted peppers, can be halved and served as appetizers. The entrées (crispy Cornish hen, braised lamb shank) are hearty and offer beautifully balanced flavors and textures. Etcetera etcetera proves that looking good does not always mean spending a fortune—the $35 prix-fixe three-course dinner is an exceptional value.

44 & X Hell's Kitchen

American

B2

622 Tenth Ave. (at 44th St.)

Subway: 42 St - Port Authority Bus Terminal
Phone: 212-977-1170
Web: www.44andx.com
Prices: $$

Lunch & dinner daily

There's a sophisticated kind of charm about this casual, delicious, and affordable neighborhood haunt. Maybe it's the carved wooden bar with intricate wrought-iron bar stools, the gorgeous chandeliers against the crisp white ceilings, or the stunning fresh flower arrangements? Or it could be those quirky religious statues perched away from the merry-makers at the bar? Whatever it is, it works and everyone seems to love it.

Snag a seat on the spacious sidewalk patio and get nibbling on Maryland lump meat crab cakes over sun dried tomato vinaigrette and roasted vegetables; or perhaps a persimmon salad with toasted walnuts, pomegranate seeds, and blue cheese. Mains include an excellent crispy sea bass over braised artichoke hearts and chanterelle mushrooms.

Frankie & Johnnie's

C4   S t e a k h o u s e   🍴

32 W. 37th St. (bet. Fifth & Sixth Aves.)

Subway: 34 St – Herald Sq
Phone: 212-947-8940
Web: www.frankieandjohnnies.com
Prices: $$$

Lunch Mon – Fri
Dinner Mon – Sat

You get a slice of history with your perfectly-seared ribeye at this storied Garment District steakhouse. The renovated townhouse–with its masculine sensibility and cozy wood-paneled library-turned upstairs dining room–used to belong to the actor John Drew Barrymore, and it is the second of three sibling restaurants that began in 1926 (the first restaurant is a stone's throw away and the third location resides in Rye, New York).

Served by a professional, all-male brigade, the food is pure steakhouse bliss: think silky Clams Casino, topped with crispy bacon and scallions; tender, bone-on ribeye, seared to rosy perfection; irresistibly crunchy hashbrowns; and buttery, flaky apple strudel, delivered with a side of fresh whipped cream.

Gallagher's

C2   S t e a k h o u s e   🍴

228 W. 52nd St. (bet. Broadway & Eighth Ave.)

Subway: 50 St (Broadway)
Phone: 212-245-5336
Web: www.gallaghersnysteakhouse.com
Prices: $$$

Lunch & dinner daily

Established in 1927 next to what is now the Neil Simon Theater, this culinary character and true New Yorker satisfies carnivores with deliciously juicy beef grilled over hickory coals. This focus is clear upon entering to face rows of assorted cuts hanging, patiently aging, in the glass-enclosed meat locker. Inside the wood-paneled dining room, charmingly gruff waiters in gold-trimmed blazers efficiently tend red-checked tables, alongside walls lined with nostalgic photographs of Broadway stars, politicians, and athletes.

While meals are not cheap, the quality shines. Classic salads and creamy desserts (a dense and creamy cheesecake) are sumptuous bookends to any meal here. The prix-fixe power lunch is an excellent option for the budget-conscious.

Gordon Ramsay at The London ✿✿

Contemporary 🍴🍴🍴🍴

A3

151 W. 54th St. (bet. Sixth & Seventh Aves.)

Subway: 7 Av
Phone: 212-468-8888
Web: www.gordonramsay.com
Prices: $$$$

Dinner Tue – Sat

Gordon Ramsay at The London NYC

To the rear of the ground floor of the beautiful London NYC, beyond Maze and The London Bar, sits the very elegant Gordon Ramsay restaurant. The formal room is nothing short of scintillating, dressed with pearl-laminated walls set aglow by ivory-shaded lamps, gleaming mirrors upon handsome wood panels, and spacious tables covered with thick linen and pristine bone china. While the staff may lack warmth, they compensate with attentive and professional service. Still, it remains that this is a place of elegant exclusivity.

Yet there is a more capricious side emanating from the kitchen. On a good night, each taste is extraordinarily classic and correct: a duo of Hudson Valley foie gras is smooth and perfectly pan-fried, with an accompanying terrine on a bed of spiced apples with thyme-infused brioche. Yet another dish may be masterful and sparked with creative zest, as in grilled venison loin complemented by a quenelle of cabbage chutney, wild dark chocolate triangles, charred romaine, crisp quark dumpling, and venison jus.

Desserts may balance every flavor, from the sweet tang to creamy richness of a mango parfait with coconut dacquoise, passion crème, and shards of chocolate meringue.

Hakkasan ✿

C2

Chinese 🍴🍴🍴

311 W. 43rd St. (bet. Eighth & Ninth Aves.)

Subway: 42 St - Port Authority Bus Terminal
Phone: 212-776-1818
Web: www.hakkasan.com
Prices: $$$$

Lunch & dinner daily

Daniel Kreiger

On the one hand, Hakkasan appears to live up to every cliché of big, corporate Asian dining: long halls and stunning blue glass doors lead to a massive mega-space smartly divided by carved marble and dark wood panels. It is so fully tricked out that the gorgeous waitstaff may have been hired for their casting-call good looks rather than menu knowledge, leaving you wondering if you've accidentally wandered into a nightclub (after all, there is no sign outside except a double "K"). On the other hand, the food here is very good; the dim sum, exceptional.

Seafood is their strong point, so begin with the likes of *shu mai* filled with chopped seafood and pork, topped with a thick slice of high quality sea scallop; or the truly excellent, silky, and tender king crab and mushroom roll. Dumplings might arrive bright green and encase delicate lobster meat, or crunchy, fried, and garlicky.

So is this authentic Chinese food? Not exactly: Hakkasan's cuisine is designed to please the high-end Western palate. It may be where Kim Kardashian would come to pose with a pair of chopsticks and a duck-stuffed pumpkin puff—but if she actually ate it, she'd probably tweet that it was "OMG fantastic."

Han Bat

Korean 🍴

53 W. 35th St. (bet. Fifth & Sixth Aves.)

Subway: 34 St - Herald Sq
Phone: 212-629-5588
Web: N/A
Prices: 💰💰

Lunch & dinner daily

Pop into this homey 24-hour K-town spot for traditional, tasty, and affordable Korean comfort food. Unlike the surrounding tearooms and barbecue joints in this energetic neighborhood, Han Bat favors a cozy, familial vibe and belly-warming specialties.

Meaty Korean standards are done especially well here and the portions are well-sized for groups. Order up sizzling clay pots of *dol sot bi bim bap* topped with beef, pickles, eggs, and the endless requisite condiments; plates of crispy and addictive *mandoo* stuffed with pork and vegetables; restorative, savory bowls of *sul run tang* waiting for you to salt them to taste; and a spicy stew of kimchi and tofu. Intrepid foodies should go on to sample the *u jok sara moo chim*—"jello" from ox legs.

Hell's Kitchen

Mexican 🍴

679 Ninth Ave. (bet. 46th & 47th Sts.)

Subway: 50 St (Eighth Ave.)
Phone: 212-977-1588
Web: www.hellskitchen-nyc.com
Prices: $$

Dinner nightly

Named for its western midtown locale, this hip and progressive Mexican eatery has been packing them in from day one with their complex, spiced-to-order food and great service to boot. Be forewarned that the vibe here can go from amiable and lively to raucous at prime times, so best to arrive early and enjoy a *cerveza*.

Everything is lovingly prepared, from starters like sweet plantain gorditas with goat cheese, salsa verde, and *pico de gallo*, to such decadent desserts as banana empanadas with chocolate sauce and whipped cream. Other highlights might include lobster-shrimp fritters with passion fruit mayonnaise and corn-tomatillo salsa, or poached artichoke quesadilla with *Idiazabal*, roasted sweet corn, and a lush poblano *crema*.

Kashkaval

C1

856 Ninth Ave. (bet. 55th & 56th Sts.)

Subway: 50 St (Eighth Ave.)
Phone: 212-581-8282
Web: www.kashkavalfoods.com
Prices: $$

Lunch & dinner daily

Kashkaval is a perfect little Mediterranean grocery/wine bar/ charming neighborhood eatery. Inside what appears to be a scruffy little storefront, the dedicated staff and gracious owners scurry to accommodate locals picking items from the front showcase that are ideal for a picnic basket; while the ever-growing lines of regulars happily wait for a precious table or stool to be vacated in the rustic and wood-beamed back dining room.

At its heart, this Mediterranean menu embodies what every diner wants: quality ingredients, careful cooking, good prices, and smiles to boot. Offerings may include the amazingly light, fresh, and tasty spinach *borek*, made with thin layers of dough, stuffed with spinach and feta, and resembling a rolled, flat cinnamon bun.

Keens

C4

72 W. 36th St. (bet. Fifth & Sixth Aves.)

Subway: 34 St - Herald Sq
Phone: 212-947-3636
Web: www.keens.com
Prices: $$$

Lunch Mon – Fri
Dinner nightly

Dating back to 1885, Keens is imbued with a palpable sense of history that sets it apart from the average midtown chophouse. A collection of dining rooms build the setting, each arranged with dark wood furnishings, linen-draped tables, and chock-full of Gilded Age charisma. A vestige of Keens' men-only, smoker's club days is displayed in their collection of long-stemmed, clay churchwarden pipes lining the ceiling.

Mouthwatering slabs of broiled meat star here; and the hand-selected prime cuts of beef are dry-aged in house. Icy platters of juicy oysters and bananas Foster are classic bookends to any feast.

The Pub Room offers lighter fare, and the bar pours one of the most extensive selections of single malt Scotch around.

Kirakuya

C4

Japanese

2 W. 32nd St. (bet. Fifth & Sixth Aves.)

Subway: 34 St - Herald Sq
Phone: 212-695-7272
Web: www.sakebarkirakuya.com
Prices: $$

Lunch Mon – Fri
Dinner Mon – Sat

Via its big pane windows hung with iridescent drapes, Kirakuya offers a rich view of K-town, vibrant with revelers and travelers. Set on the second floor of a nondescript building, this little sake bar excels for its expertly prepared mix of Japanese classics along with a few Korean favorites. The room is long, spacious, and great for groups eager to explore the array of sake and small plates. Hefty banquettes draped with red tapestries add a stamp of color.

The calm, sultry vibe is perfect for enjoying plates of pickled vegetables—each bite furnishes big flavor and fresh crunch. Arriving in ceramic vessels, other prized items include *nasu dengaku*, creamy-smoky grilled eggplant spread with sweetened miso; or thin slices of Berkshire pork tempura.

Kristalbelli

C4

Korean ✗✗

8 W. 36th St. (bet. Fifth & Sixth Aves.)

Subway: 34 St - Herald Sq
Phone: 212-290-2211
Web: www.kristalbelli.com
Prices: $$$

Lunch Mon – Sat
Dinner nightly

Turning up the heat in the dreary Garment District, Kristalbelli is a sexy harbinger of this fast-changing neighborhood. Outside, the gray slate and marble façade and impressive wooden door imply opulence; inside, crystal barbeque grills set on grey marble framed by a jolly gold monk bring table-top dining over-the-top. The fun and bling continues upstairs, in the young, hip, and hopping lounge.

Yet amid all this glitz and glam is a well-trained service team and very talented kitchen. *Banchan* opens with a superlative assortment that might include green chilies with fermented bean paste, marinated mushrooms, cold egg custard with scallions, and kimchi. A sparkling signature crystal bowl does not distract from the deeply favored, almost buttery ribeye.

Kunjip

Korean ✕

9 W 32nd St. (bet. Broadway & Fifth Ave.)

Subway: 34 St - Herald Sq
Phone: 212-216-9487
Web: www.kunjip.net
Prices: 🍴🍴

Lunch & dinner daily

Craving a cup of burdock tea and some kimchi at 2:00 A.M? Kunjip is open and ready to serve you. This place doles out traditional Korean food 24 hours a day seven days a week and the line is out the door. It's in the heart of bona fide K-town steps from Herald Square, so rest assured that it's the real deal.

Service is speedy and the place is bustling so it helps to know what to order. You can't go wrong with the restorative *dogani-tong*, a soup of simmered ox knees, which could be your stand-in for chicken noodle any day. Move on to the *goong joong dduk boki*, a thin fried rice cake of scallions and beef; or the *kam ja-tang*, an amazingly tender fall-off-the-bones meat soup. *Jok bal*, sliced pig's feet topped with a fishy sauce is refreshingly different.

La Masseria

C2

Italian ✕✕

235 W. 48th St. (bet. Broadway & Eighth Ave.)

Subway: 50 St (Eighth Ave.)
Phone: 212–582-2111
Web: www.lam.serianyc.com
Prices: $$

Lunch & dinner daily

One of the best Italian options in the area, this very authentic Theater District favorite heightens the everyday into true art. Dressed to look like an ancient farmhouse, guests are greeted by stone and stucco walls, exposed wood beams, and great old photos; not to mention the spot-on service. A few benevolent rounds of cheek-kissing and hand shaking are reserved for the chic regulars flocking in.

Yet when it comes to the food, La Masseria leaves the theatrics at the door. There are no distractions on a plate of fried zucchini named for the chef, Pino; or stuffed eggplant with smoked mozzarella. Other favorites have included calf liver sautéed with blueberry vinegar; or oven-roasted rabbit fragrant with fresh herbs and splashed with a wine sauce.

The Lambs Club

American ✗✗

C3

132 W. 44th St. (bet. Broadway & Sixth Ave.)

Subway: Times Sq - 42 St
Phone: 212-997-5262
Web: www.thelambsclub.com
Prices: $$$

Lunch & dinner daily

With its rich red leather seats, warming fireplace, and black-and-white photo-filled walls, The Lambs Club is reminiscent of its roots as a flourishing theater club. The dining room is dark, moody, and masculine; in contrast, the staff is friendly and all-around professional—it's easy to feel special here even when the volume is pumping.

This iconic building was envisioned by Stanford White, and renowned restauranteur/Chef Geoffrey Zakarian's American cuisine does the setting justice. Talent and care are palpable at this sequestered spot, in such dishes as grilled quail set over farro and tart-sweet cranberry *gastrique*; Heritage pork chop in a delicious sherry jus with crispy pork hash; and a lush lemon *baba* with limoncello and raspberries.

Landmark Tavern

American ✗✗

B2

626 Eleventh Ave. (at 46th St.)

Subway: 50 St (Eighth Ave.)
Phone: 212-247-2562
Web: www.thelandmarktavern.com
Prices: $$

Lunch & dinner daily

If you find yourself in the foodie nether regions of *rive à l'est*, here's some relief. Originally opened in 1868 as an Irish saloon that catered to local dock workers, Landmark Tavern later served time as a mediocre restaurant in desperate need of repairs. And repairs it got with its 2005 transformation into these handsome, fresh digs, replete with carved mahogany paneling, shiny beveled mirrors, and a clever menu to match. Though it's not quite the ambitious operation it was on the heels of the revamp, Landmark's commitment to high-minded pub fare is still very much intact. Try the hazelnut-crusted Scotch eggs, rolled with sausage and served over organic baby greens; or a fluffy shepherd's pie filled with buttery root vegetables and fragrant meat.

Lan Sheng ✿

C3

Chinese 🍴

60 W. 39th St. (bet. Fifth & Sixth Aves.)

Subway: 42 St - Bryant Pk
Phone: 212-575-8899
Web: www.lanshengrestaurant.com
Prices: $$

Lunch & dinner daily

MICHELIN

Lan Sheng's lip-numbing and heart-pounding hot pots are setting palates ablaze in midtown. The fact that their competent and efficient service team is as warm as a peppercorn ranks them well above their flourishing Sichuan brethren. It seems as if the culinary handcuffs have been removed from this "regional" cuisine, which shines here with excellent ingredients in simple yet skillful dishes.

Comfortable, high-backed banquettes, ornate wooden carvings, and recessed lighting impart an elegant touch to this long and narrow room. Hectic at lunch, Lan Sheng fills quickly with business diners slurping up the likes of delicious *dan dan* noodles tossed in soy and tangled with ground pork, smoky chili oil, and scallions—the apotheosis of spicy noodles. Likewise, pickled vegetables in chili oil are the perfect accompaniment to any meal.

Photos are an expedient way to navigate the expansive menu, which has included specialties like dry wok-fried green beans with spicy pork crumbles; or tea-smoked duck with marvelously crisped skin and tender, juicy meat. The house-special pork belly, thinly sliced in pan juices fragrant with ginger and paired with steamed *bao*, offers a rich and abundant experience.

La Silhouette

French ✕✕

C1

362 W. 53rd St. (bet. Eighth & Ninth Aves.)

Subway: 50 St (Eighth Ave.)
Phone: 212-581-2400
Web: www.la-silhouettenyc.com
Prices: $$$

Lunch & dinner daily

Quietly situated on the ground floor of a residential building, this little jewel shines unassumingly—one may be tempted to stroll right by. But an elegant, surprisingly sprawling interior with three distinct dining areas (and a terrace) melts away all preconceptions, as do the exceptional menu...and that saffron-infused gin.

Credit the freshly drafted chef, whose fine creations include foie gras *a la plancha* with kumquat *mostarda* and parsnip-pear mousseline; grilled white prawns over roasted Brussels sprouts and barley salad; and an outstanding lamb chop with shank *crepinette* over sweet potatoes and broccoli rabe. Among the inventive dessert offerings, go for popcorn "crème brûlée" with candied honey apples, caramel popcorn, and caramel ice cream.

Lugo Caffé

Italian ✕✕

B3

1 Penn Plaza (enter on 33rd St.)

Subway: 34 St - Penn Station
Phone: 212-760-2700
Web: www.lugocaffe.com
Prices: $$

Lunch Mon – Fri
Dinner Mon – Sat

Snagging a seat at the long, semi-circular bar is *the* best way to carouse at this spirited café, set in an otherwise drab locale. Everyone loves Lugo and awe prevails as one meanders through this vast, well-dressed space. Keeping company with quirky touches like coffee cans and Italian newspapers are more handsome elements like sky-high ceilings, massive windows, and cocooned booths.

Diners at this airy *ristorante* are here for the mood and food. Set with placemats that read like menus, tables tender the likes of irresistible homemade mozzarella paired with fiery peppers and *soppresata*; fried artichokes licked with lemon aïoli; *rigatoni all'Amatriciana* revealing salty pancetta; and classic rosemary chicken *al forno* with root vegetables and jus.

Le Bernardin ✿ ✿ ✿

Seafood 🗙🗙🗙🗙

155 W. 51st St. (bet. Sixth & Seventh Aves.)

Subway: 50 St (Broadway)
Phone: 212-554-1515
Web: www.le-bernardin.com
Prices: $$$$

Lunch Mon – Fri
Dinner Mon – Sat

Lyn Hughes Photography

There may be no better place to spend too much of someone else's money, especially now that Le Bernardin's massive renovations are complete. At last, midtown big bankers and deep-pocketed celebrants have a brand new, upscale bar and lounge in addition to the spectacular dining room that has not one bad seat. Everything looks perfect. Maybe even more.

Behind the luxe, honey-tone surrounds, the kitchen is undeniably skilled and operating with great precision under Chef Eric Ripert. However, Le Bernardin's truest devotees may find that at the end of their meals, the wow-factor was missing, as if someone tampered with the volume between each course. Such legacy dishes as hamachi-wrapped herbs and lettuce with carrot-lime *sauce vierge* combine extraordinary ingredients with Asian flavors that are uncharacteristically subtle. Yet the next course may rekindle a spark in seared langoustines over mâche and wild mushroom salad with foie gras slivers and a powerful white balsamic vinaigrette. A bright, coral-colored char may arrive visually arresting but lack vitality.

Then dessert reveals dense and deeply chocolatey Black Forest cake made refreshing with cherry-beer sorbet. The *mignardises*? Bliss.

Madangsui

Korean

35 W. 35th St. (bet. Fifth & Sixth Aves.)

Subway: 34 St - Herald Sq
Phone: 212-564-9333
Web: www.madangsui.com
Prices: $$

Lunch Mon – Fri
Dinner nightly

If the Korean-speaking waitstaff doesn't tip you off to this K-town joint's authenticity, then perhaps the mind-blowing barbecue, cooked directly at your table, will. Located about a block north of midtown's Korean restaurant hub, Madangsui's clean, glass-fronted façade offers a reprieve from the flurry outside. Inside, soothing leather banquettes and cream-colored walls promise more sanity, but the excited hum toward the kitchen divulges a restaurant that is getting its (much deserved) fifteen minutes.

Don't miss the short beef ribs bobbing in a hot broth laced with cellophane noodles; spot-on oyster pancakes, studded with green scallions; or the Metropolitan beef and pork combo, which gives delicious new meaning to dinner theater.

Mandoo Bar

Korean

2 W. 32nd St. (bet. Broadway & Fifth Ave.)

Subway: 34 St - Herald Sq
Phone: 212-279-3075
Web: N/A
Prices: ☜☜

Lunch & dinner daily

Whether steamed, fried, spicy or not, Mandoo is always Korean for "dumpling," and every kind you can dream up is served here as unique, tidy little bundles. This postage stamp-sized K-town favorite keeps its massive number of customers happy with its array of freshly made, unassuming Korean fare, dished out fast enough to keep weekend shoppers on the move.

Meals may begin with the likes of pan-fried dumplings filled with pork and vegetables (*goon mandoo*); bite-sized and boiled baby *mandoo*; or the combo *mandoo*, with fillings of seafood, vegetables, and pork. Korean-style spicy beef soup (*yuk kae jang*) and acorn or buckwheat flour noodle dishes tossed with citrus vinaigrette, sesame seeds, scallions, and cilantro are fine and worthy accompaniments.

Má Pêche

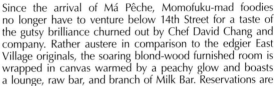

Fusion ✗✗

 B4

15 West 56th St. (bet. Fifth & Sixth Aves.)

Subway: 57 St
Phone: 212-757-5878
Web: www.momofuku.com
Prices: $$

Lunch Mon – Sat
Dinner nightly

Since the arrival of Má Pêche, Momofuku-mad foodies no longer have to venture below 14th Street for a taste of the gutsy brilliance churned out by Chef David Chang and company. Rather austere in comparison to the edgier East Village originals, the soaring blond-wood furnished room is wrapped in canvas warmed by a peachy glow and boasts a lounge, raw bar, and branch of Milk Bar. Reservations are accepted—a unique convenience.

Skill, talent, and judiciously sourced ingredients prevail throughout, especially in items like raw, thinly sliced scallops from New Jersey mingled with sweet plantain, yuzu and sesame; a steamed lobster bun with maitake mushrooms and chicharrón; or an entrée of Florida red snapper coupled with miso and bone marrow.

Marseille

French ✗✗

C2

630 Ninth Ave. (at 44th St.)

Subway: 42 St - Port Authority Bus Terminal
Phone: 212-333-2323
Web: www.marseillenyc.com
Prices: $$

Lunch & dinner daily

Marseille marries the charm of a classic French bistro with the inimitable style of New York City. The sexy, soft golden glow, convivial spirit, and superlative Theater District location make it a popular choice for everyone from tourists craving a taste of Broadway to colleagues cooling off after a day's work. The skilled and truly professional kitchen prepares an impressive cuisine bursting with pronounced, balanced flavors. From salads and seasonal specials to more French-formed entrées like steak frites, there is something for everyone. Hungry diners appreciate that the portions lean toward American sensibilities; and the budget-conscious value the prix-fixe lunch and dinner menus. Don't skip out without the frites—they may be the best in the city.

Marea ✿ ✿

Seafood XXX

240 Central Park South (bet. Broadway & Seventh Ave.)

Subway:	59 St - Columbus Circle	Lunch Sun – Fri
Phone:	212-582-5100	Dinner nightly
Web:	www.marea-nyc.com	
Prices:	$$$$	

Daniel Krieger

This city-wide gem is a slice of the upper crust that feels very much at home on Central Park South. A discreet exterior implies quiet exclusivity; the inside is calibrated to wow its A-list clientele of film stars and the business types who back them. The buzz is pervasive but never overwhelming. Be sure to admire the laminated walls sparkling against marble, onyx, and seashells; but aim for the banquettes (most comfortable seating option).

Chef Michael White displays the skill of a craftsman in deftly balancing clean tastes and textures of the sea, but what he creates is sublime pleasure. His kitchen is honest, fearless, and delves wholeheartedly into enhancing the city's appreciation of Italian food.

Starters have included plump raw prawns in a spicy-sweet marinade, atop crunchy cucumber. Simplicity is beguiling in such pasta combinations as homemade spaghetti tossed with ripe tomatoes and strong, lusty tastes of sea urchin, beneath fragrant basil and a sprinkle of semolina. Scallops are crisply roasted but still translucent in the center, served with woodsy *chiodini* mushrooms and *lardo*-studded polenta. Desserts, like a deconstructed carrot cake, bring to life each vivid flavor.

Maze at The London

151 W. 54th St. (bet. Sixth & Seventh Aves.)

Subway: 7 Av

Lunch & dinner daily

Phone: 212-468-8888

Web: www.gordonramsay.com

Prices: $$

The Maze at The London is the younger and more spirited sister of Gordon Ramsay at The London. And, since we're speaking of royalty, it's a bit like those Middleton girls, and Maze is definitely the Pippa to Gordon Ramsay's Kate. Sexy and elegant, this restaurant is less serious than its counterpart, but still attracts a well-coiffed and deep-pocketed crowd of jacket-wearing tourists and tycoons. It's chic-Paris in its smoky mirrored, teal banquetted, shimmering glass art deco glory.

Like its setting, the food is Frenchified. Roast chicken breast is glistening and topped with "potato chips"; black risotto is decadently buttery with St. Georges mushrooms; and chocolate fondant is textbook perfect coated with a green cardamom caramel for a perfect finish.

Mercato 😊

352 W. 39th St. (bet. Eighth & Ninth Aves.)

Subway: 42 St - Port Authority Bus Terminal

Lunch & dinner daily

Phone: 212-643-2000

Web: www.mercatonyc.com

Prices: $$

With greetings like "*buona sera*" and "*come stai*" flitting around, you can be assured of the honest and authentic nature of this Italian trattoria. By virtue of its location on spirited 39th Street, Mercato sees a torrent of visitors, yet it never fails to deliver a delicious blend of experiences. Most everybody here wears a sunny disposition, perhaps in response to such retro decorative touches as antique farm tools, muted walls, and vintage posters.

Over in a dimly lit corner, wooden tables are filled with eager diners awaiting gifts from the kitchen including an *amuse* of luscious lentils; tender fried artichokes with a pat of mashed anchovy; handmade gnocchi with a thick wild boar ragù; and a beautiful red snapper encased in a semolina-polenta crust.

Masa ✿ ✿ ✿

Japanese ✕✕

C1

10 Columbus Circle (in the Time Warner Center)

Subway: 59 St - Columbus Circle
Phone: 212-823-9800
Web: www.masanyc.com
Prices: $$$$

Lunch Tue – Fri
Dinner Mon – Sat

Masa

Despite its prosaic locale in the Time Warner Center, this is one of NY's most impressive restaurants. Pull back that hefty door with reverence and bow thy head, supplicant, upon entering the temple of Masa. The serene space stuns with its Zen water element, towering greenery, and imported hinoki wood counter that is sanded nightly to shine with pristine purity. There are a few tables, but that would mean missing the opportunity to face the magic and education of these spectacular students at the school of Masa—they are congenial and dedicated to the great Chef Takayama and his eponymous cuisine.

As if bearing the signature of an expat chef and his years in America, the dishes are more his unique style than traditional Japanese. The prices are exorbitant, but the quality of product and preparation is inexplicably perfect. It all begins with the finest fish that may have swum directly to the restaurant and onto the counter in worthy self-sacrifice.

Toro tartare is brilliantly simple yet lush as is the hammer fish shabu shabu. If a Kobe beef course is on offer, it's worth the splurge; while exceptional alchemy between uni and truffles elevates the simple risotto into a complex masterpiece.

Miss Korea

Korean ✕✕

10 W. 32nd St. (bet. Fifth & Sixth Aves.)

Subway: 34 St - Herald Sq   Lunch & dinner daily
Phone: 212-594-4963
Web: www.misskoreabbq.com
Prices: $$

Miss Korea ain't no pageant queen; she is in fact a sleek, smart restaurant churning out seriously tasty Korean fare. Its unique façade of rocks encased in wiring carries to the interior, which is equally striking with massive cut-stone walls. In fact, you may feel as if you are inside an ancient castle softened by greenery and a highly convivial spirit.

The deep room is enlivened by four-tops set with billowing branches shrouded with ivy and birds. Floating in a wood frame, rosy bulbs cast a gentle glow on *haemul-pajeon*, crispy seafood-scallion pancake; *samgyupsal*, pretty pink strips of barbecued pork belly kissed with salt and delicious sesame oil; and a richly complex *bullak-jeongol*, hot pot of kimchi broth filled with octopus, tofu, and *bulgogi*.

Molyvos

Greek ✕✕

871 Seventh Ave. (bet. 55th & 56th Sts.)

Subway: 57 St - 7 Av   Lunch & dinner daily
Phone: 212-582-7500
Web: www.molyvos.com
Prices: $$

Mighty Molyvos is both an attractive and applauded choice among Greek gourmands and Carnegie Hall patrons. This slender yet deep space is bright yet warm and subdued; while the décor, void of themed clichés, exudes style in the form of wood paneling, ceramics, and an elaborately patterned coffered ceiling.

From your post at a large table, glimpse a gallery of smiling family photos. Carrying this congenial spirit is Molyvos' beloved menu. The kitchen's vision and devotion can be tasted in *keftedes me saltsa domates*, spicy meatballs in cumin-infused tomato sauce; tender and meaty lamb spare ribs glossed with thyme and ouzo; and a toasted almond-vanilla cake served with vanilla-yogurt ice cream. A pre-theater menu and loaded bar keep the scene lively.

The Modern

Contemporary 𝗫𝗫𝗫

A4

9 W. 53rd St. (bet. Fifth & Sixth Aves.)

Subway: 5 Av - 53 St
Phone: 212-333-1220
Web: www.themodernnyc.com
Prices: $$$

Lunch Mon – Fri
Dinner Mon – Sat

Ellen Silverman

Sleek, sexy, and smart, The Modern does much to entice. The refined yet brightly styled space is indeed very special, with a striking glass wall separating the more casual bar area from the chic formal dining room's tall orchids and towering beauty. But what it does best is showcase those extraordinary floor-to-ceiling windows facing directly into the MoMA's sculpture garden. While The Modern may dwell within a museum, the vibe here is lively, chatty, and always fashionable.

The well-sized menu features dishes that begin with a classic idea, but this accomplished and confident kitchen spins them with contemporary flair. Clean, sharp flavors combine beautifully in a seafood trio of sliced, raw yuzu-marinated scallops; fresh tuna with American caviar; and thin salmon morsels with wasabi shoots. Expect sweetbreads that are moist and silky beneath a golden-crisped crumb coating, alongside veal-filled pasta, shredded cabbage with bacon, and finished with caper-studded tarragon mousseline.

Desserts might bring milk chocolate and hazelnut *dacquoise*, its crunchy nut base topped with smooth chocolate mousse and thick caramel sauce—that scoop of raspberry sorbet makes it an instant classic.

Mr. Robata

 A4

1674 Broadway (bet. 52nd & 53rd Sts.)

Subway: 50 St (Broadway)
Phone: 212-757-1030
Web: www.mrrobata.com
Prices: $$$

Lunch Mon – Fri
Dinner nightly

In an amusing and unexpected feat, humble Mr. Robata somehow thrives within the strip-clubby netherworld of touristy Times Square. Among discerning and discreet of-age adults, this is clearly an entertaining locale. And among foodies, it's a great stop for fusion Japanese. Inside, find two attractive dining areas: one that offers an inviting counter and an auxiliary room decked with well-sized tables.

The food is tasty but less than authentic. Still, Mr. Robata entices with friendly, adept service. Oversized platters shine with powerful flavors, as in fried tuna tacos tossed with crunchy sesame seeds. Wagyu sliders are a generous crowd-pleaser, while the "never too late" maki with soft shell crab and *robata*-grilled mushrooms and eggplant are fun finds.

New Wonjo

C4

23 W. 32nd St. (bet. Broadway & Sixth Ave.)

Subway: 34 St - Herald Sq
Phone: 212-695-5815
Web: N/A
Prices: $$$

Lunch & dinner daily

Truth be told, New Wonjo–a no-frills, turn-and-burn Korean joint nestled into bustling 32nd Street–is not going to give the reigning outer borough darlings a run for their money anytime soon. But if you're looking for some decent Korean food in midtown, you could do a lot worse than this modest, two-level eatery, fitted out with tabletop barbecue grills.

Moreover, after a management overhaul in spring of 2010, the kitchen now falls under the sights of Chef Hwang Han Joo, who reputedly boasts over 40 years of Korean culinary experience. Taste the experience in dishes like *kam ja jun gol*, a fragrant, flavorful casserole of spicy pork bone, potato, and vegetables; or tenderly marinated cuts of brisket and short ribs, grilled to succulent perfection.

Nobu Fifty Seven

Japanese ✗✗✗

 A3

40 W. 57th St. (bet. Fifth & Sixth Aves.)

Subway: 57 St
Phone: 212-757-3000
Web: www.noburestaurants.com
Prices: $$$$

Lunch Mon – Sat
Dinner nightly

The Nobu name is revered the world over, but this NYC elder dressed by David Rockwell brings a local Japanese landscape to Gotham by way of bamboo, birch trees, and rattan mats. Following this stylized sensibility is a cadre of polite and attentive staff; it may be a hectic Friday night, yet every burnished wood table is given equal respect.

A lounge with settees and a long bar beneath dramatically suspended sake barrels help placate the masses crowding these cavernous chambers. Spotlights bring out the blush in a tangy sashimi salad, while diverse ingredients come into play in crunchy and tart lobster tacos. Find other crowd-pleasing trends revealed in meaty halibut cheeks braised with wasabi-pepper sauce; and Washu beef slices with pink salt.

Orso

Italian ✗✗

 C2

322 W. 46th St. (bet. Eighth & Ninth Aves.)

Subway: 42 St - Port Authority Bus Terminal
Phone: 212-489-7212
Web: www.orsorestaurant.com
Prices: $$

Lunch & dinner daily

This intimate little restaurant–with its knowledgeable, friendly staff and antique photos–is the late-night haunt of Broadway players in search of a post-show meal. It shows off their good taste too, for the food at this Restaurant Row darling rises well above the competition.

Occupying the ground floor of a charming brownstone, Orso offers a daily menu of simple, delicious Italian classics like *raviolone* with crab, tomato, and capers in brown butter; or oven-roasted quail with a Marsala reduction. The $24 *contorni* selection of five vegetable dishes like roasted potatoes and garlic; or the tasty mélange of sweet-sour eggplant, yellow squash, and peppers is a meal in itself.

Be sure to call ahead; their pre-theater prix-fixe books quickly.

Oceana

Seafood

120 W. 49th St. (at Sixth Ave.)

Subway: 47-50 Sts - Rockefeller Ctr
Phone: 212-759-5941
Web: www.oceanarestaurant.com
Prices: $$$

Lunch Mon – Fri
Dinner nightly

Paul Johnson

Oceana, seafood purveyor extraordinaire, has settled beautifully into its illustrious home in Rockefeller Center. Enter to see a dramatic parade of pristine shellfish (maybe razor clam ceviche tinged with yuzu?) and oysters at the raw bar and be reminded of the restaurant's seriousness of purpose. The sleek and contemporary dining room, with deep blue banquettes and stunning floral arrangements, is an impeccable setting in which to savor Chef Ben Pollinger's superlative fare. A glass-enclosed private room, or chef's table by the kitchen are attractive options for power crowds hosting lunch meetings.

The superbly fresh items never falter in finding just the right global accent, as in a chilled, creamy asparagus soup enhanced by marinated salmon, sugar snap peas, and dill. The taro-wrapped dorade is unbelievably moist, served in a flavorful coconut-cilantro curry studded with baby bok choy and peanuts.

The broiled mahi is as appealing on the plate as to the palate, arriving golden brown with parsnips, Fingerling potatoes, and chestnuts in a balsamic reduction. Desserts reveal hints of inspiration, especially the boozy pink champagne cake layered with vanilla custard and grapefruit sorbet.

Osteria al Doge

Italian ✗✗

C3

142 W. 44th St. (bet. Broadway & Sixth Ave.)

Subway: Times Sq - 42 St
Phone: 212-944-3643
Web: www.osteria-doge.com
Prices: $$

Lunch Mon – Fri
Dinner nightly

Tucked into one of those theater-dominated cross streets that define this jumbled area of Times Square, the first thing Osteria al Doge has on the competition is its good looks: think sunny yellow walls, wrought-iron chandeliers, and bright Italian ceramic plates. Not to mention a long marble and wood bar where solo diners can settle into a comfortable padded stool and enjoy a little people-watching before the real show.

Back on the plates it's delicious Italian food tended to with love, like a plump tangle of fettuccine *verdi* in a silky lamb ragù dotted with lemon rind and pitted black picholine olives; thin slices of tuna carpaccio drizzled with citrus olive oil, a dash of crunchy sea salt, and herbs; or a fresh lemon tart topped with strawberries.

Osteria del Circo

Italian ✗✗

A3

120 W. 55th St. (bet. Sixth & Seventh Aves.)

Subway: 57 St
Phone: 212-265-3636
Web: www.circonyc.com
Prices: $$$

Lunch Mon – Fri
Dinner nightly

Ever fantasized about running away to join the circus? Fulfill that dream without all of the acrobatics at Osteria del Circo. This restaurant, run by the Maccioni clan of Le Cirque fame, offers a tasteful take on the Big Top. Its tent-like ceiling is complete with streaming fabric in a riot of colors and is punctuated by spinning circus performers and animal sculptures. There is a palpable buzz here—just one of the reasons there are so many regulars.

However, this menu isn't about peanuts and popcorn. Instead, look forward to deftly prepared Italian dishes like grilled branzino and milk-fed veal chops from the professional kitchen. The staff is warm and engaging—not surprising given the Maccionis' reputation for throwing open their arms to guests.

Per Se ✿ ✿ ✿

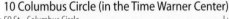

Contemporary 🍴🍴🍴🍴🍴

C1

10 Columbus Circle (in the Time Warner Center)

Subway: 59 St - Columbus Circle   Lunch Fri – Sun
Phone: 212-823-9335   Dinner nightly
Web: www.perseny.com
Prices: $$$$

Deborah Jones

Rightly recognized as one of the world's finest restaurants, Per Se is nothing short of spectacular. The entrance is serene amid fresh flowers and lounge tables for "salon" dining. Inside, high ceilings add grandeur, bright picture windows command Central Park views, and a sedate palette ensures focus on the food. The linens are thick, that china is bespoke, and your handbag will find its own footed rest by your side.

Service is formal but without pretense, thanks to a fresh-faced and personable yet polished staff. In the kitchen, Chef de Cuisine Eli Kaimeh shows talent and great adherence to the masterful Chef Thomas Keller. The fixed menu has featured marinated scallops in thick, vichyssoise-style potato cream, finished with lime beads and herb oil—intense but very complementary. Such creative flavor pairings go on to include ravioli stuffed with pristine white crab, served atop sour-sweet tomato marmalade and droplets of horseradish.

At meal's end, expect the server to present a polished wood box displaying rows of white, milk, and dark handmade chocolates. Each and every filling will be explained, for a dramatic, exacting, and perfectly whimsical reflection of dining at Per Se.

Petrossian

French 🍴🍴🍴

A3

182 W. 58th St. (at Seventh Ave.)

Subway: 57 St - 7 Av
Phone: 212-245-2214
Web: www.petrossian.com
Prices: $$$

Lunch & dinner daily

Petrossian is not hip. It is classic, continental, and a rare breed in the city. With such exemplary attributes–location, historic setting, and refined staff–this French bastion smacks of bourgeois indulgence. The exterior is unique with detailed stonework that features frolicking cherubs and griffins; a forbidding wrought-iron door guards the entrance. But, the dining room is typical with pink and black granite, a mirrored bar, and crystal sconces.

This costly (or stuffy?) *paradis* clings to the fabric of NYC dining with pleasant, comforting offerings like a tasting of foie gras terrine and smoked fish. Affluent regulars adore the pan-roasted lobster risotto with porcini and Parmesan; and a classically rich almond-apple torte with vanilla ice cream.

Pier 9

Seafood 🍴🍴

C1

802 Ninth Ave. (bet. 53rd & 54th St.)

Subway: 50 St (Eighth Ave.)
Phone: 212-262-1299
Web: www.pier9nyc.com
Prices: $$$

Lunch & dinner daily

When a hankering hits for seafaring favorites, steer your ship straight to Pier 9. This fresh and upbeat space, with whitewashed walls, aquamarine tiles, and bright colors, will instantly elevate your mood and have you feeling the wind in your hair. Sidewalk dining and an open-air back patio are breezy during warmer months, and the bar is always rollicking.

Expect barefoot, casual-style seafood, where an outstanding rendition of New England clam chowder, blackened snapper tacos, and "Chicago-style" lobster hot dogs reign. The succulent lobster roll, piled high and dressed with little more than a hint of celery seeds, will have you canceling that trip to Maine. Order a Bloody Mary and raw bar items, but pay attention to the daily specials.

pizzArte

A3

Pizza 🍴🍴

69 W. 55th St. (bet. Fifth & Sixth Aves.)

Subway: 57 St
Phone: 212-247-3936
Web: www.pizzarteny.com
Prices: **$$**

Lunch & dinner daily

If there were one dish universally loved, it would be pizza, that slice of Neapolitan bliss. While it is many things to many people, NYers rejoice at pizzArte, where pizza is baked to perfect pliability with a bit of char and topped with immaculate ingredients. Unlike its chaotic surrounds, this bi-level establishment is all opulence with whitewashed walls, marble, a well-set bar, and manicured stools.

Beyond its gentle hum of music and regal Neapolitan paintings, the handsome pizza oven is buried in the back. Here, a *pizzaiolo* stands sentry, churning out a deliciously charred Margherita with milky mozzarella. While pizza is their art, *paccheri al baccalà* with tomatoes and olives, and *penne Ferdinando* with eggplant and basil will not disappoint.

Porter House

C1

Steakhouse 🍴🍴🍴

10 Columbus Circle (in the Time Warner Center)

Subway: 59 St - Columbus Circle
Phone: 212-823-9500
Web: www.porterhousenewyork.com
Prices: **$$$$**

Lunch & dinner daily

The name says it all at Porter House, a member of the Time Warner Center's elite restaurant collection. The sprawling room is a temple to its delicious dry-aged namesake and offers a contemporary variant on the familiar steakhouse aesthetic crafted from polished cherry wood, tobacco brown leather, and stainless steel. The prime location is convenient for business folk and hungry shoppers alike.

Under the longtime charge of Executive Chef Michael Lomonaco, the expansive menu is steeped in tasty starters; and sides like tomato and onion salad dotted with Maytag blue cheese, and rich truffle-mashed Yukon Golds round out a carnivorous feast. A range of non-steak options is also offered, and the nostalgic take on dessert is worth saving room for.

Print

American 𝕏𝕏𝕏

B1

653 Eleventh Ave. (at 48th St.)

Subway: 50 St (Eighth Ave.)
Phone: 212-757-2224
Web: www.printrestaurant.com
Prices: $$

Lunch & dinner daily

From the West Side's hinterlands of car dealerships and warehouses, this revelatory spot blooms with California style. Its home, off the lobby of Ink48 hotel, impresses with oversized windows and an eco-friendly vibe. In keeping with the "green" theme, wine glasses are made from recycled glass and composting is a way of life.

Their farm-to-table ethos extends to the cuisine with extraordinary success. Gorgeous European-style copper tables become exquisite when piled with plates of goat cheese gnocchi with cauliflower in Parmesan emulsion, and grilled octopus with chorizo. Fresh flower arrangements echo the seasonality and simplicity behind a Berkshire pork chop with New York apples and Port reduction, and chocolate bread teased with honey and ricotta.

Qi Bangkok Eatery

Thai 𝕏𝕏

C2

675 Eighth Ave. (bet. 42nd & 43rd Sts.)

Subway: Times Sq - 42 St
Phone: 212-247-8991
Web: www.qirestaurant.com
Prices: $$

Lunch & dinner daily

Yes, the Times Square locale–amid tourists, chain stores, billboards, and more tourists–is hell for thoroughbred New Yorkers, yet Qi is worth a detour for its serious Thai food and flirty cocktails. The antithesis of its neon neighbor Olive Garden and with visitors at their heels, it is no wonder that this far sleeker stop (trappings include a white bar, glossy accents, low lights, and loud tunes) is always packed.

Irrespective, fried *plau tuu* fish with *nahm prikh kapi*, a spicy shrimp relish; grilled *chang mai*, sausage with crispy pork skin; and fried cured egg with basil chicken make it worthy. A fiery red curry with pork; and smoky eggplant salad laced with ground shrimp bring flavors of the East (at the hands of muddled servers) to this well-trod turf.

Radiance Tea House

Asian ✗

A3

158 W. 55th St. (bet. Sixth & Seventh Aves.)

Subway: 57 St - 7 Av   Lunch & dinner daily
Phone: 212-217-0442
Web: www.radiancetea.com
Prices: $$

Tea drinking is synonymous with Asian hospitality; the respect and harmony this tradition conjures is part and parcel of the experience had at Radiance Tea House. Open the doors and climb a few steps to enter this tranquil sanctum whose pin-drop silence is broken only by the gentle sip of tea-drinkers.
This sweet book and tea shop may offer a rather limited menu (a bit larger at dinner), but the tea selection is truly vast. The room is airy with a semi-open kitchen and wing devoted to a well-chosen book selection. Servers may be hushed but are happy to answer your queries about *unagi-don* with broiled eel and pickled radish; sticky rice and pork wrapped in lotus leaf; or a fresh salad of "tropical" salmon with mango, avocado, and five-spiced pecans.

Remi

Italian ✗✗✗

A4

145 W. 53rd St. (bet. Sixth & Seventh Aves.)

Subway: 7 Av   Lunch Mon – Fri
Phone: 212-581-4242   Dinner nightly
Web: www.remi-ny.com
Prices: $$

A convivial buzz winds through this Italian restaurant, from the lively back dining area to the glass-roofed atrium in the front that offers a gourmet breakfast and great salad selection to-go. At its center, find whimsical flying buttress archways, murals, mirrors, and glass chandeliers that recall the Veneto region.
Yet this well-orchestrated production's true draw is its delicious menu that highlights easygoing, rustic Italian specialties as in house-made pasta with lamb ragù, crowned with pillowy-soft lamb meatballs, and topped with aged buffalo milk Parmigiano. The nice offering of Remi classics is always spot-on, as in seared tuna with poppy seeds, roasted vegetables, and balsamic reduction; or *garganelli* with garlic, shrimp, and fried zucchini.

Robert

Contemporary ✗✗

D1

2 Columbus Circle (bet. Broadway & Eighth Ave.)

Subway: 59 St - Columbus Circle   Lunch & dinner daily
Phone: 212-299-7730
Web: www.robertnyc.com
Prices: $$

Behold the sweeping views of Central Park from this bright, sexy setting on the 9th floor of the Museum of Art and Design. Be sure to request seating near the north-facing, floor-to-ceiling windows. The interior is almost as pleasing to the eye: cheery splashes of fuchsia and orange perk up a sleek space, where transparent bucket seats, clear-topped tables, and contemporary art installations beautifully reflect the museum to which it belongs.

Drop in for lunch, afternoon tea, or dinner for the likes of tuna carpaccio pizza sprinkled with trout caviar, spicy aïoli, and cucumber; *tagliatelle* with juicy lamb meatballs, fresh mint, and grated *ricotta salata*; or sweet and sour braised veal breast atop mashed cauliflower dabbed with quince relish.

Russian Samovar

Russian ✗✗

C2

256 W. 52nd St. (bet. Broadway & Eighth Ave.)

Subway: 50 St (Broadway)   Lunch & dinner daily
Phone: 212-757-0168
Web: www.russiansamovar.com
Prices: $$

Which came first: the vodka or the celebs? It's hard to say when it comes to this hot spot, which caters to hockey players, Russian intellectuals, and vodka aficionados alike. Our bets are on that beautiful vodka selection, available in all kinds of flavors, qualities, and sizes (shot, carafe, or bottle). Nestled into the bustling Theater District, Russian Samovar is both quirky and elegant—with low lighting, glass panels, and musicians playing the piano and violin. The staff, both attentive and sweet, can walk you through delicious fare like a fresh salmon caviar blini, prepared tableside; *pelmeni*, tender veal dumplings served with sour cream and honey mustard; or milk-cured Baltic herring, paired with pickled onions, potatoes, and carrots.

Scarlatto

Italian ✕✕

250 W. 47th St. (bet. Broadway & Eighth Ave.)

Subway: 50 St (Eighth Ave.)　　　　　　　　　　Lunch & dinner daily
Phone: 212-730-4535
Web: www.scarlattonyc.com
Prices: $$

Done and done: this adorable trattoria is guaranteed to woo your date and finally put an end to those frustrating post-Saturday night wanderings. Dip down below street level and you'll find a lovely, exposed brick interior lined with wine bottles, mirrors, and still shots of Audrey Hepburn in *Roman Holiday*.

The menu doesn't offer too many surprises, but it does deliver solid, well-prepared Italian fare. Rosy-pink *carpaccio di manzo* arrives ultra-thin and topped with a creamy Parmesan-lemon dressing, a soft pile of arugula, and chewy slices of sourdough bread; while a bowl of *garganelli* gets a kick from osso buco enlivened with rosemary; and fresh Atlantic salmon is baked with caramelized Vidalia onions served with garlicky sautéed spinach.

The Sea Grill

Seafood ✕✕

19 W. 49th St. (bet. Fifth & Sixth Aves.)

Subway: 47-50 Sts - Rockefeller Ctr　　　　　　Lunch Mon – Fri
Phone: 212-332-7610　　　　　　　　　　　　Dinner Mon – Sat
Web: www.patinagroup.com
Prices: $$$

This seafood grill overlooking Rockefeller Center's ice skating rink boasts one of the city's most famed locations. As expected, holiday bookings start early at The Sea Grill, when skaters whizz by your windows filled with the best (and warmest) view of the Christmas tree. However, summertime is likewise charming, when the doors swing open and diners can enjoy an alfresco feel overlooking the Rink Bar. Even in winter, the dining counter is a smart choice—less of a production and better perch.

Perhaps due to its tourist-driven locale, the food can seem like something of an afterthought. Offerings may include yellowfin *a la plancha* with a delicate, lemon-caper and olive oil dressing, or more memorable desserts like their tart and creamy key lime pie.

Seäsonal ✿

Austrian ✗✗

132 W. 58th St. (bet. Sixth & Seventh Aves.)

Subway: 57 St - 7 Av
Phone: 212-957-5550
Web: www.seasonalnyc.com
Prices: $$$

Lunch Mon – Sat
Dinner nightly

Seäsonal Restaurant & Weinbar

Somehow, Seäsonal has taken its tight space and made it feel bright and airy, ensuring its status as an upscale diamond on this very drab block. The décor is comfortably spare, with a small bar pouring Austro-centric wines and serving as an ideal perch for a pre-dinner glass. Modern artwork set against white walls reminds of the menu's contemporary theme.

At midday, the quiet ambience seems ideal for talking business—which is a surprise, as the lunchtime menu (though limited) is an extraordinary value. Dinnertime offerings are much more expansive, with desserts that explore the gamut of sweet Austrian decadence.

No matter the time of day, everything at Seäsonal is beautifully presented and alive with flavor. Elegant modernity is clear in the likes of *porchiertes ei*—a softly poached egg that mingles sweetly with segments of lobster claw, sautéed hen of the woods mushrooms, lobster-mushroom foam, and a showering of pumpernickel crumbs. Their spaetzle is a hearty highlight, made fantastically creamy with an abundance of Bergkäse cheese, blending wild mushrooms and zucchini. To finish, expect pastries to recall the classics, as in Sachertorte, along with a thick scoop of *schlag*.

South Gate

Contemporary

A3

154 Central Park South (bet. Sixth & Seventh Aves.)

Subway: 57 St
Phone: 212-484-5120
Web: www.154southgate.com
Prices: $$$

Lunch & dinner daily

Tucked into the first floor of the Jumeirah Essex House, South Gate is downright splendid in its sophistication. Designed by Tony Chi, the room owns a singular light and airy sexiness, with padded leather tables, creamy swivel chairs, and mirrored glass walls.

The superlative kitchen's modern American menu elevates contemporary classics to current heights. Don't miss the creamy fried macaroni and cheese, crunchy with breadcrumbs and sporting a perfectly smoked tomato coulis; or the delicately poached lobster salad with ripe avocado and shaved fennel ribbons, beautifully tied together with a lemon emulsion. Spotty service can sometimes put a dent in an otherwise lovely evening, but a seat at the welcoming bar will certainly remedy the situation.

Staghorn

Steakhouse

B3

315 W. 36th St. (bet. Eighth & Ninth Aves.)

Subway: 34 St - Penn Station
Phone: 212-239-4390
Web: www.staghornsteakhouse.com
Prices: $$$

Lunch Mon – Fri
Dinner Mon – Sat

Does the word "steakhouse" conjure up images of old-school, slightly brusque waiters in white aprons and no frills good-old-boy décor? Well, think again. Staghorn steakhouse takes the bull by its, ahem, horns, and turns it completely on its head. The less-than-thrilling neighborhood may leave something to be desired, but inside this former warehouse is a wondrous space with an Asian-Zen ambience.

The look is modern but the food is classic, with typical sides like mashed potatoes and creamed spinach. Start with tasty baked clams or the Staghorn salad bursting with Roquefort and tomatoes. From well-aged Porterhouse steaks that ooze with juice to thick and meaty Kansas City bone-in sirloin, it's all about the beef to the chic carnivore at this temple.

Sugiyama

Japanese ✕✕

C1

251 W. 55th St. (bet. Broadway & Eighth Ave.)

Subway: 57 St - 7 Av   Dinner Tue – Sat
Phone: 212-956-0670
Web: www.sugiyama-nyc.com
Prices: $$$

On the outside, nothing screams unique about this spot. But, it is sage to never judge a book by its cover, so stay awhile. Amid construction sites, parking lots, and traffic, find warm and demure Sugiyama. Make your way inside its narrow hallway to a warm, welcoming earthy-toned haven replete with rock gardens.

Transporting you further into Japanese comfort are bamboo lamps hanging from boughs and an open kitchen starring the master Nao Sugiyama, as he moves in slow, steady precision. Perhaps observe him preparing a modern kaiseki including monkfish liver, braised baby squid, and snow crab-radish roll. Smoky toro and creamy uni are presented beside a fragrant red snapper dashi and followed by wonderful Wagyu beef paired with garlic chips.

Sushi of Gari 46

Japanese ✕✕

C2

347 W. 46th St. (bet. Eighth & Ninth Aves.)

Subway: Times Sq - 42 St   Lunch Mon – Fri
Phone: 212-957-0046   Dinner nightly
Web: N/A
Prices: $$$$

This outpost of Chef Masatoshi "Gari" Sugio's much-loved sushi trifecta doesn't quite stack up to the near-surreal omakase experience that shot the original Upper East Side prodigy to fame, but coming this close to sushi perfection in the increasingly commercial Theater District is good enough. The pay-per-piece omakase show will put a sizable, albeit worthy, dent in your wallet, but those on a budget can always hit the reasonably-priced regular menu. The place to sit is at the action-packed bar, where you can watch the staff slice and dice their way through nigiri like a nori-wrapped bundle of warm rice topped with sweet King crab meat; or gorgeous ruby red tuna, brushed with soy and topped with creamy tofu sauce and freshly grated wasabi.

Sushi Zen

C3

Japanese ✗✗

108 W. 44th St. (bet. Broadway & Sixth Ave.)

Subway: 42 St - Bryant Pk
Phone: 212-302-0707
Web: www.sushizen-ny.com
Prices: $$$

Lunch Mon – Fri
Dinner Mon – Sat

Nestled among midtown's high-rises, this jewel of a sushi restaurant is a nice respite from the Bryant Park hustle and bustle—with soothing swaths of natural light flooding a small dining room with high ceilings, and a sidewalk seating section protected by fabric panels and potted green plants.

Chef Toshio Suzuki's team doles out a host of rolls, many of them going beyond the conventional preparations to employ seasonal fish and vegetables. Kick things off with a smoky white miso soup bobbing with Asari clams; and then move on to the Bara Chirashi Sushi, or sushi Zen style. "Bara" means little things, and here that translates to a neverending style of fish, sashimi, and vegetables served over rice. Save room for the *yokan*, a sweet, jellied dessert.

Szechuan Gourmet ☺

C3

Chinese ✗

21 W. 39th St. (bet. Fifth & Sixth Aves.)

Subway: 42 St - Bryant Pk
Phone: 212-921-0233
Web: N/A
Prices: $$

Lunch & dinner daily

Despite the exquisite pain inflicted by their wok tossed green chilies, legions line up for more of Szechuan Gourmet's spicy, tasty, and authentic delicacies. Away from the usual lunch bustle, hordes hustle at this midtown haven for their devilishly delicious repertoire of Sichuan specialties.

The attempt at ambience is a touch clichéd, but the kitchen's masterful marriage of ingredients amply atones with tofu crêpes stuffed with shiitakes; crispy lamb dusted with cumin and chilies; and bass fillets swimming in a smoky soup of cabbage and cellophane noodles. Rabbit pieces glazed with a sweet, spicy oil; and conch slivers in roasted chili vinaigrette will leave you delighted.

For a quieter (more delicious?) meal, stop by its baby sis on West 56th Street.

Taboon

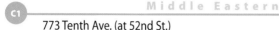

Middle Eastern ✗✗

C1

773 Tenth Ave. (at 52nd St.)

Subway: 50 St (Eighth Ave.)
Phone: 212-713-0271
Web: N/A
Prices: $$

Lunch Sun
Dinner nightly

This far western neighborhood gem offers an always pleasant vibe and enticing air courtesy of the brick-walled, wood-burning oven (*taboon*) that greets entering guests and sets the whitewashed interior aglow. The crackling logs, fronted by neatly arranged platters of produce, exude a rustic mien and fuse deftly with the food and philosophy.

Fresh from *taboon* to table, rip into the house-made focaccia and await the lot of enticing specialties. Linger abroad with the likes of charred octopus confit with hearth-roasted apples and pickled cucumber; or succulent osso buco of lamb glossed with a meaty reduction, atop a pile of bulgur wheat.

A solid dining feat, Taboon is a pioneer of sorts in fusing Middle Eastern and Mediterranean flavors.

Tang Pavilion

Chinese ✗✗

A4

65 W. 55th St. (bet. Fifth & Sixth Aves.)

Subway: 57 St
Phone: 212-956-6888
Web: N/A
Prices: $$

Lunch & dinner daily

It's not easy to be a favorite spot in a city of constant change, and Tang Pavilion has been succeeding for decades. This Chinese classic raised the bar when it first appeared on the scene and hasn't changed course since. In fact, they've garnered quite a following, but Tang shines thanks to its tasty Shanghainese fare.

Snub the regular offerings and request their menu of "Shanghai specialties," faraway and well above the passé standards. Mauve walls and banquette rows spill into a large room graced with jacketed servers carrying around plates of steamed lamb jelly infused with five-spice and other aromatics; ribbons of dried tofu tossed with crunchy soy beans and sweet, tender pork; and a giant, buttery sea cucumber frilled with dry shrimp roe.

Toloache

Mexican

C2

251 W. 50th St. (bet. Broadway & Eighth Ave.)

Subway: 50 St (Broadway) Lunch & dinner daily
Phone: 212-581-1818
Web: www.toloachenyc.com
Prices: $$

Mexican dining is at its hottest in New York, with many thanks to the unstoppable team behind the uniquely authentic Toloache, Yerba Buena, and their other rapidly expanding outposts. Here in midtown, this two-story restaurant is decked in Talavera tiles, wood-beam ceilings, and stunning copper and tin lanterns.

A pleasure from start to finish, try the outrageously good house specialty, the *chapulines* taco, filled with Oaxacan-style dried grasshoppers. Tamer tastes can chose from an array of brick oven-fired quesadillas or ceviches, perhaps followed by flan with coffee-caramel sauce and fresh berry pico de gallo.

A serious list of divine margaritas and over 100 tequilas is on offer—all worthy bar mates to more than a dozen varieties of mescal.

Trattoria Dell'Arte

Italian

A3

900 Seventh Ave. (bet. 56th & 57th Sts.)

Subway: 57 St - 7 Av Lunch & dinner daily
Phone: 212-245-9800
Web: www.trattoriadellarte.com
Prices: $$$

There's a downright contagious exuberance to Shelly Firemen's always-packed Carnegie Hall classic, Trattoria Dell'Arte. It might be the smart, confident service staff, or the overflowing, recession-be-damned antipasto bar. Maybe it's the cheeky welcome motto ("What's Italian for Carnegie Hall? Trattoria Dell'Arte."), or the Tuscan-styled rooms lined with mahogany wine racks and dripping candles, that keep people coming back again and again.

Expect to pay–perhaps a bit too steeply–for this kind of *io non lo so*, but the flaky, thin-crust pizzas and heady dishes of finely-sauced pastas do not disappoint. Save room for the irresistible Italian desserts, like an airy cheesecake wrapped in chocolate sponge cake, topped with piping-hot chocolate ganache.

21 Club

American ✗✗

A4

21 W. 52nd St. (bet. Fifth & Sixth Aves.)

Subway: 5 Av - 53 St
Phone: 212-582-7200
Web: www.21club.com
Prices: $$$

Lunch Tue – Fri
Dinner Mon – Sat

The fabled 21 Club has been in business for over 83 years, but there's nothing slowing it down. Opened originally as a speakeasy, this NYC institution has wined and dined everyone from movie stars and moguls to moneyed city folk. From its lantern-holding jockeys and townhouse exterior to its leather and wood-paneled dining room that feels like a step back in time, 21 Club is a classic through and through.

The menu is a perfect accompaniment to the setting with choices like seared foie gras tinged with mango chutney and spread atop toasted brioche; or a splendid and classic rendition of steak tartare paired with a green salad. Upstairs and in the back, the feel is formal—so for a casual bite with prettier prices, head off the main entrance to Bar 21.

Utsav

Indian ✗✗

C2

1185 Sixth Ave. (enter on 46th St.)

Subway: 47-50 Sts - Rockefeller Ctr
Phone: 212-575-2525
Web: www.utsavny.com
Prices: ⊜⊜

Lunch & dinner daily

Push past the humdrum ground-floor bar seating, and make your way up the carpeted steps for a dramatic surprise. This is Utsav ("festival" in Sanskrit)—an upscale little hideaway perched on a suspended corridor between office buildings. From here, the restaurant fashions a contemporary, vibrant, and quintessentially Indian look that is light and airy with billowing fabrics, leafy green plants, and unique views.

The gorgeous, overflowing lunch buffet and bar-area takeout options bring office workers in by the droves, with curries, soft piles of blistered, piping-hot naan, and tandoori chicken. However, the à la carte and evening menus are equally worthy, and if the *ras malai* (sweet spheres of sugary paneer bathed in milk) are available, don't miss them.

ViceVersa

Italian ✗✗

C1

325 W. 51st St. (bet. Eighth & Ninth Aves.)

Subway: 50 St (Eighth Ave.)
Phone: 212-399-9291
Web: www.viceversarestaurant.com
Prices: $$

Lunch Sun – Fri
Dinner nightly

This smart and elegant spot (pronounced VEE-chay versa) embodies everything that a European would love in Italian-American cuisine. Inside, the dining room is a haze of muted gray and taupe with a long bar for solo dining, and pretty enclosed garden area that opens in fair weather for alfresco meals. The beautifully choreographed service and attentive staff is a worthy attraction in itself.

Although the menu lists some Italian classics, the dishes themselves cater to the American palate, with creamy and boldly sauced pastas aplenty. Expect the likes of eggplant cannoli filled with ricotta over warm mixed vegetables; *farfalle verdi* with lobster, sweet onion, and a light San Marzano tomato sauce; or roasted Vermont's suckling pig infused with cumin.

West Bank Café

American ✗✗

B2

407 W. 42nd St. (bet. Ninth & Tenth Aves.)

Subway: 42 St - Port Authority Bus Terminal
Phone: 212-695-6909
Web: www.westbankcafe.com
Prices: $$

Lunch & dinner daily

This beloved Theater District mainstay has kept its head above the all-too-choppy waters of Manhattan's dining scene since 1978 by offering delicious, progressive American food at honest prices. The flocks of regulars that squeeze into this simply adorned bistro most nights of the week are proof, though some of these guests may be heading to the Laurie Beechman Theater, located inside the café.

The vibe is lively, warm, and energetic, so settle into one of the leather banquettes and let the pleasant hum of jazz enhance your meal. Try the tender and beautifully charred steak, perhaps flanked by a salty tower of beer-battered onion rings. Bargains are available after 8:00 P.M., when two courses for $25 are served to non-theatergoers each evening.

Yakitori Totto

Japanese

251 W. 55th St. (bet. Broadway & Eighth Ave.)

Subway: 57 St - 7 Av

Phone: 212-245-4555

Web: www.tottonyc.com

Prices: $$

Lunch Mon – Fri

Dinner nightly

As if it were hiding from its brassy surrounds, Yakitori Totto is discreetly set up a narrow, steep flight of stairs. Inside, this faithful *yakitori-ya* is buzzing with diners, polished wooden tables, and a soundtrack ranging from J-pop to jazz. Two glassed-in private rooms shield subdued groups from the sultry and hip vibe.

Yakitori Totto is devoutly devoted to grilled meats and treats. Tended by prompt servers, the front counter and grill station dominates with parcels of *gyoza* and *tako waso*, octopus massaged with salty wasabi. Best to arrive early for authentic and irresistible treats like *sunagimo, reba, kawa, bonchiri* (gizzard, liver, and skin crested with sea salt); *ton toro* (pork neck skewers); and *momo*, juicy chicken thighs with soy *tare*.

Look for **red** symbols, indicating a particularly pleasant ambience.

SoHo & Nolita

SoHo (South of Houston) and Nolita (North of Little Italy) prove not only that New York has a penchant for portmanteaus, but also that the downtown "scene" lives on now more than ever. What remains new and ever-changing are the subtle transformations that redefine these neighborhoods block by block. Despite the retail invasion that has taken over some of SoHo's eastern corners, it remains true to its promise of sun-drenched restaurants and open-air cafés filled with European sophisticates and supermodels lingering over salads. There are also plenty of tourists to admire them.

Shopping in SoHo

Those fortunate enough to live in what were once artists' lofts (now multimillion dollar condos) know that there are still a few foodie gems in this area. For your at-home tapas needs, **Despaña** offers Spanish foods (and rare wines next door) as well as delicacies from oil-packed tuna to mouthwatering *bocadillos*. They will even prepare a traditional tortilla Española with advance notice. A visit to **Pino's Prime Meat Market** (that carries some of the best meat in town) or **Salumè**, (a Northern Italian sandwich haunt) should be followed by a respite at the original **Dean and Deluca**, filled with some of the cities favorite cakes and coffees. While this is a true gourmet treat, be forewarned that its steep prices match the sleek location. On Hudson Square, **City Winery** gives urban wine enthusiasts a place to make their own private-label wine by providing the grapes (a selection of varietals from international vineyards), the barrels, the storage, and the expertise.

NOLITA

Farther east is Nolita—a neighborhood as cool as its name. This is where a slightly hipper and hungrier downtown set flock (judging by its many offerings). These locals aren't living the typical midtown nine-to-five life and shun the *je ne sais quoi* of SoHo in favor of smallish spots that begin with the word "café." At the top of this list is **Café Habana**, offering its casual crowds a gritty diner vibe and amazing Mexico City-style corn on the cob (also available for takeout next door at **Café Habana To Go**). Equally hip hangouts can be found at **Café Gitane**, serving French-Moroccan; or **Lani Kai** for its killer cocktails and Polynesian small plates. The ethos in Nolita is focused: Do a single thing very well. This may have been inspired by **Lombardi's**, which claims to be America's very first pizzeria (founded in 1905) and still has lines outside the door. **Hoomoos Asli**'s setting and service may be basic, but they clearly put effort into the outstanding hummus, fluffy pitas, and

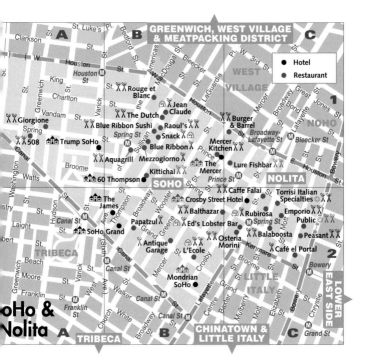

WEST VILLAGE

NOHO

NOLITA

SOHO

TRIBECA

LITTLE ITALY

LOWER EAST SIDE

SoHo & Nolita

● Hotel
● Restaurant

Rouge et Blanc
Jean Claude
The Dutch
Burger & Barrel
Giorgione
Blue Ribbon Sushi
Raoul's
Snack
508
Trump SoHo
Blue Ribbon
Mercer Kitchen
Lure Fishbar
Aquagrill
Mezzogiorno
Kittichai
The Mercer
Caffe Falai
Torrisi Italian Specialties
60 Thompson
Crosby Street Hotel
The James
Balthazar
Rubirosa
Emporio
Public
Papatzul
Ed's Lobster Bar
Peasant
SoHo Grand
Balaboosta
Antique Garage
L'Ecole
Osteria Morini
Café el Portal
Mondrian SoHo

falafels to accompany those tart, fresh lemonades. **Pinche Taqueria** is where you should head for the best fish tacos this side of California, but if whiling away the afternoon in an aromatic bakery better suits your mood, then sojourn at **Dominique Ansel's Bakery** or **Little Cupcake Bakeshop**. **Valley Shepherd Creamery** on Sullivan Street sates salt fiends with a host of expertly-crafted artisan cheeses, but to satisfy a sweet tooth in style, linger at **Pappabubble**, whose candies are created with an eye-popping sense of design. With equal ingenuity and old-school flair, **Rice to Riches** serves its celebrated bowls of rich rice pudding with creatively named toppings, like "Mischief" (buttery graham crackers) or "Nudge" (chilled espresso and cocoa). Cheesecake connoisseurs take note that **Eileen's Cheesecake** and its mind-boggling lineup of flavors has been chasing those Junior's fanatics back to Brooklyn. Even between feedings, this locale promises to nurture your inner epicurean with a visit to the Bowery for its throng of unrefined kitchen supply stores. One of the greater challenges Nolita poses is the decision of where to end the day. Tucked into these streets are cozy bars, each with its own stylish NY feel, *sans* the masses besetting other neighborhoods. Date-like places such as **Pravda** with its assortment of vodkas or **Sweet and Vicious** for stellar libations, are a fitting finale.

Antique Garage

B2

Turkish 🍴

41 Mercer St. (bet. Broome & Grand Sts.)

Subway: Canal St (Broadway)　　　　　　　　　Lunch & dinner daily
Phone: 212-219-1019
Web: www.antiquegaragesoho.com
Prices: $$

Let the sultry sounds of live jazz lure you into this little Bohemian hot spot, performed by a trio of old-school jazz cats—and absolutely free. The seduction continues inside, where exposed brick walls, high ceilings, low lighting, and a collection of charming antiques and photos make the perfect setting for a rendezvous or a quiet meal.

A nice selection of cocktails as well as Turkish white and red wines pair up perfectly with the likes of *circassian* chicken (shredded and served with tangy walnut sauce); *sarma* (thick slices of halloumi cheese topped with tomatoes and thyme and wrapped in pickled grape leaves, then grilled); or to end, dry and sweet apricots, stuffed with cream, *kaymak*, and almonds. Food is served up with genuine happiness.

Aquagrill

B1

Seafood 🍴🍴

210 Spring St. (at Sixth Ave.)

Subway: Spring St (Sixth Ave.)　　　　　　　　Lunch & dinner daily
Phone: 212-274-0505
Web: www.aquagrill.com
Prices: $$

Aquagrill is a SoHo fixture that keeps out of the spotlight. Despite its ordinary façade and snug interior, it is *the* best place in town for impeccably fresh oysters. And if that doesn't float your boat, find prawns, clams, and sea urchins on their excellent "Seafood Plateau Royale." Unique Loire valley whites complement this bivalve-centric menu that is widely adored by all who flock to this sophisticated space.

Every item of décor pays homage to the menu's focus—seafood and oysters. While it can get cramped inside and on the enclosed deck, patrons continue to queue up for steamed sumptuous whelks with a cayenne aïoli; bouillabaisse with poached Casco cod and lobster in a garlic-saffron-tomato bath; and pumpkin pie with *schlag* for a spicy finale.

Balaboosta

C2   Middle Eastern   ✗✗

214 Mulberry St. (bet. Prince & Spring Sts.)

Subway: Spring St (Lafayette St.)   Lunch Tue – Sun
Phone: 212-966-7366   Dinner nightly
Web: www.balaboostanyc.com
Prices: $$

Downtown foodies are already well aware of Israeli-born Chef Einat Admony thanks to her popular Taïm, located in the West Village and clearly marked by its lines out the door. Here at the chef's latest in Nolita, Balaboosta (a Yiddish expression meaning the perfect housewife), the menu is Sephardic in spirit and served in an attractively spare room with a petite bar area.

Small plates may feature crowd-pleasing hummus presented in a mortar and pestle, as well as *patatas bravas* with *za'atar* and roasted garlic aïoli. Dr. Dave's grilled pizza is made with carrot purée, caramelized onions, goat cheese, and cilantro; while contemporary entrées include grilled lamb chops with Persian lime sauce, smoky eggplant, and Upland watercress salad.

Balthazar

B2   French   ✗✗

80 Spring St. (bet. Broadway & Crosby St.)

Subway: Spring St (Lafayette St.)   Lunch & dinner daily
Phone: 212-965-1414
Web: www.balthazarny.com
Prices: $$$

With its legendary red awning and brassy good looks, Keith McNally's ageless downtown darling has been a joyous zoo ever since it opened its doors in 1997.

All of this means that reservations are highly recommended, though there are a few ways to dodge the prime-time problems. Bar tables are open to walk-ins; breakfast hours are lovely; and the bakery next door serves scrumptious salads, sandwiches, and pastries to-go (not to mention devastating hot chocolate). At the restaurant, classic bistro fare abounds in a rotating list of daily specials, from trout on Monday to Sunday's *choucroute*. Of course, anyone seeking that timelessly Balthazar experience should attempt the towering feast of chilled oysters and *fruits de mer*—a true must-have.

Blue Ribbon

Contemporary ✕

B1

97 Sullivan St. (bet. Prince & Spring Sts.)

Subway: Spring St (Sixth Ave.) Dinner nightly
Phone: 212-274-0404
Web: www.blueribbonrestaurants.com
Prices: $$$

It's for good reason that the Blue Ribbon family is now liberally fanned out across the city. Meet the catalyst for it all—Blue Ribbon brasserie, a New York classic tucked into Sullivan Street. The restaurant's welcoming and engaging staff is a luxury in a neighborhood more inclined to make you feel plain than cherished—which is quite interesting, considering Blue Ribbon has its own celebrity following. Namely, the city's chef circuit, that regularly swings through post-shift (the kitchen serves until 4:00 A.M.) come to indulge in a range of raw bar delights, and flavorful comfort classics like the playful *pu pu* platter or gourmet fried chicken.

So follow suit, bring a group, and dive into decadent delicacies like bone marrow with oxtail marmalade.

Blue Ribbon Sushi

Japanese ✕✕

B1

119 Sullivan St. (bet. Prince & Spring Sts.)

Subway: Spring St (Sixth Ave.) Lunch & dinner daily
Phone: 212-343-0404
Web: www.blueribbonrestaurants.com
Prices: $$$

Cooler than the traditional sushi den yet just as delicious, Blue Ribbon Sushi is yet another example of how these über-restauranteurs, the Bromberg brothers, have mastered their cultish art of the casually hip New York eatery. Here, they turn their attentions to the sea, where the team of talented chefs has but one all-important question for customers: Pacific or Atlantic? This is how the fresh-off-the-boat (or plane) sashimi and daily specials are delineated, although the spicy tuna set can tread safer waters with dishes like the crispy rock shrimp tempura.

No reservations are taken at this discreet sushi den, so aim for off-hours or lunchtime, when you can command a booth for an afternoon feast. Late hours, until 2:00 A.M., are popular among chefs.

Burger & Barrel

C1
American   🍴🍴

25 W. Houston St. (at Greene St.)

Subway: Broadway - Lafayette St
Phone: 212-334-7320
Web: www.burgerandbarrel.com
Prices: $$

Lunch & dinner daily

It should come as no surprise that Burger & Barrel is busier than a barrel of monkeys. After all, it comes from the same owners that have worked their magic with the lovely Locanda Verde and Lure. Inside, it's as tight as it is cool with a classic pub feel. You won't be able to have a private conversation, but the eavesdropping is fantastic!

Renowned burgers (like the Puebla) deserve the headline, with tasty toppings like red onion relish, roasted chili peppers, and creamy *queso fresco*, though there is more to this menu than meat. Comforting favorites go on to include fried chicken and sides like corn pudding or polenta fries. Desserts are to drool over—the salty peanut butter-brownie sundae is a perfect way to round out a heart-stopping meal here.

Café el Portal

C2
Mexican   🍴

174 Elizabeth St. (bet. Kenmare & Spring Sts.)

Subway: Spring St (Lafayette St.)
Phone: 212-226-4642
Web: N/A
Prices: 💰💰

Lunch & dinner Mon – Sat

Be thankful, residents of Nolita. Given the mass of hip, overpriced joints in the neighborhood, it's a minor miracle that this tiny, well-run charmer firing up excellent and economical Mexican food, continues to thrive. Inside, find bright kitschy walls, thumping tunes, and sweet service, so snag a spot at one of the few tables, and get noshing.

Comforting *sopa de pollo* bobbing with vegetables, cilantro sprigs, and tortilla strips is a fine way to start, followed by tasty *tacos de camaron*—corn tortillas stuffed with shrimp, shredded lettuce, *queso*, onion, and cilantro. The fiery *tinga* quesadilla will set your taste buds ablaze, with beef marinated in smoky chipotle sauce and tucked into two corn tortillas with tangy, green tomatillo sauce.

Caffe Falai

Italian Italian ✗✗

C2

265 Lafayette St. (bet. Prince & Spring Sts.)

Subway: Spring St (Lafayette St.) Lunch & dinner daily
Phone: 212-274-8615
Web: www.falainyc.com
Prices: $$

This sexy spot may have expanded but is as gorgeous as ever. While the former dessert case is gone, the same decadent pastries and cakes can be found on the menu. Sleek design notes include the monochromatic walls, white furnishings, pristine tablecloths, tiled floors, and counters lit by shimmering crystal candelabras. The bar now pours a formidable list, so summon a member of the honey-sweet (perhaps even flirtatious?) waitstaff, and order an Italian-inspired cocktail, made with the rarely found Santa Maria Novella bitters and liquors.

Plump tortelli, filled with a wonderful potato purée, in rich Bolognese ragù is a must; as is the *pollo alla Veneziana*, tender chicken breast with onion confit, earthy mushrooms, and celery root purée.

The Dutch

American ✗✗

B1

131 Sullivan St. (at Prince St.)

Subway: Spring St (Lafayette St.) Lunch & dinner daily
Phone: 212-677-6200
Web: www.thedutchnyc.com
Prices: $$$

An instant hit when it opened, The Dutch continues to be upbeat, boisterous, and hotter than ever. The bar rocks and the dining room is routinely packed, but this place is still inviting with its Roman and Williams décor and on-point staff. Keep in mind that the oyster bar is a great spot for a solo meal removed from the fray.

Chef Andrew Carmellini spins a wondrous web of Americana. The clever "Barrio" tripe is deliciously tender bobbing in a stew of beer, chilies, and hominy, topped with cool avocado and corn chips. Velvety duck breast is coated with finely chopped pecans and set atop organic dirty rice studded with andouille sausage. And that devil's food cake slathered with black pepper-boiled icing really does deserve all of its praise.

Ed's Lobster Bar

Seafood ✕

C2

222 Lafayette St. (bet. Kenmare & Spring Sts.)

Subway: Spring St (Lafayette St.)
Phone: 212-343-3236
Web: www.lobsterbarnyc.com
Prices: $$

Lunch & dinner daily

The delicacy and purity of seafood is epitomized in cute and convivial Ed's Lobster Bar. A sunny yet cool space with a good mix of food-savvy NYers, Ed's is that ideal sanctum for anyone who wishes to escape to New England for an hour.
As if to ease the no-reservations policy, this saltwater gem offers a fine choice of seafood-friendly wines and beers that go down as smoothly as the oysters. The narrow space is dotted with tables, but true cheer is found at the marble bar. While side dishes are all enticing, faves like perfectly fried calamari; creamy and luscious chowder with succulent clams; and the stellar buttery lobster roll (piled with juicy meat tossed in mayo, celery, and dill) aside crispy fries and Ed's homemade pickles are sheer decadence.

Emporio

Italian ✕✕

C2

231 Mott St. (bet. Prince & Spring Sts.)

Subway: Spring St (Lafayette St.)
Phone: 212-966-1234
Web: www.auroraristorante.com
Prices: $$

Lunch & dinner daily

Although Emporio neighbors other exciting spots, it remains a well-loved alternative to the countless cafés that dominate these SoHo blocks. This noisy yet attractive restaurant showers its pretty patrons with a warm welcome and heaps of attention. Decorative touches include a profusion of reclaimed wood, subway tiles, and a seductive glow. The requisite wood-burning oven sits in the back room outfitted with a skylight and beautiful open kitchen.
Forever focused on organically driven dishes, the kitchen turns out the likes of *le pappardelle*, ribbons of chestnut pasta tossed with mushrooms and *pecorino Sardo*; *la passera*, roasted fluke crested with fennel and Brussels sprouts; and a silky *torta di latticello* frilled with berries and maple syrup.

508

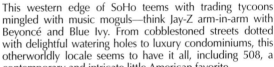

American ✕✕

A1

508 Greenwich St. (at Spring St.)

Subway: Spring St (Sixth Ave.)
Phone: 212-219-2444
Web: www.508nyc.com
Prices: $$

Lunch Sun – Fri
Dinner nightly

This western edge of SoHo teems with trading tycoons mingled with music moguls—think Jay-Z arm-in-arm with Beyoncé and Blue Ivy. From cobblestoned streets dotted with delightful watering holes to luxury condominiums, this otherworldly locale seems to have it all, including 508, a contemporary and intricate little American favorite.

It's all very quaint and casual inside with a modest décor of exposed brick, communal tables, and cozy armchairs. However, their beer list is anything but meek, and couples perfectly with a flatbread pizza spread with homemade spicy tomato sauce and wild boar smoked sausage. Goat "sloppy joe" sliders are wonderfully tender, but reach epic status when matched with short rib-stuffed peppers capped with creamy Manchego.

Giorgione

Italian ✕✕

A1

307 Spring St. (bet. Greenwich & Hudson Sts.)

Subway: Spring St (Sixth Ave.)
Phone: 212-352-2269
Web: www.giorgionenyc.com
Prices: $$

Lunch Mon – Fri
Dinner nightly

Owned and founded by jovial Giorgio Deluca (of Dean & Deluca), this long-time resident of Spring Street has become a SoHo destination, maintaining a loyal following and impressive longevity.

Excellent pastas and knock-out pizzas are spot on, but save room for the glorious array of house-made desserts. Start with a fresh fava salad tossed with crispy escarole, mint, pecorino, lemon, and olive oil; then roll up your sleeves for a choice of seasonal fresh pastas, like *garganelli con ragù di coniglio*, with its fragrant ragù of tender rabbit, tomatoes, earthy mushrooms, white wine, and the unmistakable scent of juniper berries. Finish off with a divine *crostata di albicocca*—flaky crust topped with poached apricots, almond cream, and mascarpone.

Manhattan ▶ SoHo & Nolita

Jean Claude

French ✗

 B1

137 Sullivan St. (bet. Houston & Prince Sts.)

Subway: Spring St (Sixth Ave.) Dinner nightly
Phone: 212-475-9232
Web: www.jeanclauderestaurant.com
Prices: $$

With its tight-knit tables, lived-in good looks, and soft French music quietly thrumming in the background, this romantic little bistro could be straight off of Paris' Left Bank. Luckily for Manhattan, though, the infinitely charming Jean Claude is smack in the middle of SoHo.

In winter, the room is decidedly cozy; while summer finds the front windows thrown open and couples lingering over the reasonably priced wine list, which boasts a nice carafe and half-carafe list. The French cooking is straightforward and delicious, with a solid lineup of bistro staples like tender *moules marinieres* and frites; seared hanger steak in a thyme, red wine and shallot reduction, paired with a sinful *gratin dauphinois*; and a spot-on rendition of crème brûlée.

Kittichai

Thai ✗✗

 B1

60 Thompson St. (bet. Broome & Spring Sts.)

Subway: Spring St (Sixth Ave.) Lunch & dinner daily
Phone: 212-219-2000
Web: www.kittichairestaurant.com
Prices: $$$

Good Thai food rarely doubles as a place to woo your sweetie, but dark and sultry Kittichai breaks the mold. Tucked into the trendy 60 Thompson hotel, the restaurant owns a jaw-dropping interior, replete with silk swaths, suspended orchids, and floating candles.

Thai hounds know there are more authentic places in the city to get their fix, but Kittichai makes up for the lack of heat with well-polished European touches. Try the spicy and sour oxtail soup, bobbing with Kaffir lime leaves and charred tomatoes; tender organic chicken, served in a delicious green, coconut-scented curry dancing with Thai eggplant and sweet basil; or a delicious Thai ice cream sundae with coconut jelly, passion fruit seeds, and palm seeds.

L'Ecole

French ✗✗

B2

462 Broadway (at Grand St.)

Subway: Canal St (Broadway)
Phone: 212-219-3300
Web: www.lecolenyc.com
Prices: $$

Lunch daily
Dinner Mon – Sat

Inspired and led by the dedicated students of the International Culinary Center, L'Ecole's creations are naturally insightful; even a dish that feels over-the-top illustrates their desire to succeed. It is a lovely room–welcoming and affable–with an earnest staff. Decorated with colorful walls, black-and-white photos, and circular fixtures, the space feels festive. The large glass windows overlook a bustling intersection, and people-watchers vie for these seats.

The menu features delicious classics, as promised by the surrounding "oohs and aahs." Pretty tables are set with finery, enhancing that roasted spiced monkfish atop green lentils; cured Spanish mackerel beside a warm potato salad; and a gooey chocolate almond cake laced by lemon cream.

Lure Fishbar

Seafood ✗✗

C1

142 Mercer St. (at Prince St.)

Subway: Prince St
Phone: 212-431-7676
Web: www.lurefishbar.com
Prices: $$$

Lunch & dinner daily

Housed in the basement of the popular Prada showroom, Lure Fishbar easily has some of the best digs in town. Outside, SoHo's streets might be covered in beautiful, old-school cobblestones and teeming with young gorgeous gazelles, but down here a tiki-trendy-meets-maritime motif (think tropical prints, angular porthole windows, and cozy booths) and fat seafood plates reign supreme.

A mean-looking sushi counter and raw bar lets you know how seriously they take the food, though. A plate of yellowtail carpaccio arrives fresh as can be, topped with garlic-chili sauce, sesame oil, thin slices of avocado, and crispy, deep-fried shallots; while a wickedly fresh branzino is served whole, perfectly de-boned and laced with pesto, scallions, and crunchy shallots.

Mercer Kitchen

Contemporary ✕✕

 B1

99 Prince St. (at Mercer St.)

Subway: Prince St
Phone: 212-966-5454
Web: www.jean-georges.com
Prices: $$$

Lunch & dinner daily

A-listers and Hollywood types may flock to the latest "it" restaurant, but these trendy spots often shutter long before their cool quotient becomes cliché. Mercer Kitchen is that rare NY restaurant that has retained its hot spot reputation and celebrity guestbook for what seems like eons. Showcasing a street-level bar (with stellar cocktails), a divvied up downstairs dining room, and subterranean lounge, Mercer Kitchen continues to offer well-executed and contemporary food like pizza flambée topped with smoky, fatty bacon and crème fraîche; delicately flavored tuna spring rolls with a soy purée; and baked salmon with potato salad and horseradish. Bold-faced names aren't only at the tables—Jean-Georges Vongerichten is still behind the scenes here.

Mezzogiorno

Italian ✕

   B1

195 Spring St. (at Sullivan St.)

Subway: Spring St (Sixth Ave.)
Phone: 212-334-2112
Web: www.mezzogiorno.com
Prices: $$

Lunch & dinner daily

The big, bright blue awnings of this Italian veteran are a fixture on the SoHo scene. Its 100 interior collages–each one a local artist's unique interpretation of the restaurant's logo– are a lovely reminder of when the neighborhood was more artists than agents.

The real star of the show, of course, is the beautiful wood-burning oven, which juts out into the main dining room where all can marvel at its delicious, thin-crust pies. In addition to the extensive pasta offerings, try the myriad seasonal Italian specialties like *carciofi saltati*, a plate of tender artichoke hearts paired with crunchy pistachio, and laced with lemon and parsley—this is a perfect delight when spring hits and the raised terrace opens up for prime people-watching.

Osteria Morini

Italian ✗✗

C2

218 Lafayette St. (bet. Kenmare & Spring Sts.)

Subway: Spring St (Lafayette St.)   Lunch & dinner daily
Phone: 212-965-8777
Web: www.osteriamorini.com
Prices: $$

Chef Michael White's rustic tribute to Emilia-Romagna rarely misses a beat. Once through the heavy wooden door, the cozy, oft-crowded space decorated with curios, photos, and shelves of ingredients pulses with the satisfied expectations of contented diners. An expert staff moves efficiently between the bar, the chef's counter, and the dining room.

The food is uncompromising, luscious, and hearty. The simple *polpettine*, prosciutto-and-mortadella meatballs, burst with porky goodness in a chunky tomato sauce; the *gramigna* topped with sausage ragù is elegant and full-flavored. The *affogato* is an unexpected and transporting star of the show—this cloud of zabaglione gelato resting on an ocean of espresso is reason enough to return again and again.

Papatzul

Mexican ✗

B2

55 Grand St. (bet. West Broadway & Wooster St.)

Subway: Canal St (Sixth Ave.)   Lunch & dinner daily
Phone: 212-274-8225
Web: www.papatzul.com
Prices: $$

Since its inception, Papatzul has remained a sought-after spot for tasty Mexican-American food. Just about every table holds a heaping bowl of creamy guacamole, so forget all notions of a diet. It's easy to spot this tiny SoHo storefront—look for a blue banner with the white logo fluttering above the door. Make your way through the glass doors to arrive in the cozy bar, packed with friends sipping sangrias, margaritas, and beers.

The dining room widens beyond the bar, revealing well-spaced wood tables and whitewashed walls adorned with masks. Expect such hearty fare as *sopes con calabaza* (masa cakes with zucchini and mushrooms, topped in goat cheese); *ensalada de nopalitos* with artichokes and fava beans; and churros served with a rich *cajeta* mousse.

Peasant

Italian ✗✗

194 Elizabeth St. (bet. Prince & Spring Sts.)

Subway: Spring St (Lafayette St.) Dinner Tue – Sun
Phone: 212-965-9511
Web: www.peasantnyc.com
Prices: $$

Things just keep getting better here at Peasant. A seasoned SoHo staple, this sublime spot continues to fire up terrific Italian with expert skill and consistency. Whitewashed brick walls and gorgeous wood-burning ovens stir up visions of an osteria, while the crackling hearth, complimentary bread, and sublime ricotta cheese seal the deal.

Sarde al forno–baked sardines with crispy breadcrumbs and grated lemon zest, served in a terra-cotta cassoulet–start things off beautifully. Fresh, hand-cut pastas are cooked al dente perfectly, as in the *malfatti con coniglio* in a hearty and gamey braised rabbit ragù, served with root vegetables and milky *Parmigiano*. End with apple and quince tart, flaky, sweet, and moist, topped with a scoop of gelato.

Raoul's

French ✗✗

180 Prince St. (bet. Sullivan & Thompson Sts.)

Subway: Spring St (Sixth Ave.) Dinner nightly
Phone: 212-966-3518
Web: www.raouls.com
Prices: $$$

Whether by charm or talent, this beloved bistro has survived 30-plus years in one of the fussiest parts of town, somehow remaining popular, sophisticated, and stylishly unpretentious. The authentic French fare is prepared simply, but remains impressive with top ingredients and delicious flavors—as in the steak tartare with quail egg, or seared foie gras with Concord grape purée. The menu, exquisitely handwritten on chalkboards and presented by the amiable waitstaff, still appeals to savvy diners and connoisseurs hungry for meaty steaks and crispy duck fat fries.

The energetic atmosphere in the dimly lit main room is intoxicating, but those seeking a calmer spot for quiet conversation should try the bright upstairs space or tiny covered garden.

Public ✿

Fusion XX

C2

210 Elizabeth St. (bet. Prince & Spring Sts.)

Subway: Spring St (Lafayette St.)
Phone: 212-343-7011
Web: www.public-nyc.com
Prices: $$$

Lunch Sat – Sun
Dinner nightly

AvroKO

With its series of handsome dining spaces and a scene that can best be described as "sexy," Public offers a perfect setting in which to appreciate Chef Brad Farmerie's spirited and refined cuisine. Buzzy, glowing, and always populated by bon vivants, this former factory was meticulously styled into its industrial sophistication by noted design firm AvroKO.

The chef is not shy about marrying seemingly unlikely combinations, and his menu for Public presents an enticing lineup. Delicately battered and fried Hama Hama oysters are returned to their shells for presentation and accompanied by vibrant wasabi-yuzu dipping sauce. Main courses might unveil Berkshire pork (a Sichuan spice-crusted tenderloin and voluptuous crisp-skinned belly) in a truffle-dashi broth; and venison loin perfectly cooked and brilliantly garnished by bright salsa verde and dumplings enriched with Cabrales cheese.

The drinks program deserves a concentrated once over for its collection of Australian and New Zealand wines, an after-dinner selection that includes lemon-vanilla or grapefruit-rosemary *cellos*; and sophisticated mocktails made with fresh juices and herbs, as in a blackberry, Thai basil, and yuzu smash.

Rouge et Blanc

Contemporary XX

48 MacDougal St. (bet. Houston & Prince Sts.)

Subway: Houston St
Phone: 212-260-5757
Web: www.rougeetblancnyc.com
Prices: $$$

Dinner Tue – Sun

With a burlap-covered ceiling, reclaimed wood, handcrafted pottery, lanterns, and plants, Rouge et Blanc's Indochine-influenced décor leaves no one guessing its theme. This restaurant successfully renews the romance of French-influenced Vietnam in its interior; while behind the scenes, the kitchen delivers a contemporary Asian menu that highlights pristine ingredients.

Well-charred razor clams are sweet and smoky atop leek confit; and creamy yellowtail is served with Oregon black truffles, soy jus, and ugli fruit for a fresh and citrusy finish. Rich endings, like caramelized foie gras with apples, cocoa nibs, and vanilla bean ice cream, are unusually appealing. Let the over-eager bussers know you are not in a hurry, then all can relax and enjoy.

Rubirosa

Italian X

235 Mulberry St. (bet. Prince & Spring Sts.)

Subway: Spring St (Lafayette St.)
Phone: 212-965-0500
Web: www.rubirosanyc.com
Prices: $$

Lunch & dinner daily

Boy oh boy (pardon the pun). From its adorable waitstaff (perch at the counter for *the* best flirting) to its mind-blowingly good Italian-American food, Rubirosa is one of the hotter tickets downtown. You won't know if you're swooning over the waiter, that Amaretto sour, or the intoxicating smells wafting from the oven here. Rubirosa is very Nolita, but one of the owners has ties to Joe & Pat's—a fixture in the annals of New York pizza.

This Italian-American sweet lives up to the adage about never being too rich or too thin with the Rubirosa classic, honoring its 50-year-old family recipe with a cracker-like crust, pure tomato sauce, and few distractions. The rock-your-world *sfogliatelle* are proud Neapolitan blue-collar bliss served up with a smile.

Snack

Greek ✗

B1

105 Thompson St. (bet. Prince & Spring Sts.)

Subway: Spring St (Sixth Ave.)
Phone: 212-925-1040
Web: N/A
Prices: 🍜

Lunch & dinner daily

Snack may not be that quaint, laid-back Santorini *taverna*, but there is much to love in this bustling slip of a restaurant tucked into SoHo's quiet, leafy Thompson Street. The old black-and-white photos and shelves of Greek groceries fail to conjure far-off lands, but ignore the slightly erratic interior and strive to snag one of the four dining room tables. The Hellenic fare is authentic enough to transport at first bite. Just don't stop at the meze—entrées are equally satisfying.

Despite the moniker, most of the portions here are hearty, including a generously-sized shredded lamb sandwich, topped with ripe tomatoes, roasted red onions, a smear of aïoli, and fresh arugula; or a Greek salad bursting with creamy feta, kalamata olives, and oregano.

Red=Particularly Pleasant.
Look for the red ✗ and 🏠
symbols.

Torrisi Italian Specialties ✪

Italian 🍴🍴

C2

250 Mulberry St. (at Prince St.)

Subway: Spring St (Lafayette St.)
Phone: 212-965-0955
Web: www.torrisinyc.com
Prices: $$$

Lunch Fri – Sun
Dinner nightly

Ryan Lee

Chefs Mario Carbone and Rich Torrisi sure have stepped up their game in the past year and their cleverly delicious take on old-school cooking shines even brighter. The line-out-the door-popular prix-fixe is noticeably more refined now while the recent addition of a stellar tasting menu has fans agape.

The charming room boasts lacy curtains, a white penny tile floor, and product-lined walls reminiscent of an Italian-American *alimentari*. And despite the casual look of the staff, this crew knows their stuff—be it the provenance of the milk used to make the warm mozzarella or a recommended bottle from the interesting list to carry you through the ceaseless tasting.

A palpable narrative unwinds in the menu's novel procession that marries Italian cuisine with NYC chutzpah and thus may begin with an Americano mocktail paired with mustard-dusted pretzel nuggets. The feast forges ahead with hand-chopped beef tartare capped by a "yolk" of béarnaise inspired by the legendary Delmonico's; a bowlful of meaty ragù sided by a fresh-from-the-oven semolina roll; or "Jewish lamb" in a Manischewitz reduction. Finally, a raw cow's milk cheese Danish is crowned by a slice of ripe fig grown in Brooklyn.

TriBeCa

Catering to its local clientele of creative types, trendy TriBeCa is, quite simply, a cool place to eat. Here, splurge on meals in pricey restaurants (whose reputations and namesake celebrity chefs precede them), or go for more modest gastropub fare. On sunny days, snag an umbrella-shaded table outside—TriBeCa's famously wide sidewalks are hugely accommodating and among the city's top spots for star-gazing. This stretch of cobblestoned streets, galleries, design stores, and historic warehouses converted to multi-million-dollar lofts was named in the 1970s by a real-estate agent hoping to create a hip identity for the area. The acronym–which stands for Triangle Below Canal–describes an area that is not a triangle at all, but a trapezoid bounded by Canal Street, Broadway, Murray Street, and the Hudson River. Greenwich and Hudson streets are its main thoroughfares for dining and nightlife.

Drinking and Dining

In keeping with its independence and artistic spirit, TriBeCa offers a gourmet experience for any palate (or price tag). On West Broadway, **Bubble Lounge** gives urban wine and champagne enthusiasts a place to celebrate special occasions in style. With such a massive list of hors d'oeuvres and a premium bar, it successfully seduces scores of revelers. Also beloved by wine connoisseurs is **Chambers Street Wines**. Those looking for something to enjoy with their wine will rejoice in the monthly events sponsored by **New York Vintners**, which may include free cheese tastings or lessons on making mozzarella. Luxury spa AIRE now offers rituals where one can soak in olive oil, cava, or red wine. The only downside? You can't drink it. The neighborhood is loaded with wonderful bakeries, the most popular of which includes **Duane Park Patisserie** for pastries and seasonal specialties; and **Tribeca Treats** for decadent and delicious chocolates. Part of the City Bakery family is **Birdbath** neighborhood green bakery, which is not just admired for its eco-friendly philosophy and practices, but also for its unique repertoire of breakfasts and lunches to-go, as well as desserts and specialty drinks offered all week long. **Puffy's Tavern** is a friendly hangout displaying five flat screens for sports fans, happy-hour drinks, and hearty lunchtime Italian sandwiches.

Speaking of local faves, **Bubby's** will cater to your homestyle food cravings, while **Zucker's Bagels & Smoked Fish** will remind you of *bubbe's* grub. Like every NY neighborhood TriBeCa claims its own great culinary treasures including **Korin** that boasts an array of Japanese chef knives and restaurant supplies, well-loved by many of the city's noted chefs. Speaking of Asian heaven, round up some friends

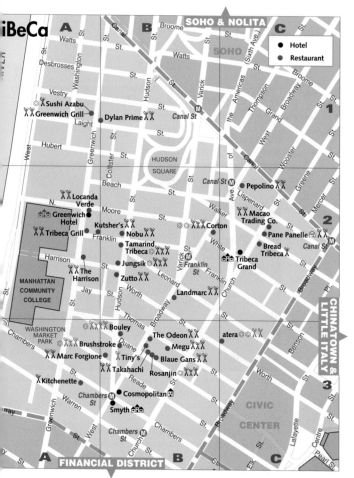

SOHO & NOLITA

SOHO

- ● Hotel
- ● Restaurant

Broome St
Watts St
Watts St
Desbrosses St
Vestry St
Washington St
Hudson St
Canal St
the Americas (Sixth Ave.)
Thompson St
Grand St
Broadway
Wooster St
Greene St
Mercer St

☼ Sushi Azabu
ХХ Greenwich Grill
● Dylan Prime ХХ
Laight St
Greenwich St
Collister St
Hubert St
West St
Beach St
HUDSON SQUARE

Canal St Ⓜ ● Pepolino ХХ
Lispenard St
Walker St
ХХ Macao Trading Co.
ХХ Locanda Verde
Moore St
ＸＸ ☼☼ ХХХ Corton
● Pane Panelle ☼ ХХ
🏨 Greenwich Hotel
Kutsher's ХХ
White St
● Bread Tribeca Х
Canal St
ХХ Tribeca Grill
Franklin St
● Nobu ХХ
Varick St
Franklin St
🏨 Tribeca Grand
● Tamarind Tribeca ☼ ХХХ
Harrison St
Jungsik ☼ ХХХ
Church St
ХХ The Harrison
● Zutto ХХ
Leonard St
MANHATTAN COMMUNITY COLLEGE
Jay St
Hudson St
Worth St
Thomas St
Landmarc ХХ
WASHINGTON MARKET PARK
☼ ХХХХ Bouley
Broadway
☼ ХХХ Brushstroke
Duane St
● The Odeon ХХ
atera ☼☼ ХХ
Benson Pl
Chambers St
ХХ Marc Forgione
Х Tiny's
● Megu ХХХ
Worth St
ХХ Takahachi
● Blaue Gans ХХ
Rosanjin ☼ ХХХ
Reade St
Х Kitchenette
Chambers Ⓜ
● Cosmopolitan 🏨
murray St
Warren St
Smyth 🏨🏨
CIVIC CENTER
Chambers Ⓜ
Greenwich St
West St
Church St
Chambers St
Lafayette St
Centre St

FINANCIAL DISTRICT

Elk St
Pearl St

CHINATOWN & LITTLE ITALY

---

to sample unique Japanese treats at **Takahachi Bakery**. Under the "dinner and a movie" category, the 2001 film *Dinner Rush* used TriBeCa as a stage. In fact, director Bob Giraldi shot this Mafia- and food-themed movie at one of his famed eateries—**Gigino Trattoria**. The plot tells the story of a night in the life of a chic TriBeCa restaurant, delving into sidelines such as food critics and ambitious chefs. Today this area is still associated with films of many stripes, thanks to the annual Tribeca Film Festival, created by Robert DeNiro and others to revitalize the area after 9/11. This world-famous springtime extravaganza hosts twelve days of great films, special events, and plenty of community camaraderie. Throngs of locals, tourists, and film fiends flock here during this time to see the movies and experience TriBeCa's many wonderful restaurants.

atera ✿✿

Manhattan ▶ TriBeCa

77 Worth St. (bet. Broadway & Church St.)

Subway: Chambers St (Church St.)
Phone: 212-226-1444
Web: www.ateranyc.com
Prices: $$$$

Dinner Tue – Sat

Nathan Rawlinson

New Yorkers love glitz and glamor, hype and buzz, but what really gets resident foodies pumped is a fresh new talent. Enter Chef Matthew Lightner, who has made us all sit up and take notice.

There's not a bad seat along this hushed 18-seat, smooth concrete counter, as each offers an up-close view of the brigade as they craft each precious bite in their gorgeous slate-clad kitchen. While eager gourmands flock to the luxurious bar stools, there is also a corner reclaimed wood table set beneath a wall of blooming herb planters.

At first, a dish may seem monochromatic, but further appreciation reveals visually arresting and stimulating cooking; their approach to food is reverent, unbridled, and delicious. A parade of trompe l'oeil dishes may begin atop rocks, bespoke ceramics, or perhaps a wood plank echoed in its presentation of a gnarled, knobby, fried sunchoke chip filled with creamy buttermilk. Such eye-popping canapés might be the prelude to diver scallops cured in gin botanicals, or dry-aged squab breast swathed in pear vinegar reduction. Freeze-dried chocolate meringue shattered into charcoal-like bits before your eyes, or truffles nestled in house-grown moss offer a strong finish.

Blaue Gans

B3

Austrian XX

139 Duane St. (bet. Church St. & West Broadway)

Subway: Chambers St (West Broadway)　　　　　Lunch & dinner daily
Phone: 212-571-8880
Web: www.kg-ny.com
Prices: $$

Blaue Gans is revered for its winning trifecta of food, drink, and vibe. This venerable space is endowed with snug tables and banquettes, while its hospitable bar is popular among the FiDi set. Find a cozier perch beside looming windows, perfect for a beer and sausage. Embellished with movie posters and a marvelous soundtrack, Blaue Gans feels at once Euro and downtown. If that doesn't scream unique, check their menu of fine wursts and schnitzels.

A bibb salad bathed in pumpkin oil offers a perfect prelude to *käsekrainer*, a fatty, cheesy sausage matched with sauerkraut; or fried *jäger schnitzel* drowned in a mushroom-bacon sauce. You'll want to save room for dessert—maybe a *schwarzwälder kirsch torte* with sour cherries and amaretto crunch ice cream.

Bread Tribeca

C2

Italian X

301 Church St. (at Walker St.)

Subway: Canal St (Sixth Ave.)　　　　　Lunch & dinner daily
Phone: 212-334-0200
Web: www.breadtribeca.com
Prices: $$

There's a kind of fresh, airy feel to this sweet place, housed in a gorgeous, historically industrial building with a white, windowed façade. Inside, indigo banquettes and chairs set against immaculate tables, rectangular light fixtures hanging from high ceilings, and pristine brick walls induce feelings of openness.

A longstanding spot, Bread Tribeca fires up the kind of simple, good stuff that keeps locals and visitors coming back time and time again. The addition of a vegetarian menu, a "cleansing program," and items like gluten-free bread draw an even wider audience. Have a go at the succulent and crisp-grilled shrimp, coated with lemon juice, olive oil, garlic, and oregano; or farfalle tossed with spicy pork sausage, broccoli rabe, and Parmiggiano.

Bouley ❀

B3

163 Duane St. (at Hudson St.)

Subway: Chambers St (West Broadway)
Phone: 212-964-2525
Web: www.davidbouley.com
Prices: $$$$

Lunch & dinner Mon – Sat

Nicole Bartelme

Luxury embraces you upon entering this extraordinary château-inspired space, richly appointed with worldly imports, chandeliers that appear to drip jewels, carved wooden doors, and fresh orchid arrangements—sometimes supervised by the eminent chef himself. Bouley's entry can be difficult to locate, but gilded arched ceilings and the scent from impossibly fragrant apples in the foyer will lure you in. It's as if the king ordered a bit of fruit. But of course, royal treatment is reserved for guests alone, as the poised and intent staff will remind you through your meal.

An experience not readily replicated, dining here is transporting and festive as evidenced by the celebrants that fill its plush berry-tinged velour chairs. Hand-painted floral walls remain true to David Bouley's classic French aesthetic and culinary foundation. He can often be seen preparing a rather contemporary menu glazed with global influences.

Starters are intriguing and exciting as in supremely tender shrimp, scallop, and ribbons of baby squid crusted with wafer-thin strands of phyllo. The subtle sweetness and vivid colors in a pumpkin soup bring wonderful complexity to fresh ricotta foam lilting with toasted *pepitas*.

Brushstroke ✿

Japanese ✗✗✗

30 Hudson St. (at Duane St.)

Subway: Chambers St (West Broadway)
Phone: 212-791-3771
Web: www.davidbouley.com
Prices: $$$$

Dinner Mon – Sat

Brushstroke/Nicole Bartelme

Brushstroke is one restaurant with two distinct dining options and no missteps. White pine plank floors, oak counters, and rice paper embellish the gorgeous main dining area, serving six- to ten-course kaiseki menus from the intensely focused exhibition kitchen helmed by Chefs David Bouley and Isao Yamada. Expect extreme professionalism and attentive service from front to back of the house.

Attention to detail and exquisite ingredients are the hallmarks of their cuisine. Small courses such as *chawan mushi* with velvety foie gras and shaved black truffles; applewood-smoked duck breast with fresh chamomile leaves; or miso-glazed black cod over a purée of broccoli rabe display an immaculate Japanese style.

The former bar/lounge area has been retooled to serve as an omakase-only sushi counter, where one will find an unwavering mastery of authentic *Edomae* sushi. Chef Eiji Ichimura's magic is on display where seats allow a virtual lesson in Japanese culinary technique. He proudly presents each bite himself, from the *baigai* (whelk) simmered, sliced, and then re-assembled in its conch-like shell, to the extraordinary parade of sushi, through a sweet-salty-tangy surprise of soy sauce ice cream.

343

Corton ✿ ✿

B2

239 West Broadway (bet. Walker & White Sts.)

Subway: Franklin St
Phone: 212-219-2777
Web: www.cortonnyc.com
Prices: $$$$

Dinner Tue – Sat

Richard Pare

Chef Paul Liebrandt invokes a certain game-changing genius that has been crammed into high-profile kitchens across the globe. Here at Corton, find young foodies with cerebral tastes and future chefs trying to gauge where their profession is heading. The contemporary cuisine is very creative, intriguing, and impressive. The service is warm, but falters if the chef is elsewhere that night.

White walls with reliefs of branches, and bits of gold leaf set the minimalist scene, while a slender pane of glass may reveal the chef's imposing form in the kitchen.

Set menus range from six to nine courses, and may begin with marshmallow-soft yuzu foam, sashimi, and paper-thin daikon topped with osetra caviar and edible blossoms. An affinity for sweetness is revealed in a dual "rouge" composition of intensely hued cabbage purée, purple artichoke heart, meringue, crunchy kohlrabi; and an accompanying bowl of black eggplant meringue, Treviso, and tart fruit sorbet. Squab is blissfully tender, with a wedge of roasted, crumb-topped carrot, caramelized potato fondant, dressed tableside in an excellent jus. Chocolate desserts–with squiggles of birch gelée and dabs of honey-sweet chestnut cream–are memorable.

Dylan Prime

American ✗✗

B1

62 Laight St. (at Greenwich St.)

Subway: Franklin St
Phone: 212-334-4783
Web: www.dylanprime.com
Prices: $$$

Lunch Sun – Fri
Dinner nightly

Set in a converted TriBeCa warehouse, Dylan Prime is a giant multi-room affair. Yet, for a quick spoil, nothing beats their ample bar encountered by aiming left upon entering the enclosed hall. Sultry spotlights set the dining room aglow; rustic, yet elegant details like exposed brick, leather upholstery, and lavish banquettes enrich the allure of this distinguished den.

Keeping company with their boisterous bar–largely populated by FiDi types–is a quiet-toned dining room graced by easy yet efficient servers. The clambake here is a summer spectacle of lobster, clams, mussels, and potatoes; while crispy artichokes tossed with walnut crumble, a dry-aged, buttery Porterhouse, and hazelnut cheesecake are clearly focused on the American side of things.

Greenwich Grill

Fusion ✗✗

A1

428 Greenwich St. (bet. Laight & Vestry Sts.)

Subway: Franklin St
Phone: 212-274-0428
Web: www.greenwichgrill.com
Prices: $$

Lunch & dinner daily

Situated upstairs from its sister spot, Sushi Abazu, this enchanting sibling marries Italian and Japanese flavors into a seasonal menu. The lovely space divides into a sultry lounge styled in round, brick red banquettes and large, low-hanging lights; and a sleek dining area with white linen-topped tables and stone accents.

Tasty features include carpaccio of sea bass topped with tobiko, served over endive and mizuna greens; Zuwai crab and caramelized leeks over *spaghettini*, tossed with *bottarga* and red pepper flakes; and scrumptious oven-roasted chicken with diced potatoes in a whole grain mustard sauce. Finish off with a *matcha* meringue roll—green tea mousse, strawberries, and banana wrapped in freshly baked meringue, served with vanilla sauce.

The Harrison

Contemporary 🍴🍴

 A2

355 Greenwich St. (at Harrison St.)

Subway: Franklin St   Lunch Mon – Fri
Phone: 212-274-9310   Dinner nightly
Web: www.theharrison.com
Prices: $$

Justifiably admired by locals and astute visitors, The Harrison is stunning in that downtown hip sort of way. The softly lit dining room is sensual and slightly jazzy, as "ribbons" of red beveled glass trim the top of every window and lend a sultry air when sunlight filters in. In keeping with the neighborhood spirit, even the floral ensembles are elaborate and fun.

The service is well-orchestrated, with the bar clearly ruling the room. Dressed with fine china, tables showcase homemade ricotta *cavatelli* enriched with braised duck, tomato, and chevre; sharp eggplant croquets with tomato chutney; and tender bites of lamb Milanese paired with sautéed greens. And whether they serve you birthday cake or not, custard-filled éclairs are a total treat.

Kitchenette

American 🍴

A3

156 Chambers St. (bet. Greenwich St. & West Broadway)

Subway: Chambers St (West Broadway)   Lunch & dinner daily
Phone: 212-267-6740
Web: www.kitchenetterestaurant.com
Prices: 💰💰

Styled after an old-school luncheonette with black-and-white floor tiles, swiveling barstools and a long Formica-topped counter, Kitchenette stops just short of kitsch when it comes to the food. This ain't your Momma's Betty Crocker, but delicious, real-deal home cooking—think freshly baked cornbread, decadent four-cheese macaroni, and silky turkey meatloaf. Washed down with a Boylan's bottled soda, a meal at Kitchenette could put a smile on the grumpiest man's face. The desserts are all made in-house and should not be missed: try the lemon and poppy seed layered cake, a fresh, mile-high slice of crumbly, buttery divinity laced with cream cheese frosting. For the Columbia crowd, Kitchenette has a sister location in Morningside Heights.

Jungsik

Korean ✕✕✕

B2

2 Harrison St. (at Hudson St.)

Subway: Franklin St
Phone: 212-219-0900
Web: www.jungsik.kr
Prices: $$$$

Dinner Mon– Sat

Why Not Smile

Jungsik dwells on the ground floor of a grand building set upon an elegant TriBeCa corner. Its grey façade blends with the landscape, but an arresting wall of windows is an instant eye-catcher. From entry to exit, warm, hospitable and never-scripted service is the norm. They even have a sense of humor—yet another boon to this tasteful and modern space.

Elusive cream and black shades paint the bar and dining room, which in turn evokes serenity with lush high-backed banquettes, large linen-topped tables, and central service tables gently illuminated by sleek pendant lights.

While playful canapés like Korean fried chicken paired with a pleasing vintage wine might distract, the arrival of *bibimbap* mingling yellow tomatoes and basil sorbet will return your senses to the table. Presentation is key at this haute Korean haven. This is especially evident when white porcelain bowls are filled with roasted mushrooms swimming in a delectably flavorful dashi broth topped with a soft-poached egg. Seaweed rice, toasted quinoa, and briny sea urchin display a delicious interplay of taste and texture when mixed together, as does the moist, beautifully crisped red snapper bathed in a spicy cilantro sauce.

Kutsher's

Eastern European ✗✗

A2

186 Franklin St. (bet. Greenwich & Hudson Sts.)

Subway: Franklin St
Phone: 212-431-0606
Web: www.kutsherstribeca.com
Prices: $$$

Lunch Sat – Sun
Dinner nightly

Who knew herring could be hip? Zach Kutsher, that's who. The name might sound familiar to a certain set of New Yorkers (it was a longtime vacation spot in the Catskills à la Dirty Dancing), but it's now becoming known more for chopped liver than campfires.

At this self-proclaimed modern Jewish bistro, you can expect your *bubbie's* food, but finished with downtown oomph. The menu showcases some serious chops (Jeffrey Chodorow is a partner) via perfectly comforting potato latkes topped with sour cream; hugely addictive duck fries double-fried in duck *schmaltz*; and simply delectable crispy artichokes. Chopped liver, pickled herring, and *kreplach* stray from the classic preparations with modern interpretations, perfect for the moneyed Bugaboo set.

Landmarc

French ✗✗

B2

179 West Broadway (bet. Leonard & Worth Sts.)

Subway: Franklin St
Phone: 212-343-3883
Web: www.landmarc-restaurant.com
Prices: $$

Lunch & dinner daily

Saunter into this bi-level beauty to find cool steel touches and warm woods mingling with slate and lavender hues, the space set a-twinkle with soft track lighting. An open fire grill cozies up the place, and on warmer days, the serene second level expands out into a breezy balcony.

Choose a half bottle of wine from the terrific selection, and absorb yourself in the comfort and pleasures of rich foie gras terrine, served with pickled red onion and toasted points; warm and savory goat cheese profiteroles, plump with *chevre*, herbs, and diced red peppers; or a delectable special such as a generous oven-roasted *boudin blanc* over celery root slaw and braised red cabbage. Top it off with a decadent chocolate-iced éclair, bursting with Chantilly cream.

Locanda Verde

Manhattan ▶ TriBeCa

A2

Italian ✗✗

379 Greenwich St. (at N. Moore St.)

Subway: Franklin St
Phone: 212-925-3797
Web: www.locandaverdenyc.com
Prices: $$$

Lunch & dinner daily

It may be inside the Greenwich Hotel, but Locanda Verde is more a hip neighborhood hangout than hotel restaurant. While this rustic Italian remains casual favoring fancy jeans over suits, the star power of owner Robert DeNiro and Chef Andrew Carmellini brings an upscale bent and downtown vibe to the crowd who looks as good as the space—right down to the fantastic alfresco dining area.

Comfort foods headline in simple sandwiches, exemplary focaccia, and blockbuster pastas that can display brilliance and talent. Daily specials might include fried chicken Mondays—hold your breath that it will become a regular treat. The thrills continue through dessert, with Chef Karen DeMasco's famous chocolate donuts with crackle glaze and oatmeal cookie sandwiches.

Macao Trading Co.

C2

Portuguese ✗✗

311 Church St. (bet. Lispenard & Walker Sts.)

Subway: Canal St (Sixth Ave.)
Phone: 212-431-8750
Web: www.macaonyc.com
Prices: $$

Dinner nightly

Hidden just behind a red light on a quiet TriBeCa block, Macao Trading Co. is one of those opium-den-like joints that stays humming until 4:00 A.M. In other words, exactly the kind of place your suburban friends *think* you hang out in all the time.

So prove them right: because unlike so many other stylish restaurants that don't deliver, Macao gives as much attention to the food as to the drinks and sexy décor. Macao belonged to the Portuguese before they handed the island over to the Chinese in 1999, and the two cultures are given equal play time on the menu: try the *bacalhau* tartare, a house-cured salt cod topped with beets, fresh horseradish, and micro greens; or tender pork and lamb meatballs with smoked paprika tomato sauce and chorizo.

Marc Forgione

American 🍴🍴

B3

134 Reade St. (bet. Greenwich & Hudson Sts.)

Subway: Chambers St (West Broadway)
Phone: 212-941-9401
Web: www.marcforgione.com
Prices: $$$

Lunch Sun
Dinner nightly

A dark awning and metal steps mark the entry to this sultry and savory TriBeCa pet. The mood is set with dusky lights (candles are a staple, naturally), backlit leather banquettes, and tables crafted from sanded wood. Between weathered planks and shelves rife with kitchenware, notice an honest yet enchanting rusticity at Marc Forgione.

Ample windows, framed mirrors, and a hopping bar harken back to the city. Wood chairs scoot up to tiny tables where fine china and cutting boards hint at what is to unfold—serious American food tinged with modern flair like agnolotti packed with uni panna cotta and finished with a spark of curry. Whether diners opt for the rowdy chocolate "blondie" tart or Lady Ashton cake, their palate is assured the gift of decadence.

Megu

Asian 🍴🍴🍴

B3

62 Thomas St. (bet. Church St. & West Broadway)

Subway: Chambers St (West Broadway)
Phone: 212-964-7777
Web: www.megurestaurants.com
Prices: $$$

Dinner nightly

One peek at Megu's menu and you can expect a pleasurable affair. A stunning blend of beauty and style, this space comes with a pretty price, but trust that it's worth it—imagine an omakase of seven courses and the rest of the puzzle will fall into place. Descend the slate stairs into the large, lofty dining room dramatically decorated with an ice Buddha and a giant bell.

As expected, Megu is perpetually packed with sake-sipping trendsters grooving to the thumping music while clamoring for inventive Japanese fare. Expect such well-balanced dishes as Kobe beef skewers paired with soy-wasabi, miso, black sesame, and soy-garlic sauces; *hoba* leaf-wrapped lamb chops grilled to tender perfection; and crab fried rice tossed with garlic mayonnaise.

Nobu

Japanese ✗✗

B2

105 Hudson St. (at Franklin St.)

Subway: Franklin St
Phone: 212-219-0500
Web: www.myriadrestaurantgroup.com
Prices: $$$$

Lunch Mon – Fri
Dinner nightly

Everything is exactly as it should be at this longtime TriBeCa success story. And yet, the décor doesn't seem aged at natty Nobu, a seasoned Japanese gem still favored for both casual and corporate gatherings. While suits with Blackberries favor their fast and friendly service, the vibe at night attracts good-looking locals. Two-tops may be packed but booths along one wall and the sushi counter are far more inviting.

Lunch serves a pared down menu, while dinner unveils almost twice as many of Nobu's signature courses. Most of these flirt with Western accents and may include bigeye and Bluefin toro tartare in a drinkable bath of wasabi-soy; squid "pasta" with crisp vegetables; sweet and tender miso cod; and excellent shiitake or eggplant tempura.

The Odeon

American ✗✗

B3

145 West Broadway (at Thomas St.)

Subway: Chambers St (West Broadway)
Phone: 212-233-0507
Web: www.theodeonrestaurant.com
Prices: $$

Lunch & dinner daily

Occupying a prime piece of real estate smack in the middle of TriBeCa, The Odeon has been going strong since the 1980's—go at the right hour these days, and you're still likely to find the lawyers and City Hall types who put the place on the map perched on their bar stools.

Between the art deco architecture, wood framed-windows, and lazy fans slowly rotating overhead, one is bound to feel as if they just walked into a lovely brasserie in Lyon. The food matches the atmosphere—charming and noisy, laid-back but never absent-minded. Try the heirloom beet salad with silky shaved fennel, aged goat cheese, and blood orange vinaigrette; or a sushi-grade yellowfin tuna burger licked with wasabi mayonnaise and tucked between a toasted sesame seed bun.

Pane Panelle

Italian   ❌❌

C2

305 Church St. (at Walker St.)

Subway: Canal St (Sixth Ave.)   Lunch & dinner daily
Phone: 212-219-4037
Web: www.panepanelle.com
Prices: $$

In 1935, owner Gerard Renny's grandparents opened Pep's Bar, the Brooklyn stalwart now resurrected as Zi Pep in the East Village. Here in TriBeCa, Pane Panelle is glorious proof of these well-worn chops, and where heart-warming, street-style Italian is dished with aplomb.

Expect wonderfully crisp *arancini* stuffed with spicy Italian sausage and mozzarella; and *panelle e melanzane*, a Palermo-style sandwich of chickpea fritters, fried eggplant, mortadella, and pecorino (also try their sandwich kiosk). Even typically uninspired fare is made here with exceptional flair, as in the chicken *al mattone*, served as a compressed block of juicy white and dark meats over a bed of rapini and potatoes. The ricotta cheesecake is absolute, irresistible perfection.

Pepolino

Italian   ❌❌

C2

281 West Broadway (bet. Canal & Lispenard Sts.)

Subway: Canal St (Sixth Ave.)   Lunch & dinner daily
Phone: 212-966-9983
Web: www.pepolino.com
Prices: $$

Head upstairs to the second floor of this bi-level fave, where diners and staff are on a first name basis and Chef Enzo Pezone amicably makes his way through the dining room. A fine array of pastas and fish specials draws crowds of locals in the know.

To whet the palate, savor the complementary tomato-basil pâté (one of the tastiest openers around), before moving onto the irresistible *taglioni gratiniati*, long flat noodles loaded with shredded *prosciutto cotto*, fontina, Parmesan, and béchamel sauce with hints of rosemary. Other hits include braised salt cod in tomato sauce with capers, peppers, garlic, and parsley; and the homemade ricotta cheesecake, mousse-like and ethereal with touches of lemon and vanilla, which makes for a superb finale.

Rosanjin ✿

141 Duane St. (bet. Church St. & West Broadway)

Subway: Chambers St (West Broadway) Dinner Mon – Sat
Phone: 212-346-0664
Web: www.rosanjintribeca.com
Prices: $$$$

♿

Peter Dressel

Rosanjin is a sanctuary for diners who appreciate the art of kaiseki: a traditional Japanese progression of courses displaying careful skill and precise technique.

Cached among the cast-iron facades of a picture perfect TriBeCa block, pay attention because Rosanjin's signage is discreet—easy to miss actually. Inside, it is serenity now, as polished yet reserved servers welcome you into this hushed haven. Rosy hues tint the serene setting complete with slate floors, fabric-covered walls, and cushioned armchairs.

Let there be no doubt that Rosanjin is dedicated to serious dining, as if the chef considers each course to be an opportunity to flaunt his restrained attention to detail and respect for tradition. At the same time, meals are refined and studious. Several options are available but keep in mind the more in-depth menus require advance notice. Expect a meal of high points like a dome of silken corn tofu dabbed with freshly grated wasabi and *tonburi* (mountain pearls); sparkling sashimi atop a pillar of crushed ice; grilled river fish with pickled *myoga*; or a pot of tile fish and sea urchin rice. Leftovers (if there are any) are ceremoniously packaged to be enjoyed at home.

Sushi Azabu ✿

A1

428 Greenwich St. (bet. Laight & Vestry Sts.)

Subway: Franklin St

Phone: 212-274-0428

Web: www.greenwichgrill.com

Prices: $$$

Lunch Mon – Fri

Dinner nightly

Sushi Azabu

Discreetly tucked in the basement of Greenwich Grill, Sushi Azabu excels in the art of subtlety. The subterranean space uses curved booths, inlaid stone floors, and slender canvasses depicting inky images of carp to fashion a snug yet elegant room. The young, moneyed crowd reflects the neighborhood, confidently ordering from the traditional Japanese menu.

The chef's omakase (a must) might begin with a single jumbo oyster, sliced into four lush, creamy morsels. The embellishments of grated daikon, green onion, and a touch of soy only enhance its fresh, mildly briny flavors. Or, find an array of sashimi ranging from fatty tuna and bright white fluke to a small cup of sea-salty uni. An undeniable highlight here is the classic *Edomae* sushi. Each piece is carefully crafted and presented on a gunmetal-grey ceramic slab stacked with fresh wasabi. These perfectly formed mouthfuls of sensational quality fish are by far the pinnacle of a meal. The chef might include the likes of rich mackerel topped with sheets of vinegar gelée, silky sea eel dabbed with *kabayaki* sauce, and raw scallop with lemon sea salt.

Desserts are petite and lovely, like house-made vanilla ice cream swirled with *marron glacé*.

Takahachi

Japanese ✗✗

B3

145 Duane St. (bet. Church St. & West Broadway)

Subway: Chambers St (West Broadway)
Phone: 212-571-1830
Web: www.takahachi.net
Prices: $$

Lunch Mon – Fri
Dinner nightly

In a neighborhood dominated by the Japanese behemoths Nobu and Megu, unassuming Takahachi is a welcome reprieve for nouveau Japanese cuisine—minus the fuss, high-flying theatrics, and exorbitant price tags. Those willing to forgo the sexier settings even find a little romance in the skylights of Takahachi's small, spare dining room come sunset.

Mainly, this is a local fave for families to gather over a delicious meal. The menu may unveil bright, velvety sashimi; fresh tangles of sesame-dressed buckwheat soba noodles studded with shiitake mushrooms and avocado; or grilled appetizers like the supremely fresh black cod marinated in nutty and irresistible miso.

For outstanding desserts and bread, head a few blocks down to Takahachi Bakery on Murray Street.

Tiny's

American ✗

B3

135 W Broadway (bet. Duane & Thomas Sts.)

Subway: Chambers St (West Broadway)
Phone: 212-374-1135
Web: www.tinysnyc.com
Prices: $$

Lunch & dinner daily

Relatively new to this pricey little enclave is the impossibly charming Tiny's, perched at the bottom of a pink-painted, Federal-style residence, amid soaring multi-loft mansions and ultra-chic shops. Plumb in the heart of a quiet TriBeCa street, it is a welcome relief from the hectic city bustle. Inside, pressed-tin ceilings, worn white terra-cotta floors, antique wood banquettes, and a wood-burning fireplace make for an enchanting atmosphere.

The kitchen's talents are clear in sensational offerings like sweet potato and apple soup with brioche croutons and maple cream; mozzarella-stuffed meatball marinara with crostini; and smoky duck breast over cashew-miso purée and wok-finished broccoli. Save room for the moan-inducing chocolate pretzel tart.

Tamarind Tribeca

Indian

99 Hudson St. (at Franklin St.)

Subway: Franklin St

Lunch & dinner daily

Phone: 212-775-9000

Web: www.tamarinde22.com

Prices: $$$$

Tamarind Tribeca

Tamarind Tribeca has been setting hearts ablaze from its impressive glass-fronted home that seats an affluent crowd. With a warming Brazilian teak-patterned floor, mesmerizing spray of orange orchids, stunning marble bar, and dainty lampshades, it is now hailed as one of the flashier lairs for haute Indian food.

A gorgeous blend of men with pressed collars (their jackets thrown jauntily over the shoulder) and women donning deadly designer stilettos frequent this bi-level space, which cost many cool millions to construct. An imposing foyer, glass-enclosed tandoori oven, and gleaming mezzanine are among the telling details

While the bar stirs up excellent cocktails, a notable wine list (displayed along another glass wall) complements the cuisine as well. Settle into a veiled booth and begin with *kaddu narial*, a silky butternut squash soup fragrant with fenugreek seeds, followed by *sufiani machli* (sea bass) that emerges from the tandoor supremely moist and creamy. The staff may be rushed or lacking in some skills, but dishes like Punjabi mutton sautéed with tomatoes, cumin, garlic, and spices; or sweet potato pudding tinged with crushed cardamom prove the kitchen's mastery of Indian cuisine.

Tribeca Grill

Contemporary ✗✗

A2

375 Greenwich St. (at Franklin St.)

Subway: Franklin St
Phone: 212-941-3900
Web: www.myriadrestaurantgroup.com
Prices: $$$

Lunch Sun – Fri
Dinner nightly

Tribeca Grill is hallowed for its proficient and well-paced service; and disciples in the know (wealthy patrons from around the way) love to seek their expert sommelier for counsel on a wine list—replete with impressive German and Austrian selections. Less suited for intimate affairs, the Grill exudes a classic quality and is a reliable destination among the elite and beautiful people of NYC.

Diners hold court amid exposed duct work, wall-to-wall windows, and a mighty bar posed in the center. To delight the palate, find rustic veal and mushroom terrine served with raisin-walnut bread and violet mustard. Seared scallops with squash-bacon risotto, subtly spiced pumpkin cheesecake, and a well-plated cheese course unveil a real love for seasonal ingredients.

Zutto

Japanese ✗✗

B2

77 Hudson St. (bet. Harrison & Jay Sts.)

Subway: Franklin St
Phone: 212-233-3287
Web: www.zuttonyc.com
Prices: $$

Lunch & dinner daily

Zutto is at the helm of serious Japanese *izakaya* entrenching themselves in the city's scene. A welcoming space with a practical yet pleasing aesthetic, this "Japanese-American pub" as the owners like to call it, has long been a TriBeCa fixture. Contemporarily fit with wooden communal tables and exposed brick, there is ample space to lounge here, likely to a background beat of Billboard's best.

While the menu meanders, a taste of such varied dishes as *chuuka manjuu* (*baos* filled with tender, fatty pork belly and miso); or *shoyu ramen*, a dish native to the north of Japan and enriched with tofu and *menma*, will have you smitten.

From pristine sushi like soft shell crab decked with fresh roe to *negi toro* with pickled daikon, the chef reveals fine pedigree.

Upper East Side

The Upper East Side is a vast, mainly residential neighborhood with many faces ranging from prominent New York families to fresh-from-college prepsters. Closest to the park are posh spots catering to the Euro crowd and ladies who lunch. Walk further east to find young families filling the latest, casual *sushi-ya* or artisanal pizzeria. Along First and Second avenues, pubs are packed with raucous post-grads keeping the party alive.

The most upper and eastern reaches were originally developed by famed families of German descent who built country estates in what has now become Yorkville. **Schaller & Weber** is one of the few remaining butchers carrying traditional Austro-German products including fantastic wursts for winter steaming or summer grilling, and the pungent mustards to match them. The Upper East Side has a greater concentration of gourmet markets than any other neighborhood in the city, most with a European feel. Each shop may be more packed than the next, yet has made processing long lines an art of inspired efficiency. **Agata & Valentina** specializes in everything Italian with a vast regional cheese selection. **Citarella** pumps its mouthwatering aroma of rotisserie chickens out the storefront to entice passersby, but the seafood selection is where they find nirvana. **Grace's Marketplace** is also a longtime favorite, loved for its cramped corners and cascading displays. Insiders frequent their trattoria replete with quality ingredients carried in the store. However, the true champion of everything uptown and gourmet, is Eli Zabar and his ever-expanding empire. **E.A.T.** has been a Madison Avenue darling since 1973, selling baked goods and takeout foods alongside its casual café. Later branches include his **Vinegar Factory** and mega-mart **Eli's**. However, there are plenty of smaller purveyors to patronize. **Lobel's** and **Ottomanelli** are among the cities best remaining butcher shops, both offering the best meats and pragmatic cooking advice. **William Greenberg** bakes NY's favorite cookie, the black-and-white, along with to-die-for *babka*. Paris' venerable **Ladurée** makes the Upper East Side even sweeter with its rainbow of pastel macarons, which also make lovely hostess gifts, while **Glaser's Bake Shop** looks and tastes of everything Old World. And on the high end, **Lady M**'s boutique and couture cakes blend right in with this chic locale. For any foodie, Kitchen Arts & Letters has the largest stock of food and wine publications in the country; and owner Nach Waxman is as good a source of industry insight as any book or blog.

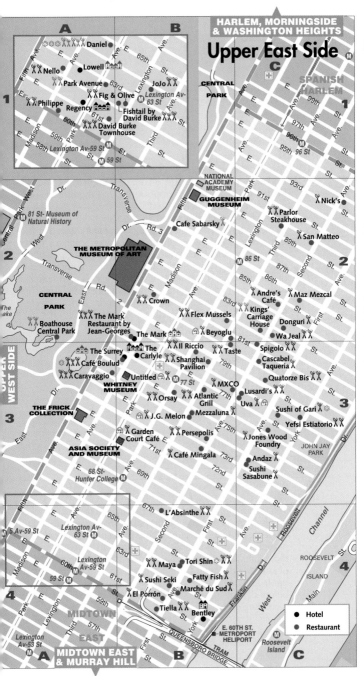

Upper East Side

A   B   C

Daniel

Nello
Lowell

Park Avenue
Philippe
Fig & Olive
JoJo
Lexington Av-
63 St
Regency
Fishtail by
David Burke
David Burke
Townhouse
Lexington Av-59 St
59 St

CENTRAL
PARK

SPANISH
HARLEM

E. 99th
97th
96 St
95th 96 St
93rd

NATIONAL
ACADEMY
MUSEUM
GUGGENHEIM
MUSEUM

81 St-Museum of
Natural History

Cafe Sabarsky

Nick's
Parlor
Steakhouse
San Matteo

THE METROPOLITAN
MUSEUM OF ART

86 St
85th
87th
83rd

CENTRAL
PARK

Crown

Flex Mussels
Kings'
Carriage
House

Andre's
Café
Maz Mezcal

Donguri
Wa Jeal

Boathouse
Central Park

The Mark
Restaurant by
Jean-Georges

The Mark

Beyoglu

Il Riccio
Taste

81st

Spigolo

The Surrey
Café Boulud
Caravaggio

The
Carlyle

Shanghai
Pavilion

Untitled
77 St

Cascabel
Taqueria
Quatorze Bis

WHITNEY
MUSEUM

MXCO

Lusardi's
Uva

Sushi of Gari

THE FRICK
COLLECTION

Orsay
Atlantic
Grill
Mezzaluna

77th
75th

Yefsi Estiatorio

J.G. Melon

Garden
Court Café

Persepolis

Jones Wood
Foundry

JOHN JAY
PARK

ASIA SOCIETY
AND MUSEUM

Café Mingala
73rd

Andaz
Sushi
Sasabune

68 St-
Hunter College

69th
72nd

L'Absinthe

67th

Roosevelt
Channel

5 Av-59 St
Lexington Av-
63 St

63rd

Maya
Tori Shin

Sushi Seki
Fatty Fish
Marché du Sud

ROOSEVELT
ISLAND

Lexington
Av-59 St
59 St

60th
61st

El Porrón

Tiella
Bentley

QUEENSBORO
BRIDGE

TRAM

E. 60TH ST.
METROPORT
HELIPORT

Roosevelt
Island

Lexington
Av-53 St

MIDTOWN
EAST

MIDTOWN EAST
& MURRAY HILL

- ● Hotel
- ● Restaurant

Andaz

C3

1378 First Ave. (bet. 73rd & 74th Sts.)

Subway: 77 St
Phone: 212-288-0288
Web: www.andaz1378.com
Prices: $$

Lunch & dinner daily

For an admirable array of traditional regional favorites, Andaz is a prudent Indian recommendation. This Yorkville treat is understated in its appearance, but the room is well-maintained and politely staffed.

Northern specialties abound in the variety of preparations including a silky mélange of fragrant but mildly spiced house-made cheese and spinach in the *saag paneer*. Southern India is well-represented with classics like a Kerala fish curry wherein pieces of flaky white tilapia are bathed in a complex sauce of tamarind water, cumin seeds, curry leaves, and enriched with coconut powder. Jumbo prawns, minced lamb rolls, and other treasures emerge from the tandoor; and a selection from the full roster of puffy breads is strongly advised.

Andre's Café

C2

1631 Second Ave. (bet. 84th & 85th Sts.)

Subway: 86 St (Lexington Ave.)
Phone: 212-327-1105
Web: www.andrescafeny.com
Prices: 🍴🍴

Lunch & dinner daily

This charming café details deliciously old-fashioned baked goods from a bakery of the same name established in Queen's in 1976. Tiny, tidy, and welcoming, the exterior proudly boasts this establishment's Hungarian heritage with a red, white, and green awning. A temptingly arranged display of sweet and savory strudels, tortes, and cakes greet guests upon entering. Table service is available in the rear, and before delving into dessert, there is a full menu of hearty old-world fare offered daily.

Weekday meal specials come complete with a salad or soup and choice of three desserts, and can include home spun traditional favorites like chicken *paprikash*, swathed in a luscious paprika cream sauce and accompanied by freshly made *nokedli*.

Atlantic Grill

Seafood 🍴🍴

B3

1341 Third Ave. (bet. 76th & 77th Sts.)

Subway: 77 St
Phone: 212-988-9200
Web: www.atlanticgrill.com
Prices: $$

Lunch & dinner daily

Swimmingly similar to its growing family including the Blue Water Grill, this handsome respite hooks a very NY clientele with a vast, Asian-accented menu focused on the sea. True to its name, Atlantic Grill's menu highlights seafood options like sushi, caviar, and raw bar offerings. Entrées can be a simple grilled salmon or a more involved affair like Mediterranean bronzini with artichokes *barigoule*, saffron potato, and Italian salsa verde.

The alluring space is frequented by a fun-loving crowd occupying two rooms—one features a nautical blue-and-white theme; and the other is sunny with a terrazzo floor and wicker chairs. Fair weather sidewalk seating is in high demand as is weekend brunch, and an efficient staff holds court at this corporate gem.

Beyoglu

Turkish 🍴

B2

1431 Third Ave. (at 81st St.)

Subway: 77 St
Phone: 212-650-0850
Web: N/A
Prices: $$

Lunch & dinner daily

Sharing may not come naturally to everyone, but when dining at Beyoglu, arrive with a crowd and prepare to pass your plates to fully experience the delicious range of Mediterranean meze that earns its praise. Most of the recipes—and some wine and beer offerings—come from Turkey, though Greek and Lebanese accents can be found throughout. Warm and tender pita bread makes a delightful accompaniment to anything on the menu. Thick homemade yogurt with spinach and garlic; grilled shrimp; and marinated octopus are a short sampling of the wide selection.

If grazing doesn't satisfy, choose from a list of larger daily specials, perhaps including *tavuk izgara*, char-grilled breast of free-range chicken, and *kilic sis*, swordfish kebabs served with rice pilaf.

361

Boathouse Central Park

American 🍴🍴

A2

The Lake at Central Park (E. 72nd St. & Park Dr. North)

Subway: 68 St - Hunter College
Phone: 212-517-2233
Web: www.thecentralparkboathouse.com
Prices: $$

Lunch & dinner daily

This unique locale offers Manhattan's only lakeside dining experience. Built in 1954, Loeb Boathouse is a pleasant multi-venue operation that includes a charming outdoor bar perched along the water and a lovely glass-walled dining room offering views of the lake, greenery, and skyline beyond—there isn't a bad seat in the house.

Highlighting American ingredients and sensibilities, the menu features an updated approach in items like steak tartare dressed with a Parmesan tuile; Muscovy duck breast with leg confit, wild rice-apple pancake, and Calvados sauce; or roasted Scottish salmon with root vegetables and pinot noir sauce.

While lunch and brunch are served year-round, note that dinner is only offered during warmer months (April through November).

Café Mingala

Burmese 🍴

B3

1393B Second Ave. (bet. 72nd & 73rd Sts.)

Subway: 68 St - Hunter College
Phone: 212-744-8008
Web: N/A
Prices: 😊😊

Lunch & dinner daily

Don't let the well-worn exterior or nearby construction craze deter you from visiting the only Burmese spot in all five boroughs. Know that Café Mingala is well worth the stop. Inside, colorful murals depicting the country's landscape deck the walls, while floral turquoise booths line one side of the narrow space, and wooden tables the other.

The traditional Burmese dishes really soar; *mohinga* is especially spot-on: rice noodles in a thick broth of puréed fish, lemongrass, and legumes, served with garnishes of deep-fried shallots, crispy yellow lentils, cilantro, and lemon. One must definitely try the *keema*—a dense "thousand layer" pancake topped with a rich ground beef-and-potato curry. Lunch specials are a great money saver.

Café Boulud

French 🍴🍴🍴

B3

20 E. 76th St. (bet. Fifth & Madison Aves.)

Subway: 77 St

Phone: 212-772-2600

Web: www.danielnyc.com

Prices: $$$$

Lunch & dinner daily

Bill Milne

Just as one might expect from the address, Café Boulud is a smart, discreet, and *très* Upper East locale, just steps from Central Park. The space itself is stylish rather than stodgy, and evokes a vintage 20s-era look through low ceilings, eye-catching art, and colorful bud vases. Tables are small and close but exude the same height of quality that has made this eponymous chef the toast of the town.

There is a pleasant, chatty hum from lunching ladies, businessmen, and even the occasional family. Greetings are warm and the service is formal, though a meal's pacing can at times be a bit off.

The menu is divided into four categories: Farmers Market, French Classic, Seasonal, and World. Meals here might begin with a simple canapé of golden-fried risotto balls with black truffles and cheese, or a starter of sliced and delicately flavored raw scallop in miso marinade with scallion vinaigrette. Entrées have revealed a plump, moist, and crisp-skinned chicken breast paired with wintery roasted Brussels sprouts, silky parsnip purée, light gnocchi, and an excellent sticky-sweet maple jus. To finish, find a puff pastry vol-au-vent topped with caramelized apple, caramel tuile, and Bourbon ice cream.

Cafe Sabarsky

Austrian ✗

B2

1048 Fifth Ave. (at 86th St.)

Subway: 86 St (Lexington Ave.)
Phone: 212-288-0665
Web: www.kg-ny.com
Prices: $$

Lunch Wed – Mon
Dinner Thu – Sun

In addition to the renowned art displayed at the intimately scaled Neue Galerie, find Chef Kurt Gutenbrunner's charming café modeled after a late 19th century Viennese *kaffehause*, complete with dark wood-paneled walls and formally attired servers. The museum, housed in a 1914 Beaux-Arts mansion, was conceived by cosmetic mogul Ronald Lauder and art dealer Serge Sabarsky to display their collections of early 20th century Austrian and German art.

The traditional menu features savory fare like sautéed bratwurst over riesling sauerkraut, along with an indulgent listing of classic sweets like apple strudel. Beverages include a very nice selection of German and Austrian wines by the glass, tremendous coffee offerings, and divine hot chocolate.

Caravaggio

Italian ✗✗✗

A3

23 E. 74th St. (bet. Fifth & Madison Aves.)

Subway: 77 St
Phone: 212-288-1004
Web: www.caravaggioristorante.com
Prices: $$$

Lunch & dinner daily

Dressy and expensive, this ambitious Italian is fittingly nestled among Madison Avenue galleries and boutiques. Caravaggio's slender dining room, decorated with silk-covered walls, sleek leather seating, and evocative, original artwork exudes a coolness that can mirror the disposition of the formal waitstaff.

The menu is enhanced by a lengthy list of daily specials that is verbally recited in minute detail. Be sure to pay attention and indulge, but the printed menu offers gems as well, like *cavatelli* with clams and unctuous, rich sea urchin. *Vitello tonnato* is a classic unto itself, braised until fork-tender, sliced paper-thin, then sauced with that wondrous combination of egg yolk, Dijon, olive oil, tuna, lemon, capers, and chives.

Cascabel Taqueria

Mexican ✗

C3

1538 Second Ave. (at 80th St.)

Subway: 77 St
Phone: 212-717-8226
Web: www.nyctacos.com
Prices:

Lunch & dinner daily

From its new, bigger home, this tasty spot still serves up quite a nice taco. The menu is concise and in keeping with the focused taqueria theme, with selections that include double layered corn tortillas filled with house-made chorizo and smoked paprika onions; roasted wild shrimp with fresh oregano, garlic, and chili oil; or chipotle-braised Amish chicken topped with chicken *chicaharrón*. Interesting (and deliciously healthful) sides include a bowl of fluffy organic quinoa topped with Cotija cheese and cilantro.

The space is a daylight-filled room complete with TV-equipped bar and dining room in zesty shades of lime green and lemon yellow, and tables topped with caddies of salsas. Upper West Siders check out the new Broadway location.

Crown

Contemporary ✗✗

B2

24 E. 81st St. (bet. Fifth & Madison Aves.)

Subway: 77 St
Phone: 646-559-4880
Web: www.crown81.com
Prices: $$$

Lunch Tue– Fri
Dinner nightly

Restaurateur John DeLucie brings his downtown brand (as in The Lion) uptown at Crown located in a 1930s mansion between Madison and Fifth. Elegant beige and brown don the multi-room setting bedecked with a zinc bar and window-walled rear dining room offering spectacular views of the block's privileged backyards. A secret room fronted by a swinging bookshelf offers very private dining.

The menu displays verve in its offering of fresh handkerchief pasta draped with decadent white Bolognese sauce; and fantastic specimens of Maine diver scallops, seared golden brown, and sided by plump escargots. Even if this crowd shuns dessert that doesn't mean you should, with treats like espresso-infused panna cotta with *fior di latte* ice cream and crushed cacao nibs.

Daniel ✿ ✿ ✿

A1

60 E. 65th St. (bet. Madison & Park Aves.)

Subway: 68 St - Hunter College
Phone: 212-288-0033
Web: www.danielnyc.com
Prices: $$$$

Dinner Mon – Sat

Bill Milne

Daniel remains the type of restaurant where one can never be overdressed. However, its ambience has a calm elegance and less aggressive exclusivity than one might expect. The room shines with art deco style and is a brilliant reflection of its clientele, who still fill the air with power and pomp, though Daniel's gleaming precision has been softened to a warm glow among servers—very good, gracious, and personable.

There are no missteps on the menu: world-renowned Chef Daniel Boulud has polished each plate to perfection, from the genius with which it was conceived to the masterful French technique it brings to life. A starter of Nantucket Bay scallops tastes as if the sea itself is blooming within pools of blood orange juice, olive oil, sea urchin, bits of celery, and a few floral leaves. The signature duo of *poularde demi-deuil* begins as a classic of poached breast and crisp, truffle-stuffed leg with roasted chestnut and black truffle purées, but becomes contemporary alongside lightly pickled savoy cabbage.

The simply named chocolate-coconut "biscuit" belies its complexity and fantastic contrast. The single gold leaf resting on top is a luxurious reminder of where you are dining.

David Burke Townhouse

Contemporary XXX

A1

133 E. 61st St. (bet. Lexington & Park Aves.)

Subway: Lexington Av - 59 St   Lunch & dinner daily
Phone: 212-813-2121
Web: www.davidburketownhouse.com
Prices: $$$

 David Burke's refreshed Upper East Side restaurant, housed in a quaint, red-bricked building with a white-furnished lounge features an elegantly appointed space dressed with handsome red banquettes amidst tall white walls adorned with Roman shaded mirrors and bright artwork.

An immaculately attired service staff might kick things off with a warm Gruyère and poppy seed popover, and then move on to Burke's signature brand of bold, contemporary cuisine (now executed by Picholine alum, Executive Chef Carmine DiGiovanni) that may reveal crisp and angry lobster; and Hudson Valley rabbit degustation with date-mustard spread and spring onions. The reasonably priced lunch prix-fixe offers all this elegance at a pretty price.

Donguri

Japanese X

C2

309 E. 83rd St. (bet. First & Second Aves.)

Subway: 86 St (Lexington Ave.)   Dinner Tue – Sun
Phone: 212-737-5656
Web: www.dongurinyc.com
Prices: $$$

The ongoing construction of the Second Avenue subway may have obscured Donguri's already unassuming location, but this intimate Japanese hideaway still draws a devout following. Its steady clientele of high-powered international bankers, neighborhood couples, and Japanese ex-pats longing for a taste of home speaks to its sophistication and authenticity.

Owned by Ito En (known for green tea products), Donguri specializes in the Kansai regional specialties of Osaka and Kyoto. Savory starters like fried sesame tofu or *tako tataki-kyuri* (octopus and cucumber in spicy sauce) lead to heartier plates such as roasted duck breast with *yuzu-kosho* pepper paste. Soba and udon noodles round out the offerings, with sashimi offered as an appetizer or entrée.

El Porrón

B4

1123 First Ave. (bet. 61st & 62nd Sts.)

Subway: Lexington Av - 59 St   Lunch & dinner daily
Phone: 212-207-8349
Web: www.elporronnyc.com
Prices: $$

The tapas movement shows no signs of ceasing anytime soon, but this welcome neighborhood addition more than does the craze justice with its energetic ambience featuring upbeat Spanish tunes; a lively crowd chugging down delicious sangria come nighttime; and finger-licking authentic Spanish cuisine.

The items churned out from the kitchen are as playful as the room itself, and gracefully dance between traditional entrées and scrumptious paellas worth the 40-minute wait. Sample the tapas *frias*, perhaps a traditional salad of roasted eggplant, red peppers, sweet onion, and salted cod; or tapas *calientas*, like quail in fig-raisin sauce with house-made potato chips. For larger appetites, try entrées like veal with wild mushrooms and Oloroso sherry reduction.

Fatty Fish

B4

406 E. 64th St. (bet. First & York Aves.)

Subway: Lexington Av - 63 St   Lunch & dinner daily
Phone: 212-813-9338
Web: www.fattyfishnyc.com
Prices: $$

Tucked away near the edge of the Upper East Side, Fatty Fish is a beacon for home-style fare that successfully melds traditional western cooking methods with eastern ingredients for an eccentric array of preparations that are not easily typified. One will find sushi, pork *gyoza*, fish and chips with ponzu aïoli, and seared salmon with coconut rice and carrot-ginger sauce among the offerings.

Come lunchtime the restaurant presents a gently priced list that may offer thick and hearty green split-pea soup with buttery croutons; tasty *yakisoba* studded with slices of Kurobuta pork sausage; and house-made almond cookies.

The graciously attended setting is low-key, save the bold orange accent wall that matches the attention-grabbing awning out front.

Fig & Olive

B1

Mediterranean ✗✗

808 Lexington Ave. (bet. 62nd & 63rd Sts.)

Subway: Lexington Av - 63 St
Phone: 212-207-4555
Web: www.figandolive.com
Prices: $$$

Lunch & dinner daily

The bounty of the Mediterranean's olive groves is not only featured on the menu of this casually elegant Upper East spot (with midtown and Meatpacking locations), but is also available for purchase in gift-worthy packaging. Each dish–from salad Niçoise to grilled branzino–is accented with a specific extra virgin oil, carefully selected to highlight their extensive stock. Dinners begin with an olive oil trio to sample (though your server will choose which ones you try).

Inside the bright, sunny space, shoppers find a soothing respite in light Mediterranean plates of ceviche, a sampling of crostini, or pastas and grilled fare. The wine list echoes the same regions of origin as the fragrant oils, with many selections available by the glass.

Fishtail by David Burke

B1

Seafood ✗✗✗

135 E. 62nd St. (bet. Lexington & Park Aves.)

Subway: Lexington Av - 63 St
Phone: 212-754-1300
Web: www.fishtaildb.com
Prices: $$$

Lunch & dinner daily

This fitting addition to Chef David Burke's oeuvre features an elegant setting through two levels of a cozy townhouse, lending a ritzy, residential feel. The first floor is an oyster bar and lounge popular with the after-work crowds, while the upstairs is a deep red dining room with accents that colorfully convey the ocean theme.

The menu focuses on fish and much is caught by the company-owned boat. Dishes are stamped with the chef's unique touch, whether as salt-baked American red snapper with smoked tomato sauce, shellfish towers, or more creative interpretations like pretzel-crusted crab cakes with lemon-poppyseed mayonnaise. Weekdays bring a three-course prix-fixe lunch. Regardless of your selection, these dishes show the hand of a skilled kitchen.

Flex Mussels

B2

174 E. 82nd St. (bet. Lexington & Third Aves.)

Subway: 86 St (Lexington Ave.)
Phone: 212-717-7772
Web: www.flexmusselsny.com
Prices: $$

Dinner nightly

Despite its strong name, Flex Mussels is actually a fun, casual, and intimate seafood shack with uptown polish. Usually packed to the gills, the slim bar area features pretty touches like flowers, slender mirrors, and a dining counter. The back dining room is spare, contemporary, more subdued, and fills up quickly.

The menu features the namesake bi-valve, hailing from Prince Edward Island, priced by the pound, steamed in more than twenty globally-inspired guises, like the "PEI" featuring lobster stock and drawn butter; or "San Daniele" with prosciutto, caramelized onions, white wine, and garlic. No matter the choice, your best accompaniment is a side of piping-hot, hand-cut skinny fries.

Flex now has a downtown sibling in the West Village.

Garden Court Café 😊

B3

725 Park Ave. (at 70th St.)

Subway: 68 St - Hunter College
Phone: 212-570-5202
Web: www.asiasociety.org
Prices: $$

Lunch Tue – Sun

Tucked into the glass-enclosed, plant-filled lobby of the Asia Society, this café is a far cry from your garden-variety museum restaurant. Though it doesn't generate much fanfare, it is worth seeking out, not only for its quiet ambience, but for the light Asian dishes that expertly fuse East and West.

Serving lunch only, from Tuesday through Sunday, the menu draws Asian inspiration in its offerings that may include herb-crusted salmon with lemongrass, Thai basil, and mint. The bento box features two chef selections along with rice and salad.

Everything here is done with quality, right down to the careful presentation and very good service—and the museum's entry fee is not required. Don't miss the museum gift shop for its wonderful wares.

Il Riccio

Italian

B3

152 E. 79th St. (bet. Lexington & Third Aves.)

Subway: 77 St   Lunch & dinner daily
Phone: 212-639-9111
Web: www.ilriccioblu.com
Prices: $$

This low-key Italian, and its smiling cadre of charming staff, is just the right spot to recharge after an afternoon perusing the fabulous neighborhood boutiques or meandering through the nearby Metropolitan Museum of Art. Inside, the space offers a cozy feel with warm ochre walls, simple furnishings, and an assemblage of photographs, though regulars know to head back to the enclosed garden to enjoy their meals.

The cooking here is fuss-free, pasta-focused, and lovingly dedicated to the Amalfi Coast. Dishes may include arugula and roasted red pepper salad with salty marinated anchovies; spaghetti with crab meat and fresh tomatoes; grilled fish dressed simply with olive oil and lemon; and a straightforward selection of dessert pastries.

J.G. Melon

American

B3

1291 Third Ave. (at 74th St.)

Subway: 77 St   Lunch & dinner daily
Phone: 212-744-0585
Web: N/A
Prices: ⬤⬤

J.G. Melon is the kind of place that parents tell their children they used to frequent when they were young in the city; nothing changes here, and that is part of the allure. It's a multi-generational watering hole for the masses, feeding Upper East Siders burgers and beers in a convivial setting that never seems to forget itself. The key here is the burger: griddled and served on a toasted bun, it's one of the best in the city. Couple this with a bowl of the crispy round fries and a cool draft and you have the answer to why this spot has been packed for years. BLTs, salads, steaks, and omelets round out the menu. Tables may be tight and the waits can be long, but the service is jovial and it's come-as-you-are and…did we mention the burger?

JoJo

B1

160 E. 64th St. (bet. Lexington & Third Aves.)

Subway: Lexington Av - 63 St   Lunch & dinner daily
Phone: 212-223-5656
Web: www.jean-georges.com
Prices: $$$

If only everybody could have a neighborhood home like this. Lodged in a lovely townhouse in an affluent area of town, JoJo sees a routine following of ritzy revelers. Two velvet-covered stools sit by the terra-cotta-covered entrance beside an antique desk where the host holds court, and fitted below the front window is a bar mixing an array of potions. Every well-heeled tourist rubbing elbows with the local crowd agrees: tiny JoJo oozes charm, snugly packed tables and all.

Keeping company with such pretty patrons is a menu of contemporary creations including roasted butternut squash purée gilded with chives; slow-baked salmon poised atop sweet corn pudding and crested with pickled onions; and a spiced pear tart drizzled with a hot milk chocolate sauce.

Jones Wood Foundry

C3

401 E. 76th St. (bet. First & York Aves.)

Subway: 77 St   Lunch Sat – Sun
Phone: 212-249-2771   Dinner nightly
Web: www.joneswoodfoundry.com
Prices: $$

The moniker of this pleasing Yorkville pub refers to when the neighborhood was merely a stretch of heavily forested land. Although that bucolic ideal has been replaced by tower-lined corridors, the eatery offers a taste of the Old World tucked away from the fray. A narrow wood bar area welcomes guests, while a pretty courtyard dining room and larger rear space offer plenty of breathing room.

Chef/partner Jason Hicks garners inspiration from his childhood in England to beget a spot-on lineup of enjoyable pub grub. A "toast" list includes a soft boiled farm egg and soldiers; steak and kidney pie is presented as golden brown pastry stuffed with a stew of chopped beef and vegetables; and a delightfully boozy sherry trifle caps off any meal here.

Kings' Carriage House

C2

Contemporary ✗✗

251 E. 82nd St. (bet. Second & Third Aves.)

Subway: 86 St (Lexington Ave.)
Phone: 212-734-5490
Web: www.kingscarriagehouse.com
Prices: $$

Lunch & dinner daily

Picture the mist rolling in when dining at this bona fide facsimile of an Irish manor, warmly run by Elizabeth King and husband Paul Farrell (of Dublin). Since 1994, this elegantly countrified setting has been an old-world rarity, complete with creaky floors, murals, linen-draped tables with lacy overlays, antique china, and vintage silverware accenting the multiple dining rooms. A collection of china teapots is even available for purchase.

The nightly prix-fixe menu offers an updated take on classically prepared cuisine that complements the romantic ambience beautifully, as in the roasted filet mignon with a medallion of tarragon-Cognac sausage and port wine demi-glace. Afternoon tea is quite popular, so be sure to reserve in advance.

L'Absinthe

French ✗✗

B4

227 E. 67th St. (bet. Second & Third Aves.)

Subway: 68 St - Hunter College
Phone: 212-794-4950
Web: www.labsinthe.com
Prices: $$$

Lunch & dinner daily

A true charmer, L'Absinthe is a uniquely enjoyable classic neighborhood bistro that can claim few peers. The warm and amiable setting boasts an authentically continental elegance that is enhanced by an understated, sophisticated clientele.

The flawless menu offers a culling of preparations that are seasonal and contemporary in theme, but the real draw here are Chef Jean-Michel Bergougnoux's "brasserie classics" like the *choucroute royale Alsacienne*, presented as a heaping platter of expertly prepared pork: garlicky sausage, *boudin blanc*, belly, and ham. Also await caraway-spiced braised cabbage and boiled potatoes. Another classic, the *baba au rhum* is deliciously done—a boozy moist cake slathered with *crème pâtissière* and *brunoise* of tropical fruits.

Lusardi's

1494 Second Ave. (bet. 77th & 78th Sts.)

Subway:	77 St	Lunch Mon – Fri
Phone:	212-249-2020	Dinner nightly
Web:	www.lusardis.com	
Prices:	$$$	

A neighborhood mainstay since 1982, brothers Luigi and Mauro Lusardi continue to run an impressive operation. Tastefully appointed with pumpkin-colored walls and deep-toned woodwork, the dining room is warmly attended by a beaming staff that suits Lusardi's comfortable elegance and old-world vibe.

Fresh ingredients and careful preparation go into the Northern Italian fare such as *crespelle Fiorentina*, a cylinder of pan-fried eggplant filled with a fluffy blend of spinach and ricotta then bathed in bright and creamy tomato sauce. Many of the preparations feature an appetizingly rustic presentation as in the *fegato alla Veneziana*—chunks of chicken liver sautéed with sweet onions and white wine, then piled onto a nest of coarse ground polenta.

Marché du Sud

1136 First Ave. (bet. 62nd & 63rd Sts.)

Subway:	Lexington Av - 59 St	Lunch & dinner daily
Phone:	212-207-4900	
Web:	www.marchedusud.com	
Prices:	✆	

Who says you can't be all things to all people? Open all day, this bakery/gourmet grocery/wine bar/restaurant seems to be wearing many hats without a glitch. Walk by the interesting imported products—you can pick up a jar of mustard on your way out. Snag a menu, printed on the back of Paris Match and other French language magazines, and you'll soon see that *Alsatian tarte flambée* is de rigueur here. Go for tradition and you'll enjoy this thin, flaky crust topped with Gruyère, bacon, and onions; or go house-style with crème fraîche, duck confit, and black truffle-foie gras.

Chef/partner Adil Fawzi hails from Morocco, so the *Marocaine*, topped with hummus, harissa, merguez, cheese, and lemon confit is a sure bet. Don't worry *cherie*, there's dessert too.

The Mark Restaurant by Jean-Georges

Contemporary 𝕏𝕏𝕏

25 E. 77th St. (at Madison Ave.)

Subway: 77 St
Phone: 212-606-3030
Web: www.themarkrestaurantnyc.com
Prices: $$$

Lunch & dinner daily

Snuggled inside the posh kingdom of the Mark Hotel, The Mark Restaurant is the true hot spot for the ladies-who-lunch crowd. This bastion of Upper East Side exclusivity hits its own mark with an eye-catching, light-filled, contemporary décor. Ladies aren't the only ones dressed to the nines—even the staff is sharply attired in black and cream uniforms.

Executive Chef Pierre Schutz is at the helm and proudly presents a varied menu that ranges from raw bar offerings to the house cheeseburger gilded with black truffle dressing and Brie. The choices are surprisingly straightforward, with crowd-pleasers like a smoked salmon pizza on an "everything" crust, grilled lamb chops with barbecue sauce, or roasted lobster with Meyer lemon risotto and basil.

Maya

Mexican 𝕏𝕏

1191 First Ave. (bet. 64th & 65th Sts.)

Subway: 68 St - Hunter College
Phone: 212-585-1818
Web: www.richardsandoval.com
Prices: $$

Dinner nightly

Maya continues to impress as one of the city's finest examples of upscale Mexican cuisine. And if that isn't luring enough, it now offers increased potential for margarita-fueled revelry with its inviting Tequileria Maya, pouring more than 200 bottles. The room is nicely attended to and features dark furnishings contrasted with soft orange-splashed walls.

Here, Mexican flavors are captured with modern flair and combine seamlessly in delicious *especialidades* such as mahi mahi *"a la talla"*—a plump piece of adobo-marinated fish set atop slivered Napa cabbage and tomato, dressed with chipotle aïoli. *Cazuelas* like beef short ribs spread with tamarind *mole* are served with warm tortillas, and even sides excite as in the poblano chile-and-potato gratin.

Maz Mezcal

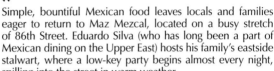

Mexican ✕

316 E. 86th St. (bet. First & Second Aves.)

Subway: 86 St (Lexington Ave.) Lunch Sat – Sun
Phone: 212-472-1599 Dinner nightly
Web: www.mazmezcal.com
Prices: **$$**

Simple, bountiful Mexican food leaves locals and families eager to return to Maz Mezcal, located on a busy stretch of 86th Street. Eduardo Silva (who has long been a part of Mexican dining on the Upper East) hosts his family's eastside stalwart, where a low-key party begins almost every night, spilling into the street in warm weather.

The flavorful fare includes an assortment of enchiladas, flautas, tostadas, and burritos to create your own Tex-Mex-style platter, or choose from the house combinations named for Mexican beach towns. Specialties may include traditional *mole* poblano made with seven distinct chile varieties and bittersweet chocolate.

Dishes are tailored to mild palates, but the kitchen is happy to accommodate those who prefer food *picante*.

Mezzaluna

Italian ✕

1295 Third Ave. (bet. 74th & 75th Sts.)

Subway: 77 St Lunch & dinner daily
Phone: 212-535-9600
Web: www.mezzalunanyc.com
Prices: **$$**

After more than 25 years in the business, this old Upper East Side cat could show the new crop of wood-burning ovens popping up across the city a thing or two. Mezzaluna (named for the crescent-shaped knife, which you'll find rendered 77 different ways on the restaurant's art-strewn walls) manages to feel both fresh and comforting to the throngs of loyal regulars who keep it packed day and night.

What's their secret? Simple, unfussy Italian food that's made with pristine ingredients and careful attention to detail—not to mention a wood-burning oven that pushes out perfectly bubbling pies; a thoughtful Italian wine list; and a warm, convivial staff bolstered by a friendly, hands-on owner who can often be found milling about his dining room.

MXCO

B3

M e x i c a n ✗

1491 Second Ave. (at 78th St.)

Subway: 77 St
Phone: 212-249-6080
Web: www.mxcony.com
Prices: 🍥🍥

Lunch Sat – Sun
Dinner nightly

Sure, those from the other coast lament the authenticity of New York's Mexican spots, but the situation is improving, thanks to the welcomed addition of this cantina. The family-friendly, casual, anytime vibe and budget-friendly pricing are all appreciated, but its biggest draw is a menu devised by consulting Chef Julieta Ballestros, from Crema in Chelsea.

The list of goodies offers a range of generously stuffed tacos, like Coca-Cola-braised *carnitas*, built upon excellent corn tortillas spread with black bean purée and accompanied by a shot of roasted tomato salsa. *Penca de nopal*, grilled prickly pear salad; and chorizo *sope*, griddled masa patties topped with fresh chorizo also populate a menu bolstered by quesadillas, burritos, and flautas.

Nello

A1

I t a l i a n ✗✗

696 Madison Ave. (bet. 62nd & 63rd Sts.)

Subway: 5 Av - 59 St
Phone: 212-980-9099
Web: N/A
Prices: $$$$

Lunch & dinner daily

Nello offers a chic and polished yet satisfying Italian dining experience, fashionably perched among pricy boutiques and astronomical real estate. The bright and airy room (resplendent with marble, ivory walls hung with black-and-white safari scenes, and thick linen-covered tables dressed with white flowers) is overseen by a well-orchestrated, suit-clad service team. Everything here radiates privilege and optimism. Even the menu's typeface appears elegant...and expensive.

While high prices and celebrity sightings do not ensure an enjoyable meal, the flavorful offerings like San Daniele prosciutto and melon; neat mounds of perfectly prepared pasta; and hearty entrées of osso buco should bring enough pleasure to help ease the potential sticker shock.

377

Nick's

Pizza ✗

C2

1814 Second Ave. (at 94th St.)

Subway: 96 St (Lexington Ave.)   Lunch & dinner daily
Phone: 212-987-5700
Web: www.nicksnyc.com
Prices: ☜☞

Due to a blockade of equipment needed for the ongoing construction of the Second Avenue subway line, Nick's may be a bit harder to spot but still ranks highly on Upper East Siders' short list of pizza favorites. This Manhattan location of the Forest Hills original, named for owner Nick Angelis, has cozy surroundings with tables overlooking the dough-tossing *pizzaiolos* and jovial service.

In addition to the excellent, bronzed, crackling thin-crust pizzas, a variety of Italian-American pastas (referred to as "macaroni") and entrées are available as full or half portions for family-friendly dining. Offerings may include veal scaloppini with lemon and butter or an enjoyable tangle of linguini with white clam sauce infused with roasted garlic cloves.

Orsay

French ✗✗

B3

1057 Lexington Ave. (at 75th St.)

Subway: 77 St   Lunch & dinner daily
Phone: 212-517-6400
Web: www.orsayrestaurant.com
Prices: $$

This Lexington Avenue corner is a classy scene through and through. The art nouveau look is so well done it may as well be an authentic tableau of hand-laid mosaic tiles, mahogany paneling, and a pewter-topped bar. When the weather warms, the chic crowd spills out onto the sidewalk, protected by a wide awning.

Chef Antoine Camin, formerly of La Goulue, has brought his celebrated cheese soufflé with him, as well as his deliciously signature touches brightened with au courant flourish. The ladies who lunch happily devour the likes of *Japonais* tartare—a cylinder of chopped tuna moistened by toasted sesame oil and flecked with tempura bits and wasabi cream. Classics like the golden brown, creamy, cheesy *croque monsieur* do this brasserie proud.

Park Avenue

Contemporary XX

A1

100 E. 63rd St. (at Park Ave.)

Subway: 59 St
Phone: 212-644-1900
Web: www.parkavenyc.com
Prices: $$$

Lunch & dinner daily

At Park Avenue, not only does the seasonally inspired menu change with the weather, so does the décor. Every three months the restaurant shutters for 48 hours and re-emerges as a celebration of spring, summer, fall, or winter; the look is produced by a series of panels that frame the room and create a fresh backdrop every season.

The kitchen's skills befit the stylish setting where an early autumn meal may bring forth salmon tartare studded with golden cherry tomatoes slow-cooked until sweet; expertly seared Montauk snapper showered with root vegetables and porcini mushroom broth; and a spiced pumpkin molasses cake gilded by sour cream panna cotta and *chai* ice cream.

The interesting array of stirring cocktails is in keeping with its seasonal concept.

Parlor Steakhouse

Steakhouse XX

C2

1600 Third Ave. (at 90th St.)

Subway: 86 St (Lexington Ave.)
Phone: 212-423-5888
Web: www.parlorsteakhouse.com
Prices: $$$

Lunch & dinner daily

This sexy, contemporary Upper East Side steakhouse, straddling a busy corner of Third Ave. and 90th St., has managed to remain under the radar. But what a shame, for this neighborhood find boasts clubby, welcoming good looks (think plush fabric and masculine dark stripes); first-class steaks cooked to juicy perfection; and a mean Belgian beer selection.

Kick your night off with one of the rotating daily specials, such as a starter of soft shell crabs, delicately fried and served with a punchy gherkin-spiked rémoulade; and then move on to the succulent bone-in ribeye, topped with roasted garlic cloves and served with a bevy of traditional sauces (béarnaise, horseradish, herb fresh lime, and red wine reduction) to choose from.

Persepolis

1407 Second Ave. (bet. 73rd & 74th Sts.)

Subway: 77 St
Phone: 212-535-1100
Web: www.persepolisnyc.com
Prices: $$

Lunch & dinner daily

Alluring cuisine served in a classic Upper East Side setting keeps this longtime neighborhood treasure on the short list of the city's finer Persian restaurants. An attractive room with red-toned wood furnishings, landscape paintings, and gracious service fashion a convivial scene in which to enjoy the range of fragrant specialties.

One bite of the house tabbouleh reveals the seriousness of the kitchen; it is neatly plated, sparked by a bright and tasty balance of lemon and garlic, and vibrant green from a profusion of fresh parsley. The array of grilled marinated meats is impressive as well, but the stews deserve particular attention, as in the *khorest gaimeh*—cubes of beef filet braised with split peas, pickled lime, tomato sauce, and hints of cinnamon.

Philippe

33 E. 60th St. (bet. Madison & Park Aves.)

Subway: Lexington Av - 59 St
Phone: 212-644-8885
Web: www.philippechow.com
Prices: $$$

Lunch Mon – Sat
Dinner nightly

This luxe Chinese is elegant but not too fancy to be delicious. Inside, the stage is set with linen-draped tables, chopsticks in wooden boxes, and celebrity sightings. The staff pairs white jackets and mandarin collar uniforms with red canvas sneakers—this whimsical departure from formality is juxtaposed by the monochromatic color scheme throughout the multi-room space.

The satisfying menu features masterfully prepared noodles and pick-your-protein lettuce wraps. Entrées, like nine seasons spicy prawns with sweet and sour sauce, are sized to share, but half-portions are offered. A supplemental listing of healthier steamed dishes includes chicken and broccoli with brown rice. Enthusiasts can visit Philippe in Miami, L.A., and even Mexico City.

Quatorze Bis

C3

French ✗✗

323 E. 79th St. (bet. First & Second Aves.)

Subway: 77 St
Phone: 212-535-1414
Web: N/A
Prices: $$

Lunch Tue – Sun
Dinner nightly

With its lipstick red façade and sunny yellow awning, Quatorze Bis easily stands out along this high-rise stretch of the Upper East. The pleasant interior, frequented by a mature, well-dressed crowd, displays a continental flair with framed vintage posters, mirrored panels painted with the wine list, and comfortable red velvet banquettes. The friendly waitstaff greets patrons with a small blackboard to present the day's specials.

The menu's roster of satisfying French classics is executed with savoir faire, as in the terrine *maison* and a savory tart of bacon, leek, and Gruyère. Grilled sirloin with light and crispy frites and decadent sauce béarnaise followed by the excellent hot apple tart is testament to the timelessness of true bistro cooking.

San Matteo

C2

Pizza ✗

1739 Second Ave. (at 90th St.)

Subway: 86 St (Lexington Ave.)
Phone: 212-426-6943
Web: www.sanmatteopanuozzo.com
Prices:

Lunch Fri – Sun
Dinner nightly

Upper East Siders have been counting their blessings since this convivial pizza newcomer moved into the neighborhood. The space is tiny and rustic, but also inviting and gracious.

More than 20 varieties of Neapolitan-style pizza temptingly emerge from the hand-built, wood-fired oven. Add to this a unique regional specialty hailing from Campania called *panuozzo*. Simply stated, it's a cross between a calzone and a panino, comprised of a puffy plank of freshly baked pizza dough stuffed with an array of fine quality ingredients such as roasted pork, mozzarella, and baby arugula for the *panuozzo di Bartolomei*. Co-owner Fabio Casella is an authority on Italian cheeses and, as one would hope, the excellent toppings here include house-made mozzarella.

Shanghai Pavilion

Chinese ✗✗

B3

1378 Third Ave. (bet. 78th & 79th Sts.)

Subway: 77 St
Phone: 212-585-3388
Web: N/A
Prices: 🍝

Lunch & dinner daily

Shanghai Pavilion may be considered upscale neighborhood Chinese, yet it rises above its many peers with attractive surroundings and service with a smile—these are your first hints that there is an underlying seriousness to the cooking here. The polished, unobtrusive staff does much to draw these well-heeled local residents, but the list of celebration-worthy, order-in-advance specialties earns their devotion.

Shanghainese and Cantonese regional favorites abound, as with the slurp-inducing steamed juicy dumplings. While enjoying these toothsome treats, the efficient servers stealthily restock your soup spoon with the next bun from the tabletop bamboo steamer. Other house specialties may include red-cooked chicken and braised beef with dried chilies.

Spigolo

Italian ✗✗

C3

1561 Second Ave. (at 81st St.)

Subway: 77 St
Phone: 212-744-1100
Web: www.spigolonyc.com
Prices: $$

Lunch Sat – Sun
Dinner nightly

Set on a generic corner of Second Avenue, Spigolo is more than a simple neighborhood gem. The façade is easily spotted by its wide-open windows, pretty planters, and red awning; likewise, the service is all ease and warmth. A tiny copper bar offers a cheerful perch to observe the scene—local denizens mingle at bare tables amid polished cork floors and food-themed art.

In the back, a glass-enclosed window lets you peek into the kitchen where the action is palpable. They are in the midst of creating the likes of chewy *bucatini* coated with a spicy squid ink marinara sauce stocked with slivers of cuttlefish. Dining alfresco is epic when paired with spinach agnolotti shimmering in a ricotta purée, trailed by a dense dark chocolate cheesecake.

Sushi of Gari ✿

Japanese ✗

402 E. 78th St. (bet. First & York Aves.)

Dinner nightly

Subway: 77 St
Phone: 212-517-5340
Web: www.sushiofgari.com
Prices: $$$

Sushi of Gari

Immaculate seafood handled with finesse should be the slogan here. Sushi of Gari is an East Side stalwart that not only boasts bites with distinct personality, but a rollicking setting attended by dead-serious chefs and polite Japanese servers. They may appear terse but are ever-obliging and assure an exceptional experience. The crowds can seem rambunctious at times, but maybe this is just everyone's glee at having scored a seat at Gari's counter.

The space itself is spare and minimalist, anchored by the sushi counter and its fleet of impeccably trained Japanese chefs. The extraordinary skill here is immediately clear from the first taste of rice: delicate, decadent, perfect. A neat cut of salmon topped with torched tomato and onion purée proves that *umami-rific* should be a real word.

While a wide variety of sushi à la carte will never disappoint, this is a place where the chef's unwritten omakase is worth the splurge—its end (signaled by waving off more food) may well induce tears. Relish the sweetness of a shrimp ceviche set atop diced red peppers, onions, and citrusy mango; shabu shabu snow crab; or scored red snapper with a lightly dressed *mizuna*-arugula salad and lotus root chip.

Sushi Sasabune

Japanese ✗

C3

401 E. 73rd St. (at First Ave.)

Subway: 77 St
Phone: 212-249-8583
Web: N/A
Prices: $$$

Lunch Tue – Fri
Dinner Tue – Sat

Ignore the unremarkable interior; this kitchen is worthy of high praise. Putting your faith in Chef/owner Kenji Takahashi and his team is inherent to a fine meal here, as patrons are regaled with blackboard signs that read, "Trust me." Indeed, this is a place where customers find mounted warnings of "No Spicy Tuna, No California Roll" as reminders that the sushi chefs are in charge. Trust *us* that it will be good.

There are no missteps once the omakase-only procession begins, preceded by the commands, "soy sauce" or "no soy sauce." Expect such gems as mackerel sashimi drizzled with ponzu sauce; nigiri of delicate amberjack on warm rice zinged by *yuzu kosho*; or a cooked trio of crisped fluke fin, butter fish, and sea eel brushed with *kabayaki* sauce.

Sushi Seki

Japanese ✗

B4

1143 First Ave. (bet. 62nd & 63rd Sts.)

Subway: Lexington Av - 59 St
Phone: 212-371-0238
Web: N/A
Prices: $$$

Dinner Mon – Sat

Beloved Sushi Seki fills up nightly with a devoted following that represents a cross section of city life: neighborhood families, business colleagues, novices looking to broaden their horizons, and even celebrity chefs enjoying a late night snack. Although the décor of this well-worn sushi den doesn't make much of an impression with its dark carpeting, simple furnishings, and unadorned walls, what goes on behind the counter is truly special.

The menu offers enjoyable appetizers and cooked fare, but sushi is where Seki shines. The original special recipe platter serves up a stellar nigiri array–rich salmon topped with warmed tomato; butter-sautéed scallop; tuna with tofu cream; and silky *amaebi*–as well as a crunchy, creamy, spicy shrimp tempura roll.

Taste

American

B3

1413 Third Ave. (at 80th St.)

Subway: 77 St
Phone: 212-717-9798
Web: www.elizabar.com
Prices: $$

Lunch & dinner daily

Located on what might be called "Eli's block," Taste is adjacent to Eli's Manhattan, the upscale food hall proffering a wide range of tempting products. This attractive dining room is appointed with a striking inlaid tile floor, tobacco brown walls, and mocha-hued furnishings. At night, tables dressed in orange Frette linens lighten the rich palette.

The impressive menu focuses on seasonality and simplicity in offerings like grilled Mediterranean sardine crostini with piquillo pepper hummus or North Carolina chicken with horseradish Yukon Golds and savoy cabbage. If offered, a slice of the famous lemon meringue cake is a must. For home indulgence, order a whole cake in advance.

Breakfast and lunch are self-service, with many items priced by the pound.

Tiella

Italian

B4

1109 First Ave. (bet. 60th & 61st Sts.)

Subway: Lexington Av - 59 St
Phone: 212-588-0100
Web: www.tiellanyc.com
Prices: $$

Lunch Mon – Sat
Dinner nightly

Although this forgotten stretch of First Ave, steps from the Roosevelt Island Tramway and Queensboro Bridge, is busy and unattractive, Tiella's Southern Italian specialties and classic hospitality are reason enough to seek it out. This neigborhood fave is housed in a room as slender as a train car, outfitted with espresso-tinted wood furnishings set against ivory walls and exposed brick.

Tiella draws its name from the petite pans used to produce wood-oven pizzas that are characterized by a uniquely delicate crust. Toppings are fresh and balanced, as in the *Caprese* with creamy mozzarella, sweet cherry tomatoes, and fragrant basil. An inventive pasta listing, several *secondi*, and starters such as a *bellisima* block of eggplant Parmigiana complete the menu.

Tori Shin ✿

Japanese 🍴🍴

1193 First Ave. (bet. 64th & 65th Sts.)

Subway: 68 St - Hunter College
Phone: 212-988-8408
Web: www.torishinny.com
Prices: $$

Lunch & dinner daily

Atsushi Kono

The smoky essence of imported *bincho-tan* (white charcoal) permeates everything at Tori Shin luring patrons inside with its aromas. The exterior is discreet; there's no need to blare, that's saved for the exuberant *Irasshaimase!* greeting guests receive upon entering this slice of Japan.

Salivating customers line the horseshoe-shaped counter surrounding the restaurant's core, downing waves of sake or draft beers while chefs patiently fan the flames under mouthwatering skewers, searing each delicacy over a menacing, slow-burning heat.

Some advice for first-timers; join the herd and go for the chef's omakase. Wary diners can opt out of the more interesting parts, but the experience won't be as authentic. Everything is organic here, and all parts of the chicken are handled with meticulous care and great skill. Skewers are sent out in a succulent succession that may include "oyster" with charred skin; juicy *tsukune* (chicken meatball); custard-soft livers; rib bone brushed with yakitori sauce; and for something a little different—fried thigh meat served with a divine, chunky tartar sauce made with diced egg, cornichon, and dill.

Simply put, Tori Shin is the best *yakitori-ya* in the country.

Untitled

American ✕

B3

945 Madison Ave. (at 75th St.)

Subway: 77 St
Phone: 212-570-3670
Web: www.untitledatthewhitney.com
Prices: $$

Lunch Wed – Sun
Dinner Fri – Sun

Operated by the Union Square Hospitality Group, this daytime dining showstopper is ensconced within the Whitney Museum of American Art. Untitled's bright setting is furnished with blond wood booths and a comfortable dining counter which faces a blackboard wall highlighting the comprehensive listing of locally sourced product.

An array of breakfast goodies are served all day, say huckleberry pancakes with homemade pork sausage; while more savory dishes can be had come lunchtime, as in a sandwich of pole caught tuna salad on rye. Dinner is served at week's end and features an à la carte listing that may include escarole with shaved fennel and blood orange vinaigrette; or pan seared red snapper fillet propped by creamy cauliflower and lemon parsley pesto.

Uva

Italian ✕

C3

1486 Second Ave. (bet. 77th & 78th Sts.)

Subway: 77 St
Phone: 212-472-4552
Web: www.uvawinebar.com
Prices: $$

Lunch Sat – Sun
Dinner nightly

A few steps away from Lusardi's is this charmingly laid-back and more boisterous member of the family, whose delectable menu is a siren song for focussed diners. The amber-hued neighborhood beacon is packed nightly and whimsically embellished with grape references.

In deftly combining fine ingredients, Uva's kitchen produces an extensive array of plates that shines a light on the Italian table. There's plenty to nibble on, say a host of dressed breads that include *carta de musica condita* (paper-thin Sardinian flatbread), or the likes of quivering *burrata* studded with marinated peppers, fava beans, and basil. Heartier still are the secondi, which may bring *vitello gratinato*—tender veal crowned by whipped eggplant and pecorino.

Wa Jeal

C2

1588 Second Ave. (bet. 82nd & 83rd Sts.)

Subway: 86 St (Lexington Ave.)   Lunch & dinner daily
Phone: 212-396-3339
Web: www.wajealrestaurant.com
Prices: 🍜

Specializing in the heated fare of the Sichuan province, Wa Jeal is spicing up the Upper East. The upscale room is comfortable with an uncharacteristically cozy atmosphere and gracious service.

The menu offers popular lunch specials and an array of regional favorites, but for a much more distinctive experience dive into the chef's menu, with its assortment of cold or hot appetizers and specialties that demonstrate the kitchen's complexity and strength. Dishes are both fresh and tantalizing, as in poached chicken dressed with soy, crushed dried red chili, and sesame oil boasting the unique, sensational tingle of Sichuan pepper; a mung bean jello salad that is at once cool and spicy; and lean strips of camphor tea-smoked duck boasting a salty-sweet allure.

Yefsi Estiatorio

C3

1481 York Ave. (bet. 78th & 79th Sts.)

Subway: 77 St   Dinner nightly
Phone: 212-535-0293
Web: www.yefsiestiatorio.com
Prices: $$

Squeeze in, grab a seat, and watch as plates fly out of the kitchen fast and furious to keep up with the demand of ravenous Yorkville residents who are counting their lucky stars for this new and tasty resident.

Chef Christos Christou hails from Cyprus, trained at the French Culinary Institute, and has headed stalwarts like Molyvos and Milos. His menu offers an array of meze like *feta sto fourno* of baked sheep's milk cheese set atop roasted eggplant; or *garides me fasolia* comprised of chopped jumbo shrimp tossed with gigante beans sauced with mastic-accented tomato purée. Expect such entrées as grilled fish or baby lamb chops with roasted lemon potatoes.

Plastered walls inlaid with gleaming wood beams and cherry wood tables furnish the cheery room.

Upper West Side

Manhattan ▶ Upper West Side

Proudly situated between two of Manhattan's most celebrated parks, home to venerable Lincoln Center, and the beloved Natural History Museum, the family-friendly Upper West Side is one of the city's most distinct neighborhoods. It has a near-cultish belief in its own way of doing things–whether it's because they boast some of the best cafés namely **Épicerie Boulud** that has it all from breakfast, sandwiches, soups, and salads, to coffee, pastries and *gelati*, or that life here means constantly tripping through the sets of *Law and Order*–these residents cannot imagine being elsewhere.

First and foremost, the Upper West is a neighborhood for strolling. Its sidewalks are lined with quaint brownstones, frequently featured in cherished flicks as well as in popular and primetime TV shows. Imagine rambling apartments filled with bookish locals arguing with equal gusto over the future of opera, or whether the best sturgeon is at **Murray's** or **Barney Greengrass**. If a scene from *Hannah and Her Sisters* comes to mind, you are beginning to understand this neighborhood. What is on offer at **Indie Food and Wine** are delightfully simple sandwiches that deliver ample pleasure to film- and theater-lovers alike. These are usually book-ended by lush chocolates from **Mondel** or baked madeleines at **La Toulousaine**.

Medley of Markets

This enthusiasm extends to all aspects of life—particularly food. For shopping, the **Tucker Square Greenmarket** is popular and anchored on West 66th Street (aka "Peter Jennings Way"). Equally celebrated is the original **Fairway**, filled with reasonably-priced gourmet treats. Intrepid shoppers should brave its famously cramped elevator to visit the exclusively organic second floor.

No visit to the Upper West Side is complete without **Zabar's**–home of all things gourmet and kosher–to ogle the barrels of olives and grab a few knishes. Another cyber haunt that cradles everything is the thekoshermarketplace. com. If planning an Italian themed evening, visit Cesare Casella's **Salumeria Rosi**. This local darling offers an excellent choice of cured meats as well as tasty bites. Finally, get your sweet and refreshment fix on at famous and much frequented **Soutine Bakery**. This quiet little storefront struts its stuff with jaw-dropping cakes, but for the legendary chocolate chip cookie, **Levain**'s is a must. Of course, one of **Magnolia**'s (many) outposts is sure to gain a quick cupcake following. Too much sugar? Grab a "Recession Special" savory snack at **Gray's Papaya**—the politically outspoken (check the window slogans) and quintessentially Upper West hot dog chain.

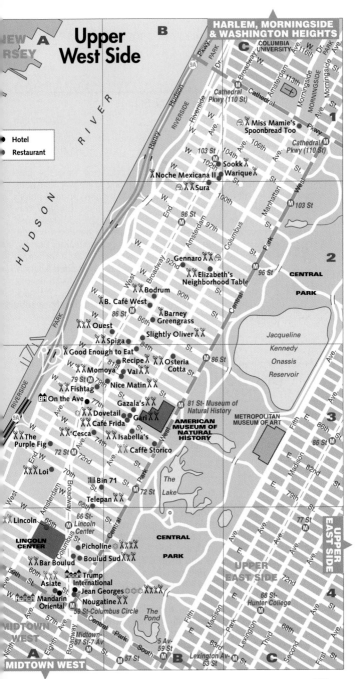

Upper West Side

NEW JERSEY

HUDSON RIVER

- ● Hotel
- ✗ Restaurant

COLUMBIA UNIVERSITY
Cathedral Pkwy (110 St)
Cathedral
113th
Morningside Ave.
Cathedral Pkwy (110 St)
Miss Mamie's Spoonbread Too
103 St
104th
Soookk
Warique
Noche Mexicana II
Sura
103 St
96 St
Gennaro
Elizabeth's Neighborhood Table
96 St
Bodrum
B. Café West
Barney Greengrass
Ouest
Slightly Oliver
Spiga
Good Enough to Eat
Recipe
Osteria Cotta
86 St
Momoya
Vai
Fishtag
Nice Matin
On the Ave
Gazala's
Dovetail
Gari
Café Frida
Cesca
Isabella's
The Purple Fig
Caffè Storico
Loi
Bin 71
Telepan
72 St
Lincoln
LINCOLN CENTER
Picholine
Boulud Sud
Bar Boulud
Trump International
Asiate
Jean Georges
Nougatine
Mandarin Oriental
59 St-Columbus Circle
Midtown-57 St-7 Av
5 Av-59 St
57 St
Lexington Av-63 St

CENTRAL PARK

81 St- Museum of Natural History
AMERICAN MUSEUM OF NATURAL HISTORY
Jacqueline Kennedy Onassis Reservoir
The Lake
METROPOLITAN MUSEUM OF ART
86 St
82nd
79th
77 St
68 St-Hunter College
The Pond
63rd

UPPER EAST SIDE

Asiate

F u s i o n 🍴🍴🍴

A4

80 Columbus Circle (at 60th St.)

Subway: 59 St - Columbus Circle   Lunch & dinner daily
Phone: 212-805-8811
Web: www.mandarinoriental.com
Prices: $$$$

There may be no finer Central Park view than the jaw-dropping vista through floor-to-ceiling windows at Asiate, an elegant fusion restaurant on the Mandarin Oriental hotel's 35th floor. Yet this natural beauty, set against the New York skyline, is in fact rivaled by Asiate's own splendor fashioned with walls of wine, stylized branches suspended from the ceiling, shimmering fabrics, and semi-private leather booths. Nonetheless, Asiate proves its own worth as a restaurant with a masterful waitstaff and impeccably trained kitchen. Mediterranean sensibilities are expressed with Asian flavors, as in the *étuvée* with bay scallops, langoustine, Littleneck clams, and hearts of palm with coconut-herb broth; or soba noodles with osetra caviar and wasabi cream.

Bar Boulud

F r e n c h 🍴🍴

A4

1900 Broadway (bet. 63rd & 64th Sts.)

Subway: 66 St - Lincoln Center   Lunch & dinner daily
Phone: 212-595-0303
Web: www.danielnyc.com
Prices: $$$

The birth of Bar Boulud ensured Chef/owner Daniel Boulud's compelling foothold in the Upper West of Manhattan. As its name attests, this "bar" pours sizeable and rare bottles in the airy, warm-toned dining lair. To further tease wine pundits, the room–narrow and deep with a rounded ceiling–mimics a barrel's interior, decked with abstract images of wine spills. Whether you nestle into a booth or bar stool, be sure to begin with an impeccable charcuterie plate. It may even wholly consume you, so save room for thrills like *lapin garigue*, tender rabbit layered with fragrant herbs and carrots. Entrées like sautéed Quinault sturgeon followed by *tanin*, an intense dark chocolate tart filled with cocoa mousse, will keep you lilting well into the night.

Barney Greengrass

 B2

541 Amsterdam Ave. (bet. 86th & 87th Sts.)

Subway: 86 St (Broadway)
Phone: 212-724-4707
Web: www.barneygreengrass.com
Prices: 💸

Lunch Tue – Sun

New York's venerable "Sturgeon King" has earned its title and position as an Upper West Side institution.

In addition to serving breakfast and lunch until 5:00 P.M., they do double duty as a vibrant carry-out business and now take Internet orders. The place is darling, whether eating in or taking out; the deli sandwiches–piled high with pastrami or homemade egg salad, and served with a big, bright, crunchy pickle–are among the best in the city.

Their food is the real thing so order a heaping plate of sturgeon, house-cured gravlax, or clear, flavorful bowl of matzoh ball soup at this Formica-clad jewel and take a trip back in time. Service without ceremony but unique NY attitude makes a trip to Barney Greengrass an authentic and essential experience.

B. Café West

 B2

566 Amsterdam Ave. (bet. 87th & 88th Sts.)

Subway: 86 St (Broadway)
Phone: 212-873-0003
Web: www.bcafe.com
Prices: $$

Lunch Sat – Sun
Dinner nightly

It used to be that finding a good spot along this Upper West stretch was like looking for a needle in a haystack. Well, needle found! B. Café West (the original "East" is on the Upper East Side) is now a go-to spot. This postage stamp of a restaurant stands out for its charming style, seemingly endless selection of Belgian-only beers, and delicious comfort food that is authentic and satisfying. The rustic, faux traditional style may feel a bit cliché, but no one seems to mind.

First, choose from their impressive beer list (you can't go wrong), then slurp some *moules* swimming in savory broth, and crunch those addictively crispy frites. From beef croquettes to smoked ham-wrapped endive with béchamel and Gruyère, this is Belgian comfort food to the hilt.

Bin 71

Italian

237 Columbus Ave. (bet. 70th & 71st Sts.)

Subway: 72 St
Phone: 212-362-5446
Web: www.bin71.com
Prices: $$

Lunch Tue – Sun
Dinner nightly

Is it a wine bar? Espresso bar? Italian *assaggini* (small plates) joint? It's all three, and more. The Upper West has a snazzy little number on its hands, where locals can nibble on the likes of Jonah crab *raviolo* before skipping over to Lincoln Center for a night of culture. Charm oozes at every corner, from the flower-topped marble bar, to the dark wood stools, to the French doors that open up onto sparkly Columbus Avenue.

The solid selection of wines would excite any oenophile—over thirty are offered by the glass, and double that by the bottle. Try gnocchi with beef and veal Bolognese studded with carrots, celery, cream, and smoky pancetta; or the heavenly pork, beef, and lamb meatballs stewing in a sumptuous sauce of white wine and lemon.

Bodrum

Turkish

584 Amsterdam Ave. (bet. 88th & 89th Sts.)

Subway: 86 St (Broadway)
Phone: 212-799-2806
Web: www.bodrumnyc.com
Prices: $$

Lunch & dinner daily

This Upper West Side Turkish restaurant is the very definition of a cozy and comfortable neighborhood spot. Regulars pack the place throughout the day for its inviting, Mediterranean feel; warm-weather sidewalk seating; and the delicious, well-priced fare.

Though not a traditional feature of Turkish cuisine, there's a wood-burning oven for thin, crafty pizzas, which are a popular choice among chatting locals. The bulk of the appealing menu features traditional Turkish specialties like crunchy and fresh shepherd salad with a smattering of sumac, and grilled chicken *Baharat*. Flavorful and healthy dishes keep the neighborhood coming back for more, as do the lunch and dinner specials that are as light on the wallet as they are on the waistline.

Boulud Sud

 Mediterranean

 A4

20 W. 64th St. (bet. Broadway & Central Park West)

Subway: 66 St - Lincoln Center

Lunch & dinner daily

Phone: 212-595-1313

Web: www.danielnyc.com

Prices: $$$

Courtesy of Chef Daniel Boulud, this local haven has been a hit since its inception. While the private area downstairs may seem a labyrinth of sorts, the dining room is still abuzz with suits and socialites. Vaulted ceilings, wood-paneling, and sun-splashed prints are a perfect preface to their unapologetically Mediterranean cooking.

Accurately reflective of the delicious areas of North Africa, Greece, and Italy, Boulud Sud's cuisine is warm and inviting. Chefs from the well-run, semi-open kitchen hover over a fresh version of *vitello tonnato* wrapped around cornichons, and chicken tagine sweetened with preserved lemon. Finish with such sweet treats as grapefruit *givré* topped with thin strands of halvah, and thank Chef Boulud for pushing the envelope.

Café Frida

 Mexican

 B3

368 Columbus Ave. (bet. 77th & 78th Sts.)

Subway: 81 St - Museum of Natural History

Lunch & dinner daily

Phone: 212-712-2929

Web: www.cafefrida.com

Prices: $$

Sporting bright fuchsia walls, pretty wrought-iron chandeliers, and cozy wooden tables, this pretty little hacienda manages to be festive, classy, and rustic all at the same time. Add in the fluffy handmade tortillas; fresh organic produce; and intricate Mexican specialties, and you'll think you've died and gone to Puebla.

The gorgeous spectrum of homemade margaritas and serious tequila list only lulls you deeper into the dream. Café Frida's menu, served up by a friendly and knowledgeable staff, might reveal a fragrant and comforting chicken soup bobbing with tender white hominy, potatoes, and tomatillo; or *enchiladas suiza*, stuffed with juicy shredded chicken and draped in a tart tomatillo purée and cool lick of *crema*.

Caffè Storico

Italian ✗✗

170 Central Park West (at 77th St.)

Subway: 81 St - Museum of Natural History
Phone: 212-485-9211
Web: www.caffestorico.com
Prices: $$

Lunch & dinner Tue – Sun

Philadelphia restaurateur Stephen Starr can sniff out an opportunity better than a hound chasing summer truffles. And voila: his Caffé Storico is born to the freshly revitalized New York Historical Society. Lovely and bright, the space is flooded with natural light bouncing from white walls to marble tables laid bare, as if to match that glorious, windowed sculpture arcade.

Brass chandeliers seem as if they are suspended in thin air, but all eyes remain firm on the open kitchen, preparing the likes of silky *baccalà mantecato* laced with caperberries. Wonderfully thick sourdough spread with some of the city's best liver pâté and trailed by *garganelli* enrobed in cauliflower purée and studded with *bottarga* showcase a successful marriage of ingredients.

'Cesca

Italian ✗✗

164 W. 75th St. (at Amsterdam Ave.)

Subway: 72 St
Phone: 212-787-6300
Web: www.cescanyc.com
Prices: $$

Dinner nightly

Tucked into 75th Street, just off Amsterdam Ave., the sexy 'Cesca keeps perfect company with a spate of new condos that were built into this Upper West Side nook over the last few years. The space is stylish and sprawling, with dark, low-ceilings, deep brown velvet banquettes, and iron chandeliers; while the waitstaff is attentive, professional, and eager to please. Everyone is in good spirits at 'Cesca, it would seem.

But how's the food, you wonder? Not wildly innovative, but very fresh and very well-made. Witness a luscious *minestra* studded with cubes of sweet, aromatic *cotecchino*, chard, chickpeas, tomato, and herbs; chewy orecchiette humming with homemade lamb sausage, pecorino, and rainbow Swiss chard; and tender, slow-roasted Long Island duck.

Dovetail ❀

B3

103 W. 77th St. (at Columbus Ave.)

Subway: 81 St – Museum of Natural History
Phone: 212-362-3800
Web: www.dovetailnyc.com
Prices: $$$

Lunch Sun
Dinner nightly

© Nathan Rawlinson

A muted façade and iron-framed door lead to the easygoing sophisticate, Dovetail. Welcoming you inside is an entire wall dedicated to wine and the mouthwatering aroma of freshly baked cheddar-corn bread.

The decor is delightfully spartan as quiet colors dominate the scene and maple veneer panels decorate the walls. Nothing distracts from the star of the show—an upscale, soft leather-bound, seasonally focused American menu. Service is easygoing and embodies an effortless hospitality, ensuring that every guest feels well looked after.

Vegetables are the kitchen's forte and Chef John Fraser's flair shines through a Brussels sprout salad with salty Mangalista ham, rich Manchego, and sweet yali pears in a delicate cauliflower purée. Two elongated batons of rabbit and foie gras terrine *en croute* are presented with a purée of romaine, mushrooms, truffles, topped with diced quince and just a hint of the sweetness of dried prunes. Three swordfish lobes set upon a marvelous chowder of clams and smoky-hot chorizo underline terrific composition. Desserts might present a terrine of soft crêpes with apple butter accompanied by candied walnuts, persimmon, thyme, and Bourbon-brown butter ice cream.

Elizabeth's Neighborhood Table

American ✗✗

B2

680 Columbus Ave. (at 93rd St.)

Subway: 96 St (Broadway)   Lunch & dinner daily
Phone: 212-280-6500
Web: www.elizabethsnyc.com
Prices: $$

Sadly, the northernmost reaches of the Upper West Side lack a definitive character. Call it dreary or ho-hum, but it's typically not a nabe that is worthy of sticking around too long. That is until the arrival of Elizabeth's Neighborhood Table. Whitewashing with a picket fence-feel, Elizabeth's looks like it would be more at home on beautiful Cape Cod.

Inside, butcher-block tables, aquamarine walls, and vivid artwork lend a classic New England vibe. The menu is as all-American as apple pie. The kitchen has a solid farm-to-table focus tinged with nostalgia—think of mac and cheese with manchego and white cheddar; steamed mussels with whole grain mustard aïoli and white wine; or plump, perfectly sweet pork chops with garlic mashers and braised red cabbage.

Fishtag

Seafood ✗✗

A3

222 W. 79th St. (bet. Amsterdam Ave. & Broadway)

Subway: 79 St   Lunch Sat – Sun
Phone: 212-362-7470   Dinner nightly
Web: www.fishtagrestaurant.com
Prices: $$$

If the handle of this popular dining room hasn't given it away, the name certainly will—Fishtag is all about seafood. Set on the ground floor of a townhouse, this parlor boasts a convivial bar and a slender white-walled dining room, arranged around a center island used to display an arresting selection of cheeses.

Delightfully sharable, Fishtag's menu underscores Chef Michael Psilakis' modern Greek accent and is organized by style from light to heavy. One may start off with scallop ceviche brightened by pomelo and *aji amarillo* before moving on to crisp-skinned salmon atop finely chopped cucumber, tomato, and onion awash in red wine vinaigrette; then decadent sheep's milk dumplings draped in tomato *fonduta* and nuggets of homemade *loukaniko* (pork sausage).

Gari

J a p a n e s e ✗✗

370 Columbus Ave. (bet. 77th & 78th Sts.)

Subway: 81 St - Museum of Natural History   Lunch & dinner daily
Phone: 212-362-4816
Web: N/A
Prices: $$$

The Columbus Avenue outpost of Sushi of Gari (there are three in Manhattan) fashions a hip aesthetic with contemporary Asian décor and large glass windows facing the sidewalk.

While ingredients are top quality and everything is made to order, there is strong focus on mass appeal here, as more guests order à la carte rather than put themselves in the skillful hands of the sushi chefs and try the highly recommended omakase, where the true beauty of Gari lies. A fine mix of sushi, including signatures by Chef Masatoshi "Gari" Sugio, and cooked dishes are all prepared with a modern touch. European influences are evident in items like duck and lamb chops.

Offering a well-chosen list of sake and wine, plus professional service, Gari is packed nightly.

Gazala's

M i d d l e   E a s t e r n ✗✗

380 Columbus Ave. (at 78th St.)

Subway: 81 St - Museum of Natural History   Lunch & dinner daily
Phone: 212-873-8880
Web: www.gazalasplace.com
Prices: $$

This is Gazala Halabi's second creation (Hell's Kitchen holds the original) but kid sister is quite the hit. Ample, well-run, and attractive, Gazala's churns out tasty Middle Eastern eats with an eye toward Druze specialties. Set in a notable building across from the venerable Museum of Natural History and Central Park, Gazala's has become its own destination.

Focus is clearly on the food in this two-fold dining space, with a tiny kitchen set front and center. A slim room features a communal table, while a larger, sun-lit room has wood tables laden with wafer-thin *sagg*, an ideal vessel for scooping up smoky baba ghanoush. A sesame seed-crested *mankosha* pie is unique and rich with spinach and goat cheese, while dense date cookies are plain outstanding.

Gennaro

B2

665 Amsterdam Ave. (bet. 92nd & 93rd Sts.)

Subway: 96 St (Broadway)
Phone: 212-665-5348
Web: www.gennaronyc.com
Prices: $$

Dinner nightly

Gennaro is as true as a trattoria can be in NYC. This comfortable space is a master of consistency, despite having expanded the dining room to include a wine bar. Its décor is delightfully unchanged and the pasta dishes remain hearty and delicious. The bench is still parked out front and for good reason—Gennaro gets seriously crowded and patrons are glad for a seat.

The casual setting features golden yellow walls hung with ceramic plates and rustic wood shelves displaying wine bottles. Daily specials are a great complement to their homemade menu of *involtini di pesce spada* (swordfish stuffed with breadcrumbs and pine nuts atop peppery arugula); silky *orechiette* with broccoli rabe and sharp provolone; and tiny cannoli filled with rich ricotta cream.

Good Enough to Eat

B3

483 Amsterdam Ave. (bet. 83rd & 84th Sts.)

Subway: 79 St
Phone: 212-496-0163
Web: www.goodenoughtoeat.com
Prices: $$

Lunch & dinner daily

The title of the place pretty much says it all—it's good enough to eat here, all right, and you could do so from morning 'till night if you wished. This family-friendly comfort food haven offers breakfast, lunch, and dinner (not to mention takeout), and the Upper West Side locals, for one, can't get enough of Chef/owner Carrie Levin's simple, but mouthwatering renditions of tender, home-cooked meatloaf; flaky fish and chips; and crunchy stacks of buttermilk-fried onion rings.

The homey atmosphere matches the food, with a whimsical mix of folk art, cow accents–lots of 'em–and large "candies" hanging from the ceiling. A cozy area in front offers a great solo meal—add a little frost on the window, and you'll dream you've gone home for the holidays.

Isabella's

Mediterranean ✗✗

B3

359 Columbus Ave. (at 77th St.)

Subway: 81 St - Museum of Natural History
Phone: 212-724-2100
Web: www.isabellas.com
Prices: $$

Lunch & dinner daily

For over two decades, this popular NY dining institution has boasted and rightfully earned some of the area's best sidewalk real estate. Lovely interiors and Mediterranean flavors make Isabella's a worthwhile legacy. However, bi-level dining, outdoor seating (weather permitting), and competition from its neighbor, Shake Shack, does nothing to ease long waits for tables, especially during weekend brunch which features a variety of Benedicts, from crab to BLT-inspired.

Music keeps tempo with the bustling activity, while the charming and professional staff tends to diners relishing the likes of herb-roasted chicken. Regulars know two things: For a small corkage fee, they may BYOB; and always save room for the generous warm brownie sundae.

Lincoln

Italian ✗✗✗

A4

142 W. 65th St. (bet. Amsterdam Ave. & Broadway)

Subway: 66 St - Lincoln Center
Phone: 212-359-6500
Web: www.lincolnristorante.com
Prices: $$$$

Lunch Wed – Sun
Dinner nightly

Set amidst the newly refreshed Lincoln Center campus, this aptly named dining room is frequented by families, Upper West Siders, and date-night duos. The gleaming two-story setting is a dramatic production, wrapped in glass and crowned by a sloping turf-topped expanse; its ethereal color scheme and polished mahogany is the distillation of contemporary refinement.

Kick off the evening with a cocktail; a sip from the Prosecco bar (or Negroni bar) is an imperative before diving into the carte of seasonally hued Italian creations. Primi, such as *malfatti* (beet green and ricotta dumplings) dressed with a supple sauce of orange flower water flecked with poppy seeds, share the spotlight with entrées such as Pekin duck breast and leg with farro and giblet jus.

Jean Georges ✿ ✿ ✿

A4

1 Central Park West (bet. 60th & 61st Sts.)

Subway: 59 St - Columbus Circle   Lunch & dinner daily
Phone: 212-299-3900
Web: www.jean-georges.com
Prices: $$$$

Thomas Loof

In a city that is never silent, in an opulent dining room so close to Columbus Circle that you could practically hit a cab with a champagne cork, a hush has befallen Jean Georges. Even the curvaceous leather chairs, round-backed booths, and thick carpeting with earth-toned striations seem styled to soothe. Oversized windows dressed in sheers flood the room with natural light. Everything here exudes class—note that jackets are required only at dinner.

All of this serves as a backdrop for Chef de Cuisine Mark Lapico's precise and fine-tuned preparations of the eponymous Jean-Georges Vongerichten's globally inspired cuisine.

Meals here might begin with beautiful bowls of chopped buttery, orange-fleshed sea trout and raw oysters seasoned with horseradish, sea salt, and pumpernickel toasts. Perhaps next, find sweet and supple shrimp cooked to the exact moment of doneness, with shaved water chestnut, bits of smoky chipotle pepper, and a saffron sauce that suggests the existence of alchemy. Be sure to indulge in the memorable *mignardise*, a grand finale featuring yuzu and sesame macarons, house-made chocolates, and pillow-soft vanilla marshmallows.

Prix-fixe lunch menus offer extraordinary value.

Loi

Greek ✗✗✗

A3

208 W. 70th St. (bet. Amsterdam & West End Aves.)

Subway: 72 St   Dinner nightly
Phone: 212-875-8600
Web: www.restaurantloi.com
Prices: $$$

Greek TV personality, cookbook author, and restaurateur, Maria Loi, is a known powerhouse. At her eponymous spot, this favorite chef gives her homeland's cuisine an upscale kick, while maintaining a comforting touch. The airy, elegant main room evokes the country's gorgeous landscape through white leather booths, bright lighting, and colorful photo murals of the Corinthian Gulf. Back-lit wine walls and stunning floral arrangements complete the sophisticated scene.

Dig into delights like sea urchin accompanied by crispy pita chips; baked goat cheese croquets topped with fig and apricot compote; tender grilled octopus with capers, chickpeas, almonds, and fresh herbs; or the *psari se krousta alatiou*—fresh whole fish baked in a sea salt crust.

Miss Mamie's Spoonbread Too

Southern ✗

C1

366 W. 110th St./Cathedral Pkwy. (bet. Columbus & Manhattan Aves.)

Subway: Cathedral Pkwy/110 St (Central Park West)   Lunch & dinner daily
Phone: 212-865-6744
Web: www.spoonbreadinc.com
Prices: 🞉🞉

This venerable Morningside Heights institution doesn't coast on its reputation as a homey Southern haven just north of Central Park. The food is as good as ever, the atmosphere is easygoing and welcoming, and the music is soulful yet unobtrusive.

Fresh and expertly made classics rule the menu, but the daily specials board offers gems that should not be ignored. Here, find the likes of crazy chicken, perfectly fried and juicy with a generous helping of three sides and gravy. The smothered pork chops are tender and wonderfully tangy; the yams are soft and spicy; and the banana pudding is the stuff of dreams. Sit back and soak in a super-sweet iced tea or the Spoonbread punch and relax—food made with such care can take its time getting to your table.

Momoya

427 Amsterdam Ave. (bet. 80th & 81st Sts.)

Subway: 79 St   Lunch & dinner daily
Phone: 212-580-0007
Web: www.momoyanyc.com
Prices: $$$

For a glimpse of the sushi-making prowess, slip into a seat at the sexy, white marble counter and watch these pros do their thing. Blond woods, cream leather booths, slate floors, sultry lighting, and careful orchid arrangements combine subdued masculinity with feminine touches at Momoya, a cool yet bright little spot with a second outpost in Chelsea.

Start off with warm mushroom salad tossed in yuzu-soy vinaigrette, or a special tuna roll done up with grilled yellow tail and almonds. Try the cold soba, bobbing in fragrant broth with spicy tempura rock shrimp; or the tender, flaky miso cod atop wilted, yuzu spinach. The *matcha*-dusted *mille* crêpes, delicately layered with green tea ice cream and cream anglaise, are a triangular slice of heaven.

Nice Matin

201 W. 79th St. (at Amsterdam Ave.)

Subway: 79 St   Lunch & dinner daily
Phone: 212-873-6423
Web: www.nicematinnyc.com
Prices: $$

So well-loved is this local favorite that Nice Matin has gained an everyday roster of ladies lunching, freelance junkies, and stroller-pushing moms. It paints a lively scene on a cold, rainy day, luring everyone in with their warm, worn-in, pseudo-French vibe and years of popularity. In keeping with its easy style, the brasserie also boasts a massive Mediterranean menu coupled with soft prices and a big-time wine list.

The service is not spot-on, but with round-the-clock diners nibbling away on exquisitely simple plates of poached leeks topped with egg mimosa or crunchy beets kissed with *chevre*, it's easy to feel the love. A grilled herb-marinated chicken and arugula sandwich is massive, but blissful when paired with their thin, crispy frites.

Noche Mexicana II

Mexican ✗

B1

842 Amsterdam Ave. (at 101st St.)

Subway: 103 St (Broadway)
Phone: 212-662-6900
Web: www.noche-mexicana.com
Prices: $$

Lunch & dinner daily

Sequels are usually better known for missing the mark rather than hitting it, but Noche Mexicana II bucks the trend. This Upper West Side pearl known for its fluffy tamales moved to bigger and brighter digs this year, closing its original some blocks north. These higher reaches of Amsterdam Ave. aren't the prettiest, but once inside this bright, upbeat spot, you'll never look back.

Moist corn meal tamales with succulent pork and green *mole* sauce; spicy *camarones Mexicana*; tempting *guajilio* chili with tender chicken—you can't go wrong. Other surefire hits include *tingas*, *taco cesina* (preserved beef), and the *pipian de pollo*, shredded chicken served with toasted pumpkin and sesame seeds and cooked with jalapeño and *guero* chile peppers...*muy bueno!*

Nougatine

Contemporary ✗✗

A4

1 Central Park West (at 60th St.)

Subway: 59 St - Columbus Circle
Phone: 212-299-3900
Web: www.jean-georges.com
Prices: $$

Lunch & dinner daily

Prestigiously set on the ground floor of the Trump International Hotel, Nougatine proves to be nothing short of lavish. The recently refreshed look is clean and contemporary bathed in light reflected from its large, unencumbered windows—a world away from the crowded plazas and blaring cabs outside.

Minimalist touches like plush leather banquettes, gleaming light fixtures, and a brushed metal bar convey gentility, making Nougatine an otherworldly spot to rest your weary, globetrotting feet over an aperitif or quick bite. A bowl of verdant green pea soup crested with crispy croutons and Parmesan foam is an elegant standout among other items like succulent skate with aromatic black beans; or a dense slice of sour cream cheesecake with passion fruit compote.

Osteria Cotta

Italian 🍴

B3

513 Columbus Ave. (bet. 84th & 85th Sts.)

Subway: 86 St (Broadway)
Phone: 212-873-8500
Web: www.cottanyc.com
Prices: $$

Lunch Sun
Dinner nightly

This neighborhood newcomer is already the go-to spot for those NYers who are tired of trendy and seek a taste of home without the hassle. Osteria Cotta is decidedly more comfortable than chic, featuring wood beams, wrought-iron banisters, exposed brick walls, and wood-framed glass doors that open out to Columbus Avenue to define its rustic look.

There's a roaring oven for pizza that also turns out a truly perfect roasted chicken. For some old-fashioned comfort, try the lasagna Bolognese: rich, creamy, with thick sheets of chewy pasta, satiny pillows of cheese and kissed with the flavors of fennel and pork—it might be more than poor *nonna's* heart can bear. Don't miss the Nutella- and ricotta-filled dessert calzone for a little sachet of heaven.

Ouest

Contemporary 🍴🍴🍴

B2

2315 Broadway (bet. 83rd & 84th Sts.)

Subway: 86 St (Broadway)
Phone: 212-580-8700
Web: www.ouestny.com
Prices: $$$

Lunch Sun
Dinner nightly

Ouest is not sexy; it is sultry. But in this area, baby, you've got to have more than looks to last. The Upper West Side may not swarm with important eateries, but Ouest's elevated and serious cuisine has made it a magnet for celebrities, media moguls, and locals for more than a decade. The slender front bar is adored for sipping; under its grand ceiling lamps are red leather banquettes packed with eager guests.

Bustling with capable servers, the large back dining room is a masculine yet elegant, balconied space. From here, the open kitchen presents plates of silky cauliflower custard beside buttery lobster knuckles; sumac-crusted tuna with a white bean purée and red pepper compote; and a distinctly flavorful peanut butter-chocolate bombe.

Picholine

Mediterranean ☒☒☒☒

A4

35 W. 64th St. (bet. Broadway & Central Park West)

Subway: 66 St - Lincoln Center

Phone: 212-724-8585

Web: www.picholinenyc.com

Prices: $$$$

Dinner Tue – Sat

Picholine

Picholine has been hailed as an Upper West grande dame since its inception. A rounded etched glass awning hints of the Parisian metro, while every interior detail is immensely sophisticated and comfortable. This bar is a famously pretty seat from which to enjoy a pre-theater drink or sample the delightfully exquisite cheese program—note the climate-controlled cart parading about. Beyond this, the plush dining room showcases ornate chandeliers dangling in a serene setting that has recently received a well-earned face-lift by designer David Rockwell. No detail is lost on the stylish crowd whose pockets are either deep or deeper.

Limoges porcelain plates introduce Chef Terrance Brennan's tasteful French-accented fare, which might begin with a wintery salad tossing wafer-thin, crisp flavors of pink radishes, purple carrots, and turnips atop artistically composed butternut squash mousse. Meals go on to include butter-poached day boat lobster paired with an assertive smoked ricotta-potato mousseline and sautéed cepes; or wild striped bass fillets with a lush romesco mousse.

Apple *pain perdu* is a burst of freshness and complexity, drizzled with caramel ice cream and a dense rum raisin sauce.

The Purple Fig

A3

250 W. 72nd St. (bet. Broadway & West End Ave.)

Subway: 72 St
Phone: 212-712-9823
Web: www.thepurplefignyc.com
Prices: $$$

Lunch & dinner daily

The Purple Fig is quietly tucked through a deep-set arched doorway, beyond the slightly dark yet inviting bar offering premium spirits and sultry jazz. Leather booths and linen-topped tables beautify the rear of this rather romantic dining room, where walls are festooned with colorful photographs of their praiseworthy dishes.

There are many gustatory pleasures to be had at The Purple Fig, perhaps starting with a grilled scallop laid beside poached apple slices and a warm pea velouté. Other dishes include a wild salmon fillet, cured and smoked pastrami-style, masterfully matched with Dijon and dill-pickled fruit as well as ginger-cucumber-wasabi crème fraîche; or a warm Valrhona chocolate cake crowned with a quenelle of pistachio ice cream.

Recipe

B3

452 Amsterdam Ave. (bet. 81st & 82nd Sts.)

Subway: 79 St
Phone: 212-501-7755
Web: www.recipenyc.com
Prices: $$

Lunch Sat – Sun
Dinner nightly

Listen here, Upper West Siders. Put this twenty-six seat oasis on your list of must-visits, if you haven't already. Fantastic food (a brunch favorite) and an enthusiastic staff are Recipe's ingredients for success, so get in on the action. Soft grey walls, white brick, and natural, unfinished wood tables comprise the simple space, which gets a sprinkling of cool, reclaimed items like a chicken-wire screen from the former New York Times building.

Scrumptious seared duck breast atop wild rice, sweet corn, and braised kale; or toothsome beef cheek tortellini with tomatillo salsa and sunflower seeds are just few of the tasty options. For the sweet-lovers, the chocolate *pignoli* tart with caramel, almond crust, and chocolate sorbet makes the heart soar.

Slightly Oliver

Gastropub

B2

511 Amsterdam Ave. (bet. 84th & 85th Sts.)

Subway: 86 St (Broadway)
Phone: 212-362-1098
Web: www.slightlyolivernyc.com
Prices: $$

Lunch Sat – Sun
Dinner nightly

Slightly Oliver is a welcome departure from the usual suspects on this stretch of Amsterdam Ave. Rife with playful drinks, this gastropub's "Commonwealth-inspired" menu also promises to lift your spirits amid the homey space featuring faux bookshelves, low lights, and high tables.

Cozy duos head up a few stairs to romantic booths shrouded in lace curtains; while the "apothecary style" bar–featuring a glass-enclosed area packed with distilling elements–is truly unique. The menu meanders, but an informed staff deftly steers you through such good pub grub as puffy flats spread with figs and artichokes. Cool beginnings (roasted butternut squash tossed with frisée) or big plates (flaky steak and kidney pie) are ace when followed by a soft malva pudding.

Sookk

Thai

B1

2686 Broadway (bet. 102nd & 103rd Sts.)

Subway: 103 St (Broadway)
Phone: 212-870-0253
Web: www.sookkrestaurant.com
Prices: $$

Lunch & dinner daily

From the hip folks behind the downtown lounge, Room Service, this tiny Thai joint draws Upper West Siders in droves—and it's not hard to see why. Unique dishes are cooked up in the style of Yaowarat (a district in Northwest Bangkok) which marries Thai, Sichuan, and Cantonese cuisines. Warm up with savory white lemongrass soup of poached chicken, chili oil, and mushrooms; or the delectable chicken pumpkin curry in spicy coconut milk. The mussel turnip cake may sound like an acquired taste, but plump green mussels stir fried with ginger and tamarind, with pan-fried turnips, eggs, and bean sprouts are a funky crowdpleaser.

Bedecked in bright colors, mesh lanterns, and red banquettes, the space is attractive top to bottom (check out the restrooms).

Spiga

Italian ✕✕

B2

200 W. 84th St. (bet. Amsterdam Ave. & Broadway)

Subway: 86 St (Broadway)
Phone: 212-362-5506
Web: www.spiganyc.com
Prices: $$$

Dinner nightly

When neighborhood residents want to treat themselves to a memorable Italian meal, they head to Spiga. Replete with shelves lined in wine bottles, a beamed ceiling, and affable service, the handsome setting also claims a creative kitchen turning out a heap of specialties influenced by Puglia and the northern reaches of the country.

Kick things off with a salad of mixed beans studded with the crunch of celery and slivered red onion—stunning in its simplicity. Then move on to herb-crusted lamb chops, coated with a flurry of fresh rosemary made fragrant by the hot oven, accompanied by sautéed broccoli rabe and a block of creamy potato gratin. Finish with the apple and pear strudel enrobed in a tender crust and paired with a scoop of ginger ice cream.

Sura 😊

Thai ✕✕

B2

2656 Broadway (bet. 100th & 101st Sts.)

Subway: 103 St (Broadway)
Phone: 212-665-8888
Web: www.surathaikitchen.com
Prices: 🐵🐵

Lunch & dinner daily

Sura brings a dose of heat to the spice-challenged Upper West Side. The interior is unexpectedly upmarket with a smoky slate grey palette and shimmering accents. In contrast, white marble-topped tables line the slender setting and the neat culinary presentations enhance the stylish air.

Sura's outstanding preparations indicate that this kitchen is much more serious about its representation of Thai cuisine that many of its ilk. Indulge in standouts such as fresh and flavorful duck *larb*; or blue crab-studded fried sticky rice with egg and scallion. The *khao soi*—slender egg noodles bathed in a house-crafted rich and aromatic coconut curry topped with a peak of crunchy fried noodles and pickled mustard leaves—is a technically superb specialty.

Telepan

American ✗✗

A3

72 W. 69th St. (bet. Central Park West & Columbus Ave.)

Subway: 66 St - Lincoln Center
Phone: 212-580-4300
Web: www.telepan-ny.com
Prices: $$$

Lunch Wed – Sun
Dinner nightly

Sitting on one of the prettiest area blocks, a plush awning and cheery hostess welcomes diners to this excellent and trailblazing NY mainstay. Inside, the room is relaxing and warm with splashes of green everywhere. While the floors and tables are carved from hard wood, candles and fireplaces soften the mood. A glass-enclosed wine case is a serious showstopper only to be matched by their unpretentious and seasonal offerings.

Chef Bill Telepan's devotion to deliciousness manifests itself in calamari "pasta" tossed with arugula pesto; and moist veal meatballs. Tender *mezzaluna* stuffed with tart and milky *burrata*; or wild Sockeye salmon bathed in a lemon-thyme dressing and paired with olive oil-potato gratin are why this prized respite is perpetually packed.

Vai

Mediterranean ✗✗

B3

429 Amsterdam Ave. (bet. 80th & 81st Sts.)

Subway: 79 St
Phone: 212-362-4500
Web: www.vairestaurant.com
Prices: $$

Lunch Wed –Sun
Dinner nightly

Happily, Vai is back in the neighborhood, after having lost its former 77th Street digs. The new space is thankfully bigger, but maintains the same alluring style with bare, dark wood tables, brown leather seating, and a curved marble bar illuminated in sultry candlelight. Potted flowers and framed mirrors add a lovely touch.

Jean Georges alum, Vincent Chirico, continues to lead the charge in the kitchen, firing up dynamite *assaggi* for the small plate-loving crowd. Get on board with sautéed Gulf shrimp atop root vegetable soffrito, herbs, and smoky chorizo; pan-roasted Arctic char, flanked by sweet onion confit and drizzled in warm pancetta vinaigrette; and green and white asparagus topped with snowy shavings of *ricotta salata* and truffle essence.

Warique

Peruvian ✗

B1

852 Amsterdam Ave. (bet. 101st & 102nd Sts.)

Subway: 103 St (Broadway)
Phone: 212-865-0101
Web: N/A
Prices: $$

Lunch & dinner daily

Warique is located in the *way* Upper West Side–you'll need to travel until you hit the triple digits–but this casually comfortable restaurant is worth the trek if only for their stick-to-your-ribs comfort food from Peru.

While some of the classic hits (tripe, braised intestines, guinea pig) are missing here, rest assured as Warique doesn't miss a beat when it comes to delivering knock-your-socks off flavors. The *causa Peruana*, a mix of mashed potatoes, avocado, and shrimp, is doused in a hell-breathing sauce of *aji amarillo*, while those who seek less spicy, but amazingly delicious, should opt for the juicy and tender *pollo a la brasa* (chicken with crispy skin dripping with sweet fat) served with *salchipapa* (fries studded with deep-fried sausage).

Avoid the search for
parking. Look for 🚗.

John Peden/The New York Botanical Garden

The Bronx

The Bronx

The only borough attached to the mainland, the Bronx is marked by contrasts. Although abandoned apartment buildings and massive housing projects once overran the borough's south section, private foundations and grassroots movements are successfully revitalizing these areas. As always, grand mansions and lavish gardens still characterize the northern areas of Riverdale and Fieldston. And, with such a plethora of organic farms cropping up (Green-Up is a program run by the NY Botanical Gardens and organizes tours of these lush lands), it is no wonder that this borough is now a hotbed of culinary gems—even **Sabatino Tartufi**'s tantalizing truffles have arrived on the scene.

BELMONT

Hispanics, African-Americans, Irish-Americans, West Indians, and Albanians comprise much of the current population. Though a host of Italians once settled in the Belmont area, today they only reside as shop proprietors. Thanks to the 19th century journalist John Mullaly, who led a movement in the late 1800s to buy and preserve inexpensive parcels of land, 25 percent of the Bronx today consists of parkland. This includes Pelham Bay Park, with its sandy Orchard Beach. Once here, step into pizza paradise–**Louie and Ernie's**–for a slice of heaven.

Beyond, City Island is a gem of a coastal community with its quaint inns and seafood spots. During the summer, stroll down City Island Avenue, and into **Lickety Split** for a scoop of silky ice cream. Belmont's most renowned street and Italian food mecca, Arthur Avenue, lures from far and wide. Tear into warm, freshly baked breads from **Terranova** or **Addeo**—the choices are plenty. Dive into a ball of warm and creamy mozzarella at **Joe's Deli** (open on Sundays!). The pistachio-studded mortadella from **Teitel Brothers** or *salumi* from **Calabria Pork Store** are also perfect salt licks.

Gourmet Getaway

Don't forget to check out **The Arthur Avenue Retail Market**, a covered oasis built by Mayor LaGuardia to prevent pushcart vendors from crowding busy streets. The dwindling vendors inside sell quality Italian pasta, homemade sausage, olive oil, notorious heroes, heirloom seeds, and hand-rolled cigars. Although the Belmont section is now mainly known as Little Mexico and Ecuador, it has a world of Eastern European treats. Visit **Tony & Tina's Pizza**, but skip the Italian stuff. Instead, devour Albanian or Kosovar *burek*—these flaky rolls are packed with pumpkin purée and are *sine qua non*. **Gustiamo**'s warehouse will delight with simple Italian specialties including a variety of regional oils and vinegars;

pastas and rice; San Marzano tomatoes; and other appealing items. In the same vein, **Honeywell Meat Market** (their butchers in particular) can teach newbies a thing or two about breaking down a side of beef. Bronxite's will revel in the heart-satisfying *chicharrón de cerdo* at pork-central **El Bohio Lechonera** in nearby Crotona Park. Take yourself out to a ball game at the Yankee Stadium and snack from **Lobel's** cart (the ultimate butcher shop); or if you're lucky enough to have premium seats, enjoy one of their expertly dry-aged steaks.

Comfort Foods

The Eastchester, Wakefield, and Williamsbridge sections of the Bronx cradle a number of communities and their tasty eats and treats. The spicy, smoky tidbits of the Caribbean have become a local staple. Visit Vernon's **New Jerk House** for mouthwatering jerk chicken, and end with something sweet from **Kingston Tropical Bakery**. Craving some Italian? Drop by **G & R Deli** for big flavors in their homemade sausages or rich meaty sauce sold by the quart. End at **Sal & Dom's** for flaky *sfogliatelle*.

Asia comes alive at **Pho Saigon No.1**—peek in to discover that authentic Vietnamese food has officially arrived in the Bronx. And Cambodian delights abound at **Phnom Penh-Nha Trang Market** across the street. The hamburger craze continues uptown at the **Bronx Ale House** and **Bruckner Bar & Grill**. In need of a beer with your meaty treats? **Bronck's Beer** and **Bronx Brewery** are always frolicking with rich selections.

A Latin Affair

A unique blend of Latin American hangouts populates the South Bronx, with the largest concentration hailing from Puerto Rico. On Willis Avenue, Mott Haven's main drag, bright awnings designate Honduran diners, Mexican bodegas, and Puerto Rican takeout. Vital to New York's food business is the **Hunts Point Food Distribution Center**, a 329-acre complex containing a mass of food wholesalers, distributors, and food processing businesses.

This mega complex includes **The Hunts Point Meat Market**, **Hunts Point Terminal Produce Market**, and **The Fulton Fish Market**, a wholesale triumvirate where the city's restaurateurs and market owners come to pick their goods. Such delicious browsing can only lead to a bigger appetite, which should be whetted at **Mo Gridder's BBQ** in Hunts Point—this is a classic haunt for barbecue and exudes potent doses of unique Bronx flavor.

RIVERDALE

Riverdale may not be widely known for its dining culture and culinary gems, but it continues to comfort its local clusters at the primped **Mother's Bake Shop**, famed for their traditional *babkas* and challahs. **Skyview Wines** carries a rare selection of kosher wines, thereby completing your sweet escapade with a touch of spirit. Hop, skip, and a jump from the last stop on the 1 line, follow your nose (cause it always knows) to **Lloyd's Carrot Cake** for one or several slices of their divine carrot cake.

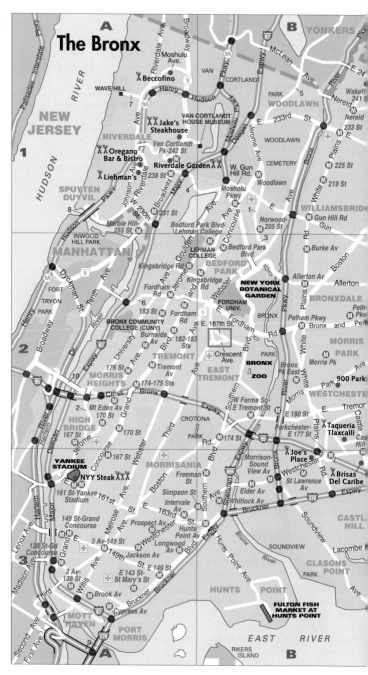

The Bronx

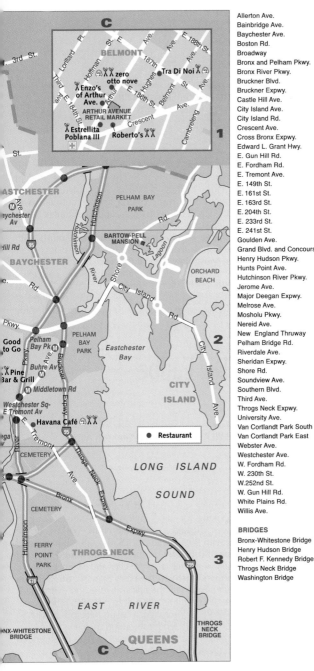

Beccofino

A1

Italian

5704 Mosholu Ave. (at Fieldston Rd.)

Subway: Van Cortlandt Park-242 St
Phone: 718-432-2604
Web: N/A
Prices: $$

Dinner nightly

Tucked into the quaint, family-oriented Bronx neighborhood of Riverdale, Beccofino sets a pretty, idyllic stage straight away—with large inviting windows overlooking a leafy, residential street and a rustic osteria interior outfitted with exposed brick walls, terra-cotta floors, and a handful of tables topped with deli paper.

Beccofino's menu is pure Italian-American comfort, with hand-crafted dishes that prioritize fresh ingredients over inventiveness. Most nights, you'll find a healthy list of hand-written daily specials, along with dishes like cappellini primavera with fresh, plump shrimp, vegetables, a touch of cream, and grated Parmesan; a very homey rendition of fettuccine Alfredo; and pineapple sorbet served in the freshly frozen fruit.

Brisas Del Caribe

B3

Puerto Rican

1207 Castle Hill Ave. (bet. Ellis & Gleason Aves.)

Subway: Castle Hill Av
Phone: 718-794-9710
Web: N/A
Prices:

Lunch & dinner daily

This popular eatery stays packed to the rim day and night with those looking for solid Puerto Rican fare at bargain basement prices. Tucked into a multi-ethnic enclave of the Bronx dotted with 99 Cent stores, 1950s coffee houses, and Korean grocers, Brisas Del Caribe's waiters bounce around the bright, airy room at a good clip and seem to like it when you can woo them with a bit of Spanish. But don't be dissuaded if you don't talk the talk—anyone and everyone is welcome here. It just might take a little longer to order is all.

Don't miss the spot-on *mofongo*, a crispy, delicious mountain of plantain studded with tender shredded chicken; or the killer Cubano sandwich, stuffed with sweet and salty shredded pork, cheese, sliced pickles, and mayo.

Enzo's of Arthur Ave

Italian

2339 Arthur Ave. (bet. Crescent Ave. & 186th St.)

Subway: Fordham Rd (Grand Concourse)   Lunch & dinner daily
Phone: 718-733-4455
Web: N/A
Prices: $$

With its old-fashioned tiled floors, bistro tables, and pressed-tin ceiling, this offshoot of the original Enzo's might look like your average red-sauce joint, but Enzo's takes comfort cooking to a new level.

Yes, it's informal with casually dressed Fordham students here for everyone's favorite cavatelli with broccoli rabe and spicy sausage, but others come from afar, to shop and sate themselves on some of the city's better clams oreganata. Owner Enzo DiRende (whose father co-founded legendary Dominick's) improves every standby with his devotion to sourcing from local vendors—a smart thing when your 'hood is teeming with killer Italian markets. Fresh, crusty ciabatta, delish cured meats, and the vanilla-scented cheesecake are all made around the corner.

Estrellita Poblana III

Mexican

2328 Arthur Ave. (bet. Crescent Ave. & 186th St.)

Subway: Fordham Rd (Grand Concourse)   Lunch & dinner daily
Phone: 718-220-7641
Web: N/A
Prices:

The smallest of its brethren, this adorable Arthur Avenue spot serves up the same mouthwatering Mexican as the other two, but in sweeter surroundings. The sparkling room is like a tiny, immaculate jewel box with powder blue walls, wood wainscoting, and purple hand-cut flowers atop each table.

At the heart of this local favorite is the food—homemade, fresh, honest, and satisfying. Though the friendly staff speaks little English, the menu is clear and the specials delicious. Start with the likes of *budin Azteca*, corn tortillas with layers of shredded chicken, cheese, and chile with a spicy-nutty *mole* sauce. Specials punctuating the menu may include their fantastic *pozole* of tender hominy and pork.

Take note: tamales are available on weekends only.

Good to Go

C2

1894 Eastchester Rd. (near Morris Park Ave.)

Subway: E 180 St (& bus BX 21)　　　　　　Lunch & dinner daily
Phone: 718-829-2222
Web: N/A
Prices: $$

With its friendly vibe and plates of belly-pleasing comfort, Indian Village locals love Good to Go. Smack in the heart of bustling Eastchester Road and surrounded by teaching hospitals and commercial enterprises like Starbucks and Dunkin' Donuts, it brings a welcome bit of warmth to the landscape. The lively interior sports exposed brick, caramel-colored walls, and chocolate brown tables glowing under soft track lighting.

Italian-American classics are tasty and well done, as in baked clams—the chopped mollusks tossed with garlicky breadcrumbs, hot chili flakes, and parsley. The decadent *lasagna rustica* is made with heaping layers of meatballs, ricotta, pecorino, mozzarella, and meat sauce, and is sure to keep neighborhood denizens satisfied.

Havana Café 😊

C2

3151 E. Tremont Ave. (at LaSalle Ave.)

Subway: N/A　　　　　　Lunch & dinner daily
Phone: 718-518-1800
Web: www.bronxhavanacafe.com
Prices: $$

Located in the Schuylerville section of the Bronx, Havana Café is a welcoming, well-run, and comfortable find. Beyond the cream-colored façade, palm trees, and outdoor dining, find a charming interior decked with a dark wood bar and marble-topped tables. Quaint posters, tropical fronds, and lazy ceiling fans evoke a sense of old Havana.

Don't be surprised to see that every single table is probably topped with their wonderful "Cuban pizza" flatbread, served on a wooden plank and topped with fat, sweet shrimp and a garlicky piquillo pepper sauce. More traditional but equally tasty dishes include mounds of tender-juicy braised flank steak piled high on fluffy rice and beans, or pork sautéed with caramelized and crispy tobacco-onions.

Jake's Steakhouse

Steakhouse ✗✗

A1

6031 Broadway (bet. Manhattan College Pkwy. & 251st St.)

Subway: Van Cortlandt Park-242 St   Lunch & dinner daily
Phone: 718-581-0182
Web: www.jakessteakhouse.com
Prices: $$$

Got baseball on the docket but beef on the brain? This multi-level, 126-seat Bronx steakhouse might be one of the best-kept secrets for Yankees fans headed north after the game. Located across from Van Cortland Park, just off the last stop of the 1 train, Jake's Steakhouse offers superior steaks for reasonable prices, in a warm, masculine interior.

Kick things off with the tender house crab cake, chockablock with fresh lump meat; and then move on to the star of the show—a hand-selected, wet-aged slab of premium T-bone, sliced off the bone and laced in natural beef jus. Any cut can be gussied up with melted Gorgonzola, crunchy frizzled onions, and port wine sauce, but with steak this good, you might not need the bells and whistles.

Joe's Place

Puerto Rican ✗

B3

1841 Westchester Ave. (at Thieriot Ave.)

Subway: Parkchester   Lunch & dinner daily
Phone: 718-918-2947
Web: www.joesplacebronx.com
Prices: $$

The Bronx loves its hometown heroes: J. Lo, Dave Valentin, Sonia Sotomayor, and Joe Torres. Who? If you have to ask, you're not from the Bronx. That's because Torres owns one of the top spots in the Bronx for delicious Puerto Rican/Dominican food.

From children to Congressmen, they're all here, and Joe chats up with them all. This place draws regulars who all come to catch up with the jovial proprietor and for the classic dishes. Begin with *sopa de pollo*, that lovely hot mess of chicken and noodles that tastes just like *papi* ordered. Move on to the *mofongo* with shredded pork and a mash of deep-fried green plaintains. *Pastelillo* is a flaky, crusty triumph and the *bacalao guisado*, a flavorful cod stew with pimiento-stuffed olives and capers, is a surefire hit.

Liebman's

Deli

552 W. 235th St. (bet. Johnson & Oxford Aves.)

Subway: 231 St
Phone: 718-548-4534
Web: www.liebmansdeli.com
Prices:

Lunch & dinner daily

Some things never change (phew!) and Liebman's is definitely one of those things. This iconic kosher deli has been stuffing sandwiches and ladling bowls of matzoh ball soup for over 50 years. Residents wax poetic about the place, but it's nothing special, just a true-blue deli. Walk in and it's like a Smithsonian set for a Jewish deli—a neon sign in the front window, the grill roasting hot dogs, and meat slicing machines.

The food is classic and soulful as in stuffed veal breast, potato latkes, pastrami and tongue sandwiches on nutty rye bread paired with tangy pickles...and even that old standby—noodle pudding. Order to-go, or take a load off and grab a seat at one of the booths. Just don't forget about that bowl of "cure-all" matzoh ball soup.

900 Park

Italian

900 Morris Park Ave. (at Bronxdale Ave.)

Subway: Bronx Park East
Phone: 718-892-3830
Web: www.900park.com
Prices: $$

Lunch & dinner daily

Easy, breezy, beautiful...900 Park. It might be located in the "other" Little Italy (Morris Park), but this stylish spot goes well beyond just fresh *cavatelli*. More St. Barts than Calabria, 900 Park hums with a great vibe and packed crowd spanning everyone from children to their grandparents.

Save the skinny jeans—these family-style meals will stuff you to the gills. Still, overindulging never felt so good with delicious starters like seafood-topped pizza and mussels *fra diavolo*, but keep that fork at the ready. Wrap your noodle around this: the pasta is delish! Don't know Caroline or Michael? Who cares. The pasta dishes named for them are so good you'll be blowing *baci*. Got room? Tuck into the grilled veal chop before retiring near the fireplace.

NYY Steak

Steakhouse ✗✗✗

A3

1 E. 161st St. (in Yankee Stadium)

Subway: 161 St - Yankee Stadium
Phone: 646-977-8325
Web: www.nyysteak.com
Prices: $$$$

Lunch Wed – Fri
Dinner Wed – Sat

Yes, it's tucked inside Yankee Stadium, but you won't find any ballpark franks here. Instead, this steakhouse hits it out of the park with its traditional décor mixed with serious Yankee pride (the autographed walls are Kodak worthy).

You don't need to don a pinstriped suit but definitely skip the Sox, since this place is Yankee heaven. Even the steaks are branded with the interlocking NY. There's certainly plenty of room—these tender, dry-aged, and perfectly seared steaks are monsters but oh-so-good. Sides like lobster mac and cheese and onion rings are home runs and the A+ wine list will have you yelling "beer not here!" A natural during games (when tickets are necessary), NYY Steak keeps the party going even when the boys of summer aren't home.

Oregano Bar & Bistro

Latin American ✗✗

A1

3524 Johnson Ave. (bet. 235th & 236th Sts.)

Subway: 231 St
Phone: 347-843-8393
Web: www.oreganolb.com
Prices: $$

Lunch Sat – Sun
Dinner nightly

Oregano Bar & Bistro's arrival on the scene seems to have brought about many smiles. Adorned with brass, bistro chairs, red-and-blue banquettes, antique mirrors, and a stunning carved wood bar, it is no wonder that locals love it. Large French doors open to the sidewalk decked with potted plants and invite pedestrians to this room abuzz with cocktail-loving cliques.

Add that to the live music, and it's a party complete with hefty portions of French-Latin fare. Expect the likes of *poitrine de poulet à la moutarde*, nicely charred chicken pieces finished in a mustard sauce tinged with tarragon; *paella maison* absolutely loaded with tender strips of duck, seafood, and vegetables; or an intensely rich and moist rum cake swept with a thick layer of icing.

Pine Bar & Grill

Italian 🍴🍴

C2

1634 Eastchester Rd. (at Blondell Ave.)

Subway: Westchester Sq - Tremont Av   Lunch & dinner Mon – Sat
Phone: 718-319-0900
Web: www.pinebargrill.com
Prices: $$

This hot younger sister to the always-bustling F & J Pine Restaurant used to be called Pine Tavern #2, but is now a destination in its own right. This bar and grill is not a typical Italian-American red sauce joint, but a decidedly spiffier spot with dark wood, coffered ceilings, and slick black-and-white photographs.

Since the Bastones do Italian so well, indulge in their perfect *pizzette* decked with milky-white fresh mozzarella and hearty *lasagne* that layer rich ground meat ragù with sweet ricotta and freshly made sheets of egg pasta. No need to meander off point with Latin notes like empanadas or coconut shrimp. If Frankie's in the back, he'll whip up practically anything you want. You want the spaghetti *pomodoro*? You get the spaghetti *pomodoro*!

Riverdale Garden

Latin American 🍴🍴

A1

4576 Manhattan College Pkwy. (at Broadway)

Subway: Van Cortlandt Park-242 St   Lunch Sun
Phone: 347-346-8497   Dinner nightly
Web: www.newriverdalegarden.com
Prices: $$

As you walk up curving 242nd Street toward this tucked-away Bronx gem, listen for strains of Cuban jazz wafting through the night air. Follow it to the newly renovated Riverdale Garden, where you can throw back a *Cuba libre* or a mojito at the roomy bar (special prices on Havana Thursdays), then escape to the unexpected and leafy tranquility of the back garden terrace.

Charmingly folksy service delivers Afro-Latin treats like tender African stuffed chicken, rolled around sweet plantain and Serrano ham; or the *Rabo*, a Cuban oxtail stew accompanied by steamed yucca and a bright lime-cilantro-garlic mojito sauce. You may want to skip dessert and opt for another round of mojitos to sip as you savor the sweet fact that you're not in Manhattan anymore.

Roberto's

Italian ✗✗

C1

603 Crescent Ave. (at Hughes Ave.)

Subway: Fordham Rd (Grand Concourse)
Phone: 718-733-9503
Web: www.roberto089.com
Prices: $$

Lunch Mon – Fri
Dinner Mon – Sat

This highly regarded Bronx favorite is most luminescent when its patriarch (Roberto Paciullo) stands sentry. Leading into a spanking new dining room, the dark wood bar still serves an opulent parade of grappas. The tables are still country chic—dark, supple, and bare. Bathed in candlelight, Roberto's seduces crowds into prolonging their Italian love affair, even after scouring Arthur Avenue's treats.

Keeping company with classic Italian-American food in this rustic yet elegant space are a gramophone, tasteful paintings, and velvet drapes. Specials like breaded octopus may not star every night, but *radiatore* pasta tossed with grilled lamb and pecorino; thin swordfish steaks marinated in lemon and herbs; and ricotta-rich cannolis are solid standards.

Taqueria Tlaxcalli

Mexican ✗

B2

2103 Starling Ave. (bet. Odell St. & Olmstead Ave.)

Subway: Castle Hill Av
Phone: 347-851-3085
Web: N/A
Prices:

Lunch & dinner daily

It's the little touches at Taqueria Tlaxcalli (the fuchsia ribbon tied around the cutlery, the tortilla basket topped with a colorful painted lid, the myriad sauces served for each and every taco ordered) that make a visit up to this Parkchester taqueria worth the hike. That the food is complex, authentic, and lip-smacking good is just the icing on the cake.

Locals pour into the tiny, crayola-bright space to begin their days with *huevos rancheros*, served sunny side up with refried beans, ham, and spicy red or green sauce. Later on, day-trippers join in, pop open a beer to the strum of contemporary Mexican music, and tuck into tortas slathered with beans, mayonnaise, avocado, tomatoes, chipotles, jalapeños, and whatever else your tastes may desire.

Tra Di Noi

 Italian ✗

C1

622 E. 187th St. (bet. Belmont & Hughes Aves.)

Subway: Fordham Rd (Grand Concourse)   Lunch & dinner Tue – Sun
Phone: 718-295-1784
Web: N/A
Prices: $$

Standing proudly amid time-honored Italian markets and delis, Tra Di Noi radiates the kind of nostalgic warmth found only in the most authentic places and is really *the* place to escape the crowds on Arthur Ave. Loyal locals flock here for Chef Marco Coletta's (he was also Sophia Loren's personal chef for a brief time) deliciously satisfying Italian-American dishes, while his wife showers all with big doses of Abbruzzi-style hospitality.

The lasagna and *pizzaiola* alone are reason enough to dine here, but food lovers far and wide return for mouthwatering pasta *carbonara*, pounded veal chop, or fresh swordfish Siciliana. The jovial atmosphere hums with bits of bilingual banter rising from the tables—further evidence of a true Italian-American experience.

zero otto nove

Italian ✗✗

C1

2357 Arthur Ave. (at 186th St.)

Subway: Fordham Rd (Grand Concourse)   Lunch & dinner Tue – Sun
Phone: 718-220-1027
Web: www.roberto089.com
Prices: $$

♧ Named for the area code back in Chef/owner Roberto Paciullo's Italian hometown of Salerno, zero otto nove feels like the real deal—with the affable Paciullo (who also runs the popular Roberto's around the corner) hustling around the rustic, brick-lined interior from table to oven and back again, shaking hands with customers and overseeing his kitchen with an eagle's eye.

The Salerno-style dishes, served homestyle big with an excellent wine list for matching, include mouthwatering pizzas (sporting unique toppings like fresh butternut squash, pancetta, and smoked mozzarella); delicious baked pastas; and oven-baked meats and fish. Don't miss the *mafalde con ceci*, perfectly cooked wide ribbons of pasta with chickpeas, tomato, and crispy pork belly.

Brooklyn

Brooklyn

Forage Brooklyn's trellis of neighborhoods and discover an exciting dining destination characterized by mom-and-pop stores, ethnic eateries, and trendy hot spots. Credit the influx of enterprising young chefs–many trained at Manhattan's top restaurants–for ushering in a new level of dining, while sedate establishments maintain the borough's rugged authenticity. The sustainable food movement has taken root as eco-conscious communities expand, and local artisans gain popularity for their high-quality, handcrafted goods. Locavores, want to support your neighbor's garden? Check out the handy website (www.eatwellguide.org) which offers a citywide directory of "green" gastronomy—family farms, farmers' markets, et al.

WILLIAMSBURG

Williamsburg, traditionally an Italian, Hispanic, and Hasidic neighborhood, is now home to hipsters and artists. Here in "Billyburg," artistic food endeavors abound: Find upscale diners in former factories, and an artisan chocolate line handcrafted from bean to bar at **Mast Brothers Chocolate**. Be sure to bring a big appetite to **Smorgasburg**, Williamsburg's open-air, all-food market held on the waterfront from spring through fall. If interested in learning how to pickle, bake a great pie, or ferment kombucha. Sign up for a cooking class at the **Brooklyn Kitchen**.

Over on Metropolitan Avenue, cute takeout shop **Saltie** offers a short yet delish list of tempting sandwiches and sweets, to be chased down by a cuppa' at **Blue Bottle Coffee Co.** Famous **Fette Sau** stokes legions of fans with its dry-rubbed smoked meats and sides; while **Pie 'n' Thighs** has returned to comfort with heaps of down-home goodness. Inspired by the art of butchery, **Marlow & Daughters**, boasts locally sourced meats, house-made sausages, and a delightful spectrum of artisanal dry goods.

If meat and cheese are your daily staples, a visit to the boutique pizzeria **Best Pizza** is a must. In keeping with the mien of this neighborhood, their space may appear a bit disheveled (slate-topped tables are scattered throughout the small room), yet patrons come in droves for their two varieties—a sliced cheese pizza embellished with pickled vegetables, and a sliced white pizza with dabs of creamy mozzarella and rich ricotta.

DUMBO

Besides DUMBO's breathtaking views, stroll down cobblestoned Water Street and into **Jacques Torres** for a taste of chocolate heaven. Bordering Prospect Park, verdant Park Slope boasts blocks of tony trattorias and cafés, catering to an army of stroller-rolling parents, including **Four & Twenty Blackbirds**—a charming bakeshop churning out a deluge of incredible pies.

The **Park Slope Food Coop** is a member operated and owned cooperative selling locally farmed produce, fair trade products, grass-fed meat, free-range poultry, and more. It is the largest of its kind in the country, and membership is offered to anyone willing to pay a small fee and work a shift of less than three hours each month. Carroll Gardens, a historically Italian neighborhood, offers shoppers a bevy of family-owned butchers and bakeries along Court Street. **D'Amico** is coffee-lovers' nirvana, while **Caputo's** has sandwiches worth the wait. As Court Street blends into family-friendly Cobble Hill, find **Staubitz Market**, the friendliest butcher around. Continue the stroll to Atlantic Avenue with its Middle Eastern goodies at **Sahadi's** and **Damascus Bakery**.

RED HOOK

On Brooklyn's waterfront rests Red Hook, attracting action with its large spaces and low rents. Industrious residents are transforming the neighborhood's aged piers and warehouses into cool breweries, bakeries, and bistros. Speaking of which, the **Red Hook Lobster Pound** is a treasured hangout for lobster lovers, but if in the mood for a sweet treat, head to **Baked**, **Steve's Authentic Key Lime Pie**, or **Cacao Prieto's**—courtesy of the Prieto family whose very own Coralina Farms provides the entire cacao for their chocolates and spirits. The **Red Hook Farmer's Market** features produce grown on Red Hook Community Farm. Both ventures are operated by Added Value, a mentoring

organization that teaches urban youth how to till, sow, and harvest. On weekends from May through October, the ever-popular trucks and tents that line the Red Hook Ball Fields cater to hordes of New Yorkers in the know with their selection of homemade Latin American and Caribbean street food.

The Global Highway

Saunter to Fort Greene for a taste of African delicacies: Ethiopian at **Bati's** and South African at **Madiba**, where the sidewalk offers some great alfresco dining. Land at Sunset Park, and be tantalized by the vibrant Mexican food and flavors as you bite into a *pambazo* from **Tacos Xochimilco**. Slightly south, Mexico meets China, and this fusion is best expressed in rare culinary offerings. Sidewalks teem with vendors steaming fresh tofu and fishmongers selling offbeat eats—bullfrog anyone? Chinatown encroaches into Bay Ridge where the dim sum is delicious and Asian markets aplenty. In a flock of Kosher restaurants, **Di Fara** is an unorthodox pizzeria and has called Midwood home for decades, and every few weeks **North Carolina Country Store** delivers to its locals a parade of home-style Southern staples. At the end of Brooklyn, Brighton Beach is best known for its borscht and blintzes. **Café Glechik** is an Ukranian *bijou* replete with faithful fare—beef tongue chased by *syrniki*? And there is no confusing the Chesapeake with Sheepshead Bay, but **Randazzo's Clam Bar** will provide you with a similar stellar seafood experience.

Brooklyn

- ● Hotel
- ● Restaurant

A

B

1

NEW JERSEY

HOLLAND TUNNEL
TOLL

MANHATTAN

HUDSON RIVER

Broadway

Canal St.

West St.

Delancey St.

Houston St.

14th St.

Chrystie St.

First St.

EAST RIVER

Ẋ Anella
Ẋ Paulie Gee's
Ẋ Karczma
🏠 Ẋ Calyer
Ẋ Ẋ Reynar
🏠 Wythe
See inset

Kent Ave.

Bedford Av

Metropolitan
Grand

See inset II

Marcy Av Ⓜ

2

LIBERTY
STATE
PARK

ELLIS
ISLAND

UPPER
NEW YORK
BAY

LIBERTY
ISLAND

GOVERNORS
ISLAND

BATTERY
PARK

FDR

TOLL

Flushing Ave.

**BROOKLYN
HEIGHTS**

Myrtle Ave.

Fulton St.

Atlantic Ave.

DeGraw St.

Court St.

Smith St.

Lafayette Ave.

Gates Ave.

Putnam

Franklin Ave.

Washington Ave.

Classon Av Ⓜ

Classon Ave.

**RED
HOOK**

RED HOOK
RECREATION
AREA

Van Brunt St.

Hamilton Ave.

9th St.

11th St.

4th Ave.

15th St.

**PARK
SLOPE**

Prospect Park West

**BROOKLYN
MUSEUM**

Ⓜ Fra

Botanic
Garden

3

LOWER
NEW YORK
BAY

Gowanus
Bay

278

23rd St.

25th St.

7th

Prospect Expwy

PROSPECT

Prospe
Pk

PARK

15 St–
Prospect Pk Ⓜ

Flatbush Ave.

Ⓜ Parksi

McDonald Ave.

Fort
Hamilton
Pkwy Ⓜ

27

Caton Ave.

Ⓜ Church Ave.

Ⓜ Church
Ocean

Beverly Rd

Cortelyou Rd Ⓜ

Ⓜ 36 St

Ẋ Maria's Bistro
Mexicano

GREENWOOD
CEMETERY

Ẋ Am Thai Bistro

Ⓜ 45 St

**SUNSET
PARK**

53rd St

47th St

Ⓜ 9 Av
Church Av Ⓜ

39th St

Coney Island Av

Cortelyou Rd

Purple Y

4

Ẋ Petit
Oven

Bay Ridge
Av Ⓜ

Ẋ Lucky Eight

Ⓜ 59 St

Ẋ Ẋ Pacificana

Ⓜ 44 St

🏛 Mimi's Hummus

Ẋ Ẋ The Farm
on Adderly

Picket Fen

Ẋ Ẋ East Harbor
Seafood Palace

Ẋ Tanoreen

Ẋ Ẋ The
Pearl Room

77 St Ⓜ

86 St Ⓜ

Bamboo Garden Ẋ

8 Av Ⓜ

Fort Hamilton
Pkwy

Ⓜ 55th St

Ⓜ 50 St

Ⓜ 62 St

Ⓜ New Utrecht Av

Ditmas
Av

Ⓜ 18th Av

Ⓜ 18 Av

**BOROUGH
PARK**

Newkirk Av

Ⓜ Av H

**BROOK
COLLE**

Ⓜ Av J

Shore Pkwy

Bay
Pkwy

Ẋ Eliá Ⓜ

Ẋ Dish

5th

3rd

86th St

95 St Ⓜ

4th

7th

14th

New Utrecht Av

62 St

18 Av

71 St Ⓜ

Ⓜ 20 Av

Bay Pkwy

Island

Ⓜ Av M

Ẋ Mtskheta Café ● ●

Ẋ Spicy Bampa ●

Ẋ Cupola Samarkanda ●

● Taci's Beyti Ẋ, Win

434

Inset I

Mill Basin Kosher Delicatessen

435

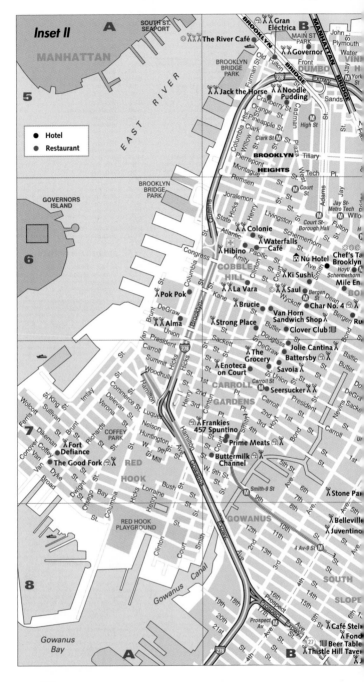

Inset II

A · B

SOUTH ST. SEAPORT

MANHATTAN

✿ ✕ ✕ ✕ The River Café
✕ ✕ Gran Eléctrica
MAIN ST PARK
John
Plymouth
Water
✕ ✕ Governor

BROOKLYN BRIDGE
Old Fulton
Front
DUMBO
Expwy
Sands
York St M

BROOKLYN BRIDGE PARK
Furman
Cranberry St.
Orange St.
Cadman Plaza
High St M

● Hotel
● Restaurant

✕ ✕ Jack the Horse
✕ ✕ Noodle Pudding

Pineapple St.
Clark
Clark St. M
Pierrepont
Willow

EAST RIVER

BROOKLYN HEIGHTS
Tillary
Pl.
Tech
Jay
Adams

GOVERNORS ISLAND

BROOKLYN BRIDGE PARK

Montague
Remsen
Joralemon
State
Congress
Columbia

St.
Court St M
Jay St-Metro Tech M
Fulton
Willo

6

Atlantic
✕ ✕ Colonie
✕ Waterfalls Café
Court St- Borough Hall M
Schermerhorn

✕ Hibino
Pacific
Amity
COBBLE HILL
Clinton
✿ ✕ ✕ Ki Sushi
Nu Hotel ✿
Hoyt/ Schermerhorn M
Chef's Ta Brooklyn
Mile En

✕ Pok Pok
Kane
✿ ✕ ✕ La Vara
✕ Brucie
✕ ✕ Saul
Wyckoff
Dean
Bergen St M
Char No. 4 ✕
Bergen Ru

DeGraw
Van Horn Sandwich Shop ✕
BO

✕ ✕ Alma
Union
✕ Strong Place
Butler
● Clover Club ▤

President
Carroll
Summit
Woodhull
Sackett
✕ The Grocery
DeGraw
Douglass
✕ Jolie Cantina ✕
● Battersby ✿ ✕
Baltic

✕ Enoteca on Court
Union St.
● Savoia
Butler

CARROLL GARDENS
Carroll St M
✕ ✕ Seersucker
President
Carroll

2nd Pl.
1st
✕ Frankies 457 Spuntino
3rd Pl.
2nd St.
1st St.
Bond
Nevins St
Carroll

COFFEY PARK
W. 9th St.
✿ ✕ Prime Meats
✕ Buttermilk Channel
4th St.

✕ Fort Defiance
● The Good Fork ✿ ✕
RED HOOK
W. 9th St.
Smith-9 St M
9th
✕ Stone Pa

RED HOOK PLAYGROUND
Bush St.
Lorraine
GOWANUS
10th St.
11th
12th St.
13th St.
4 Av-9 St M
5th
✕ Belleville
✕ Juventino

SOUTH
SLOPE

Gowanus Canal
16th St
18th
19th
20th
21st
Prospect
Prospect Av M
14th St.
15th

Gowanus Bay

✕ Café Stei
✕ Fond
▤ Beer Table
✕ Thistle Hill Taver
✕

A · B

436

C

Navy
Yard
Basin

egar
House

BROOKLYN NAVY YARD

INDUSTRIAL PARK

D

Broadway

Flushing Av

St.

Flushing

Flushing

Queens

Ave.

Myrtle
Willoughby Aves

FORT
GREENE

FORT
GREENE
PARK

SoCo

Umi Nom

Black
Swan

Bedford-
Nostrand Aves

The General
Greene

Roman's

CLINTON HILL

Clinton Av-
Washington Av

Classon Av

Speedy
Romeo

Berlyn

No. 7

Do or Dine

BROOKLYN
ACADEMY

Atlantic Terminal (LIRR)

Lafayette
Av

Locanda
Vini & Olii

Atlantic Av

Atlantic Av

Clinton Av-
Washington Av

Fulton
Nostrand Av

PROSPECT

The
Vanderbilt

Thirstbarávin

ooklyn
n Camp

Franny's

James

HEIGHTS

606 R & D

Santo
di Là

PARK

Grand Army
Plaza

Chavela's

SLOPE

Moim

Bar Corvo

Eastern Pkwy-
Brooklyn Museum

Franklin Av-
Botanic Garden

Nostrand Av

Sterling St

BROOKLYN
MUSEUM

BROOKLYN
BOTANIC
GARDEN

lewood

PROSPECT

PARK

C

D

437

Al di Là

Italian ✗

248 Fifth Ave. (at Carroll St.)

Subway: Union St   Lunch & dinner daily
Phone: 718-783-4565
Web: www.aldilatrattoria.com
Prices: $$

This Park Slope fixture serves up delectable Venetian-inspired cuisine in an unbeatably charming setting run by husband-and-wife team Emiliano Coppa and Chef Anna Klinger.

Church pew seating, a blown glass chandelier, and a scattering of whimsical touches dress the high-ceilinged room where neighborhood folk and foodies from afar dine on the likes of shaved wintry white vegetables–celery root, parsnip, cauliflower, and endive–tossed with champagne vinaigrette, a vibrant hit of black pepper and *castelmagno* cheese; or pastas such as dense and chewy ricotta *cavatelli* dressed with Parmesan, lemon, wilted radicchio, kale, and crowned by a dollop of whipped ricotta.

Around the corner, Al di Là Vino proffers a wine bar experience with a similar menu.

Allswell

Gastropub ✗

124 Bedford Ave. (at N. 10th St.)

Subway: Bedford Av   Lunch & dinner daily
Phone: 347-799-2743
Web: N/A
Prices: $$

Allswell's menu changes nightly and offers solid, often vibrant cooking that would be an attraction all its own, even if the chef weren't known for having previously manned the stoves at the Spotted Pig. This comfortable Williamsburg tavern boasts walls embellished with a patchwork of vintage wallpaper framed by polished wood slats, a communal table prettied with flowers, and a wall-mounted blackboard menu. Small plates might range from showcasing seasonal vegetables, as in cardoon and kale toast to a whole grilled quail slicked with red chili and rosemary vinaigrette, perched atop a nest of shredded purple cabbage and batons of green garlic. Larger entrées have included pork *piccata* doused with lemon and caper-sparked butter sauce.

Alma

Mexican ✖✖

A6

187 Columbia St. (at Degraw St.)

Subway: Carroll St
Phone: 718-643-5400
Web: www.almarestaurant.com
Prices: $$

Lunch Sat – Sun
Dinner nightly

It might be a hassle to get to Alma via public transportation, but this contemporary Mexican charmer is well worth the hike to its increasingly food-savvy Carroll Gardens-meets-Red Hook Brooklyn neighborhood, with priceless views of lower Manhattan and area ship yards.

Duck into the Degraw St. entrance (the Columbia St. entrance takes you through the rollicking bar), and head upstairs. There, a sangria jar welcomes you to the whimsically appointed dining room with wide-plank floors and enormous rooftop dining area (covered in winter). After you start with a generous helping of the guacamole chockablock with avocados, move onto *hongos*—pan-fried, thickly sliced mushrooms with caramelized onions, chili, and *hoja santa* leaves, topped with Oaxaca cheese.

Am Thai Bistro

Thai ✖

B3

1003 Church Ave. (bet. 10th St. & Stratford Rd.)

Subway: Church Av (18th St.)
Phone: 718-287-8888
Web: www.amthaibistro.com
Prices:

Lunch & dinner daily

Despite the many flourishing Thai restaurants in the city, the choices in this gentrifying nook of Brooklyn are few. So, when this sweet and attractive spot showed up, people took notice. The decor is spare with dark walnut tables and a dash of modern Asian accents, but toward the back, a festive spirit looms large via fuchsia lights set against a silver background tracing an outline of Thailand in gold.

The traditional, well-crafted Thai menu may unveil the likes of *yum yum* shrimp tossed with pickled garlic, peanuts, fish sauce, and fresh herbs that deliver a spectrum of sour, sweet, tart and pungent flavors; fluffy bistro *roti* with massaman curry; or grilled *e-sarn* pork, crunchy, decadent, and deliciously offset by a chili-lime glaze.

Anella

Contemporary 🍴

B1

222 Franklin St. (bet. Green & Huron Sts.)

Subway: Greenpoint Av   Lunch & dinner daily
Phone: 718-389-8100
Web: www.anellabrooklyn.com
Prices: $$

Tucked away in Greenpoint, just a few blocks from the East River, Anella hosts diners in an intimate rough and tumble space boasting a sliver of a dining room, a charming back patio, and a welcoming bar fashioned out of a reclaimed work bench from the Steinway & Sons piano factory.

The kitchen is on display and sends forth a menu of ambitious creations, beginning with a loaf of bread freshly baked and served in a clay flowerpot. Smoke was a recent inspiration as seen in a slice of brisket afloat in a lusciously fluid risotto of spinach and garlic. Other preparations have included seared striped bass paired with lentils and cauliflower that was roasted and whirled into a purée; and a finale of apple *crémeux* atop almond cake sided by rum ice cream.

An Nhau

Vietnamese 🍴

C3

172 Bedford Ave. (bet. N. 7th & N. 8th Sts.)

Subway: Bedford Av   Dinner nightly
Phone: 718-384-0028
Web: N/A
Prices: 💰

Set along busy Bedford Avenue, this everyday Vietnamese restaurant is located alongside sister spot Banh Mi, a takeout shop specializing in the famed namesake sandwich. An Nhau offers table service in a room outfitted by wooden shutters, mirrors, and a wall decked with a big, delightful mural of a Vietnamese street scene.

Begin the affair with rolls and salads and make your way through the menu's home-style cooking featuring enjoyably aromatic preparations as well as numerous variations of the classic *pho*. Other delectable entrées include *bun*—lemongrass, garlic, and mint scented meats served over cool rice vermicelli; and pork belly braised in a sweet and savory coconut water-based broth, served with a hard boiled egg and pickled mustard greens.

Applewood

Contemporary

C8

501 11th St. (bet. Seventh & Eighth Aves.)

Subway: 7 Av (9th St.)
Phone: 718-788-1810
Web: www.applewoodny.com
Prices: $$

Lunch Sat – Sun
Dinner Tue – Sat

 Skillfully prepared cuisine and a dainty setting reflect the seriousness of Applewood's owners, David and Laura Shea. The pair is committed to promoting the work of organic and local farmers in a changing menu of small plates and entrées dedicated to reflecting the seasons.

The spare yet comfortable dining room, set in a century-old townhouse on a tree-lined street, is furnished with honey-toned wood tables and spindleback chairs. When in use, a working fireplace warms the light-colored room, accented by the work of local artists.

Starters like house-made charcuterie with garlic crostini and stone-ground mustard set the tone for an enjoyable meal that might feature Vermont lamb with French green lentils, Delicata squash, and buttermilk vinaigrette.

Aurora

Italian

C3

70 Grand St. (at Wythe Ave.)

Subway: Bedford Av
Phone: 718-388-5100
Web: www.auroraristorante.com
Prices: 🍝🍝

Lunch & dinner daily

 This charming trattoria has long been a popular dining choice for residents of this dynamic stretch of Williamsburg. Stocked with wood furnishings, the rustic brick and plaster room is dressed up with vintage knickknacks and features a pretty ivy-covered outdoor area that doubles the seating capacity of the corner setting.

Aurora's enjoyable Italian cuisine speaks to the power of simplicity with minimally dressed market greens, expertly prepared pastas, and roasted meats. One can't go wrong with a meal of plump house-made sausage with lightly sautéed broccoli rabe and pickled Calabrian pepper; silky agnolotti stuffed with ricotta, spring peas, and fresh mint; or *affogato* with chocolate-crumb-coated vanilla gelato, all offered at impressive value.

Baci & Abbracci

Brooklyn

Italian ✗

C4

204 Grand St. (bet. Bedford & Driggs Sts.)

Subway: Bedford Av
Phone: 718-599-6599
Web: www.baciny.com
Prices: $$

Lunch Sat – Sun
Dinner nightly

This upbeat Williamsburg eatery features Italian cuisine with a wholehearted emphasis on pizza. With more than twenty permutations of pies baked in their wood-burning oven from Naples, these smoky-chewy crusts may be the foundation for sauce and freshly made mozzarella, or even *focaccia tartufata*—two thin layers filled with robiola cheese and topped with truffle oil. Beyond this, the adept kitchen also boasts homemade bread, enjoyable pastas, and an impressive short-list of *secondi* like juicy lamb chops with a crisp potato-rosemary crust.

The intimate space sports a contemporary design framed by a concrete floor, sleek furnishings, and glazed-tile accents. A charming little patch of backyard makes an especially popular setting for weekend brunch.

Bamboo Garden

Chinese ✗

A4

6409 Eighth Ave. (at 64th St.)

Subway: 8 Av
Phone: 718-238-1122
Web: N/A
Prices:

Lunch & dinner daily

This bustling establishment confirms that there is impressive dim sum to be found in Brooklyn. The large setting may look a bit tattered but it is clean and boasts a generous number of large, round, linen-draped tables; during the day the space is jam-packed with a gregarious flock of local residents.

The tables are attended to by Cantonese-speaking ladies, dressed in fuchsia blouses and red vests, pushing carts of steaming treats through the hungry hordes. Resist the urge to stock your table all at once; survey the delicacies and pace yourself for a spectrum of fresh, delish dumplings, buns, and pastries. The feast also includes some refreshingly unique preparations (perhaps braised tofu with salted fish?) that steer away from the standard lineup.

Bar Corvo

Italian

D8

791 Washington Ave. (bet. Lincoln & St John's Pls.)

Subway: Eastern Pkwy - Brooklyn Museum
Phone: 718-230-0940
Web: www.barcorvo.com
Prices: $$

Lunch Sat – Sun
Dinner nightly

Bar Corvo brings an inspired Italian menu to this rather bleak Brooklyn stretch. A comfortable marble-topped bar is a great place from which to watch this theatrical show of flaming kitchen burners. However, the exterior is anything but flashy. Peek through glass panes for signs of the deliciousness that waits inside.

Diners line the slim entrance in anticipation of a seat within this outdated yet jaunty nest. Quirky touches like distressed wall paper and floors crafted out of pretty penny tiles serve to elevate the pleasure after a warm salad tossing farro, roasted cauliflower, and Brussels sprouts; or ricotta *cavatelli* robust with wild mushrooms. Braised lamb shank with fava beans makes for a fantastic comfort food finale.

Battersby

Contemporary

B7

255 Smith St. (bet. Degraw & Douglas Sts.)

Subway: Bergen St (Smith St.)
Phone: 718-852-8321
Web: www.battersbybrooklyn.com
Prices: $$

Dinner Tue – Sun

Squeezed within the bevy of options lining well-endowed Smith Street, this new kid on the block has swiftly made its presence known. Run by a pair of culinary school buddies, each with his own impressive pedigree, the petite dining room is minimally dressed but boasts finer touches: a confidently versed staff and excellent china show off the accomplished cooking and give the setting palpable sophistication.

The crew works in a tight yet tidy corner, sending forth savory preparations such as silken polenta soup poured tableside into rock shrimp and sofrito; veal sweetbreads meunière astutely paired with luscious Caesar dressing and whole romaine leaves; and chocolate-caramel tart with perfectly whipped local cream. Each dish glows with creative charm.

Beer Table

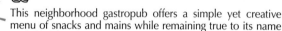

B8 · Gastropub 🍴

427 B Seventh Ave. (bet. 14th & 15th Sts.)

Subway: 7 Av (9th St.)
Phone: 718-965-1196
Web: www.beertable.com
Prices: 😊

Lunch Sat – Sun
Dinner nightly

This neighborhood gastropub offers a simple yet creative menu of snacks and mains while remaining true to its name and focus with a rotating selection of draft beers. The attentive staff offers sage advice about the extensive and wisely organized beer list (lighter at the top, darker towards the bottom). The charming space is dominated by three communal tables and shelves of house-made pickles.

The menu is heavy on beer-friendly nibbles designed to pair nicely with rare brews from a spicy Belgian Christmas ale to the hoppy pale ales. Beer Table may host events like Date Night and Family meal during the early part of the week, but this cozy establishment consistently pleases with the likes of roasted corn with lime mayonnaise; *posole*; or grasshopper pie.

Belleville

B8 · French 🍴

330 5th St. (at Fifth Ave.)

Subway: 4 Av - 9 St
Phone: 718-832-9777
Web: www.bellevillebistro.com
Prices: 😊

Lunch Sat – Sun
Dinner nightly

With windows that fly open to sidewalk seating along Brooklyn's bustling Fifth Avenue; a gaggle of closely nuzzled tables with mismatched wooden chairs; and vintage mirrored walls, Belleville could easily be plucked straight off the streets of the Parisian neighborhood it's named after. Luckily for us, it's right here in Park Slope—serving up delicious bistro staples like duck confit and steak frites to neighborhood families.

Kick things off with a fresh beet salad drizzled with tart vinaigrette and topped with crumbles of soft, creamy goat cheese; and then move on to a spot-on coq au vin with plump lardons and tender sautéed mushrooms plated with a fluffy pile of mashed potatoes; or creamy lemon custard served in a dainty espresso cup.

Berlyn

German   🍴

C6

25 Lafayette Ave. (bet. Ashland Pl. & St. Felix St.)

Subway: Atlantic Av   Dinner Tue – Sun
Phone: 718-222-5800
Web: www.berlynrestaurant.com
Prices: $$

Follow the trail of breadcrumbs straight into Berlyn for a taste of something spaetzle. This German restaurant charms with a dark wood bar, moody blue walls, creaky floors, and gnomes (yes, gnomes) decorating the place. A year-round patio is an added bonus. The mood is upbeat, due in large part to the pre-theater crowds (BAM is directly across the street), so those seeking a leisurely pace best check theater times to avoid the masses rushing to catch a show.

The food is equally cheery with such favorites as juicy fried meatballs slathered in a rich sweet onion and briny caper gravy, and the *käsespaetzle*, which may well be the German equivalent of mac and cheese. Get your Gretel on and go for the gingerbread pudding—moist and redolent of warm spices.

Black Swan

American   🍴

D6

1048 Bedford Ave. (bet. Clifton & Lafayette Sts.)

Subway: Bedford - Nostrand Avs   Lunch & dinner daily
Phone: 718-783-4744
Web: www.blackswannyc.com
Prices: $$

This hot spot on an up-and-coming stretch of Bedford Avenue in Bed-Stuy is more than just a neighborhood pub. It has all the makings of a beloved bar–the comfort, warmth, and good vibes–but rocks a fantastic menu to boot. Slip into one of the dark wood booths or hang at a communal table and let the food and beer begin.

A good starting place is a bowlful of delectable mussels, plump and cooked in a mustard-cream sauce, served with crispy fries; or perhaps a plate of soul-comforting mac and cheese, with orecchiette pasta and jalapeño. Burger lovers are in for a serious treat: this excellent rendition, made with Piccini Brothers beef and available with all manner of sides (bacon, avocado, goat cheese, fried egg) is one of the best bets around.

Blanca ✿

C2

261 Moore St. (bet. Bogart & White Sts.)

Subway: Morgan Av

Dinner Wed – Sat

Phone: 646-703-2715
Web: www.blancanyc.com
Prices: $$$$

Anthony Falco

From ham-and-pineapple pizza to crispy veal sweetbreads with savory key lime custard, Chef Carlo Mirarchi has come a long way. Ensconced within the burgeoning Bushwick compound that is Roberta's, Blanca is an entirely separate destination. This test kitchen-cum-fabulous dining counter seats twelve and offers each a close-up exhibit of some pretty amazing skill and ingenuity.

The servers are just as passionate as the kitchen, and appropriately chillax in accordance with the establishment's locality. And how's this for ambience? Guests at *chez* Mirarchi are invited to choose their own tunes from a stack of vinyl records that can be played on the stereo turntable.

Initially, diners were asked to keep this place under wraps, but it was nearly impossible not to croon about the tasting menu that sprang forth in the form of raw Japanese needlefish clutching slivers of green almond; seared sablefish slicked with pumpernickel and *oro blanco* grapefruit vinaigrette; explosive *nduja*-filled ravioli sparked by orange, chili, and mint; and roasted *poulet rouge* draped in a deliciously crisped skin. Chickpea shortbread and goat's milk ice cream with rhubarb marmalade brings the meal to a stellar finish.

Bozu

Japanese

296 Grand St. (bet. Havemeyer & Roebling Sts.)

Subway: Bedford Av   Dinner nightly
Phone: 718-384-7770
Web: www.oibozu.com
Prices:

An enticing selection of Japanese tapas–with many pleasing vegetarian options–is buttressed by a gracious staff and laid-back vibe at this upbeat, hip, and tasty spot. The slim wood and brick space is dressed in grey and installed with an L-shaped counter, a row of tables, and back patio. Brings friends and order a lot.

The sushi bar tempts with the yakko roll filled with silken house-made tofu and green onion; spicy mushroom roll dabbed with tomatillo puree; and *gunkanzushi* topped with sweet sea scallop and plump salmon roe alongside soy sauce pre-seasoned with wasabi. Cooked dishes bring on the likes of deep fried *gyoza* filled with tomato, and fantastically intense nuggets of fried chicken thigh marinated for 48 hours in garlic and soy sauce.

Brooklyn Fish Camp

Seafood

162 Fifth Ave. (bet. Degraw & Douglass Sts.)

Subway: Union St   Lunch & dinner daily
Phone: 718-783-3264
Web: www.brooklynfishcamp.com
Prices: $$

Inspired by the simplicity of rural Southern fish shacks, this Park Slope offshoot of Mary's Fish Camp reveres its mighty seafood, made with downhome talent.

The welcoming bar upfront leads to a dining room furnished with little more than warm-hued wood tables topped with brown paper mats and bags of oyster crackers. Out back, picnic tables and folding chairs make a fine setting for a summertime meal, accompanied by movies shown on a whitewashed wall. Servers are engaging and rockabilly-chic.

The new chef's fresh hand preserves the sanctity of the house classics (like lobster roll), while introducing tasty creations like crisp-skinned Walleye pike paired with bacon- and chicken liver-studded dirty wild rice and a pan sauce of Tabasco, butter, and citrus.

Brooklyn Star

D4

593 Lorimer St. (at Conselyea St.)

Subway: Lorimer St - Metropolitan Av

Phone: 718-599-9899

Web: www.thebrooklynstar.com

Prices: $$

Lunch Sat – Sun
Dinner nightly

Hooray for Brooklyn Star 2.0. The demise of the original was gut-wrenching—this hand-built restaurant was razed by a fire in 2010. But, perhaps a blessing in disguise? Because a just as alluring incarnation has sprouted nearby. The fresh setting heralds diners with a bar and dining room enlivened with a brick red terrazzo floor, eggshell walls, and chunky blonde wood tables topped with hot sauce, pepper vinegar, and wild flowers.

Chef Joaquin Baca's love letter to old-fashioned, down home specialties may reveal a green bean casserole coalesced by mushroom béchamel and showered with buttery crumbs and fried shallots; a hunk of a sandwich—warm bacon-wrapped meatloaf stuffed between thick slices of Pullman bread; and excellent buttermilk biscuits.

Brucie

B6

234 Court St. (bet. Baltic & Kane Sts.)

Subway: Bergen St (Smith St.)

Phone: 347-987-4961

Web: www.brucienyc.com

Prices: $$

Lunch & dinner Tue – Sat

With its nostalgia-hued vibe, Brucie is a welcome addition to the neighborhood. Housed in a former sushi den, the space now sports a considerably rustic scene devised by communal seating, a copper dining counter, and a corner designated for pasta prep.

The menu's old-world inspiration bears a new-world sensibility in its range of Italian specialties that reflect a product-driven commitment. "Smalls" feature olive oil-packed tuna crostini fashioned from slices of Caputo bakery bread, aïoli, and orange *fritti*. "Biggies" include a hearty hunk of lasagna—like a seasonal layering of ground lamb, butternut squash, and Parmesan-seasoned béchamel.

The Cobble Hill spot also functions as a market, proffering an assortment of goodies to take home.

Buttermilk Channel

American ✗

B7

524 Court St. (at Huntington St.)

Subway: Smith - 9 Sts.
Phone: 718-852-8490
Web: www.buttermilkchannelnyc.com
Prices: **$$**

Lunch Sat – Sun
Dinner nightly

Glossy, dark paint and large windows emanating a warm glow give this establishment an inviting, turn-of-the-century maritime feel. This befits its name, which references the (once crossable) strait separating Brooklyn from Governor's Island. The butter-yellow dining room attracts a lively and diverse crowd; regardless of one's tastes, the menu is bound to please, thanks to this very serious team of experienced professionals.

The menu begins with snacks like handmade mozzarella with basil and warm anchovy sauce, house-made charcuterie, and farmstead cheeses—perfect accompaniments to a local brew. The full offering of seasonal comfort food complements a separate (equally impressive) menu devoted to vegetarians. Mondays offer three courses for $25.

Cadaqués

Spanish

C4

188 Grand St. (bet. Bedford & Driggs Aves.)

Subway: Bedford Av
Phone: 718-218-7776
Web: www.cadaquesny.com
Prices: **$$**

Lunch Sat – Sun
Dinner nightly

Named for the Costa Brava town where legendary Spanish artists, including Dalí, Picasso, and Miró sojourned, this Williamsburg tapas bar exhibits talent and creativity in its array of plates that are alluded to as modern Catalan. The copious selection snares hungry eyes and pleases sharp palates with a tasty show of skill: *plancha*-griddled *pan con tomate* rubbed with garlic and topped with freshly grated tomato; decadently thick, ivory white *sopa de almendras* drizzled with olive oil and balsamic vinegar; fried artichokes capped by fennel pollen aïoli; and delightfully tender octopus dressed with a pool of ink and crunchy, cool avocado fritters. The slender room is chic; done up with a galvanized metal ceiling (hung with linen pendants) and reclaimed wood.

Café Steinhof

B8

Austrian ✗

422 Seventh Ave. (at 14th St.)

Subway: 7 Av (9th St.)
Phone: 718-369-7776
Web: www.cafesteinhof.com
Prices: 🍴🍴

Lunch Tue – Sun
Dinner nightly

Austrian flavors abound at this winsome Park Slope café. Dominating the space is an affable bar, where a selection of beers on draught, generously measured libations, and fruit brandies are poured; and any of these would be a fine accompaniment to the traditional and hearty Central European cooking. Dark wood furnishings and old-timey signage promoting Austrian provisions hung on the walls frame the space. The scene is more laid-back during the day but just as enjoyable.

Small plates and house specialties, all imbued with old world relish, include the likes of golden chicken consommé with crepe slivers and chives; black sausage strudel; tender bread dumplings with wild mushroom fricassee; and chicken in paprika-seasoned cream sauce.

Calyer 🐣

B1

Contemporary ✗

92 Calyer St. (at Franklin St.)

Subway: Greenpoint Av
Phone: 347-889-6323
Web: www.calyerbrooklyn.com
Prices: $$

Lunch Sat – Sun
Dinner Wed – Mon

Run by the team behind Anella, this welcome Greenpoint arrival serves up an unabashed menu of small plates in a provincial tavern, styled to evoke the neighborhood's history of wood shipbuilding.

An amuse bouche of fried plantain chips with spicy tomatillo salsa and pickled mustard seeds is an enthusiastic nod to the chef's native Puerto Rico and provides a stimulating start. The menu conveniently progresses from lighter to heavier dishes, perhaps beginning with poached parsnips with smoked yogurt and savory granola—bold yet finessed. Shards of *chicharrónes* slicked with anchovy vinaigrette adrift in white bean purée might lead into a trio of chicken: braised thigh, grilled livers, and crisply rendered skin with pickled peppercorn-spiked jus.

Celestino

Seafood 🍴

C2

562 Halsey St. (at Stuyvesant Ave.)

Subway: Utica Av
Phone: 347-787-3564
Web: N/A
Prices: $$

Dinner Tue – Sun

Those on Brooklyn's culinary vanguard know about Celestino and its trailblazing owner Massimiliano Nanni, but the secret is now getting out. Not many would pick this seemingly out-of-the-way spot in Bed-Stuy with its barely burgeoning restaurant scene, but one bite and naysayers are forgotten.
The whitewashed brick walls sparsely decorated with lobster traps and fishing nets suit the concise, piscine-focused menu. Italian servers shuck oysters at the bar and shuffle dishes that begin with simple and classic plates of prosecco-marinated sardines, tender cuttlefish over creamy polenta, and spaghetti topped with mussels in a white wine broth. Light and delicious crêpes are ingenious when filled with a wonderfully unique and rich seafood ragù.

Char No. 4 😊

Gastropub 🍴

B6

196 Smith St. (bet. Baltic & Warren Sts.)

Subway: Bergen St (Smith St.)
Phone: 718-643-2106
Web: www.charno4.com
Prices: $$

Lunch Fri – Sun
Dinner nightly

More shrine than pub, this Smith Street watering hole offers a massive listing of whiskey, half of which are devoted to Bourbon—a must for all "brown" fans. All are available in one or two ounce pours, allowing a civilized examination of the elixir's varied styles. The comfy bar radiates warmth with its wall of amber-filled bottles; and the slender dining room in the back, also dressed in brown, fits the mien.
The Southern-flecked menu unveils such decadent delights as grilled flatiron steak with warm bacon-poblano salad and onion-beer marmalade. Weekend brunch brings an inexpensive prix-fixe, perhaps a poached egg trimmed with house-smoked brown sugar ham, buttermilk biscuit, and cheddar grits. Coffee and tea are included (but not Bourbon).

451

Chavela's 😋

Mexican ✗

D7

736 Franklin Ave. (at Sterling Pl.)

Subway: Franklin St
Phone: 718-622-3100
Web: www.chavelasnyc.com
Prices: 😊😊

Lunch & dinner daily

Behold the gorgeous, sea-green dome perched on a sparse corner of Franklin Avenue, directly above the wrought-iron entrance that leads into this lively gem of a spot. Inside, a burst of colorful Mexican tiles blanket the dark wood bar, where wrought-iron candle chandeliers dangle from high tin ceilings. Exposed brick and deep red walls showcase ceramic butterflies, iron mirrors, and gold window hangings.

Perfectly made Mexican classics are the name of the game here at Chavela's, which is slowly emerging as a neighborhood treasure. Scrumptious *papas con chorizo*–corn tortillas stuffed with potato, chorizo, shredded cabbage, pickled jalapeños, and *crema fresca*–are a good starting place. Or try the *sopa de tortilla*, a robust soup of chicken and tomatillos.

Clover Club

American 🍽

B6

210 Smith St. (bet. Baltic & Butler Sts.)

Subway: Bergen St (Smith St.)
Phone: 718-855-7939
Web: www.cloverclubny.com
Prices: $$

Lunch Tue – Sun
Dinner nightly

A former shoe store is now an atmospheric Smith Street rest stop that fashions a spot-on vintage vibe with mosaic tiled floors, glove-soft leather banquettes, and pressed-tin ceilings dangling etched-glass pendants that glow as warmly as single malt. The glossy mahogany bar (furnished with leather-upholstered bar stools) is overseen by a natty bartender artfully shaking and pouring a stellar selection of libations like the namesake Clover Club—a mixture of gin, dry vermouth, lemon, and raspberry syrup.

An excellent menu of savory bites is a perfect counterpoint to such liquid indulgences, with herb-marinated hanger steak over toasted baguette with horseradish cream, duck fat-fried potato crisps, oysters on the half-shell, or an American caviar service.

Chef's Table at Brooklyn Fare ✿ ✿ ✿

Contemporary ✗✗

B6

200 Schermerhorn St. (bet. Bond & Hoyt Sts.)

Dinner Tue – Sat

Subway: Hoyt-Schermerhorn
Phone: 718-243-0050
Web: www.brooklynfare.com
Prices: $$$$

Emma Chao

This Chef's Table is something of a wonderland, though here your journey begins behind the Wizard's curtain, at the dining counter and face-to-face with Chef Cesar Ramirez. Authoritarian, bespectacled, and brilliant, he is not so much running a restaurant as a professional kitchen worth every one of the million dollars that built it. The space sparkles with copper pots, stainless steel counters, and the beatific smiles of 18 very lucky patrons.

Seating is communal, there are no menus, and descriptions are minimal at best. Whether the barrage of dishes results from the chef's stream of consciousness or divine rapture is unclear, but each taste seems untouchable and classic. The opening salvo may be a rich, foamy shot of soup layering orange and yogurt, or a signature, the sardine and sage "potato chip." Following this, sample a head-spinning array of seafood-focused plates, from arctic char with fresh roe and the tiny explosion of finger lime beads, to a dashi-simmered bite of octopus and heart of palm dabbed with a mouth-numbing touch of *sansho* pepper.

Some moments may tempt you to halt your meal, linger, and preserve each taste, but stay strong. There may be twenty more courses to come.

Colonie

 B6

127 Atlantic Ave. (bet. Clinton & Henry Sts.)

Subway: Borough Hall
Phone: 718-855-7500
Web: www.colonienyc.com
Prices: $$

Lunch Sat – Sun
Dinner nightly

Among Atlantic Avenue's flurry of Middle Eastern fare, tavern grub, and faux Mexican is this shining jewel serving up mouthwatering goodies to the fine folks of Brooklyn Heights and points beyond. Flickering candles, exposed brick, and distressed wood set the scene in the row-house slender room that is routinely packed tight with a devoted crowd. It may be loud but the service team is outstanding.

The kitchen is on display for all to see, and those seated at the counter will feel especially up close. Get to it with some snacks like oysters or some crostini, say Maine shrimp with lemon oil and chives before moving on to smoked ricotta *gnudi* with deep-fried broccoli florets and pinto beans; or seared tilefish with wilted kale and *bottarga*.

Cupola Samarkanda

 B4

1797 McDonald Ave. (at Ave. P)

Subway: Avenue P
Phone: 718-375-7777
Web: N/A
Prices: $$

Lunch & dinner Tue – Sun

To say that this feels like a glitzy invention by Tony Manero–the star character from *Saturday Night Fever* with a fancy for Brooklyn discos–is surely no exaggeration. Nor is it an exaggeration to claim that here you'll find some of the most memorable *mantes* in the city. The lights are flickering, the keyboard wants tuning, and the back-up singer is wobbly, but this is precisely what makes Cupola Samarkanda so desirable and bizarre and fun.

Among the local Georgians, Uzbeks, and Azerbaijani denizens, this gem offers perfect bites of home in the form of *cheburek*, plump, subliminal layers of flaky dough filled with cheese; and *geez-beez*, a classic sauté of tender, shining liver served in a "bowl" of cracker-like dough and crowned with onion rings.

Diner

American ✗

C4

85 Broadway (at Berry St.)

Subway: Marcy Av
Phone: 718-486-3077
Web: www.dinernyc.com
Prices: $$

Lunch & dinner daily

Do not let Diner's impossibly hip crowd and rather ramshackle setting deter you. Beneath all that plaid are ordinary folk who appreciate the renovated 1920s Kulman Diner setting and an impressively unfussy kitchen that knows how to make a perfect block of head cheese. Originally founded by the pioneering restaurateurs and publishers of *Diner Journal*, this establishment has been run with heart and personality since 1998.

Grass-fed steaks and burgers are a mainstay, but the bulk of the impressively prepared menu is inspired by the season and changes daily. The kitchen uses spot-on technique in dishes such as rabbit confit salad with rabbit pâté toast; or lamb steak with charred leek purée, fennel potato salad, and horseradish crème fraîche dressing.

Dish

Japanese ✗

A4

9208 3rd Ave. (bet. 92nd & 93rd Sts.)

Subway: Bay Ridge - 95 St
Phone: 718-238-2323
Web: www.dishbayridge.com
Prices: $$

Lunch Sat – Sun
Dinner Tue – Sun

Here in Bay Ridge, people just like this place. Attractive, with a classically minimalist Japanese design, Dish is easy to love. It turns out that bamboo grows in Brooklyn; stalks decorate one side of the dining room.

At first glance, the menu looks standard Japanese, with starters like negimaki and yakitori, but there are a few departures, such as barbecue scallop skewers with bacon. Starters like hot and spicy seafood soup showcase their very fine tuna, jumbo shrimp, and mackerel in a clear, piquant broth. Sushi features the usual suspects and rolls are creative, if at times slightly too much so. They also fire up the stove to prepare the likes of lobster teriyaki, Chilean sea bass with miso, and filet mignon with red wine sauce.

455

Do or Dine 😬

D6

1108 Bedford Ave. (bet. Lexington Ave. & Quincy St.)

Subway: Bedford - Nostrand Avs
Phone: 718-684-2290
Web: N/A
Prices: $$

Lunch Sun
Dinner nightly

It's like the mafia of Michelin-starred runaways at Do-or Dine, where made men from The Modern and Daniel have decamped to slum it, Bed-Stuy-style. Finding this place will try the patience of a saint, but here's a hint: look for the awning heralding West Indian takeout. This renegade establishment is bedecked with decoupage tabletops, black and white mosaic tile floor, and a disco-ball spinning above.

The "one fish two fish" charred sardine starter pitched with capers, toasted hazelnuts, and mizuna; and "pork renderloin", cooked in duck fat, fanned across sweet-and-sour braised red cabbage and paired with roasted apple ensconced in wasabi marshmallow are just two examples of the *buonissima cucina* that emerges from the tiny kitchen.

DuMont

D4

432 Union Ave. (bet. Devoe St. & Metropolitan Ave.)

Subway: Lorimer St - Metropolitan Av
Phone: 718-486-7717
Web: www.dumontrestaurant.com
Prices: $$

Lunch & dinner daily

DuMont–which got its name from a salvaged neon sign for the pioneering television network–epitomizes its neighborhood's relaxed, edgy, and creative vibe. The multi-room space is warm and comfortably worn, with dark wood tables topped in brown paper, vintage tile floor, and leather seating handmade by the owner, Colin Devlin. There is also a backyard with elevated seating called "the treehouse."

Executive Chef Polo Dobkin (of Dressler) fuels crowds of Billyburg hipsters who clamor for his near-addictive comfort food menu. Favorites may include lamb meatballs with braised Tuscan kale; roasted chicken with red wine sauce; and of course, the DuMac and cheese. Brunch keeps weekends groovy.

For a quick burger and a beer, try nearby DuMont Burger.

Dressler ✿

C4

149 Broadway (bet. Bedford & Driggs Aves.)

Subway: Marcy Av
Phone: 718-384-6343
Web: www.dresslernyc.com
Prices: $$

Lunch Sun
Dinner nightly

Stephanie Lempert

Dressler is a study in contrasts, yet remains a lovely experience from start to finish. The décor of this haute Williamsburg restaurant is at once masculine and minimal with dark wood furnishings, brick walls, and low lighting; yet feminine and ornate amid elaborate chandeliers, floral etchings, and mosaic-tiled floors.

Touches of Americana, whiffs of the Mediterranean, and a foundation of classic French cuisine weave a delightful tale that is the menu of Chef Polo Dobkin. Inspired appetizers reveal a tentacle of Portuguese octopus, tender chalk-white flesh against a crisped mauve exterior, propped amid tiny beluga lentils studded with finely diced bits of chorizo and sauced with a dash of decadent romesco. The Scottish salmon presented seared skin side up is seasonally streaked with the likes of pan-roasted Brussels sprout leaves, caramelized cauliflower florets, sautéed wild mushrooms, and finished with curry-infused beurre blanc.

Desserts remain a highlight. Try the fresh-from-the-oven financier, delicately crumbly yet moist and super almond-y, laden with slow-roasted apple, crowned by a scoop of toasted almond ice cream, and swelled by a smear of lip-smacking huckleberry purée.

457

East Harbor Seafood Palace

A4

Chinese ✗✗

714-726 65th St. (bet. Seventh & Eighth Aves.)

Subway: 8 Av
Phone: 718-765-0098
Web: N/A
Prices: $$

Lunch & dinner daily

Come for dim sum to this behemoth that rocks with joyful chatter and gleeful moans from tables devouring impressive morsels. *Cha siu bao* (barbecue pork buns); *cha siu soh* (barbecue pork puff pastry); *zha liang* (fried crullers wrapped with *cheung fun* skin); and other treats are stocked on steaming carts that constantly circulate the room.

However, come sundown the setting is sparsely occupied. But that shouldn't deter you from making dinner here a consideration; quite the contrary in fact. The warm welcome is genuine, and suggestions are forthcoming when requested. They may reveal tender stir-fried beef tossed with long beans and cashew nuts; or a succulent sea scallop gently steamed in its shell and topped with chopped garlic-studded glass noodles.

Egg 😊

C3

American ✗

135 N. 5th St. (bet. Bedford Ave. & Berry St.)

Subway: Bedford Av
Phone: 718-302-5151
Web: www.pigandegg.com
Prices: 😊😊

Lunch daily

Boasting that famously laid-back Brooklyn personality, old-fashioned Southern soul, and a daily breakfast that lasts until 6:00 P.M., Egg's slender dining room seems to serve as a remote office for Williamsburg's work-from-home set. We may never know how many bestsellers were conceived here, while downing cups of sustainably-grown coffee or doodling with crayons provided on the paper-topped tables. On weekends, the wait for a table can be lengthy—jot your name on the flipchart stationed outside and be patient.

Days here begin with house-made granola, braised-duck hash, or fresh-baked buttermilk biscuits (perhaps the city's best), slathered in sawmill gravy flecked with pork sausage crumbles, or a vegetarian option with pan-seared mushroom gravy.

El Almacen

Argentinian

D3

557 Driggs Ave. (bet. N. 6th & N. 7th Sts.)

Subway: Bedford Av
Phone: 718-218-7284
Web: www.elalmacennyc.com
Prices: $$

Lunch Sat – Sun
Dinner nightly

This Argentinian grill is a carnivore's delight with its menu of meaty entrées from the grill (*de la parilla*) like the *parrillada* featuring short ribs, ribeye, and chorizo with truffle fries; or the "kitchen" offerings (*de la cocina*) which might include malbec-braised short ribs with sweet potato purée and Brussel sprouts. These hearty offerings are best followed by *dulce de leche* in one of its several guises.

El Almacen, which means general store in Spanish, boasts a dark, rustic, and atmospheric setting replete with creaking wood furnishings, shelves of bric-a-brac, and cast iron skillets mounted on a brick wall. The bar is inviting, amply stocked with wine bottles, and set against a backdrop of creamy white tile warmed by the candlelit room.

Eliá

Greek

A4

8611 Third Ave. (bet. 86th & 87th Sts.)

Subway: 86 St
Phone: 718-748-9891
Web: www.eliarestaurant.com
Prices: $$

Dinner Tue – Sun

Oh my , Mykonos? Nope, it's Bay Ridge, but Eliá's weathered plank floors and whitewashed walls decorated with wooden shutters will have you convinced otherwise. And that's before you have even seen the charming backyard patio.

This sure isn't a weak Greek with plenty of top-of-mind classics (grilled shrimp, octopus) and a few newbies (house-made ravioli filled with shredded braised lamb) thrown in for good measure. Appetizers, like the tender pork ribs marinated in ouzo and roasted with Greek spices, are large enough to count as entrées, but with so many tempting choices, don't stop there. Definitely go for the pan-seared sheep's cheese *saganaki*, doused with a shot of ouzo for (ta-da!) flaming fun. Who doesn't love dinner and a show?

El Mio Cid

50 Starr St. (at Wilson Ave.)

Subway: Jefferson St
Phone: 718-628-8300
Web: www.elmiocidrestaurant.com
Prices: $$

Lunch & dinner daily

Right on a lovely corner in the middle of Bushwick, El Mio Cid is a pleasant surprise. This Spanish charmer dresses up the block with its polished presence—exposed brick walls covered with artist-painted murals of Spanish landscapes. The bar's wraparound seating is definitely a come-and-see-me magnet. Yes, those glass containers filled with addictive sangria blends are definitely calling your name.

Cold and hot tapas run the gamut from tender artichoke hearts and crispy sweetbreads, while stuffed chicken with spinach and cheese is delicious. *Paella Valenciana* is brimming with seafood like mussels, squid, clams, and monkfish as well as a few unusual suspects like lobster and shelled peas thrown in for good measure. Is this Bushwick or Barcelona?

Enoteca on Court

347 Court St. (bet. President & Union Sts.)

Subway: Carroll St
Phone: 718-243-1000
Web: www.enotecaoncourt.com
Prices: ⊕⊕

Lunch & dinner Tue – Sun

From the folks who run the old-school but newly renovated Marco Polo Ristorante located just next door, comes this fresh-hearted take on *la cucina Italiana*. The wine bar-inspired room dishes out wood and brick details and serves as a cozy spot in which to enjoy a long line of snacks that include Italian cheeses, panini, and *marinati* (olives, roasted peppers, or eggplant).

The wood-burning oven is used to prepare the majority of offerings that include baked pastas; *carciofo ripieno* (stuffed artichokes); and an array of pizzas topped with a regionally influenced composition of ingredients. The *spiedini* are worthy of consideration—meaty skewers filled with the likes of house-made sausage, onions, and peppers, finished with red wine reduction.

The Farm on Adderley

American ✗✗

B4

1108 Cortelyou Rd. (bet. 12th St. & Stratford Rd.)

Lunch & dinner daily

Subway: Cortelyou Rd
Phone: 718-287-3101
Web: www.thefarmonadderley.com
Prices: $$

Lots of love flows from breakfast to dinner into this trailblazing Ditmas Park hotspot, where streams of devotees and a whip-smart team with a soaring vision and eco-conscious philosophy keep the place humming. The welcoming digs are decked in exposed brick, wood-paneled walls and simple bare wood tables, while the sweet outdoor garden is punched up with murals and greenery.

Try the likes of homemade tagliatelle, lightly coated with a creamy pesto of mushrooms, walnuts, and parmesan; the signature Farm burger, topped with cheddar, on a toasted English muffin alongside fries and pickles; or the fantastic pan-roasted fluke with baby carrots, spinach, and cumin-butter. End with the delightful goat-cheesecake ganache, topped with red wine-poached pears.

Fonda

Mexican ✗

B8

434 Seventh Ave. (bet. 14th & 15th Sts.)

Lunch Sat – Sun
Dinner Tue – Sun

Subway: 7 Av (9th St.)
Phone: 718-369-3144
Web: www.fondarestaurant.com
Prices: $$

Bright colors and bold artwork adorn this cheery Park Slope favorite for creative Mexican cooking. The staff radiates hospitality, and speaking of warmth, when the sun is out, the tiny dining room is augmented by seating out back, which regulars know is *the* place to be.

Fonda's menu is endowed with a skilled spin, evident in items like a refreshing salad of diced watermelon and cucumber embellished with mild yet creamy *queso fresco* and the crunch of crushed *pepitas*. A lighter take on *chile relleno* reveals roasted poblanos stuffed with spinach, raisins, and pine nuts, and dressed with a tomato-chipotle sauce and knob of epazote-seasoned goat cheese.

Chef Roberto Santibañez lets Manhattan in on the fun with the arrival of his offshoot in the East Village.

Forcella

D4

485 Lorimer St. (bet. Grand & Power Sts.)

Subway: Lorimer St - Metropolitan Av
Phone: 718-388-8820
Web: www.forcellaeatery.com
Prices:

Lunch & dinner daily

 A domed wood-fired oven with glossy black tile is the heart of Williamsburg's Forcella, where pizza falls under three headings: *rosse*, *bianchi*, and *fritte*. In addition to puffy, smoke-imbued disks topped with the likes of imported tomatoes, house-made mozzarella, and fresh basil, some of Forcella's 'zas take a dip in hot oil for a distinctive take on the familiar.

The *montanara* is fried before being decked and baked as a traditional Margherita, while the fully-fried *ripieno classico* stuffs a belly-busting pocket with ricotta, mozzarella, and soppressata. *Pizza alla carbonara* for brunch or *alla Nutella* for dessert demonstrates the versatility of everybody's favorite Italian export.

Forcella Bowery offers a more spacious setting and identical menu.

Fort Defiance

American

A7

365 Van Brunt St. (at Dikeman St.)

Subway: Smith - 9 Sts (& bus B77)
Phone: 347-453-6672
Web: www.fortdefiancebrooklyn.com
Prices: $$

Lunch daily
Dinner Wed – Mon

 If you build it, they will come. Maybe that's what the owners were thinking, since this spot way out in Red Hook isn't exactly a hop, skip, and a jump away. But once you're tucked inside, expect to jump for joy over the very tasty and gussied up Southern-inspired food on the concise menu—think pimento cheese and Ritz crackers; deviled eggs; and shrimp and grits.

Plan on coming for more than just the food, since the drinks are out-of-this-world. From nods to old-world Waldorf=Astoria cocktails to new creations with literary namesakes (like Correspondence) and an ever-changing beer menu, there's something to quench the thirst of those true-blue artists, counter-culture denizens, and yes, even a few wealthy Wall Streeters, who populate Red Hook.

Frankies 457 Spuntino

Italian

B7

457 Court St. (bet. 4th Pl. & Luquer St.)

Subway: Smith - 9 Sts
Phone: 718-403-0033
Web: www.frankiesspuntino.com
Prices:

Lunch & dinner daily

The ever-expanding empire of Frank Castronovo and Frank Falcinelli (the Franks) has its origins in this hands-down Carroll Gardens favorite.

Loosely translated as "snack", the menu of this home-styled Italian spot offers a selection of deliciously fuss-free fare. Headliners include fresh salads like shaved Brussels sprouts poked with diced Castelrosso cheese and slicked with the house's golden-hued olive oil; the signature meatballs studded with pine nuts and raisins; and sublime pastas like sweet potato-filled ravioli in Parmesan broth.

Cooking is initially done in the basement kitchen, but dishes are finished upstairs behind stacks of charcuterie and crusty breads gracing the utterly charming brick-lined and wood-furnished space.

Franny's

Italian

C7

295 Flatbush Ave. (bet. Prospect Pl. & St. Marks Ave.)

Subway: Bergen St (Flatbush Ave.)
Phone: 718-230-0221
Web: www.frannysbrooklyn.com
Prices: **$$**

Lunch Sat – Sun
Dinner nightly

Run by husband-wife team Francine Stephens and Andrew Feinberg and their contagious passion for sustainable agriculture, Franny's is always an inviting spot. An affable staff, stirring cocktails, and a stack of highchairs in the back demonstrate all are welcome here.

The open kitchen's centerpiece is a wood-burning brick oven churning out a tandem of puffed and crispy pizzas. Their clam pie finished with chilies and parsley is the stuff of legends; while other luscious plates have featured marinated cucumbers with crushed black olives, slivers of summer onions, and fragrant herbs; and pasta perfection as in penne mingled with pork sausage and sprouting broccoli.

Soon, there will be even more to love when Franny's moves to bigger digs just up the street.

The General Greene

American 🍴

C6

229 DeKalb Ave. (at Clermont Ave.)

Subway: Lafayette Av
Phone: 718-222-1510
Web: www.thegeneralgreene.com
Prices: $$

Lunch & dinner daily

The rustic American revolution marches on with The General Greene. This solidly ensconced Fort Greene restaurant taps the talents of an acclaimed kitchen which cooks up a creative, Southern-inflected menu guaranteed to steal the hearts of the upscale bohemian crowd that floods this neighborhood. Its unkempt good looks and hip waitstaff only seal the deal.

The seasonal menu may include a silky chicken liver pâté dusted with sea salt; or their signature fried chicken accompanied by sweet potato and andouille hash, as well as braised collard greens. Or go for comfort with the 3 cheese mac n' cheese followed by homemade ice cream.

Also visit their attached country store for old-school goodies that range from house-rendered lard to candies.

The Good Fork

Contemporary 🍴

A7

391 Van Brunt St. (bet. Coffey & Van Dyke Sts.)

Subway: Smith - 9 Sts (& bus B77)
Phone: 718-643-6636
Web: www.goodfork.com
Prices: $$

Lunch Sat – Sun
Dinner Tue – Sun

A Red Hook pioneer and adored destination, The Good Fork is truly worth the excursion to this vibrant and food-centric neighborhood. The setting has a rarified intimacy and regardless of where you sit, inside or out, diners are adeptly coddled and cared for. Framed in honey-hued wood veneer and hand-built by Ben Schneider, the dining room is reminiscent of a train car from a bygone era.

His classically trained wife, Sohui Kim, keeps the kitchen wheels churning as it gleefully trots the globe and flaunts a deliciously diverse sensibility. Try the grilled squid packed tight with quinoa, dressed with refreshing mango salsa, and sauced with silken squid ink as a starter. Entrées include roasted local chicken gently kissed by a fermented black bean sauce.

Governor

Contemporary ⚒

B5

15 Main St. (bet. Plymouth & Water Sts.)

Subway: High St
Phone: 718-858-4756
Web: www.governordumbo.com
Prices: $$

Dinner Mon – Sat

Governor has been bestowed with many gifts: a capable chef and skilled cadre to master the various contemporary twists on their farm-to-table fare; an iconic location on Brooklyn's waterfront; and a convivial vibe. The two levels of this young and very modern spot sprawl with dark wood, metal accents, sleek glass, and hints of greenery to soften.

The menu is a veritable tribute to quality ingredients that show up in the likes of beautifully charred romaine *à la plancha*, topped with peeled and roasted grapes, creamy yogurt, and an herbaceous "bread salad." Also try strips of tender beef tongue braised for a day-and-a-half, served with a bone marrow popover; or a brioche-flavored macaron topped with red berries and *cajeta*- and brown butter-sauce.

Gran Eléctrica

Mexican ⚒

B5

5 Front St. (bet. Dock & Old Fulton Sts.)

Subway: High St
Phone: 718-852-2700
Web: www.granelectrica.com
Prices: $$

Lunch Sat – Sun
Dinner nightly

Craving an excellent assortment of Mexican tidbits within a mellow locale? Gran Eléctrica will feed your desire. With a growing roll of tech firms in DUMBO, Gran Eléctrica beckons to these brains in a menu of diverse plates cradling the likes of a cool, bright mackerel ceviche topped with creamy avocado and briny green olives.

Add that to a clear vision and hard-hitting resumes (the chefs have passed through such top-notch kitchens as Per Se and Fat Duck), and it is no wonder this multi-room gem is ever-packed. A lovely back garden set directly under the iconic Brooklyn Bridge is a perfect spot for relishing such soulful concepts as deep-fried *tortita de huauzontle* floating in a spicy salsa; or crispy, straight-from-heaven cinnamon-flecked churros.

The Grocery

American ✗

288 Smith St. (bet. Sackett & Union Sts.)

Subway: Carroll St
Phone: 718-596-3335
Web: www.thegroceryrestaurant.com
Prices: $$

Dinner Tue – Sat

There's plenty to love about Smith Street's quintessential neighborhood restaurant. Open for more than a decade, The Grocery's longevity is commendable. And justly so— the quaint space framed by sage green walls is an always-welcoming scene, though regulars know to make a beeline for the luxuriant backyard when the weather warms.

Co-chefs Charles Kiely and Sharon Pachter attend to the kitchen and take turns venturing out into the dining room to chat up the devoted clientele. The vibe is unmistakably cordial. Sit back and relish the facile cooking that renders appetizing items like a salad of sautéed squid, shaved fennel, and kalamata olives dressed with a lemon-scallion vinaigrette; or tender and flavorful slow-roasted duck with red wine sauce.

Gwynnett St.

Contemporary ✗✗

312 Graham Ave. (bet. Ainslie & Devoe Sts.)

Subway: Graham Av
Phone: 718-889-7002
Web: www.gwynnettst.com
Prices: $$

Dinner nightly

Intriguing and ambitious cooking awaits you at this earnest Williamsburg newcomer. The comfortable dining room has a casual mien, with wood furnishings, brown-paper placemats, and wine storage on display. The well-managed staff adds a level of polish that complements the noteworthy efforts of the kitchen.

Diners can start off with whiskey bread and cultured butter before moving on to a meal that might include a toasty roasted maitake mushroom set on creamy, rosemary-scented onion and topped by warmed through strips of *lardo*; or crisp-skinned striped bass with golden potatoes, fennel fronds, and thick cream reduced with smoked oysters. Vegetarians get some notable attention too, with an entrée of almond tofu, sunchokes, and preserved lemon.

Hibino

Japanese 🍴

 B6

333 Henry St. (bet. Amity & Pacific Sts.)

Subway: Borough Hall
Phone: 718-260-8052
Web: www.hibino-brooklyn.com
Prices: 💸

Lunch Mon – Fri
Dinner nightly

This Cobble Hill treat is demure in appearance, but the warm welcome provided by a gaggle of female servers is a fitting prelude to the hospitality that will unfold. Once seated, a small blackboard is brought tableside where guests peruse the list of *obanzai* (Kyoto-style tapas). The evening may bring marinated and fried chicken thigh with tartar sauce; *chikuzen ni* (simmered chicken); or roasted oysters with spicy gazpacho. The menu changes daily but their tastiness remains constant.

Hibino's regional dedication is also evident in its offering of Osaka's traditional *hako* sushi. This box-pressed sushi dish might be served as a layering of excellent quality rice, shiso, *kanpyo* (preserved gourd), and fresh salmon.

The menu is pared-down at lunchtime.

Jack the Horse

American 🍴🍴

 B5

66 Hicks St. (at Cranberry St.)

Subway: High St
Phone: 718-852-5084
Web: www.jackthehorse.com
Prices: $$

Lunch Sun
Dinner nightly

Jack the Horse is named after a lake in Minnesota. If that doesn't tell you how much the chef loved fishing, their seafood bounty will. Brooklyn Heights boasts oldtime dining gems and this younger statesman follows suit. Featuring exposed brick walls decked with quaint clocks and bookshelves, banquettes overflowing with pillows, and a soundtrack belting the classics, this American bistro is loved for its tasty treats and quenching cocktails—note the syrups, tinctures, and bitters.

The scene is blithe with windows overlooking a historic street. Crowds cackle over plates of oysters paired with wakame and a sweet chili sauce; slow roasted duck posed atop fluffy farro and anise-tinged sorrel; or a steamed persimmon pudding with cinnamon crème anglaise.

467

James

C7

American

605 Carlton Ave. (at St. Marks Ave.)

Subway: 7 Av (Flatbush Ave.)
Phone: 718-942-4255
Web: www.jamesrestaurantny.com
Prices: $$

Lunch Tue – Sun
Dinner nightly

A Prospect Heights fixture, James is charming, upscale, and comfy. Whether here for Monday Burger night featuring a classic lamb, slow-roasted pork, or lentil burger, or simply to sample this solid American food, James romances you with a Dutch Lucite chandelier, pressed-tin ceilings, tufted leather banquettes, and silver bowls of fragrant citrus.

This surefooted husband-wife team lives upstairs and grows most of the herbs used in the kitchen on their rooftop. The result? A parade of such fresh creations as *cavolo nero* mingling red quinoa, smoked almonds, *ricotta salata*, and poached egg; an expertly prepared Berkshire pork chop with ribbons of fat and creamy beans; or a grilled lemon pound cake topped with strawberry rhubarb, Thai basil, and yuzu cream.

Java

B8

Indonesian

455 7th Ave. (at 16th St.)

Subway: 7 Av (9th St.)
Phone: 718-832-4583
Web: N/A
Prices:

Lunch Mon – Fri
Dinner nightly

Meet Rofia, the delightful owner and chef here at Java, whose loving hospitality infuses this adorable spot with huge doses of charm. Get all cozy in the tiny dining room and prepare to get your Indonesian nosh on. Bamboo skewers of charbroiled lamb served with *kepac manis* are a delectable start; followed by velvety *semur*—thin slices of beef simmered in a rich garlicky sauce. The terrific *cumi baker* (baked tender squid topped with an aromatic ginger sauce) is a must try; but don't try to get the delicious details, as the tight-lipped chef won't divulge her secrets.

Bring a buddy and partake in the famous *Rijsttafel*, a feast of fifteen dishes plus dessert for under forty bucks. Note to the booze crowd: no alcohol is served.

Jolie Cantina

International ✗

B7

241 Smith St. (at Douglass St.)

Subway: Bergen St (Smith St.)   Lunch & dinner Tue – Sun
Phone: 718-488-0777
Web: www.joliecantina.com
Prices: $$

 Fans of the old Jolie, which stood for years on Atlantic Avenue, will remember a graceful Mexican accent that worked its way onto the menu of classic French specialties. And now, as one can gather from the re-christened moniker, a full-on Mexican spirit is at play in this new location on a Cobble Hill corner.
The kitchen's skilled fusion yields creations such as velvety black bean purée poured over gently poached lobster pieces and cassis-red onion chutney; duck confit enchilada; or soothing *chilaquiles* glammed up by honey-tinged tomatillo salsa and nuggets of king crab. If dessert is not your thing, opt for the cheese plate stocked with curds procured from neighboring cheesemonger Stinky Brooklyn in lieu of the *churros y dos salsas dulces*.

Juventino

Contemporary ✗

B8

370 Fifth Ave. (bet. 5th & 6th Sts.)

Subway: 4 Av - 9 St   Lunch daily
Phone: 718-360-8469   Dinner Tue – Sun
Web: www.juventinonyc.com
Prices: $$

Park Slopers should feel fortunate to have such an invitingly sweet spot in the neighborhood. Tables are lacquered with pages from old cookbooks, and the space is stocked with book-filled shelves and a generally countrified look.
Chef Juventino Avila offers brunch daily; eye-openers include homemade granola and cage-free truffled eggs. Heartier preparations embrace seasonality and product as in Berkshire pork loin with heirloom beans, early spring vegetables, and caramelized apple jam. While others plates share a south-of-the-border accent in items like a block of pan-seared cod cresting a flavorful mound of Mexican-style rice; and an offering of *tacos de mama*—over-stuffed handmade tortillas accompanied by a trio of salsas.

Karczma

Polish Polish ✗

136 Greenpoint Ave. (bet. Franklin St. & Manhattan Ave.)

Subway: Greenpoint Av   Lunch & dinner daily
Phone: 718-349-1744
Web: www.karczmabrooklyn.com
Prices: ☜☜

Located in a slice of Greenpoint that still boasts a sizeable Polish population, Karczma offers a lovely old-world ambience that may belie its age (opened for five-plus years) but perfectly matches its very traditional, budget-friendly menu. Hearty offerings may include peasant-style lard mixed with bacon and spices, or the plate of Polish specialties that heaps on pierogies (three varieties, steamed or fried, topped with sliced onions and butter), kielbasa, potato pancakes, hunter's stew, and stuffed cabbage. Grilled plates can be prepared for two or three, while others, like the roasted hocks in beer, could easily feed as many.

The charming, farmhouse-inspired interior is efficiently staffed by smiling servers in floral skirts and embroidered vests.

Ki Sushi

Japanese ✗

122 Smith St. (bet. Dean & Pacific Sts.)

Subway: Bergen St (Smith St.)   Lunch Mon – Sat
Phone: 718-935-0575   Dinner nightly
Web: N/A
Prices: $$

Count sushi among Smith Street's wealth of dining options. At Ki, the quality of fish and talented kitchen offer plenty to please its devoted fans who are here to relish the raw and the cooked in this Zen-chic space fitted-out with a gently flowing wall of water and potted plants.

The cheerful sushi team works from a counter stocked with a tempting array of pristine fish. The sushi and sashimi are excellent, as is the whimsical and visually appealing maki, like the Fashion Roll of chopped tuna, jalapeño, and yuzu *tobiko* wrapped in slices of raw scallop. Dishes like rock shrimp tempura drizzled with a creamy spiced mayonnaise emerge from the small kitchen located in back.

The friendly and attentive service adds to the charm of this Boerum Hill favorite.

La Superior

Mexican ✗

C4

295 Berry St. (bet. S. 2nd & S. 3rd Sts.)

Subway: Bedford Av
Phone: 718-388-5988
Web: www.lasuperiornyc.com
Prices: 🕸🕸

Lunch & dinner daily

Truly a superior taqueria, this south of the border fave located on Williamsburg's south side proffers a lip-smacking selection of inexpensive tacos made from high quality ingredients and filled with deliciousness. Expect the likes of shredded chicken in a cloak of lush *mole negro*, or turkey escabèche topped with pickled red onion on a black bean purée-slathered tortilla. A rainbow of margaritas–tamarind, *guayaba*, and hibiscus–or a Cube Libre made with Mexican Coca-Cola washes down this most satisfying array that also includes snacks like street-style quesadillas and made-to-order guacamole.

The restaurant's name is scrawled tattoo-like across its painted brick façade, alluding to the carefree décor within made up of chile red walls and movie posters.

La Vara

Spanish ✗✗

B6

268 Clinton St. (at Verandah Pl.)

Subway: Carroll St
Phone: 718-422-0065
Web: N/A
Prices: $$

Lunch Sat – Sun
Dinner nightly

Alex Raij and Eder Montero (the duo behind Chelsea's Txikito and El Quinto Pino) have expanded to Brooklyn with a bang at this tapas-style restaurant that blends Moorish, Jewish, and Spanish influences with terrific results. Via a façade of picture windows framed in slate blue-painted wood frames, La Vara invites you to come inside and sample away.

From the *berenjena con miel*–fried eggplant drizzled with honey and served with cheese–to braised chickpeas and spinach in a savory broth, or a tender stuffed rabbit loin, plates are well-crafted and exude huge flavor. Artichokes served with aïoli; cumin-roasted lamb; and creamy cuttlefish strips in a milky almond-based broth are other instances of how the kitchen keeps it coming at this warm and lively spot.

Locanda Vini & Olii

Italian 🍴

D6

129 Gates Ave. (at Cambridge Pl.)

Subway: Clinton - Washington Avs
Phone: 718-622-9202
Web: www.locandany.com
Prices: $$

Dinner Tue – Sun

Ensconced in a restored century-old pharmacy, Locanda Vini & Olii is trimmed with a weathered white tiled floor and rustic furnishings. See-through cabinets stocked with colorful glass and curios flank the room and the kitchen is fronted by the original pick-up window. This lovely Italianate spot recently celebrated its tenth anniversary and experienced a change in ownership resulting from founding owners Francois and Catherine Louy handing over their pride and joy to the charge of Chef Michele Baldacci, Sommelier Rocco Spagnardi, and GM Michael Schall.

The cooking stays the course and continues to delight with the likes of *pappa al pomodoro*—slick, almost fluffy bread and tomato soup; or silky, parsley-flecked *fazzolettini* with shrimp and fish ragù.

Lucky Eight

Chinese 🍴

A4

5204 Eighth Ave. (bet. 52nd & 53rd Sts.)

Subway: 8 Av
Phone: 718-851-8862
Web: N/A
Prices:

Lunch & dinner daily

Eat well for a Cantonese song at Lucky Eight, though first you'll need to find it buried among Chinese pastry shops, grocers spilling goods onto the sidewalk, and the throng of pedestrians populating this stretch of Eighth Avenue south of Sunset Park.

Everything is small and bustling. A front counter proffers the menu to go, while those who dine in are swiftly greeted, ushered to a table (or empty seat) and presented with a laminated menu displaying an array of dim sum that is a departure from the standard set (think fish skin dumplings and pork knuckles). The Cantonese line-up offers barbecued meats over rice; a savory tangle of noodles like *e-fu* noodles tossed with XO sauce and dried scallops; and vegetables like *choi sum* steamed to emerald green.

Maria's Bistro Mexicano

 Mexican ✗

886 Fifth Ave. (bet. 37th & 38th Sts.)

Subway: 36 St   Lunch & dinner daily
Phone: 718-438-1608
Web: www.mariasbistromexicano.com
Prices: $$

Head to Sunset Park for some great Mexican cuisine—those who call this vibrant Brooklyn pocket home consider themselves lucky to have such a bright spot in the neighborhood. The cozy space, complete with backyard seating, pops with color and is warmed by the genuinely hospitable light cast by Maria herself.

Dig into a hearty bowlful of *pozole* or tortilla soup before delving into the array of appetizing preparations like a thick-cut grilled pork chop with *salsa roja Oaxaqueño* or *enchilada mi bandera* topped with a trio of sauces. The *chile poblano* combo is a delicately fried one-two punch: one plumped with a savory combination of cheeses, the other stuffed with a beguilingly sweet mixture of chicken, almonds, diced plantains, and apple.

Marlow & Sons

 Gastropub ✗

81 Broadway (bet. Berry St. & Wythe Ave.)

Subway: Marcy Av   Lunch & dinner daily
Phone: 718-384-1441
Web: www.marlowandsons.com
Prices: $$

This always enticing dusky den is manna for the denizens of Williamsburg's gastronomes who come for a taste of Marlow & Sons deliciously fuss-free fare at breakfast, lunch and dinner. In the front find strong coffee and sweet treats as well as some interesting sundries. The back room presents a minimally worded carte that offers lunchtime sustenance like a refreshingly chilled yellow squash purée revved up with curry powder and a swirl of yogurt–the perfect antidote to a hot summer afternoon–or smoked trout, a salad-y composition of silken infused fish with warm potato wedges, and creamy dill dressing. Dinner features the succulent, bronze-skinned brick chicken, a menu mainstay as well as oysters, cheeses, and an oft-changing list of specials.

Mesa Coyoacán 😋

D3

372 Graham Ave. (bet. Conselyea St. & Skillman Ave.)

Subway: Graham Av
Phone: 718-782-8171
Web: www.mesacoyoacan.com
Prices: $$

Lunch Wed – Sun
Dinner nightly

Not that Brooklyn is wanting for exciting dining options, quite the opposite exactly, but Chef Ivan Garcia's tempting establishment has been greeted with open arms, and mouths. The Mexico City native ruled the roost previously at Barrio Chino and Mercadito, and now takes up residence in a glass fronted slab where wolfish appetites are sated.

It's not just the swank interior, fitted out with richly-patterned wallpaper, snug banquettes, and communal tables, but the mouthwatering Mexican food that makes this place such a jewel. Partake in tacos, perhaps the *carnitas*—braised Berkshire pork D.F.-style stuffed into handmade tortillas; or a choice from the *platos fuertes* that include *enchiladas de mole*, made from the chef's secret family recipe.

Mile End 😋

B6

97A Hoyt St. (bet. Atlantic Ave. & Pacific St.)

Subway: Hoyt-Schermerhorn
Phone: 718-852-7510
Web: www.mileendbrooklyn.com
Prices: 😋😋

Lunch & dinner daily

The star of the show at this gem of a spot is Montreal-style smoked meat: pasture-raised brisket that is spice-rubbed, then cured, oak-smoked, steamed, and finally hand cut onto slices of mustard-slathered rye. It's a revelatory sandwich, exactingly prepared, and has few peers in the city. Dinner brings further competition for your appetite with the likes of *poulet Juif*, a tantalizingly smoky, bronze-skinned chicken with wilted escarole and warm schmaltz-enriched vinaigrette. The petite room is rarely quiet. Beyond the handful of tables, there is a dining counter facing the white-tiled kitchen, accented with a blackboard of specials and treats such as Hungarian shortbread. To enjoy the goodness at home, walk up to the sidewalk window for takeout.

Mill Basin Kosher Delicatessen

Deli

C4

5823 Ave. T (bet. 58th & 59th Sts.)

Lunch & dinner daily

Subway: N/A
Phone: 718-241-4910
Web: www.millbasindeli.com
Prices: $$

This thirty-eight-year-old Brooklyn treasure is as old school as it gets, and though it's a bit of a trek to Mill Basin, anyone looking for a real Jewish deli won't think twice. Part deli counter, part artsy dining room, and part party hall, Mark Schachner's beloved spot serves up all the classics from beef tongue sandwiches to gefilte fish.

The wildly overstuffed sandwiches (all served with homemade pickles and coleslaw) are a homerun, as in the pastrami, which is steamed not once but twice, leaving the meat juicy yet hardly fatty. Dive into a Rueben—an open-face and intense pile of juicy corned beef, Swiss cheese, and tart sauerkraut on toasted rye bread, topped with a Russian dressing. The pastrami eggroll is a serious, cultish favorite.

Mimi's Hummus

Mediterranean

B4

1209 Cortelyou Rd. (bet. Argyle & Westminster Rds.)

Lunch & dinner daily

Subway: Cortelyou Rd
Phone: 718-284-4444
Web: www.mimishummus.com
Prices:

Think snack-taverna and imagine this adorable, warm spot in Brooklyn's ever-changing Ditmas Park. It may be teeny-tiny, but excellent design and wise use of space give Mimi's a modern holistic feel—with large windows bringing natural light by day, and an open kitchen adding a cheerful ambience come nightfall.

The menu is simple, super-fresh, and perfectly spiced, as in dishes of made-to-order hummus; a meaty version with ground beef and pine nuts; chunky Moroccan-style tomato stew with a wonderfully plump poached egg and Israeli salad; or irresistibly thick and creamy *labne*, laced with fragrant herbs. At dinner, the menu expands, and takeout is available. For cheeses, coffee, chocolates, and more, visit their very well-stocked market next door.

Miranda

C3

80 Berry St. (at N. 9th St.)

Subway: Bedford Av
Phone: 718-387-0711
Web: www.mirandarestaurant.com
Prices: $$

Lunch Sat – Sun
Dinner Wed – Mon

 Run by husband-wife team Sasha and Mauricio Miranda, this welcoming establishment is located in a charmingly rustic Williamsburg building dating back to the 1800s, and accented with straw seat chairs, vintage crockery, and exposed brick walls. The duo has an impressive resume that shines through at this corner-side location.

The cuisine here fuses Italy and Latin America flavors for a creative and vibrant menu. Starters include *arancini* and empanadas; pastas (portioned as appetizers or entrées) are made in house as in the pappardelle with mole-braised lamb ragu; main dishes include pan-seared Long Island duck with creamy polenta, Tuscan kale, and chile de arbol sauce. Finish with a selection of European farmhouse cheese.

Moim

C8

206 Garfield Pl. (at Seventh Ave.)

Subway: 7 Av (Flatbush Ave.)
Phone: 718-499-8092
Web: www.moimrestaurant.com
Prices: $$

Lunch Sat – Sun
Dinner Tue – Sun

 Set among an assemblage of bucolic brownstones, Moim serves a fresh take on Korean cuisine. Like its menu, the setting bears a contemporary vibe in a room of concrete grey and dark wood details. Moim translates as "gathering" and encourages sharing with oversized tables to be topped with any number of plates, small or large.

The kitchen rises above the pack with an array of items that begin with tapas such as stir-fried eggplant, and organic soft tofu in seasoned soy sauce. Small plates are also featured and include puffy steamed buns filled with a mixture of chopped pork and kimchi. Heartier plates and bowls offer the likes of *dak bok-kum*, a Korean-style *pot-au-feu* of rice wine-braised chicken, spicy chili soy, and Korean potato gnocchi.

Momo Sushi Shack

Fusion ✗

C1

43 Bogart St. (bet. Grattan & Thames Sts.)

Subway: Morgan Av
Phone: 718-418-6666
Web: www.momosushishack.com
Prices: $$

Lunch & dinner daily

Feeling nostalgic for the days of Manhattan before its Disneyfication? Look no further than this Brooklyn 'hood, where tattooed bike-toting artists rule the roost and graffiti isn't a nuisance, it's an art form. Momo Sushi Shack is packed with hipsters all dancing to a different beat. There's nothing ersatz about its loading dock look, since it's not made to look warehousy—it is! Inside is true-blue industrial with cement floors and corrugated steel.

Wagyu beef "sushi" topped with crispy garlic and seaweed and a trio of flavored soy sauces made in-house is scary good. From the minced fresh scallops and the pressed tofu with basil-infused soy sauce, to the cold udon noodles swimming in shiso vinaigrette, it's a total tongue-teasing flavor bonanza.

M Shanghai

Chinese ✗

C4

292 Grand St. (bet. Havermeyer & Roebling Sts.)

Subway: Bedford Av
Phone: 718-384-9300
Web: www.newmshanghai.com
Prices: ⌾⌾

Lunch & dinner daily

Inspired by the cooking of owner May Liu's grandmother, M Shanghai's menu begins with a range of excellent steamed or fried dumplings filled with pork, vegetables, or seafood. A host of other Shanghainese specialties might include *siu mai* stuffed with flavorful sticky rice or double-sautéed pork belly. Even the less regionally specific dishes are intriguing, like the *kung pao* chicken tossed with dried red chillies, whole peanuts, and green onion. Don't forget to order some greens—sautéed morning glory in black tea sauce is gloriously smoky.

Wood flooring and whitewashed brick walls feel contemporary while honey-toned slats above and ceiling lights fashioned from bamboo birdcages lend a distinctly Chinese feel that is attractive and free of kitsch.

477

Mtskheta Café

A4

Central Asian ✕

2568 86th St. (bet. Bay 41st St. & Stillwell Ave.)

Subway: 86 St
Phone: 718-676-1868
Web: N/A
Prices: 💰

Lunch & dinner Thu – Tue

Central Asians have made this nabe their home, and following suit, are scores of eateries where these locals can live and play. While their cuisine may not be firmly planted on the NY soil, Mtskheta Café's presence has done much to alter this landscape of food and culture. Inside the dining room, faux exposed brick walls are painted a mossy green and matching the jungle theme are green tablecloths and paper napkins.

If a TV streaming music videos feels gimmicky, the menu written in Russian should relieve all qualms. Let affable servers direct you to the classics, which may include eggplant rolls stuffed with walnut sauce and an eggplant purée; *khachapuri*, creamy pan-fried cheese bread; or *bozbashi*, a mutton and rice soup frilled with fresh onions.

Noodle Pudding

B5

Italian ✕✕

38 Henry St. (bet. Cranberry & Middagh Sts.)

Subway: High St
Phone: 718-625-3737
Web: N/A
Prices: $$

Dinner Tue – Sun

Locals are head over heels in love with this comfort-centric Italian star. The service is sincere; the staff is versed; and the ambience is quaint—Noodle Pudding embodies it all and is a point of pride. Inside this earthy den, kick back and relax to the warm croons of Etta James resounding through terra-cotta floors and a dark wood bar.

With no reservations, arrive early to nab your nook. Like other diners, find yourself sopping up every last drop of *polpo* (tender, chewy octopus in a chunky tomato sauce), or a fresh *sarde* special. The kitchen gets the details right in *rigatoni alla Siciliana* crested with feathers of *ricotta salata*; while *straccetti* (grilled pounded beef served with mushrooms tossed in truffle oil) has been drawing droves for decades.

Northeast Kingdom

American ✗

  C2

18 Wyckoff Ave. (at Troutman St.)

Subway: Jefferson St   Lunch & dinner daily
Phone: 718-386-3864
Web: www.north-eastkingdom.com
Prices: $$

 You don't have to say goodbye to American pie at Northeast Kingdom, since this place is revered for its heavenly pot pies. It's a little taste of Americana-style food in the heart of warehouse-heavy and mega organic supermarket-enhanced Bushwick. Sure, it's a bitty gritty, but it has a burgeoning culinary scene, and Northeast Kingdom is running with the big dogs.

From fried green tomatoes and Vermont cheddar-stuffed pierogi to fricassee of wild mushrooms made silky with cream and sitting atop favas, carrot purée, and new potatoes, Northeast Kingdom's chef, Kevin Adely takes the best of the farmstand and brings it to life. Dishes like ginger-mint dressed pan-roasted duck are proof that it isn't your average country cookin', so leave Billy Bob behind.

No. 7 🐶

American ✗✗

C6

7 Greene Ave. (bet. Cumberland & Fulton Sts.)

Subway: Lafayette Av   Lunch Sat — Sun
Phone: 718-522-6370   Dinner Tue — Sun
Web: www.no7restaurant.com
Prices: $$

Apparently seven is the luckiest number. It's sprouting up all over—there is even a No. 7 sandwich spin-off in the über-hip Ace Hotel. But, this restaurant doesn't look like the corner deli (think distressed mirrors, marble tiles, banquettes, and an open kitchen).

Start with the signature fried broccoli, grapefruit, and black bean hummus appetizer—it's the perfect opener for this slightly offbeat but oh-so-good menu. The General Tso fillet-o-fish sub pairs crispy white fish with cilantro and American cheese, slathers it with a roasted tomatillo-chili mayo, and stuffs it with pickled cabbage into a plush sub bun. Grab a fork for the comfort of the turkey and goose meatloaf and the bitter bliss of the chocolate and blood orange tart.

Brooklyn

1 or 8

C4   Japanese ✗✗

66 S. 2nd St. (at Wythe Ave.)

Subway: Bedford Av   Dinner Tue – Sun
Phone: 718-384-2152
Web: www.oneoreightbk.com
Prices: $$

Taking it's moniker from the Japanese gambling expression that means all or nothing, this atelier of food is a sure thing for an impressive meal. The lofty space features a blank canvas frame accentuated by high-backed white booths surrounding tables set aglow under pendant lamps.

A glass-enclosed kitchen and tempting sushi counter keep the artsy patrons sated with serious raw offerings and unique cooked items. Showing the hands of a skilled team are fluke carpaccio dressed with a bead of ponzu and grapefruit; the *ebisen* maki, wrapped in rice paper and filled with seasoned rice, shrimp, and mango; or steamed *asari* bobbing in a red miso broth. A recent dessert special featured rice flour madeleines filled with red bean paste and dusted with *matcha*.

Osteria il Paiolo

C3   Italian ✗✗

106 N. 6th St. (bet. Berry & Wythe Sts.)

Subway: Bedford Av   Lunch & dinner daily
Phone: 718-218-7080
Web: www.ilpaiolonyc.com
Prices: $$

Williamsburg's Osteria il Paiolo rocks a slick and urbane vibe in this hipster 'hood. Step in and find a dark wood bar against a backdrop of polished copper (*paiolo* refers to a copper cooking pot) and linen-covered tables prettied by bright flowers. But this is Brooklyn after all, so exposed brick and concrete flooring are part of the deal.

The Italian cuisine bears a northern accent and offers a spectrum of cheeses coupled with homemade jams; house-made pastas like *spaghetti alla chitarra* twirled with a vibrant arugula pesto; and heirloom polenta topped with shrimp and rosemary. For a satisfying *secondi*, you can't go wrong by ordering the *osso buco alla Milanese*, classically paired with a dollop of delicious saffron-infused risotto.

Pacificana

Chinese

813 55th St. (at Eighth Ave.)

Subway: 8 Av
Phone: 718-871-2880
Web: N/A
Prices: $$

Lunch & dinner daily

You can thank Sunset Park's growing Asian population for the influx of excellent Chinese restaurants into this far-flung pocket of Brooklyn. Among the best of the lot is Pacificana, a bright, airy restaurant–think vaulted ceilings, jumbo windows, and an open kitchen sporting floor-to-ceiling fish tanks–tucked into a second floor space off bustling Eighth Avenue.

Dim sum carts packed to the gills roll by like temptations-on-wheels and dinner guests tuck into traditional fare like the rich, fragrant South China duck casserole alongside other treats like crispy pork over jelly fish, and tender shrimp dumplings. Chicken with crunchy mustard greens, paired with preserved black beans and a steaming bowl of fluffy white rice is nothing sort of heart-warming.

Palo Santo

Latin American

652 Union St. (bet. Fourth & Fifth Aves.)

Subway: Union St
Phone: 718-636-6311
Web: www.palosanto.us
Prices: $$

Lunch Sat – Sun
Dinner nightly

Nestled among Park Slope's brownstones, Palo Santo's ground floor space feels delightfully homey. Handmade wood furnishings, tiled flooring, and an amber-hued counter set the warmly shaded scene. The kitchen, stocked with neatly arranged produce, is set behind the counter and accented by copper pots and colorful pitchers.

The eclectic Latin cuisine utilizes local ingredients gathered from the Grand Army Plaza Greenmarket as well as those grown in the rooftop garden. The day's *anticuchos* has featured skewers of rich, grilled pork liver dusted with spices; and entrées list a hearty plate of pan-roasted bluefish accompanied by sweet plantain roasted whole in the skin and garnished with shredded cabbage slaw dressed with red wine vinegar and jalapeño.

Parish Hall

 Brooklyn

American ✗

C3

109A N. 3rd St. (bet. Berry St. & Wythe Ave.)

Subway: Bedford Av

Phone: 718-782-2602

Web: www.parishhall.net

Prices: $$

Lunch & dinner daily

From the team behind brunch spot-extraordinaire Egg comes Parish Hall, a delectable addition to this reputedly flavorsome neighborhood. Located merely steps from the Mast Brothers chocolate shop and factory, Parish Hall's concrete floors and white-on-white décor screams industrial-chic.

The menu expertly melds a New York state of mind, an exploratory sense, and the southern leanings of proprietor George Weld to construct a list of offerings that may reveal a salad of roots and tubers (raw carrots, radish, roasted parsnips, and pickled beets) drizzled with sweet pecan milk; seared Montauk tilefish atop creamy Carolina Gold rice studded with bits of country ham and polished with green garlic broth; or toasted rye cake crowned with frozen maple mousse.

Paulie Gee's 😊

Pizza ✗

B1

60 Greenpoint Ave. (bet. Franklin & West Sts.)

Subway: Greenpoint Av

Phone: 347-987-3747

Web: www.pauliegee.com

Prices: 🍸🍸

Dinner Tue – Sun

Owner Paul Gianonne, aka Paulie Gee, channeled a lifelong love of pizza into this charmingly delicious spot that feels as if it has been around forever. Rustic in appearance, the room's cool concrete and brick are warmed by the glow of the wood-burning pizza oven imported from Naples. From here, Gianonne and son work their magic.

The addictive crust is beguilingly moist and chewy, perfumed with smoke, and adroitly salted. Killer wood-fired pizza dominates the menu with tempting combinations, excellent ingredients, and whimsical names. Offerings may include the Harry Belafontina—fontina, tomatoes, beefy meatballs, crimini mushrooms, and golden raisins. Vegans get respect here, with an added menu of vegan cheese and house-made vegan sausage.

The Pearl Room

Contemporary ✗✗

A4

8201 Third Ave. (at 82nd St.)

Subway: 86 St

Phone: 718-833-6666

Web: www.thepearlroom.com

Prices: $$

Lunch & dinner daily

With its jumbo garden and bright, sun-streaked dining room, this Brooklyn steady is a solid choice year-round. Most days, you'll catch a glimpse of the charming Chef/owner Anthony Rinaldi floating around, working his magic back in the kitchen and out in the dining room.

The Pearl Room is known for its vast seafood spread, and Rinaldi's wheelhouse is intricately designed fish plates like pan-fried, pine nut-crusted lemon sole or ravioli stuffed with Maine lobster, ricotta, and fresh herbs in cream sauce. But don't discount his other offerings—the menu boasts starters like house-made mozzarella with roasted peppers and marinated golden tomatoes, vegetarian and meat dishes ample enough to split, as well as a few tongue-wagging desserts.

Petit Oven

French ✗

A4

276 Bay Ridge Ave. (Ridge Blvd. & Third Ave.)

Subway: Bay Ridge Av

Phone: 718-833-3443

Web: www.petit-oven.com

Prices: $$

Dinner Wed– Sun

Unassuming but worth your attention, this little Bay Ridge site offers a petit, tidy room that is simply done and fills quickly. The ambience here brings a gracious welcome, and the air wears a palpable note of authenticity.

Chef/owner Katarzyna Ploszaj styles her agreeable and refreshingly relaxed cuisine through a classic French lens, with appetizers that may include a novel riff on Greek salad composed of thinly shaved Brussels sprouts mingled with diced feta, a handful of black olives, sliced red onion, and a sprig of fragrant oregano all licked with olive oil and a bright hit of lemon juice. Expect entreés like an impressively cooked duck breast, crisped and rosy, with red onion-ginger marmalade, and duck fat-roasted potatoes scented with thyme.

Peter Luger ✿

C4

178 Broadway (at Driggs Ave.)

Subway: Marcy Av

Phone: 718-387-7400

Web: www.peterluger.com

Prices: **$$$**

Lunch & dinner daily

Even with its imposing pane windows and gleaming walls, Peter Luger remains ever-historic. The waiters are not gruff, they are focused. Dining here is not a meal; it is a right of passage. And these steaks are not just good—they are probably going to be the best you ever have. This is the reason why Peter Luger has been receiving paramount praise since first opening to a very different Brooklyn in 1887.

In a room reminiscent of old New York and early German ale-houses, an unabashedly male crowd of tourists and tycoons sit elbow-to-elbow, not worrying themselves with perusing a menu. When that steak for two (or three or four) arrives, slow yourself and take a long, hot look to appreciate its every perfection. The marbling is a thing of beauty, and is all the more appetizing when presented sliced and sizzling with drippings. Take a few mouthfuls before even considering the house sauce. It may be tasty, but c'mon, this steak is already nirvana in its nakedness.

Let your eyes stray from the prize long enough to dig into their emerald green and savory creamed spinach or thick, hand-cut fries. For dessert, the silky sour cream cheesecake is utterly delicious, *mit schlaag*, of course.

Picket Fence

B4

American

1310 Cortelyou Rd. (bet. Argyle & Rugby Rds.)

Subway: Cortelyou Rd   Lunch & dinner daily
Phone: 718-282-6661
Web: www.picketfencebrooklyn.com
Prices: $$

This warm, welcoming Ditmas Park family favorite is the go-to spot for some rib-sticking, good old, all-American comfort food. Inside the tiny café, bare wood tables and white chairs perch on well-worn floors, while spring-green banquettes, rattan furnishings, and colorful throw pillows add touches of hominess. On a sunny day, grab a kid-friendly seat in the lovely garden.

Tuck into a tasty plate of farfalle, bursting with juicy jumbo shrimp, crumbled Italian sausage, and fresh herbs in tomato sauce; or the tender, grilled pork chop, with oven roasted butternut squash, fluffy couscous, and applesauce. Swing by on a Thursday night for half-priced bottles of wine, or over the weekend for brunch that includes free-flowing mimosas for all of nine dollars.

Pok Pok

A6

Thai

127 Columbia St. (bet. Degraw & Kane Sts.)

Subway: Carroll St   Dinner nightly
Phone: 718-923-9322
Web: www.pokpokny.com
Prices: $$

Andy Ricker's eagerly anticipated offshoot of the famed Portland original has finally landed on the edge of Brooklyn's growing Columbia Waterfront District. Reservations are not accepted so plan on waiting. No matter—the staff is friendly, and the space is alive with fun.

Inspired by northern Thai specialties, Pok Pok uses excellent ingredients to concoct succulent charcoal-grilled eats boasting fresh, spicy, and tart flavors. Two (of many) stunners include *laap plaa duuk yaang Isaan*, a charcoal-roasted catfish salad sparked by fragrant mint, galangal, red chili, and toasted rice powder; and luscious *muu kham waan*—Mangalista pork neck liberally seasoned with garlic, coriander root, black pepper, and a sweetened soy glaze.

Potlikker

American ✗

338 Bedford Ave. (bet. S. 2nd & S. 3rd Sts.)

Subway: Bedford Av
Phone: 718-388-9808
Web: www.potlikkerbrooklyn.com
Prices: $$

Lunch Sat – Sun
Dinner Tue – Sun

Despite the down-home handle, Chef Liza Queen's newest venture shows a breadth of inspiration in its menu of well-crafted creations. The relaxed bar is a great spot to chat with the staff while enjoying a beer, and the dining room is bright and welcoming—pistachio green furnishings poised against lemon yellow walls.

In the back, the kitchen is on display and the crew may look intense. But that's for good reason; they're turning out a winning menu. Enjoy the likes of a Dutch baby pancake with goat cheese, raw honey, and fragrant thyme; freshly made cannelloni stuffed with summer squash-studded ricotta; and other big hits such as slow-cooked pork ribs neatly brushed with rhubarb gastrique and sided by a rhubarb-topped corn muffin and tender collards.

Prime Meats

European ✗

465 Court St. (at Luquer St.)

Subway: Smith - 9 Sts.
Phone: 718-254-0327
Web: www.frankspm.com
Prices: $$

Lunch & dinner daily

Spreken ze...yummy? Don't worry about brushing up on your German to visit Prime Meats. Niceties aside, your mouth will be otherwise occupied.

It all starts with house-pickled vegetables and soft pretzels served with spicy hot mustard and continues with a cavalcade of carnivorous delights. Roasted bone marrow with gremolata, pickle-brined Amish chicken, and oh yes, sausages. *Sürkrüt garnie* is a threesome of meats with pork belly, calf tongue, and bratwurst for a very harmonious affair. Finish it with a piece of sea salt dark chocolate—so wunderbar.

Prime Meats doesn't just know how to suck out all the marrow of life, it looks good too. With dark woods, tall wooden booths, and wood-framed glass windows, it nails that classic brasserie look.

Purple Yam

Asian 🍴

B4

1314 Cortelyou Rd. (at Rugby Rd.)

Subway: Cortelyou Rd
Phone: 718-940-8188
Web: www.purpleyamnyc.com
Prices: $$

Lunch Wed – Sun
Dinner nightly

Ditmas Park, a lovely Brooklyn enclave, is extoled for its restored Victorian homes. Catering to its upper-crust tastes is Purple Yam, with an interior that features soothing colors, plush banquettes, and wood-bamboo accents. Drenched in a soft glow, Purple Yam pays homage to (of course) the namesake and adored tuber.

These may be show up as succulent *tocino* (sugar-cured pork) sliders in purple yam *pan de sal*, or *buko*, a flaky crust filled with *macapuno* custard. Either way, the results are just plain excellent. Deviating from the Philippines are exciting versions of *bibimbap* with burdock, though oxtail *kare-kare* has that remarkable richness and brilliant funk from pungent shrimp paste that proves the kitchen's authentic touch—perfect with a San Miquel.

Reynard

American 🍴🍴

B1

80 Wythe Ave. (at N. 11th St.)

Subway: Bedford Av
Phone: 718-460-8004
Web: www.reynardsnyc.com
Prices: $$

Lunch & dinner daily

Servicing Williamsburg's Wythe hotel is this inviting dining room, run by Brooklyn restaurateur Andrew Tarlow (of Diner and Marlow & Sons). The signature ramshackle-y mien of those two aforementioned spots has been dressed-up a bit here, to fashion a chic setting that is sexy enough for date-night yet suitably relaxed for those with kids in tow. Original details abound throughout the space and feature a mosaic tile floor, cast iron columns, and parchment-colored walls.

A trusted lieutenant has been charged with sending out an intriguing set of creations like wood-oven warmed olives; flatbread slathered with Mornay sauce and topped with caramelized radicchio; or lamb meatballs dressed with harissa-spiked yogurt and red rice-orzo pilaf.

The River Café ✿

B5

1 Water St. (bet. Furman & Old Fulton Sts.)

Subway: High St

Phone: 718-522-5200

Web: www.rivercafe.com

Prices: $$$$

Lunch & dinner daily

Noah Kalina/The River Café

From the outside, the Brooklyn Bridge appears to protect and cradle this twinkling local landmark. From the inside, its soaring height leads over the East River to the Manhattan cityscape and instantly conveys just why Buzzy O'Keefe first opened The River Café on the rather sketchy waterfront in 1977. Today, gardens, waterfalls, and a cobblestone drive gild its timeless beauty. Arrive by water taxi from Fulton Street for an inexpensive sightseeing ride that docks next to the restaurant.

Amid such splendor, the service remains attentive from start to finish and the kitchen once a launching pad for A-list chefs, sends forth food that is equally focused, serious, and ambitious.

Starters like Maine peekytoe crab soup with coconut milk, lemongrass, and Thai basil offer Southeast Asian accents. Market-fresh North Carolina red snapper–the pristine fillets delicately pan-fried and enhanced with fish fumet–is artistically presented with artichoke leaves and balanced by beurre blanc and verjus. Homemade cheesecake highlights undeniably superb ingredients. By the time it is finished tableside with passion fruit purée, this becomes another elevated classic, a world away from its humble beginnings.

Roberta's

Contemporary 🍴

C2

261 Moore St. (bet. Bogart & White Sts.)

Subway: Morgan Av
Phone: 718-417-1118
Web: www.robertaspizza.com
Prices: $$

Lunch & dinner daily

There's no denying Roberta's is cool. Housed in a former garage, the barebones interior is brilliantly raw and rustic; the rooftop garden, backyard dining area, and internet-based Heritage Radio Network broadcasts, keep everything loud, cool, and fun.

A roster of whimsically dubbed pizzas emerge from the fire-engine red oven, like the Tracy Patty revealing a white pizza frilled with caramelized cabbage, *boquerones*, and cracked pepper atop a divine, wood-smoke scented crust. From the kitchen comes a peerless, seasonally driven bill of fare: Nantucket Bay scallops with crispy trout skin and squeeze of Meyer lemon; house-made squid ink tagliatelle with plump mussels and sea urchin; and a brilliant parsley sponge cake with caramel-fennel ice cream.

Roebling Tea Room

Contemporary 🍴

C4

143 Roebling St. (at Metropolitan Ave.)

Subway: Lorimer St - Metropolitan Av
Phone: 718-963-0760
Web: www.roeblingtearoom.com
Prices: $$

Lunch & dinner daily

The moniker is rather nondescript, but this venue offers plenty of razzle-dazzle on the plate. Starters like pan-seared monkfish cheeks with quince, golden raisins, and lightly cooked tomato; and entrées such as gloriously roasted young chicken with creamy almond butter, roasted celery root, and pea shoot pistou are but just two fine examples of the intriguing and eclectic dinnertime cooking bristling with creativity.

Perched on a laid-back Williamsburg corner, the lofty dining hall combines an open layout and industrial edge. The room feels attractively hip with rough-hewn wood furnishings, metal chairs, and glazed tile—all softened by candlelight. The beverage selection pours creative cocktails, a full range of teas, and a daily kombucha.

Roman's

C6

243 DeKalb Ave. (bet. Clermont & Vanderbilt Aves.)

Subway: Lafayette Av
Phone: 718-622-5300
Web: www.romansnyc.com
Prices: $$

Lunch Sat – Sun
Dinner nightly

Your *mamma* didn't give you much of a choice for dinner, and neither will Andrew Tarlow and Mark Firth—at least not at Roman's. But have faith, young Brooklyn: this is the brilliant duo behind Diner and Marlow & Sons, two wildly successful Williamsburg restaurants that helped put this borough's distinct cuisine on the map.

Small and warm, with candlelight bouncing off white-tiled walls, and blazing color mosaic tiles dotting the room, Roman's is truly lovely and insanely packed. The daily-changing, Italian menu is true to its inspiration, offering a handful of simple, but delicious courses that might include spaghetti with garlicky mussels or striped bass with salsify and cardoons. Daily cocktails–one bitter, one dry–are a memorable start to meals.

Rucola

B6

190 Dean St. (at Bond St.)

Subway: Bergen St (Smith St.)
Phone: 718-576-3209
Web: www.rucolabrooklyn.com
Prices: $$

Lunch & dinner daily

Eat your greens and buy them too at Rucola. This Boerum Hill beauty has a Berkeley-meets-Brooklyn vibe. Inside, it's barn-like, with details like milk bottle chandeliers and Pennsylvania reclaimed wood, but it's really all about the veggies. These streets are lined with enviable, classic townhouses, whose residents flock to Rucola, sidle up to a table, and tuck into such heavenly fare as a farm fresh zucchini salad served cold with flecks of *ricotta salata*, mint, and cucumbers; or house-made, perfectly cooked shells topped with tomato and shaved *baccalà*. Even the dayboat Chatham cod is loaded with greens in all their fresh and crispy glory.

You've been so good and ate all your vegetables, so reward yourself with a slice of that excellent chocolate torte.

Rye

American ✕

C4

247 S. 1st St. (bet. Havemeyer & Roebling Sts.)

Subway: Marcy Av
Phone: 718-218-8047
Web: www.ryerestaurant.com
Prices: **$$**

Lunch Sat – Sun
Dinner nightly

Rye's Classic Old Fashioned–a carefully crafted swirl of liquid amber–is the perfect personification of Chef Cal Elliott's beloved establishment. Like the signature pour (strong, satisfying, and comforting), the mien of this discreetly marked spot follows suit with a space that is anchored by a reclaimed mahogany bar and accented by creaky plank flooring and exposed filament lighting.

The succinct menu boasts adept touches reflecting the kitchen's chops. A recent entrée of skewer-grilled shrimp and scallops dressed with a spicy Thai-inspired vinaigrette and set upon a salad of avocado and grapefruit revealed a highly enjoyable inspiration. For dessert, molten chocolate cake was another classic that was lovingly represented with pistachio ice cream.

The Saint Austere

Contemporary 🍽

D4

613 Grand St. (bet. Leonard & Lorimer Sts.)

Subway: Lorimer St - Metropolitan Av
Phone: 718-388-0012
Web: www.thesaintaustere.com
Prices: 🆎

Lunch Sun
Dinner Mon – Sat

Sometimes all one needs is a nice glass of wine and a little snack (or three). For this, The Saint Austere fits the bill nicely. Platings bring on far-flung influences—as in the *banh Mi(lano)*, pork terrine, thinly-shaved mortadella, and house-pickled vegetables sandwiched into a toasted baguette moistened by chili-flecked dressing. However, the menu's truest muse is a general coupling of Italian and Spanish flavors, such as pork belly *croquetas* accompanied by a dipping sauce of crushed chicken livers; or slow-cooked polenta topped with sweet onions caramelized in sausage drippings.

The spartanly adorned room offers a hospitable bar in addition to three communal tables. And the wine list offers a gently priced selection of mostly European labels.

Brooklyn

Samurai Mama

Japanese 🍴

205 Grand St. (bet. Bedford & Driggs Aves.)

Subway: Bedford Av
Phone: 718-599-6161
Web: www.samuraimama.com
Prices: 😊😊

Lunch & dinner daily

Chef Makoto Suzuki (also of Momo Sushi Shack and Bozu) dishes up an appetizing composition of mostly cooked fare at this whimsical Williamsburg gem. The Japanese vibe and flavor are quaint and impressively authentic, and diners tend to partake in preparations that include *konbu dango* (deep-fried seaweed and soybean croquettes); chewy, salty flying fish jerky topped with magenta shards of pickled daikon; or salmon *negi* sushi "taco" cradled in a sheet of toasted nori.

A series of quirky paintings frame the seasonally dressed communal table which may unveil such delicacies as *kinoko tsukejil* "dipping-style" udon, featuring handmade noodles crafted from California-milled flour bobbling alongside rustic wild mushrooms in a rich and complex savory broth.

Saraghina

Pizza 🍴

435 Halsey St. (at Lewis Ave.)

Subway: Utica Av
Phone: 718-574-0010
Web: www.saraghinabrooklyn.com
Prices: $$

Lunch & dinner daily

Saraghina, named for a character in a Fellini film, may have lost its original owners but it hasn't lost any of its appeal. Bicycles are aplenty outside this building on a charming Bed-Stuy street lined with brownstones and Victorians. It's kitschy cute...old butcher signs, chairs hanging from the ceiling, and marmalade jars define the look, and there's even a leafy garden in the back for nice summer days.

This all-day spot is known for the pizza, which like the *capocollo* (topped with thick and searingly spicy *coppa* and buttery mozzarella) is definitely a don't-miss, but wait, there's more. Creamy risotto studded with sweet sausage; striped bass perfectly seasoned and simply cooked; even a grilled apple salad with tart goat cheese...it's all so *buono*!

Saul ✿

B6

140 Smith St. (bet. Bergen & Dean Sts.)

Subway: Bergen St (Smith St.)   Dinner nightly
Phone: 718-935-9844
Web: www.saulrestaurant.com
Prices: **$$$**

Tyson Reist

This Smith Street pioneer has enjoyed impressive longevity and today is just as worthy of serious fawning as it was when it opened back in 1999. Although aging tends to conjure negative imagery, let's say Saul has matured gracefully through the years, settling in nicely and securing a place deep in the hearts of the countless diners who've supped here.

Found along a tree-lined stretch amid shops and cheery playgrounds, the charming room is an inviting respite that combines hardwood floors, brick-lined walls, and a pressed-tin ceiling for that iconic, casually chic ambience.

Chef Saul Bolton gives American cooking an inspired turn in creations that commence with an elegant amuse-bouche—perhaps a shot of carrot purée swirled with cilantro yogurt? Mediterranean sardines are house-cured in a mixture of extra virgin olive oil, white balsamic vinegar, thyme, and lemon peel, then layered with eggplant caponata; and skate is pan-roasted and tucked atop tender rings of local calamari, diced smoked sausage, wilted kale, and an intense lobster broth. Desserts are never an afterthought here: warm apple crumble covering rum-soaked dried sour cherries and a scoop of cream cheese ice cream.

Savoia

B7

Italian 🍴

277 Smith St. (bet. Degraw & Sackett Sts.)

Subway: Carroll St   Lunch & dinner daily
Phone: 718-797-2727
Web: www.savoiarestaurant.com
Prices: $$

With its young at-home moms, lunching construction crews, and savvy foreign visitors, all walks of life are drawn to this Smith Street charmer, pastorally furnished with wooden tables and straw-seat chairs. Exposed brick and colorful tiles complement the two-room setting equipped with a wood-burning pizza oven. Fittingly, Savoia devotes a large portion of its menu to manifold pizza offerings made in the Neopolitan tradition. Still, there is also an ample selection of gratifying homemade pastas, like the organic buckwheat *maltagliati* with porcini mushrooms, *bresaola*, and truffle oil; as well as heartier items like the roasted pork chop with eggplant caponata and grilled *orata* with sun dried tomatoes. Affable service adds to Savoia's casual vibe.

Sea

C3

Thai 🍴

114 N. 6th St. (bet. Berry St. & Wythe Ave.)

Subway: Bedford Av   Lunch & dinner daily
Phone: 718-384-8850
Web: www.seathainyc.com
Prices:

Peel away the passive greeting at the door, the thumping soundtrack, that lounge-y décor, and Williamsburg's outpost of the multi-branded chain offers a reasonably priced array of tasty Thai standards. The cavernous space pulsates, thanks to its popularity among everyone from young families to after-work groups. The concrete-framed setting is broken up into alcoves arranged around a golden, Buddha-crowned reflecting pool.

The extensive menu boasts an assortment of starters, like Thai sour sausages in green cabbage cups, propped on slivered red onion, toasted peanuts, and fresh ginger. Also find a full range of pick-your-protein noodles, curries, and stir-fries, as well as specialties like crispy whole fish with a tamarind-chili sauce.

Seersucker

American XX

B7

329 Smith St. (bet. Carroll & President Sts.)

Subway: Carroll St   Lunch & dinner daily
Phone: 718-422-0444
Web: www.seersuckerbrooklyn.com
Prices: $$

Folks have little difficulty guessing this concept, but here are a few clues: shaved country ham on a warm buttermilk biscuit; pan-fried sweetbreads with red eye gravy and spring peas; and crisp-skinned trout with risotto-style Carolina rice, favas, and mint. This is proudly Southern cooking with a sophisticated flair. For groups, the snack tray is loaded up with deviled eggs, pimento cheese, and homemade chips.

The graciously attended to setting is neat and tidy, done in a cool palette of pale gray, and the kitchen of Arkansas-born Chef /owner Robert Newton showcases a colorful and enticing display of pickled produce. Dapper yet comfortable, this 30-seat Smith Street spot is everything that one would hope to get from a place named Seersucker.

Sensation

Chinese X

 C4

208 Grand St. (bet. Bedford & Driggs Aves.)

Subway: Bedford Av   Lunch & dinner daily
Phone: 347-335-0063
Web: www.sensation-sh.com
Prices:

Sensation hones in on the specialties of Shanghai in a contemporary room that eschews the traditional decorative trappings found in many Chinese spots. The dark grey and burgundy setting offers generously sized tables and a view of the tidy kitchen in back.

These tempting dishes are sure to put a smile on your face, especially if you happen to hail from Shanghai and have a hankering for rich, juicy pork and crab buns—an absolute must. A light touch and fresh flavors typify the cooking here as in neat slivers of tofu sheets tossed with julienned carrot, green onion, and sauced with a mild broth; lightly spiced house-made noodles glistened by fermented soybean paste and studded with diced tofu; or strips of lean pork stir-fried with crunchy wild rice roots.

606 R & D

C7

American ✕

606 Vanderbilt Ave. (bet. Prospect Pl. & St. Marks Ave.)

Subway: 7 Av (Flatbush Ave.)   Lunch & dinner Tue – Sun
Phone: 718-230-0125
Web: www.606vanderbiltbklyn.com
Prices: $$

Lush green and earthy colors welcome you into this charming newbie on Vanderbilt Ave. The space is narrow but alluring in front, where it functions as a dairy market and bake shop serving coffee and pastries to a handful of tables. Beyond this, find a bar flanked by mirrors and a bustling open kitchen, where patrons watch the action over a glass of kombucha.

For a more relaxed seat, retreat to the rear made marvelously cushy with espresso-hued tiles, weathered planks, and planter boxes. A kimchi omelette sauced with *sriracha* vinegar reaches epic proportions when paired with a wonderfully fatty and well-seasoned broccoli rabe sausage; while the juicy rotisserie chicken served with watercress and cool yogurt is a signature for good reason.

SoCo

D6

Southern ✕✕

509 Myrtle Ave. (bet. Grand Ave. & Reyerson St.)

Subway: Classon Av   Lunch Fri – Sun
Phone: 718-783-1936   Dinner Tue – Sun
Web: www.socobk.com
Prices: $$

This sleek newcomer brings down-home sophistication–with Asian flavors and a slightly Nordic aesthetic–to its hipster home at the center of the Clinton Hill-Bed Stuy-Fort Greene triangle. Its cheeky name opposes its sexy, industrial-chic vibe: SoCo is the portmanteau for a viciously sweet liqueur more popular in college dorm rooms than here, among a gorgeous display of backlit bar spirits.

Chef Kingsley John's Southern-fusion menu might begin with pouches of sweet crawfish and collard green dumplings set in a wonderfully spicy coconut green curry. Larger plates of tender short ribs braised in a blissful coconut-molasses-ginger sauce, or jumbo shrimp and lobster knuckles in tomato broth with creamy white cheddar grits will never disappoint.

Speedy Romeo

American ✗

D6

376 Classon Ave. (at Greene Ave.)

Lunch & dinner daily

Subway: Classon Av
Phone: 718-230-0061
Web: www.speedyromeo.com
Prices: $$

Speedy Romeo (named after co-owner Todd Feldman's family's racehorse) is a fun and fab spot located in the far reaches of Clinton Hill. Housed in an old auto parts store, the building's façade (with the shop's name emblazoned in blue) lures from afar. Bypass the nonfunctioning neon "LIQUORS" sign that still hangs over the dark framed door to enter.

Smart and striking, this tavern-meets-roadside grill is fitted with funky industrial-age relics. But, closer scrutiny reveals such solid, inventive dishes as long Italian green peppers stuffed with *sopressata*; or a Casey Moore pizza with baked clams, spinach, and béchamel. Monkfish cheek skewers infused with *puttanesca* flavors display enjoyable twists that bear little likeness to their Italian predecessors.

Spicy Bampa

Chinese ✗

B4

6920 Eighteenth Ave. (bet. Bay Ridge Ave. & 70th St.)

Lunch & dinner Mon – Sat

Subway: 18 Av
Phone: 718-236-8088
Web: N/A
Prices: $$

What was once Bamboo Pavilion is now Spicy Bampa. This much more appropriate and enticing handle signals authentic Sichuan fare offered inside this neat spot located in Brooklyn's burgeoning Chinatown. The space remains the same, rather nondescript but gingerly beautified by bamboo-etched wallpaper and pale yellow walls; large tables host hungry families.

Bubbling hot pots are a house specialty and bring trays of soft noodles, succulent meats, leafy greens, and a brew of chili oil steeped with Sichuan peppercorns. Other signatures unveil Chengdu hometown chicken featuring chilled, sliced pieces on the bone dressed with scallions and a smoky red chili vinaigrette; or deep-fried chunks of tender pork chop strewn with smoky cumin and ground fennel seeds.

497

St. Anselm

D4

355 Metropolitan Ave. (bet. Havemeyer & Roebling Sts.)

Subway: Bedford Av
Phone: 718-384-5054
Web: N/A
Prices: $$

Dinner nightly

Look to this roughhewn Williamsburg newcomer for a meal of grilled, meaty satisfaction. Loud and proud carnivores, this one's for you.

The perpetually rollicking kitchen embraces grilling as its preferred method of cooking to turn out a commendable bill of fare. Razor clams, sardines, artichokes, or *haloumi* comprise the offering of sizzling "smalls," while "bigs" are founded on cuts of hormone-free meats procured from small ranches, and have included a dinner plate-sized lamb blade steak–scorched, enjoyably fatty, and deliciously salted–topped with a coin of mint-gremolata butter. Other options can include a sweet tea-brined chicken; sides like decadent spinach gratin; or Mason jar of chocolate *pot de crème* topped with *fleur de sel* and whipped cream.

Stone Park Cafe

B7

324 Fifth Ave. (at 3rd St.)

Subway: Union St
Phone: 718-369-0082
Web: www.stoneparkcafe.com
Prices: $$

Lunch Tue – Sun
Dinner nightly

At this corner location, large windows peer onto Park Slope's vibrant Fifth Avenue thoroughfare and small namesake park, attracting neighborhood couples and families seeking worldly and creative fare.

A three-course, $34 prix-fixe Market menu offers excellent value and admirable cooking. Expect small plates like grilled baby octopus with Spanish chorizo, fingerling potatoes, and preserved lemon; fresh pastas; and hearty entrées such as grilled hanger steak with black pepper spätzle and balsamic-veal reduction.

The light, airy interior has exposed brick, pale sage walls, a long bar near the entrance for pre-dinner cocktails, and a candlelit, sunken dining room with linen-topped tables. Weather permitting, alfresco sidewalk seating is available.

Strong Place

Gastropub ✗

B6

270 Court St. (bet. Butler & Douglass Sts.)

Subway: Bergen St (Smith St.)
Phone: 718-855-2105
Web: N/A
Prices: $$

Lunch Fri – Sun
Dinner nightly

Fronted by a welcoming bar area that is unapologetically devoted to beer (more than 20 labels are served on tap bolstered by an additional selection of fifteen bottles), Strong Place invites everyone to kick back and unwind. The vibe is chill, as chunky wood tables and metal seating render a vaguely industrial look. An open kitchen and raw bar station embellish the amiable atmosphere.

Snacks such as deviled eggs, boiled peanuts, and waffle fries with onion dip serve as perfect partners for a frosty brew; while entrées offer market-focused pub-grub with a French accent. Dishes include fluke carpaccio with shaved fennel and pomegranate seeds, crispy duck leg confit, and a luscious spice-rubbed nugget of pork with black eye peas and baby bok choy.

Tabaré

Latin American ✗

C4

221 S. 1st St. (bet. Driggs Ave. & Roebling St.)

Subway: Bedford Av
Phone: 347-335-0187
Web: www.tabarenyc.com
Prices: $$

Lunch Sat – Sun
Dinner nightly

Spanish tuna and black olive empanadas, homemade pastas, and the market-driven likes of a summery chilled soup made of cubanelle peppers all deliciously co-exist at the charming Tabaré, where the cuisine of Uruguay headlines the delightful roster. Attractively rustic, the compact dining room is lined by slats of unpolished wood, and provides seating along a colorful fabric-covered banquette. The bar–like the back patio–is an inviting roost.

Tabaré's cooking uses local product and represents the Italian-Spanish influences that color the kitchen's creations. This includes *malfatti*, luscious ricotta dumplings adorned with squash blossoms wilted under a drizzle of hot butter and white truffle oil; or grass-fed skirt steak sided by savory *chimichurri* sauce.

Taci's Beyti

B4

1955 Coney Island Ave. (bet. Ave. P & Quentin Rd.)

Subway: Kings Hwy (E. 16th St.)
Phone: 718-627-5750
Web: N/A
Prices: $$

Lunch & dinner daily

Be prepared to sit among smiling strangers here at Taci's Beyti, where neat rows of tables filled with families and laughing patrons create a comfortable and relaxed atmosphere as waiters spring to and fro, balancing golden, fresh, and fragrant platters. This Midwood favorite serves tasty Turkish bites spun with hearty doses of knowledge and care.

Some of the simplest delights include a perfect shepherd's salad of thinly sliced *kasseri* cheese with fresh cucumbers and tomato; or crisp triangles of feather-light spinach pie. Deep flavors shine through the tangy, sweet-spicy, and delectable pan fried eggplant sautéed with tomatoes, peppers, and garlic; and the chopped lamb kabob, grilled and gently seasoned with paprika.

Reserve ahead for weekends.

Talde

C8

369 Seventh Ave. (at 11th St.)

Subway: 7 Av (9th St.)
Phone: 347-916-0031
Web: www.taldebrooklyn.com
Prices: $$

Lunch Sat – Sun
Dinner nightly

Headed by Chef Dale Talde, who previously spun his magic at glitzy pan-Asian spots like Morimoto and Buddakan, this fresh venture brings a tasty dose of flavor to a sweet Park Slope corner. It is family-friendly but still rocks a sexy vibe with an abundance of carved wood pieces displayed throughout, high-backed booths, an open kitchen, dining counter, and boisterous ring.

The menu conjures the flavors of China, Japan, Thailand, Korea, and the Philippines for an appetizing melange that may reveal crispy-chewy pretzel dumplings filled with nuggets of pork and chives, served with tahini-enriched mustard; fried oyster- and bacon-*pad Thai* sided by hot sauce and Filipino-style infused vinegar; or shrimp toast with fried egg and Chinese sausage gravy.

Tanoreen

Middle Eastern

A4

7523 Third Ave. (at 76th St.)

Subway: 77 St
Phone: 718-748-5600
Web: www.tanoreen.com
Prices:

Lunch & dinner Tue – Sun

In a roomy setting with glassed-in sidewalk dining and jewel-toned sconces, Tanoreen impresses with its extensive menu of Middle Eastern home-style specialties. Chef/owner Rawia Bishara may have started her career with dinner parties, but today she runs this popular foodie destination with her daughter.

Meals graciously commence with bowl of pickled vegetables and basket of pita and crisp flatbreads topped with *za'atar*. The array of hot and cold appetizers is tempting, but Tanoreen's entrées and grilled preparations command equal attention. Expect baked eggplant layered with lamb, potatoes, tomatoes, and spices; fried fish with tahini dipping sauce; or a combination of grilled chicken, ground and cubed lamb, seasoned with the house spice blend.

Thirstbarávin

French

D7

629 Classon Ave. (at Pacific St.)

Subway: Franklin Av
Phone: 718-857-9227
Web: N/A
Prices: $$

Dinner Tue – Sat

Crown Heights is fast changing into a vibrant area. Landing here is the charming and friendly Thirstbarávin, whose minimalist, industrial décor (white brick walls, concrete floors, lofty windows, and solid block tables) and long, welcoming wine bar fits in seamlessly.

The very unfussy French menu has many favorites, but the likes of eggs mayonnaise, halved hard-boiled eggs draped in homemade mayo with a hint of smoky paprika, are among the most praised. Dishes may go on to include fava bean panzanella with crusty olive oil-coated bread, mint, and shaved pecorino; outstanding slices of rosy roast beef paired with potato-and-sorrel gratin; or a truly memorable and expertly prepared almond cake with crème fraîche and tart strawberry-rhubarb compote.

Thistle Hill Tavern

B8

441 Seventh Ave. (at 15th St.)

Subway: 15 St - Prospect Park
Phone: 347-599-1262
Web: www.thistlehillbrooklyn.com
Prices: $$

Lunch Sat – Sun
Dinner nightly

In South Slope, this relative newcomer conjures that classic tavern ambience usually found in longtime neighborhood favorites. The corner location is flanked by sidewalk seating for a leisurely alfresco lunch; inside, exposed brick and chocolate-brown wainscoting paint a warm and inviting scene.

Brunch is a mostly savory affair, while evenings might begin with snacks like salt and pepper fries or charred endive with Gorgonzola vinaigrette to go with a house cocktail or beer. Dinners are a hearty expression of seasonal, locally sourced dishes, such as Maine mussels steamed in Brooklyn-brewed pilsner, leeks, Dijon mustard, and tarragon; or braised beef short ribs with smashed fingerling potato salad and pickled horseradish crème fraîche.

Traif

C4

229 South 4th St. (bet. Havemeyer & Roebling Sts.)

Subway: Marcy Av
Phone: 347-844-9578
Web: www.traifny.com
Prices: $$

Dinner nightly

Rocking an affinity for pork and shellfish, this rollicking Williamsburg eatery serves up a vibrant array of flavor-packed small plates. The restaurant's moniker translates to "forbidden" in Yiddish, and the extensive menu offers more than 20 eclectic, global creations prepared by Chef/owner Jason Marcus and his team from a sliver of open kitchen that is brightly tiled and equipped with a single Vulcan range.

The team rises to the challenge, sending forth the likes of crispy salt and pepper shrimp with a *sriracha*-spiced salad of pineapple, cucumber, watermelon and Thai basil; Catalan-style black *fideos* with nuggets of octopus, escargot, and drizzles of creamy green garlic sauce; and warm bacon doughnuts with *dulche de leche* and coffee ice cream.

Umi Nom

A s i a n

D6

433 DeKalb Ave. (bet. Classon Ave. & Taaffe Pl.)

Lunch & dinner Mon – Sat

Subway: Classon Av
Phone: 718-789-8806
Web: www.uminom.com
Prices: $$

Tons of fun and quite an adventure, Umi Nom sexes up this drab stretch of DeKalb Ave, edging closer to Bed-Stuy than to Fort Greene. Just around the corner from the Pratt Institute's lovely campus, Chef King Phojanakong (of Kuma Inn) is giving King's County a taste of his unique Thai-Filipino-influenced delights.

Classics like *Pancit canton* (egg noodles stir-fried with shrimp, chicken, peas, peppers, and fish sauce) share the menu with spicy, mouthwatering mackerel; and outstanding pork sliders with a sweet, peanutty sauce and tart pickles. Get lucky and dine on a day when *adobo* is the special—silky, fatty pork belly rubbed with spices, slowly cooked for three hours, then grilled. Quench your thirst with a refreshing sweet and sour *kalamansi* juice.

The Vanderbilt

C o n t e m p o r a r y

C7

570 Vanderbilt Ave. (at Bergen St.)

Lunch Sat – Sun
Dinner nightly

Subway: 7 Av (Flatbush Ave.)
Phone: 718-623-0570
Web: www.thevanderbiltnyc.com
Prices: $$

Chef Saul Bolton's yummy venture, opened in partnership with Ben Daitz, is the perfect contrast to his beloved namesake dining room on Smith Street. This lively and loud Prospect Heights spot, clad in reclaimed wood and marble-topped communal tables, is great for boisterous groups or a quick solo bite at the bar offering a worldly assemblage of thirst-inducing snacks.

Start with hush puppies with smoked garlic mayonnaise, blistered shishito peppers, or spicy fried chicken wings; then wash it down with a craft beer or blackboard listing of well-mixed cocktails, like the house Pimm's cup made with sweet basil and bitter lemon. The more substantial list of menu items includes house-made sausages and Chatham cod *a la plancha* with red curry.

Van Horn Sandwich Shop

Southern

231 Court St. (bet. Baltic & Warren Sts.)

Subway: Bergen St (Smith St.)
Phone: 718-596-9707
Web: www.vanhornbrooklyn.com
Prices: $$

Lunch & dinner Tue – Sun

Emanating a charmingly old-timey appearance and dishing up Southern-inspired fare, this Cobble Hill spot deliciously typifies au courant Brooklyn dining. The menu of hot and hearty sandwiches is fashioned from local ingredients in combinations that feature freshly prepared buttermilk-fried chicken on a sesame-seed bun and North Carolina-style pulled pork. The BLP slathers toasted sourdough slices with pimento cheese, makes a decidedly high-brow substitution of garlic aïoli for plain mayonnaise, then tops it off with crisp bacon and tender butter lettuce.

Side dishes like baked mac and cheese, jalapeño hushpuppies, craft beers, and cocktails round out a down-home menu that tastes even better when enjoyed seated outside in the backyard.

Vinegar Hill House

American

72 Hudson Ave. (near Water St.)

Subway: York St
Phone: 718-522-1018
Web: www.vinegarhillhouse.com
Prices: $$

Lunch Sat – Sun
Dinner nightly

With sustainable fish and meats procured from Fleisher's in upstate NY, and dishes created in a fiery wood-burning oven, Vinegar Hill House gets an extra leg-up with its interesting cheese list. The locale may seem off the radar, yet Vinegar Hill is knee-deep in crowds hungering for their comfort fare. Inside, find a retro hodgepodge that includes a framed portrait of JFK overlooking the snug space.

The ultra-busy kitchen swarms with a young, thoughtful staff. Charred toasts with anchovy mayonnaise and sardines are a lovely opener for braised squid with chickpeas, cauliflower, and *muhammara*. An exquisitely textured peanut butter ice cream is the crowning glory.

For a lighter bite in a more casual setting, head to Hillside Cafe, located merely steps away.

Waterfalls Café

Middle Eastern ✗

B6

144 Atlantic Ave. (bet. Clinton & Henry Sts.)

Lunch & dinner daily

Subway: Borough Hall
Phone: 718-488-8886
Web: N/A
Prices:

Deliciously uncompromised, made-to-order Middle Eastern food: what's not to love at the Waterfalls Café, a little café that rises above the rush of Arabic diners that cluster along this stretch of Atlantic Avenue? Perhaps the service, which can be a bit stilted and off-the-mark from time to time—that said, you'll soon realize that patience is a mighty big virtue here.

The reward is in the spectacularly creamy hummus; light-as-air falafel, fresh and crackling from the fryer; moist stuffed grape leaves; perfectly-spiced *moujadarra*, spiked with tender caramelized onions; and supremely tender chunks of lamb *shawarma*, served with fresh pita. No alcohol is served, but fragrant teas and Arabic coffee finish the meal and takeout is available.

Winly

Chinese ✗

B4

1217-1221 Ave. U (bet. E. 12th St. & Homecrest Ave.)

Lunch & dinner daily

Subway: Avenue P
Phone: 718-998-0360
Web: N/A
Prices: $$

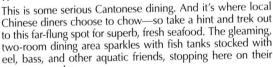

This is some serious Cantonese dining. And it's where local Chinese diners choose to chow—so take a hint and trek out to this far-flung spot for superb, fresh seafood. The gleaming, two-room dining area sparkles with fish tanks stocked with eel, bass, and other aquatic friends, stopping here on their way to your plate.

The ample menu offers the likes of braised *yee mein* with shiitake, black foot, and white beech mushrooms; sliced pork, mustard greens, and salty duck egg soup; or bean curd stuffed with chopped shrimp, water chestnuts, and egg, served alongside sautéed conch and scallops. Flavorful classics include pork intestines with tangy fermented cabbage.

A bona fide Cantonese affair, this might be a good time to brush up on your language skills.

Zenkichi

C3

Japanese 🍴🍴

77 N. 6th St. (at Wythe Ave.)

Subway: Bedford Av
Phone: 718-388-8985
Web: www.zenkichi.com
Prices: $$

Dinner Tue – Sun

Beyond a rather daunting wood-armored exterior, Zenkichi's small entryway is practically camouflaged. Once inside however, warm greetings ensue as groups small and large are escorted through the dim, three-level *izakaya* to private booths. Service is serious here; when ready to order, summon the staff with the tabletop button.

The menu features an assortment of Tokyo-style small plates designed to be enjoyed with alcohol, and lots of it. Set your own course or choose the well-priced omakase: an eight-course seasonal feast that may start with a chilled plate of pristine fish and then close with roasted honey-soy duck. Start off with some sake and oysters at adjacent Bar Akariba.

Return visits are inevitable—just remember to reserve.

Feast for under $25 at all restaurants with 🍜.

Queens

Queens

Nearly as large as Manhattan, the Bronx, and Staten Island combined, the borough of Queens covers 120 square miles on the western end of Long Island. Thousands of immigrants arriving here each year make Queens the most culturally diverse county in the country. They are all drawn to the relatively affordable housing, a familial quality of life, and the tight-knit cultural communities formed by extended immigrant families. Such a unique convergence results in the borough's largely international flavor, drawing throngs of NYers eager to dine on affordable, ethnic eats.

ASTORIA'S GLOBAL BUFFET

Stroll through Astoria, a charming quarter of brick row houses and Mediterranean groceries. Discover grilled octopus and baklava at one of the many terrific Greek restaurants; then make your way to Little Egypt on Steinway Street for a juicy kebab; or chow on Czech kielbasas at the local *biergarten*. Along global lines, **La Boulangerie** in Forest Hills is introducing locals to divine French treats— imagine crusty, piping hot baguettes. And what goes best with beautiful bread? Cheese naturally, available in myriad selections at **Leo's Latticini**. The iconic *pasticceria*, **La Guli**, has been open since 1937 and dishes out a tandem of cakes, pastries, cookies, and biscuits to everyone's heart's content. **Terminal C** at La Guardia Airport is now a wonderful food destination with outposts courtesy of Andrew Carmellini, Michael Lomonaco, and many more gourmands. On any lazy day, beer-lovers should frequent Astoria's newest beer havens. For an intimate setting with a serious selection head to **Sweet Afton**; and for the ultimate alfresco experience, **Studio Square** is *the* place! Order a dish from their Garden Grill menu and find yourself floating for the rest of the night. If not, entertain friends with a karaoke night and peruse the unique beer offerings at **Mingle Beer House**.

FIERY FLUSHING

Flushing still reigns as Queens' most vibrant Asian neighborhood. Drop in for dim sum, Henan specialties (beef dumplings bobbing in a tangy soup?), or slurp an avocado shake and a savory bowl of hot *pho* like you'd find street side in Saigon. Food vendors at Flushing's mini-malls offer a feast for the ravenous that's light on the pockets with delights from every corner of China. You'll find anything at these stalls including hand-pulled noodles, fiery Sichuan chili oil dishes, Peking duck pancakes, *bings*, and buns in a bustling setting that's right out of a Hong Kong alley. And the Chinese offerings don't stop here. If in the mood for vegetarian kosher Chinese delights, forge ahead on Main Street to **Buddha Bodai**. En-route to JFK, stop by **Warung Kario** on Liberty Avenue for unique Indonesian-Surinamese cuisine. Traveling east is the **Queens County Farm Museum**. Considered one of the largest working farms in the city, it supports sustainable farming, offers farm-to-table meals, and is replete with livestock, a greenhouse complex, and educational programs.

ELMHURST

Vivacity and diversity personify Elmhurst, the thriving hearth to immigrants primarily from China, Southeast Asia, and Latin America. The Royal Kathin, a celebration that occurs at the end of Thailand's rainy season, pays homage to the spirit of the monks. The Elmhurst adaptation may lack the floods, but offers a bounty of faithful Thai treats. Whitney Avenue houses a restaurant row with a range of tiny Southeast Asian storefronts. Indulge your *gado gado* craving at **Minangasli** or **Upi Jaya** and get your *laksa* on at **Taste Good**. Elmhurst spans the globe, so if the powerful and pungent flavors of Southeast Asia aren't your thing, dive into an Argentinean *parilla* for a shift from Asia to the Americas.

Jackson Heights is home to a distinct South Asian community. Take in the *bhangra* beats blaring from cars rolling along 74th Street—a dynamic commercial stretch of Indian markets, Bengali sweet shops, and Himalayan-style eateries. Some favorites include Indian tandoor

specialties and Tibetan *momos*. Latin Americans from Colombia, Ecuador, Argentina, Uruguay, Peru, and Mexico also make up a large part of the demographic here. Catering to their tastes, Roosevelt Avenue sizzles with a sampling of enticing taquerias, aromatic Colombian coffee shops, and sweet Argentinean bakeries. The commercial thoroughfare connects several neighborhoods, shape shifting from country to country.

WANDERING THROUGH WOODSIDE

Follow the Avenue west to Woodside, where Irish bars commingle with spicy Thai spots. Once home to a large Irish population, Woodside now shares its blocks with a small Thai and Filipino community. The kelly green awnings of decade-old pubs dot the streets, and clover-covered doors advertise in Gaelic. Here **Donovan's** has one of the best (and juiciest) burgers in all the five boroughs. Alongside is Little Manila, an eight-block stretch of Roosevelt Avenue, where you can find Filipino groceries and restaurants galore. The opening of **Jollibee**, an ultra-popular fast-food chain, has folks lined up for a taste of home. On Queens Boulevard in Sunnyside (one of the most divergent 'hoods), eat your way through Korea, Columbia, Mexico, Romania, China, and Turkey. Of course, not in one day! In late June, check out The New York City Food Film Festival where food and film lovers gather to view screenings of food films while noshing on a variety of lip-smacking nibbles.

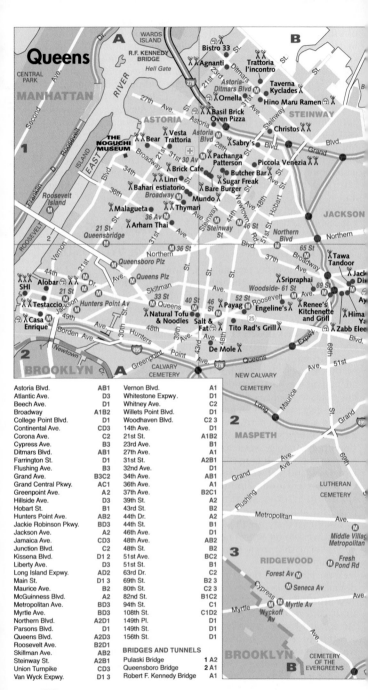

Street	Grid		Street	Grid
Astoria Blvd.	AB1		Vernon Blvd.	A1
Atlantic Ave.	D3		Whitestone Expwy.	D1
Beech Ave.	D1		Whitney Ave.	C2
Broadway	A1B2		Willets Point Blvd.	D1
College Point Blvd.	D1		Woodhaven Blvd.	C2 3
Continental Ave.	CD3		14th Ave.	D1
Corona Ave.	C2		21st St.	A1B2
Cypress Ave.	B3		23rd Ave.	B1
Ditmars Blvd.	AB1		27th Ave.	A1
Farrington St.	D1		31st St.	A2B1
Flushing Ave.	B3		32nd Ave.	D1
Grand Ave.	B3C2		34th Ave.	AB1
Grand Central Pkwy.	AC1		36th Ave.	A1
Greenpoint Ave.	A2		37th Ave.	B2C1
Hillside Ave.	D3		39th St.	A2
Hobart St.	B1		43rd St.	B2
Hunters Point Ave.	AB2		44th Dr.	A2
Jackie Robinson Pkwy.	BD3		44th St.	B1
Jackson Ave.	A2		46th Ave.	D1
Jamaica Ave.	CD3		48th Ave.	AB2
Junction Blvd.	C2		48th St.	B2
Kissena Blvd.	D1 2		51st Ave.	BC2
Liberty Ave.	D3		51st St.	B1
Long Island Expwy.	AD2		53rd Dr.	C2
Main St.	D1 3		63rd Dr.	C2
Maurice Ave.	B2		69th St.	B2 3
McGuinness Blvd.	A2		80th St.	C2 3
Metropolitan Ave.	BD3		82nd St.	B1C2
Myrtle Ave.	BD3		94th St.	C1
Northern Blvd.	A2D1		108th St.	C1D2
Parsons Blvd.	D1		149th Pl.	D1
Queens Blvd.	A2D3		149th St.	D1
Roosevelt Ave.	B2D1		156th St.	D1
Skillman Ave.	AB2			
Steinway St.	A2B1		BRIDGES AND TUNNELS	
Union Turnpike	CD3		Pulaski Bridge	1 A2
Van Wyck Expwy.	D1 3		Queensboro Bridge	2 A1
			Robert F. Kennedy Bridge	A1

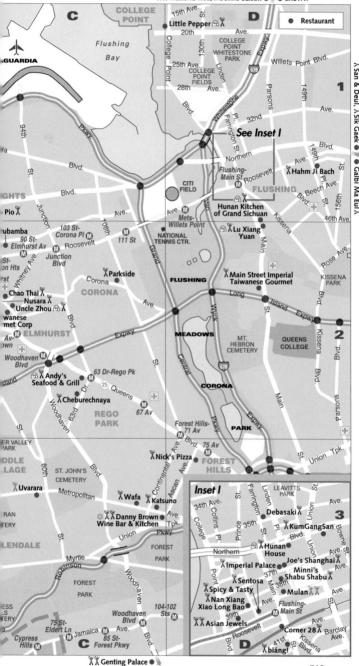

XX Trattoria Neo, X Bonne Saison ● ● ● eXo XX

COLLEGE POINT

C

D

● Restaurant

Flushing Bay

15th Ave.
20th
Little Pepper ⊕X

130th St.

College Point

25th Ave.
28th Ave.

COLLEGE POINT WHITESTONE PARK

COLLEGE POINT FIELDS

✈ GUARDIA

Ave.

I-678

Willets Point Blvd.

149th

1

Parsons

32nd Ave.

X San & Deul, X Sik Gaek ● ● X Galbi Ma Eul X

94th St.

Blvd.

Whitestone Expwy

Farrington Pl.

149th Pl.

156th

Blvd.

Beech Ave.

46th Ave.

GHTS

Blvd.

Blvd.

Junction

103 St-Corona Pl

108th St.

CITI FIELD

Ave.

Northern

Flushing-Main St Ⓜ

Roosevelt

X Hahm Ji Bach

FLUSHING

Van Wyck

Ave.
Mets-Willets Point Ⓜ

Hunan Kitchen of Grand Sichuan

Kissena

Pio X

ubamba

90 St-Elmhurst Av ●

Roosevelt

111 St Ⓜ

NATIONAL TENNIS CTR.

⊕X Lu Xiang Yuan

Rose Ave.

St-on Hts

Junction Blvd

X Parkside

Corona

FLUSHING

KISSENA PARK

Whitney Ave.

CORONA

Ave.

X Main Street Imperial Taiwanese Gourmet

Chao Thai X
—Nusara X
Uncle Zhou ⊕X

Blvd.

Long

Island

Expwy

Kissena

rst

wanese met Corp

Blvd.

Av-own

ELMHURST

Expwy

MEADOWS

Wyck

MT. HEBRON CEMETERY

QUEENS COLLEGE

2

⊕
Woodhaven Blvd Ⓜ

X Andy's Seafood & Grill

63 Dr-Rego Pk
Ⓜ
Queens ㉕

CORONA

Central

I-678

Main

Blvd.

island

X Cheburechnaya

Blvd.

67 Av

REGO PARK

Forest Hills-71 Av Ⓜ

Pkwy

PARK

Expwy

Parsons

ER VALLEY PARK

80th

Blvd.

75 Av

Union Tpk.

DDLE LAGE

X Uvarara

ST. JOHN'S CEMETERY

Metropolitan

Continental Ave.

Ascan Ave.

X Nick's Pizza

FOREST HILLS

Inset I

LEAVITTS PARK

RAN TERY

St.

X Wafa X Katsuno

XXX Danny Brown Wine Bar & Kitchen

Ave.

Tpk.

Union

34th Ave.

Collins

35th

Farrington

Linden

Ave.

Debasaki X

3

LENDALE

Myrtle

FOREST PARK

Prince St.

College St.

Northern

X KumGangSan

Blvd.

Bowne St.

Ave.

Robinson

FOREST PARK

Woodhaven Blvd Ⓜ

104-102 Sts Ⓜ

⊕X Hunan House

X Imperial Palace

37th Ave.

Main St.

Joe's Shanghai X

Minni's Shabu Shabu

38th

ESS S TERY

75 St-Eldert Ln Ⓜ

Jamaica

Cypress Hills Ⓜ

85 St-Forest Pkwy Ⓜ

X Sentosa

X Spicy & Tasty
X Nan Xiang Xiao Long Bao

XX Asian Jewels

Roosevelt

39th

X Mulan XX

Flushing-Main St Ⓜ

Ave.

Corner 28 ●

Kissena

Barclay Ave.

Blvd.

41st

X biáng!

D

XX Genting Palace ● 🍴

513

Agnanti

B1

Greek ✗✗

19-06 Ditmars Blvd. (at 19th St.)

Subway: Astoria - Ditmars Blvd   Lunch & dinner daily
Phone: 718-545-4554
Web: www.agnantimeze.com
Prices: $$

This adorable Astoria outpost (the original is in Brooklyn) oozes with provincial charm and spins out hearty Greek goodness while boasting killer views of the midtown Manhattan skyline. Inside, ornate linens drape the tables, old-world photos hang on terra-cotta walls, and a flickering fireplace intensifies the coziness.

Grab a spot on the bucolic terrace and fill up on delights like Santorini fava beans mashed with olive oil and topped with chopped red onion, parsley, and dill; a *ntakos* bread salad with tomatoes, olives, capers, and oregano; or *baccalao skordalia* of battered and fried cod topped with a savory potato-garlic sauce. The *halvah politiko* is a must try—halvah slices dripping with syrup and blueberry compote.

Alobar 😊

A2

American ✗✗

46-42 Vernon Blvd. (bet. 46th Rd. & 47th Ave.)

Subway: Vernon Blvd - Jackson Av   Lunch & dinner daily
Phone: 718-752-6000
Web: www.alobarnyc.com
Prices: $$

Stained glass accents, antiques, copper light fixtures, and slate floors festoon this spacious Long Island City gem envisaged by Chef Ian Kapitan. Thankfully, he also has the chops, literally, to make this tavern a perennial neighborhood favorite—his kitchen displays superb skill in turning out hearty nose-to-tail eats crafted from products butchered in-house and raised within a radius of 150 miles from the city.

One divine example is the Amish pig tails that are given the royal treatment—braised, baked, deep-fried, and brushed with tomato and brown sugar. Maple bacon popcorn- and ginger-glazed baby back ribs are succulent snacks; and entrées include braised beef short ribs served with homemade Worcestershire sauce and bone marrow-Yorkshire pudding.

Andy's Seafood & Grill

Chinese ✕

C2

95-26 Queens Blvd. (bet. 63rd Ave. & 63rd Dr.)

Subway: 63 Dr - Rego Park   Lunch & dinner daily
Phone: 718-275-2388
Web: N/A
Prices: 💷

Rising from a diverse pack of Rego Park restaurants is Andy's—a seafood haven and grill that cooks up equally authentic Taiwanese and Sichuan specialties. The owner and staff are warm and engaging, which is helpful as the vast bill of fare requires their navigation. The room feels muted, with beige walls displaying delicate artwork on one side and explosively colored photographs on the other.

Seafood is the star in this menu, but variety can run the gamut. Highlights might include meaty oyster mushrooms tossed with basil and yam noodles; a whole steamed flounder laid on a bed of fragrant pickled *majack* fruit; braised abalone in a soft yet rich oyster sauce; or surprisingly light noodles stir-fried with dry shrimp, ground pork, bean paste, and scallions.

Arharn Thai

Thai ✕

A1

32-05 36th Ave. (bet. 32nd & 33rd Sts.)

Subway: 36 Av   Lunch & dinner daily
Phone: 718-728-5563
Web: www.thaiastoria.com
Prices: 💷

Just a block off the N train along this busy stretch of Astoria, Arharn Thai appears to be a fairly non-descript operation: clean, relatively unadorned, with Thai-inspired artifacts dotting the walls. However, the vibrant Thai specialties that swiftly land upon the minimally dressed tables immediately break up the blandness of the room.

Each dish deftly balances the sweet, salty, spicy, bitter and sour elements that define the country's cuisine. While the heat is given the usual Western taming, there is still a great deal left to satisfy in plates like *mook ka prow*, sautéed pork with basil leaves and chili; crisp roasted duck with red curry; or *buad shee*, a dessert of banana steamed in coconut milk served with a warm coconut-banana soup.

Asian Jewels

✕✕

D3

133-30 39th Ave. (bet. College Point Blvd. & Prince St.)

Subway: Flushing - Main St   Lunch & dinner daily
Phone: 718-359-8600
Web: www.tunseng.com
Prices: $$

Asian Jewels is beloved by the crowds who flock here—they come not for the frills, but for the lovely and expansive dim sum. Requisite details like columns draped in red and gold, veneered wood, and glitzy chandeliers fit the bill in this ample space set with round tables and banquet chairs.

Uniformed servers are all smiles and skill as they guide you through some of the best offerings in town. Each dish vies to top the last, from beef stew with sweet-sharp black lily bulbs to cubes of steamed tofu with preserved vegetables. Dungeness crab is a star here, steamed with garlic and served with Japanese eggplants. Still, dim sum like steamed rice rolls with honey-roasted pork, or the chef's specialty of salt and pepper-fried anchovies are irresistible.

Ayada 😊

✕

B2

77-08 Woodside Ave. (bet. 77th & 78th Sts.)

Subway: Woodside - 61 St   Lunch & dinner daily
Phone: 718-424-0844
Web: N/A
Prices: $$

Bright from the outside and warmly lit indoors, Ayada's warm vibe and friendly, family-run spirit has a knack for making all diners feel at home.

Neon lights work here and glow atop closely spaced dark wood tables. Purists who aren't happy unless they're crying should take the menu's "spicy" selections with a grain of salt, as there is a paltry use of Thai chilies (they're sorely missed in the otherwise delicious crispy catfish salad). But, Ayada boasts an impressive roster of delicious à la carte like the *kang som* sour curry which is redolent of tamarind and lime and tastes as if it were straight out of Bangkok. Sautéed Chinese broccoli with crispy pork, and deep-fried whole red snapper topped with green mango reveal top product and ace technique.

Bahari estiatorio

Greek

31-14 Broadway (bet. 31st & 32nd Sts.)

Subway: Broadway
Phone: 718-204-8968
Web: www.bahariestiatorio.com
Prices: $$

Lunch & dinner daily

It's all about fresh and traditional Greek classics with a hint of rusticity at this serene Astoria spot. The appealing space sports two airy, wide rooms—one styled in calming whites and blues; the other in rustic tones with exposed brick, a quirky collection of window shutters, and high wood-beamed ceilings

Check out a few of these must-mentions: *tyrokafteri*—feta cheese and spicy pepper spread, whipped to heavenly creaminess, and served with pita points; or *fasolakia yahni*, string beans cooked in fresh, chunky tomato sauce. Their mousaka is light and deeply flavored, layering eggplant, potatoes, and ground beef with creamy béchamel sauce; and *arni psito* is an exquisitely tender braised lamb served with stewed peas and artichokes in lemon sauce.

Bare Burger

American

33-21 31st Ave. (at 34th St.)

Subway: 30 Av
Phone: 718-777-7011
Web: www.bareburger.com
Prices: $$

Lunch & dinner daily

Funky chandeliers made out of spoons; spare, clean tables; and a whole lot of bustle welcome you to Bare Burger, a fast-growing burger "chain" set among Astoria's thriving food scene. But burgers you can feel good about? Now that's a tasty idea.

This sustainable-minded gem occupies a well-exposed corner near the elevated train station. Once inside, customers have their choice of filling (everything from straight-up beef to elk, bison, and grilled pineapple); and the fun is just getting started. With salads and organic milkshakes in flavors like pistachio and raspberry, you'd be hard-pressed to find a more appealing place for the young foodies moving into the hood. Don't miss the addictive dipping sauces like curry ketchup and spicy chipotle mayo.

Basil Brick Oven Pizza

Italian ✗

28-17 Astoria Blvd. (bet. 28th & 29th Sts.)

Subway: Astoria Blvd   Lunch & dinner daily
Phone: 718-204-1205
Web: www.basilbrickoven.com
Prices: $$

Set amid a residential block in Astoria is this true-blue Italian gem. Basil Brick Oven Pizza is a multi-room arena, dominated by a domed wood-burning oven. Look beyond this to find a narrow hallway that leads diners to an adjacent and more ample dining space. The rooms' embellishments are suitably minimal and rustic, with exposed brick walls and dark wood tables.

The chef and cadre keep their focus on such tasty items as *impepata di cozze*—New Zealand mussels sautéed in San Marzano tomatoes, fresh basil, and olive oil, and served with a slice of crusty focaccia. The *pizzucca* topped with an herbed pumpkin-walnut sauce is excellently crisped, charred, and delicious; while the *Regina Margherita* strewn with Parmiggiano Reggiano reflects master skill.

Bear

Contemporary ✗✗

12-14 31st Ave. (bet. 12th St. & 14th Sts.)

Subway: Broadway   Lunch Sun
Phone: 917-396-4939   Dinner Tue – Sun
Web: www.bearnyc.com
Prices: $$

From its hangar door façade to the quirky décor (picture dark, shimmery walls hung with framed odds and ends and sexy, curvy banquettes), Bear strays from the pack.

Haute cuisine is the last thing some expect tucked away on a side street in residential Long Island City, but it delivers just that. It's clear that the husband-and-wife team behind this keeper is bullish on cutting-edge cooking. From fried brats nestled in wonton wraps served with sharp mustard, to cheesecake enrobed in a crispy shell and kissed with strawberries, Bear takes the traditional and turns it on its head. Slow-roasted duck is artfully plated amid stewed apples, currants, and set atop a potato purée for a standout dish.

All this and service without a growl make Bear a local fave.

biáng!

Chinese ✗

41-10 Main St. (bet. 41st Ave. & 41st Rd.)

Subway: Flushing - Main St
Phone: 718-888-7713
Web: www.biang-nyc.com
Prices: $$

Lunch & dinner daily

Jason Wang's Xi'an outpost went viral after Anthony Bourdain declared his lamb buns were amazing. That proclamation has since spawned biáng!, Mr. Wang's latest success story housed amid Flushing's crammed streets. But, biáng! is a bona fide destination where the vibe is boisterous and the narrow space is moody yet handsome with flattering lights and dark brown walls.

The fantastically funky, regional menu reveals the likes of *má là shuàn níu du*, tripe "cigars" slathered with spicy fermented tofu sauce and chili oil; or *zi rán yáng ròu jia bái jii mó*, succulent and wonderfully messy lamb slices sautéed with cumin and peppers tucked between crisply griddled flatbreads. Unique salads include piney fiddleheads with Sichuan pepper oil and black vinegar.

Bistro 33

Fusion ✗

19-33 Ditmars Blvd. (at 21st St.)

Subway: Astoria - Ditmars Blvd
Phone: 718-721-1933
Web: www.lilbistro33.com
Prices: $$

Lunch Sat – Sun
Dinner nightly

Located a few blocks from scenic Shore Blvd., Bistro 33 is home to Chef Gary Anza. This perfect little neighborhood spot serves a fusion cuisine that marries the chef's classic training with his experience in the art of sushi–he is a graduate of the French Culinary Institute and an alum of Bond Street– for a unique dining experience that does this borough proud. The resulting menu is well-prepared, neatly presented, and delights the palate with an array of sushi like freshly rolled maki topped with creamy, chopped lobster; as well as contemporary offerings that have included excellent pan-seared scallops sauced with warm, smoky-bacon dressing; and slow-cooked pork belly sweetened with an intriguing reduction of black cherry soda and palm sugar.

Bonne Saison

Thai ✗

40-04 Bell Blvd. (at 40th Ave.)

Subway: N/A
Phone: 718-224-6188
Web: N/A
Prices: $$

Lunch & dinner daily

Consider it your *bonne chance* to have dined at this bright yet warm restaurant on Bell Boulevard. Steakhouses, wine bars, and barbecue dens may line these streets, but what they lack, Bonne Saison delivers with aplomb. The white interior is set with two rows of tables, a flat-screen, and bustling glass-enclosed kitchen preparing Franco-Thai treats. Quaint sepia photos of France, holiday lights, and a marble floor form most of the ambience, but really, everyone's here for the warm service and superior food.

A bona fide French section in the menu features faithfuls like *filet de boeuf au poivre*, while entrées like tofu with Thai basil sauce; *escargots de Bourgogne*; and tender duck lacquered with tangy tamarind are sure to sate your senses.

Brick Cafe

Mediterranean ✗

30-95 33rd St. (at 31st Ave.)

Subway: Broadway
Phone: 718-267-2735
Web: www.brickcafe.com
Prices: $$

Lunch Sat – Sun
Dinner nightly

The food is simple and the service sweet at Brick Cafe, where locals rave about the brunch and the outdoor area is flooded come summer. With its chunky wood tables, reclaimed flooring, and farm bric-a-brac, the interior will transport you straight back to that little restaurant you can never remember the name of in Carcassone—and who couldn't use a little rustic romance on a corner of Queens usually reserved for Greek diners and thumping Euro clubs?

Best not to fight this kind of momentum and join the crowds digging into Southern French-and-Italian style dishes like grilled Maya shrimp, zucchini, and portobello mushroom caps tossed in a cilantro-garlic olive oil. The brunch menu carries the usual omelets and French toast, but also octopus carpaccio.

Butcher Bar

B1

Barbecue

37-08 30th Ave. (bet. 36th & 37th Sts.)

Subway: 30 Av
Phone: 718-606-8140
Web: www.butcherbar.com
Prices: $$

Lunch & dinner daily

Got grass? That's not a question but rather the cheeky motto of this startlingly delicious smoke joint, as evinced by T-shirts hanging on their walls. Flanked by old-time butcher shops, Butcher Bar aims to pay respect to these nostalgic cleaver-wielding geniuses by showcasing their first-rate finds: ruby red and marbled steaks, sausage links, and thick pork chops. Suitably Spartan, the space is simple with mirrors set atop banquettes, bright lights, and a bustling, open kitchen. Plain wood tables are topped with squeeze bottles of "original" and "sweet & spicy" sauces that are best with barbecue treats like a juicy pulled chicken sandwich. Spicy beef chili is a mere teaser before delectable mains like a smoked pork belly sandwich served with slaw.

Casa Enríque

A2

Mexican

5-48 49th Ave. (off Vernon Blvd.)

Subway: Vernon Blvd - Jackson Av
Phone: 347-448-6040
Web: N/A
Prices: $$

Dinner nightly

The Aguilar brothers know how to throw a flavor fiesta. Don't be fooled by the blank canvas interior design–it's white, white, white, plus a little shiny steel on the bar–because the sizzle is all behind the scenes.

The kitchen concocts rich, complex, and amazing food that masterfully blends upscale inventions with nods to *mamá* (many of the recipes are a nod to the Aguilars' mother). Tuck into flaky, sweet crab in a crispy tortilla; or savor the traditional tastes of classic Mexican staples like *rajas con crema* with just the right amount of heat, and the buttery deliciousness of pastel-hued *tres leches*. But nothing matches the *mole de piaxtla*—this exceptional dish delivers stimulating results with its intoxicating scent and eruption of flavors.

Chao Thai

C2

85-03 Whitney Ave. (at Broadway)

Subway: Elmhurst Av
Phone: 718-424-4999
Web: N/A
Prices: 🐛

Lunch & dinner daily

This Thai treasure is not only a friendly escape from the cacophony of the LIRR, but a lovely culinary gem. Teeming with Asian diners, Chao Thai rises above its competition with earnest authenticity. The menu is manifold with classics, but most dishes hail from the North like *moo pad phrik ging*, juicy pork and crisp string beans stir-fried in a fragrant curry paste. It would be remiss to skip the daily specials (in Thai), so ask a waiter to explain.

All tables are dotted with complex, richly scented sauces that blend sublimely with classics like *massaman* curry (chicken and potatoes in a pungent coconut gravy); and grilled eggplant salad with ground pork and shrimp. The "potato chip bags" with deep-fried salted fish are a thrilling countertop takeaway.

Cheburechnaya

C2

92-09 63rd Dr. (at Austin St.)

Subway: 63 Dr - Rego Park
Phone: 718-897-9080
Web: N/A
Prices: 🐛

Lunch Sun – Fri
Dinner Sat – Thu

The service can be halting, the halogen lighting is brutal, and the blaring Russian music videos don't exactly scream date-night. But this boisterous Rego Park restaurant's inconveniences fade when the dining room's open grill lights up–crackling and sizzling with juicy kebabs–and gorgeous plates of food start flying out of the kitchen (sometimes all at once). On cold nights, nothing placates like a bowl of their chicken soup with *pelmeni*.

Their unique take on kosher food, which caters to the local Bukharan Jewish population, emphasizes roasted meat and hearty, comforting dishes. Every single part of a lamb that can be cooked can be found on the menu (ribs, fat, etc). For a unique ending, try the *chak chak*—Chinese noodles bound with honey and aromatics.

Christos

Steakhouse ✗✗

B1

41-08 23rd Ave. (at 41st St.)

Subway: Ditmars Blvd   Dinner nightly
Phone: 718-777-8400
Web: www.christossteakhouse.com
Prices: $$$

A dark red awning dips down over windows promising hearty portions of dry-aged beef while neat hedges line the entrance to this beloved Astoria institution. Inside, a front area serves as both bar and butcher shop, beautifully displaying their range of house-aged chops. Hardwood floors, warm tones, and mahogany tables draped in white linens complete the traditional setting.

But what sets Christos apart from its chophouse brethren is the uniquely Greek influence of the food: *taramosalata* and salads of Greek sausage over *gigante* beans share the menu with standards like roast chicken, lobster, and ribeye. Expertly prepared sides like tart and tender dandelion greens (*horta*) tossed in lemon juice and olive oil bring fresh flavors to steakhouse dining.

Corner 28

Chinese ✗

D3

40-28 Main St. (at 40th Rd.)

Subway: Flushing - Main St   Lunch & dinner daily
Phone: 718-886-6628
Web: N/A
Prices: $$

Straddling a busy corner of Flushing is the bright, double-decker goliath, Corner 28. Note that the left door leads to a chaotic takeout joint, serving one-dollar Peking duck from early morning until 2:00 A.M. The restaurant entrance is to the side, away from Main Street, and leads up to the second floor, where a sunlight-flooded room finds diners flipping through glossy menus at dark-wood tables.

Friendly servers hustle to and fro with heaping platters of Chinese broccoli with garlic, or snow pea leaf and oyster mushroom casserole. The space can get crowded quickly and the Chinese music can jangle the nerves, but oh-how-soothing it is to finally tuck your chopsticks into squid in XO sauce, perfectly sautéed, delicate, and fanned over crunchy peapods.

Danny Brown Wine Bar & Kitchen ❀

Mediterranean 🍴🍴

104-02 Metropolitan Ave. (at 71st Dr.)

Subway: Forest Hills - 71 Av

Phone: 718-261-2144

Web: www.dannybrownwinekitchen.com

Prices: $$

Dinner Tue – Sun

Fixed in a residential neighborhood that seems more festive with each visit, this refined and prosperous dwelling follows suit. After an initial salute by a warm, earnest, and dedicated staff, one gets a sense of the sophistication that is about to unfold at Danny Brown. From start to *finis*, he scintillates within a space swathed in muted colors and tasteful furnishings.

This Queens native resembles that classic, well-loved French bistro with its high ceilings, expertly spotlighted artwork, and deep-backed, cushioned wood chairs. Well-spaced tables afford a wonderful level of privacy; and with such sultry beats humming in the background, it is no wonder that Danny Boy is such a treasure among couples both young and old.

Their well-stocked bar and open kitchen work tirelessly to ensure an excellent experience during meals that may reveal slices of smoky grilled chorizo with parsnips and meaty Manzanilla olives; or silky eggplant *rollatini* joined luxuriously with creamy mascarpone and posed atop a fennel velouté. Diners savor the delicacy in Spanish mackerel tartare kissed with crème fraîche and plump caviar. The dark, dense rum raisin cake is a comforting and delicious finale.

De Mole

Mexican ✗

 B2

45-02 48th Ave. (at 45th St.)

Subway: 46 St - Bliss St
Phone: 718-392-2161
Web: www.demolenyc.com
Prices:

Lunch & dinner daily

If the words sweet, competent, clean, and Mexican come into mind, you're most likely thinking of this heart-warming haunt for delightful Mexican. Albeit a tad small, with a second dining room in the back, rest assured that De Mole's flavors are mighty, both in their staples (burritos and tacos) and unique specials (seitan fajitas anyone?)

This Mexican pearl rests on a corner of low-rise buildings where Woodside meets Sunnyside, yet far from the disharmony of Queens Boulevard. Fans gather here for hearty *enchiladas verdes con* pollo, corn tortillas smeared with tomatillo sauce and *queso blanco*. Crispy chicken *taquitos* are topped with rich sour cream; steamed corn tamales are surprisingly light but filled with flavor; and the namesake *mole* is a must.

Debasaki

Japanese ✗

 D3

33-67 Farrington St. (bet. 33rd & 35th Aves.)

Subway: Flushing - Main St
Phone: 718-886-6878
Web: www.debasaki.com
Prices: $$

Lunch & dinner daily

Surrounded by chop-shops and industrial outlets, this sexy Korean/Japanese chicken joint in Flushing gets a bit isolated after 8:00 P.M., though those who know where they're headed are in for a treat. Inside, you'll find a slick, stylish interior fitted out with cushy, high-backed striped booths, thumping Korean pop beats, and an intimate back bar that manages to be even darker than the restaurant.

The soups are notable at Debasaki, but it's the chicken that keeps this restaurant packed all hours of the night. Don't miss the deliciously deep-fried *gyoza*; fried chicken wings stuffed with shrimp, corn, cheese, hot peppers, and corn kimchi; boneless barbecue chicken topped with crunchy fish roe; or the tart kimchi fried rice with cheese.

Engeline's

B2

58-28 Roosevelt Ave. (bet. 58th & 59th Sts.)

Subway: Woodside - 61 St   Lunch & dinner Tue – Sun
Phone: 718-898-7878
Web: N/A
Prices: 😌

Admittedly, Filipino cuisine is not for the faint of heart (pig blood, beef hearts, fried chicken skin), but those with a daring spirit or simply longing for a taste of the homeland will do well by visiting Engeline's. This part bakery and part full-fledged restaurant is loved for its top-shelf goods and cadre of amiable staff.

Specialties like the sizzling *sisig*, made with deep-fried pork belly and topped with a just-broken egg; or *rellenong talong* comprising eggplant, pork, and the idea of an omelet are two must-try items. Go for the *pata* and don't be put off by the serrated knife stuck in the middle of this deep-fried pork knuckle. Desserts like cookies steamed in banana leaves and topped with caramel are great to enjoy in-house or to-go.

eXo

D1

15-16 149th St. (at 15th Rd.)

Subway: N/A   Lunch & dinner daily
Phone: 718-767-4396
Web: www.exorestaurant.com
Prices: $$

Exo, from the Greek word for "outside," is a most apt epithet for the gorgeous garden flanking this very casual and very Mediterranean canteen. The colors and heft of the enclosed area point to a sunny locale. When the clouds part, dine alfresco under the moonbeams.

Settled on a quiet, leafy corner of a bucolic enclave, find eXo's diners relishing, in the garden or rich sunset-yellow dining room, the aromas wafting from dishes like lamb roast (they can also bring it home to you); *keftedes, halloumi*-stuffed meatballs with *tzatziki; horiatiki,* a stellar toss up of vegetables, olives, and feta; and a slow-cooked pork shank with sautéed escarole. On balmy nights, the whole spit-roasted animal is excellent, and perfect for ravenous groups.

Galbi Ma Eul

D1

194-03 Northern Blvd. (bet. 194th & 195th Sts.)

Subway: Flushing - Main St (& bus Q12)   Lunch & dinner daily
Phone: 718-819-2171
Web: N/A
Prices: **$$**

While Flushing has a good number of Korean spots, the lines outside Galbi Ma Eul never seem to fade. Locals and visitors gather here around tabletops equipped with traditional wood-burning charcoal barbeque pits clamoring perhaps for their tantalizing house-specialty, *galbi*—a mountain of perfectly marinated beef short ribs and pork belly with an array of tasty sides. Other than these tabletop feasts, the space itself is nondescript, with large planters and a blaring TV.

The menu goes on to offer an excellent second specialty, *agoo jjim*, a gargantuan pot of spicy monkfish stew with spring onions and bean sprouts in a perfect balance of sweet, salty, spicy flavors. *Banchan* include octopus in *gohujang* sauce and crab in chili sauce.

Genting Palace

C3

110-00 Rockaway Blvd. (at 110th St.)

Subway: 111 St   Lunch & dinner daily
Phone: 718-215-3343
Web: www.rwnewyork.com
Prices: **$$**

This luxurious and modern Chinese restaurant is set in a most unusual space—on the third floor of Ozone Park's Aqueduct Racetrack, a vast entertainment and gambling center. Genting Palace is palatial, sound-proofed, and offers views of the racetrack, making it a mecca for big spenders and moneyed gamers.

Their menu is detailed but focuses on southern China and Canton with tasty dim sum like steamed dumplings filled with shrimp and pork, sticky rice and dried scallops steamed in lotus leaves, and pork spare ribs with a black bean paste. Also find a delicate rendition of shrimp *egg foo young* set in a marvelous French demi-glace; and a full menu offers the likes of poached chicken and vegetables flavored with holy basil; or fried rice studded with seafood.

Hahm Ji Bach

D1

41-08 149th Pl. (bet. Barclay & 41st Aves.)

Subway: Flushing - Main St

Lunch & dinner daily

Phone: 718-460-9289

Web: www.hahmjibach.com

Prices: $$

A healthy assortment of *banchan* (small plates including kimchi, spicy mackerel etc) is usually a good indicator of a serious Korean restaurant, and you'll find no shortage of them at Hahm Ji Bach—a delicious Korean barbecue restaurant buried down a nondescript side street in the blossoming K-town that's sprung up near Queens' Murray Hill LIRR station.

The unassuming Hamjibak won't woo you with it's plain-Jane décor, but scores major points for the patient, oh-so-knowledgable waitstaff service, and masterful Korean specialties like *daeji bulgogi*, a plate of marinated pork ribs in chili-garlic sauce sprinkled with bright green scallions; or *boyang jeongol*, a traditional hot pot of lamb, dumplings, and vegetables swimming in a rich, spicy beef broth.

Himalayan Yak

B2

72-20 Roosevelt Ave. (bet. 72nd & 73rd Sts.)

Subway: 74 St - Broadway

Lunch & dinner daily

Phone: 718-779-1119

Web: www.himalayanyakrestaurant.com

Prices: ⬤⬤

From the intricately carved doors and furnishings to the exposed brick and sultry sienna walls lined with masks and miniature yaks, the broadly appealing and exceptionally friendly Himalayan Yak is a place of care, restraint, and dining adventure.

The menu may be best described as Indian-light, a hybrid that draws specialties from several cuisines including Nepali, Indian, Bhutanese, and most heavily Tibetan. Begin a culinary tour with *tsam thuk*, a thick, porridge-like soup served at room temperature, and bobbing with soft cubes of yak cheese; large beef dumplings in a rich, hot, and savory soup of tender greens and diced carrots; or a vegetarian tray which includes pickled mango strips, chutneys, greens, jasmine rice, and Indian pepper "paper bread.".

Hino Maru Ramen

Japanese

B1

33-18 Ditmars Blvd. (bet. 33rd & 34th Sts.)

Subway: Astoria - Ditmars Blvd   Lunch & dinner daily
Phone: 718-777-0228
Web: www.hinomaruramen.com
Prices: $$

Everybody in this residential neighborhood seems to love Hino Maru Ramen. This Japanese "gastropub" takes its job very seriously, and although the menu is diverse, their ramen promises to rock your world. The décor is nothing flashy, but it is a large, comfy space with hefty seats and serious feasting. A huge blackboard lists daily specials (like astoundingly fresh oysters topped with a granita comprised of yuzu, mirin, and dashi); while *hiromaru ramen* is a deliciously dark and stormy staple featuring fiery meatballs in a rich pork broth brimming with garlic and mushrooms. Other items include *miso nasu* (silky eggplant with sweet miso and bonito flakes); or shrimp fried rice studded with pickled red ginger, daikon, and topped with a fried egg.

Hunan House

Chinese

D3

137-40 Northern Blvd. (bet. Main & Union Sts.)

Subway: Flushing - Main St   Lunch & dinner daily
Phone: 718-353-1808
Web: N/A
Prices:

This quieter stretch of Northern Boulevard is NY's rising (and reigning) Chinatown and is sure to fire up any spice-seekers willing to brave the trek. Here, Hunan House is a plain but tidy spot serving heart-warming Hunanese fare, and reminding all of its phenomenal complexity. The menu reads like a textbook of this region's cuisine; its authenticity is paramount.

Many dishes, like braised fish head, are seafood-centric, though they often share Sichuan's affinity for chilies. Expect the likes of steamed spare ribs, thick and lean, in a hollowed bamboo branch brimming with a powerful sauce of fermented black beans and red chili oil. White chili-preserved beef is an ingenious dish of dried bean curd and a mix of five-spice and star anise, and beefy broth.

Hunan Kitchen of Grand Sichuan

42-47 Main Street (bet. Blossom & Franklin Aves.)

Subway: Flushing - Main St
Phone: 718-888-0553
Web: www.thegrandsichuan.com
Prices: 🍜

Lunch & dinner daily

As New York's Sichuan renaissance continues apace, this pleasant and unpretentious Hunanese spot has popped up on Flushing's Main Street. The look here is tasteful and uncomplicated; the cooking is fiery and excellent.

The extensive menu of Hunan specialties includes the likes of the classic regional dish, pork "Mao's Style" simmered in soy sauce, Shaoxing wine, oil, and stock, then braised to tender perfection. Boasting heat and meat in equal amounts, the spicy-sour string bean with pork expertly combines rich and savory aromatics, vinegary beans, and fragrant pork with tongue-numbing peppercorns. The barbecue fish Hunan-style is a brilliant menu standout.

Smaller dishes, like winter melon with seafood soup, round out an expertly prepared meal.

Imperial Palace

136-13 37th Ave. (bet. Main & Union Sts.)

Subway: Flushing - Main St
Phone: 718-939-3501
Web: N/A
Prices: $$

Lunch & dinner daily

Grab a group of your fellow chowhounds and hop the 7 train to Flushing for plates of scrumptious classic Chinese cuisine. You'll be needing your nosh buddies to help you tackle the ample menu, which is jam-packed with delectable offerings like crunchy snow pea shoots with garlic; flavorful squid with chives; and fragrant preserved meat (sausage) with tart mounds of spinach. But the claim to fame at this frequented spot is the sticky rice and crab...did we say Dungeness? Oh, yes. Juicy, plump, sweet crabmeat served in a leaf-lined steamer with sublime bits of crisp, golden rice, along with black mushrooms, ginger, scallions, and dried shrimp.

Large, banquet style tables dot the dining space where the lively atmosphere brims with a prominently Asian crowd.

Jackson Diner

Indian ✕

37-47 74th St. (bet. Roosevelt & 37th Aves.)

Subway: Jackson Hts - Roosevelt Av   Lunch & dinner daily
Phone: 718-672-1232
Web: www.jacksondiner.com
Prices:

Jackson Diner is quite a trendsetter. When it trashed the tacky lights, sparkly chandelier, and flat-screen, the venerable Indian institution transformed itself into a sleek and mod eatery—and the neighborhood followed suit. While the inside has changed, the food is still the same: unapologetically simple and consistently solid.

Queens is dotted with the most marvelous, colorful fare, but Jackson Diner remains the favored spot for honest, authentic, and moderately priced *desi* food. Fans flock here for their tried-and-true preparations including garlicky *achari* mushrooms infused with ginger and turmeric; a gamey bone-in goat curry deliciously fragrant with ginger, tamarind, and a faint hint of coconut; or the classic *dal makhani* spiced with coriander.

Joe's Shanghai

Chinese ✕

136-21 37th Ave. (bet. Main & Union Sts.)

Subway: Flushing - Main St   Lunch & dinner daily
Phone: 718-539-3838
Web: www.joeshanghairestaurants.com
Prices: $$

Ah, Joe's Shanghai, how well you seduce with your deliciously delicate soup dumplings, perhaps with a wad of crab or pork sticking out the top. You may not be large, yet you soar with fans and not a table to spare. Such is the norm at the original Flushing hot spot, which may be a touch dated but is mighty trim and tidy. Two massive flat-screens dominate this room, yet diners remain riveted by the Asian delights churned out of the kitchen.

Swift and sweet servers attend to round and sturdy tables armed with hefty chairs. Robed in matching uniforms, they present the likes of meaty Sichuan beef tendon soup with silky noodles; eggplant and shredded pork glistening with garlic sauce and scallions; and sautéed baby shrimp paired with slices of tangy kidney.

531

Katsuno

C3

103-01 Metropolitan Ave. (at 71st Rd.)

Subway: Forest Hills - 71 Av

Phone: 718-575-4033

Web: www.katsunorestaurant.com

Prices: $$

Dinner Tue – Sun

In Katsuno's tiny kitchen, find Chef Seo whipping up extraordinarily authentic Kyoto home-style (*obanzai*) cooking. The snug space is simple and clean, with touches of artwork on green walls, and a hidden, semi-private dining room in the back. The setting is modest, but the cuisine soars. Among the delights, discover a supremely delicate and smoky soup with tender baby clams and a fragrant leaf of cilantro bobbing on the surface. The chef's signature squid is always a highlight, pearly white and perfect in texture served simply atop a shiso leaf and side of *natto*. More adventurous eaters will seek the likes of *shiokara* sushi—hailed as a rare flavor for sophisticated palates. Cold *somen* and warm soba noodles round out the menu with hearty satisfaction.

KumGangSan

Korean

D3

138-28 Northern Blvd. (bet. Bowne & Union Sts.)

Subway: Flushing - Main St

Phone: 718-461-0909

Web: www.kumgangsan.net

Prices: $$

Lunch & dinner daily

Lip-smacking Korean fare flows 24-7 from the kitchen of KumGangSan—a bright, busy restaurant tucked into Queens' bustling Northern Blvd. By day, customers pile into the dark wood tables or angle for a seat at the sushi bar, where big, windowed walls offer streams of sunlight and a nice view of the garden.

An excellent assortment of *banchan*, including grilled needlefish, kicks off a meal that might include seafood *pa jun*, a wonderfully crispy rice flour pancake with tender seafood, vegetables, and scallions, and served with sesame seed-studded soy sauce; or sweet and tender eel, carefully broiled and fanned out over a rich and earthy house sauce redolent of the sea.

Later, stock up on pre-made treats to take home at Janchi Janchi next door.

Linn

Japanese 🍴🍴

A1

29-13 Broadway (bet. 29th & 30th Sts.)

Subway: Broadway
Phone: 718-204-0060
Web: www.linnrestaurant.com
Prices: $$

Lunch Wed – Sat
Dinner nightly

Tasty little Linn brings Tokyo via Chelsea to Astoria—enter to find yourself amid an art gallery offering the finest fish. Simply dressed in dark tile floors and white walls, Linn revolves around its L-shaped bar, as if to ensure that sushi and sashimi are the way to go—oysters mingled with mushroom nigiri are a minute in your mouth, but forever on your mind.

The staff is average at best, but the chef (who hails from Masa) shines in his handling of first-rate fish. While most order à la carte, others dive into an omakase that opens with a bowl of dashi brimming with *kombu* and cod flakes, followed by tender pork belly in a sweet mirin glaze. Two cubes of fresh tofu are full of flavor when topped with a plum-soy sauce and caramelized white miso paste.

Little Pepper 😊

Chinese 🍴

D1

18-24 College Point Blvd. (bet. 18th & 20th Aves.)

Subway: Flushing - Main St (& bus Q20A)
Phone: 718-939-7788
Web: N/A
Prices: 💰💰

Lunch & dinner Fri – Wed

The exquisite Little Pepper housed in College Point boasts a delicate and faithful rendition of Sichuan cooking. Add that to the fresh and clean interior dressed-up marble tiled floors, immaculate white walls adorned with "frescoes" created by the owner's son, and a small service bar, and it is no wonder that this is such a big hit.

But the focus here is surely on their sublime, honest cuisine, which thankfully has not changed. Some irresistible faves include fresh cucumber with mashed garlic sauce; thinly sliced, blanched ox "organs" tossed in an intensely flavorful chili oil; and glass noodles in a heavenly pool of stir-fried pork, scallions, and Sichuan peppercorns. Need some crispy treats? The deep-fried whole fish topped with pickles is bliss.

Lu Xiang Yuan 😊

D2

42-87 Main St. (bet. Blossom & Cherry Aves.)

Subway: Flushing - Main St   Lunch & dinner daily
Phone: 718-359-2108
Web: N/A
Prices: 😊

Exciting and unfamiliar regional Chinese cuisine is flourishing in Flushing. A relative newcomer to this chill stretch of Main Street, Lu Xiang Yuan is firing up outstanding dishes—Quingdao style. The clean but ordinary space and ambience may lack character; yet it is memorable for the food's extraordinary balance and interplay of hot, sour, and sweet tastes.

Subtle smokiness and tangy flavors headline the jaw-dropping selection, featuring the likes of a brilliantly textured mixed-bean jelly with pickled leafy greens, crisp cucumber, and vinegar sauce; or a purple-red Chinese radish and shrimp soup. Pork tendon is toffee-rich and unforgettable. The mountain yam stir-fried with lily bulb, and the silk melon with clam meat are beguiling and elegant.

Main Street Imperial Taiwanese Gourmet

D2

59-14A Main St. (bet. 59th & 60th Aves.)

Subway: Flushing - Main St (& bus Q44)   Lunch & dinner daily
Phone: 718-886-8788
Web: N/A
Prices: 😊

With its impossibly long name and simple, Zen-like interior, this Taiwanese joint isn't trying to woo anyone to Flushing for ambience. You can find that anywhere, after all. It's all about the food at this compact gem sporting a clean space and walls simply adorned with large framed Chinese characters.

Rest assured it's worth it for the stinky tofu alone. The staff speaks little English, but with a dash of ingenuity you'll soon be on your way to exquisite delights like bamboo pork, served together in a hot cast iron vessel with scallions and a mouthwatering sauce; wildly fresh oyster pancakes sporting caramelized edges and a tantalizingly sweet sauce; and tender cuttlefish tossed with minced pork, crunchy Chinese celery, and seared green peppers.

Malagueta

A1

Brazilian ✗

25-35 36th Ave. (at 28th St.)

Subway: 36 Av   Lunch & dinner daily
Phone: 718-937-4821
Web: www.malaguetany.com
Prices: $$

For a mainstay that has stood still for many years, Malagueta's Brazilian menu loves to meander north of the country. The captain of the kitchen must clearly be inspired by his homeland, as he pays homage to such authentic items as *feijoada completa*, served on Saturdays only. It may not be the only Brazilian gem in town, but it is one that offers a meal minus the stupefying slices of meat.

The bright walls are judiciously covered with oils and make for excellent views from tables set with flowers and crisp linen. Soft tunes invite one to take time enjoying a classic *caldo verde* soup with chorizo; *corvine com vatapa*, roasted pollock strewn with a spicy shrimp cream sauce and breadcrumbs; or a sweet corn pudding frilled with cinnamon sugar.

Minni's Shabu Shabu

D3

Chinese ✗

136-17 38th Ave. (bet. Main & Union Sts.)

Subway: Flushing - Main St   Lunch & dinner daily
Phone: 718-762-6277
Web: www.minnishabushabu.com
Prices: $$

Always hopping, this shabu-shabu lair underwent a recent facelift; now both the food and setting are the better for it. The contemporary exterior is a sign of what to expect—a Taiwanese hot-pot spot bringing serenity with cool slate floors, tall windows, thick glass doors, and wood beams. A long hallway leads to a sprawling, three-tiered room of white walls and high ceilings.

Packed with families and solo diners, the shimmering expanse keeps the hordes hovering aound a sauce bar of unique condiments. These are a zesty introduction to the spectrum of flavors found in tripe and beef shabu-shabu in a spicy kimchi broth floating with udon noodles and dumplings; or fried pork "chop" presented sliced on a lettuce leaf tinged with a sweet-spicy dipping sauce.

535

Mulan

D3

136-17 39th Ave. (at Main St.)

Subway: Flushing - Main St

Lunch & dinner daily

Phone: 718-886-8526

Web: www.mulan-restaurant.com

Prices: $$$

Sheltered amid wedding boutiques and Asian pottery shops on the third floor of the Queens Crossing shopping mall, this dazzling spot is one of the prettiest Chinese restaurants around. The chic room is fitted with white high-backed chairs, mahogany wood floors, and silk branches of cherry blossom as window dressings, then partitioned by another seating area smack at its center—a raised platform enclosed within four glimmering water "curtains."

Mouthwatering dishes have included coconut soft shell crab, pan-seared and paired with mango *coulis*; vegetable fried rice, intriguingly pearly and nutty, with sweet whole shrimp; sea bass in a five spice broth with pickled soy beans, and wood ear mushrooms; or tender rack of lamb spiced with cumin and anise.

Mundo

A1

31-18 Broadway (at 32nd St.)

Subway: Broadway

Dinner Thu – Tue

Phone: 718-777-2829

Web: www.mundoastoria.com

Prices: $$

Like the eclectic neighborhood it resides in, this Astoria charmer purveys its unique mix of global fare in a setting that showcases new resident artists every three weeks. The crowds respond with unflagging loyalty, and anyone who is lucky enough to accidentally wander in will find a bustling dining room filled with regulars lapping up the gracious hospitality and humor of Mundo's spirited host, Willy.

Kick things off with a classic Peruvian *causa*, highlighting fiery mashed potatoes, or the "Nile's Flower" made with artichoke bottoms simmered in olive oil, served with scallions, fluffy potato cubes, and broad beans fragrant with dill. End with a warm semolina *helva*, with pine nuts, pistachio, walnuts, and a dollop of cool vanilla ice cream.

Nan Xiang Xiao Long Bao

 D3

Chinese 🍴

38-12 Prince St. (bet. 38th & 39th Aves.)

Subway: Flushing - Main St
Phone: 718-321-3838
Web: N/A
Prices: 🐚🐚

Lunch & dinner daily

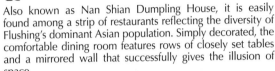

Also known as Nan Shian Dumpling House, it is easily found among a strip of restaurants reflecting the diversity of Flushing's dominant Asian population. Simply decorated, the comfortable dining room features rows of closely set tables and a mirrored wall that successfully gives the illusion of space.

This enjoyable and interesting menu focuses on noodle-filled soups, toothsome stir-fried rice cakes, and the house specialty, juicy pork buns. These are made in-house and have a delicate, silky wrapper encasing a flavorful meatball of ground pork or crab and rich tasting broth. Eating the specialties may take some practice, but take your cue from the slurping crowd: puncture the casing on your spoon to cool the dumplings and avoid scalding your mouth.

Natural Tofu & Noodles

 A2

Korean 🍴

40-06 Queens Blvd. (bet. 40th & 41st Sts.)

Subway: 40 St
Phone: 718-706-0899
Web: N/A
Prices: $$

Lunch & dinner Wed – Mon

Natural Tofu & Noodles may appear nondescript, but peek through the large window panes to discover that the kitchen is in full display and perpetually in motion with noodle pulling, sauce ladling, and pots bubbling. A small army of chefs hovers over stoves of aromatic and heartwarming Korean fare.

The long and narrow dining room is simply embellished with gleaming wood tables. Away from the kitchen's mayhem, diners usually opt for the house-specialty tofu, silky and custard-like, perhaps in a cauldron of fragrant broth with mixed seafood. *Dolsot bibimbap* is a hot casserole of rice topped with a pyramid of minced beef, chicken, and seasoned vegetables enriched with an egg yolk and red chili sauce to taste. Kimchi pancakes are a classic at their best.

Nick's Pizza

D3

Pizza ✗

108-26 Ascan Ave. (off Austin St.)

Subway: 75 Av
Phone: 718-263-1126
Web: N/A
Prices: ⊗⊗

Lunch & dinner daily

Pizza couldn't be hotter in New York right now, but this quiet little Forest Hills pie joint was kicking it long before the recent influx of newcomers. Located a stone's throw from the legendary Forest Hills Gardens, a lovely neighborhood featuring stunning Tudor homes, the pizzeria boasts a Norman Rockwell charm, with big glossy windows, a marble pizza counter, and cushy soda shop booths made for dinner with the family.

The menu is straightforward, with pizza, calzones, and a near-perfect cannoli, but don't be fooled by the simplicity—this is some of the city's finest pizza, its perfectly pliant crust lightly charred and laced with a lick-your-fingers red sauce, then loaded with toppings like crumbly sausage, fresh prosciutto, or tart anchovies.

Nusara

C2

Thai ✗

82-80 Broadway (at Whitney Ave.)

Subway: Elmhurst Av
Phone: 718-898-7996
Web: www.nusarathaikitchen.com
Prices: $$

Lunch & dinner daily

The surroundings–a multi-use mall anchored by a massive supermarket–leave much to be desired, but step inside Nusara and the busy environs of Elmhurst disappear. The dining room is bright and inviting, and the attractive décor is defined by vibrant photos of fruit from Southeast Asia.

The warm welcome doesn't end there. The menu is filled with traditional Thai hits as well as a few unusual selections thrown in for good measure. Wonderful and flavorsome grilled pork; tender char-grilled Siam chicken; sticky and spicy spare ribs; and fried soft shell crab served with a green mango salad are among the choices. Sweet or sour? Don't choose and get two for one with the roasted duck served beside juicy pineapple, cilantro, red chili, and lime vinaigrette.

Ornella

 Italian ✗

B1

29-17 23rd Ave. (bet. 29th & 31st Sts.)

Subway: Ditmars Blvd
Phone: 718-777-9477
Web: www.ornellatrattoria.com
Prices: $$

Lunch & dinner daily

The walls are warm in color but dressed with vibrant sconces, and the menu is all about tasty, honest Italian-American food. The team behind Ornella clearly has an innate sense of providing the best in Italian hospitality, palpable both here and for those looking to escape to the Viterale's estate in the Catskills for a food-centric weekend.

Knowing that the farm (usually) supplies Ornella its unique batch of herbs and greens, peek at the menu and find yourself craving a taste of everything. Although classic in mien, witness some surprises on the menu like duck meatballs glossed with an orange-brandy reduction; handmade chestnut pasta gliding in a lemon-pistachio pesto; and a thick pork chop with a "pocketful" of mushrooms, prosciutto, and cheese.

Pachanga Patterson

Mexican ✗

B1

33-17 31st Ave. (at 34th St.)

Subway: 30 Av
Phone: 718-554-0525
Web: www.pachangapatterson.com
Prices: $$

Lunch Sat – Sun
Dinner nightly

 You don't need a lot of change in your purse to enjoy a good meal at Pachanga Patterson. Astoria's 31st Street, once known as Patterson Avenue, is quickly becoming a go-to spot for great food at even better prices, and Pachanga is one of its stand-outs.

 Tacos stuffed with *moo shu* duck or Vietnamese pork shoulder offer something to tip your sombrero at. Pachanga is no typical Mexican restaurant, though the tortillas from Tortilleria Nixtamal are serious, the salsas are pretty darn good, and there's nary a burrito in sight. Unconventional dishes can be a bit wonky (think pork belly enchiladas with chocolate-laced fig sauce) but are tasty nonetheless. The food is matched only by the incredibly warm service. Small plates, small prices, and big smiles.

Parkside

C2

107-01 Corona Ave. (bet. 108th St. & 51st Ave.)

Subway: 103 St - Corona Plaza
Phone: 718-271-9871
Web: www.parksiderestaurantny.com
Prices: $$$

Lunch & dinner daily

Enter this warm, convivial Corona landmark and immediately feel welcomed by all—from hostess and bartender, to server and chef. A contagious, celebratory spirit fills the enthusiastic diners enjoying well-priced, old-fashioned, Italian-American classics of yesteryear in a perennially packed, multi-room space. Its brick arches, soft music, twinkling white lights, rattan chairs, and hanging foliage conjure a glassed-in gazebo, staffed by tuxedo-clad waiters.

Take a seat among the family-friendly patrons and order a plate of perfectly prepared pork chops with vinegar peppers; sliced, aged Prime steak *pizzaiola* with tomato, garlic, olive oil, and oregano; or *fedelini marechiaro* with shrimps, clams, and fresh garlic bathed in a hearty sweet red sauce.

Payag

Filipino ✗

B2

51-34 Roosevelt Ave. (at 52nd St.)

Subway: 52 St
Phone: 347-935-3192
Web: N/A
Prices: $$

Lunch & dinner Wed – Mon

The dearth of soulful, authentic Filipino food in the boroughs has been remedied to the tune of one restaurant: Payag. Here, owner Rena Avendula succeeds not just in satisfying hunger, but spirit as well. A *payag* is a simple Filipino hut, and the design of the dining room–airy and bright–is meant to evoke home. Calming touches of sea shells, bamboo, and rattan abound.

The food, which blends Spanish, Chinese, and Malay influences, is equally homey and hearty; portions are gargantuan and carefully presented. The classic Filipino stew, *kare-kare*, is full of tender, succulent oxtail and tripe in a peanut based sauce. The crispy *pata*, a deep-fried pig's knuckle, is almost overwhelmingly rich; juicy, crackling skin gives way to the fork-tender pork underneath.

Piccola Venezia

Italian ✗✗

B1

42-01 28th Ave. (at 42nd St.)

Lunch & dinner daily

Subway: 30 Av
Phone: 718-721-8470
Web: www.piccola-venezia.com
Prices: $$$

Piccola Venezia deserves its landmark status: This old-time idol has been going strong ever since opening in 1973. With Italian-American cooking now so rampant in the city, it is wholly refreshing to happen upon a NY classic of such welcoming comfort. The décor is outdated, but the white tablecloths are clean and crisp. The glasses gleam at the prospect of great wine varietals, and the walls are adorned with watercolors depicting Venetian scenes.

With a distinctly macho mien and crowd, well-versed waiters follow suit, making you nostalgic for *yota*, a heart-warming bean-and-cabbage soup loaded with bacon; *fusi* swirled in a grappa- mushroom- and Grana-sauce; or *trippa alla Triestina*, succulent tripe in a light tomato sauce served with smashed-fried potatoes.

Pio Pio

Peruvian ✗

C1

84-02 Northern Blvd. (at 84th St.)

Lunch & dinner daily

Subway: 82 St - Jackson Hts
Phone: 718-426-4900
Web: www.piopionyc.com
Prices: ⊖⊖

The Peruvian rotisserie chicken joint that spawned a mini-empire (there are more than 8 locations now) moved from its colorful, exposed brick digs in Queens, but they didn't go far. Located just across the street from the old spot, Pio Pio is a sprawling, street level operation featuring a pleasant little garden and jumbo photos of the mother land.

The menu remains blissfully similar, with Peruvian goodies like crispy empanadas stuffed with sweet, fragrant chicken and a wicked salsa *criolla* (a house specialty that, when it appears on the menu accompanying any dish, should scream "order me"); or the *arroz con mariscos*, a Peruvian paella chockablock with fresh scallops, octopus, mussels, shrimp, and squid in a terrific red sauce.

Renee's Kitchenette and Grill

B2

69-14 Roosevelt Ave. (bet. 69th & 70th Sts.)

Subway: 69 St   Lunch & dinner Wed – Mon
Phone: 718-476-9002
Web: N/A
Prices:

Don't come for the setting–a rather utilitarian room located on a stretch of Roosevelt by the Grand Central Parkway overpass–but if you're looking for bang for the buck, you've found it. Renee's is a favorite among Filipinos who come for a taste of their homeland. The fact that you might be the only gringo here is just one more sign that this is the real deal.

Follow the next table's lead and start by slurping one of Renee's signature smoothies. You can't go wrong with classic Filipino staples like chicken *adobo* (in vinegar and soy sauce) and *tinolang manok* (a tart chicken soup with spinach); while items like *paksiw na lechon* (pork in liver sauce) are better suited for the adventurous palate. When you leave, your stomach will be as full as your wallet.

Sabry's

B1

24-25 Steinway St. (bet. Astoria Blvd. & 25th Ave.)

Subway: Astoria Blvd   Lunch & dinner daily
Phone: 718-721-9010
Web: N/A
Prices: **$$**

 See that piping hot, fresh pita bread coming out of the oven? It's headed straight to your table with a side of their deliciously smoky baba ghanoush, and a plate of tender grilled sardines dressed with vinegar, cumin, and oregano.

This comfortable, every-day Egyptian eatery is set smack in the heart of Astoria's "Little Egypt" and serves superbly fresh seafood in a relaxed environment. Try the whole grilled red snapper, cooked in garlic, cumin, red pepper, parsley, and olive oil—tender, aromatic, and delicious. Or give the *taojine* a whirl, a version of a tagine with rich tomato sauce, onions, garlic, cumin, and cardamom, studded with calamari and shrimp.

Note to the drinkers: no alcohol is allowed at this strictly observant spot.

Salt & Fat 🏠

✗

A2

41-16 Queens Blvd. (bet. 41st & 42nd Sts.)

Subway: 40 St   Dinner Tue – Sun
Phone: 718-433-3702
Web: www.saltandfatny.com
Prices: $$

♿ Oh, Sunnyside. Are you the next big foodie destination? Chef Daniel Yi seems to think so, springing open this brilliant and unique yet unpretentious little spot right in the heart of Queens Boulevard. Inside, dark wooden tables line exposed stone walls, and framed black-and-white photos perch on cream-colored wooden panes.

Here at Salt & Fat, beloved American classics are whipped up with global flare. Behold the braised short rib buns slathered in apricot mustard; outstanding oxtail terrine served with hon shimeji mushrooms; "crack" and cheese, topped with béchamel, and fatty, smoky bacon; Hampshire pulled pork sliders in *sriracha* barbecue sauce; and tender hanger steak served over *kobacha* purée. What are you waiting for? Hop on the 7 train stat.

San & Deul

✗

D1

251-05 Northern Blvd. (bet. 251st St & Browvale Ln.)

Subway: Flushing - Main St (& bus Q12)   Lunch & dinner daily
Phone: 718-281-0218
Web: N/A
Prices: $$

At the edge of the Queens' border, where the borough starts to meet Long Island, along a wide boulevard known as 25A, sits San & Deul—a Korean restaurant where the cooking is done table-top with real wood, the *panchan* is delightful, and the service is lovely.

If the décor (a clean, bright room with large windows overlooking the street) is a little on the functional end, you can probably look the other way. Food like this is ambience enough: A mashed soybean casserole is dotted with veggies and fresh clams; deep-fried dumplings are stuffed with pork, shiitake mushrooms, fish sauce, and tofu; and tender prime beef short ribs are cooked over a wood burning grill, then served with red rice, kimchi, and red-leaf lettuce for wrapping.

Sentosa

D3

39-07 Prince St. (at 39th Ave.)

Subway: Flushing - Main St

Phone: 718-886-6331

Web: www.sentosausa.com

Prices: 💰

Lunch & dinner daily

Sentosa is a nirvana of sorts for die-hard Southeast Asian food fans. Set at the base of a building where the foot traffic never ceases, this Malaysian marvel is firmly planted amid Chinese banquet halls and eateries hawking Cantonese roast meats and Vietnamese *pho*. The inside is immaculate, airy, and modern in a muted sort of way with natural light bouncing from teak walls to stone-tiled floors.

The courteous and friendly staff is eager to educate and delight you with any number of dishes from the well-explained menu, from firm and fiery pickled vegetables to the refreshing watermelon juice. Expect *poh piah* packed with jicama, tofu, and bean sprouts; or the ever-authentic *nasi lemak* mingling coconut rice, anchovies, chicken curry, and hard-boiled eggs.

SHI

A2

47-20 Center Blvd. (bet. 47th & 48th Aves.)

Subway: Vernon Blvd - Jackson Av

Phone: 347-242-2450

Web: www.shilic.com

Prices: $$

Dinner nightly

After decades of work, Long Island City is now a residential gem rife with delicious eats. SHI is one such treat, set on the street-level of a lovely high-rise on the banks of the East River. The views from its rooftop are special and the moment you walk through their wood-carved doors, find yourself upon a dramatic stage. Floor-to-ceiling windows frame the Manhattan skyline while the sleek lounge is set with a fine bar, white leather chairs, and plush banquettes.

Stop here or wander on to the stunning dining room lit by crystal chandeliers, where diners nibble on Cointreau prawns exuding sweet and salty flavors. Singapore noodles mingled with sesame oil and curry, and a sweet corn chicken soup pocked with fresh scallions leave a lusciously lasting taste.

Sik Gaek

Korean

D1

161-29 Crocheron Ave. (bet. 161st & 162nd Sts.)

Subway: Flushing - Main St (& bus Q12)   Lunch & dinner daily
Phone: 718-321-7770
Web: N/A
Prices: $$

When David Chang and Anthony Bourdain have sunk their pincers into some far-flung outer borough joint, you know you're in for a treat. Sik Gaek, a Korean restaurant in Auburndale, is a riot of a place: think corrugated metal roofs, blaring rock music, neon aquariums, and flashing traffic lights, and you only start to get a picture.

But the fun atmosphere is only the beginning. Kick things off with a piping hot bowl of fish broth bobbing with thin noodles, fish cake, vegetables, boiled egg, and scallions; and then move on to the money shot: an enormous paella-style pan heaped with fresh vegetables, loads of shellfish, and a live—yes, live—octopus, which will probably try to make a run for it. Thankfully, there's not a yellow cab in sight.

Spicy & Tasty

Chinese

D3

39-07 Prince St. (at 39th Ave.)

Subway: Flushing - Main St   Lunch & dinner daily
Phone: 718-359-1601
Web: www.spicyandtasty.com
Prices:

Spicy & Tasty has found its home in this bustling pocket of Queens, where a dizzying array of restaurants, bakeries, and stores jockey to win the favor of Flushing's booming Asian population. Its local love is clear in the diverse ethnicities scattered across the clean, contemporary, and spacious dining room, as well as in the cuisine—though it does seem to restrain its punchy Sichuan heat for fear of scaring the newbies.

Nonetheless, this food is thoroughly enjoyable. It is likewise fun to watch the warm, knowledgeable staff walk first-timers through steaming plates of dumplings, plump with a spicy red chili sauce and minced meat; broad noodles in a powerful, rich, meaty sauce dancing with scallions and peppers; or tender and fiery cold tripe salad.

Sripraphai

B2

64-13 39th Ave. (bet. 64th & 65th Sts.)

Subway: Woodside - 61 St
Phone: 718-899-9599
Web: www.sripraphairestaurant.com
Prices: ∞∞

Lunch & dinner Thu – Tue

A few years ago, this local favorite set off a critical firestorm for delivering killer, authentic-as-it-gets Thai food, then smartly expanded into roomier digs. In the current space, you'll find a large, elegant dining room with an enormous backyard garden, replete with gurgling fountain.

But with the flood of Westerners hovering like wolves outside the front door, has this beloved Woodside restaurant tamed her fiery ways? She has, but the bland food still remains quite popular regardless of diminished quality. The menu may feature bright green papaya salads; tender roasted duck over a bed of greens; fluffy Thai-style frittatas studded with ground pork; or fresh soft shell crab, lightly fried and pooled in delicious coconut-laced green curry.

Sugar Freak

B1

36-18 30th Ave. (bet. 36 & 37th Sts.)

Subway: 30 Av
Phone: 718-726-5850
Web: www.sugarfreak.com
Prices: $$

Lunch Sat – Sun
Dinner Tue – Sun

It's easy to see what's to like about Sugar Freak. This cute and comfortable spot plays up its Big Easy roots at first glance with a wrought-iron façade proudly fixed with a fleur-de-lis in the center. Inside, it's slightly hodge-podge, with its own rendition of recycled-chic (lights fashioned from milk bottles, lots of reclaimed woods, and retro Formica-and-steel high bar tables).

A husband-and-wife team runs the show here, where the menu highlights classic New Orleans-style cuisine (rich crawfish étouffée?) with inventive twists—maybe deviled eggs topped with fried chicken skin? Oh, and with this name, you bet the desserts are good. Diners freak out for the chess pie, a chocolate pie with peanut butter crumble baked in-house inside a Mason Ball jar.

Taiwanese Gourmet Corp

Chinese

84-02 Broadway (at St. James Ave.)

Subway: Elmhurst Av
Phone: 718-429-4818
Web: N/A
Prices:

Lunch & dinner daily

A spotless semi-open kitchen is one of the first signs that this Taiwanese restaurant is just a little bit different than the other kids. Straddling a corner of Elmhurst, Taiwanese Gourmet is a bright spot on Queens' Chinatown circuit, with jumbo windows flooding the dining room with daylight and beautifully framed ancient warrior gear flanking the walls.

The menu reads minimalist, but the staff can be quite helpful if you approach them with questions. Skip the unimpressive oyster pancakes, and dive into dishes like shredded beef and dried tofu, stir-fried in a complex, dark sauce; a delicate, beer-infused duck hot pot teeming with juju beans and Chinese herbs; or a scrumptious clam and chicken hotpot bursting with flavor from smoky bonito flakes.

Taverna Kyclades

Greek

33-07 Ditmars Blvd. (bet. 33rd & 35th Sts.)

Subway: Astoria - Ditmars Blvd
Phone: 718-545-8666
Web: www.tavernakyclades.com
Prices:

Lunch & dinner daily

Years of non-stop service to a loyal and diverse clientele have only enhanced the classic patina of this small, but warm, boisterous, and beloved Greek tavern. Headed by a dedicated chef/owner and staff, Taverna Kyclades continues to serve fresh fish daily, grilled or fried (note the showcase refrigerator in the semi-open kitchen), along with perfect portions of *tzatziki* or *taramosalata*. Expect straight-up traditional foods, like *horta*, and remember that lemon potatoes, roasted and bathed in tangy oil, should accompany any dish here.

The setting here is no frills, but it is a perfect spot to dine family style, elbow-to-elbow at simple wood chairs, or year-round in the enclosed garden area. Service here is cool, helpful, and without attitude. *Opa*!

Tawa Tandoor

Indian

B2

37-56 74th St. (bet. Roosevelt & 37th Aves.)

Subway: Jackson Hts - Roosevelt Av   Lunch & dinner daily
Phone: 718-478-2730
Web: www.tawatandoorrestaurants.com
Prices: $$

Tawa (Hindi for metal grill) Tandoor is long, dark, and handsome with wood floors, sumptuous leather chairs, and banquettes. Burrowed inside a recessed ceiling are modern light fixtures that shine upon a stunning fish tank and small service bar that keeps the crowd happy. Many of them are here for the hugely favored Indo-Chinese delicacies like *hakka* chicken and chicken *Manchurian*.

Beyond the specialties, let the ace staff keep you happy with expected classics such as vegetable *jalfrezi* dotted with black pepper; *kaleji masala* (mutton livers sautéed with onions, ginger, chilies, and cilantro); and *tawa*-grilled garlic naan that deliciously soaks up *navaratan* korma—vegetables married with fragrant spices in a silky almond sauce.

Testaccio

Italian

A2

47-30 Vernon Blvd. (at 47th Rd.)

Subway: Vernon Blvd - Jackson Av   Lunch & dinner daily
Phone: 718-937-2900
Web: www.testacciony.com
Prices: $$

Safe to say, Testaccio makes a lovely first impression—attractive and elegant with cream runners, votive candles, and antique mirrors. Its large rooms are endowed with wood tables and amphoras. Frascati wines are well-represented in the bar out front, while a beautiful refrigerated wine-stacked case separates its dining room from the mezzanine.

Leather banquettes cradle a stylish sea of disciples who come to devour their focused yet tasty Italian fare like a rich, flavorful *zuppa* served with focaccia and goat cheese. Classic and rightly balanced, *spaghetti alla carbonara* gets an extra kick from *guanciale*; *pizza con funghi* is made special with truffles; and *baccalà* in a fragrant tomato broth offers an excellent and accurate Roman experience.

Thymari

Greek ✗✗

A1

32-07 34th Ave. (bet. 32nd & 33rd Sts.)

Subway: Broadway
Phone: 718-204-2880
Web: www.thymari.com
Prices: $$

Lunch Sat – Sun
Dinner Tue – Sun

Thymari brings Greek classics back to life in their dainty Astoria home. Drawing you in is an impeccably clean and inviting bar area adorned with plush pillows. Beyond, an archway leads to the main dining room flooded with fuss-free tables, striking photos, and fresh air from wide-open windows.

Shaded with Mediterranean colors, Thymari is the sort of place that fosters relaxation and conversation, perhaps about sweet dolmades filled with rice, apricots, and pine nuts; or sesame-crusted *arahova* feta, pan-fried and topped with strawberry-raspberry compote. The kitchen loves its contemporary twists, patent in *loukaniko*, homemade pork sausage seasoned with fennel, sundried tomatoes, and orange; or flaky baklava soaked in fragrant lavender honey.

Tito Rad's Grill

Filipino ✗

B2

49-12 Queens Blvd. (bet. 49th & 50th Sts.)

Subway: 46 St - Bliss St
Phone: 718-205-7299
Web: www.titorads.com
Prices:

Lunch & dinner daily

When your breakfast coffee arrives with sardines and garlic fried rice, you'll know you're not really in Queens anymore. The welcome may be frosty and the Filipino-only crowd may wonder if you know what you're in for, but settle into one of the tightly packed tables and be rewarded.

First and foremost, Tito Rad's barbecue specialties are not to be missed. From tuna jaw to supremely tender pork, the barbecue presents the perfect yin and yang flavor combo of salty and sour. Be sure to sample some *menudo*, a pork-based stew, and the spicy tuna belly cooked in coconut milk, served soupy with bits of bitter melon and explosive heat. Tito's delight is the perfect finish with a trio of rich *leche* flan, cassava cake, and *ube*, a dense cake made from purple yam.

Trattoria l'incontro

Italian ✗✗

21-76 31st St. (at Ditmars Blvd.)

Subway: Astoria - Ditmars Blvd
Phone: 718-721-3532
Web: www.trattorialincontro.com
Prices: **$$**

Lunch & dinner Tue – Sun

Take the N train to the last stop to track down this feel-good Italian mainstay. Throngs of serious foodies flood this local favorite nightly; yet no matter how busy they get, Abruzzi native Tina Sacramone and her son, Rocco, always find time to pour on the hospitality.

In the back, a brick oven churns out a host of savory pies (as well as a chocolate-stuffed one for dessert), as endearing (if gushy) servers circulate the tranquil, well-appointed dining room, reciting a dizzying array of daily specials—there may be a half-dozen salads alone, not including those made with seafood. Outrageously generous pasta dishes highlight Italian-American sensibilities, with hearty amounts of everything from black, inky linguini with seafood to gnocchi with rabbit ragù.

Trattoria Neo

Italian ✗✗

15-01 149th St. (at 15th Ave.)

Subway: N/A
Phone: 718-767-1110
Web: www.trattoria-neo.com
Prices: **$$**

Lunch & dinner daily

Set on a leafy corner, right off the Cross Island Parkway, Trattoria Neo is a perfect match for its little enclave. Framed by large wooden doors and windows, the inside is cozy and welcoming with wood ceiling beams, Venetian plaster covering columns and walls, and sconces gently lighting the room.

Just as the wrought-iron candelabras recall classic Italy, so does its menu. From the marble bar, expect inventive cocktails to go with *arancini di riso*, saffron rice balls stuffed with ragù Bolognese; or *braciola di maiale*, a huge oven-roasted pork chop with an intense vinegared cherry pepper sauce, paired with buttery potatoes. Wednesday is pasta (and live music!) day so insist on the likes of *stringhetti*, tossed in tomato sauce with fresh basil and Parmesan.

Uncle Zhou

C2

Chinese ✕

83-29 Broadway (at Dongan Ave.)

Subway: Elmhurst Av
Phone: 718-393-0888
Web: N/A
Prices:

Lunch & dinner daily

Bare tables, walls adorned with pictures of the food you're about to devour, and a mini-mall location don't typically bode well, but what Uncle Zhou lacks in frills, it more than makes up for in flavor.

Food here is incredibly executed. Peruse the menu for perennial favorites like paper-thin beef and hand-pulled noodles laid to rest under a fiery broth flavored with Sichuan peppercorns; or just point to the wall—that big tray of chicken in the photo isn't on the menu but appears mighty flavorful in its chili broth. You can order noodles how you like them (in a brick red soup bobbing with lean slices of lamb), while regulars opt for the whole tilapia, fried to golden perfection and baked with chewy noodles in a zesty sweet and sour sauce.

Urubamba

C2

Peruvian ✕

86-20 37th Ave. (at 86th St.)

Subway: 82 St - Jackson Hts
Phone: 718-672-2224
Web: N/A
Prices: $$

Lunch & dinner daily

Far from the high-end Peruvian cuisine flowing through Manhattan, Urubamba (named for a river in Peru) is rustic, homey, and made to satisfy the soul with its own answer to comfort food classics. Inside, the deep and narrow space feels like a petite hacienda, adorned with wood shutters, a windowed banquette, and whitewashed brick walls covered with Peruvian artefacts and paintings.

Urubamba's delicious *desayuno* is served only on weekends and is adored by its constant crowd. Also find patrons salivating over *cau cau*, cubes of honeycomb tripe stewed in a turmeric-flecked sauce; *chupe de camaron*, a thin shrimp chowder with potatoes, rice, and *choclo*; or traditional *alfajores*, sugar-dusted biscuits filled with thick and decadent *dulce de leche*.

Uvarara

Italian Italian

C3

79-28 Metropolitan Ave. (at 80th St.)

Subway: Middle Village - Metropolitan Av (& bus Q54)
Phone: 718-894-0052
Web: www.uvararany.com
Prices: $$

Dinner Tue – Sun

It's not just part of the marketing campaign—*mamma* really is cooking in the kitchen here, and she is all heart. Uvarara isn't putting on any airs and its setting, complete with mismatched, wobbly chairs and a genuinely sweet staff, feels just like your Aunt Milly's house.

The only difference? The food is better. Whether it's simple yet wonderfully seasoned grilled vegetables or linguini with clams and squid in a light marinara, the kitchen delivers on its promise of honest-to-goodness Italian cooking at a great price point. *Fagottino* with chopped tomatoes, mozzarella, and basil; and *pizzetta*, filled with onions, olives and anchovy cream are made to order, so they're always on point. Wash it down with an Italian red or white from the vast wine list.

Vesta Trattoria

Italian

A1

21-02 30th Ave. (at 21st St.)

Subway: 30 Av
Phone: 718-545-5550
Web: www.vestavino.com
Prices: $$

Lunch Sat – Sun
Dinner nightly

Vesta is the Roman God of the hearth; in Queens, it is the home to revered Italian delicacies and a unique wine list rife with special blends from Long Island producers. Such local love is undeniably delightful, as is Vesta's simple space with sage-green banquettes, thought-provoking canvases, dark wood floors, and gentle lighting to suit the diminutive room. Maneuvering into your seat may take some effort, but a whiff of their Italianized classics (maybe a soulful chicken soup bobbing with noodles and fennel) and you will be besotted. A thin-crust, whole-wheat pizza slathered with crispy kale, sweet currants, and salty Grana Padano evokes a healthy dictum, while rigatoni tossed in a blue cheese cream and topped with herbed breadcrumbs is pure decadence.

Wafa

C3

100-05 Metropolitan Ave. (bet. 70th Ave. & 70th Rd.)

Subway: Forest Hills - 71 Av   Lunch & dinner Wed — Mon
Phone: 718-880-2055
Web: www.wafasfood.com
Prices: $$

Wafa is loved largely for her delicious and homemade Lebanese cuisine. Having moved into newer quarters, she now sports a lime green décor that is totally rudimentary and wholly suited to her timeless nabe. Flanked by red sauce joints and solid Japanese respites, Wafa is an ideal refuge for those seeking authentic, diverse fare.

Named after her leading lady, Wafa Chami, who can be seen ruling the roost from the open kitchen, Wafa is genuinely warm and bold on authenticity. The kitchen displays a clear grasp of ingredients and flavors when creating a sinfully smoky baba ghanoush infused with lemon and tahini. *Shish tawook* (kebabs) become more enticing when paired with pickles and garlic paste, as does the lamb shawarma doused in pomegranate juice.

Zabb Elee 😊

✗

B2

71-28 Roosevelt Ave. (bet. 70th & 72nd Sts.)

Subway: 74 St - Broadway   Lunch & dinner daily
Phone: 718-426-7992
Web: www.zabbelee.com
Prices: 😊😊

There is nothing gussied up about Zabb Elee. This tiny Thai storefront is skimpy on style (decked with fluorescent lights and narrow seats where the 7 train roars overhead), but the patrons aren't flocking here for looks. Nope, they're here for really good and truly authentic Thai cooking.

The heat is on at Zabb Elee, where the food isn't dumbed down for blander American palates. It is equal parts sour, sweet, and spicy, though the staff is happy to alter the level of heat. Whether you sink your teeth into marvelously seasoned grilled chicken gizzards with tamarind sauce, or the delightfully sour *esarn* Thai sausage, do ensure you snack on the addictive bits of caramelized pork strewn amid swamp cabbage, or slurp the dreamy broth of the *tom yum* soup.

DEPT. OF TRANSPORTATION $Staten$

Staten Island

Staten Island

Unless you live there, chances are that Staten Island is different from the perception. Think of ports, shores, and waterfronts perched at the gateway to New York Harbor. Then, consider that, in some ways, much of what enters the city has first passed through this most secluded borough. It is only fitting that the bridge that opened it up and may have ended its previously bucolic existence be named for Giovanni da Verrazano, the Italian explorer who first arrived here in 1524. This is particularly apt, because one of the strongest and most accurate generalizations of Staten Island is that it is home to a large Italian-American population. No self-respecting foodie would consider a visit here without picking up a scungilli pizza from **Joe and Pat's**, or at least a slice from **Nunzio** and maybe **Denino's**, too!

Display of Deliciousness

Beyond this, Staten Island continues to surprise with its ethnically diverse localities. Take a virtual tour of the eastern Mediterranean at **Dinora** or **Nova Food Market** for imported olives, cheeses, and freshly butchered meat. Or, visit the old-world Polish delis, many of which seem to comfortably survive based on their large takeout business and those mouthwatering homemade jams. Sri Lankan devotees can rejoice in the area surrounding Victory Boulevard for its storefront diners and restaurants serving a range of this spicy and flavorsome cuisine, with perhaps a stop at **Lakshmi's**. Speaking of South Asia, this region is also home to the unique and tranquil Jacques Marchais Museum of Tibetan Art, which presents the art and culture of Tibet and the Himalayas. Close by these Asian thrills are a few authentic taquerias, as well as the **St. George Greenmarket**, where one can find produce grown locally at S.I's very own Decker Farm. Historic Richmond Town also organizes the family-focused festival *Uncorked!*, featuring the best and finest in professional and homemade wine and food, offering recipes of traditional favorites. For rare and mature wines, visit **Mission Fine Wines**.

Food, Fun, and Frolic

Keeping all this in mind, it should be no surprise whatsoever to learn that the Staten Island of the future includes plans for a floating farmer's market, aquarium, and revamped waterfronts. So sit back and have a drink at one of the vibrant bars along Bay Street, and lament the world's myopic view of this much maligned borough. Drive through some of the city's wealthiest zip codes, boasting splendid views of Manhattan and beyond. Whether here for delicious Sri Lankan fish buns from **New Asha**; to glimpse the world's only complete collection of rattlesnakes at the S.I. Zoo; or to seek out the birthplaces of stars such as Christina Aguilera and Joan Baez, a visit to Staten Island is sure to surprise.

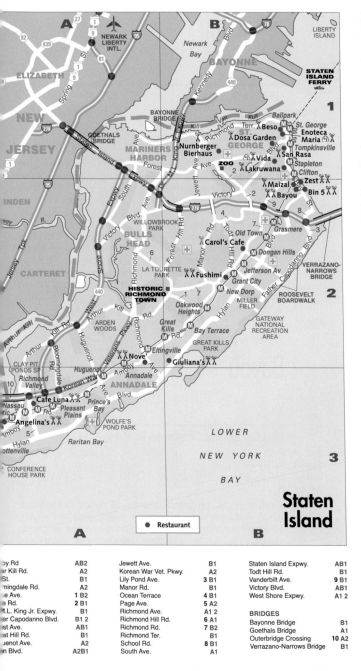

Staten Island

● Restaurant

A

B

Angelina's

Italian ✕✕

A3

399 Ellis St.

Subway: N/A
Phone: 718-227-2900
Web: www.angelinasristorante.com
Prices: $$$

Lunch & dinner Tue – Sun

Angelina's may live beside a railroad depot, but gauging from its perpetual crowd and packed parking spaces, it is safe to assume that locals and visitors continue to be smitten with this Italian pinup. Poised atop the island's tip, the view from this striking multi-level Victorian home armed with hefty windows is stunning, especially at sunset.

Speaking of day's end, it is also *the* hot spot for live music, stirring drinks, and appealing eats. Grilled asparagus topped with sweet crabmeat and doused in truffle oil is a terrific teaser, chased by hearty helpings of *trenette nere ai frutti di mare*, pasta coated in a chunky tomato sauce studded with shrimp, mussels, and scallops. A delicate *sfogliatella* bursting with ricotta is served hot to sate the soul.

Bayou

Cajun ✕✕

B2

1072 Bay St. (bet. Chestnut & St. Marys Aves.)

Bus: 51, 81
Phone: 718-273-4383
Web: www.bayounyc.com
Prices: $$

Lunch & dinner daily

N'awlins via Staten Island? You heard right. This longtime borough favorite now presents a hugely polished space–featuring everything from a marble-lined bar area and linen-covered tables, to gleaming mirrors and sumptuous chandeliers–in which diners relish their solid and satisfying treats. Add live music during the week, and you've got one heck of a reason to stay on the island after dark.

Bayou's menu rounds the usual Creole-Cajun bases, but does so with panache: Cajun-seasoned alligator bites arrive grilled and served over chewy ciabatta bread, with Stella bleu cheese and tomato salad; while Steak Louie–a New York strip steak seasoned with Cajun spices–is served with a crunchy stack of onion rings and a side of chunky blue cheese and tomato.

Beso

Spanish ✗

11 Schuyler St. (bet. Richmond Terrace & Stuyvesant Pl.)

Subway: N/A

Phone: 718-816-8162

Web: www.besonyc.com

Prices: $$

Lunch & dinner daily

With its pan-Castillian décor (a Spanish shawl for curtains, adobe walls, portraits of Flamenco dancing beauties), and sweet, helpful staff, this wildly popular spot–a stone's throw from the Staten Island ferry–is an excellent choice for big, lively groups or adventurous Manhattanites up for visiting their neighbor to the south.

Settle into one of the massive, intricately carved tables, order a glass of sangria, and let the grazing begin. Start with *relleno de gambas*, plantain stuffed with tangy shrimp, red peppers, onions, and garlic, with a sweet, tart sauce; and then move to *pollo Española*—sautéed chicken breast in mushroom sauce, served with yellow rice and pigeon peas. The house-made flan, served room temperature, is a lovely finale.

Bin 5

Contemporary ✗✗

1233 Bay St. (bet. Maryland & Scarboro Aves.)

Bus: 51, 81

Phone: 718-448-7275

Web: N/A

Prices: $$

Dinner nightly

Bin 5 lives in this unique outer borough, enjoying an upswing with revitalized waterfronts and food treasures brimming with action. Amid both residential and commercial structures, Bin 5 is a local favorite for its terrific trifecta of genial service, a charming space, as well as their playful and consistently flavorful bill of fare.

Under the glint of original tin ceilings and amid snug wood tables covered in crisp linen, patrons relish starters like grilled, silky eggplant *rollatini*, wrapped around tart but creamy goat cheese over an arugula and chopped tomato salad. Larger plates include penne sautéed with sweet Italian sausage, fennel seeds, tomatoes, and hot cherry peppers; or slices of moist veal scaloppini drenched in a creamy Dijon sauce.

Cafe Luna

Italian ✗✗

A3

31 Page Ave. (bet. Boscombe Ave. & Richmond Valley Rd.)

Bus:	74	Lunch Mon – Fri
Phone:	718-227-8582	Dinner nightly
Web:	www.cafelunanyc.com	
Prices:	$$	

Some places are synonymous with ethnic identities: Brighton Beach is known for Russian immigrants; Jackson Heights is an Indian enclave; but nothing says Italian-American quite like Staten Island. This place is straight up, no apologies Tony Soprano-style joint and the red-sauce Italian restaurants that serve the population generously dole out these hefty standards.

With its whitewashed-stucco exterior, neon sign, and mini-strip mall locale, Café Luna echoes the borough's take-me-as-I-am attitude and is one of the best of the bunch with its homemade pastas and grilled fish. Even seemingly simple items like stuffed artichokes drizzled with olive oil; *anelletti* with meat ragù; or a creamy Italian cheesecake are well-made and boast super-fresh fixings.

Carol's Cafe

American ✗

B2

1571 Richmond Rd. (at Four Corners Rd. & Seaview Ave.)

Bus:	74, 76, 84, 86	Dinner Wed – Sat
Phone:	718-979-5600	
Web:	www.carolscafe.com	
Prices:	$$	

This is the kind of place that you'd only find in New York and in particular, Staten Island. Carol's Café is a local institution and there really is a Carol here. She warmly entreats you to try her Neapolitan-style fried ravioli appetizer filled with ricotta, Parmesan, mozzarella, and salty *sopressata*, before moving on to a hearty plate of rigatoni tossed with wild mushrooms and spinach in a creamy Gorgonzola sauce.

While these are great choices and ideal for sharing, Carol's spin on sautéed broccoli rabe (with the addition of roasted garlic and candied lemon wedges) makes eating your greens a delightful proposition. Quirky selections like Dr. Lou Gianvito's fish (Who is he? Who cares...the dish is great!) add to the charm of this unique mainstay.

Dosa Garden

B1

323 Victory Blvd. (bet. Cebra Ave. & Jersey St.)

Bus: 46, 48, 61, 66
Phone: 718-420-0919
Web: www.dosagardenny.com
Prices: $$

Lunch Tue – Sun
Dinner nightly

Tucked into a Staten Island neighborhood slowly filling with Sri Lankan, Indian, and other South Asian restaurants, Dosa Garden cuts a warm but minimalist figure, with a few colorful wall murals, East Asian décor, and soft ethnic music playing in the background.

But with a kitchen manned by Tamil chefs from the Chettinad region of India (close to Sri Lanka), Dosa Garden's fare is a cut above the competition. The main draw is the irresistible *dosas* and *uthappams* made to order. The rest of the lengthy menu might unveil crispy lentil doughnuts soaked in a mildly-spiced yogurt and topped with fried green chilies and fragrant curry leaves; or *chettinadu curry*, silky lumps of fresh fish in an amazingly fragrant dark curry studded with mustard seeds.

Enoteca Maria

B1

27 Hyatt St. (bet. Central Ave. & St. Marks Pl.)

Subway: N/A
Phone: 718-447-2777
Web: www.enotecamaria.com
Prices: $$

Dinner Wed – Sun

Enoteca Maria adeptly conjures images of *bambini* being welcomed home by a comforting meal prepared by *nonna*. Updated and fresh, it is a cut above its neighbors featuring such requisite details as exposed duct work, marble "brick" walls, and a bustling open kitchen—this space could easily land in the Village. A walnut cabinet stocked with wines is a lovely sight and blends perfectly with the aromas wafting from the kitchen.

Expect artichoke-packed *ravioli ai carciofi* simmered in a creamy and lush mascarpone sauce; *insalata di finocchi*, crunchy fennel slices mingled with fruit in champagne vinaigrette; and *involtini di vitello di Giuseppina*, rolls of veal packed with prosciutto, asparagus, and fontina cheese, sautéed in butter and Marsala wine.

Fushimi

B2

2110 Richmond Rd. (bet. Colfax & Lincoln Aves.)

Bus: 51, 81
Phone: 718-980-5300
Web: www.fushimi-us.com
Prices: $$$

Lunch & dinner daily

Seeking a quiet space for a one-on-one dinner date? Don't come to Fushimi. This Asian-leaning restaurant should be saved for nights when you want to rev things up. It's sexy and dramatic, if a little bit big on all the decorative bells and whistles. Red, black, and gold dominate the design of the three dining spaces, while the sushi bar is set against a wall covered in shiny river stones.

The food is equally flashy, but well-made and very fresh. Lemongrass hot and sour soup bobbing with shrimp and scallions; crunchy beef *negimaki*; and a crispy duck salad lean more toward Asia, while the cream cheesy-blue crab fajita is fusion all the way. Staten Islanders take their pick from a large, sometimes silly-sounding (the out-of-control roll?) sushi menu.

Giuliana's

B2

4105 Hylan Blvd. (at Osborn Ave.)

Bus: 54, 78, 79
Phone: 718-317-8507
Web: www.giulianassi.com
Prices: $$

Lunch & dinner Tue – Sun

Hylan Boulevard's bakeries, cafés, grocers, and bridal shops paint the perfect picture of Italian-American culture, Staten Island's largest demographic. On this corner, framed in twinkling lights, is a lovely spot known for fresh-made mozzarella and toothsome Italian specialties.

Inside, framed photos of local diners, sports legends, and pop culture icons line the walls, setting an "everybody knows your name" kind of vibe. White linens drape wooden tables and walls are painted in warm golden hues. For a taste of a tried-and-true Sicilian dish, dig into the exquisite and authentically made *perciatelle con sarde*—piping hot pasta topped with flaky sardines, tender fennel, golden raisins, a touch of saffron, and crispy toasted breadcrumbs.

Lakruwana

Sri Lankan

B1

668 Bay St. (at Broad St.)

Bus: 51, 76
Phone: 347-857-6619
Web: www.lakruwana.com
Prices:

Lunch & dinner Tue – Sun

It might be New York's most Italian-American borough, but Staten Island is home to a zillion Sri Lankan joints. Up until recently though, enjoying this country's food meant hunkering down in eateries that looked more like bodegas. No more: with the recent relocation of Lakruwana, the Sri Lankan food scene has officially arrived.

The over-the-top space is filled with wood masks, clay pots, and gold plaques, but the meticulously prepared food brings you home. Don't miss fish *lamprais*—banana leaf pouches of aromatic and nutty yellow rice laced with silky fish, cashews, and hard boiled egg; a moist fish croquette blending potato, onion, and mint served with a pepper sauce; or string hoppers, frilly pancakes of rice flour and coconut milk paired with curry.

Maizal

Mexican

B2

990 Bay St. (bet. Lynhurst & Willow Sts.)

Bus: 51, 81
Phone: 347-825-3776
Web: www.maizalrestaurant.com
Prices: $$

Lunch Tue – Fri & Sun
Dinner Tue – Sun

If you've graduated beyond the thinking that Mexican food is just about burritos and nachos, then you're ready for Maizal. This lovely Staten Island restaurant is proof positive that you don't need to drink out of a sombrero-shaped cup to enjoy the flavors of our south-of-the-border ally.

Sure, there are some traditional items on the menu, and you definitely can't go wrong with classics like chicken enchiladas with ancho chile sauce, and *enchilada de mole poblano*; but opt for one of the specials and you'll be in for a treat. From silky beef tongue with green tomatillo sauce to *pollo Patron*, chicken smothered in tequila and topped with *guajillo* chile sauce, mushrooms, and cream, the kitchen highlights the many, delicious dimensions of Mexican cooking.

Nové'

A2

3900 Richmond Ave. (bet. Amboy Rd. & Oakdale St.)

Lunch & dinner Tue – Sun

Bus: 59, 79
Phone: 718-227-3286
Web: www.noveitalianbistro.com
Prices: $$$

Nové is Staten Island to a tee. Take a look around the room and see couples wearing sunglasses (even at night), dressed-to-the-nines. They are moneyed, mostly Italian-American, and all seem to know each other. Despite the elegant setting, the uninitiated may feel a bit like they're dining at the wrong cafeteria table. Then again, from coffered ceilings to carved wood moldings to a custom-made wine cabinet, no expense was spared in this opulent dining room, and that's exactly how this crowd wants it.

The menu varies from simple, unadorned pastas, like rigatoni with prosciutto and mozzarella cubes, to carefully constructed veal scaloppini with prosecco sauce. The offerings may sometimes seem bizarre, but it is just what the diva ordered.

Nurnberger Bierhaus

B1

817 Castleton Ave. (at Regan Ave.)

Lunch & dinner daily

Bus: 46, 96
Phone: 718-816-7461
Web: www.nurnbergerbierhaus.com
Prices: $$

This paen to the German art of stuffing yourself and throwing back beers is proof that despite its Italian connections, Staten Island proudly flies the flag of other culinary cultures.

There's no glitz with this schnitz. The feel is timeless, waitresses sport *dirndls*, and there's a requisite collection of beer steins. The crowd is raucous, due in large to the ever-flowing beer, and covers everyone from little ones to old men packed around platters of meat. Meanwhile, their warm soft pretzels will forever ruin a hankering for the street cart variety. After tucking into *jagerschnitzel*, hearty goulash, and the menu's crowing jewel, *wusterller mit allem drum* and *dram* (with its four types of sausage piled high with sauerkraut), you'll be rolling out of here.

San Rasa

Sri Lankan

226 Bay St. (bet. Hannah St. & Victory Blvd.)

Subway:	51	Lunch & dinner Wed – Mon
Phone:	718-420-0027	
Web:	www.sanrasa.com	
Prices:	😋😋	

San Rasa may require both a ferry ride and an open mind, but this authentic Sri Lankan favorite is absolutely worth it—and absolutely delicious. Conveniently situated just a short walk from the ferry landing, this ace location doesn't exactly mind its appearence (the décor can seem busy with odd gadgets and carved items; the views nonexistent). Focus on the smells and tastes of the feast before you.

Ideally, go with a group to explore the menu and savor the likes of *lamparis*, banana leaf purses filled with fragrant yellow rice and silky chicken. *Appams*, made from flour and coconut milk, are best for sopping up a fiery goat curry infused with turmeric, chilies, and cumin seeds. The Sunday lunch buffet is an extraordinary bargain for intrepid foodies.

Vida

American

381 Van Duzer St. (bet. Beach & Wright Sts.)

Bus:	78	Lunch Fri – Sat
Phone:	718-720-1501	Dinner Tue – Sat
Web:	www.vidany.com	
Prices:	$$	

If you have a hankering for fresh food in a bright little interior, you're going to flip for Silva Popaz's charming Vida. An entryway filled with dried poblano braids leads to a sunny yellow room dotted with orange stools and wrought-iron café chairs, often filled with devoted locals and day-trippers in the know.

Popaz's extensive travels inform the menu, which dances across so many regions it's hard to define. Let a gorgeous bowl of vegan lentil soup, served with toasted country bread, do the talking; then move onto tender pulled pork and chicken, wrapped in a pair of pristine corn tortillas and topped with sharp cheese, tangy green onion, and a lick of salsa; or wildly fresh mussels and linguini dancing with Korean chili paste and shallots.

565

Zest

B2

French ✕✕

977 Bay St. (bet. Lynhurst & Willow Sts.)

Bus:	51, 81
Phone:	718-390-8477
Web:	www.zestrestaurant.com
Prices:	**$$**

Dinner Tue – Sun

Staten Island dwellers need not hop the ferry for a nice evening out. Instead, just pick up the phone and make a reservation at Zest. Dark wood paneling, jazzy portraits, and crisp white linens lend a supper club feel to the charming ambience of this pleasing spot.

From foie gras to rack of lamb, expect French classics all the way; and do not be tempted to veer from the wonderfully traditional dishes by their less successful, more complicated choices (shrimp and crab roll?). Desserts like crêpes Suzette, with apricots poached in a fresh Grand Marnier sauce, folded into warm triangles with a quenelle of vanilla ice cream, is pure pleasure.

The staff isn't speedy, but like the above-mentioned crêpe, you'll be enveloped in a warm and comfortable feeling.

Craving Chinese light bites? Look for our dim sum symbol 🥢.

Where to Stay

Eventi

851 Sixth Ave. (bet. 29th & 30th Sts.)

Subway: 28 St (Broadway)
Phone: 212-564-4567 or 866-996-8396
Web: www.eventihotel.com
Prices: $$$

237
Rooms

55
Suites

If life imitates art, then Eventi is the sincerest form of flattery. This hip Kimpton hotel, located merely steps away from the city's ever-bright Theater District, captures the creative spirit of Chelsea both indoors and out. The nabe's galleries are given a run for their money at this block-long hotel where nighttime exterior lights look like a Rothko canvas. Inside, it's post-modern posh with red marble floors, rich walnut floors, and gleaming bronze and chrome accents.

The look is hot, but the feel is homey inside the plush rooms and suites. From custom Frette linens to state-of-the-art technology, luxury is in the details of these sleek and soothing accommodations. And it's not just for the adults—from four-legged family members to kids, Eventi welcomes one and all with a bevy of services like spa treatments and 24-hour fitness.

Think alfresco dining in New York means a plastic chair crammed on a busy sidewalk? Not here, where the great outdoors is celebrated in Eventi's 12,000-square-foot Plaza, where you can catch a flick on their big screen. When the weather behaves, make your way outside to sample to your heart's (or stomach's) content at Chelsea's myriad gourmet restaurants.

Manhattan ▶ Chelsea

Hilton Fashion District

C2

152 W. 26th St. (bet. Sixth & Seventh Aves.)

Subway: 28 St (Broadway)
Phone: 212-858-5888
Web: www.f26nyc.com
Prices: $$$

280
Rooms

Hilton Fashion District

Say *auf wiedersehen* to humdrum Hilton and run away straight into this Fashion District star. You don't need a degree from nearby FIT to see that this hotel is all dressed-up and going places.

Just off Seventh Avenue, this is an accurate showcase of sleek, contemporary design. The spacious guest rooms and suites feature a crisp sophistication with uncluttered lines, dark wood furnishings, geometric-patterned wallpaper, and rich blue carpeting. Plenty of amenities and comforts (pillow-topped beds with Frette linens, for one) keep the divas from dialing down to the front desk. The lobby, with its shiny chrome- and neon-accented lighting, could easily double as a music executive's crash pad or cool nightclub. And it does—this place is a magnet for pretty young things. The Rare Bar and Grill lures Barbies and Kens with its carnivorous delights (Kobe burgers and succulent steaks). Just go ahead and try to squeeze into that LBD after partaking in that deep-fried Oreo (it's OK, there's a 24-hour fitness center to work it off *mañana*, baby).

Mingle with the beautiful people or just enjoy the view at The Rare View Rooftop Lounge, which pulses with a vibrant beat, especially on the weekends.

Manhattan ▶ Chelsea

Hôtel Americano

518 W. 27th St. (bet. Tenth & Eleventh Aves.)

Subway: 23 St (Eighth Ave.)
Phone: 212-216-0000
Web: www.hotel-americano.com
Prices: $$$

56
Rooms

It might not be the Latin lover you envisioned, but you'll definitely fall for Hôtel Americano. This looker is the first foray north for Grupo Habita, a collection of hip hotels that are ultra handsome and mod.

Set near the High Line in Chelsea, this paean to sleek and spare sophistication is everything the locality promises. It all starts with that impossibly chic chrome netting exterior, but the high-wattage looks don't stop there. Hôtel Americano is a clubhouse for bright young things and it's debatable whether the staff, bedecked in custom Loden Dager-designed uniforms and sporting model good looks, or the clientele—a bevy of models, photographers, and Euros—is better looking. Oh, and that high-minded interior design (the contempo-cool lobby filled with furnishings by Jasper Morrison, Antonio Citterio, and Poul Kjaerholm, for one) isn't anybody's sloppy seconds.

The guest rooms are at once spare and sumptuous. Cement floors, platform beds, and the abundant use of natural materials feel eco-Asian, while everything from high-tech amenities to plush creature comforts up the luxe factor. As if it couldn't get any cooler, ride the elevator to La Piscine, a rooftop pool, bar, and lounge.

Manhattan ▶ Chelsea

The Maritime

363 W. 16th St. (at Ninth Ave.)

Subway: 14 St - 8 Av
Phone: 212-242-4300 or 800-466-9092
Web: www.themaritimehotel.com
Prices: $$$

123
Rooms

3
Suites

Alex La Cruz

Sure, Manhattan is more high rises and honking taxis than coconuts and swaying hammocks, but it's still an island, and there's no better place to feel the, ahem, wind in your hair than at The Maritime Hotel. This landmark building, once home to the National Maritime Union, delivers a ship-shape experience in the heart of Chelsea. The aromas from Chelsea Market will tempt from across the street, or hop aboard one of the hotel's bicycles for a two-wheeled journey past neighboring galleries and shops.

From the porthole-like windows, teak paneling, and nautical light fixtures to the platform beds and royal blue furnishings, it's smooth sailing in the cabin-like guest rooms. While in the suites, the feel is refined-retro with copies of vintage *National Geographic* lining the shelves. Even the saltiest dog will warm to the outdoor showers, featured in the terrace suites.

There's a rocking social scene at The Maritime as city-chic patrons feast on rustic Italian indoors in the brasserie or outside on the sunny terrace at La Bottega. One port of call that simply can't be missed is the easy, breezy, and oh-so-beautiful rooftop Cabanas, flooded with hipsters grooving to their sultry beats.

Manhattan ▶ Chelsea

The Bowery Hotel

335 Bowery (at 3rd St.)

Subway: Astor Pl
Phone: 212-505-9100 or 866-726-9379
Web: www.theboweryhotel.com
Prices: $$$$

128 Rooms

7 Suites

These days, the East Village is much more boho-chic than La Boheme. Evidence that this formerly scrappy neighborhood cleans up quite nicely? Make your way to the warm and inviting Bowery Hotel. In case the red coat- and top hat-wearing doormen haven't convinced you, the crackling fireplace and clubby interiors will certainly encourage you to sit and relax awhile. The ambience is slightly European blended with an old New York vibe.

The intimate rooms and suites are natty–think polished wood floors and furnishings offset by crisp white linens–while industrial-style floor-to-ceiling windows frame downtown views. Marble baths and ceiling fans complete the residential look and feel. Take a suite with a terrace to enjoy an outdoor shower.

The private lobby bar, complete with a grand piano and signature drinks, makes cocktail hour happy indeed, but Gemma fits the bill with pitch-perfect rustic Italian cooking. Inside it is quite simply the Italian countryside come to life. Ceilings are strewn with baskets, while walls are hung with copper pots. Wood-paneled walls, simple rough-hewn wooden tables...it's all so terrifically Tuscan and available for all-day dining and 24-hour room service.

Andaz Wall Street

B3

75 Wall St. (at Water St.)

Subway: Wall St (William St)
Phone: 212-590-1234 or 877-875-5036
Web: www.andaz.com
Prices: $$$

249
Rooms

4
Suites

Andaz Wall Street

The address may read Wall Street, but there's nothing buttoned-up or stuffy about the Andaz. Instead, this stylish spot designed by David Rockwell turns the traditional hotel experience on its head. Glide past the doors and make yourself comfortable in the lobby-cum-living room. The reservations desk is a vestige of the past here, where you are greeted instead by a tablet-toting host who sees to it that you find your place. Everything from the 24-hour fitness facility to the seasonal farmers markets has been designed to lend the impression of a residence, rather than a temporary stay.

Dark oak floors, bleached wood, and sleek black tile bathrooms show off a spare sophistication in the rooms and suites. From cushioned window seats and custom-made textured wallpaper, to four-sided personal closet valets, these accommodations are fitted with thoughtful details.

Take a look around and it's clear that Andaz is bullish on sustainability. There's recycled oak flooring in Wall & Water, while locally sourced and organic materials are used in both the spa and the kitchen. The seasonally driven menu here is a sensation, though the impressive contemporary design is a close second.

Manhattan ▶ Financial District

Best Western Seaport Inn

33 Peck Slip (at Front St.)

Subway: Fulton St
Phone: 212-766-6600 or 800-937-8376
Web: www.seaportinn.com
Prices: $$

72
Rooms

Slip into something very comfortable at the Best Western Seaport Inn. Smack dab in the South Street Seaport and within walking distance of the Financial District, WTC memorial, and the Statue of Liberty, the Best Western's superior waterfront address means that visitors can hop aboard a ferry to see the sights, ride up to Yankee Stadium to catch a game, or make it to their meetings right on time.

Normally location, location, location means money, money, and more money, but not at the Best Western. This hotel bucks the trend of charging sky-high prices for a first-rate location, and throws in a few extras along the way. The cherry on top is the complimentary delicious buffet breakfast. And that smell? It's the freshly baked cookies served every afternoon.

Traditional early American décor defines the classic interiors (think of emerald green splashes, abundant floral patterns, and nautical-themed prints), but it's their views that are postcard worthy. The Brooklyn Bridge isn't for sale, so it's perfectly fine if it steals your heart from the guest room window. Go ahead and splurge on a terrace room—the glorious vistas from the panoramic balcony terraces are worth the price of admission.

Gild Hall

 B2

15 Gold St. (enter on Platt St.)

Subway: Fulton St
Phone: 212-232-7700 or 800-268-0700
Web: www.thompsonhotels.com
Prices: $$$

116 Rooms

10 Suites

Thompson Hotels

The market's fluctuations have been known to make a grown man cry, but you're not swayed by the talking heads debating winners and losers. That's because you've got all your money on gold, er, gild, that is, at Gild Hall.

This place has serious chops as the sister property to hipper-than-thou 60 Thompson and its singular style is at once quirky and sophisticated. Wood-paneled walls, handsome 60s-ish furnishings, and a few antler chandeliers thrown in for good measure give the lobby a ski chalet-meets-city loft look, while upstairs, lipstick red hallways lead to cozy-chic guest rooms. Clubby but with a mod edge, these rooms might have tartan blankets and leather headboards, but there's nothing grandpa about them.

Nosh on Dean & Deluca goodies in your fluffy robe within the privacy of your suite or retire to the bi-level Library Bar for a drink, or three, where you'll likely rub shoulders with masters of the universe. If all that talk of bulls has you hankering for a steak, just pop over to The Libertine. This fresh interpretation of the classic English tavern doesn't take itself too seriously but hits the spot with such tasty pub grub as lobster clubs, oysters, and cheesecake.

Manhattan ▶ Financial District

The Ritz-Carlton, Battery Park

 A2

2 West St. (at Battery Pl.)

Subway: Bowling Green
Phone: 212-344-0800 or 800-241-3333
Web: www.ritzcarlton.com
Prices: $$$$

259
Rooms

39
Suites

The Ritz-Carlton New York, Battery Park

It's located at the southern tip of Manhattan, but The Ritz-Carlton, Battery Park, is definitely on top. This luxurious modern hotel has all the bells and whistles...sleek interior design, top-notch services, and oh, those views! Lady Liberty and the New York Harbor seem close enough to reach out and touch. You might even find a lump in your throat as you swell with patriotic pride. Wall Street and the Financial District are at your doorstep, while downtown's historic sites are steps away.

Inside, the look is art deco with a modern punch, thanks to the art collection comprised of New York-based artists. The rooms and suites are exceedingly comfortable, and with everything from Frette linens and plush towels to state-of-the-art gadgets, guests want for nothing. Book the harbor view rooms for inspiring views—made even better with the addition of telescopes. Club level rooms deliver the customary Ritz-Carlton extras like added privacy and seemingly endless treats.

Bliss out at the Carita Spa or pencil in a workout at the fitness center. 2 West is the embodiment of a "room with a view" with its floor-to-ceiling windows, but the American bistro menu is far from a concession prize.

Wall Street Inn

B3

9 S. William St. (bet. Beaver & Broad Sts.)

Subway: Wall St (William St.)
Phone: 212-747-1500 or 877-747-1500
Web: www.thewallstreetinn.com
Prices: $$

46 Rooms

The Wall Street Inn

Expense reports should not elicit fear. Stay at the delightful Wall Street Inn and you won't have visions of Sarbanes-Oxley dancing in your head, or for that matter, anyone from accounting beating down your door. Elegance and comfort come at a palatable price here, where downtown Manhattan's rich history comes alive.

The Inn is tucked inside a historic building that was the one-time home of Lehman Brothers. This 46-room inn is a gem in the heart of the Financial District and feels worlds away from the hustle and bustle. Steal away from the cacophony of the nearby Stock Exchange to the peace and quiet of the charming guest rooms. Furnished in a classic early American style, the look is a nod to history. The distinctive touches (fresh flowers and cozy bedding) and a warm, hospitable spirit make converts out of first-time guests.

It's small, but the Wall Street Inn doesn't miss a beat and offers conference facilities, a full-service business center, and a well-equipped fitness center complete with a sauna and steam room. There is no on-site restaurant, but don't worry since you'll be treated to a continental breakfast and can dial down for in-room dining courtesy of nearby Smörgas Chef.

Manhattan ▶ Financial District

Ace Hotel New York

parmesan

20 W. 29th St. (at Broadway)

Subway: 28 St (Broadway)
Phone: 212-679-2222
Web: www.acehotel.com/newyork
Prices: $$$

262
Rooms

3
Suites

Guitar propped against the wall? Check. Old trunk posing as a nightstand? Check. Quotes and funky posters on the wall? Check. Is this your college dorm room? Nope. It's the Ace Hotel, and it's a winner. In the middle of it all, you can quite literally get anywhere from here, but pull up a chair and stay awhile.

It's the real deal, nailing that beatnik sensibility, and it even comes with a past. Formerly known as The Breslin, this turn-of-the-century hotel welcomed a cast of characters from Diamond Jim Brady to artist Harry Smith. The "come as you are" attitude and creative vibe is alive and well today, but don't worry if you can't strum a guitar or draw a straight line—you're still welcome here. Save some Benjamins by staying in the so-called "cheap" rooms or bring along the pals and sleep bunk bed-style.

The Ace may attract an indie crowd, but these artists certainly won't be starving. Mongolian tofu, pork and shrimp chorizo...No. 7 Sub Shop's sammies break the mold. And Starbucks? So bourgeois. Get that caffeine fix instead at Stumptown Coffee Roasters, where everything from the tweed newsboy cap-wearing staff, to the Red Hook-roasted coffee is steeped in an oh-so-downtown vibe.

Manhattan ▶ Gramercy, Flatiron & Union Square

The Carlton

B1

88 Madison Ave. (at 29th St.)

Subway: 28 St (Park Ave. South)
Phone: 212-532-4100 or 800-601-8500
Web: www.carltonhotelny.com
Prices: $$$

294 Rooms

23 Suites

The Carlton Hotel

Plenty of spots try to capture the glamour of a bygone era, but not The Carlton. This hotel doesn't have to try to be old New York—it is old New York. First opened in 1904 as The Seville, this place has plenty of juicy stories. Legend has it that Groucho Marx perfected his act while working here as a bellboy.

A century later, this old gal's still got it (with a little help from design wiz David Rockwell). Reincarnated as The Carlton, this hotel celebrates a stylish blend of old and new. The gleaming lobby is a showpiece of handsome art deco styling, but proof that this hotel never forgets its roots is the oversized historic photo of the original hotel hanging front and center in the lobby. From distressed mirrored furnishings and leather headboards to polished nickel and rich walnut details, the rooms and suites are havens of luxury. Get in a true NY state of mind by booking an Empire Suite with memorable views of the Empire State Building.

Don't be surprised if the social scene feels a bit like a Fitzgerald novel. The Carlton's purported speakeasy past lends a mysterious and seductive flavor to Salon Millesime and Bar Millie, where performers tickle the ivories of the baby grand piano.

Manhattan ▶ Gramercy, Flatiron & Union Square

Gramercy Park Hotel

2 Lexington Ave. (at 21st St.)

Subway: 23 St (Park Ave. South)
Phone: 212-920-3300 or 866-784-1300
Web: www.gramercyparkhotel.com
Prices: $$$$

140 Rooms

45 Suites

Sorry Hemingway, but even you couldn't have written a better storyline than this. Built on the site where homes to Edith Wharton and architect Stanford White once stood, the Gramercy Park Hotel first welcomed guests in 1925. And my, what guests walked through these doors. Humphrey Bogart was married here. Babe Ruth imbibed at the bar. It doesn't get much better than that, but wait, it has. It's tough to improve on a legend, but the Gramercy Park Hotel has done it.

Mike Bloomberg may not give you a key to the city, but the front desk can give you a key to exclusive Gramercy Park—Manhattan's only private park. And that's not the only special access you'll get. From the bold lobby to the playful rooms, works of art are shared with guests throughout the hotel. Red velvet curtains, black-and-white tiled floors, chartreuse walls...it has an Alice in Wonderland-meets-sexy boudoir quality that would give your Waspy aunt the shakes.

Stiletto-clad socialites and pop icons gather at the Rose and Jade Bars, ruled by a moody and slightly outré ambience. Drops of sunshine and greenery drench the Gramercy Terrace rife with city scenesters sippin' and suppin' on Danny Meyer's reputed range of treats.

Inn at Irving Place

56 Irving Pl. (bet 17th & 18th Sts.)

Subway: 14 St - Union Sq
Phone: 212-533-4600 or 800-685-1447
Web: www.innatirving.com
Prices: $$$$

12
Rooms

Roy Wright

With leafy Gramercy Park to the north and quaint streets lined with 19th century townhomes all around, it would be easy to confuse The Inn at Irving Place with a Hollywood set for a Henry James novel. Surprisingly, it's not inspired set design—these two impeccably restored townhomes dating to 1834 are the real thing. Distinguished and genteel, this posh area continues to reign as one of New York's most privileged addresses. Luckily, you don't need a dowry to taste the high life; a reservation at the Inn at Irving Place works just fine.

It is the age of elegance here, where a dainty dozen accommodations await guests. Brimming with antiques and period furnishings, these intimate rooms are perfect for a romantic getaway. The unique country-in-the-city atmosphere is a delightful distraction from the busy streets.

Turn back time and enter a rarefied world of white gloves and tea parties at the very proper Lady Mendl's Tea Salon. There is perhaps no better way to spend an afternoon than nibbling on finger sandwiches and sipping tea in this Victorian-style room. Prefer something stronger than Darjeeling? Cibar Lounge mixes martinis and other classic cocktails in an upscale setting.

Manhattan ▶ Gramercy, Flatiron & Union Square

NoMad Hotel

1170 Broadway (at 28th St.)

Subway: 28 St (Broadway)
Phone: 212-796-1500
Web: www.thenomadhotel.com
Prices: $$$

154 Rooms

14 Suites

The name of this hotel articulates many different things. First, it conveys the address—North of Madison Square Park. This area, which sits at the juncture of the Flatiron, Gramercy, Chelsea, and midtown districts, is one of the city's hottest new neighborhoods. But, the NoMad's name isn't just shorthand for its locale. It also happens to perfectly sum up the sexy style of this worldly, eclectic hotel designed by renowned tastemaker Jacques Garcia.

Housed in the 1903 Beaux-Arts Johnston building, the NoMad is hip without the hurt. Embossed black leather walls and glossy black-and-white mosaic floors define the intimate lobby that reeks of seduction. Upstairs, the guest rooms share a distinctly residential ambience with such stellar features as polished maple flooring, chests resembling antique steamer trunks, and walls hung with a treasured collection of architectural drawings, maps, postcards, and other vintage-style items. Finesses like custom Côté Bastide bath amenities, Frette linens, and Sferra bathrobes are all here.

Nomads in need of a nosh find Gilded Era glory in a series of rooms run by dynamic duo chef Daniel Humm and general manager Will Guidara of Eleven Madison Park.

Manhattan ▶ Gramercy, Flatiron & Union Square

W - Union Square

201 Park Ave. South (at 17th St.)

Subway: 14 St - Union Sq
Phone: 212-253-9119 or 877-782-0027
Web: www.whotels.com
Prices: $$$$

270 Rooms

18 Suites

W-New York

Isn't it a tad ironic that the fun W New York-Union Square occupies the onetime home of Guardian life insurance? However, it does attract the most corporate crowd in town, for whom life insurance is much more than a mere twinkle in their eyes. Age shares the spotlight with beauty at the W, where the good bones of the original 1911 Beaux-Arts building are fused with the striking, contemporary David Rockwell design.

The place is always slammed with a bevy of urban yuppies toasting to the success of their tech start-ups–the nabe has been nicknamed Silicon Alley for a reason–and people-watching is a serious sport here. The suitably named Living Room is a hotbed of canoodling, cocktail-swilling bright young things. Later, it's all about the action and the groovy beats at the underground nightclub, Lilium, where the action almost never ends.

If all this elbow-rubbing has you craving some personal space, head upstairs to one of the rooms or suites. With overstuffed velvet armchairs and pillowtop mattresses, comfort is king at the W. Crisp white linens set against the moody mocha-colored furnishings are serenity wow, but you can always dial up some Zen with an in-room spa treatment.

Manhattan ▶ Gramercy, Flatiron & Union Square

Gansevoort

18 Ninth Ave. (at 13th St.)

Subway:	14 St - 8 Av
Phone:	212-206-6700 or 877-462-7386
Web:	www.hotelgansevoort.com
Prices:	$$$$

166 Rooms

21 Suites

There is perhaps no better Cinderella story in NYC than the Meatpacking District. The streets of this gritty, tough-as-nails neighborhood once ran red with blood from freshly butchered meats. Today, designer dresses and radical art hang from the spots where meats were hung to dry, due in large part to the Gansevoort Hotel.

Forever fresh and hip, the Gansevoort got in on the ground floor and has ridden the wave ever since. Their striking rooms and attractive suites show off a thoroughly modern vibe with an understated luxury. Pops of vibrant color and contemporary artwork add a little razzle-dazzle to the otherwise serene setting. Speaking of serenity, get your relaxation on at Exhale Spa, known for its mind-body therapies and Core Fusion fitness program.

Occupying a prime location on cobblestoned Ninth Ave., the trendy boutiques, nightclubs, and restaurants are all within a stiletto's throw. Then again, with much talked-about dining at Toy, teaming Jeffrey Chodorow's China Grill Management and Nightlife Impressarios Derek and Daniel Koch, sunny days at the buzzing rooftop pool with its 70s-style lounge, and sultry nights at Provocateur, there's a convincing argument to simply stay put.

The Standard

848 Washington St. (at 13th St.)

Subway:	14 St - 8 Av
Phone:	212-645-4646
Web:	www.standardhotels.com
Prices:	$$$

337
Rooms

Nikolas Koenig

What do you do when railroad tracks run right through your land? If you're The Standard, you take the high road. Literally. This architecturally impressive hotel straddles the High Line, the rusty tracks-cum-glorious public park that many are calling the most important public project in generations.

There's certainly nothing typical about The Standard. Known for providing über-hip surroundings and elegant accommodations, this collection of hotels appeals to everyone from hipsters to hedge funders. They know to come with high expectations, since sacrifice is not part of the deal. The views from all 337 rooms of this cantilevered building are simply spectacular. Floor-to-ceiling glass windows show off the Big Apple in all her glory. The rooms are the very definition of clean and uncluttered contemporary design sprinkled with the sexy styling of the 1950s.

If you can tear yourself away from your deep-soaking bathtub with a view, The Standard invites you to socialize in style at the seasonally appropriate and ever-popular Biergarten (but don't break out the lederhosen just yet since this sunny spot is more hip than Heidi), or ice skating rink-slash-open air café, Standard Plaza.

Manhattan ▶ Greenwich, West Village & Meatpacking District

Aloft Harlem

2296 Frederick Douglass Blvd. (bet. 123rd & 124th Sts.)

Subway: 125 St (Frederick Douglass Blvd.)
Phone: 212-749-4000 or 877-462-5398
Web: www.starwoodhotels.com/alofthotels
Prices: $$

124
Rooms

Despite a rich history, an Ivy League university, and a pulsing entertainment scene, Harlem was a largely overlooked neighborhood for hotels until recently. Not anymore. Nothing says gentrification quite like a brand spanking new hotel, and Aloft is the first to be built in Harlem in 40 years. Welcome to the *new* Harlem Renaissance, where Starwood's trendy Aloft brand is making waves.

Step inside where you'll get the distinct feeling you're boarding a spaceship. Mod furnishings, neon lights...it's all very tech-chic for the new millennium. Fun and upbeat, Aloft doesn't take itself too seriously, but it does offer some serious comforts. The rooms and suites feel extra airy with oversized windows and nine-foot ceilings, while the technology keeps you and your many gadgets running smoothly. And speaking of smooth, Bliss Spa products are available on hand in the walk-in showers.

Got the munchies? Aloft has something to satiate any appetite. Re:fuel is the antidote to the vending machine with its healthy and tasty array of sweet and savory snacks. For those with more time on their hands, w xyz(SM) is just the spot for shooting the breeze with a glass of wine and bite to eat.

The Hotel on Rivington

B2

107 Rivington St. (bet. Essex & Ludlow Sts.)

Subway: Delancey St
Phone: 212-475-2600 or 800-915-1537
Web: www.hotelonrivington.com
Prices: $$$

89 Rooms

21 Suites

Hotel on Rivington

Times Square is squeaky clean, the Meatpacking District is all gussied up, and Harlem is hot again. Has the city finally lost its appeal? Not if you're in the Lower East Side, where vibrant visitors (hello Snooki!) dominate the scene and gentrification hasn't quite caught up (yet).

The Hotel on Rivington, a 21-story gleaming glass tower, is the haute hippie's hotel of choice. Its edgy design stitched together by design talents from around the world satisfies the cool quotient, while creature comforts like fabulous bathrooms with heated floors, steam showers, and Japanese-style soaking tubs ensure supreme relaxation. Don't throw any rocks since you're definitely living in a glass house in these rooms—floor-to-ceiling glass walls account for drop-dead views. Of course, if you want to improve how the world sees you, head downstairs to the Platinum Salon for a new 'do.

To the diner go the spoils at Viktor and Spoils, the hotel's Mexican taqueria and tequila bar. CO-OP Food and Drink has that inimitable Lower East Side, slightly off-center aura. Just like the photo collage piecing together various celebrities, the menu is a wacky and creative blend of sushi and gourmet American bistro food.

Manhattan ▶ Lower East Side

The Benjamin

B3

125 E. 50th St. (bet. Lexington & Third Aves.)

Subway: 51 St
Phone: 212-715-2500 or 866-222-2365
Web: www.thebenjamin.com
Prices: $$$$

112
Rooms

97
Suites

The Benjamin is really and truly a snooze. Sleep, not only yours–but your kids' and dog's too–is a matter of utmost importance at this midtown marvel that employs a sleep concierge, offers a dozen different pillows, and even schedules pet psychics to lull your pooch to sleep. But don't keep your eyes closed for the whole time, since The Benjamin is even more impressive during daylight hours.

Midtown Manhattan hotels are notorious for their cramped quarters, but The Benjamin bucks the trend with a spectrum of spacious rooms and suites equipped with full galley kitchens. There is plenty of space to stretch out, get some work done, and even enjoy a little downtime (especially on the terraces in deluxe one bedroom and VIP suites). For additional relaxation, sojourn at the third-floor Wellness Spa, also known for their rejuvenating skin and body therapies.

And if all this indulgence leaves you famished, rest assured as Iron Chef Geoffrey Zakarian shepherds the stoves at The National. The warm and classic American bistro atmosphere prevalent here is the perfect complement to their seasonally based, locally sourced cuisine. And don't worry, Zakarian can even make you breakfast in bed.

Manhattan ▶ Midtown East & Murray Hill

Elysée

60 E. 54th St. (bet. Madison & Park Aves.)

Subway:	5 Av - 53 St
Phone:	212-753-1066 or 800-535-9733
Web:	www.elyseehotel.com
Prices:	$$$

87 Rooms

13 Suites

Library Hotel Collection

Maybe you can have the best of both worlds...if you stay at Hotel Elysée. This gracious hotel is situated in the heart of midtown, yet it maintains a distinguished "tucked away from it all" air. The Elysée has been greeting guests with open arms since the 1920s. This hidden gem has long been a favorite of visiting artists and business figures who return time and again for the exceptional comforts and conveniences. Guests are more than just a room number here, where complimentary breakfast and a daily afternoon wine and cheese reception are just two instances of the niceties.

There are only 100 rooms at this intimate hotel. Take a room with a view of 54thStreet for a front row seat to all of the action, or ask for a quieter back room for added privacy. The rooms and suites share a classic European influence and some rooms boast unique features like terraces, solariums, and kitchenettes.

Of course, Hotel Elysée is perhaps most famous as the home of that legendary New York institution, The Monkey Bar. This famed bar has certainly seen its fair share of monkeying around—it's been open since the Great Depression. From its steakhouse-style menu to its convivial atmosphere, it's a classic.

Manhattan ▶ Midtown East & Murray Hill

Four Seasons New York

57 E. 57th St. (bet. Madison & Park Aves.)

Subway: 59 St
Phone: 212-758-5700 or 800-487-3769
Web: www.fourseasons.com
Prices: $$$$

305 Rooms

63 Suites

You've always wanted all of New York at your feet, and while it may seem like a pipe dream, the city is quite literally at your feet at the Four Seasons. Its location in the belly of the midtown beast belies its serene interiors. Open the doors to the breathtaking lobby, where a backlit onyx ceiling and impressive limestone columns create a dramatic, temple-like appearance.

This prestigious sanctum, the city's tallest luxury hotel, commands jaw-dropping views in its plush rooms and suites. Simple sophistication reigns in these accommodations fit for modern-day moguls. English sycamore and leather furnishings, marble baths, and one-touch technology are among the "standards" here. Skip the breakout session and indulge in some personal time at the oasis-like spa before brokering a deal over breakfast.

The Four Seasons has long functioned as a boardroom of sorts for the city's high-flying business transactions. Walk in any day of the week and the hotel's venues like highly rated dining rooms, The Bar, TY Lounge, and Calvisius Caviar Lounge, are like a who's who of industry. Listen closely over that martini and you might just pick up an insider's tip or a juicy tidbit of *Post*-worthy gossip.

Hotel 57

B1

130 E. 57th St. (at Lexington Ave.)

Subway: 59 St
Phone: 212-753-8841
Web: www.marriott.com
Prices: $$

183
Rooms

19
Suites

Cris Molina

Tuck an extra bag or two in your luggage if you're staying at Hotel 57. Its enviable address, just steps from the flagship Bloomingdale's store, is a shopper's paradise, and it's a sure thing that a few "little brown bags" will find their way back to the room. Hotel 57 looks like a boutique hotel but functions like the Marriott/Renaissance that it is. Designer Jordan Mozer has crafted an of-the-moment look that rivals the designer finds in area shops.

Hardwood floors, exposed brick walls, unique artwork, and high ceilings give the rooms a true residential feel. Throw in top-notch amenities like marble bathrooms, custom linens, and high-tech services and you'll be moving in in no time. Hotel 57 even lets guests in on little-known area secrets with its curated tips from in-the-know staff.

Classic styling and scenic views of the Chrysler Building are par for the course at the rooftop lounge, American. That cheering you hear? It's coming from Opia Bar & Lounge, where locals gather to watch international soccer and rugby games. Opia Restaurant takes the cake with its enticing setting and French menu. Good thing that Hotel 57 features a gym where you can work off that second croissant.

Manhattan ▶ Midtown East & Murray Hill

Library

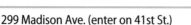

299 Madison Ave. (enter on 41st St.)

Subway:	Grand Central - 42 St
Phone:	212-983-4500 or 877-793-7323
Web:	www.libraryhotel.com
Prices:	$$$

60 Rooms

Shh! Keep your voice down or everyone will find out about the delightful Library Hotel. This place is one-of-a-kind and offers a different slant on harried midtown east.

The Library doesn't employ your average run-of-the-mill guest room categorization. Nope. Instead, each of the ten floors corresponds to one of the different classification systems of the Dewey Decimal system (translation—there are floors for topics like Religion, History, Math & Science, etc.). Pick a floor and you'll get a cozy room brimming with books on that subject. Nota bene: don't go for Erotica when you're bringing Mom along. Plush Egyptian cotton linens and sleek flat panel televisions...this definitely isn't your grandfather's library.

Bury your nose in a book but don't hole up entirely, since the Library also offers a bevy of distractions. Amble over to the Reading Room, which hosts a complimentary breakfast buffet along with evening wine and cheese receptions, or book a table at the American-focused bistro and international wine bar, Madison & Vine. Guests can also try their hand at writing the great American novel in the lovely, flower-filled Poet's Garden or fireside in the Writer's Den.

New York Palace

455 Madison Ave. (enter on 50th St.)

Subway: 51 St
Phone: 212-888-7000 or 800-697-2522
Web: www.newyorkpalace.com
Prices: $$$$

813
Rooms

86
Suites

The New York Palace

Pack a tiara and point the carriage straight to the New York Palace. Reigning over midtown, this princely haven is truly fit for a queen. Gloriously marrying the landmark 1882 Villard Houses with a modern 55-story tower, the New York Palace takes a legend and makes it au courant. From the grand marble lobby and impressive Palace Gate courtyard, to the delightful American bistro Istana and drop-dead gorgeous Gilt Bar, this hotel really puts on the dog (and lets you bring yours along, too). It's good to be king at their 7,000-square-foot wellness center, where luxurious spa treatments are all the rage.

Go for old-school European refinement or opt for a modern flair in their updated yet classic rooms and suites, which boast ample space, style, and service. Accommodations in the Towers truly take luxury to another level. This exclusive hotel-within-a-hotel offers unparalleled privacy and added features, plus jaw-dropping views from its prestigious perch on the tower's top 14 floors.

No matter the choice, guests count their blessings from this elegant respite that just so happens to look out over famed St. Patrick's Cathedral (along with that temple of retail, Saks Fifth Avenue).

Manhattan ▶ Midtown East & Murray Hill

595

Roger

131 Madison Ave. (at 31st St.)

Subway: 33 St
Phone: 212-448-7000 or 888-448-7788
Web: www.therogernewyork.com
Prices: $$$

191
Rooms

2
Suites

Following a $10 million makeover, the graceful Roger Williams hotel has dropped its last name but has picked up oodles of style, making it a revered and sought-after lodging that can hold its own among the chic spate of accommodations dotting this burgeoning enclave just north of Madison Square Park.

The soaring ceilings capping the ground floor of this boutique property create a serene atmosphere; while whitewashed walls, streams of daylight, and bright furnishings fashion a carefree lounge-like feel that's utterly conducive to planning your day or meeting with friends. Need to unwind? Enjoy a cocktail at the intimate corner bar, or head up to the mezzanine café, The Parlour, where visitors to the Big Apple can nosh on Manhattan faithfuls like pastries from Ceci-Cela and cheeses from Murray's.

The Roger's guest rooms also sport a fresh face. A classy blue and brown palette dominates the quarters that are given added luxury with croc-embossed furnishings, romantic black-and-white prints of Central Park, and C.O. Bigelow bath products in the functional bathrooms. Some rooms are even snazzier, featuring sizable terraces prettied by potted flowers and views of the Empire State building.

70 park avenue

70 Park Ave. (at 38th St.)

Subway:	Grand Central - 42 St
Phone:	212-973-2400 or 877-707-2752
Web:	www.70parkave.com
Prices:	$$$

201
Rooms

4
Suites

Kimpton Hotels & Restaurants

On the more mellow end of posh and pricey Park Avenue lies the stately 70 park avenue. Just a little bit funky and a whole lot of fresh, 70 park avenue shakes things up for its young and trendy patrons. The hospitable service staff engineers a pleasant stay at this well-priced hideaway located merely a few blocks from bustling Grand Central Terminal. Business services, fitness facilities, in-room spa services, and the lively Silverleaf Tavern with a popular happy hour are among the perks available to guests.

Low lighting, shimmery, geometric-printed fabrics, and even fresh bowls of fruit show off a tranquil sophistication in the lobby. It's the first sign that this definitely isn't Grandma's Park Avenue.

But wait, there's more. Rich, dark espresso hues blend with regal purples and sexy silvers for a dramatic look in the rooms and suites. Mirrored lacquer side tables and punchy modern art further enhance the chic ambience, while fresh flowers and plentiful amenities elevate the comfort factor. Good looks come without a catch here, where there's not a single trace of that dreaded too-cool-for-school attitude and everyone from tykes to tycoons is welcomed with arms wide open.

Manhattan ▶ Midtown East & Murray Hill

597

The St. Regis

 A2

2 E. 55th St. (at Fifth Ave.)

Subway: 5 Av – 53 St
Phone: 212-753-4500 or 800-759-7550
Web: www.stregis.com/newyork
Prices: $$$$

164 Rooms

65 Suites

Even if your last name doesn't appear in the Social Register, live like it does (at least temporarily) at the grand and glorious St. Regis. This hotel specializes in all-out refinement.

Built by John Jacob Astor and perfected by his son Vincent (who went down with the Titanic), the St. Regis has since lost its claim as the tallest hotel in New York, but it's never lost any of its luster. This landmark glitters at every turn and brings the best of all worlds to guests. Take tea in the Astor Court or toast Bloody Marys (invented here) and discover the secret of the Maxfield Parrish mural in the King Cole Bar. Luxuriate in the princely pampering at Remède Spa, or schedule a fitness session with a personal trainer. Of course, the ultimate taste of how the other half lives is the St. Regis' highly acclaimed butler service. Butlers have been attending to the needs of privileged guests for over a century now, so expect nothing short of spectacular service.

The posh public facilities are reason alone to stay here, but the breathtaking accommodations run a close second. Classic and crisp Edwardian details exude elegance, while specialty and designer suites inject a bit of wit and whimsy.

Manhattan ▶ Midtown East & Murray Hill

Avalon

16 E. 32nd St. (bet. Fifth & Madison Aves.)

Subway: 33 St
Phone: 212-299-7000 or 888-442-8256
Web: www.theavalonny.com
Prices: $$

80 Rooms

20 Suites

Vinci Avalon

Right around the corner from the well-tread Empire State Building, Penn Station, and Madison Square Garden, this boutique property indulges business travelers with six meeting rooms and mini-bars plus refrigerators in each guest room. Leisure travelers and theater lovers profit from the Avalon's setting, a short walk from Times Square and the bright lights of Broadway.

All appreciate large "Superior" rooms, each of which flaunt 27-inch flat-screen TVs, ample closet space, velour robes, and Irish cotton linens. Dark hardwood floors, earth tones (soft green, brown, and rust), and Italian marble baths accentuate the décor. At the top tier of room types, the 20 executive suites average 450 square feet and come with Jacuzzi tubs, fax machines, sofa beds, and Bose Wave radios.

Just off the elegant lobby, which is set about with pillars and paneling, the Library/Club room is a den-like area outfitted with a personal computer. Guests here will enjoy thoughtful and warm service from the affable staff, as well as passes to the nearby Equinox gym and fitness center. The SerRa Mediterranean Bistro serves a scrumptious spread for breakfast every morning and American fare for lunch and dinner.

Manhattan ▶ Midtown East & Murray Hill

599

The Waldorf=Astoria

B3

301 Park Ave. (bet. 49th & 50th Sts.)

Subway: 51 St
Phone: 212-355-3000 or 800-925-3673
Web: www.waldorfastoria.com
Prices: $$$$

1085
Rooms

331
Suites

The Waldorf=Astoria isn't a hotel—it's an icon. As much a part of New York culture as hot dog vendors and the Statue of Liberty, no other hotel has captured the imagination of filmmakers, composers, and authors quite like the Waldorf. Glamorous balls...society weddings...this hotel has hosted them all. It's no wonder that countless numbers of people have taken the line "meet me at the Waldorf" to heart.

If these walls could talk they'd put US Weekly out of business. Everyone from movie stars to every sitting U.S. President has stayed here. It's easy to see why, with a prime location and standard-setting services, the hotel even lays claim to creating 24-hour room service. Belles of the ball will find the Guerlain Spa and famed Kenneth Salon just right for primping and pampering.

From its grand ballrooms to traditional rooms and suites, The Waldorf is the big daddy of Old World grandeur. And the lobby? They just don't build them like this anymore. It is the ultimate spot for whiling away the afternoon while people-watching. Some things never change, and the Waldorf's three restaurants (Oscar's, Bull & Bear, and Peacock Alley) are as much a part of old New York as the hotel itself.

Algonquin

59 W. 44th St. (bet. Fifth & Sixth Aves.)

Subway:	42 St - Bryant Pk
Phone:	212-840-6800
Web:	www.algonquinhotel.com
Prices:	$$$

156 Rooms

24 Suites

The Algonquin Hotel

It is just not up for discussion: the Algonquin is a living, breathing piece of history. This storied landmark, home of the famed Algonquin Roundtable, is the ultimate culture club (sorry George Michael). Known as a hotbed of intellectual and artistic curiosity and creativity, everybody who was anybody in the arts and letters has passed through these doors. Don't go thinking this literary landmark is for stuffed suits and fuddy duddys, though.

Thanks to a recent transformation by design superstar Alexandra Champalimaud, the Algonquin earns top marks from both fashionistas and culture vultures alike. Despite the jazzy new look, the restoration spiced things up without stripping any of its unique character. Case in point: the longstanding tradition of keeping a house cat, Matilda. The latest feline resident is even given an annual birthday party!

Rich jewel tones, Edwardian furnishings, and writing desks (peect for penning pithy postcards) lend a moody, seductive air to the elegant lobby. Once famous for its debates, the Round Table is now equally famous for its retro-style dishes, while the Blue Bar is a veritable museum of Broadway-themed drawings from longtime regular, Al Hirschfeld.

Manhattan ▶ Midtown West

The Blakely

136 W. 55th St. (bet. Sixth & Seventh Aves.)

Subway: 57 St
Phone: 212-245-1800 or 800-735-0710
Web: www.blakelynewyork.com
Prices: $$

63
Rooms

55
Suites

Seeking that special place in Gotham City that feels more like a private residence than an impersonal hotel room? Join the club, at The Blakely that is. With its discreet awning and elegant brick façade, this gem of a hotel is easy to mistake for a refined service apartment or prestigious club, but you won't need a down payment or a letter of recommendation to get inside.

The midtown location is as good as it gets. In life, you might get to Carnegie Hall with practice, practice, practice, but if you're a guest of The Blakely, you can also get there with just a few steps. The venerated Museum of Modern Art is also merely a stone's throw away and the enticing shops of Fifth and Madison avenues are all within easy reach. But, if you want to really feel like a New Yorker and connect with the locals, go for a run in nearby Central Park. The Blakely makes it all part of the experience.

Cherry furnishings, rich oak baseboards, and marble-tiled bathrooms with deep-soaking bathtubs give the rooms and suites a comfortable appeal. Fully equipped kitchenettes, perfect for whipping up yummy snacks and light meals, add to the livability of these classically comfortable accommodations.

Manhattan ▶ Midtown West

Casablanca

C3

147 W. 43rd St. (bet. Broadway & Sixth Ave.)

Subway: 42 St - Bryant Pk
Phone: 212-869-1212 or 888-922-7225
Web: www.casablancahotel.com
Prices: $$

43
Rooms

5
Suites

Library Hotel Collection

Walk east of tourist-central Times Square along 43rd Street and find yourself being transported away from the hubbub of midtown and into the magic of Morocco. Casablanca brings the mystery and romance of this unique country to the nerve center of New York City.

From the colorful tiles and tapestries to such graceful archways and decorative moldings, the attention to detail makes this hotel stand apart from the pack. The rooms and suites have a mood-lifting design—think of sand-hued walls and sunny orange fabrics. Even the bath products crafted from olive oil and orange essence, share the spirit. Mingle with other guests at the nightly cocktail and hors d'oeuvres reception, or linger over The New York Times while enjoying the bountiful (and complimentary) European-style breakfast buffet at Rick's Café.

Warm, hospitable service and an unparalleled intimacy make this 48-room hotel a true find. The vibrant lights of Broadway are just a block or two away, but the Casablanca is a world away from the cacophony of touristy Times Square. Of course, another reason to fall head over heels for this place is its amazingly affordable rates. After all, a dollar isn't just a dollar these days.

Manhattan ▶ Midtown West

Chambers

B4

15 W. 56th St. (bet. Fifth & Sixth Aves.)

Subway: 57 St
Phone: 212-974-5656 or 866-204-5656
Web: www.chambershotel.com
Prices: $$$$

72 **Rooms**

5 **Suites**

Evan Joseph

New Yorkers love to debate the various merits of uptown versus downtown (and vice versa), but the ever-chic Chambers begs the question—why choose? This hotel may look straight out of SoHo, but it's smack dab in the middle of it all in midtown, just off Fifth Avenue. Museums, world-class shopping, and fine dining are just outside the door.

The Chambers exudes a dressed-up downtown vibe, courtesy of designer David Rockwell's Midas touch. The rooms and suites wed a modern and industrial style that may feel like home to some and a warehouse to others. These loft-life accommodations are light-filled and airy...oversized terraces on two suites are exceptional...and art is everywhere. Sure you can drop $20 on admission to the nearby MoMA (and you should), but at the Chambers, you can live with more than 500 original works of art. Since real artists can't be confined to a frame, admire the gorgeous hallway mural with its red raspberries and delicate hummingbirds, and wonder if this is the Garden of Eden or the way to your room?

From decadent shakes (blended with soft serve mixed with organic whole milk), cakes, and whole pies (perhaps the candy bar?), Momofuku Milk Bar does a body good.

The Chatwal

130 W. 44th St. (bet. Sixth & Seventh Aves.)

Subway: Times Sq - 42 St
Phone: 212-764-5900 or 888-524-2892
Web: www.thechatwalny.com
Prices: $$$$

50
Rooms

26
Suites

The Chatwal, A Luxury Collection Hotel, New York

It's not a surprise that The Chatwal is an absolute showstopper. It does have some serious chops as the onetime clubhouse of The Lambs Club, the first professional theater organization.

Set within a landmark Stanford White-designed building, The Chatwal really pulls out all the stops. Designed by the in-demand Thierry Despont, this hotel is the embodiment of all things debonair and dapper. The luxurious rooms and suites are havens of high design with plush details like ultrasuede-covered walls and glossy leather built-in cabinets, while exquisite art deco accents harken back to the glamour of the 1930s. From a signature scent and a celebrity chef-curated minibar to hand-tufted mattresses, the meticulous attention to detail is simply unparalleled.

Bliss out at the Chatwal Spa by Kashwere, where all of the senses are engaged with a variety of Eastern- and European-inspired holistic therapies. The Chatwal effortlessly plays the part of gracious host, especially in the Lambs Club Bar. Once the watering hole of silver screen legends like Charlie Chaplin and Spencer Tracy, today this sexy and spirited establishment earns rave reviews for its sultry scene and curated cocktails.

Manhattan ▶ Midtown West

City Club

55 W. 44th St. (bet. Fifth & Sixth Aves.)

Subway: 42 St - Bryant Pk
Phone: 212-921-5500
Web: www.cityclubhotel.com
Prices: $$$

62
Rooms

3
Suites

Matthew Hranek

Feel like a member of an exclusive club while staying at the stylish City Club. With prestigious neighbors like the Harvard Club and the New York Yacht Club, a prime location with proximity to Grand Central and Times Square, and a swanky feel, the City Club makes lifetime members out of first-time guests.

Completed in 1904, the City Club was once home to an exclusive gentleman's political club. The legacy remains in part–petite rooms once housed club members' butlers–but there's no debating that its rebirth as a luxury boutique hotel is nothing short of sensational. The 65 rooms bear the inimitable touch of American designer Jeffrey Bilhuber. Hand-drawn plaster walls, waxed cork flooring, crisp white linens, and polished bronze details all contribute to the tailored, fresh sensibility. Vintage New York maps, Playbills, old books, and vinyl records serve as unique pieces of art. It's never too-hip-it-hurts, though. Snuggle in and enjoy one of the many page-turners thoughtfully included in each room.

Not everyone can put their feet up and feast on in-room dining from award-winning chef, Daniel Boulud. Membership, ahem, temporary residence at the City Club certainly has its privileges.

Ink48

B1

653 Eleventh Ave. (at 48th St.)

Subway: 50 St (Eighth Ave.)
Phone: 212-757-0088 or 877-843-8869
Web: www.ink48.com
Prices: $$

203 Rooms

19 Suites

Ink48

It shouldn't really come as a surprise that Ink48 is making big news. After all, this hotel occupies a former printing house. And yes, while it may be housed in the far reaches of the west side of Manhattan, the boutique Ink48 hotel makes its mark with a sultry and industrial-meets-chic décor. Its 11th Avenue location is busy, busy, busy (and often loud) but inside the hotel, the mood is relaxing and inviting.

The lobby and public spaces are infused with a rich, seductive design (think red velvet and cobalt blue furnishings, gleaming polished woods, and moody lighting), while upstairs, the guest rooms are sun-filled, bright, and airy with high ceilings, large windows, and tasteful, fashionable décor. Lucky guests who book westward-facing rooms have drop-dead, spectacular river views.

Kimpton loyalists know that this chain pampers guests and A+ amenities like a posh spa, celebrity-studded rooftop lounge, and in-demand restaurants appropriately named Press and Print are all part of the luxe experience. The service has literally gone to the dogs, with a canine-centric service menu offering everything from doggie day care and spa services to boutique finds for your four-legged friend.

Manhattan ▶ Midtown West

InterContinental Times Square

300 W. 44th St. (at Eighth Ave.)

Subway: 42 St - Port Authority Bus Terminal
Phone: 212-803-4500 or 877-331-5888
Web: www.interconny.com
Prices: $$$

603 Rooms

4 Suites

Michael Kleinberg/InterContinental

Want to be in the middle of it all? Go big and book the InterContinental Times Square. Rising 36 stories above the city, this glittering glass tower pulses with the infectious energy of its locale. Steps from New York institutions like Sardi's and lit by the glow of the nearby Theater District, the InterCon gives guests a front row seat to all of the action, but it's not just what's outside that makes this stunning hotel a winner.

Step off the street into the striking lobby, where sleek lines and a contemporary verve set a stunning tone, but nothing captures the eye like the serene courtyard garden behind reception. From the tall trees to the reflective pool to the modern sculptures, it is a breath of fresh air in the middle of the city.

From business and fitness to Todd English's Ça Va Brasserie and Ça Va Marche, the facilities are first-rate. Ride the elevator to the seductive hush of the elegant rooms and suites and it's clear that the InterContinental dresses to impress. The accommodations are the last word in contemporary-chic, but oh, those views. Floor-to-ceiling glass window walls frame million-dollar views that stretch from Times Square all the way to the Hudson River.

Jumeirah Essex House

160 Central Park South (bet. Sixth & Seventh Aves.)

Subway: 57 St - 7 Av
Phone: 212-247-0300 or 888-645-5697
Web: www.jumeirahessexhouse.com
Prices: $$$$

439
Rooms

70
Suites

Jumeirah Essex House

The Jumeirah Essex House is a masterpiece. The construction of this landmark began just before the stock market crash of 1929, but nothing can keep a good hotel down, and this one opened its doors to great fanfare in 1931. The elegant Essex House has been making New York history ever since. In fact, Sunday brunch was originated here in the 1930s.

Located on exclusive Central Park South, the hotel served as a gourmet finishing line for Sunday strollers who completed their Central Park constitutionals. Of course, the Essex House has always been more than just a destination for dining—sipping a delicious cocktail amid the stunning room can be quite a thrilling experience.

This art deco icon has been a favorite of visiting celebrities and dignitaries. As in years past, today's guests flock here for its premier location, sophisticated services, and quiet luxury. Featuring the latest high-tech amenities, the rooms and suites are handsomely appointed with custom furnishings, alligator-print leather, and glossy, honey-toned wood veneers. Nothing beats a room with dramatic views of Central Park, but get an ever better, up-close look at the greenery with the hotel's unique guided tours.

Manhattan ▶ Midtown West

Le Parker Meridien

118 W. 57th St. (bet. Sixth & Seventh Aves.)

Subway: 57 St
Phone: 212-245-5000 or 800-543-4300
Web: www.parkermeridien.com
Prices: **$$$$**

719
Rooms

7
Suites

If midtown is the heart of Manhattan, then 57th Street is its major artery. This street is home to flagship boutiques from leading luxury brands, world-renowned concert halls and museums, to headquarters of some of the top companies, so it's fitting that Le Parker Meridien also calls it home.

This sophisticated hotel brings you the world quite literally, (there's a 24-hour translation service) without any of the fuss. Stylish in an updated kind of way, it also feels incredibly warm and inviting. Work, play, sleep—it's all a pleasure here in these ergonomically inspired rooms and suites where expansive desks with Aeron chairs, oversized cedar-lined baths and showers, and sleek amenities are part and parcel.

Working out is never a chore at the fabulous Gravity Fitness and Spa. Shoot hoops, play racquetball, swim in the penthouse pool, or spa-ah at this 15,000-square-foot temple of wellness that has outsiders begging for a day pass. Breakfast is the most important meal of the day at Norma's, where waffles and frittatas go all day long, but nothing beats the slightly secretive (ask in the lobby) but oh-so-good (made to order with all the fixings) burger and fries from the burger joint.

The London NYC

A3

151 W. 54th St. (bet. Sixth & Seventh Aves.)

Subway: 7 Av
Phone: 212-307-5000 or 866-690-2029
Web: www.thelondonnyc.com
Prices: $$$$

552 Rooms

10 Suites

The London Hotels

Samuel Johnson once quipped "when a man is tired of London, he is tired of life." The same holds true of the stylish London NYC hotel. This ever-sleek hotel delivers space, style, and a fantastic location all rolled into one gorgeous package.

No disrespect to Johnson, but there are some times in life when you are just plain tired. For those times, The London is just right. Sink into one of their spacious suites, where a bed dressed in luxurious Fili d'Oro Italian linens and piled high with handwoven throws awaits. Interior designer David Collins used soft grays and blues together with crisp furnishings to craft a style that is tailored as a Savile Row suit. With bathrooms by luxury brand Waterworks and cutting-edge technology, this hotel doesn't miss a trick in the book. The look may be London, but the view (across the city to Central Park) is all New York.

Brit bad boy Gordon Ramsay was the brains behind the London Bar so it's no surprise this super-swank, suede-ceilinged space isn't just for canoodling over cocktails. Smoked salmon scrambled eggs and buttermilk pancakes at breakfast, classic afternoon tea, and dolled-up bar food in the evening—it redefines all-day dining.

Manhattan ▶ Midtown West

Metro

45 W. 35th St. (bet. Fifth & Sixth Aves.)

Subway: 34 St - Herald Sq
Phone: 212-947-2500 or 800-356-3870
Web: www.hotelmetronyc.com
Prices: $$

161 Rooms

18 Suites

Finding a good hotel in the heart of the Fashion District is a snap at the Metro. With its convenient location, casual comforts, and a price that still leaves some change in the pocket, this hotel has it all sewn up.

Guests never feel the squeeze at this warm and hospitable respite where continental breakfast, Internet, business services, and access to the fitness center are just some of the services they graciously provide at no charge. Ideal for business travelers seeking an expense report-friendly spot, Metro's location near the world-renowned Theater District also appeals to leisure travelers.

Don't expect to sacrifice good looks here just because the price is right. Metro's rooms and suites are as stylish as they are inviting. Sand-colored walls, tufted headboards, and Mandarin-hued furnishings blend for a sunny sophistication. The Metro Grill restaurant and bar specializes in American dishes throughout the day, and the charming Library is a great spot for sipping a cup of tea by the fireplace. The rooftop garden terrace is Metro's crowning glory. Spend a warm, sunny day atop the hotel, where the views of the nearby Empire State Building look like a postcard come to life.

The Michelangelo

152 W. 51st St. (at Seventh Ave.)

Subway: 50 St (Broadway)
Phone: 212-765-1900 or 800-237-0990
Web: www.michelangelohotel.com
Prices: $$$

123 Rooms

55 Suites

James Stankman/Starquest Media LLC

The Michelangelo delivers Italian refinement in a New York minute. This elegant hotel sits at the intersection of all that makes Manhattan marvelous. Everything–from shopping and sightseeing to award-winning entertainment–is literally at their doorstep.

The Michelangelo's sumptuous interiors are proof that it has no trouble living up to its namesake. With its abundant use of gleaming marble, glittering crystal chandeliers, and shimmery silk-upholstered furnishings, this hotel is indeed a work of art. The lobby makes a glorious first impression, while the guest accommodations elevate expectations with supremely elegant settings. Staying in the big city for more than a month? Move in to one of the Michelangelo's fully equipped guest residences, located next door to the hotel. Service (literally) goes the extra mile by offering a complimentary private car service to Wall Street. The concierge also offers a wealth of knowledge and a helping hand.

Italian designer Andrea Auletta hit all the marks with seductive red silks and plush furnishings at every corner. If you overdid the snacking while strolling the city, make sure to work off those calories at their well-equipped fitness center.

Manhattan ▶ Midtown West

The Peninsula New York

700 Fifth Ave. (at 55th St.)

Subway: 5 Av - 53 St
Phone: 212-956-2888 or 800-262-9467
Web: www.peninsula.com
Prices: $$$$

185 Rooms

54 Suites

Mark Wieland Photography

The Peninsula doles out good old-fashioned glamour. This palatial hotel stands sentry at the corner of Fifth Avenue and 55th Street in one of the most enviable locations in the city. Its grand columns and Beaux-Arts façade commands a powerful presence, while inside, the lobby knocks your socks off with its sparkling crystal chandelier suspended from the coffered, wedding cake-like ceiling. The sweeping staircase looks the part for a grand Hollywood entrance. It's just one of the many reasons that celebrities and other discerning travelers make this hotel their city base.

While the public spaces pour on the glitz, The Peninsula's rooms and suites offer a subdued sophistication. Far from fussy, the haven-like spaces are defined by soft, soothing earth tones and simple furnishings, and the marble bathrooms are deliciously deluxe.

Go ahead and hit the roof. With a stunning pool, fitness center, and spa, plus outdoor drinking at the 1930s Shanghai-styled Salon de Ning, the rooftop is tops. Afternoon tea is just the thing at the traditionally elegant Gotham Lounge, while morning, noon, and night, business deals are high-fived in high style at the signature Fives restaurant and bar.

The Plaza

768 Fifth Ave. (at Central Park South)

Subway: 5 Av - 59 St
Phone: 212-759-3000 or 888-850-0909
Web: www.theplaza.com
Prices: $$$$

180
Rooms

102
Suites

The Plaza

The esteemed Plaza is neck and neck with the Waldorf=Astoria in the race for New York's most recognizable hotel, but one thing is for certain—this Beaux-Arts landmark wins the hearts of its guests from the moment they walk through the door. The Plaza has witnessed, and made, New York history since 1907. Bookended by Bergdorf Goodman and Central Park and reigning over Fifth Ave., it just doesn't get any better than this location.

Louis XV furnishings and 24kt gold-plated faucets in the rooms and suites—it's all so unabashedly over the top. The Plaza outdoes itself at every turn. Loosen up at the Caudalíe Spa, brighten up your tresses at the celebrity-favorite Warren-Tricomi Salon, or sweat like a star at The Plaza fitness center.

The Plaza is beloved by visitors and treasured by residents. Its Palm Court and storied hallways have been a rite of passage for generations of city slickers. Relive the glamour of a bygone era at these spots, listen to jazz at the Rose Club, sip champagne in the Champagne Room, or go casual at The Plaza Food Hall by Todd English. For an "only at The Plaza" memory, pint-sized guests play dress up and take tea just like their favorite character, Eloise.

The Ritz-Carlton, Central Park

B3

50 Central Park South (at Sixth Ave.)

Subway: 5 Av - 59 St
Phone: 212-308-9100 or 866-671-6008
Web: www.ritzcarlton.com
Prices: $$$$

212
Rooms

47
Suites

In stark contrast to its edgier downtown sibling, The Ritz-Carlton, Central Park, doles out a fancy look and feel. Horse-drawn carriages clomp past this posh hideaway where elegantly attired doormen wait to open the doors to these hushed interiors. The lobby, with its gleaming wood-paneled walls, antique rugs, and bountiful fresh flowers, epitomizes clubby elegance. Is that sound the gentle strains of a harp? It sure is.

Sunlight streams into the airy rooms and suites, where soft shades of lemon, cream, and white add a feminine touch to the classic styling. It's all very posh, without being pompous and provided that you live in a gracious estate, you'll feel right at home. The Star Lounge is the hotel's go-to for all-day dining and afternoon tea (accompanied by that harp). The Central Park Side Car and The Shining Star are just two of the specialty cocktails mixed to perfection by the resident bartender, while the kitchen glams up classics (think truffle mac and cheese).

Switzerland's famed La Prairie beauty company has set up its first shop stateside here at The Ritz-Carlton. Diamond perfection body treatments...platinum and caviar facials... this spa specializes in luxurious decadence.

The Setai

400 Fifth Ave. (at 36th St.)

Subway: 34 St - Herald Sq
Phone: 212-695-4005 or 877-734-3028
Web: www.setaififthavenue.com
Prices: $$$$

157 Rooms

57 Suites

The Setai Fifth Avenue/a Capella Hotel/Robert Reck

Are you a landmark or are you just tucked inside one? New York is full of hotels that are nestled inside buildings designated as historic landmarks, but how many can say their building serves as a landmark? The Setai wins that argument every time. This modern masterpiece is a beacon of beauty. Soaring 60 stories above Fifth Avenue in lower midtown, this sky-reaching hotel's striking design and crown of lights cut a swath across the city skyline.

Indeed, The Setai is a tall glass of water. Moody and seductive, the hotel's interiors lure guests away from the gray city streets. The mocha-hued furnishings set against gleaming marble floors create a chic cocoon in the seating areas off the lobby and in the Bar on Fifth, where you can soak up some libations and sultry jazz tunes. Make a grand entrance by climbing the lobby's sweeping staircase. Retreat to the sleek Auriga Spa or beautify at the French-inspired Julien Farel Salon before a big night out on the town.

After a long day, nothing satisfies quite like The Setai's supremely comfortable and stylish rooms and suites. These accommodations, outfitted with exotic materials and custom finishings, are the ultimate urban escape.

Manhattan ▶ Midtown West

6 Columbus

6 Columbus Circle (at 58th St.)

Subway: 59 St - Columbus Circle
Phone: 212-204-3000
Web: www.sixcolumbus.com
Prices: $$

72
Rooms

16
Suites

Don't feel like a hamster running on a wheel. Step away from the standard and try something different at 6 Columbus. Steps away from historic Columbus Circle, this fresh and upbeat hotel brings a downtown verve to this bustling area. It should come as no surprise that 6 Columbus is shaking things up. Part of the burgeoning Thompson Hotels Group, 6 Columbus shares the groups funky and feisty spirit.

Take a look at the lobby's shag-style rug, leather couch, and photos of vintage airplanes for a taste of what's to come. Imbued with a 1960s modern-meets-new millennium sensibility, the rooms and suites are retro yet refined. Artwork by Guy Bourdin, custom-made Sferra linens, Waterworks bath fixtures, and even goodies from Dean & Deluca...6 Columbus might share a vintage feel but this luxurious boutique property is no dusty thrift shop.

Blue Ribbon Sushi Bar & Restaurant pops its head up north at 6 Columbus and gives foodies a reason to put away their Metro cards. Above 6 might just be the best thing going—subscribing to the theory that a good view isn't just for sunny days, this sky-high terrace's retractable roof means that a rooftop happy hour is possible any day of the year.

Sofitel

45 W. 44th St. (bet. Fifth & Sixth Aves.)

Subway: 47-50 Sts - Rockefeller Ctr
Phone: 212-354-8844 or 877-565-9240
Web: www.sofitel-newyork.com
Prices: $$$$

346
Rooms

52
Suites

Sofitel

Midtown's Sofitel brings a bit of French flair without any of the fuss or frou frou. This 30-story tower of limestone and glass shimmers and sparkles on busy 44th Street. Avant-garde and elegant, the Sofitel makes it so easy to catch a show, wander through a world-class museum, or make it to an important meeting right on time.

The rooms and suites feature an appealing blend of art deco accents with a French *je ne sais quoi*. Lipstick red- and zebra-print chairs and splashy art lend a dramatic air, while fluffy bedding and luxuriously-fitted bathrooms make the living really good. Conference facilities, meeting rooms, and business services are wide-ranging at the Sofitel and attract a global following.

The Sofitel is surrounded by countless dining selections ranging from casual bites to award-winning haute cuisine, but for a taste of France, visit the art deco-inspired Gaby Restaurant. Once inside, it is an explosion of color, with jewel-toned chairs and oversized canvases lining the walls, but the mood is defiantly relaxed and serene. For a more convivial atmosphere, head over to Gaby Bar for a dark chocolate martini featuring Godiva Chocolate Liquor and Bailey's & Cream.

Manhattan ▶ Midtown West

619

Washington Jefferson Hotel

318 W. 51st St. (bet. Eighth & Ninth Aves.)

Subway:	50 St (Eighth Ave.)
Phone:	212-246-7550 or 888-567-7550
Web:	www.wjhotel.com
Prices:	$

135 Rooms

♿

♿

📶

Imagine being surrounded by all that midtown has to offer—Radio City Music Hall; Times Square; Rockefeller Center; even Central Park and Lincoln Center. Now, are dollar bills coming out of your ears? If they are, you're not staying at the Washington Jefferson Hotel. This causally sophisticated hotel is a gem in the heart of it all with a comfortable price that lets you enjoy dinner and a show.

Its simple elegance offers a respite from the sensory overload of the neighborhood's "look at me" neon lights. One glance at the crisp white walls, hung with only a flat-screen television and a small, simply framed picture, and it's clear that the Washington Jefferson gives you everything you need without anything you don't. Penny pinchers love the petite rooms (suitable for single occupancy only), but no room is a budget buster.

The staff aims to please, whether it's pressing an item of clothing or suggesting a sightseeing tour. The fitness center is open 24 hours to accommodate busy travelers. Shimizu Sushi & Shochu Bar has been slicing and dicing fresh fish for two decades. If sushi doesn't float your boat, amble over to Triomphe Restaurant, which shares owners with the hotel.

Manhattan ▶ Midtown West

Crosby Street Hotel

79 Crosby St. (bet. Prince & Spring Sts.)

Subway: Prince St
Phone: 212-226-6400
Web: www.firmdalehotels.com
Prices: $$$$

75 Rooms

11 Suites

Firmdale Hotels

Just because they love you in London doesn't mean they'll sing your praises in New York. Unless you're the artsy and one-of-a-kind Kit Kemp. The tour de force behind some of London's hottest boutique hotels, Kemp hopped across the pond and jumped right in with the Crosby Street Hotel. It's a splashing success.

Situated on a cobblestoned street in fashionable SoHo, the Crosby Street Hotel has you at hello. The lobby is like a living room-cum-art gallery filled with unexpected surprises. The hodgepodge of mixed mediums travels across all times and results in a wacky, but wonderful result. But wait, there's more. The 86 individually designed rooms and suites have that oh-so-British blend (think florals mixed with stripes).

Crosby Street Hotel may look eccentric, but it functions seamlessly. There's a screening room for film buffs as well as a Sunday night film club to beat those end of weekend blues. The Crosby Bar & Terrace echoes the little bit of this and that design sense with its fusion menu and its funky/flirty ambience. It might be SoHo, but Crosby Street doesn't forget its roots. Afternoon tea is a staple here and is served with such traditional treats as cakes and scones.

The James

27 Grand St. (at Sixth Ave.)

Subway: Canal St (Sixth Ave.)
Phone: 212-465-2000 or 888-526-3778
Web: www.jameshotels.com
Prices: $$$$

109 Rooms

5 Suites

If you build it, they will definitely come. If you're The James hotel, that is. Located at the corner of Thompson and Grand, The James was a ground-up new construction hotel that is imbued with the artistic spirit that has made SoHo world famous. Urban with a breath of fresh air is the best way to describe this hotel that is so far just two-of-a-kind (there is a sister James in Chicago). Sun-filled and airy, the Sky Lobby looks out over the adjacent garden, where a spa cabana is on hand for alfresco massages.

The guest rooms are the very essence of SoHo sophistication. Reclaimed wood floors are a nod to the hotel's eco-minded practices, while niceties like rain showers and customized toiletries are proof positive that this hotel never forsakes life's little luxuries. Warm and rich color tones set a relaxed mood, but with views like these from the floor-to-ceiling windows, your attention will be directed elsewhere.

The city slicker-meets-country barn setting at David Burke Kitchen is just right for its gussied up down-home cooking. For a more SoHo spirit, ride up to the roof where the shimmering pool makes a beautiful backdrop for the sexy glass-enclosed bar and lounge, Jimmy.

Manhattan ▶ SoHo & Nolita

The Mercer

147 Mercer St. (at Prince St.)

Subway: Prince St
Phone: 212-966-6060
Web: www.mercerhotel.com
Prices: $$$$

67 Rooms

8 Suites

Thomas Loof

The Mercer caused a stir when it debuted on the SoHo scene. Sister to Chateau Marmont in Los Angeles and conceptualized by hotel magnate André Balazs, The Mercer was the original boutique hotel. It spoke to travelers seeking something different; something a bit more like home, only cooler. The Mercer stood out from the crowd and inspired plenty of copycats. Imitation is the sincerest form of flattery, but there's still only one Mercer hotel.

The 75 rooms are pure SoHo in all its glory. Loft-like, with abundant light, high ceilings, and exposed brick, they wear a slick modernist design courtesy of Christian Liaigre. Views of Mercer Street or the bamboo courtyard add to the residential vibe of this low-key luxe hotel that is a magnet for movie stars and artists. On-call personal trainers, massage therapists, and yoga or Pilates instructors are also available for extra indulgence.

Another key element of that "just like home" feel is The Mercer's 24-hour food and bar service in the lobby. From the look (African wenge woods, 14-foot ceilings, and an overflowing floor-to-ceiling, 50-foot bookcase) to the loungers (is that who I think it is?), it delivers warm and fuzzy for the fabulous.

Manhattan ▶ SoHo & Nolita

Mondrian SoHo

B2

9 Crosby St. (bet. Grand & Howard Sts.)

Subway: Canal St (Broadway)
Phone: 212-554-6120 or 800-697-1791
Web: www.mondriansoho.com
Prices: $$$$

264
Rooms

6
Suites

The Mondrian definitely wouldn't play in Peoria. This hotel is what SoHo is all about. It's also what happens when you give a designer carte blanche. Luckily it worked out for the Morgans Hotel Group, which has been to this rodeo before with other one-of-a-kind boutique properties. This flight of fancy, the brainchild of designer Benjamin Noriega-Ortiz, is imaginative and inspired. It is Jean Cocteau's *La Belle et la Bête* come to life.

The lobby is awash in periwinkle and white with a Greek islands-meets-sexy French girl sensibility. Furry lamps, oversized wing chairs, and textured urns all lend a Dali-esque feel. Upstairs, the rooms and suites share a more sedate interpretation. Royal blue carpets, white lacquered platform beds, blue-and-white toile pillows are fresh and feminine. iPads in every room, Malin + Goetz bath amenities, in-room spa services, an onsite fitness center, plus passes to Equinox are evidence that it's not just about good looks at Mondrian SoHo.

The dramatic décor filled with eclectic Asian accessories makes Mister H seem like a stage set. It might borrow its inspiration from SoHo's neighboring Chinatown, but this sexy bar/nightclub is more *noir* than noodletown.

60 Thompson

60 Thompson St. (bet. Broome & Spring Sts.)

Subway: Spring St (Sixth Ave.)
Phone: 212-431-0400 or 877-431-0400
Web: www.60thompson.com
Prices: $$$$

87 Rooms

10 Suites

Thompson Hotels

It's the address, not its shoe size. 60 Thompson oozes cool and epitomizes Bohemian chic. Just steps away, SoHo's celebrated galleries, cafés, and shops beckon. With its unique brand of laid-back luxury, it is exactly the kind of place rock stars suffering from "exhaustion" would go to rest, but mere mortals love it too.

Designed by SoHo's favorite son Thomas O'Brien, this hotel's success story launched an entire collection of Thompson Hotels. While not quite an "oldie," it's definitely a goodie, and this mainstay continues to function as the living room and cafeteria for the neighborhood's hipsters. This hotel pulses with the vibrant energy of this creative capital, but upstairs in the rooms and suites, the mood is soft and serene. Sferra linens, Frette robes, Kiehls products, and marble bathrooms with mosaic floors are among the luxurious details, while suites with private balconies are always in demand.

Of course, the reason to stay at 60 Thompson is its social scene, so head downstairs to the lobby for some excellent people-watching, slip into the seductive Thom Bar with groovy beats, or hang out at the private rooftop lounge A60, where a guest key serves as the secret password.

Manhattan ▶ SoHo & Nolita

Soho Grand

310 West Broadway (bet. Canal & Grand Sts.)

Subway: Canal St (Sixth Ave.)
Phone: 212-965-3000 or 800-965-3000
Web: www.sohogrand.com
Prices: $$$$

361 Rooms

2 Suites

Everybody likes to make a discovery, be the first on the scene, and set trends instead of following them, but not many can do it. The Soho Grand is a trailblazer and the granddaddy of them all. Opened in 1996, it was the first hotel built in the SoHo district in nearly a century. While plenty would follow suit, nobody has taken the shine off the Soho Grand.

It is exquisite down to every last detail. From the hand-painted silver leaf ceiling and the magnificent glass bottle staircase to the intricate cast iron, the Soho Grand is a celebration of artistry and workmanship. Blending 1870s Gilded Age-era elegance with a funky 1970s feel, the hotel pays homage to the neighborhood in its sensational interiors.

Rising 17 stories above downtown, the rooms are gifted with glorious views. Gadget geeks love the high-tech goodies like pre-loaded MacBooks, but the Grand is a fashionista fave (in-room services from Laurent Dufourg's salon are just one reason). Perhaps the best place to soak up the Soho Grand lifestyle is at one of its bars and restaurants. The Club Room and Grand Bar have an appealing old-world allure, while the Salon has a lighter feel. The Yard is a delight during summer months.

Trump SoHo

246 Spring St. (at Varick St.)

Subway: Spring St (Sixth Ave.)
Phone: 212-842-5500 or 877-828-7080
Web: www.trumpsohohotel.com
Prices: $$$$

245
Rooms

146
Suites

Phillip Ennis Photography

There are a million and one reasons to stay at Trump SoHo. This glamorously modern hotel really and truly rises above the crowd as it reaches skywards 46 stories above the SoHo streets. The views of the city and the Hudson River are unmatched, but don't turn all of your attention outwards or you'll miss some of this hotel's magic.

Trump SoHo's rooms and suites showcase a contemporary Italian élan. Furnished by Fendi Casa, the accommodations are dripping with a luxurious feel. Whether it's side tables or stereo systems, the mantra here is modern, modern, modern. From the quiet and au courant Library stocked with Taschen art books, to the stunning alfresco setting at Bar d'Eau (a 6,000-square-foot pool bar brimming with groovy tunes, thrilling cocktails, and a range of light bites), the hotel boasts something to fit your every mood.

Cut out of Grandpa's will? It's all good, since you'll feel like a million bucks after a visit to the Spa at Trump. This luxurious bi-level facility seduces spa-fiends with its Middle Eastern-inspired décor, and Trump SoHo even has the distinction of being the only spot in New York City with Turkish hammams. Soaking it all in never felt so good.

Manhattan ▶ SoHo & Nolita

Cosmopolitan

95 West Broadway (at Chambers St.)

Subway: Chambers St (West Broadway)
Phone: 212-566-1900 or 888-895-9400
Web: www.cosmohotel.com
Prices: $

129
Rooms

TriBeCa is the playground of film stars and finance whiz kids, so what's a regular Joe to do? Book a room at the Cosmopolitan, naturally. Set within the charming cobblestone streets of TriBeCa, where an endless parade of buzz-worthy bars and restaurants are vying for attention, the Cosmopolitan serves up style without the sticker shock. And it turns out that you don't have to be a local heartthrob or grande dame to enjoy the many pleasures of TriBeCa after all.

Fresh flowers, comfortable beds, colorful artwork, and ceiling fans give the guest rooms a cheerful and upbeat ambience. Incredibly quaint but clean and utilitarian at the same time, the Cosmopolitan's amenities may be limited to a business center and room service courtesy of the cool and casual Cosmopolitan Café. But, who really cares when some of the city's finest and most flavorful restaurants are just outside the door, thereby making this a great location, accessible to all that is unique in Lower Manhattan.

Consult their helpful concierge for invaluable advice on area sights like the World Trade Center Memorial, Statue of Liberty, and South Street Seaport, which is now ever-buzzing with a host of bars and cafés.

Manhattan ▶ TriBeCa

Greenwich Hotel

377 Greenwich St. (at N. Moore St.)

Subway: Franklin St
Phone: 212-941-8900
Web: www.thegreenwichhotel.com
Prices: $$$$

75 Rooms

13 Suites

Herbert Ypma

You know those people who travel the world only to fill their homes with an impressive array of well-collected items? They've come home to roost at The Greenwich Hotel. The tailored brick façade belies the treasures held within this hip hotel that just so happens to be backed by TriBeCa's own Robert De Niro. From the Drawing Room to the Italian-inspired courtyard, there's a jazzy juxtaposition of jewel-toned English-style furnishings with a seemingly timeworn collection of antlers, shells, baskets, and vases.

The Greenwich really struts its stuff in the rooms. Cookie cutter it's not, as each of the hotel's suites has something different to offer. From Moroccan tiles and Italian Carrara marble to hand-loomed Tibetan silk rugs and Swedish Duxiana beds, it is a veritable United Nations of design. Oh, and there's room service from white-hot chef Andrew Carmellini.

Take to Shibui Spa for a dip in the lantern-lit pool. This dreamy space is set under the roof of a 250 year-old wood-and-bamboo farmhouse, that was painstakingly recreated in the hotel by Japanese craftsmen. The spa even features a traditional shiatsu room with tatami mats and a series of time-honored Japanese bathing rituals.

Manhattan ▶ TriBeCa

Smyth

B3

85 West Broadway (at Chambers St.)

Subway: Chambers St (West Broadway)
Phone: 212-587-7000 or 888-587-6984
Web: www.thompsonhotels.com
Prices: $$$

96
Rooms

4
Suites

Mr. and Mrs. Smith is the often-used name for stars when they're seeking anonymity. It conveys regular, average, even maybe a bit boring. There's a new Smyth in town in TriBeCa at the Smyth hotel, and this one isn't a bit bland; in fact, it has a young, jazzy appeal.

Yabu Pushelberg pushes the envelope with a vaguely vintage and completely original look (maroon ostrich-embossed leather walls are just one feature). Marble bathrooms with translucent floor-to-ceiling showers sex things up in these rooms and suites, some of which feature private terraces to go with those floor-to-ceiling city views.

Mix and mingle at the Smyth Bar, just off the lobby, or grab your night by the horns at the Toro Lounge. Located below ground in the cellar, Toro is the definition of Spanish-flavored sophistication. Smyth's prizewinner is famed restaurateur Frederick Lesort's Plein Sud. Whitewashed interiors and wood-paneled ceilings manage to feel at once industrial and rustic, but it's the brasserie food with even more palatable prices that keeps the cool kids coming back. Sunday brunch is a particular favorite for those who partied til the wee hours and need a *croque monsieur* to revive their senses.

Manhattan ▶ TriBeCa

Tribeca Grand

2 Sixth Ave. (at Church St.)

Subway: Canal St (Sixth Ave.)
Phone: 212-519-6600 or 877-519-6600
Web: www.tribecagrand.com
Prices: $$$

186 Rooms

15 Suites

GrandLife Hotels

This is yet another superstar, brought to you by the same folks behind the Soho Grand. This dynamic duo have done it again, and the Tribeca Grand lives up to its lineage, its name, and even its neighborhood. The building's triangular shape echoes the district's acronym (triangle below Canal).

Mid-century modern design influences the public and private spaces. Designer William Sofield refreshed the décor while maintaining its integrity. Guest rooms are residential-style retreats featuring the latest in luxurious amenities, like Egyptian cotton linens, custom furnishings, and toiletries from local apothecary Malin + Goetz. Guests can even take a bite out of the Big Apple with an Apple, since this hotel stocks iPods, iPads, and MacBooks preloaded with the carefully curated tours of downtown.

The eight-story atrium is the focal point of the hotel, while its Church Bar is its beating heart. It offers a classic take on the traditional New York bar, and the swanky Lounge captures the vivacious downtown spirit. The hotel's private screening room is where they really show off. Home to a weekly film series starring cult classics, new releases, and favorite TV shows, it's TriBeCa to a "t."

Manhattan ▶ TriBeCa

Bentley

500 E. 62nd St. (at York Ave.)

Subway: Lexington Av - 59 St
Phone: 212-644-6000 or 888-664-6835
Web: www.bentleyhotelnyc.com
Prices: $$

161
Rooms

36
Suites

Does the Upper East Side have you conjuring up images of upper crusty Park Avenue matrons, stiff upper lipped gentlemen donning dark suits, and ladies who lunch? If so, you're obviously not familiar with the Bentley. This fashion-forward hotel flies in the face of the curmudgeonly rumors.

Prepare to be wowed by its dazzling interiors. Zebra-printed carpets, sienna-colored bed throws, houndstooth pillows, and even gleaming marble bathrooms with Spa Therapy products by Lather all make the intriguing rooms and suites extend beyond the ordinary. Incredibly spacious, the accommodations bring the city indoors with striking skyline and East River views.

Enjoy convenient services including a business center, 24-hour front desk, and fitness facility privileges. The Bentley's rooftop restaurant and bar spotlights a lavish continental buffet breakfast as well as Italian-American cuisine for dinner. Enclosed by glass on three sides, this 21st Floor respite also proffers a breathtaking and panoramic perspective of midtown and beyond.

The best part about The Bentley? You don't need to have a Park Avenue-sized trust fund to sleep in sophisticated style with the city right at your feet.

The Carlyle

B3

35 E. 76th St. (at Madison Ave.)

Subway: 77 St
Phone: 212-744-1600 or 800-227-5737
Web: www.thecarlyle.com
Prices: $$$$

124 Rooms

64 Suites

The Carlyle, A Rosewood Hotel

The Carlyle is Upper East Side elegance at its best. Perfectly sited on Madison Avenue and surrounded by leading boutiques and galleries, this hotel is equal parts exclusive hideaway and world-class hotel. Perhaps that's why it was a favorite of Princess Diana and was purportedly the love nest for Marilyn Monroe and John F. Kennedy.

The Carlyle is crisp and cool. The intimate lobby's glossy ebony floors, creamy white walls, and mandarin-colored sofas epitomize the sleek lines and out-and-out elegance of art deco design. The Carlyle's interiors have been crafted by everyone from Dorothy Draper and Mark Hampton to today's reigning queen of design, Alexandra Champalimaud. In contrast to the handsome details of the public spaces, the accommodations share a softer, more feminine side. Floral patterns, dreamy color schemes, and to-die-for Central Park views are part of the plush life at The Carlyle.

The bejeweled Sense Spa and the Yves Durif Salon are favorites of trendsetting New Yorkers, but it is The Carlyle's restaurants and bars that have hosted residents for generations. Socialites flock to the Carlyle Restaurant, but Café Carlyle and Bemelmans Bar are true-blue New York institutions.

Manhattan ▶ Upper East Side

The Lowell

 A1

28 E. 63rd St. (bet. Madison & Park Aves.)

Subway: Lexington Av - 63 St
Phone: 212-838-1400 or 800-221-4444
Web: www.lowellhotel.com
Prices: $$$$

23
Rooms

49
Suites

Lovely, charming, and delightful, The Lowell is a slice of the English countryside in the heart of the Upper East Side. Settled just off Madison Avenue, the hotel occupies a perfectly manicured tree-lined street. Just 49 suites and 23 rooms are behind these doors, and guests are treated to unprecedented levels of individualized attention and service. The accommodations throw open their arms with a romantic ambience. Some boast working fireplaces, winsome canopy beds, and terraces for a true taste of a pied-a-terre.

Everything bears evidence of going the extra step...even the fitness center is decorated with framed contemporary prints for an added touch of elegance.

Don't miss the orange vanilla-infused French toast or a number of other unique Euro-Asian inspired culinary creations at the Pembroke Room. The hotel offers teas to the tune of 20 different blends at its traditional afternoon tea. If fresh scones topped with Devonshire cream and delicate tea sandwiches are simply too dainty for your taste, The Post House will have you licking your chops. This American steakhouse is the real McCoy with that red-blooded gentleman's club feel and superior aged, Prime cuts of beef.

The Mark

25 E. 77th St. (at Madison Ave.)

Subway: 77 St
Phone: 212-744-4200
Web: www.themarkhotel.com
Prices: $$$$

100 Rooms

50 Suites

Todd Eberle

From Gucci to the Guggenheim, Chanel to the Cooper-Hewitt, and Michael Kors to the Met, the upper reaches of the Upper East Side delight style seekers and tastemakers alike. Privileged guests have been making their mark at this esteemed hotel since 1927, but thanks to a recent top-to-bottom restoration, it's no worse for the wear. The exterior reads Upper East Side formality, but inside, this hotel screams exuberance. French designer Jacques Grange has revved up the interiors with an eye-catching avant-garde design. It may be shades of gray outside, but at The Mark, it's black-and-white all over. The geometrically patterned floors are more than dazzling—they're the Mark's signature (take home a striped umbrella as a souvenir).

Grange toned it down a bit for the largely serene rooms and suites, but the sophistication still comes shining through with chic, contemporary French furnishings and modern prints.

The Mark hits all the right marks when it comes to white-glove services. Sweat like a celeb at the fitness center, overseen by trainer-to-the-stars, John Sitaras. Getting glam (or goldielocks) was never so easy, since the renowned Frederic Fekkai salon is headquartered here.

Manhattan ▶ Upper East Side

The Regency

540 Park Ave. (at 61st St.)

Subway: Lexington Av - 59 St
Phone: 212-759-4100 or 800-233-2356
Web: www.loewshotels.com
Prices: $$$$

267 Rooms

86 Suites

Loews Hotels & Resorts

The Loews Regency Hotel may have a coveted and prestigious Park Avenue address, but there's not a shred of pomposity present in this well-run mainstay. The Regency has always appealed to business travelers who appreciate its comprehensive services and updated facilities like state-of-the-art meeting and function spaces (not to mention its proximity to city businesses). With the shops of Madison and Fifth avenues just a block or two away and with extras like dog walking and kid's programs, The Regency is fun for the whole family.

The casually elegant guest rooms and suites make everyone feel right at home. Ergonomic chairs roll up to granite-topped desks looking out over the city, and plush linens ensure a good night's sleep. Take a break with a complimentary workout at Browning's Fitness, then wind down with a massage in the privacy of your guest room. Nico Salon offers the full gamut of hair, skin, and nails beauty services.

540 Park, the hotel's signature restaurant, offers a rare peek inside New York's power scene. Considered the originator of the "power breakfast," it is still morning's best. At night, the cabaret-styled Feinstein's delivers its dose of dinner and a show.

The Surrey

20 E. 76th St. (at Madison Ave.)

Subway: 77 St
Phone: 212-288-3700 or 800-978-7739
Web: www.thesurrey.com
Prices: $$$$

157 Rooms

32 Suites

The Surrey Hotel

Don't miss one fabulously curated minute—get to The Surrey in a hurry! This stylish hotel has a past (Bette Davis, JFK, and Claudette Colbert all stayed here) but it's the present that is making real history. The Surrey's location may be knee-deep in the old-monied world of the Upper East Side, but its quietly elegant flair is as new as a spring lamb.

The simplistic beauty of black-and-white photography is not only an inspiration for the design palette; it is woven into the entire experience. The impressive original works of art are displayed throughout public and private spaces. The rooms are packed with features like oversized desks, deep-soaking tubs, and hand-painted wardrobes. Some boast fireplaces and private terraces for an added level of luxury.

The Surrey's sensuous style is a feast for the eyes. Even the Spa dishes out a heaping serving of style, but this hideaway also presents a spread for the palate. Settle into a banquette next door at Bar Pleiades, where quilted walls and black-and-white lacquer finishes are smart and sexy, and the bar menu is crafted by none other than Daniel Boulud. For a breath of fresh air, head up to the exclusive rooftop garden on the 17th Floor.

Manhattan ▶ Upper East Side

Mandarin Oriental

 A4

80 Columbus Circle (at 60th St.)

Subway: 59 St - Columbus Circle
Phone: 212-805-8800 or 866-801-8880
Web: www.mandarinoriental.com
Prices: $$$$

202
Rooms

46
Suites

East meets the West (Side, that is) at the sensational Mandarin Oriental. Perched atop the Time Warner Center and hovering above bustling Columbus Circle, the Mandarin is a vision unto itself. Of course, those panoramic views of glorious Central Park aren't too tough to take either.

The rooms and suites reflect the hotel's Asian heritage with shimmering silks, festive splashes of red and orange, and decorative objects. All accommodations come with floor-to-ceiling views of the city skyline and Central Park or the mighty Hudson River. The cutting-edge technology creates a home theater-like experience for entertainment, while the Italian linens and marble baths are perfect for sybarites. Leave it all behind at the sumptuous Asian-inspired spa crafted of bamboo, stone, and gold leaf. Fitness facilities, including a lap pool, are first class.

Dining and drinking are elevated to an entirely new level here. The hotel's own MoBar and Lobby Lounge are always up for a good time. Additionally, as part of the Time Warner Center, Mandarin guests are treated to a seemingly limitless selection of haute cuisine hot spots and gourmet dining outposts—all quite literally at their doorstep.

On the Ave

2178 Broadway (at 77th St.)

Subway: 79 St
Phone: 212-362-1100 or 800-509-7958
Web: www.ontheave.com
Prices: $$

274 Rooms

8 Suites

On the Ave

The Upper West Side is a true New Yorker's neighborhood. Lined with the requisite brownstones, trendy boutiques, and popular restaurants, it looks straight out of a Woody Allen film. Wait, it is straight out of it. But really, who can think straight with all that clutter? On the Ave is to the rescue! This light-filled, loft-style boutique hotel delivers downtown cool with an uptown address. The Museum of Natural History is just two blocks away and Central Park is only three. This is the Upper West Side at its very best.

On the Ave is polished but with just a hint of pop. Bright orange and yellow make an appearance in the sleekly styled rooms and suites. Every conceivable amenity from flat-screens, ergonomic Herman Miller desk chairs, a fully-stocked minibar, and crisp cotton linens all combine to create immensely comfortable havens from the hustle and bustle of the city streets.

There is a 24-hour business center and two plant-filled balconies for taking in the view and catching a few rays. Oh, and one other thing...they also provide you with passes to the Equinox Fitness Center where you can work off those dreaded carbs. What, you've heard of it? On the Ave is right on the money.

Trump International Hotel & Tower

1 Central Park West (at Columbus Circle)

Subway: 59 St - Columbus Circle
Phone: 212-299-1000 or 888-448-7867
Web: www.trumpintl.com
Prices: $$$$

47
Rooms

129
Suites

The battle cry of Trump International Hotel & Tower might as well be "go big or go home." Rising from its Central Park West address and reaching skyward, the Trump truly towers head and shoulders above the rest. It brings the best together under one (exceptionally tall) roof.

Style and substance live happily ever after at this hotel, where there isn't a trace of The Donald's signature swagger. The elegant rooms and suites are a little bit modern and a little bit classic, but the features are all of the moment. Fully equipped kitchens come with Sub-Zero refrigerators, while 55-inch flat-screen televisions hang on the walls. But nothing takes the eyes away from those views. Floor-to-ceiling glass frames jaw-dropping views—you'd have to board a helicopter to get a better sight.

Stressed out? Not anymore. The 6,000-square-foot spa and fitness center caters to masters of the universe in need of some serious tender, loving care with a bevy of tension-taming treatments. Don't worry if rejuvenating facials and detoxifying body wraps have you running for the hills. The fitness center and 55-foot indoor pool ensure that guests remain in the lap of luxury even while working out.

Nu Hotel

85 Smith St. (bet. Atlantic Ave. & State St.)

Subway: Hoyt - Schermerhorn
Phone: 718-852-8585
Web: www.nuhotelbrooklyn.com
Prices: $

90 Rooms

3 Suites

Gridley & Graves Photography

Did you know there are actually five boroughs that make up New York City? Perhaps much to the chagrin of many, there is more to life than Manhattan, and giving it a run for its money is the über hip borough of Brooklyn.

If all you know about Brooklyn is its famous bridge, then it's time to cross the river. This borough's avant-garde demeanor and eclectic style is best seen at the trendy Nu Hotel. The Nu brings together the best of Brooklyn in one spot. Three distinct neighborhoods–the brownstones and bistros of Boerum Hill, the old-world shops and gardens of Cobble Hill, and the Italian flavor of Carroll Gardens–all converge right here in downtown Brooklyn. How wonderfully convenient it all is, plus it's easy to get to downtown Manhattan if need be.

Stay in one of the 93 loft-like rooms that share a laid-back vibe mixed with just a hint of Brooklyn badass (Basquiat drawings, found objects from area landmarks, stenciled quotes from famous residents). Yes, there's a distinct hippie mien, but Nu pulls it together and offers the real deal with a 24-hour fitness center, complimentary Continental breakfast, and even evening tapas and cocktails. Norman Mailer never had it this good.

Brooklyn

Wythe

80 Wythe Ave. (at N. 11th St.)

Subway: Bedford Av
Phone: 718-460-8000
Web: www.wythehotel.com
Prices: $$

72
Rooms

The Wythe is located in Williamsburg and beautifully repurposes a former waterfront cooperage built in 1901 into an über-hip 72-room place to stay. The vibe isn't luxe—there's no spa, chocolate on your pillow at turndown, or room service—but the hotel is swank on its own terms, offering a thing or two its Manhattan peers would be hard-pressed to provide.

The lobby flaunts a sitting area stocked with reading material and board games; while rooms achieve a lofty mood by employing an industrial-chic design that features polished concrete floors, original masonry details, bespoke wallpaper, and high timber ceilings. Similarly, bathrooms are comfortable and contemporary outfitted with locally made all-natural bath products in eco-friendly packaging. An abundance of windows frame the twinkling city beyond, but for an even better view, ride up to the sixth floor rooftop lounge, The Ides.

When Reynard and the rooftop bar are in full swing, security politely sifts through the crowd so guests can return to their rooms with no fuss whatsoever. Finally, getting in and out of Manhattan is also delightfully easy from the Wythe—the hotel is just minutes away from midtown and LaGuardia airport.

Brooklyn

● Where to **Eat**

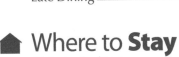 Where to **Stay**

Alphabetical List of Restaurants

647

N

Restaurants by Cuisine

Contemporary

Jamaican

Japanese

Korean

Latin American

A Casa Fox	❌	200
Coppelia	🐫 ❌	20
Hudson River Cafe	❌❌	191
Macondo	🍴	207
Oregano Bar & Bistro	❌❌	425
Palo Santo	❌	481
Rayuela	❌❌	209
Riverdale Garden	❌❌	426
Tabaré	❌	499
Yerba Buena Perry	❌❌	183

Lebanese

al Bustan	🐫 ❌❌	220
Almayass	❌❌	96
Balade	❌❌	49
Naya	❌❌	244

Malaysian

Fatty Crab	🐫 ❌❌	147
New Malaysia	🐫 ❌	39
Nyonya	🐫 ❌	40
Sentosa	❌	544

Mediterranean

Aldea	✿ ❌❌	95
Apiary	❌❌	48
August	🐫 ❌❌	137
Barbounia	❌❌	97
Bistro de la Gare	❌	139
Boulud Sud	❌❌❌	395
Brick Cafe	❌	520
Cédric	❌❌	188
Danny Brown		
Wine Bar & Kitchen	✿ ❌❌	524
Extra Virgin	❌	146
Fig & Olive	❌❌	369
Hearth	❌❌	59
Isabella's	❌❌	401
Kashkaval	❌	286
La Promenade des Anglais	❌❌	24
Mimi's Hummus	🍴	475
Nice Matin	❌❌	404
Picholine	✿ ❌❌❌	407
Vai	❌❌	411
Vareli	❌❌	196

Mexican

Agua Fresca	❌	187
Alma	❌❌	439
Añejo	❌	264
Café el Portal	❌	325
Café Frida	❌❌	395
Casa Enríque	🐫 ❌	521
Cascabel Taqueria	❌	365
Chavela's	🐫 ❌	452
Crema	❌❌	20
De Mole	❌	525
El Parador	🐫 ❌❌	231
El Paso Taqueria	🐫 ❌	189
Empellón Cocina	❌❌	56
Empellón Taqueria	❌❌	145
Estrellita Poblana III	❌	421
Fonda	❌	461
Gran Eléctrica	🐫 ❌❌	465
Hecho en Dumbo	🐫 ❌	153
Hell's Kitchen	❌	285
La Camelia	❌	157
La Esquina	❌	38
La Superior	❌	471
Maizal	❌	563
Maria's Bistro Mexicano	❌	473
Maya	❌❌	375
Maz Mezcal	❌	376
Mercadito Grove	❌	163
Mesa Coyoacán	🐫 ❌	474
Mexicana Mama	❌	163
MXCO	❌	377
Noche Mexicana II	❌	405
Pachanga Patterson	❌	539
Pampano	❌❌	245
Papatzul	❌	332
Rocking Horse Cafe	❌	27
Rosa Mexicano	❌❌	247
Sueños	❌	29
Taqueria Tlaxcalli	❌	427
Toloache	❌❌	316

Middle Eastern

Balaboosta	❌❌	323
Gazala's	❌❌	399
Taboon	❌❌	315
Tanoreen	🐫 ❌❌	501
Wafa	❌	553

Cuisines by Neighborhood

Indexes ▶ Cuisines by Neighborhood

669

Indexes ▶ Cuisines by Neighborhood

Indexes ▶ Cuisines by Neighborhood

677

Indexes ▶ Cuisines by Neighborhood

681

Indexes ▶ Cuisines by Neighborhood

683

Starred Restaurants

*W*ithin the selection we offer you, some restaurants deserve to be highlighted for their particularly good cuisine. When giving one, two, or three Michelin stars, there are a number of elements that we consider including the quality of the ingredients, the technical skill and flair that goes into their preparation, the blend and clarity of flavours, and the balance of the menu. Just as important is the ability to produce excellent cooking time and again. We make as many visits as we need, so that our readers may be assured of quality and consistency.

A two or three-star restaurant has to offer something very special in its cuisine; a real element of creativity, originality, or "personality" that sets it apart from the rest. Three stars – our highest award – are given to the choicest restaurants, where the whole dining experience is superb.

Cuisine in any style, modern or traditional, may be eligible for a star. Due to the fact we apply the same independent standards everywhere, the awards have become benchmarks of reliability and excellence in over 20 countries in Europe and Asia, particularly in France, where we have awarded stars for 100 years, and where the phrase "Now that's real three-star quality!" has entered into the language.

The awarding of a star is based solely on the quality of the cuisine.

Bib Gourmand

😋 This symbol indicates our inspectors' favorites for good value. For $40 or less, you can enjoy two courses and a glass of wine or a dessert (not including tax or gratuity).

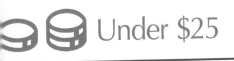

Under $25

Indexes ▶ Under $25

Brunch

Late Dining

Alphabetical List of Hotels

Indexes ▶ Alphabetical List of Hotels

Notes

Notes

Notes

Notes

YOU ALREADY KNOW THE MICHELIN GUIDE,
NOW FIND OUT ABOUT THE MICHELIN GROUP

he Michelin Adventure

all started with rubber balls! This was the product made by
small company based in Clermont-Ferrand that André and
ouard Michelin inherited, back in 1880. The
others quickly saw the potential for a new
eans of transport and their first success
as the invention of detachable pneumatic
es for bicycles. However, the automobile was
provide the greatest scope for their creative talents.
hroughout the 20th century, Michelin never ceased developing
nd creating ever more reliable and high-performance tires,
ot only for vehicles ranging from trucks to F1 but also for
nderground transit systems and airplanes.

om early on, Michelin provided its customers with tools
nd services to facilitate mobility and make travelling a more
leasurable and more frequent experience. As early as 1900,
ne Michelin Guide supplied motorists with a host of useful
nformation related to vehicle maintenance, accommodation
nd restaurants, and was to become a benchmark for good
ood. At the same time, the Travel Information Bureau offered
ravellers personalised tips and itineraries.

he publication of the first collection of roadmaps, in 1910,
vas an instant hit! In 1926, the first regional guide to France
vas published, devoted to the principal sites of Brittany, and
before long each region of France had its own Green Guide. The
collection was later extended to more far-flung destinations,
ncluding New York in 1968 and Taiwan in 2011.

In the 21st century, with the growth of digital technology, the
challenge for Michelin maps and guides is to continue to develop
alongside the company's tire activities. Now, as before, Michelin
is committed to improving the mobility of travellers.

MICHELIN TODAY

WORLD NUMBER ONE TIRE MANUFACTURER
- 69 production sites in 18 countries
- 115,000 employees from all cultures and on every continent
- 6,000 people employed in research and development

Moving

for a worl

Moving forward means developir
tires with better road grip ar
shorter braking distances, whatev
the state of the road.

CORRECT TIRE PRESSURE

 RIGHT PRESSURE

- Safety
- Longevity
- Optimum fuel consumption

 -0,5 bar

- Durability reduced by 20% (- 8,000 km)

-1 bar

- Risk of blowouts
- Increased fuel consumption
- Longer braking distances on wet surfaces

orward together
vhere mobility is safer

also involves helping motorists take care of their fety and their tires. To do so, Michelin organises ill Up With Air" campaigns all over the world to mind us that correct tire pressure is vital.

WEAR

DETECTING TYRE WEAR

MICHELIN tyres are equipped with tread wear indicators, which are small blocks of rubber molded into the base of the main grooves at a height of 1.6 mm. When tread depth is the same level as indicators, the tyres are worn and need replacing.

Tyres are the only point of contact between vehicle and the road, a worn tyre can be dangerous on wet surfaces.

NEW TIRE

WORN TIRE
(1,6 mm tread)

The photo shows the actual contact zone on wet surfaces.

Moving forward
means sustainable mobility

By 2050, Michelin aims to cut the quantity of raw material used in its tire manufacturing process by half and to have developed renewable energy in its facilities. The design of MICHELIN tires has already saved billions of liters of fuel and, by extension, billions of tons of CO2.

Similarly, Michelin prints its maps and guides on paper produced from sustainably managed forests and is diversifying its publishing media by offering digital solutions to make travelling easier, more fuel efficient and more enjoyable!

The group's whole-hearted commitment to eco-design on a daily basis is demonstrated by ISO 14001 certification.

Like you, Michelin is committed to preserving our planet.

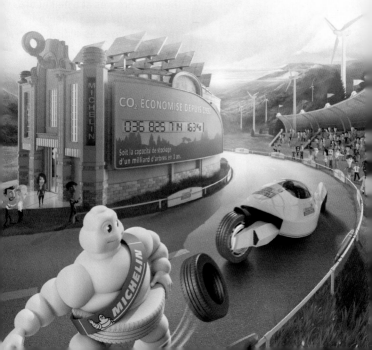

at with Bibendum

michelin.com/corporate/fr
ut more about Michelin's
v and the latest news.

QUIZ

lin develops tires for all types of vehicles. See if you can
the right tire with the right vehicle…

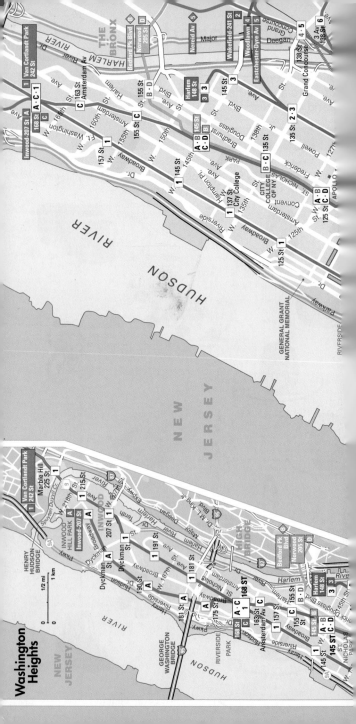